D1073914

Probability and literary form

Probability and literary form

*Philosophic theory and literary practice in
the Augustan age*

DOUGLAS LANE PATEY

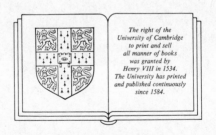

The right of the
University of Cambridge
to print and sell
all manner of books
was granted by
Henry VIII in 1534.
The University has printed
and published continuously
since 1584.

CAMBRIDGE UNIVERSITY PRESS

Cambridge

London   New York   New Rochelle
Melbourne   Sydney

Published by the Press Syndicate of the University of Cambridge
The Pitt Building, Trumpington Street, Cambridge CB2 1RP
32 East 57th Street, New York, NY 10022, USA
296 Beaconsfield Parade, Middle Park, Melbourne 3206, Australia

First published 1984

Printed in Great Britain at
the University Press, Cambridge

Library of Congress catalogue card number: 83–7819

British Library cataloguing in publication data
Patey, Douglas Lane
Probability and literary form.
1. English literature – 18th century – History and
criticism   2. English literature – 19th century
– History and criticism
I. Title
820.9′006   PR447
ISBN 0 521 25456 6

CE

TIMOTHY KEEGAN

Hic mens subsedit, cum fecerit undique gyrum,
Inque suis dandis te praetulit omnibus unum:
Totum posse suum tibi destinat.

Contents

Contents

PART III
PROBABILITY AND THE MEANING OF AUGUSTAN NARRATIVE

Preface

It is no accident that conventional divisions by period in the histories of philosophy and of literature overlap. Writers of the past have often aligned literary innovation with philosophic change, while modern scholars explain the prevalence in any given period of specific literary practices by reference to a climate of thought hospitable to such practices. It is easy to forget that the historiography of philosophy which shadows that of literature, a pattern of development mapped by Hegel in his lectures of the 1820s, arose at a time when *bonnes lettres* had only just been exchanged for *belles lettres* – that is, when literature had only just been made to suffer its modern separation from the rest of thought.[1] (We are still surprised how often Hegel's history of philosophy calls upon "literary" evidence.) Now that the movement to isolate literature from history and from the history of thought is dead – a movement which began with the birth of "aesthetics" in the eighteenth century, and reached its self-conscious apogee in modern formalist criticism – we hear once again what the author of the *Essay on Criticism* knew well, that "the historical study of literature is a necessary condition for any literary analysis,"[2] and study of the historical relations of literature and philosophy prospers.

This book is an attempt to make available to the student of seventeenth- and eighteenth-century literature a largely neglected body of thought which was crucially important to Augustan literary theory and practice. In three parts, it treats: the historical development and affiliations of the concept of probability until the eighteenth century; the role of the concept in Augustan literary theory, in its general accounts of the nature and structure of literary works; and the more specific ways in which literary and philosophic concepts of probability affected literary practice in giving shape to particular works. Although my focus is the period 1660–1800, this is also a book about change: about the shift from Renaissance to Augustan notions of the probable; about the ways in which a theoretical term changes its meaning as it migrates from one conceptual context to another; and, within the Augustan period, when the kinds of interrelations enjoyed by literature and philosophy remained fairly stable, about the ways shifts in philosophic theory alter literary practice.[3]

As might be expected of any such foundational category of thought, concepts of probability shape endeavors in many disciplines. Yet despite its pervasive importance in the Augustan conceptual framework – or perhaps because of it – only a handful of literary scholars have treated the subject. Before about 1975, only Hoyt Trowbridge could be heard to argue that "probable reasoning ... was not nearly so characteristic of the preceding and following periods," and to suggest "that an understanding of this way of reasoning might illuminate the actual processes of thought in many fields during the eighteenth century."[4] Rarer still are diachronic studies: since the time of Aristotle's *Poetics* it has been understood that "probability" (or "verisimilitude") may be a test of literary works, but the notion has seemed transparently commonsensical, so much so as to have no history, but only periods of greater or less ascendance. But by treating probability as a stable category native wholly to literary criticism, as one that does not change and that can be understood without reference to larger contexts, literary studies cannot grasp or explain the phenomena they discuss. The term *probability* conceals varied and shifting commitments, both critical and philosophic; we must examine its meaning and use in the centuries before 1660 if we are to understand its Augustan manifestations. Nor can we restrict our attention to materials solely "literary"; medicine, law, and theology (as well as rhetoric and philosophy) all contribute in the genesis of Augustan probability, its characteristic uses, and the language in which it typically is dressed.

Our task is complicated by recent developments in the history of philosophy itself. It has long been known that the mathematical theory of probability, with which this book is only very little concerned, came to flower with surprising suddenness during a few years in the mid-seventeenth century; in his massive *History of the Mathematical Theory of Probability*, Isaac Todhunter devotes only a few pages to the precursors of Pascal and Fermat. Might our idea of the probable itself, contrary to all expectation, be no older? Michel Foucault advances such a radical thesis in *Les Mots et les choses* (1966), and Ian Hacking has made Foucault's case much more persuasively in his exciting study of *The Emergence of Probability* (1975). Foucault and Hacking argue not merely that in only about 1660 did the term "probability" take on its modern meanings, but that previously our very concept of probability did not exist; its coming at once marked the end of the Renaissance and made possible the mathematical doctrine of chances. Literary critics have been quick to adopt such views.[5] If correct, the Foucault–Hacking hypothesis must in altering the historical process by which probability evolved alter also its Augustan product; by positing radical intellectual discontinuity, the hypothesis would render unintelligible much of what the Augustans themselves understood as the continuity of their own literary theory with that of the past. Chapter I presents an alternative to Foucault and Hacking's account, while in appendix A, I criticize the hypothesis itself.

Chapter II develops, by examining arguments made in a number of disciplines, the theoretical vocabulary in which Augustan thinking about probability was conducted. Only by understanding the doctrines of "probable signs" and "probable circumstances," elements in a schematization of inference from effect to cause, can we come to see how notions of probability function in Augustan literary thought. Assisted by such knowledge, part II, on literary theory, attempts to clarify old issues and raise new ones. Chapter III sorts out differing connotations of literary "probability" and "verisimilitude," while chapter V addresses the explicit use of "probability" in the Augustan critical lexicon (as a term used in the effort to mediate competing critical demands placed on the literary work). Beyond these explicit uses of the term, however, notions of probability constitute the age's very understanding of literary structure itself. It is well known that Restoration and eighteenth-century critics typically discuss works by applying, in order, the familiar Aristotelian categories of moral, fable, character, sentiments, language, and spectacle; chapter IV explains this seemingly hidebound and arbitrary critical procedure as the embodiment of a special view of literary structure. The categories refer to what the Augustans understood to be the "parts" of literary works, the parts of which literary wholes are constructed. Within a literary whole, these parts are organized hierarchically: the old categories refer to levels within a hierarchy, and their ordering becomes intelligible once we recognize that these levels are related one to another as are signs and effects in contemporary models of probable inference.

If notions of probability lie at the heart of the Augustans' theoretical understanding of the nature and structure of literature, how do those ideas affect the ways in which particular works in fact were written? To the extent that literary meaning depends on (is generated from) works' structure, how do these ideas affect our readings of particular works? Part III shows how concepts of probability are embodied in and help us to understand narrative fiction from Fielding to Sterne. In such works most of all does philosophy illuminate literary practice. Where literary works are understood to be structures of probable signs, there will be a fundamental similarity between the philosopher's account of probable inference and literary accounts of the ways "parts" of works unite into "wholes." Moreover, because the Augustans understood the process of interpretation to be, in large measure, the mental process of joining such parts into wholes in the process of reading, Augustan theories of reading and interpretation also share important similarities with contemporary accounts of probable inference. Chapter VII lays the groundwork of this isomorphism in Augustan accounts of inference, structure, and interpretation, and explores the ways it is enacted in narrative. Here we are assisted by the didactic intentions of most Augustan fiction: in these works, authors quite consciously demand of their readers certain procedures of probable inference; these procedures not only reflect contemporary thinking about the probable, but are embodied and dramatized in literary form; and the procedures of interpretation required, if these works are to be understood, are precisely the habits of thought which their authors mean explicitly to teach. For the Augustans, it is in its probability that the intelligibility of a literary work resides – the intelligibility of each part of the work, and of joinings of parts into wholes; didactic function resides in the same probability, as readers make their way through the hierarchic structures presented to them, learning certain habits of inference in the very act of exercising such inference.

The historical roots and affiliations of Augustan notions of probability are so varied and encompass so many disciplines not usually the concern of the literary critic that I cannot hope in this book to have done more than open ground on which others, more skilled in special fields than I, may build more securely. But while the necessity of treating, in addition to literary texts, contemporary systems of medicine or epistemology increases the possibility of error, it also adds to the happy burden of acknowledgements I gratefully make for the assistance of other scholars.

But for the continuing generosity and humbling intelligence of Irvin Ehrenpreis, who supervised my initial treatment of this subject in a doctoral dissertation, this book would scarcely exist. Ralph Cohen introduced me to the problems of Augustan literary history and change; to him and to my other teachers, Martin Battestin, Peter Heath, and E. D. Hirsch, Jr., I owe a debt that all who know their works will understand. Gordon Braden, Leo Damrosch, Nora Jaffe, William Little, Eric Reeves, John Richetti, Harold Skulsky, and John P. Wright read various stages of the manuscript and made a number of helpful suggestions. For answers to specific questions, I am happy to thank A. C. Crombie, Allen Debus, Brian Holly, Lester S. King, Angela Mirenda, and Alan Wiesenthal; for assistance in preparing the manuscript, Jennifer Heath, David Marshall, and Marjory Zaik. For the time and freedom necessary to write, I am grateful for fellowships from the American Council of Learned Societies, the National Endowment for the Humanities, and the William Andrews Clark Memorial Library (University of California at Los Angeles).

Part I

Stages in the history of the idea of probability

I

From rhetoric to science

Sollicite cura te ipsum probabile exhibere Deo. (Vulgate)
Studie to shewe thy selfe approved unto God. (Authorized Version)
2 Timothy 2: 15

... et probabilis in conspectu omnium virorum.
Liber filii Jesu Sirach

A primary sense of *probabilis* in Latin is *worthy of approbation* or *approval*, in an evaluative, even a moral sense. Samuel Parr, reputedly among England's greatest classicists in the late eighteenth century, discovered how many of the Latinists of his day had forgotten this meaning of *probabilis* when he was chosen to write Samuel Johnson's epitaph. Although a veteran in the genre, Dr. Parr at first balked at the assignment; persuaded by Malone and Sir William Scott, however, he composed an inscription that began:

SAMUELI JOHNSON
GRAMMATICO ET CRITICO
SCRIPTORUM ANGLICORUM LITTERATE PERITO
POETAE PROBABILI

Parr chose the adjective *probabilis*, he says in a letter, "in conformity to the rule I had laid down for avoiding all rhetorical phraseology," that is, to avoid overblown praise; he recounts the term's critical reception: "In arms were all the Johnsonians: Malone, Steevens, Sir W. Scott, Windham and even Fox, all in arms ... They do not understand it." To explain his usage, Parr sent Fox a list of illustrative passages from Cicero, Quintilian, and others. Parr's critics debated the lukewarmness of the epithet; at last, Parr himself suggested a revision that the Johnsonians approved:

POETAE LUMINIBUS SENTENTIARUM
ET PONDERIBUS VERBORUM ADMIRABILI

Parr confided to a friend that this new formula filled him with a "secret and invincible loathing," but the classicist, painfully aware of the possibilities of modern misreading, must have enjoyed the heavy touch of his second line.[1]

3

English use of *probable* long retained the Latin evaluative sense. In *Roxana* (1724), Defoe's heroine reflects on the new establishment her first catch has provided her:

This was the first View I had of living comfortably indeed, and it was a very probable Way, I must confess; seeing we had very good Conveniences, six Rooms on a Floor, and three Stories high.

Here *probable*, like *likely* in expressions still in use ("a likely lad"), means worthiness not of belief but approval.[2]

More often the English word carries the familiar sense of worthiness of belief or credit. Until the Renaissance, however, the grounds of such credit were most commonly understood to be authoritative testimony – so much so that for many, *probability* itself simply meant backing by authority. As we shall see, the Renaissance paradigm for explaining probability comes from rhetoric, and more directly from the "place" of "external" or "inartificial" proofs, that is, proofs which come from the testimony of more or less authoritative (and hence *probable*) witnesses. It is in this sense that so many generations of moral theologians understood a "probable opinion" to be one held by some "probable doctor" of the Church.[3] Witnesses whose testimony was formally admissible in court were "probable witnesses," and apt requests were "probable demands"; for Richard Hooker, the authority of the *vox populi* was society's "probable voice":

So that of peace and quietness there is not any way possible, unlesse the probable voice of everie intier societie or bodie politique over-rule all private of like nature in the same bodie.[4]

(1) PROBABILITY AND THE TESTIMONY OF AUTHORITY

And let them know that I am Machevil,
And weigh not men, and therefore not men's words.

Marlowe, *The Jew of Malta* (1589–90)

Renaissance use of *probable* reflects a millennium of philosophic doctrine. A selective reading of Aristotle common in the Middle Ages found in the *Prior Analytics* that "A probability is a generally approved proposition," and in the *Topics* that "opinions are 'generally accepted' which are accepted by every one or by the majority or by the philosophers – i.e., by all, or by the majority, or by the most notable and illustrious of them."[5] This interpretation of probability remains central through the seventeenth century:

4

Probable logic is concerned with propositions which, to all or to many men, or at least to the wise, seem to be valid ... A proposition is probable if it seems so to a person of good judgment ...

John of Salisbury, *Metalogicon* (1159)

Probabilia autem dicuntur, quae sunt magis nota vel sapientibus vel pluribus.

Aquinas, Commentary on *Posterior Analytics* (c. 1270)

Second, whenever he is dealing with the subject he brings in the testimony of the ancients, which is the way of one who is out, not to demonstrate, but to recommend according to probabilities [*probabiliter persuadentis*].

Aquinas, *Summa theologiae* (1265–73)

But a topical syllogism is from probable premises. And probable premises are those which appear to be true to all or to the majority or to the wisest; and this description is to be understood thus, that probable premises are those which are true and necessary but not known *per se* and not syllogistically demonstrable from premises known *per se*, and which, further, are not evidently known through experience, nor demonstrable from such – but which, on account of their truth, appear to be true to all or to the majority or to the wisest.

Ockham, *Summa totia logicae* (c. 1320)

Things probable according to *Aristotle*, are these that seeme true to all men, or to the most part of men, or to all wise men, or to the moste parte of wise men, or els to the most approved wise men: whereby it appeareth that things probable may be said five manner of waies.

Thomas Blundeville, *The Art of Logike* (1599)

That Axiome is probable which seemes so to all, to many, or them that are wise ...

Thomas Spencer, *The Art of Logick* (1628)

All tradition and history, everything in short that concerns the past, whether it be true or false, good or evil, possesses for us only probability, since it depends on the authority of the narrator.

Herbert of Cherbury, *De Veritate* (1624)[6]

The doctrine of the logicians inevitably informs less technical uses of the word. Hooker, whose *Laws of Ecclesiastical Polity* has been called "an extended essay on probabilities," frequently finds need, in his attempt to steer clear of both Puritan and Catholic excesses, for distinctions between probable and demonstrative knowledge; his probabilities rest clearly on authority:

For the publike approbation given by the body of this whole Church unto those things which are established, doth but make it probable that they are good...

Howbeit in defect of proofe infallible, because the minde doth rather follow probable perswasions, then approve the things that in them have no likelihood of truth at all; surely if a question concerning matter of doctrine were proposed, and on the one side no kinde of proofe appearing, there should on the other side be alleaged and shewed that so a number of the learnedest divines in the world have ever thought; although it did not appear what reason or what scripture led them to be of that judgment somewhat a reasonable man would attribute, notwithstanding the common imbecilities which are incident into our nature.[7]

So may the adverb *probably* mean "with authority," as in Sir Thomas Browne's *Pseudodoxia Epidemica* (1646), a work intended to explain the causes of error and so the proper grounds of belief:

So [with caution] are we to read the leaves of Basil and Ambrose, in their books entitled *Hexameron*, or *The description of the Creation*; Wherein delivering particular accounts of all the Creatures, they have left us relations sutable to those of Aelian, Plinie and other naturall Writers; whose authorities herein they followed, and from whom most probably they desumed their narrations.[8]

"Authority" in this discussion carries the old sense of *auctoritas* – origination (authoring), just as *auctoro* could mean "stand surety to"; authorities are the sources of testimony, so that mediaeval disputants habitually called the authorities whose testimony they cited *auctoritates*; the term by extension could refer to the testimonies themselves.[9] What is most important for our purposes is to recognize that ancient rhetoricians and lawyers (often the same people) attempted to lay down rules by which the proper weight to be given to the testimony of any authority (or witness) might be judged; because the probability of opinions was usually measured by reference to the authority that backed them, these rules continued into the Renaissance to be the most common, and sometimes the only explicit canons in terms of which the probability of any claim might be judged.

That this should have been so can be seen by examining those contexts in which we should most expect other, more modern canons of probability to have arisen. In jurisprudence, for instance, we would expect there to have been a continuous effort to formulate canons for judging the credibility of testimony; many modern legal historians have argued, however, that this was not the case, and indeed that more often in question was not the credibility of testimony but of witnesses themselves. As Theodore Waldman has shown in his study of the "Origins of the Legal Doctrine of Reasonable Doubt," it was not until the mid eighteenth century that English jurists worked out what we would now recognize as a system of rules of evidence. What rules had earlier been accepted, and which came in the Augustan period to be scrutinized and reduced to method, were those of the logicians and rhetoricians. It is significant that Baron Geoffrey Gilbert, in the first English work on the subject, his posthumous *Law of Evidence* (1753), borrows his canons from John Locke. (In 1752 had appeared Gilbert's *Abstract of Mr Locke's Essay on Human Understanding*.) Gilbert pillages especially Locke's discussions in book IV of "Probability" and of the "Degrees of Assent" (chapters 15 and 16); as we shall find, Locke's own attempt to give a general philosophic account of the degrees of probability amounts to little more than a repetition of older canons for judging the reliability of witnesses.

Sir William Holdsworth explains the late development in England of rules of evidence by reference to the gradual change between about 1500 and 1700 in the composition of English juries. Earlier juries contained members chosen because they could be expected to have most previous knowledge of the case being heard; later ones, members without such prior knowledge.

> The change in the character of the jury, which made the presence of . . . witnesses necessary, had an effect upon the law of evidence as profound as it had upon the law of pleading. Now that the verdict was based, not upon their own knowledge, but on the evidence produced to them in court, some law about this evidence became necessary.[10]

As Sir John Fortescue had put it in 1460, in rebutting the charge that English courts defied the Biblical injunction that no man be convicted on the testimony of a single witness, there are always in the jury twelve more witnesses to the case.[11]

In Europe, where most criminal cases were tried not before juries but by magistrates (who, lacking prior knowledge of cases, had to call witnesses), there developed in the Roman-canon legal tradition a complex quasi-mathematical system for evaluating testimony. Various kinds of testimony were given numerical values according to the degree of probability with which they incriminated the defendant; in some versions, a total of three points justified a verdict of "guilty" (and mere appearance before the court was presumptive evidence of guilt worth half a point).[12] This system grew from Biblical, Roman, and mediaeval practice; it is largely a system for evaluating witnesses and their authority rather than evidence. More witnesses would be required to secure conviction of a noble than a commoner; greater number of witnesses constituted weightier proof; and for centuries, the mere taking of an oath put the substance of a witness' testimony beyond dispute. One English judge stated in 1632, "A judge is bound ever to give sentence *secundum probata*, not *probabilia*."[13]

The survivals in France of this system were to appall Voltaire, who made a special study of the rules of evidence: in the *Dictionnaire philosophique* he deplores the view that legal guilt can be established as can a theorem in geometry, and in his later *Essai sur les probabilités en fait de justice* (1772), he attempts an analysis of what we recognize as the probability of evidence.

Presque toute la vie humaine roule sur des probabilités... Cependant il faut prendre un parti, et il ne faut pas le prendre au hasard. Il est donc nécessaire à notre nature faible, aveugle, toujours sujette à l'erreur, d'étudier les probabilités avec autant de soin que nous apprenons l'arithmétique et la géométrie.

Cette étude des probabilités est la science des juges: science aussi respectable que leur autorité même, puisqu'elle est le fondement de leurs décisions.

Un juge passe sa vie à peser des probabilités les unes contre les autres, à les calculer, à évaluer leur force. (496–97)

Previous simple additive methods avoided the real work of *weighing* probabilities (instead of counting authorities); also, they took into account only marks of guilt, not of innocence. "Il se peut que vingt apparences contre lui soient balancées par une seule en sa faveur." Making wry reference to the disreputable school of moral theology called "probabilism," which was supposed to have held that a "probable opinion" backed by only a single authority (however many might be cited to the contrary) may properly be taken as a maxim for action, Voltaire continues, "C'est là le cas, et le seul cas, de la doctrine de probabilisme." (J. H. Wigmore has noted that the Code Napoléon was designed to wean juries away from the view that more witnesses and oaths means more probability and evidence.)[14]

In England, Matthew Hale can speak in his *History of the Pleas of the Crown* (posthumously published in 1736) of the "probability or improbability, credibility or incredibility of the witness and his testimony"; as Barbara Shapiro has noted, the paired terms are not synonymous, for Hale is distinguishing "legal" witnesses (those whose testimony is formally admissible) from those who can be believed.[15] As late as 1751, in *Amelia*, Henry Fielding protests the legal confusion of the admissible with the believable:

In truth this matter was no less than what the law calls forgery, and was just then made capital by an act of Parliament. From this offence, indeed, the attorney was acquitted, by not admitting the proof of the party, who was to avoid his own deed by his evidence, and therefore no witness, according to those excellent rules called the law of evidence; a law very excellently calculated for the preservation of the lives of his Majesty's roguish subjects, and most notably used for that purpose. (VII, 256)

(2) PROBABILITY, OPINION, AND KNOWLEDGE

A demonstrative syllogism is one that produces scientific knowledge on the basis of necessary premises and the most certain reasons for the conclusion. A dialectical syllogism, however, is one that produces opinion on the basis of probable premises. Finally, a sophistical syllogism is one that either syllogizes on the basis of seemingly probable premises or seemingly syllogizes on the basis of probable premisses; in either case it is strictly aimed at glory or victory.

William of Sherwood, *Introductiones in logicam* (1235–50)[16]

William's tripartite division comes directly from Aristotle and is typical of logical works through the seventeenth century. Aristotle's distinction between opinion (*endoxa*), the realm of the probable, and the scientific certainty of *episteme*, or knowledge in its fullest sense, remains standard philosophical usage even through the Augustan period (though the boundaries of each may vary), as Locke and his follower Isaac Watts testify:

Probability is likeliness to be true... The entertainment the Mind gives this sort of Propositions, is called *Belief, Assent,* or *Opinion,* which is the admitting or receiving any Proposition for true, upon Arguments that are found to perswade us to receive it as true, without any certain Knowledge that it is so.

Uncertain or *dubious Propositions,* that is *Opinions,* are distinguished into *probable,* or *improbable.*[17]

Scholastic writers could use *probabilia* to mean simply the opinions of the authors they cited.[18]

It hardly required a Locke or a Butler, then, to point out that, in the words of John of Salisbury's *Metalogicon,* "probabilities" – opinions – "comprise most of human knowledge" (201). In the central Western tradition from late antiquity to the Augustans, the ideal of knowledge – *scientia,* "science" in its pre-nineteenth-century sense – was demonstrative knowledge, especially of the causes of things. *Scire est cognoscere per causas* runs the familiar tag: true knowledge is of necessary connections, demonstrative arguments linking causes to effects with certainty. By definition, *scientia* excluded all nondeductive, nondemonstrative proofs – all probability – locating these in the subordinate fields of dialectic and rhetoric. After dividing logic into "demonstration, probable proof, and sophistry" (again following Aristotle's division of the Organon into *Analytics, Topics,* and *On Sophistical Refutations*), John of Salisbury says of demonstration that "it rejoices in necessity. It does not pay attention to what various people may think about a given proposition," for what people may think is probability, whose sphere is "dialectic and rhetoric." "Demonstration does not calculate to elicit assent" (*probabilitatem non habet demonstratio*) (79–80). Containing no concept of evidence short of the deductive, *scientia* excludes probability: in science confirmation is always complete. As Aquinas notes, it excludes most of what we "know"; most of the time we must be satisfied with rhetoric: "In human affairs it is not possible to have demonstration

and infallible proof; but it suffices to have some conjectural probability such as the rhetor uses to persuade."[19]

The proper form of demonstration is the demonstrative syllogism,
distinguished from other sorts of syllogisms less in its form than in
the demands placed upon its premises. These must be either the
conclusions of other demonstrative ("scientific") syllogisms, or be
first principles arrived at by demonstrative induction (a process
different from the problematic induction of modern science).[20] Such
premises must of course be true; they must moreover be necessary
(*de omni*), essential (*per se*), commensurately universal (*qua ipsum*),
prior to and better known than the conclusion, and most signally (at
least in the minds of Aristotle's commentators), they must be causes,
since "to have reasoned knowledge of a conclusion is to know it
through its cause."[21]

The demand that demonstrative premises be necessary means
that they must be always and in every case true; that they be
essential, that they state a connection between universals. "Knowledge is of the necessary, opinion of the contingent," or, as Thomas
Spencer put it in his *Art of Logick*, "A true axiom is Contingent,
when it is such sort true, that it may also at some time be false. This is
called opinion" (157). Strictly then, knowledge and opinion are not
just different degrees of certainty with respect to the same information, but actually have different objects. The *Metalogicon*
explains, science can answer the question "What is whiteness?" but
cannot through a connection of universals tell whether a given object
is white; to answer this question, "one is compelled to digress to
corporeal things" (159). There is thus no science of the contingent,
either in the sense of the particular, or of propositions sometimes
true, sometimes false – no science of "changeable things":

no attribute can be demonstrated nor known by strictly scientific knowledge to
inhere in perishable things. The proof can only be accidental, because the
attribute's connection with the perishable subject is not commensurately universal but temporary and special... the conclusion can only be that a fact is true at
the moment – not commensurably and universally.[22]

The senses, then, give only opinion, not knowledge.[23] Of Grosseteste's acceptance of these demands on demonstrative premises
A. C. Crombie remarks, "From this it followed that 'chance or luck'
were not subjects for science."[24]

The demand that demonstrative premises be causes means both
that premises in a demonstrative syllogism refer to the causes in
nature of the effects mentioned in the conclusion, and that the
premises themselves be causes of their conclusion. In this way, for
instance, Thomas Spencer can define "cause" as "a proposition,

whereof another doth follow" (280). The middle term in demonstration is in particular to be the cause of the conclusion. Following the model of Greek mathematics, wherein properties of a geometrical figure are explained by showing that they follow from the definition of the figure, scientific explanation was to show that effects to be explained follow from the nature of the objects which change. When we have a sufficiently good definition of a thing, we have as well the explanatory grounds – the necessary and sufficient causes – of changes in it; causation and definition are opposite sides of a single coin. "It is all one... to know the nature of a thing, and to know the cause of the nature" (*Art of Logick*, p. 280). Demonstration thus requires all the knowledge needed to explain natural phenomena deductively.

Such is the "knowledge" from which probable "opinion" is for centuries distinguished. In the Middle Ages and Renaissance, only what might be called the "high" sciences were agreed truly to embody knowledge: the list changes, but theology, metaphysics, and mathematics are nearly always on it, astronomy, optics, and physics usually, and a host of others sometimes, when a given writer wishes to defend his discipline or to make a polemical point. The "low" sciences – medicine, mineralogy, meteorology, alchemy, astrology – consisted only of "opinion." Representatives of the low sciences frequently held views unorthodox both philosophically and theologically, and so contributed to the bad odor surrounding the word *opinion* in the sixteenth and seventeenth centuries. *Opinion* bore connotations of singularity, faction, and even heresy:

These times are dangerous for men to write, much more to write opinions.

Learned without opinion, and strange without heresy.

Where most power of the gospel, most prodigies of heresies and opinion.

A heretic, said Bossuet, is a man who has an opinion; according to Malebranche, "Les devots ne sont donc pas opiniâtres."[25] English usage followed French, so that stubborn adherence to opinion is *opiniatrety*, as it is to Locke:

What in them was Science, is in us but Opiniatrety, whilst we give up our Assent only to reverend Names, and do not, as they did, employ our own Reason to understand those Truths, which gave them reputation;

"'tis time," announces *The Vanity of Dogmatizing*, "for the opinionative world, to lay down their proud pretensions."[26]

The survival of *scientia* even into the Augustan age has never been sufficiently attended to by literary scholars. When Pope, for instance, writes in the *Essay on Man*, "Why has not Man a microscopic eye? / For this plain reason, Man is not a Fly" (I. 193–94), he is giving an Aristotelian demonstrative syllogism in the second figure, one which depends on the suppressed premiss that being a fly and having a "microscopic eye" are, in the language of Aristotelian logic, commensurately universal; he was giving a kind of explanation that, however unilluminating today, made good sense within the older theory of science. Spencer discusses the same logical paradigm in his *Art of Logick*:

In a demonstration that showeth what a thing is, sometimes also the medium is placed without the extreames, as when we say, why doth not the wall breath? Wee answer, because it is not a living creature: and these Syllogisms are always made in the second figure; after this sort: whatsoever doth breath, is a living creature: But the wall is not a living creature. Therefore a wall doth not breath.[27]

Within the system that made knowledge and opinion so radically distinct, probabilia and the objects of science were to be known through the use of different mental processes and the application of different faculties. Thus, to a mind differently constituted from the human, what to us is only probable might be the object of science. In the Middle Ages and Renaissance, these reflections notoriously made themselves felt in the debate over the quality of Adam's prelapsarian epistemic state. Aquinas, for example, says that in Eden Adam had nearly no opinions ("penitus nulla opinio"); the Fall altered his mind, so that what once he could *know*, he could later only form opinions about.[28] Abraham Cowley interprets the Fall in this way in his poem of 1656, "The Tree of Knowledge: That There Is No Knowledge Against the Dogmatists." Here the Tree is

> That Right Porphyrian Tree which did true Logick shew,
> Each Leaf did learned Notions give,
> And th' Apples were Demonstrative.

By eating of the Tree, man did not gain knowledge; "the only Science Man by this did get" was the condemned state in which he "searches Probabilities, / And Rhetorick, and Fallacies."

"Before the fal of Adam," writes Thomas Wilson in the first vernacular English logic, his *Rule of Reason* (1551), "his knowledge was perfeicte, but through offence, darknesse folowed, and the bright light was taken awaie. Wisemen therefore ... inuented this Arte" of logic, for, as Spencer writes in his *Art*, using the same strategy, "hereby (in some sort) is healed the wound received in our reason by *Adams* fall" (8–9; Preface). For these logicians, all probability is finally "mere" probability. Common usage follows; Bacon contrasts "pretty and probable conjectures" with "certain and demonstrative knowledge," and Thomas Nashe speaks in *The*

Terrors of the Night (1594) of the distance between probability and truth:

> Will you have the summe of all: some subtill humorist, to feed fantasticke heads with innovations and novelties, first invented this trifling and childish glose uppon dreams and phisiognomie; wherein he strove onely to boast himself of a pregnant probable conceipt beyond philosophie or truth.[29]

(3) HUMANISM AND THE REVIVAL OF CICERONIAN SKEPTICISM

> As for Ciceronians and suger-tongued fellowes, which labour more fore fineness of speech, then for knowledge of good matter, they oft speake much to small purpose, and shaking foorth a number of choise words and picked sentences, they hinder good learning, wyth their fond chatte.
>
> Ralph Lever, *The Arte of Reason* (1573)

"Probable evidence," writes Bishop Butler, "is essentially distinguished from demonstrative by this, that it admits of degrees." In the main tradition of Aristotelian demonstrative science, *scientia* always and alone possesses certainty, which is all or nothing. There may be degrees of conviction (assent) over the uncertain – the probable – but probabilities have no place in science.[30] But how much of our knowledge is really science? Few scholastics would have disagreed with Aurelio Brandolini, writing in *The Human Condition* (1488) that "There is no certainty in human affairs, everything is probable, the arrogance of affirmation should be avoided in all things"; but fewer still would have been in accord with those humanists who believed, with Juan Luis Vives in his *De Tradendis disciplinis* (1531), that "All philosophy is based entirely upon opinions and probable conjectures."[31]

Contemporary enemies of humanism, such as Ralph Lever, commonly condemned that movement as mere cultivation of Latin eloquence, and it is not unusual today to be told that the humanists' main interest was in the "subordination of logic to rhetorical values."[32] The humanists themselves contributed to this impression; Lorenzo Valla, for instance, proudly denied that he was a philosopher and repeatedly elevated rhetorical persuasion above the "mere proofs" of logic.[33] But recent pioneering work, taking seriously its claims to a Ciceronian union of wisdom and eloquence, has found in humanism an intellectual core: "not a shift from respectable dialectic to the 'soft option' of rhetoric, but a shift from certainty to probability as the focus of intellectual attention," through revival of certain elements of ancient skepticism.[34] The skeptical project had advanced so far by 1555 that even a humanist such as Ramus could complain in his *Dialectique*, his contemporaries clearly in mind, of "the Pyrrhonians and the New Academicians," who misuse dialectic "to overthrow certitude and science" (Preface). The resources of such skepticism came both from ancient texts recently rediscovered (Cicero's *Academica*, the works of Sextus) and from doctrines ignored or rejected by the architects of *scientia*; these doctrines suggest an alternative history of probability.

The distinction between knowing for certain and mere surmise is already clear in Homer, while that between knowledge and opinion (or conjecture) appears in Xenophanes and Parmenides; without defining his terms, Parmenides distinguishes the necessity of truth from the "Way of Opinion," which comprises only the likely (εικότα).[35] Working out of the methods of probable argument – argument from εικός – came in the fifth century BC with the birth of rhetoric itself. According to ancient accounts still accepted, rhetoric and its scheme of probable argument arose at a particular time and place in response to specific practical needs: in Sicily, where, after the overthrow of the tyrants and the establishment of democracy, orators had special need to plead in courts of law (which often kept no relevant written records) about contested matters of property and citizenship, and citizen members of popular assemblies, no longer courtiers advising a king who made final decisions, had to argue and decide uncertain matters of public policy.[36] Pride of place here is usually given to Corax of Syracuse, who practiced and taught an art of persuasion after the fall of Hiero (465 BC), and to his pupil Tisias (who may have been the teacher of Isocrates in Athens). In the *Phaedrus*, Plato cites Tisias and Gorgias as founders of rhetoric; he equates rhetoric with arguments from εικός, which he says its practitioners defined as "what people think," that body of commonly held opinion to which the orator must appeal in his attempt to persuade the masses (266b–67d).

Plato thus distinguishes εικότα from true knowledge; for him, even the natural sciences could attain only to probability – in Sambursky's phrase, a "likely story" about nature. According to Simplicius, "Aptly did Plato call natural science (φυσιολογία) the science of the probable (εικοτολογία)," for both the scientist and orator rely in persuasion on commonly held views that are like truth (the root sense of εικός) but are not truth itself.[37] Aristotle is the first explicitly to define probability and integrate it into a larger theory of knowledge. In the *Posterior Analytics* and the *Rhetoric*, εικότα are what is usually the case; from a faith that the truth will appear, Aristotle could all but equate them with opinion.[38] In Aristotle's system, necessary (changeless) truths are the stuff of science (ἐπιστήμη), whose instrument is demonstration, while what is true for the most part is the material of dialectic. What is merely plausible or probable (πιθανός), and so may happen to persuade, is that of rhetoric. Something like this division of what had been two aspects of probability remains standard through most of the Middle Ages.[39] But in the ancient world after Aristotle the career of probability becomes more complex, especially among the skeptics.

The grouping of schools collectively called skeptic (from the Greek meaning inquirer or observer, a term used as early as the Pyrrhonians themselves) represents a discontinuous tradition including the early Pyrrhonists (Pyrrho of Elis himself and his student Timon, c. 375–225 BC); the New Academy of Arcesilaus (315–240 BC) and Carneades (214–129 BC); the work of Aenesidemus (a mysterious figure whose origins we do not know and who may have lived at any time from 80 BC to AD 130); and that of Sextus Empiricus (AD ?150–250, location again unknown).[40] Whereas Pyrrhonism, essentially a practical doctrine, denied that any truth may be known and advocated a thorough-going suspension of judgment in all matters, the Academics (who saw themselves as maintaining the tradition of the Academy) developed a doctrine of probability and methods of argument for justifying assent based on probabilities. Carneades was the school's greatest teacher, Cicero its best-known ancient exponent.

Academic skepticism arose in opposition to Stoic claims to certain knowledge of the external world based on the way reality imprints itself on (creates impressions in) the mind. Carneades – the first to make clear the distinction between a definition and a criterion of truth – argued that no impression gives certainty about reality; impressions are only credible (πιθανός) or implausible (ἀπίθανος). But assent to the uncertain is not arbitrary: Carneades devises three tests of impressions – that they be credible, consistent, and proven in experience – three criteria of probability which, as Charlotte Stough explains, can be "ranked according to their capacity to produce conviction," and so constitute a "doctrine of evidence" (57, 62). (Since for the Academics truth cannot itself be known, while yet there are standards of credibility, they do not use the term εἰκός.)

Carneades introduced as well a practical method (*ratio argumentandi*) for establishing probabilities. Aristotle had given this task to dialectic; famous as a debater for arguing both sides of any question (like the rhetoricians Plato condemned), Carneades developed the method of argument *in utramque partem*, a procedure best known to the Renaissance through the theory and practice of Cicero. Cicero defends the practice in the *Academica*:

The sole object of our discussions [*disputationes*] is by arguing on both sides [*in utramque partem dicendo*] to draw out and give shape to some result that may be either true or the nearest possible approximation to the truth. Nor is there any difference between ourselves and those who think that they have positive knowledge except that they have no doubt that their tenets are true, whereas we hold many doctrines as probable [*probabilia*], which we can easily act upon but can scarcely advance as certain. (II. 3. 7–8)

In the same dialogue, creating a Latin vocabulary for the transmission of Greek thought, Cicero coins the phrase *veri simile* to mean what, as he defines *verisimile* elsewhere, is most like truth in being "that which usually occurs in such and such a way"; as Lisa Jardine explains, Cicero means verisimilitude to render the Greek εἰκός, which he understands as the highest degree of the πιθανός.[41] In fact, what Cicero has done here is to create a rapprochement between dialectic (εἰκός) and rhetoric (πιθανός) for deliberating under uncertainty, as well as a philosophical justification for such deliberation's literary instrument, the dialogue. Here, too, are the grounds of his famous project of uniting eloquence with wisdom: in the "dubia materia" of law and policy as in more strictly philosophical matters, orator and Academic skeptic follow one *ratio argumentandi*.[42]

Charles Schmitt has found after extensive research that "the continuity of [ancient skepticism] with the Middle Ages was practically nil"; interest was to revive only in the fifteenth century in Italy, then in Northern Europe in the sixteenth – when, as it happens, Cicero's *Academica* and the works of Sextus were rediscovered. (The Latin word *scepticus* appears only once in classical texts, in Aulus Gellius, and only twice in the Middle Ages, in two little-known texts of Sextus; it and its vernacular forms became popular only in the 1400s.)[43] Better known to the Middle Ages was Augustine's discrediting of skepticism in his *Contra Academicos*; with its rejection of argument *in utramque partem* as inimical to faith, Augustine's work changed the way dialogue was written and was the first text to be reckoned with by Petrarch and Leonardo Bruni when they revived dialogue in Ciceronian form.[44] Skepticism was reborn, moreover, quite independently of Aristotelianism, which remained the dominant tradition in philosophy until well into the seventeenth century.

At the philosophic core of humanism are its classics of reformist dialectic: the *Dialecticae disputationes* of Lorenzo Valla (1439), Rudolph Agricola's *De Dialectica inventione* (1479), and later formulations such as Philip Melanchthon's *Erotemata dialectices* (1548) and the works of Ramus. The intellectual inspiration of such works was recognized in their own time; for instance, the Aristotelian Bartholomeo Viotti, in his *De Demonstratione* (1560), finds the attempts of Agricola and Melanchthon to replace "science" with a "dialectic of probabilities" to savor of Pyrrhonian and Academic skepticism.[45] The kind of teaching which these writers wished to displace is typified by the *Summulae logicales* (1246) of Peter of Spain (later Pope John XXI), which had remained the standard text in dialectic for nearly three centuries.[46] Peter could define dialectic as an art that "reasons with probability (*probabiliter disputat*)," but his emphasis is on deductive arguments nonetheless. Scientific demonstration depended on syllogisms whose premises contained necessary connections of universals and were either the conclusions of other scientific syllogisms or were principles arrived at by induction; when these stringent conditions were not met, an argument was to be classed as at best dialectical.

Valla and his followers voice continued doubt about our ability to have true knowledge of universals, and Aristotle's notoriously mysterious doctrine of induction had already been the grounds of voluminous commentary and complaint.[47] Thus when Agricola defines dialectic as "the art of discoursing probably [*ars probabiliter disserendi*] on any subject, insofar as the nature of the subject is capable of creating conviction [*fidei*]," the familiar formula betrays a new emphasis.[48] Agricola is uniting logic and dialectic into a single art not of disputation but of discourse generally; the conflation is completed by Ramus, who defines dialectic as "the art of discoursing well [*ars bene disserendi*], and in the same sense it is called logic." "Logique is an Arte to reason probably" echoes Thomas Wilson in the first vernacular English logic.[49] In building a reformed dialectic, the humanists moreover had not merely blurred the distinction between logic and dialectic; they had so plundered rhetoric of its tools of persuasion that little was left for rhetoric but ornament and embellishment; humanist rhetoricians admit that much of what they have to say has been covered in works on dialectic, as does Wilson in his *Arte of Rhetorique* (1553):

Therefore I wish that every man should desire, and seeke to have his *Logique* perfit, before he looke to profite in *Rhetorique*, considering the ground and confirmation of its causes, is for the most part gathered out of Logique. (113)

From this blurring of Aristotelian distinctions emerges finally the "single method" of Ramus.

The most important persuasive techniques transferred from rhetoric to dialectic were the rhetorical topics; moreover, within dialectic itself, which had always been understood to consist of both a *pars inveniendi* (including dialectical topics) and a *pars iudicandi*, whereas in the Middle Ages judgment had received most attention, Renaissance works stress invention. Agricola himself treats only invention in his treatise on dialectic; a proposed continuation on judgment was never written. In a common Renaissance formulation, he defines a topic: "A place [*locus*] is nothing other than a certain common mark of a thing, with which it is possible to discover [*inveniri*] what is probable [*probabile*] of it."[50] Valla had already elevated epicheireme (nondeductive argument) above syllogism, and constructed a scale of the *verisimile* from the merely *credibile* to the *semiverum*; Agricola blurs the very distinction between probable and certain knowledge; and later writers on topical argument, such as Vives in his *De Instrumento probabilitatis*, conflate dialectical and rhetorical topics with Aristotle's categories themselves.[51]

"He who is concerned with the discovery of the probable is called an *Inventor*," writes Vives in the *De Tradendis disciplinis*, "and he who passes judgment on what has been discovered by probability is called a critic [*censor*]."[52] Topical argument in general and its presentation by argument *in utramque partem* in particular leave open a problem: how in practice are such arguments to be weighed? C. J. R. Armstrong finds that in Ciceronian dialogue, judgment "is left to someone outside the discussion itself: to you and me, to readers, to Brutus to whom the dialogue has been sent as to a judge ('iudex') who will adjudicate ('diiudicaberis') in the debate," while David Marsh traces in the revival of dialogue in the Renaissance a movement from similar open-endedness to a less probabilistic form in which one speaker typically pronounces his decision on the evidence accumulated.[53] Just as rhetoric itself was born in the need of orators and lawyers to devise persuasive arguments which would later be judged by others, humanist writers described the act of judgment as a forensic process and frequently use legal practice as a model for dialectic.[54] Dialectic must provide canons of probability by which to judge evidence; Vives writes in the *De Tradendis*:

> In the close investigation of truth, which has become so obscured to us, the judgment is advanced by a canon of probability; in forming an opinion which is based on conjecture, the instrument of dialectic is useful. It is called an examination as to the true [*censura veri*]. (40)

Craig Walton describes the formation of such canons: "The rhetorician's art of judgment is internalized, so to speak; rather than an art used in persuading oneself or others, judgment becomes an art of evaluating interrelationships between discoveries."[55]

Because the probable had for so long been understood largely in terms of what is commonly believed – the beliefs to which orator or lawyer must appeal – the first such canons to be codified concerned the relative weight to be given to the testimony of various witnesses or authorities. Following ancient ideas still common in the Renaissance, the most important of common opinions are the most universal: the εννοιαι κοιναι or *notiones communes*, which are central, for instance, to dialectic as conceived by Vives and Melanchthon, to the appeals to ordinary belief which fill Ciceronian dialogues, and to the appeals to ordinary linguistic usage that Valla made famous.[56] According to Vives, only after we have exhausted the *notiones communes* need we turn, in the familiar Aristotelian formulation, to "the testimony of the best, the most talented."[57]

It is worth pointing out before we consider the canons of probability in more detail that in the seventeenth century arguments such as this began to meet widespread resistance. If for Vives "We will accept as true whatever is recognized as such by the totality of mankind because, even after the original fall of man, God left in our minds as much light as is needed for our pilgrimage," a Malebranche can counter: "If we were fully enlightened, universal approbation would be an argument, but just the opposite is the case."[58] The disagreement here is not merely theological. In works such as the *Vérité des sciences, contre les sceptiques* (1625) of Mersenne begins a new project of restoring certainty to knowledge, a project most notably adopted by Descartes, who from the time of his *Regulae ad directionem ingenii* (1628) repeatedly and explicitly rejects all dependence on probability.[59] Because many writers continued to understand probability as resting on opinion (authority), the familiar seventeenth-century posture of rejecting previous authorities is less often the rallying cry of those wishing to clear away past errors to make room for a new probabilistic experimental science than of those seeking to clear away Renaissance probabilism to make room for a new philosophic and scientific certainty. Indeed, in the works of such scientists as Kepler and Galileo we now recognize an attempt to defend scientific certainty against the humanist skepticism of the Renaissance.[60]

(4) TOPICAL ARGUMENT AND THE CANONS OF PROBABILITY

In adopting or rejecting opinions, we must not choose on the basis of our like or dislike of those who have advanced them ... but we must be persuaded by the more certain, that is, follow the opinion of those who have arrived more certainly at the truth.

Aquinas, Commentary on Aristotle's *Metaphysics*

Probable argument in the guise of argument from authority reached in the Middle Ages a peak of importance and subtlety. In Aquinas, authority is measured by the distance of its source from divine illumination. In practice, Aquinas establishes two traditions of authority, secular and inspired, and an ascending hierarchy of particular authorities: common men, philosophers ("the wise," among whom Aristotle is wisest), doctors of the Church, saints, and at the pinnacle, scripture itself, the word of God. All opinions fall somewhere in the hierarchy; he says of Paul's use of the testimony of Aratus:

> Yet holy teaching employs such authorities only in order to provide as it were extraneous arguments from probability [*probabilibus*]. Its own proper authorities are those of canonical Scripture, and these it applies with convincing force. It has other proper authorities, the doctors of the Church, and these it looks to as its own, but for arguments that carry no more than probability.[61]

It was from such rankings of testimony by degree of their sources' authority that later philosophical accounts of the degrees of probability were to be formulated.

How are secular opinions to be weighed? Rhetoricians since the Greeks have known in what department of their field to classify the question: in the doctrine of topics, under the heading of "external" proofs. Cicero reduced Aristotle's places to system, dividing them first into "intrinsic" and "extrinsic" grounds of proof; he lists sixteen kinds of intrinsic places, but all extrinsic loci are arguments from testimony and authority. (Later writers mark the distinction with the terms "inward" and "outward," or "artificial" and "inartificial" proofs.) William of Sherwood, for example, defines authority in his *Introductiones* as "the confirmed opinion of some wise men, or, alternatively, a saying worthy of imitation"; "arguments from authority or from judicious opinion (which is the same thing)" are the first kind of "Arguments from Extrinsic Grounds" (it should be noted that William's definitions of authority and of probability are nearly identical). Arguments from extrinsic grounds, finally, are those wherein the middle term "lies outside the subject or predicate of the problem," that is, where information is brought to bear on a problem from sources external to the objects themselves under consideration (93). Nearly all Renaissance writers on logic make similar distinctions; among the best such accounts of the nature and ranking of authorities can be found in Blundeville's *Logike* of 1599.[62]

Secular writers began by following the theologians, as does Ramus in his *Logicke* of 1574:

The artificial argumente being expounded followeth consequently the unartificiall. The argument unartificiall or without arte is an argument which prouvethe or disprouvethe not of his owne nature, but by the strengthe which it hathe of some argument artificiall. And therefore when the matter is deaplie considered, it hathe but a lytle strengthe to prouve or disprouve. In civil and temporall affaires, the authoritie of the disputer gevethe no little creditte ther unto yf he be wyse, vertuous, and have the benevolence of the auditour: all these by one name may be called a testimonie. The Testimonie is parted into a devine and a humaine. (65)

Occasional texts such as Ralph Lever's *Art of Reason* add a third kind: "The witnesses upon whose authority proofes are grounded, are either heavenly, earthly, or infernall" (197). As it had been for Aquinas, divine testimony and it alone is beyond question, as Abraham Fraunce testifies in his *Lawiers Logike* (1588):

God is to be believed without exception, because God spake it; but men are so much either more or lesse credited, by how much their behavior & learning is more or lesse esteemed. (66v)

Innumerable writers proceed from this distinction to list canons whereby the testimony of human witnesses may be judged; the following from among Zachary Coke's "Canons of humane Testimony" (1654) are typical:

2. Proper, or ones own testimony of things, done or not done, especially on the worser part, if it be not wrong out of force, is counted for firm.
3. Publike testimonies of publick seals are firm.
4. Testimony of publick and long-lasting fame is also to be esteemed for meanly firm.
5. Old testimony is worth more than new.
8. Testimonies historical, of approved Historians, are firm.
9. Testimonies Theoretical of some great and received Author, alledged after reasons of a Theoretical conclusion, have great force.
10. Testimonies of many Wise men and Famous, is to be preferred before the testimony of one and obscure man.[63]

But argument from authority – argument drawn from external places – does not exhaust the kinds of argument catalogued by rhetoricians. *Intrinsic* places are the seats of arguments grounded not in testimony but, as Richard Sherry explains in his *Treatise of Schemes and Tropes* (1550), in "the thynge it selfe that is in question," or better, in the nature of things (78). Intrinsic places thus provide internal evidence for a conclusion. Where internal proofs are less than demonstrative, furthermore – where dialecticians proceed not by the single definitive argument but by that much more common Renaissance procedure both of argument and of literary structure which Sherry calls "a copious heaping of probacions" – they provide probable evidence for a conclusion. And the kinds of arguments most discussed by ancient skeptics and Renaissance humanists – and excluded by Scholastics and, later, Cartesians – are arguments from internal places.

That a topical logic may be the instrument of a dialectic genuinely grounded in the nature of things (rather than in authorities) is an obsession of Ramus from the time of his early *Aristotelicae animadversiones* (1543). He claims there: "ars dialectica est imago naturalis dialecticae ... vera ut dixi, legitimaque disserendi doctrina, est imago et pictura naturae." Invention, the power of finding probable arguments, Ramus derives from the Latin *in rem venire*, a laying open of the arguments which reside in things themselves. These arguments arise to invention in a natural order, an order which is itself an echo of the larger order of nature: the *arguments* which are the stuff of dialectic are simply the *relations* which obtain in nature, made present to the mind. Invention thus becomes a kind of natural reasoning, a kind of memory even, since according to Ramus its following out of the connections which reside in nature is in large part a remembering of the same patterns already encountered in other circumstances.[64]

In the *Topica*, the first cataloguing of the kinds of places, Cicero lists among the internal *loci*: definition, enumeration of parts, etymology, cognate words, genus, species, similarity or analogy, difference, contraries, adjuncts, antecedents, consequents, contradictions, efficient causes, effects, and comparison with events of greater, lesser, or equal importance. All these are classes of information which is in some sense in the object; several will become central to this book, and a history of arguments drawn from each place would be a not inadequate history of probability. In chapter II, we shall examine a doctrine of probable evidence known as the theory of probable signs; as effects which point with probability to their causes, such signs, though first developed in ancient medicine and always part of medical theory, were readily assimilated to the rhetorical model of the internal topics of cause and effect. From the place of "adjuncts" emerged another, related species of non-demonstrative evidence not grounded in testimony, known as "probable circumstances." For other writers, such as John Locke, to whose work we next shall turn, the ground of probable arguments not stemming from testimony is the internal place of "similarity or analogy." Locke understands analogy to be the ground of connection between all the objects of our knowledge which are related by a probability other than that of testimony: a *proposition* is probable if the state of affairs it describes resembles another state known more certainly to be the case; putting the same point another way – a way entailed by the limitations placed on our knowledge by Locke's theory of ideas – an *idea* is probable if it resembles another idea, one more securely grounded.

The best-known discussion of probability in the eighteenth century was Locke's in the *Essay concerning Human Understanding* (1690). Yet the sources of Locke's treatment have drawn the attention of nearly none of his commentators. Philosophers, such as Richard Aaron, find Locke on probability "disappointing," and so have little to say on the subject. In a passage that foreshadows Bishop Butler's maxim that "probability is the very guide of life," Locke declares that "He that in the ordinary Affairs of Life, would admit of nothing but direct plain Demonstration, would be sure of nothing, in this World, but of perishing quickly" (4. 11. 10). After such a statement, we expect a thorough analysis of the concept. But Locke's discussion is cursory, leading Leibniz to complain in the *New Essays*:

As for the inevitability of the result, and degrees of probability, we do not yet possess *that branch of logic* which would let them be estimated. And most casuists who have written on probability have not so much as understood the nature of it: they have sided with Aristotle in founding it upon authority, rather than upon likelihood [*vraisemblance*] as they ought to have, authority being only one of the reasons for something's likelihood. (II. xxi. 66)

Leibniz' criticism has not been sufficiently attended to. He understands not only that Locke's chapters on probability are cursory, but that they are derivative from rhetoric and theology.[65]

In his early *Essays on the Law of Nature*, Locke presents no account of probability at all, although he discusses belief and knowledge, and the degrees of assent. He does, however, devote space to "tradition" as a "way of knowing," a discussion that survives in Draft A of the *Essay* in his examination of such knowledge as we gain from "report of others" and the "testimony of historians"; as von Leyden notes, these passages are the germ of Locke's final treatment of probability itself in the *Essay* of 1690.[66]

Probability then, being to supply the defect of our Knowledge, and to guide us where that fails, is always conversant about Propositions, whereof we have no certainty, but only some inducements to receive them for true. The *grounds of it* are, in short, these *two* following:

First, The conformity of any thing with our Knowledge, Observation, and Experience.

Secondly, The Testimony of others, vouching their Observation and

Experience. In the Testimony of others, is to be considered, 1. Their Number. 2. The Integrity. 3. The Skill of the Witnesses. 4. The Design of the Author, where it is a Testimony out of a Book cited. 5. The Consistency of the Parts, and Circumstances of the Relation. 6. Contrary Testimonies. (4. 15. 4)

These are fully traditional canons; compare Locke's third with Coke's fourth. Locke occasionally improves on his sources; where Coke had "Old testimony is worth more than new," Locke enters a caveat:

the more hands the Tradition has successively passed through, the less strength and evidence does it receive from them. This I thought necessary to be taken notice of: Because I find amongst some Men, the quite contrary commonly practised, who look on Opinions to gain force by growing older. (4. 16. 10)

At a time when discussion of probability and testimony was inevitably also a contribution to religious controversy, Locke's target here includes Catholicism.[67] All Locke's canons are rooted in testimony, our own or others'; he even distinguishes divine testimony from human, calling the former "one sort of Propositions that challenge the highest Degree of our Assent, upon bare Testimony," because, in Cartesian fashion, "the Testimony is of such an one, as cannot deceive, nor be deceived" (4. 16. 14).

One of the earliest systems of mathematical probability in England was a quantification of Locke's canons of testimony. In 1699 John Craig published his *Theologiae Christianae Principia Mathematica* as well as a digest of its first two chapters, "A Calculation of the Credibility of Human Testimony" (in the Royal Society's *Transactions*). In addition to providing a method for calculating decrease with time in the credibility of oral or written testimony, the longer work argues that Christ will return to the earth in the year 3153, when the probability of the Biblical account of His first appearance will have dropped nearly to zero. It is perhaps Craig that Hume had in mind in the *Treatise* when, considering the question whether the credibility of all ancient history must have disappeared because testimony loses force with time, he writes,

Before I answer this objection I shall observe, that from this topic there has been borrow'd a very celebrated argument against the *Christian Religion*; but with this difference, that the connexion betwixt each link of the chain in human testimony has been there suppos'd not to go beyond probability, and to be liable to a degree of doubt and uncertainty.[68]

One of Locke's canons, "The Consistency of the Parts, and Circumstances of the Relation," is especially important to us because of the independent life it led in literary criticism; so often was this canon cited on its own that it became nearly a separate theory of probability. The criterion of consistency is of course not new; we have heard Carneades invoke it, and all ancient rhetoricians knew that testimony gains in force if it is consistent not only with other recognized opinion but with itself. In 1479 Agricola frames the point as a divergence from Aristotle:

the probable in discourse is not simply that which is truly probable, such as Aristotle defines it, as that which is seen to be so by all, by the many, or by the wisest . . . to us that will be probable, which is apt and congruent with the matter that has been proposed.[69]

Agricola may make an exception for consistency because it is clearly not an external proof like testimony, but an internal property; three centuries later George Campbell would suggest that mere consistency, because it is not clearly a relation to external evidence, be called not probability but "plausibility."[70]

Consistency was isolated from the other canons of probability for use in what we would call (although the Renaissance drew no such distinction) literary discussion. Campbell introduces "plausibility" in a treatment of criticism, and suggests as even a better word for it *verisimilitude*, to be understood, he says, as the French critics understand *vraisemblance*, as the consistency of narration. Agricola himself expands Aristotle's definition in order to discuss literature, and in particular fictional narrative, as a mode of teaching.[71] But how, to choose what has always been a difficult example, does a property of texts such as style *teach*? Quintilian writes in the *Institutes*:

Therefore we must not expect any speech to be ornate that is not, in the first place, acceptable [*probabilis*]. An acceptable style is defined by Cicero as one that is not over elegant. (8. 3. 42–43)

One of the means by which traditionally literature is to teach is its observance of decorums, appropriate relations of such properties of works as form and matter; and it turns out that observance of decorum is the way critics understood consistency, and so why consistency received treatment on its own.

When Thomas Wilson comes in his *Rhetorique* to his section "Of Narration," requiring there that a narrative be "Briefe," "plaine," and "probable," in order that "hearers may remember, understand, and beleeve" it (106), his account of the sources of probability in narration mixes together the need for backing by authoritative opinion and the need to observe decorums:

We shall make our sayings appeare likely, and probable: if we speake directly as the cause requireth. . .
The Narration reported in matters of iudgement, shall seem to stand with

reason, if we make our talk to agree with the place, time, thing, and person, if we shall shewe that whatsoever wee say, the same by all likelihoods is true, if our coniectures, tokens, reasons, and arguments be such, that neither in them, there appere any fabling, nor yet that any thing was spoken, which might of right otherwise be taken, and that we not onely speake this, but that divers other of good credite will stand with us in defence of the same, all which reporting may sone be liked, and the tale so tolde, may be thought very reasonable.

Decorums secure probability by guaranteeing that the "tale so tolde" will be consistent not only with accepted opinion, but with the ordinary pattern of nature (what happens most often). They do so precisely because decorums are formulations of such ordinary regularities as surround the topics of "place, time, thing and person." Wilson continues:

Yay, wee shall make our doings seeme reasonable, if we frame our worke to natures will, and seeke none other meanes but such onely, as the honest and wise have ever used and allowed, bringing in and blaming the evil alwayes, for such faultes chiefly, whereunto they most of all are like to be subject, as to accuse a spende all, of theft: a whoremonger, of adulterie: a rash quarreller, of manslaughter: and so of other. (107)

Decorums are "natures will" as the wisest have come to understand it, and so consistency is really an external place: it is backing by the highest authority, nature itself.

But probability understood in this way is also value-laden: it is consistency with nature's will rather than its constant practice. This comes clear in the debate between Lorenzo Valla and Bartholomeo Facio over Valla's *History of King Ferdinand of Aragon*. Valla had portrayed a king laughing, joking, and falling asleep, which to Facio was "contra precepta narrationis, ac verisimilitudine." Levity in a king is not "probabilis." Valla responds to Facio: "I am no poet."[72]

We shall be able to understand the relevance for literary thinking of this nexus of probability with decorum only when we have investigated a further element in it, that form of natural testimony known as the probable sign (the "coniectures" and "tokens" of which Wilson speaks). What we should understand now is that observance of decorums guarantees consistency (probability) by creating an *analogy* between a narration and the world outside. Whereas the strict definition of probability demands that claims be backed by specific testimonies, this wider definition allows for a much more general relation between claim and evidence, between work and world: a general relation that the Augustans were to invoke under the name of "the Analogy of Nature," and one of whose principal champions was John Locke.

In the *Essay*, Locke distinguishes the probability of "matters of fact" from what, for lack of a better label, have been called matters of "speculation" (4. 16. 5–12). The grounds of the first are "humane Testimony," especially that of "fair Witnesses"; matters of speculation, however, are such "that falling not under the reach of our Senses, they are not capable of Testimony" (4. 16. 12). (Testimony is here the direct confirmation of a conclusion, such as the senses provide in a visual report.) The sole ground of probability in matters of speculation is "*Analogy*." Matters not directly confirmable gain probability through analogical consistency. The probability of matters of fact is the probability of history; that of matters of speculation is the probability of scientific hypotheses, such as the physico-theology of a Butler in his *Analogy of Religion* (1736).

(5) LOCKE AND THE TWILIGHT OF PROBABILITY

When did ever any truth settle it self in any ones minde by the strength and authority of its own evidence? Truths gaine admittance to our thoughts as the philosopher did to the Tyrant[:] by their handsome dresse and pleaseing aspect, they enter us by composition, and are entertained as they suite with our affections ... Men live upon trust and their knowledg is noething but opinion moulded up betweene custome and Interest, the two great Luminarys of the world.

Locke, Letter to Tom (?Thomas Westrowe), 20 Oct. 1659

Despite its manifest debts to earlier treatments, Locke's *Essay* does present an original theory of probability, or rather, of the relation of the probable to the rest of our knowledge. A long line of seventeenth-century thinkers had placed the items of our knowledge on an ascending scale from merest probability to infallible certainty, but this was a scale only of the degrees of assent different kinds of propositions warrant, not a continuous scale based on similar ways of knowing propositions. Locke's distinctive contribution is his attempt to show that probable and certain knowledge arise from the same kinds of mental operation, and hence are epistemologically continuous; they differ in degree rather than kind. His position is the more remarkable when we recall that in Locke's favorite sources for the *Essay* – Descartes' early writings and the Port-Royal *Logic* – probability is radically different from genuine knowledge.

Book Four of the *Essay* presents an essentially Cartesian theory of knowledge. "*Knowledge* is nothing but *the perception of the connexion and agreement, or disagreement and repugnancy of any of our Ideas*" (4. 1. 2.). We perceive such agreement or disagreement by immediate intuition, wherein the mind "perceives the Truth, as the Eye doth light" (2. 1); Locke's assumption here is the very old one that however we may err about external states of affairs, we have incorrigibly certain awareness of our own mental contents. Demonstration provides knowledge only because each step in a demonstration rests on intuition. "The next degree of Knowledge [after intuition] is, where the Mind perceives the Agreement or Disagreement of any *Ideas*, but not immediately":

In this Case then, when the Mind cannot so bring its *Ideas* together, as by their immediate Comparison ... it is fain, by the Intervention of other *Ideas* (one or more, as it happens) to discover the Agreement or Disagreement, which it searches; and this is that which we call *Reasoning* ... Now, *in every step Reason makes in demonstrative Knowledge, there is an intuitive Knowledge* of that Agreement or Disagreement, it seeks, with the next intermediate *Idea*, which it uses as a Proof. (4. 2. 2, 7)

All knowledge, then, rests finally on intuition, either between ideas directly or by the intervention of other ideas ("proofs"), and on such intuition "depends all the Certainty and Evidence of all our Knowledge" (4. 2. 1). Without it, the mind "remains in Ignorance, and at most, gets no farther than a probable conjecture" (2. 2). Our field of true knowledge is thus "very narrow" (15. 2); most of what we know is merely probable, particularly what we know of the external world:

Indeed, some few of the primary Qualities have a necessary dependence, and visible connexion one with another, as Figure necessarily supposes Extension, receiving or communicating Motion by impulse, supposes Solidity. But though these, and perhaps some others of our *Ideas* have: yet there are so *few* of them, that have a *visible Connexion* one with another, that we can by Intuition or Demonstration, discover the co-existence of very few of the Qualities are to be found united in Substances: and we are left only to the assistance of our Senses, to make known to us, what Qualities they contain. (4. 3. 14)

For this and other reasons, "Because the highest Probability, amounts not to Certainty; without which, there can be no true Knowledge," Locke suspects that "natural Philosophy is not capable of being made a Science."[73]

The "Faculty" whereby the mind "is undoubtedly satisfied of the Agreement or Disagreement of any Ideas" is "Knowledge," or, alternatively, reason; "The Faculty, which God has given Man to supply the want of clear and certain Knowledge in Cases where that cannot be had, is *Judgment*" (4. 14. 4, 3). Judgment, then, is the faculty of probability, or nondemonstrative connections of ideas. Locke defines probability:

As Demonstration is the shewing of the Agreement, or Disagreement of two *Ideas*, by the intervention of one or more Proofs, which have a constant, immutable, and visible connexion one with another: so *Probability* is nothing

28

but the appearance of such an Agreement, or Disagreement, by the intervention of Proofs, whose connexion is not constant and immutable, or at least is not perceived to be so, but is, or appears for the most part to be so, and is enough to induce the Mind to *judge* the Proposition to be true, or false, rather than the contrary. (4. 15. 1)

His first example of such a proof is one of testimony: we may work through a mathematical proof ourselves, thus gaining knowledge, or we may take the conclusion from "a Mathematician, a Man of credit," depending on "the wonted Veracity of the Speaker in other cases, or his supposed Veracity in this."

The definition immediately raises difficulties. Just as one can ask for the grounds of the "semblance" that constitutes *vraisemblance*, one must ask Locke what is an "apparent" agreement of ideas. Sometimes he gives this a frequency interpretation:

Judgment, is the thinking or taking two *Ideas* to agree, or disagree, by the intervention of one or more *Ideas*, whose certain Agreement, or Disagreement with them it does not perceive, but hath observed to be frequent and usual. (4. 17. 17)

But this interpretation, really an appeal to the old dialectical topics, much as it accords with several of Locke's canons for judging propositions more probable, the more testimonies in their favor, does not make sense of an "appearance" of agreement. We may question further how Locke can speak, as he occasionally does, of an "apparent probability" (e.g., 16. 14), which would be a redundancy. The question is critical, for it is on the basis of his notion of apparent agreement of ideas that Locke's argument for placing probability in the scale of knowledge rests. To understand such "appearance," we must examine the *visual* basis of his theory of knowing.

"Knowing is seeing," declares *Of the Conduct of the Understanding*. "The Perception of the Mind," claims the *Essay*, is "most aptly explained by words relating to Sight."[74] Vision provides Locke with more than a metaphor for the processes of knowledge, however, for it is just this analogy with sight that is necessary to make sense of many of his claims for intuition and judgment, faculties which testify, respectively, to "the *visible or probable* agreement or disagreement of ideas" (*Conduct*, p. 117). Knowledge, Locke says again and again, depends on a *visible* connection of ideas.

Vision and certainty are connected because, for Locke as for Descartes, we can be certain of those ideas we perceive clearly and distinctly, under the "natural light" of the mind. Locke defines clarity and obscurity in ideas "by reflecting on what we call *Clear* and *Obscure* in the Objects of Sight" (4. 2. 19, 2–4). Descartes too likens the natural light of "evident intuition and necessary deduction" to "the perception of the eyes."[75] The "Degrees of our Knowledge" – and here Locke departs from Descartes – are "the degrees of its Evidence" and "clearness" (4. 2. 1). The light of demonstration, for instance, "is not altogether *so clear* and bright ... as in *intuitive* knowledge," which has the highest "evident lustre" (4. 2. 4, 6). In reasoning through proofs, though all steps rest in intuition, the light of reason is relatively "dim":

like a Face reflected by several Mirrors one to another, where as long as it retains the similitude and agreement with the Object, it produces a Knowledge; but 'tis still in every successive reflection with a lessening of that perfect Clearness and Distinctness, which is in the first, till at last, after many removes, it has a great mixture of Dimness, and is not at first Sight so knowable, especially to weak Eyes. (4. 2. 6)

As important in this passage as the notion that objects are seen more "dimly" in lesser degrees of knowledge, as if at a distance, is the phrase "similitude and agreement": ideas agree or disagree for Locke as they have a perceivable (mentally visible) *resemblance* to one another.

The language in which Locke discusses probability makes clear that the probable is related to true knowledge by being a further stage of dimness than characterizes demonstration; it is in this way, and this way only, that we can understand what Locke means by the "appearance of such an Agreement" between ideas in probable proofs as occurs in demonstrations. He later speaks of "the twilight ... of *Probability*" (14. 2), wherein we "determine of the Agreement or Disagreement of two *Ideas*, as it were by a view of them as they are at a distance" (14. 3). The metaphor of distance persists even in judging among different degrees of the probable: "any Testimony, the farther off it is from the original Truth, the less force and proof it has" (14. 10). Indeed, it is only by understanding probability in this way – as the clarity with which resemblances of ideas appear to the mind – that Locke is justified in placing probability and knowledge in a single epistemic scale. He envisages a scale of the degrees of knowledge "from the very neighbourhood of Certainty and Demonstration, quite down to Improbability and Unlikeliness, even to the Confines of Impossibility"; he distinguishes this list of degrees of logical connection from another scale of the "degrees of *Assent* from full *Assurance* and Confidence, quite down to *Conjecture, Doubt*, and *Distrust*" (15. 2). To the extent that probability deserves a place on the first list at all, and not merely on the second, it must genuinely mark some relation between ideas, a relation that holds independently of our knowledge of it. The appearance of agreement is "similitude," dim resemblance: vision, then, is more than a metaphor for knowing.[76]

It is all too clear that as an account of probability, Locke's doctrine of the resemblance of ideas is defective: it cannot be cashed in unless we have some rules to govern the appearances and degrees of resemblance, and he nowhere provides these. Since everything, and so also every idea, resembles everything else in some respect, we might on Locke's grounds prove anything to be probable on the basis of whatever evidence we chose. Nor would this criticism have seemed unreasonable to his contemporaries: George Rust, in a remarkable essay of 1651, attempts to lay down certain rules for the handling of resemblances and relations lest "every Argument can be made a proportioned *Medium* to prove every Conclusion" and "any thing may be a suitable Means to any end."[77] Locke does not see, and so makes no attempt to avoid the nightmare vision of a world in which everything proves everything; perhaps he thought his theory of ideas as signs, because sign-relations had long been subject to analysis, would yield the necessary rules of resemblance.

The degree of resemblance between ideas is for Locke the degree of "evidence" possessed by their connection. He repeats that between probability and certainty, between opinion and knowledge, the difference is one of degree, in particular, of degree of "evidence" (4. 2. 1; 4. 11. 14). The *Essay* consistently uses *evidence* in a sense descended from the Greek ἐνάργεια which throughout the Augustan period was its main philosophic meaning. It is the same sense Boyle invokes when he writes of that "clear light, or evidence of perception, shining in the understanding, [which] affords us the greatest assurance we can have (in a natural way) of the truth of judgments we pass upon things," and which Reid invokes in writing, "for surely no kind of evidence can go beyond that of consciousness."[78] What we mean by evidence, Locke calls "grounds"; his "evidence" is a shining forth to the mind whose opposite is *obscurity*, and whose direct ancestor is scholastic *evidentia*, a term which never lost its etymological connection with seeing (*videre*) and hence with light.[79] Newer senses of the term mingled with old even as Locke wrote, as, for instance, *evidence* in our sense entered the lexicon of jurisprudence, replacing its older names, *indicium* and its synonyms.[80]

Conceived before the birth of "epistemology" as we know it, *evidence* in its older sense refers to a phenomenon we would now locate somewhere between logic and psychology; a cognate ambiguity governs *opinion*, *probability*, and *certainty*, which in the context of the new theories of knowledge of the seventeenth century betray more clearly than ever before double senses, one logical, the other psychological. Cardinal Newman writes to William Froude: "We differ in our sense and our use of the word 'certain.' I use it of minds, you of propositions. I fully grant the uncertainty of all conclusions in your sense of the word, but I maintain that minds may in my sense be certain of conclusions which are uncertain in yours"; upon little more than this ambiguity rests Newman's criticism in his *Grammar of Assent* of Locke's theory of the degrees of assent.[81] "Certainty," writes Watts in his *Logick*, "according to the Schools, is distinguished into *Objective* and *Subjective*. *Objective Certainty*, is when the Proposition is certainly true in itself; and *Subjective*, when we are certain of the Truth of it. The one is in *Things*, the other is in our *Minds*" (176). In the Aristotelian tradition, this distinction is marked by the notions "better known to us" and "better known to nature."[82] Probability, in the same way, appears on Locke's two scales.

The double senses of these terms originate, of course, in a theory of knowledge in which logic and psychology are already united: one in which certain faculties take truth as their object and do infallibly deliver truths, and in which error arises not from any fault in them but from the interference of other faculties (particularly the will). To Locke, for instance – and we should recall that he has called "Knowledge" a "faculty" – "Knowledge being to be had only of visible certain Truth, *Errour* is not a Fault of our Knowledge, but a Mistake of our Judgment giving Assent to that, which is not true" (4. 20. 1). In theories such as this, knowledge is guaranteed by its pedigree, not simply by its logical backing: Locke's "Historical, plain Method" is meant to provide such guarantees (as is Bacon's method of induction, if we can avoid interference from the Idols, the sources of error). It is finally on the authority of testimony – the testimony of our faculties, designed by God, the ultimate authority – that our knowledge rests.

I do not mean merely to point out how frequently Locke uses phrases such as "the Testimony of my Eyes" or "the testimony of our Senses," revealing as these phrases are (4. 11. 2, 8). "Evidence and that alone gives the attestation of truth," he writes in the *Conduct* (103), because it is a light that comes from "the Testimony of GOD (who cannot lye)," and to whom our faculties are "witnesses," in a sense heavy with theological overtones (*Essay*, 4. 18. 5; 4. 5. 1). The testimony of the senses is to be judged by canons like those applied to human witnesses. Their testimony gives most certainty when objects are present to them (11.9), just as the best witnesses are those who have actually seen the events they testify to; different senses may "in many cases bear *witness* to the

Truth of each other's report" (11. 7), just as that testimony is stronger in which more witnesses concur. Locke's assimilation of the deliverances of sense to the testimony of witnesses – "le témoignage des yeux et le témoignage des hommes," in Buffier's phrase – was to become increasingly important to British empiricism. In his first philosophical work, *An Inquiry into the Human Mind* (1764), for instance, Thomas Reid would argue that "There is a much greater similitude than is commonly imagined, between the testimony of nature given by our senses, and testimony of men given by language," (210) for both are utterances in languages in which we must become fluent. Reid elaborates the assimilation in detail in his section "Of the Analogy between Perception, and the Credit we Give to Human Testimony," where, having isolated in men an innate "principle of veracity," he finds in nature the counterpart: a divinely ordered system of natural signs susceptible to trustworthy human induction.

It has often been remarked that nowhere in his discussion of probability does Locke make reference to the new mathematical theory of chances, nor does he even quantify probability, as does the Port-Royal *Logic*. (He does give an account of Pascal's wager, but in the form outlined in the *Essay*, Pascal's argument is distorted, and is not valid.)[83] It is impossible that Locke was unaware of these developments, and unlikely that the student of Wallis was so hampered by his much remarked on improficiency in mathematics as not to understand them; but his practical rules for weighing probabilities – "all the arguments, after having been examined on both sides, must be laid in balance one against the other" (*Conduct*, p. 52) – could come from Cicero. How is this supposed backwardness to be explained?

The *Essay* gives an explicit answer to the question. Locke deplores any attempt to quantify probability as he conceives it:

The difficulty is, when Testimonies contradict common Experience, and the reports of History and Witnesses clash with the ordinary course of Nature, or with one another; there it is, where Diligence, Attention, and Exactness is required, to form a right Judgment, and to proportion the *Assent* to the different Evidence and Probability of the thing; which rises and falls, according as those two foundations of Credibility, *viz.* Common Observation in like cases, and particular Testimonies in that particular instance, favour or contradict it. These are liable to so great variety of contrary Observations, Circumstances, Reports, different Qualifications, Tempers, Designs, Over-sights, *etc.* of the Reporters, that 'tis impossible to reduce to precise Rules, the various degrees wherein Men give their Assent. (4. 16. 9)

To be able to reduce the vagaries and diversities of testimony to a science would be to erect demonstration where, *ex hypothesi*, there are only probabilities; the best we can hope for is a general ordinal (rather than cardinal) ranking of them:

This only may be said in general, That as the Arguments and Proofs, *pro* and *con*, upon due Examination, nicely weighing every particular Circumstance, shall to any one appear, upon the whole matter, in a greater or less degree, to preponderate on either side, so they are fitted to produce in the Mind such different Entertainment, as we call *Belief, Conjecture, Guess, Wavering, Distrust, Disbelief*, etc.

For Locke, moreover, number and quantity, and mathematics itself, are inhabitants of the realm of certain knowledge, not of probable opinion (4. 2. 9); this is the seventeenth century's rejection of the Aristotelian view that number and quantity are only accidental properties of things, and so are rarely the objects of knowledge. Locke's judgments of probability concern truths that are immersed in matter and "circumstances" – though this did not prevent followers such as John Craig from quantifying a probability defined precisely as Locke had done.[84]

II

Probability and signs:
reasoning from effect to cause

For that we cannot enter into a mans heart, and view the passions or inclinations which reside there and lie hidden; therefore, as Philosophers by effects find out causes, by proprieties essences, by rivers fountaines, by boughes and floures the kore and rootes; even so we must trace out passions and inclinations by some effects & external operations.

Thomas Wright, *The Passions of the Minde in Generall* (1601)

"Probable signs" are effects which lead the mind to infer to their causes; probable signification, we might say, is a causal relation in reverse. Until well into the eighteenth century, it was through probable signs that reasoning from effect to cause, from the "manifest" (outer) properties of objects to their "occult" or "hidden" (inner) properties was understood. Probable signs licensed inferences from macroscopic nature to what was called "the internal constitution" of objects; from body to mind; and, at a variety of levels, from literary form to meaning. These signs were the creation of ancient medical theorists, and spread from medicine to other "low" sciences and to rhetoric. Ancient rhetoricians classed arguments from signs as *internal* rather than external proofs, that is, with proofs that arise from the nature of the matter proposed, rather than from external authority ("probability" in its commonest mediaeval definition). If probable signs are testimony in any sense, they are – according for instance to the Stoic theory defended by Quintus Cicero in the *De Divinatione* – the testimony of the gods.

In the Augustan age probable signs were a staple not merely of rhetoric and the sciences, but of the theory of education, history, and even theology, where they formed the groundwork of the enterprise known as physico-theology. "Conjecturing," as probable inference was called, came to be subject to explicitly formulated rules, rules especially concerning signs: conjecturing must take account not only of the clear signs that may indicate a conclusion, but also of the modifying "circumstances" of each case; skill in sorting out the signs so modified is "sagacity." In rhetoric and especially in moral theology (casuistry), finally, modifying "circumstances" become signs in their own right, and under the name "probable circumstances" they pass in the seventeenth century into the lexicon of literary criticism.

(1) SIGNS, SEMEIOTICS, SIGNATURES, AND CONJECTURES

> Omnis mundi creatura
> quasi liber et pictura
> nobis est in speculum,
> nostrae vitae, nostrae mortis
> nostrae status, nostrae sortis
> fidele signaculum.
>
> Alain of Lille, "Omnis caro fenum" (twelfth century)

> ... a play
> That wears the *facies hippocratica*
> Strong lines of death, signs dire of reprobation.
>
> John Armstrong, "Taste: An Epistle to a Young Critic" (1753)

In the final chapter of the *Essay*, Locke considers the old question of the "Division of the Sciences"; working from the traditional divisions of physics, ethics, and logic, he divides "All that can fall within the compass of Humane Understanding" into "natural Philosophy," "Ethicks," and a third category that is new. In an earlier partition to be found in the Memorandum Book for 1660–61, Locke had added to physics and ethics the category of "Dialectic."[1] In the *Essay*, dialectic becomes *semeiotics*:

Thirdly, the Third Branch may be called σημειωτική, or *the Doctrine of Signs*, the most usual whereof being Words, it is aptly enough termed also λογική, Logick; the business whereof, is to consider the Nature of Signs, the Mind makes use of for the understanding of Things, or conveying its Knowledge to others. For since the Things, the Mind contemplates, are none of them, besides it self, present to the Understanding, 'tis necessary that something else, as a Sign or Representation of the thing it considers, should be present to it: And these are *Ideas*. (4. 21. 4)

Ideas are "a Sign or Representation" of their objects; the whole of Locke's study of ideas which is the *Essay* itself, then, is to be classed as an exercise in semeiotics. Logic becomes in Locke the study of signs, as it had been to European writers such as Gassendi, but in a new way; so it remains at least until the time of the Baron de Gerando's very interesting sequel to the Port-Royal *Logic*, his *Des Signes et de l'art de penser* (1800).[2]

Locke's "Historical, plain Method" in tracing the origin and combination of ideas, as has often been remarked, is partly the product of the "histories" of natural phenomena enjoined by Bacon, and more specifically, of the histories of diseases compiled by his friend and teacher, Thomas Sydenham. *Semeiotics*, furthermore, despite the attempts of Bishop Wilkins to appropriate the word to refer to his system of sign-language in such works as *Mercury, or the Secret and Swift Messenger* (1641), was for any late seventeenth-century writer a term borrowed from medicine.[3]

In ancient philosophy, "the impulse to the formation of a theory of signs came from the medical schools," and was transmitted to later ages through the *Prognosticon* of Hippocrates (the "father of semeiotics") and the work of such physicians as Galen and Sextus Empiricus.[4] More specifically, in the words of Friedrich Hoffmann's influential *Fundamenta Medicinae* (1695), "Diagnosis consists in the precise knowledge of disease and its causes, by means of signs," and so is called "semeiotics" (83). Galen had divided medicine into six branches, physiology, etiology, pathology, hygiene, semeiotics, and therapeutics; as Lester King has shown, the same division, minus the discussion of etiology, was followed by books of medical institutes until well into the eighteenth century. For these later writers, physiology and pathology treated medicine insofar as it was a science, incorporating recent developments in natural philosophy; the last three divisions treat medicine as it is an art, dependent on the "sagacity" of its practitioners (here superiority is frequently ceded to the ancients). With the rise in the Augustan period of the mechanical philosophy, textbook treatments of semeiotics, hygiene, and thera-peutics grow shorter, those of pathology and physiology longer.[5] But diagnostics of course remains a part of medicine, and as late as 1809 can be found separate works with such titles as Landré-Beauvais' *Séméiotique, ou traité des signes des maladies*.

To Landré-Beauvais, a "symptom" is simply a perceivable state of affairs which does not point beyond itself; symptoms are noticeable by laymen. It is the task of the trained physician to "convert" these symptoms into "signs," that is, to see in them evidence of the "hidden" medical causes that give rise to them.[6] This sharp distinction between signs and symptoms is not typical of seventeenth-century writers, although Hoffmann sometimes follows it ("The signs of scorbutic fevers are scorbutic symptoms": 88); to most, these terms, as well as *mark, notice, token*, and a number of others, are synonymous. What is common to all these writers is a pattern of reasoning from effect to cause, from evident to nonevident, via the indicator which is the sign. The causal process whereby nature imprints signs in natural objects, notes Walter Charleton in a chapter of his *Physiologia* (1654) called "Occult Qualities made Manifest," is "Sigillation"; from this vocabulary comes as well that use of the adjective *signal* which makes a "signal example" one that lends especially strong probability to an inductive generalization.[7]

Diagnostic signs may further be predictive if, having successfully inferred from effect to cause, the physician can then infer (by analogy with like cases) to the future course of the disease. William Battie titles a section of his *Treatise on Madness* (1758): "The Diagnostic Signs of Original and Consequential Madness; and the Prognostic arising therefrom" (59). The most famous of these predictive signs, and one whose name remains in the medical lexicon, is the *facies hippocratica*, a condition of the face which is a sure *signum morbis* (sign of impending death).[8] Galen divided signs into those whose objects are in the past, present, and future; later writers on medical topics preserve the distinction, as we find Thomas Lodge doing, for instance, in his *Treatise of the Plague: Containing the nature, signes, and accidents of the same* (1603): "Of the signes of the Plague, both impendent and present, with the good and evil signes appearing in pestiferous sicknesses..."; Lodge also speaks of "mortall signes." Other writers on the plague such as Dekker and Defoe also concern themselves with the art of reasoning forward and backward from signs and tokens.[9]

These Galenic distinctions passed easily into the hands of dialecticians; in his *Arte of Reason*, for example, Ralph Lever says of signs (which he calls *commers*):

Commers are a general place, containing forecommers, aftercommers, and withcommers.

For some things comming after hand, are signes and warnings of that which is to come: some things folowing after, are remembrances and monumentes of that which hath bene: and divers things using to chance at once, are witnesses and assurances one of another. (189–90)

Thus terminology medical in origin comes to the service of non-demonstrative argument. The evidence signs provide is a kind of authority ("witnesses and assurances") for probable inference: "If [the signs] chance often, or for the more parte: then are the arguments taken of them likely and probable" (190–91). The very definition of the topics had traditionally been framed in terms of signs, as in the definitions in terms of *notae* cited above (p. 18 n50); the "general place" Lever discusses is standardly included under the topic "adjuncts of the thing," and hence also under the heading of *internal* proofs: the authority of nature has been assimilated completely into the logical notion of likelihood.[10]

Topical writers did not always recognize that they had conflated elements of both external and internal proofs. Richard Sherry, in *A Treatise of Schemes and Tropes* (1550), is careful to explain that signs properly arise from "the thynge it selfe that is in question," yet insists that proofs drawn from such signs are "unartificial," external proofs like the testimony of human witnesses:

Of proues some be artificiall, some unartificial. Unartificial be, foreiudgementes, rumoures, tormentes, tabelles [i.e., written depositions], othe, wytnesses, diuinacion, oracles. To these be referred whych the Greekes cal *Symeia* or sygnes: For they also commonlye are not set by the wytte of hym that disputeth, but are ministred otherwyse. They are called signes properlye, whyche rysynge of the thynge it selfe that is in question come under the sences of menne, as threatninges, whych be of the time that is paste cryinge herde oute of a place, whyche is of the tyme presente, palenesse of hym whyche is ared of the murther [*aread*: to foretell], whyche is of the tyme folowynge, or that bloud leapte oute of the bodye latelye slayne, when he came that dyd the murther. (78–79)

Diagnostic signs were classed not only temporally, but also by degrees of corroboration: signs are "fallible" (or "probable," or "accidental"), or they are "infallible" ("certain," "essential"). For Hoffmann, "The signs or symptoms that indicate disease are either essentials inseparable from the disease, called pathognomic; or they are accidental and concomitant, or separable" (83). Richard Sherry's discussion continues: "Also of signes some bee necessary, as that he liueth whiche dothe breathe, and some probable, as bloude in the garmente, whych myghte also come oute of the nose, or otherwyse." Shakespeare uses signs in the same sense and example (in fact a commonplace among ancient writers) in *2 Henry VI* when Warwick, judging from various manifest indications that a murder has been committed, remarks, "The least of all these signs were probable" (III. ii. 178). Shakespeare intimates a procedural rule for the interpretation of probable signs that is to be heard over and over in the literature of signs, witnesses, and testimony; Hoffmann makes it explicit: "When investigating the nature of a disease, we should attend to all the signs and symptoms. They should not be considered in isolation but rather in combination with each other" (83). On this principle John Downame consoles the Christian uncertain of his election in *The Christian Warfare* (1604): "The oft changing of Sathans temptations [is] a probable signe that he doth not preuaile" (96). As these examples suggest, signs were also the stuff of probable proofs in law; in the Renaissance there appeared a steady flow of treatises in jurisprudence with titles such as Giacomo Menochio's *De Praesumptionibus, conjecturis, signis, et indicijs commentaria* (1587–90).

Though obviously not confined to medicine, the logic of signs long kept a fundamental connection with it. Many of Aristotle's examples of signs in the *Rhetoric* are medical and some, like those of the relation between paleness and giving milk to fever and pregnancy, are repeated by countless later writers even when the context is not at all medical. In *The Rule of Reason*, for example, Wilson gives as instances of "Things chauncing, called *contingentia*" cases of medical diagnosis: "paleness, maie chaunce before sicknesse"; "Oft fetchying of winde, declares a sicknesse of the Lunges" (118, 119): Blundeville, in his *Logike*, illustrates the "Enthimeme" (which, though understood not in the Aristotelian way but in the Boethian sense of an argument part of which has been omitted, yet retains its Aristotelian connection with probability and signs):

From whence are such kinds of arguments gathered?
They are gathered for the most part from signes, which if they be necessary, then the Enthimeme is also necessary, as thus: The woman giveth milke, *ergo* she hath had a child, or is with childe: if the signes be probable, then the Enthimeme is also probable, as thus: This man is a night gadder, *ergo* he is a thiefe. (151)[11]

It was to ancient medical theory, and to Galen in particular, that many Renaissance logicians owed their schematizations of inference from effect to cause. Galen's distinction between *demonstratio causae* (cause to effect) and *demonstratio signi* (effect to cause, via the sign) occupied the greatest logicians of the period.[12] Once again, the medical history of such doctrines surfaces in their exposition by dialecticians; in his *Erotemata dialectices*, for instance, Melanchthon distinguishes resolution and composition:

Resolution is, for example, when from the signs of a disease we seek its seat, affect, and causes. Composition, on the other hand, is in initially describing the parts of the body, then the causes of diseases, then finally their signs. (243)

More generally, of course, the transference from medicine to rhetoric was complete in ancient times; most of the vocabulary of sign-inference can be found in Quintilian:

There are other nonnecessary signs, which the Greeks call εἰκότα; these may not be sufficient in themselves to remove doubt, but may yet be of the greatest value when taken in conjunction with other indications. The Latin equivalent of the Greek σημεῖον is *signum*, a sign, though some have called in *indicium*, an indication, or *vestigium*, a trace. (v. 9. 8–10)

In the same passage Quintilian explains the use of signs in rhetoric, not merely in building arguments (*inventio*), but also in rhetorical delivery (*pronunciatio*). To the student of rhetorical delivery, Quintilian commends that science of signs he calls "chironomy," "the law of gesture," the actor's skill in manifesting appropriate gestural signs (especially of the passions). His term was to serve as title for such works as John Bulwer's *Chirologia* (1644) and Gilbert Austin's *Chironomia* (1806). The vocabulary and assumptions of this part of rhetoric come from that branch of ancient medicine known as physiognomics.[13]

Physiognomics was to remain a permanent resource of rhetoric. Thomas Wright, in his study of both fields, *The Passions of the Minde in Generall* (1601), finding "that by externall phisiognomy and operations," one may "divine what lyeth in the heart," advises the orator:

Orators, whose project is perswasion, have two principall parts wherewith they endeuour to compasse their purpose, *Ornate dicere, & concinne agere*, To speake eloquently, and to act aptly: That consisteth specially upon proper words and sound reasons this in a certaine moderation of the voice & qualifications of gestures. Wee said aboue, that externall actions as voice, and gestures were signes of internall passions; and there we taught, how thorow those windowes a man might passe with the sight of his understanding, & discouer the secret affections of anothers heart. (27, 172)

Physiognomics was useful to the orator because it provided a schematization of yet another kind of inference from occult to manifest properties, in this case from mind to body. Nor did this application of physiognomic signs lose its scientific status as a branch of medicine until well after the Augustan period.

In the *De Augmentis*, Francis Bacon treats physiognomics in his discussion of "the doctrine concerning the League or Common Bond between the soul and body." The doctrine has two parts, one the effects of the soul as seen in the body, the other on the effects of the body as these appear in the soul: the first of these Bacon calls "Indication," the second, "Impression" (IV, 375–76). Indication includes "Physiognomy" and "the Interpretation of Natural Dreams"; Bacon finds that both Indication and Impression are of special interest to medicine, and is at pains to distinguish the well-grounded science of physiognomics from the "vain imposture" of "chiromancy," which has no physiological theory to back it up. In the course of his discussion, Bacon makes a number of shrewd observations; he criticizes the pseudo-Aristotelian *Physiognomicon* (a work not recognized as spurious until the nineteenth century) for limiting its account of physiognomic signs to those provided by the face and body when at rest:

but the structure of the body when in motion (that is the gestures of the body) he has omitted; which nevertheless are equally within the observation of his art, and of greater use and advantage. For the lineaments of the body disclose the dispositions of the mind in general; but the motions and gestures of the countenance and parts do not only so, but disclose likewise the seasons of access, and the present humor and state of the mind and will.

Between the time of Aristotle and that of Bacon, theorists of the arts came to realize that proper interpretation of facial expression depends on seeing the face in motion; a frozen expression often appears as a misleading distortion of a smile, for example.[14]

Augustan physicians who treated the relation of mind to body understood inference from one to the other as a process of reading signs. Jerome Gaub's address of 1763, the *De Regimine mentis*, uses the same metaphor of the "window" we have seen in Thomas Wright's section, "External and Internal Changes in the Body Produced by the Emotions":

Are any of you unaware, gentlemen, of the extent to which a disturbed mind can affect the outward appearance of the body? Of the manner in which different affections, whatever their nature, lead to one kind of change or another in the face, eyes, forehead and the other outward parts, each one picturing itself abroad with its own particular characteristics, so that there is no need to wish for a little window in the breast to observe what the unquiet mind conceals beneath?

Gaub proceeds without Momus' glass to analyses of the effects visible in those feeling anger, grief, terror, and joy, explaining the capacity of each to impair and restore health.[15] Like medicine itself, physiognomics involves stages of diagnosis and prognosis: Johnson's *Dictionary* contains the entry: "*Physiognomy*: the art of discovering the temper, and foreknowing the future by the features of the face."

In the Augustan period physiognomics had to defend not its connection with medicine, but, like medicine itself, its right to be called a science. We may take as a late text summarizing the results of this dispute John Evelyn's contribution to the huge literature about ancient medals, *Numismata. A Discourse of Medals ... To Which is Added a Digression concerning Physiognomy* (1697). Citing as sources works by Spon and papers in the *Transactions* of the Royal Society, Evelyn declares his purpose as that of defending the "scientific" status of physiognomy: it is a "Science, not altogether ... so vain, fallacious, and uncertain, as some imagine," though the inferences it licenses are of varying degrees of probability: "Our Design being in this Treatise only, to give a brief Account of the Conjectures which are made ('tho some as very probable only, temporal and transitory, others almost infallible, fixt, and inherent)" (334, 337). In the manner of Bacon condemning chiromancy, Evelyn distinguishes those true "Conjectures ... made of Capacities" based on "the various *Phaenomena*, Characters, and *Indices* legible in the Countenance" from unscientific "Physiognomical Divination" (294, 334). True physiognomic science can be reduced to a "Semeiotics" of "Notes, and Characters" which reveal both "the Affections, Passions, and Inclinations of the Mind" and, for medical use, the "Constitution of the Body" (332, 338).

Physiognomics had to defend its status as a science because the scientific status of medicine itself was in doubt. Like astrology or mineralogy, medicine was a "low" science of signs rather than a demonstrative science of causes. To Renaissance proponents of demonstrative science, medicine provided a prime example of a defective study, as it did for Ramus, or, because of its ancient connection with skepticism, an example for use in attacks such as Mersenne's *Vérité des sciences, contre les sceptiques.* The reputation of medicine was not helped when skeptics themselves, such as La Mothe le Vayer, took it to be the model for all knowledge. In the *Logique du Prince*, written for the duc d'Orléans, having warned that "il n'y a rien de si temeraire, que de prendre avec les Dogmatiques les vrai-semblances pour des veritez," La Mothe discusses medicine as a science that proceeds by the interpretation of "marques" and "signes"; he adds, "les autres parties de la Philosophie ne sont pas moins conjecturales que la Médecine."[16] The physician long remains the paradigm of the man who can read signs, as we shall find in discussing the novels of Smollett.

Those writers, like Friedrich Hoffmann, who saw in recent anatomy and physiology grounds for elevating medicine to the status of science, had to assimilate it to the familiar model of a demonstrative study of causes, and thus to play down its use of inference from signs. "Hitherto," argues the *Fundamenta*, "there has prevailed nothing but a refined empiricism, disguised with eloquence and talent, but lacking in true knowledge" (2); behind this complaint we hear the common charge that all attempts at science short of the demonstrative are mere rhetoric. This for instance is the insult the Aristotelian Thomas White throws at Joseph Glanvill in his *Exclusion of Scepticks from all Title to Dispute* (1665), an attack on the probabilism of *The Vanity of Dogmatizing*:

Did not the same persons strein, as enviously as possible, to defame *Aristotle*, with all manner of *Contumelies*; that the ignominy of that one man may make way for them to tear *Science* it self out of the hands of the Learned, and throw it into the dirt of *Probability*. For, he alone, of all the *Ancients*, has left any Monument of Demonstration in *Metaphysicks* and *Physicks*. The *Academicks*, where they leave the *Peripateticks*, were *Orators*, not *Philosophers*. For, *Socrates* himself was meerly a Disputer and a Doubter. *Plato* propos'd to himself, with his wholy-divine Wit and purest Eloquence, to set out *Probability*, and make himself admir'd for speaking specious things concerning the Principles necessary to Human life. (55–56)[17]

The Aristotelian defender of "experiment" rails in particular at the ready acceptance among proponents of the new science of hypothetical entities. It is precisely such entities to which Hoffmann appeals in his claim to have "provided what is true, what can be demonstrated and is supported by the principles of physics and mechanics," and thus to have avoided "any nauseous collection of opinions" and "controversies" (3, 2). Of semeiotics, he allows that although the ancients' skill in prognosis was not "knowledge," yet it should be taught.

Champions of probable methods such as Locke, Sydenham, and Mandeville, however, sought polemically to preserve medicine's old status. To Mandeville, following Locke, medicine must trust to the method of "observation, plain observation," for "Physicians, with the rest of mankind, are wholly ignorant of the first principles and constituent parts of things."[18] Sydenham in the *De Arte medica* (1669) throws back at the rationalist physician his very complaint against the empiric:

He that in Physick shall lay downe fundamentall maximes and from thence drawing consequence and raising dispute shall reduce it into the regular forme of a science has indeed done something to enlarge the art of talkeing and perhaps laid a foundation for endless disputes. But if he hopes to bring men by such a system to the knowledg of the infirmities of mens bodys, the constitution nature signes changes and history of deseases with the safe and direct way of their cure, he takes much what a like course with him that should walke up and downe in a thick wood overgrowne with briers and thornes with a designe to take a view and draw a map of the country. These speculative theorems doe as little advantage the physick as the food of men.[19]

The reference to food in the final sentence is not gratuitous; elsewhere in the essay, Sydenham likens the proponent of his theory of medicine to a "cooke" able to produce a "wholesome and savoury meale," contrasting this cook to "the profound philosopher and acute disputant":

Let not any one be offended that I ranke the cooke and the Farmer with the Schollar and Philosopher, For speakeing here of the knowledg of naturall bodys, the end and benefit whereof can be noe other then the advantages and conveniencys of human life, all speculations in this subject however curious or refined or seemeing profound and solid, if they teach not their followers to doe something either better or in a shorter and easier way then otherwise they could, or else leade them to the discovery of some new and usefull invention, deserve not the name of knowledg, or soe much as the wast of time our idle howers to be throwne away upon such empty idle phylosophy. (82–83)

The rhetorical strategy of these references to cooking is complex. Notoriously, Plato had compared the rhetorician to a cook; Sydenham understands that his kind of medicine has been accused of being mere rhetoric, and means to glory in the comparison with the cook. Embracing it, he finds that the proponents of "scientific" medicine are bad cooks – and, arguing in Baconian terms for the usefulness of cooking, makes cooking a symbol of those efforts that are not only humanely useful but which also possess a fruitful method of "invention" (discovery). To forward this art, he proposes his histories of diseases, that physicians might learn their signs and, by analogy with similar cases, their cure.

From medicine use of signs spread (in Vico's phrase) to "its offspring, pharmacological chemistry."[20] Thus plants bore "signatures," analogical likenesses to the organs they might cure, as for instance "the extract of the heart-shaped leaves of the fox-glove is called the specific for angina pectoris." In Paracelsian iatrochemistry this system of signate relations is particularly well developed.[21] To his influential text of 1609, the *Basilica Chymica*, the Paracelsian Oswald Croll appends a treatise on signatures whose full title makes clear the kinds of analogy in which signatures are grounded: *Tractatus de signaturis internis rerum, seu de vera et viva anatomia majoris et minoris mundi.*[22]

Croll ends the *Basilica* with an intriguing hymn to silence, significant according to one commentator of his Paracelsian view that medicine – the medicine to be learned from books and even that which is expressible in human (post-lapsarian) language – cannot capture the signate truths that nature speaks, so that the scientist should be silent himself in order to "listen" to those signs that are God's Word incarnate in nature.[23] Hacking has analyzed Paracelsian signatures as the authoritative testimony of God; because signatures, like signs, license further prediction, and just as the term *indicium* had in the seventeenth century a primary sense of "witness" in law (and French law through the eighteenth century used a calculus of *indices probables*, *indices prochains*, and *indices éloignés*), signatures themselves could be construed as a kind of legal evidence. In 1629, for example, Peter Ostermann presented a defense of the "signatures" of witches as probative evidence of legal guilt; he was criticized a year later on the grounds that mere signatures are not conclusive proof.[24]

Belief in signatures persisted through the seventeenth century, especially in botany, where they appear for instance among the "sensible probabilities" of John Gerarde's *Herball*.[25] It was a work on the "signs" in nature that betray God's presence, *The Wisdom of God manifested in the Works of the Creation* (1691) by the botanist John Ray, that is best known for having disposed of signatures as part of the baggage of the old low sciences. Ray calls signatures "fancied potencies or resemblances" like those invoked by demonology or witchcraft; earlier, in his *Cambridge Catalogue* (1660), he had also excoriated "the foolishness of the Chymists who chatter and boast so loudly of the signatures of plants":

We have paid close attention to the matter and are moved to assert that the signatures are not indications of natural qualities and powers impressed on plants by nature. Of the plants specifically said to be appropriate to a particular portion of the body or to a disease far the greater number have no signature. Different parts of the same plant have signatures not merely different but contradictory... There is such a vast number of plants that, even if they had come into existence altogether at haphazard, any ingenious and imaginative person could have found as many signatures as are known today.[26]

Yet as late as 1730, Bailey's *Dictionarium Britannicum* contains the entry, "SIGNATURE (in *Physicks*) the Resemblance that a Plant or Mineral bears to a Man's Body, or any Part of it," and in 1709, Vico has:

Having observed the similarity which exists between the various phenomena of the human body and those of chemistry, the healing art has been able, not only to hazard guesses [*conjicit*] concerning many physiological functions and disorders, but to make these plainly visible to the human eye. (10)

Even after the spagyrists' quasi-religious doctrine came under attack, the term *signature* remained in use as a synonym for *sign* or *mark*. In Bacon, the shift in meaning is conscious: for him, the universe is a "labyrinth" full of "deceitful resemblances of objects and signs," yet he describes his own method as one which goes beyond "common notions" to the "hidden parts of nature" – from manifest to hidden – thus arriving at "the true signatures and marks set upon the works of creation" (IV, 12, 51). Such statements are typical of Bacon's habit of taking up terminology from theories of which he disapproves and giving it a congenial interpretation in light of his own system; in this way, he can call his own method the "interpretation of Nature" (IV, 51). As Lisa Jardine has noted, what Bacon accepts of the doctrine of signatures is embodied in his theory of those "prerogative instances," or prescientific clues, that he calls "*Instances Conformable, or of Analogy*; which I also call *Parallels*, or *Physical Resemblances*"; these are surface similarities that genuinely indicate deeper ones, and thus guide the mind in discovery.[27]

Ray's own work is full of signs and marks which form the basis of probable arguments, most notably arguments for the existence and beneficence of God. The criticism of signatures had in fact begun long before his work, but at issue was not the reading of signs in nature but only what kinds of signs nature actually contains. As McGuire has argued very well, the microcosmic–macrocosmic relation, so important to Paracelsus and Croll in identifying signatures, forms the basis as well for such seventeenth-century uses of the "Analogy of Nature" in scientific inference from manifest to hidden properties ("transduction") as fill the works of Henry Power, Locke, and Newton.[28] Among those who, though opposed to the literal doctrine of signatures, continue to use the term are Glanvill and Power; Power describes those unlucky enough to live before the invention of the microscope: "(alas!) those sons of Sense were not able to see how curiously the minutest things of the world are wrought, and with what eminent signatures of Divine Providence they were inrich'd and embellish'd, without our Dioptrical assistance."[29] The term does, however, always retain its sense of signs impressed by and hence indicative of a designing *mind*: thus Thomas Reid can speak of the "clear marks and signatures of wisdom, power, and goodness, in the constitution of the world" which argue God's presence, and literary critics such as John Ogilvie and William Duff can seek "to mark the signatures" in literary works by which readers may come to understand the minds of human authors.[30]

Argument from signs long remains for writers on logic the paradigm for probable inference, even after signs' medical and scientific connotations have been rejected or forgotten. In his *Logick*, Isaac Watts does not discuss probable signs or signatures at all, but only the signs of verbal language; when he wants to give an example of an inference that is only probable, however, he produces what is, though he does not say so, an argument from a probable sign:

Arguments are either *certain* and *evident*, or *doubtful* and *merely probable*.

Probable Arguments, are those whose Conclusions are proved by some probable Medium; as, *This Hill was once a Church-yard, or a Field of Battle*, because *there are many human Bones found here*. This is not a certain Argument, for human Bones might have been conveyed there some other way. (308)

Historians, too, such as Thomas Hearne in his *Ductor historicus* (1698), find that in their field, whose status is only probability, where trustworthy testimony is lacking, historical reconstruction must be by signs.[31]

The common term for inference from probable signs is *conjecture*: Ralph Lever writes of the weakest kinds of "forecommers," "If they chance but seldome, and misse as oft as they hitte: then the reasons gathered of them are coniecturall, and prognosticallike, as oft false as true" (191). From 1500 to 1900, no noun is more often found beside the adjective *probable* than *conjecture*. Its popularity in the Renaissance comes mainly from Cicero's use of *coniecturalis* to refer to any argument from probabilities or signs;[32] in English, *conject* originally meant to prognosticate by signs, as it does in the Rheims Bible: "Some (have) presumed to calculate and coniect by the starres" (2 Thessalonians 2: 2). An example of 1652 has "Vaticinators, Coniectors, Aruspects"; Thomas Nashe uses the word this way in *Christs Teares Over Ierusalem* (1593) in a paragraph which begins, "If we would hunt after signs and tokens... No certainer cōiecture is there of the ruine of any kingdom then theyr revolting from God," while elsewhere he uses "more coniecturall" to mean more probable.[33]

By the eighteenth century the word's meaning has entirely changed. Johnson defines *conjecture* and its forms simply as "guessing," and he makes no mention of the evidence on which such guesses are founded. One of his citations is particularly telling; it is from Robert South's sermon "All Contingencies under the Direction of God's Providence" (1685). The text of South's rhetorical masterpiece is the line from Proverbs, "The lot is cast into the lap, but the whole disposing of it is in the Lord"; its burden is to enjoin political quietism in the form of a reliance on Providence in worldly affairs. South maintains that wealth and preferment come more often than not by chance, which is really God's Providence, and thus seeks to reconcile his audience to the existing distribution of these goods. Toward the end of the first division of the sermon, he remarks, "And in some things, as here in the casting of lots, a man cannot, upon any ground of reason, bring the event of them so much as under conjecture." In South's hands and by extension Johnson's, *conjecture* has entirely lost its sense of divinatory prognostication, of which the casting of lots was a familiar example.[34]

Between the time of Nashe and that of Johnson had appeared J. Bernoulli's essay on probabilities titled *Ars coniectandi* (1713), another sequel to the *Ars cogitandi*, the Port-Royal *Logic* of 1662. Bernoulli was among many in taking advantage of the connection of probability and *conjecture*; an *indice*, Voltaire was to say, "is merely a conjecture," and *conjecture* was in the Augustan period the term for any probable inference.[35] Seventeenth-century usage wavers, sometimes identifying conjectures with weakly probable inferences (*mere* probability), sometimes with highly probable ones. Locke himself wavers: sometimes he places conjecture near the bottom of the scale of "degrees of assent," just above the terms that mark suspension of judgment ("degrees of *Assent* from full Assurance and Confidence, quite down to *Conjecture, Doubt,* and *Distrust*"); elsewhere he gives it a higher ranking, listing in descending order "*Belief, Conjecture, Guess, Doubt, Wavering, Distrust, Disbelief.*" The distinction is less a philosophic than an honorific one. In the less honorific sense, Henry Power says in the *Experimental Philosophy*, again speaking of optical instruments, "Without some such Mechanical assistance, our best Philosophers will prove but empty conjecturalists, and their profoundest Speculations herein, but glass'd outside Fallacies" (Preface); in the second sense, a host of scientific writers (Power included) defend their theories as "probable conjectures." In this sense the term has been reinvigorated in our time by Karl Popper, in such works as *Conjectures and Refutations: The Growth of Scientific Knowledge* (1962), where conjecture stands for the hypothetical, or, to use Peirce's term, the abductive side of the hypothetico-deductive method.[36]

Locke's belief that medicine (and the rest of natural philosophy) cannot be made a science – that it is doomed always to be conjectural – is one with his view that students of nature are condemned to the use of signs. Causes reside in a level of reality that is permanently nonevident; unlike a Power or a Charleton (but like Glanvill), Locke believes that even could optical instruments be so developed as to see into the world of atoms, the mere co-presence of physical properties we might find there would still not constitute knowledge of their necessary connection (*Essay* 4. 3. 11–26). Moreover, ideas themselves are merely a "Sign or Representation" of their objects; simple ideas, like Paracelsian signatures, are put in steady correspondence to objective states by God (2. 21. 2; 2. 32. 14, 16; 4. 4. 4). We treat ideas as natural signs, but they are really arbitrary signs established by God (4. 3. 28, 29). Ideas of secondary qualities are in particular only non-resembling signs of the unknowable microscopic texture of objects.

For our Senses failing us, in the discovery of the Bulk, Texture, and Figure of the minute parts of Bodies, on which their real Constitutions and Differences depend, we are fain to make use of their secondary Qualities, as the characteristical Notes and Marks, whereby to frame Ideas of them in our Minds, and distinguish them one from another. (2. 23. 8)

In contrast to the scholastic theory wherein essences actually enter the mind, Locke insists that we know only signs, and that signs alone cannot provide knowledge of real essences (3. 6. 5).

"Though we see, and feel, and continuously converse with" matter, writes Glanvill, "yet its constitution, and inward frame is an *America*, a yet undiscovered *Region*"; because "*Nature* works by an *Invisible Hand* in all things," we have no genuine knowledge of the physical world:

We cannot know any thing of *Nature* but by an *Analysis* of it to its *true initial causes*: and till we know the first springs of natural motions, we are still but ignorants. These are the *Alphabet* of Science, and Nature cannot be *read* without them. Now who dares pretend to have seen the *prime motive causes*, or to have had a view of *Nature*, while she lay in her *simple Originals*? we know nothing but *effects*, and those but by our senses.

Glanvill reinterprets the old question of the quality of Adam's prelapsarian knowledge, arguing that "the accuracy of his knowledge of natural effects" arose "from his sensible perception of their causes"; for him there were "no occult qualities." But for fallen man all knowledge of nature and of other men must be by signs, and so can attain only to probability.[37]

(2) SIGNS, CIRCUMSTANCES, AND CASUISTRY

For though I telle nought his propre name,
Men shal wel knowe that it is the same
By signes and by othere circumstaunces.

Chaucer, *Pardoner's Prologue* (c. 1395)

CIRCUMSTANCES, the incidents of an event, or the particularities that accompany an action.

CIRCUMSTANCES (with *Moralists*) such things, that tho' they are not essential to any action, do yet some way affect it.

CIRCUMSTANCES *properly moral* (in *Ethicks*) are such as do really influence our actions, and render them more good or evil than they would be without such circumstances. Which writers of *Ethicks* sum up in this verse.

Quis, quid, quibus auxiliis, cur, quomodo, quando.

Bailey, *Dictionarium Britannicum* (1730)

In law, "circumstantial evidence" is indirect evidence which lends probability to a conclusion; it is opposed to direct or "real" evidence. The name comes from that general term which logicians, rhetoricians, and moralists have traditionally divided into the circumstances of time, place, manner, occasion, and various other attendant "incidents of an event." More specifically, circumstances fall in topical logic under the third of the "predicables," usually listed as *Quid nominis, Quid rei, Qualis sit,* and *Propter quid sit;* the predicable *Qualis sit,* explains Thomas Wright, "demandeth to know the proprieties of the thing," which are themselves divided into classes known as "predicaments." Under the predicament of "action and passion" fall circumstances:

Considering the predicament of action and passion, in regard they may be affected with sundrie circumstances, which better or impaire them; therefore I thought good to set downe this rule, which in generall distinguisheth their otherwise inuolued confusion.

Quis, quid, ubi, quibus auxilijs, cur, quomodo, quando.

Who, what, what time, and where,
How, why, what helpes were there. (189)

Circumstances qualify the nature of an action, and by extension provide signs by which we may know the true nature of that action. They are thus signs to be used in probable proofs, such as proofs in law. "One witness is not sufficient to convict a man of perjury," said

Lord Hardwicke in 1736, "unless there were very strong circumstances."[38] The legal use of *circumstances* became so prevalent in
the eighteenth century that Johnson gives as his second definition of
the word, "The adjuncts of a fact, which make it more or less
criminal; or make an accusation more or less probable."

Circumstances, then, are a kind of sign; moreover, they were
understood and discussed as signs. Blundeville, the scientist and
historian whose *Art of Logike* (1599) was so popular as nearly to
displace Wilson's *Rule of Reason*, treats "Probable Accidents, Coniectures, Presumptions, Sygnes, and Circumstances" in a section
worth quoting at length:

How may we reason from Probable Accidents?

From Probable Accidents you may reason Affirmatively thus: The feast of
Bacchus is this day celebrated, *ergo* there will be many drunken this day. The
generall Sessions are holden this day, *ergo* there will be some hanged.

What be the maxims of this place?

If the latter be, it is likely that the former went before, and if the former bee,
it is like enough the latter may follow: but you must beware in reasoning from
this place, that you fetch not your argument from such Accidents as chance but
seldome, or be indifferent, for such be neither necessarie nor probable, but
sophisticall and fallible, as to reason thus. Shee is a fayre woman, *ergo* she is
unchast.

Whereto serveth the place of common Accidents?

In the Judiciall kinde it helpeth greatly to prove the fact. In the Demonstrative kinde to praise or dispraise. In the Deliberative kinde to perswade or
disswade, and to gather together all Coniectures meete for the purpose, and
therefore this place is much used of naturall Philosophers to prove thinges by
natural signes, or by Physiognomie: also of Astrologers to prove dearth,
mortalitie, and such like, by wonders, and monsters, as by blasing starres, and
such like impressions. Also it is much used of Chiromancers, Southsayers, and
such as use to iudge by Coniectures, and therefore this place extendeth very far,
and serveth many uses. Hitherto also are referred the places of circumstances,
and chiefly of time and place, from whence good arguments may be fetched.
(87–88)

Circumstances are probable *accidents* in the sense that they are
accidental properties which, functioning as signs, suggest essential
ones (such as an action's true moral or legal character). We have
already heard Wright argue the use of signs in finding out "by
proprieties essences"; in this sense Wright can divide those "accidents" which "qualifie the thing" into "separable" and "inseparable"; the former are probable signs of essence, the latter certain
(187).[39] Different authors may or may not class "circumstances"
with "accidents," depending on whether they see the two as standing in the same relation to essence, but in their capacity as causal
clues (signs), the two receive nearly the same analysis.

Quintilian explains what makes circumstances such an important sort of sign:

Such in the main are the usual topics of proof as specified by the teachers of rhetoric, but ... whereas we derive what is common to all cases from general rules, we have to discover for ourselves whatever is peculiar to the case which we have in hand. This type of argument may reasonably be described as drawn from circumstances [*ex circumstantia*], there being no other word to express the Greek περίστασις, or from those things which are peculiar to any given case. (v. 10. 99–100)

By providing a logic for those affairs in which "circumstances alter cases," circumstances compel what might be called a casuistry of belief: circumstantial signs are more precise than others, and help especially to decide ambiguous cases, those in which ordinary signs might lead to conflicting conclusions. As such, it is in casuistry itself – in moral theology – that argument from circumstances finds one of its greatest uses; we may note that Bailey's definitions of the technical senses of the term are said to be drawn from "Ethicks" rather than from logic proper.

Among works of casuistry, one that can teach us most about the use of circumstances as signs has not in fact been understood to be a text in moral theology: the Port-Royal *Logic*. The final four chapters of the *Logic* contain that work's discussion of probability; their authorship has been disputed, and there is evidence that they may be the work of neither Arnauld nor Nicole. Most modern commentators would agree with J. M. Keynes, that these chapters contain the first treatment of "the logic of probability in the modern manner," but leaving aside the ambiguous evidence of those very few occasions on which the authors quantify probability, such a view cannot be justified.[40] *L'Art de penser* is not conceptually innovative in its treatment of probability, but rather consolidates doctrines from a variety of sources. What is most interesting in this treatment is not its tentative mathematical formulations, but its explicit analysis of probability in terms of circumstances, and of these as signs. And as is often the case in philosophic discussions of probability in this period, the Jansenist authors of Port Royal, under the guise of exposition of logical doctrine, are defending a polemical position in moral theology.

The authors begin with a surprisingly traditional definition of probability, as backing by authority. Quoting Augustine's maxim, "Quod scimus, debemus rationi; quod credimus, auctoritati" ("What we know, we owe to reason; what we believe, to authority"), they announce that "all we have said so far concerns science and the knowledge that is founded on the evidence of reason. But before closing, we should speak of another sort of knowledge, one which is often no less certain and evident: the knowledge we gain from authority."[41] The discussion includes not merely belief based on human testimony but also, as the chapter heading announces, "that which we know through faith, either human or divine" – as it turns out, the whole of our religious knowledge, excluding only that of the existence of God (355). Discussion of miracles follows; from the start, the authors link their treatment of probability to problems in theology.

The *Logic* proceeds to distinguish internal from external grounds of proof, framed as a distinction between kinds of circumstances. The authors present a "maxim" for weighing probabilities:

In judging the truth of an occurrence and deciding whether or not to believe in it, one must not consider the event nakedly and in itself, as one would a proposition in geometry; one must take account of all the circumstances that accompany it, both interior and exterior. I call *circonstances interieures* those which are part of the thing itself, and *exterieures* those which concern the testimony which leads us to believe in it. If all the circumstances of a thing are such that it never or rarely happens that like circumstances signify falsehood, the mind is naturally led to believe the thing true, and that there is reason to do it, especially since the conduct of life requires no greater certainty than moral certainty and must often settle for the highest probability. (363)

The passage repays attention. Internal and external proofs have become internal and external circumstances. Signs have become circumstances; the general point of the passage is no different, for example, from Lever's in his treatment of "commers." Third, judgments of probability are required in those fields wherein facts are immersed in qualifying circumstances; hence the opposition to geometry, which treats figure abstracted from matter. Finally, the author's emphasis is on practice, not merely on oratory or contemplation of what is likely: "moral" certainty is assurance sufficient to guide action.

Like signs, circumstances are either "certain" or "probable"; the *Logic* divides them also into "common" and "particular."[42] Common circumstances are those which "are met with in many instances," while special circumstances are a more direct and precise evidence of particular cases (376–78). This distinction should remind us of Quintilian's doctrine of the need to refine on the general theory of places with those more particular signs which are circumstances. The main point of the *Logic*'s "maxim" for weighing probabilities is that we must consider events in relation to their circumstances: "Il faut joindre les circonstances, & non les separer" (375–76). Emphasis on the specific circumstances of an action is part of the *Logic*'s larger attack on topical argument and the old dialectic in general; earlier, the authors take an entire chapter to argue that the method of commonplaces "est de peu d'usage" (239–45). In the final section of the work, we find that we must "not be carried away by the commonplaces, which, though they have general validity, are misleading in many specific instances, which is one of the greatest sources of human error" (382). It is ironic that circumstances, which are the indirect progeny of the topics themselves, should become the instruments of an attack on topical argument.

When even moral certainty is unattainable, the moral agent must act on the most probable maxim:

> If they [*circonstances communes*] are not counterbalanced by other, special circumstances which weaken or destroy the grounds of belief drawn from the common circumstances, we have reason to believe if not with certainty, then at least with high probability, which suffices when we are obliged to judge. For as we must content ourselves with moral certainty in those things not susceptible of metaphysical certainty, so also when moral certainty is not to be had the best we can do when choice is necessary is to embrace the more probable, since it would be irrational to choose the less probable.[43]

These are the concerns of moral theology; at the same time the *Logic* was being written, Jeremy Taylor was arguing that acting on less probable maxims is not only irrational but sinful, in a text not on logic but casuistry: the *Ductor Dubitantium: or, The Rule of Conscience* (1660).

Such a doctrine of circumstances is of course not unique to moral theology, but may be called upon in any field wherein circumstances alter cases. The Renaissance way of describing the qualification of a fact by circumstances is to say that a fact or discipline is "immersed in matter." According to Bacon, for example, "Civil knowledge is conversant about a subject, which of all the others is most immersed in matter, and with most difficulty reduced to axioms" (v, 32). In Jean Bodin's topical art of history, the *Method for the Easy Comprehension of History* (1566), while natural history "presents an inevitable and steadfast sequence of cause and effect," human history is otherwise, since it is "deeply embedded in unclean matter" (12). Bodin divides history into four kinds: human, natural, mathematical, and divine; the first is "uncertain and confused," the second "definite, but sometimes uncertain on account of contact with matter," the third "more certain, because free from the admixture of matter" (compare the Port-Royalists on geometry), and the fourth "most certain" (19). The more immersed in matter a field, the more necessary is the method of "analysis" (*resolutio*) in understanding its significant relations: analysis 'shows how to cut into parts and how to redivide each part into smaller sections and with marvellous ease explains the cohesion of the whole and the parts in mutual harmony" (20); Bodin's "analysis" is a casuistry of history. Contemporary writers repeatedly make clear the need for such analysis of the circumstances of human actions. Innocent Gentillet, in his response to Machiavelli, the *Discours sur les moyens de bien gouverner* (1576), argues that no politician or theorist can infer successfully from "causes and maxims" to "knowledge of effects and consequences" without taking into account the "circumstances, dependencies, consequences, and antecedents," which are "usually highly various and contrary, such that however similar two states of affairs might be, it will be impossible to judge or act upon them according to the same rule or maxim, because of the diversity of their adjuncts" (2).

Only, indeed, by attention to circumstances can argument from analogy proceed: Bacon calls circumstances "Adventitious Conditions or Adjuncts of Essences" (IV, 430), and in his rhetoric he is quick to point out the usefulness of such circumstances in argumentative uses of "example":

And it contributes much more to practice, when the discourse or discussion attends on the example, than when the example attends on the discourse. And this is not only a point of order, but of substance also. For when the example is laid down as the ground of the discourse, it is set down with all the attendant circumstances, which may sometimes supply it, as a very pattern for imitation and practice; whereas examples alleged for the sake of the discourse, are cited succinctly and without particularity, and like slaves only wait upon the demands of the discourse. (V, 56)

In the "attendant circumstances" of the example are the grounds for reasoning to other cases of relevantly similar kind, "for knowledge drawn freshly and in our view out of particulars knows best the way back to particulars again"; the casuist would find in this a method for discriminating relevantly similar cases of conscience.

All these examples, with their frequent reference to practice, betray their Renaissance origins; though typical in moral theology, the Port-Royal *Logic*'s distinction between intrinsic and extrinsic grounds of judgment does not in itself prove that the *Logic* is in more than a very loose sense a text in casuistry.[44] Attention to the context of its appearance, however, will show that the *Logic* is a contribution to the debate in moral theology between contending positions that have come to be known as "probabilism" and "probabiliorism."

Casuistry, or, in the term more congenial to Anglicans, case-divinity, is a product of the Counter-Reformation; it applies general moral rules to particular cases, for the use especially of confessors.

The extent of the literature, both Catholic and Protestant, is immense. Best known in Protestant England were the works of the immensely popular preacher William Perkins, especially his *Whole Treatise of the Cases of Conscience* (1608), the *De Conscientia* (1630) of his student William Ames, and Taylor's *Ductor Dubitantium*, but every major divine of the period wrote or spoke on conscience. Protestant and Catholic casuistical texts generally differ in two related matters: in the main use to which casuistry is to be put, and in the status accorded to arguments from authority (external proofs). Peter Talbot puts the Catholic case in 1658: "to believe in God, and consequently to serve Him in His own way, it is necessary to repair to an infallible guide, which is no other but the Roman Catholic Church."[45] The Puritan William Ames explains "To the Reader" of his *De Conscientia* that while "The Papists have laboured much this way, to instruct their Confessors," he writes that he "might doe something, whereby the unlearned, and such as are destitute of better helpe, might somewhat be helped." In general, Protestants appeal more often than Catholics to laymen, and much less often to extrinsic grounds of judgment. In Kenneth Kirk's somewhat biassed formulation, "It is generally assumed by Roman Catholic writers that no layman can decide the *intrinsic* probability of any opinion; he must leave this to the experts, and must rest content with an extrinsic probability based on the concurrence of their considered judgment" (195).

The range of positions in moral theology – Tutiorism (Rigorism), Probabiliorism, Aequiprobabilism, Probabilism, Laxism, not to mention such post-seventeenth-century developments as "Compensationism" – is great and the distinctions among competing views often so minute that, pressed into precision, schools fade into one another. When Alphonsius of Liguori (1696–1787), the last casuist to be made a doctor of the Church, was canonized in 1839, the Holy See declared his works free from error; contending schools hurried to find their views confirmed in his writings, but to this day, debate continues whether Alphonsius died a probabilist, a probabiliorist, or an aequiprobabilist. Modern Catholic writers frequently claim "we are all probabilists now," but, interpreting the same evidence, others make the same case for probabiliorism.[46] Seventeenth-century debate on these doctrines, finally, is intimately bound up with larger debates concerning the nature of grace and contrition, and the authority of the Church to make judgments on matters of fact as well as of right, issues on which we shall not trespass.[47] Our concern is only with the senses of *probability* and *circumstances* at use in what was one of the greatest paper wars of the age.

The central problem of casuistry is that of converting a "speculative" conscience, or theoretical knowledge of the moral law, into a "practical" conscience, a moral judgment that fits the circumstances of the given case. In this discussion "conscience" means, in Taylor's formulation, "the mind of man, governed by a Rule, and measured by the proportions of good and evil according to practice," while "speculation" is the faculty that "considers the nature of things abstractedly from circumstances" (1, 109). Conscience then is at once law (it brings to bear a natural knowledge of the moral law), witness (it brings to bear circumstances), and judge (as casuist, it chooses the maxim that best fits the given choice). "In *a right and sure* conscience the speculative and the practical judgment are always united," but such certainty in the application of the moral law is not always possible. In a "probable or thinking conscience," defined by Taylor as "an imperfect assent to an uncertain proposition, in which one part is indeed clearly and fully chosen but with an explicit, or implicit notice that the contrary is also fairly eligible" (89), choice of maxims comes only from careful weighing of contrary opinions.

Probabilism was born in the fifteenth and sixteenth centuries among the Dominicans of Salamanca; it is usually said to have reached its clearest formulation in the works of Bartholomew of Medina (1528–81), who held in his commentary on Aquinas that "if an opinion is probable it is lawful to follow it, even if the opposing opinion is more probable."[48] Since probabilism only arises when decisive evidence is lacking, Bartholomew's probability means largely backing by opinion; probabilists usually reckoned the number of authorities necessary to make an opinion probable at five or six, but Bartholomew himself claimed that "the probability of a single doctor of the Church, provided that it was probable, was sufficient justification for an action, even if more probable opinions could be alleged on the other side."[49]

Probabilism came quickly to be identified with the Jesuits; their enemies the Jansenists found in probabilism an invitation to lax practice, and accused it of being a form of laxism. Arnauld complains in 1643:

There is almost nothing that the Jesuits do not permit to Christians in reducing all matters to probabilities and teaching that one may depart from the more probable opinion (which one believes to be true) to follow the less probable – maintaining meanwhile that an opinion is probable as long as two Doctors teach it, or even just one.[50]

Pascal rhapsodizes satirically in his sixth *Provinciale*:

Reverend Fathers, how lucky is the Church to have you as its defenders! How useful are these probabilities! I never knew why you took such pains to establish that just one Doctor, *if he is weighty*, can render an opinion probable; that the contrary may be probable as well; and that one can opt for the pro or the con just as one pleases, as long as one doesn't imagine that it is true – and with such safety of conscience, that a Confessor who refused to give absolution to one of such casuistical faith would be in a state of damnation. (*Oeuvres*, v, 35)

Whether the Jansenists should be classed as probabiliorists is a matter of debate; Protestants usually hold them to be so, but Catholics often call them rigorists. In either case, their view appears to be nearly identical with what is generally accepted to be probabiliorism: in William Ames' words, "every one ought to follow that opinion, which (after due diligence to search the truth) he judgeth to be probable out of the nature of the thing and the Law of God compared together" (86) – that is, he should follow the *more* probable opinion.

Jeremy Taylor, an undisputed probabiliorist, explains the position in his Fifth Rule of the Probable Conscience: "The greater probability destroys the less"; "If we look upon two probable propositions, and consider them naturally, they are both consonant to reason in their appearencies, though in several degrees," but "it is not in moral things as it is in natural; where a less sweet is still sweet" (111). Writing the *Ductor* during the interregnum and dedicating it on its publication in 1660 to Charles II, Taylor criticizes probabilism:

If it were lawful and safe to follow the less probable opinion, and reject the greater, then ... it were lawful to choose any thing that any one of them permits, and every probable Doctor may rescind all of the Laws in Christendom, and expound all the Precepts of the Gospel in easie sences [laxism], and change discipline into liberty, and confound interests, and arm Rebels against their Princes. (113)

It has appeared that the dispute between probabilists and probabiliorists turns primarily on the senses that each gives to the term *probable*. According to Ian Hacking, Jesuit probabilists *mean* by probability, backing by authority, while Jansenist and other probabiliorists *mean* likelihood; thus he calls probabilism "a doctrine which," had it not been overthrown, "would have precluded rational probability theory."[51] There is no evidence, however, that for either side authority is more than a more-or-less important criterion of probability – for neither is authority its definition. Looking more carefully at statements like Taylor's, others argue that "in ordinary English, the word *probable* means *more likely than otherwise*, which is not the signification of the Latin *opinio probabilis*."[52] It is of course true that we sometimes use the word this way; thus Watts has in the *Logick*: "When the Evidence of any Proposition is greater than the Evidence to the contrary, then it is a *probable Opinion*: Where the Evidence and Arguments are stronger on the contrary Side, we call it improbable" (176). But this is beside the point; probabilists use a more technical (but equally common-sense) notion of probability as having degrees; in an uncertain matter, one opinion may be more probable than another, without the second losing all force. Debates between probabilists and probabiliorists do not stem simply from equivocation on a central term.

The real difference between probabilism and probabiliorism is the audience for which each is intended, and the amount of moral intelligence that can be expected of them. A look at a defense of probabilism will help make this clear. In his *Traité des premières vérités* (1724), the Jesuit Buffier devotes four chapters to *vraisemblance*; predictably, treatment of logical matters turns into moral-theological polemic. Buffier produces a list of canons for judging testimony (borrowed from Locke), explicitly calling this a table of *circonstances*; he addresses the relation of authority to action, arguing that we should take care to sort out those instances in which it is best to follow authority from others in which it is not.[53] The real issue in probabilism, in Buffier's view, is whether laymen may be justified in following an "opinion moins probable" when they are (understandably) ignorant of the strength of contrary, frequently complex opinions. He points out first that the entire debate has for all probabilists to do only with matters of lesser importance than those on which depends our salvation, in gaining which we are to use certain, not probable means. (Of course, Jansenists saw this as a much more contracted range than did Jesuits.) Buffier continues, addressing "the famous question of the *probable opinion*, which all the world talks of and few understand":

I answer that the mind can choose those parts of such an opinion that approach the truth, without choosing the opinion itself; for a *less probable* opinion is one which presents to the mind a greater appearance of falsehood than of truth. If, when one judges, the appearances of falsehood present in an opinion are not present to the mind, then that opinion is not really what one chooses; one chooses merely the appearances of truth that one has found in it... (69)

Any other view, for Buffier, would put impossible demands on the layman; probabilism is a system for guiding those who have neither leisure nor training to pursue moral questions with the tenacity and learning of an Escobar or a Sanchez. Thus the criticism of the Jansenists as rigorists.

It is of course true that many probabiliorists reject authority to a degree most Catholics found scandalous. According to William Ames, "It is never lawfull to doe against our owne opinion, whether it be certaine, or probable, for respect to other mens authority" (16). But such sweeping claims can be found only in the most radical Puritan casuists. Jeremy Taylor, for example, though he posits in his Ninth Rule of the Probable Conscience that "Multitude of Authors is not ever the most probable inducement, nor doth it in all cases make a safe and probable conscience" and that "Truth is to be weighed by argument not by testimony" (118), yet finds important use for arguments based solely in authority. Though we should follow "our own *reason* before the *sayings* of others," Taylor recognizes that an ill-applied probabiliorism may also lead to "*schism*, or *rebellion*, or *disobedience*, or *heresie*"; his final view is a compromise which holds that "though great reason may be stronger than authority, yet no private authority is greater than the publick" (121, 122). Specifically, argument from authority, though "the proceeding is inartificial and casual," is "fit to lead the ignorant," though "not the learned" (120). Here Taylor uses not only the language of rhetoric ("inartificial") but, more important, he appeals to the general conception of rhetoric as a method of communication by the learned to the vulgar. He proceeds to list (presumably for the use of the vulgar) eight rules for judging authorities, canons drawn from similar lists to be found in the rhetorical handbooks.

It is true as well that probabilist writers in general depend much more heavily than Protestants on arguments from human authorities, rather than reasoning directly from scripture or from that storehouse in the conscience of natural moral knowledge often called *synteresis*. This is perhaps why Taylor calls probabilism "this academicall or rather sceptic theology" (xi). Protestants are generally credited with replacing the mediaeval "external forum" of conscience (that is, the institutionalizing of conscience through confession, penance, etc.) with an "internal" forum wherein individuals exchange public authority for subjective certainty in moral matters, although predictably the rhetorical and skeptical culture of Italian humanism has been argued to partake of neither alternative.[54] At least one scholar, arguing that positions in moral theology are indicative of commitments to a broader "logic of decision" which encompasses not merely theology but the sciences as well, claims a correlation between (in Catholic countries) probabilism and belief that scientific theories are merely probabilities (hypothetical fictions which though operationally useful cannot claim to be realistic accounts of nature), and on the other hand (in Protestant lands) between probabiliorism and scientific claims to realism and certainty.[55]

We can now place the Port-Royal *Logic* more securely in the context of moral theology. The very traditional definition of probability with which its final chapters begin is a seeming concession to the probabilist opponent and an announcement that this will be a discussion suitable for laymen. The sections that follow, as they widen the kinds of testimony that comprise authority (especially through the doctrine of circumstances as here outlined), are designed to lead the reader to probabiliorism. The authors' emphasis is everywhere on moral practice; these chapters and the work as a whole conclude not with a defense of the *Logic* as an instrument of science, but with a probabilistic argument rooted in Pascal's wager for the importance of acting in such a way as to produce a rational expectation of salvation, and with the hope that the *Logic* will have helped readers to achieve this goal (387–88).

The usefulness of "circumstances" to all these writers on casuistry is the same: to provide precise causal clues to the nature of an action or event. In the *Numismata*, Evelyn presents a resolutely probabiliorist rule for judging from physiognomic signs: we must judge not "from any single or solitary Mark ... but by collating, and duely comparing the several Notes together, and how they consent, agree with, or thwart one another, or over-vote in number and weight" (338). Circumstances are signs that supervene on other signs, as do the *circonstances particulières* of the Port-Royal *Logic*. Translated into the language of circumstances, Evelyn's rule becomes Buffier's: "Probability grows, and approaches truth, by such degrees as the surrounding circumstances appear in greater number or in a more express manner."[56] Rules for the application of circumstances cannot be made more specific than the standard lists of who, what, where, when, etc., for to do so would be to ignore the reason for which circumstances were devised and to return to a general theory of places. Taylor's rules for their application are typical: "When two opinions seem equally probable," we must turn to "accidents, circumstances, and collateral inducements" (113). Taylor describes the process of weighing circumstances in language that recalls Samuel Johnson's famous reference in the *Life of Dryden* to 'scattered atoms of probability": though "ten thousand millions of *uncertains* cannot make one *certain*," yet moral certainty can be had if "there are a whole Army of little People, heaps of probable inducements which the understanding amasses together"; "Probable arguments are like little stars" which we must join into "constellations."[57]

Through the eighteenth century and beyond, logicians and rhetoricians describe this method of reasoning as one wherein, as John Lawson puts it in his *Lectures concerning Oratory* (1758), one may "gather in Circumstances, collect Probabilities; and from the Union and Combination of these, form an aggregated Argument" (132). From rhetoric the doctrine of circumstances as signs passes into Augustan literary theory. As we have already seen in Thomas Wilson (above, p. 26), the circumstances of "place, time, thing, and person" provide a web of rules of probability that govern decorum in narrative; the details of these circumstances presented in narrative are understood as signs – "coniectures" and "tokens."[58] As codified by critics such as Le Bossu in his doctrine of *circonstances probables*, these circumstances come to be understood as the material of which literary works are composed, signs which guide interpretation from the details of literary form to meaning. The work comes to be understood as a hierarchical structure of probable signs, referred to by critics as "probable circumstances."

(3) SAGACITY VS. CERTAINTY: AN EDUCATIONIST DEBATE

Alas how few can judge of probabilities! of them that can, how few will take pains to weigh and consider?

Obadiah Walker, *Of Education* (1673)

"The quickness of the mind in the discovery of demonstration, or in the invention and application of mediums," writes William Sharpe in 1755, "is noted in Mr. *Locke* by a fixed appellation, sagacity"; this sagacity is manifested especially in "a quicksightedness into men and things," and "a penetration into moral or sciential truth." The passages of the *Essay* to which Sharpe refers clearly identify sagacity as a form of invention in "finding out" proofs.[59] In probable inference these proofs are signs, the indicators which provide the basis for the quick inferences from outer to inner that Sharpe mentions; organized study of such signs at use in human affairs is, as we have seen, study of the topics. Sagacity, then, is skill in finding out and using signs; as such, it is for instance the virtue of skilled physicians, so that it is no accident that Vives, defender of both probabilism and education in the topics, spends more time in the *De Tradendis disciplinis* discussing medicine than any other field of study.[60] Sagacity is most needed where signs are modified by circumstances; thus according to Battie's *Treatise on Madness*, choice of the "different methods of cure in such Consequential Madness must be left to the sagacity of the Physician; it being impossible to lay down any general direction in a matter attended with so great a variety of unforeseen accidents" (82–83). The physician's skill in reading signs serves as a model for wisdom generally, so that for instance Robert Boyle can write in the 1640s, in an essay on moral theology:

There be hid in the Bosome of all humane actions, certain secret Axioms & Principles of Wisdom, the skill of whose extracting were possibly worth that of making the so coveted Elixir. And there are certain Hints ... which to discerning Eyes (as Plants do to Physitians by their Signatures reveale their Propertys;) discloze much of what they conceale.[61]

Such practical wisdom is also called *prudence*. Vives speaks in the *De Tradendis* of another field which aids in "the discovery of the probable" ("invention"), history:

Practical experience in life, gained through the examples of our ancestors, together with the knowledge of present-day affairs makes a man, as the Greeks name him, a *Polyhistor* as much as to say multiscius (a many-sided man). Such a man, however, we, following a better nomenclature, term a man of practical wisdom (*prudens*) and his province we call practical wisdom (*prudentia*). (42–43)

Thus Boyle refers in his essay "Of the Study of the Booke of Nature" (1649) to the way Providence, through "his greate Substitute Nature," "moves to his ends with the compleatest Prudence imaginable," as "the Sagacity with which [Nature] foresees stratagems" and 'steals to the Accomplishment of hir Desseins."[62]

The Augustans, like Locke, usually named these related skills in the use of signs simply *judgment*, and understood the primary job of the educator to be the inculcation of such judgment into his students. The most popular educationist treatise of the Restoration, Obadiah Walker's *Of Education* (1673) – a work which reached six editions before 1700, and was later the model for Walter Shandy's *Tristrapaedia* in *Tristram Shandy* – explains that the main aim of education is "bettering the Judgment," thereby to instill "*Wisdome* or *Prudence*" (173). Walker defines his terms:

Judgment, is the deliberate weighing and comparing of one object, one appearance, one reason, with another; thereby to discern and chuse true from false, good from bad, and more true and good from lesser... Its parts consist 1. in *circumspection*, or consideration, of all circumstances, advantages, accidents, &c. 2. In *Sagacity*, or collecting much from little hints; which requires both a great vivacity, serenity, and subtilty of spirit; all these together make up *Solertia*. 3. In *caution* or weighing all things for, and against, the subject. And 4. *Providence*, or prevision of futures, what may, and what may not, most probably fall out; which is the height of human wisedome. (125)

Elsewhere he defines *solertia* as "rational conjecturing of what is likely to succeed," and *circumspection* as attention to "all the circumstances of time, place, and all other opportunities" (174). To induce these skills, the educator relies most heavily on languages, poetry, and history – the topical arts. Walker defends use of the commonplaces against the Port-Royal *Logic*, and in mnemonics defends even the system of places of Ramon Lull (133–34).

Walker's essentially humanist educational programme was a response to the growing prestige of new Continental theories. Descartes had notoriously given up "books," claiming that his own schooling had taught him nothing of value; he scorned "rhetoric," assuming a style of ostentatious plainness; he rejected as worse than useless study of the topics (for instance, in his letter to Voetius of 1643).[63] Explicitly rejecting all appeal to probability (and authority), Descartes devised a new method which is at once a method of discovery (invention) and an educational programme, one which seeks certainty and uses as its criterion evidence (clearness and distinctness). The Cartesian approach to rhetoric is clear in such works as Pascal's "De l'art de persuader," part two of his "De l'esprit géométrique" (1656–57); its application in general to the conduct of thought inspires such works as the Port-Royal *Logic* and Spinoza's *Tractatus de intellectus emendatione*, which pointedly ousts from the realm of properly scientific uses of mind all "Perceptions arising from hearsay or from some sign."[64] But only after Cartesianism had penetrated the actual teaching of the schools of Port-Royal and the Oratory could it appear full-blown as an educational method in such works as Bernard Lamy's *Entretiens sur les sciences* (1683), whose full title continues, *dans lesquels on apprend comment l'on doit étudier les sciences, & s'en servir pour se faire l'esprit juste, et le coeur droit.*[65]

"Nous sommes faits," begin the *Entretiens*, "pour connoitre la verité." At the moment, scientific truth is only a distant goal; in natural philosophy, for instance, "the ancients knew almost nothing," and even still, of the objects of science "we scarcely see the internal constitution. What can the physician do but conjecture?"[66] In nature we know manifest but not hidden properties; it is at the imperceptible level of the hidden that causes must be sought, so that as yet we have not knowledge but conjecture. We must regard even Descartes' physics "not as the truth, but as *conjectures raisonnables*" (261). Here as in all things, however, we must not be satisfied with "what is merely *vraisemblable*"; we must convert our hypotheses into clearly and distinctly perceived facts, and like Henry Power, Lamy thinks this can be done with improved observational instruments.[67] We are not to be satisfied with a science merely of signs.

In the early dialogues, Eugène and Aminte discuss the educational programme which will best fit children to achieve such high goals.

Eugène defends older, more rhetorical methods of teaching, arguing that "no *science* compares with *bon sens* ... in whose formation logic is little useful: I've learned from experience that logic spoils rather than improves the mind" (67). But it is Aminte, speaking for Lamy, who wins the point: "Close reasoning and demonstration are the same thing," he responds, and so it is with logic that the student must begin.[68] At this point Lamy himself interrupts the dialogue to interpose a treatise on logic (the "Idée de la Logique"). Teaching itself will be a deductive process whose model is mathematics, another initial study; "The art of teaching consists only in paying particular attention to first truths and in pointing out the consequences which can be drawn from them, one after another."[69] Later the student will learn about rhetoric, primarily so that he may communicate with and manipulate the unlearned. "We have excellent models of eloquence in our language. We have treatises on mathematics, physics, and ethics written with exactitude" (143). Lamy has nothing to say of the topics, though later Cartesian educationists such as Crousaz pause to attack them.[70]

Lamy's Cartesian rejection of sagacity and judgment in favor of mathematical demonstration is essentially the programme also of Arnauld, Nicole, Pascal, Malebranche, Le Clerc, and Crousaz, as contemporary observers such as John Clarke recognized. Obadiah Walker is perhaps the first to criticize Cartesianism in education, but its most learned and spirited opponent was an author unknown in England, Giambattista Vico, particularly in his inaugural address of 1708, published in 1709 as *De Nostri temporis studiorum ratione*. A latter-day humanist for whom the highest studies are the probable arts of law and medicine, Vico attacks Cartesianism under the name "philosophical criticism," and finds it disastrous both as a method of teaching and in its psychological after-effects; in its place he recommends an education centered in topical argument.

"Critique could rout the skepticism even of the New Academy"; it is to the Academics and especially Carneades that Vico swears allegiance (9, 17). "Nature and life are full of incertitude," but "the philosophical critics disdain any traffic with probability" (15, 19). In taking as its object only certain truth, criticism limits severely its usefulness; moreover in rejecting all "ideas which are based on probability alone," criticism is "distinctly harmful ... to the education of adolescents." It is precisely "common sense" – which "arises from perceptions based on verisimilitude" – that criticism "stifles" (13). Promoting an "abnormal growth of abstract intellectualism," criticism produces "odd or arrogant behavior when adulthood is reached." Like Walker, Vico attacks Cartesianism not merely because it cannot teach us to manage uncertainty; he also finds it false to the order in which the mind's faculties appear in youth. Memory and imagination develop before the power of reasoning, so that the studies which call most on these faculties – "painting, poetry, oratory, jurisprudence" – should be pursued first (14). In his autobiography, Vico details the fruit of Cartesian inversion of the order of the mind's unfolding:

The intensive training in logic which they receive at the start of the educational process prematurely leads our young men to criticism. There is an inversion of the natural course of the mind's development... The result is that we raise a youth incapable of expressing himself except in a devastatingly arid and jejune way; a generation of non-doers, who, disliking action, sit up in judgment about all matters.[71]

Vico puts the same point another way when he argues that "the invention of arguments is by nature prior to the judgment of their validity" (14). Invention is taught by the *ars topica*, which Vico equates with "eloquence," "wisdom," and "prudence," but which criticism "utterly disregards." [72] Only through study of the topics does the student learn to weigh probabilities; the topical art taught by the Academic skeptics alone fosters prudence (14, 34). The longest sections of the *Study Methods* treat medicine (currently hampered by criticism's refusal to proceed by "attention to signs") and law (wherein Vico enjoins learning not through abstract principles but by cases, through what he calls an *ars topica juridicalis*) (32–33, 48).

Vico thus rejects the Cartesian notion that there is only one method, that of logic; in the realm of the probable, he rejects the Cartesian criterion of evidence, substituting "common sense supported by erudition."[73] At the root of this polemic is the view that criticism nourishes powers of discrimination at the expense of those of discovery and good judgment: "it is apt to smother the student's specifically philosophic faculty, i.e., his capacity to perceive the analogies existing between matters lying far apart and, apparently, most dissimilar" (24) – the powers which identify signs. His ideal is the "sagacious observer of analogous phenomena" (59), the master of signs.

That no Englishman after Walker felt compelled to make Vico's case is due in large part to the influence throughout the eighteenth century of John Locke's educationist treatises, *Some Thoughts concerning Education* (1693) and *On the Conduct of the Understanding* (1697). After 1700, in fact, Walker's *Of Education* was not reissued until the twentieth century. In general, Locke steers a middle course between Vico and Descartes (albeit closer to the latter), a course made possible by his new theory of probability.

Locke's debt to Descartes is clearest in the *Conduct*, intended originally as an appendix to the *Essay*. From the start Locke recommends study of mathematics as providing a single method that students can "transfer ... to other parts of knowledge as they shall have occasion," "for in all sorts of reasoning every single argument should be managed as a mathematical demonstration" (52). "Evidence and that alone gives the attestation of truth" (103). In a single paragraph, Locke rejects together "testimony," "probable topics," and "variety of plausible talk" (69). Those who are most "assiduous in reading" often merely "make all they read nothing but history to themselves" (65). More specifically, he argues in his section on "Bottoming":

Most of the difficulties that come in our way, when well considered and traced, lead us to some proposition which, known to be true, clears the doubt and gives an easy solution to the question; whilst topical and superficial arguments, of which there is store to be found on both sides, filling the head with variety of thoughts and the mouth with copious discourse serve only to amuse the understanding and entertain company without coming to the bottom of the question. (123)

Meanwhile, in spite of his rejection of topical argument and acceptance of a single method and criterion, Locke is always careful to make room for those matters "not capable of demonstration" which "therefore must be submitted to the trial of probabilities, and all the material arguments pro and con be examined and brought to a balance" (69). He appears in such passages to propound a double method. To a Vico Locke's position would be contradictory; it is made consistent by his doctrine that "certain or probable connections" of ideas (84) are different only in degree, not in kind. If probability rests in a resemblance between ideas, topical argument is no longer necessary.

But it was really Locke's *Thoughts* which shaped Augustan opinion on the education of the young, and here the Cartesian (indeed, the epistemologist) is scarcely detectable. The *Thoughts* is a more practical handbook than any we have mentioned, treating health and diet, discipline, choice of tutors, and foreign travel. Like Walker and Vico, Locke in the *Thoughts* recognizes that any educational scheme must take account of the stages in a child's intellectual growth; at each stage, elements of both the Cartesian and humanist programmes are called on to contribute to this growth. Locke nowhere pauses to consider the seventeenth-century educationist debate or to explain the grounds of his mediation.

(4) PROVIDENCE AND PROBABILITY

Let us consider God's Government of accidental Causes, or what we call Chance and Accident, which has a large Empire over human Affairs: not that Chance and

Accident can do any Thing, properly speaking; for whatever is done, has some proper and natural Cause which does it; but what we call Accidental Causes, is rather such an Accidental Concurrence of different Causes, as produces unexpected and undesigned Effects... Such events as these are the properest Objects of God's Care and Government; because they are very great Instruments of Providence: many times the greatest Things are done by them, and they are the most visible Demonstration of a superior Wisdom and Power which governs the World.

William Sherlock, *A Discourse concerning the Divine Providence* (1694)

How do we come to the knowledge, asks Thomas Reid in his *Lectures on the Fine Arts*, that there are other minds? "This is a question which philosophers have much disputed." Reid's answer is that we do so through probable signs, through those 'several things pertaining to the body which are the signs of things pertaining to the mind" (30). In the Augustan period, the same pattern of argument underpins what was the main argument for the existence of a divine mind: the argument from design. When in his *Essay on the Nature and Immutability of Truth* (1770), for example, Reid's student James Beattie comes to his chapter "Of Reasoning from the Effect to the Cause," his sole example of such reasoning is "the most important argument that ever employed human reason; I mean that which, from the works that are created, evinces the eternal power and godhead of the Creator."[74] From signatures and signs proceed inferences to the existence and beneficence of God in a series of works by Christian virtuosos with such titles as Ray's *Wisdom of God Manifested in the Works of the Creation* (1691) and William Derham's *Physico-Theology: or a Demonstration of the Being and Attributes of God from his Works of Creation* (1712, followed in 1715 by an *Astro-Theology*). In Europe Bernard Nieuwentijt produced a popular and often translated *Religious Philosopher* (1717), and F. C. Lesser his remarkable works of the 1730s, *Insectotheologie* and *Lithotheologie*. For the Augustans, inference from matter to mind, from form to meaning, was by signs.

Probability came to the support of Providence, however, not merely through its doctrine of signs, but also through the theory of chances. Despite the attempts of authors such as Jean Le Clerc in his *Reflections Upon what the World Commonly call Good-Luck and Ill-Luck, With Regard to Lotteries* (1699) to break the popular association of the extraordinary with the divine, seeming *im*probabilities as often as probabilities were called on as signs of divine management. As Francis Hutcheson explains in his *Inquiry* of 1725, "the recurring of any Effect oftner than the Laws of Hazard determine, gives the Presumption of Design ... and that with superior probability, as the multitude of Cases in which the contrary might happen, surpass all the Cases in which this could happen" (1. 5. 8). Our very failure to discover probable signs becomes itself a probable sign.

In his sermon on *Time and Chance*, taking as his text the verse from Ecclesiastes, "but time and chance happeneth to them all" (9: 11), Laurence Sterne finds human life to be "a series of contingencies equally improbable," yet argues that events which "run counter to all probabilities" most securely "give Testimony to providence in governing the world."[75] Sterne's claim rests on the argument that our very failure to be able to predict events proves divine influence in them. Man sees his affairs running "contrary to all his guesses and expectations," indeed 'so contrary to all our reasoning, and the seeming probabilities of success" that "the most likely causes disappoint and fail of producing for us the effect which we wished and naturally expected from them"; "conjecture" is as often wrong as right, so that "we vainly calculate" probabilities. From this dismal vision Sterne draws solace:

Some, indeed, from a superficial view of this representation of things, have atheistically inferred, – that because there was so much lottery in this life, – and because mere casualty seemed to have such a share in the disposal of our affairs, – that the providence of God stood neuter and unconcerned in their several workings, leaving them to the mercy of time and chance to be furthered or disappointed as such blind agents directed. Whereas in truth the very opposite conclusion follows. For consider, – if a superior intelligent Power did not sometimes cross and overrule events in this world, – then our policies and designs in it would always answer according to the wisdom and stratagem in which they were laid, and every cause, in the course of things, would produce its natural effect without variation. Now as this is not the case... (131)

Sterne's argument, patently fallacious as it appears to us, gained plausibility in its own time from several Augustan articles of faith on which it rests. It depends first of all on the late eighteenth century's extraordinary faith in the methods and results of science, a faith that extended so far as to hold that where methods of prediction go wrong, science itself possesses a mechanism of self-correction for setting them right again.[76] It depends further on the common Augustan understanding of chance not as the unpredictable or uncaused but as that which issues from mechanical, *nonintelligent* causes (Sterne's "blind agents"), no matter how rule-governed that mindless pattern of causation may be.[77]

As Hutcheson's formula makes clear, Sterne's argument – what we might call the argument from improbable signs – is easily susceptible of mathematical formulation. Among the results of the seventeenth-century's scrutiny of the notion of probability, historians of logic and rhetoric tell us, was a greater and greater demand for precision and rigor in probabilistic argument.[78] Such precision often meant quantification; arguments from mathematical probabilities came very quickly to be applied in a great diversity of fields. "Numbers are applicable even to such things as seem to be governed by no rule, I mean such as depend on chance," wrote Dr. Arbuthnot in an anonymous *Essay on the Usefulness of Mathematical Learning* (1701). He had made the same point in his earlier, anonymous *Of the Laws of Chance* (1692), an essay largely translated from Huyghens. Both works begin with a study of games – Arbuthnot was a devoted card-player – and proceed to apply mathematical probabilities to other branches of "civil affairs" traditionally the realm of the probable, including politics. (The very term *statistics* is a seventeenth-century coinage meaning the quantified study of affairs of *state*.)

Perhaps these works were anonymous because Arbuthnot did not think such inquiries the fitting activities of a gentleman (Swift published all but three of his works anonymously, more often for this reason than from political prudence). But in 1710 Arbuthnot published under his own name in the Royal Society's *Transactions* what was to become his and the age's most famous essay on probabilities, "An Argument for Divine Providence, taken from the Constant Regularity observ'd in the Births of Both Sexes." Arbuthnot's argument was immediately taken up by Addison in essays in the *Spectator* (no. 289) and *Guardian* (no. 136); by William Derham, the clock-maker turned natural theologian, in his *Physico-Theology*; and by Johann Peter Sussmilch in his great demographic work, *Die göttliche Ordnung* (1741). Bernoulli attacked it in two letters published in 1713, and Abraham de Moivre defended a modification of Arbuthnot's position against Bernoulli in his *Doctrine of Chances* (1718). Mandeville turned the argument to satirical purposes in the *Fable of the Bees*.[79]

Arbuthnot's argument has two parts. Reproducing the previous 82 years' bills of mortality for the city of London, he finds that in each year, more males were born than females, and in a fixed proportion. Supposing even that the odds of a male or female birth were $\frac{1}{2}$, he argues, the chance of 82 "male years" occurring in succession would be $(\frac{1}{2})^{82}$, or one in 4,856,000,000,000,000,-000,000,000. Such odds are so low that we can attribute the facts only to God's design. As Addison was to observe in the *Spectator* (no. 543, 1712), in a review of arguments from design,

I think we may lay this down as an incontested principle, that chance never acts in a perpetual uniformity with itself... And that the like chance would arrive in innumerable instances, requires a degree of credulity that is not under the direction of common sense.

Arbuthnot's second argument finds "the wise Oeconomy of Nature" at work as well in the fact that, though more males are born each year than females, yet "there is a very remarkable exact Ballance that is maintained between the Numbers of Men and Women":

to judge the wisdom of the Contrivance, we must observe that the external Accidents to which Males are subject (who must seek their Food with danger) do make a great havock of them, and that this loss exceeds far that of the other Sex... To repair that Loss, provident Nature, by the Disposal of its wise Creator, brings forth more Males than Females.

He concludes as a "Scholium" that polygamy is unjustified, for "where Males and Females are in equal number, if one Man takes Twenty Wives, Nineteen Men must live in Celibacy."

Arbuthnot's critics have not often enough kept these arguments separate. The second argument is not really mathematical, but is simply an application of the view that where there is order, there must be an orderer. So ultimately too is the first, though Arbuthnot overlays on the simple argument from design an invalid mathematical argument which is a version of our argument from improbable signs. The mathematical proof is invalid for the reasons Bernoulli pointed out, and with which de Moivre was to agree: the existence in nature of a stable statistical distribution is a fact to be explained, perhaps through an appeal to design; but once the distribution is known to exist, it becomes more, not less, likely that one will find it again in future samplings. Arbuthnot has confused the odds of an event's occurring with the odds that *some* event will occur, no matter which.

Despite Bernoulli and de Moivre, the Augustan argument from improbable signs persists. Perhaps the most extravagant version of Arbuthnot's mistake is to be found in Hutcheson's *Inquiry* of 1725; it is the clearest, because the most generalized possible version of the error. His argument runs: consider the way the world is (one way); consider the ways in which it might have been different (an infinity of ways, or since according to Hutcheson matter has five "modes," infinity to the fifth power ways). What then are the chances that the world should be as it is? $1/\infty^5$ – far too remote a chance for our world to be anything but the product of divine choice (51–52).

Arbuthnot had in fact borrowed both his data and some of his conclusions from an earlier work, *Natural and Political Observations ... made upon the Bills of Mortality* (1662). The *Observations* has been claimed variously for Sir William Petty and John

Graunt; it is a study in "political arithmetic," wherein actuarial data are taken as "an effect or sign" indicative of underlying states of affairs; the inferences from manifest effects to hidden causes licensed by these mathematical signs are supposed to establish their conclusions with "Moral certainty."[80] (Petty explains the aim of this kind of study in his *Political Arithmetic, concerning the Growth of the City of London* (1683) as the removal of obstacles which "hinder the operations of Authority"; as Peter Buck has argued, the author of the *Observations* assembles data on male and female births in order to give "evidence against 'universal liberty' in sexual conduct." The equality of men and women is used as an argument against polygamy, just as the publication of accurate information on the high incidence of venereal disease is used to discourage promiscuity.)[81]

The author of the *Observations* habitually argues that we should gauge our hopes, fears, and actions according to a rational expectation of the probable outcome of events. He assembles statistics on death by "notorious Deseases" such as leprosy, lunacy, starvation, and "Dead in the Streets" in order that "the respective numbers, being compared with the total," citizens "may the better understand what hazard they are in" (350). This kind of argument from improbable signs was among the earliest and most common uses of the new mathematics of probability; in the same year, the Port-Royal *Logic* argues in the same fashion about fear of death by lightning:

These reflections appear trivial, and they are if we rest here; but one can put them to the service of more important ends, principally to render us more reasonable in our hopes and fears. There are many, for example, put into an excessive fright when they hear thunder. If the thunder makes them think of God and of death and judgment, we shouldn't pause over this. But if it is only the danger of death that causes their extraordinary fear of thunder, it is easy to make them see that this is not reasonable. For of two million people, it is rare for even one to die in that manner. (386)

Examples such as lightning, of course, by their very rarity, are familiar signs of providential intervention into the natural order; Defoe writes for instance in his *Journal of the Plague Year*:

I know that some even of our physicians thought for a time that those people that so died in the streets were seized but that moment they fell, as if they had been touched by a stroke from heaven, as men are killed by a flash of lightning, but they found reason to alter their opinion afterward; for upon examining the bodies of such after they were dead, they always had tokens upon them or other evident proofs of the distemper having been longer upon them than they had otherwise expected. (167)

The growth of probability theory required, as did the newly powerful physical sciences themselves, to be made consistent with religious beliefs about the workings of Providence. The late seventeenth and early eighteenth centuries saw a vast outpouring of works on Providence, a fact which advances in mechanistic science (as well as the political use of appeal to Providence) may themselves help to explain. Authors on scientific subjects felt compelled, as did Bishop Burnet in his *Sacred Theory of the Earth* (1681), to argue that their speculations did not endanger belief; in his chapter "Concerning Natural Providence," Burnet offers the usual strategy of arguing that it is "a great Error" to "oppose the course of Nature to Providence," because "The Course of Nature is truly the Will of God." The position received influential support from writers such as Samuel Clarke and William Sherlock. William Law writes in *A Serious Call* (1728): "Could we see a miracle from God, how would our thoughts be affected with an holy awe and veneration of His presence! But if we consider everything as God's doing, either by order or permission, we shall then be affected with common things, as they would be who saw a miracle" (324). The reader of *Robinson Crusoe* can hardly fail to recall as an instance of such an everyday miracle designed, in Law's phrase, to "exercise and improve our virtue" (322), Crusoe's first harvest of corn from a few seeds carelessly shaken out of a bag; after some difficulties in interpreting the plague as at once naturally caused and a sign of divine displeasure, Defoe came to share this view even of the events of 1666.

Probability theory posed special difficulties in part because, although it did not propose to give causal explanations of phenomena, it proposed rational prediction to be possible concerning precisely the sorts of events most typically thought to be providential (plague, death by lightning). We have already heard South's view, expressed in a sermon on Providence, that the outcome of events such as the casting of lots cannot so much as be brought under conjecture. "It is no Heresy to believe," Arbuthnot argues on the other side in *Of the Laws of Chance*, that "Providence suffers ordinary Matters to run in the Channel of second causes"; Arbuthnot feels it necessary to write this in preface to a discussion of predicting, given available odds, whether an unborn child will be a boy or a girl. At at time when population figures were not gathered in part because census-taking was thought to be sinful, such disclaimers are more than formulaic gestures.[82]

It was only later in the period, however, that Providence and probability came explicitly to be made adversaries. Hume demolished the argument from improbable signs, especially in relation to the most important of special providences, miracles. Hacking writes of the Port-Royal *Logic*'s distinction between internal and external grounds of proof: "Hume was able to turn this chapter of the *Logic* on its head. In his essay *On Miracles* [*sic*] he argued that no external circumstances could ever suffice to render probable an event improbable enough to be called a miracle."[83] Yet long after Hume's death, Paley and the authors of the Bridgewater Treatises continued to infer to Providence from probabilities and signs, while logicians such as Whately tried to turn Hume's own arguments against him.

PART II

Probability in Augustan Literary Criticism

III

Vraisemblance, probability, and opinion

Here is the bottom and ground work of all Dramatick Poems; many talk
of it, but few understand it; but this is the general touchstone, by which
all that comes to pass in a Play is to be tryed and examin'd, and it is the
very Essence of the Poem, without which nothing rational can be done or
said upon the Stage... Poetry and other Arts, founded on Imitation,
follow not Truth but the common Opinion of men... Probability, which
is always the principal Rule, and without which all the others become no
Rules at all.

François Hédelin, Abbé d'Aubignac, *The Whole Art of the Stage* (1657)

That art imitates nature, but does so by presenting not truths but
probabilities, is a commonplace of centuries of criticism. The
formula appears transparent – until we begin to unpack the notion
of probability being invoked. Of necessity, there are as many ways
of understanding probability as there are of construing the relation
of art to nature. Renaissance criticism turns so often to problems
surrounding the ancient antithesis of fiction to truth that many
historians have found in its handling of these problems a guiding
principle for understanding the period as a whole.[1] Following the
recovery of Aristotle's *Poetics*, the terms of this debate become the
familiar ones, "truth" and events arising from "probability or
necessity." Italian theorists variously render Aristotle's εἰχός as
verisimile or *probabile*, but most frequently follow mediaeval rhetoric in choosing the former; French classical critics with near
unanimity prefer in discussing poetry *vraisemblance* to *probabilité*.[2]

In England, scarcely a critical work written during the Restoration fails to invoke and enjoin "probability" and to qualify the
proper use of its opposite. Neither *probability* nor the problems it
was used to address make such a showing in England before 1660;
the term's extraordinary vogue resulted from English reading and
translation of such French Aristotelians as Rapin, d'Aubignac, and
Le Bossu. Rymer's translation (1674) of Rapin's *Réflexions sur la
poétique d'Aristote*, with a preface of his own, led the way. After
Rymer launched the fashion, *probability* found its way from its
traditional rhetorical contexts first to those literary genres to

which Aristotle had applied it in the *Poetics* (epic, tragedy, comedy), then to all the literary kinds and even to other arts. In the eighteenth century, even landscape gardening – a highly literary art, in an age when a garden might be organized in imitation of an epic – made appeal to the standard of what William Gilpin called "a probable Nature."[3]

Verisimilitude had never been a common term in English criticism, and though during the Restoration, in an atmosphere congenial to the importation of French words, some critics might opt to use the word *vraisemblance*, stylistic and critical nationalism soon intervened. The French word began to sound pompous and pedantic, as it does in the mouth of Phoebe Clinket in *Three Hours After Marriage*.[4] By 1776, George Campbell could write in his *Philosophy of Rhetoric*:

This the French critics have aptly enough denominated in their language *vraisemblance*, the English more improperly in theirs *probability*. In order to avoid the manifest ambiguity there is in this application of the word, it had been better to retain the word *verisimilitude*, now almost obsolete. (82)

Campbell raises (but does not answer) an important question: were the linguistic forms of *verisimilitude* and *probability* ever really synonymous? Can we make their meanings sufficiently precise to discriminate between them?

Wesley Trimpi argues for synonymity, on the ground that "the Latin word *verisimilis* means 'probable'."[5] But we have seen enough of the ambiguities of *probability* to find such an argument unilluminating. Baxter Hathaway, discussing the Italians, remarks of "verisimilitude" that it "may or may not mean probability in a given critic's vocabulary," but does not attempt to distinguish the two.[6] His own use suggests that the probable was psychologically credible, the verisimilar objectively like truth, a reading reinforced by the frequency with which critics use phrases such as "probable, because verisimilar." But the truth is somewhat different; both terms come to the Renaissance not directly from Aristotle or the Roman critics but through the logical and epistemological contexts we examined in Part I.

The term *vraisemblance* was itself hardly univocal. As René Bray notes, the notion of *vraisemblance*, used in France to protect poetic fictions from the criticism that they are not truths, became in French classicism the tool whereby fiction was wedded more closely than ever to an ordinary, everyday kind of truth.[7] This development was the result of a systematic ambiguity which we have encountered before. Just as in mediaeval and Renaissance writers knowledge and opinion might have different objects, or refer to different ways of knowing the same object, with the result that terms such as *probability, evidence,* and *certainty* take on double senses, *vraisemblance* holds an objective and a subjective sense in uneasy tension. Objectively, the *vraisemblable* is what is most like truth, either in that it resembles truth or that it happens most frequently (as Dryden put it in 1679, "which succeeds or happens oftener than it misses"); subjectively, *vraisemblance* is simply credibility, which in turn is generally analyzed as congruence with previously held opinion.[8] As a result, the *vrai* and the *vraisemblable* may by different writers be seen as opposites, or merely as contraries; in different hands, the two classes may be wholly distinct, may overlap partly, or one may be wholly comprehended in the other. Boileau stands with the majority in positing partial overlap: "Le vrai peut quelquefois n'être pas vraisemblable." This is the view most faithful to Aristotle's discussion of improbable possibles in *Poetics* 24. Heinsius, on the other hand, is the best-known adherent of the third view: for him, the true is always verisimilar, a claim which Bray interprets as a misunderstanding of Aristotle's dictum that the true is always possible.[9]

Subjective and objective *vraisemblance* came into direct collision in the critical battle engendered by Corneille's *Cid*. For Jean Chapelain, whose views were to become those of the French Academy, *vraisemblance* is credibility, a belief or faith in what the work narrates necessary that the work can move us, and thereby instruct.[10] In his 1623 preface to Marino's *Adone,* Chapelain held that the true has a place in poetry only insofar as it is verisimilar; the ancients, for instance, recognizing that real events often result merely from chance, and that chance, by its variety of event, yields no ground for belief in any given event that might result from it, wisely ousted truth from poetry: "judging that because of the fortuitous and uncertain pattern of chance occurrences, the truth (which stems from chance) would spoil their efforts, they agreed to banish truth from their Parnassus."[11] Historical truth must be converted by the poet into *vraisemblance*; if he cannot find previous poetic models from which to take his treatment of historical events, he must perform the conversion himself, "without regard to truth."[12]

Corneille, in contrast, held a conception of heroic tragedy which led him to choose characters which, though historically real, raised admiration, through behavior reprobated by contemporary critics as more marvellous than probable: heroic actions, he claimed, "should always go beyond *vraisemblance.*" In the first of the *Discours* which he published in 1660 to defend his practice, Corneille directly challenges the Academy: "It is a false maxim that the subject of a tragedy must be *vraisemblable.*"[13]

Though Corneille and Chapelain appear to be contradicting one another, they are actually in considerable agreement. Both want literary works to be credible, and for the same reasons; Corneille, however, understands by *vraisemblance* not credibility but objective likeness to truth: heroic action is not the kind of thing that happens most frequently. Both writers agree, moreover, on the grounds of credibility, whether or not that credibility be called *vraisemblance*: both locate these grounds in decorum, and especially in opinion.

In the first *Discours*, Corneille explains that his inverisimilar events would never be believed but that they are "avouched either by the authority of history, which infallibly persuades, or by previously held opinion [*par la préoccupation de l'opinion commune*], which renders our spectators persuaded already" (I, 15). He derives this principle from Aristotle himself: "Aristotle gives the poet his choice of founding his fable either on historical truth, or on common opinion, or on *vraisemblance*" (I, 82). His text here is the notoriously difficult chapter 25 of the *Poetics*; the relevant passages are rendered by Thomas Twining (1789):

The *Impossible*, in general, is to be justified by referring, either to the end of *Poetry* itself, or to what is best, or to opinion... To *Opinion*, or what is commonly *said to be*, may be referred even such things as are impossible and absurd.[14]

Twining and Corneille correctly recognize that Aristotle does not mean here to identify *vraisemblance* with "what is said to be" or "common opinion," but merely to license certain extraordinary incidents by reference to it – incidents that Chapelain and the Academy were not willing to license. Yet it is just such an identification that will provide us with the grounds for the Renaissance distinction between *vraisemblance* and probability proper.

The earliest Renaissance expositors of the *Poetics* made a clear distinction between, on the one hand, probability and verisimilitude, and on the other, probability and, in Robortello's phrase, notions "quae receptae iam sunt in opinionem vulgi." In his edition of the *Poetics* (1548), Robortello ranks the various orders of discourse in traditional fashion, giving the logical status of each:

demonstratoria	verum
dialectice	probabile
rhetorice	suasorium
sophistice	speciem probabilis, sed verisimilis
poëtice	falsum, seu fabulosum

The "fabulous" includes much that has been enshrined by common opinion and hence is usable in poetry, but as such a hierarchy makes clear, for Robortello the logical status of poetry is neither probability nor verisimilitude.[15]

Very soon, however, two shifts occurred: verisimilitude came to be identified with "common opinion"; and, because probability as traditionally defined is that which is backed by the opinions of "all, or of many, or of them that are wise," verisimilitude came to be understood as a weak form of probability. We see the first shift taking place, for instance, in a passage of 1585 in which Salviati speaks of events' being verisimilar either "through opinion," or "through semblance of truth," or "through the reconciliation of a divided sense."[16] Fillip Sassetti's Aristotelian *Sopra Dante* (1573) testifies to the second shift:

A probable proposition is verisimilar, so that in order to know the nature of the latter it is necessary to know that of the probable. Those things are probable which are in agreement with the opinion of all men or of the most or of the wisest, so that truth is of no concern in this matter of verisimilitude... Since, then, verisimilitude depends upon the opinions of men, it is absolutely necessary that, as these change, the probable should also change.[17]

By the time Vossius writes his *De Artis poeticae* (1647), the shift is complete; by defining verisimilitude in terms of the traditional formula for probability, Vossius makes clear the connection between the two:

The verisimilar is to be understood not only as that which is seen as such by the wise, or by all, or by the most, or especially by the most distinguished, but also as what is seen as such by the vulgar. It is enough, therefore, for the poet that the vulgar concur.[18]

The most common Renaissance distinction between probability and verisimilitude is that of Vossius: probability takes as its backing the opinions of the wise or learned; verisimilitude, common opinion, the views of the "vulgar." To Rapin in the *Réflexions*, "*Vraisemblance* is whatever conforms to the opinion of the public"; Le Bossu, after reducing *vraisemblance* "to several Heads," according "to Divinity," "Morality," "Nature," "Reason," "Experience," and "vulgar Opinion," concludes that the last kind is the most important: "But the principal sort of *vraisemblance*, and that which we nam'd last, is the *vraisemblance* according to *common-received Opinion*." (It turns out that all these "kinds" rest finally on commonly received opinion, freeing the poet from the need for specialized knowledge of each field.)[19]

It was only in the later seventeenth century – when the works of Rapin and Le Bossu were translated into English – that *probability* and *verisimilitude* came to be synonyms. In the later seventeenth century rhetoric came no longer to be understood as merely the instrument of learned communication to the vulgar, but became a canon for learned communication generally;[20] at the same time literary verisimilitude comes to be grounded in the opinions not of the vulgar but the wise, and so collapses into probability. Rymer once again leads the way, writing in his preface to Rapin: "*Poetry* has no life, nor can have any operation without *probability*: it may indeed amuse the People, but moves not the *Wise*, for whom alone (according to *Pythagoras*) it was ordain'd."[21] But until the late 1600s, by far the more common preference is for the vulgar, for what at its most extreme is that "rough multitude" to which the cynical Castelvetro argues poets should address themselves.[22] (Sometimes canons of probability are said to be different in different genres, so that tragic probability depends on the opinions of the vulgar, epic on those of the wise.)

The older preference assumes a wider audience and one with less specialist knowledge. The common spectator, lacking specialist knowledge, for instance, of medicine, will not protest an event on stage that the physician would find medically improbable; addressing such an example, Antonio Riccoboni comments in 1585 that the medically improbable event is nonetheless "possible and verisimilar in the opinion of the multitude (to which the poet adapts himself), which does not penetrate so readily into the causes of things."[23] Le Bossu makes the same point about verisimilitude "according to *vulgar Opinion*"; Aristotle is, as usual, his authority (136).

In a final particularization of the Renaissance notion of *vraisemblance*, then, we may say that it refers to a range of propositions bounded at the top by the probable (what is backed by the opinion of the wise), and at the bottom by "mere possibility," or rather by what is seen as such by the vulgar. (Possibility itself is rarely at issue in Renaissance criticism, because recognizing actual possibility – a scientific judgment – once again requires knowledge foreign to the common audience.)[24] Sixteenth-century Italian theorists, perhaps because they were closer to the notion of philosophical probability and recognized that the probable and the verisimilar invoke different bodies of opinion, sometimes attempted to erect and name a middling grade of certainty between the possible and the probable to which the verisimilar might refer. Guarini named this range the *persuasibile*, while others chose terms such as *credibile* and *opinabile* (both distinct from *probabile*) to mark the distinction.[25]

As a development upon older notions of the probable, verisimilitude was susceptible of the same specifications as probability. Chapelain, appealing to those codifications of common opinion called decorums (*convenances*), produces a verisimilitude which incorporates criteria we have already found in rhetoric:

Faith, by which we mean an inclination of the imagination to believe that a thing is rather than that it is not, arises from two sources: one weak and imperfect – the mere testimony of historians or others; I call this weak, because we do not know men's sincerity, so that the least difficulty will put their testimony in doubt. The other, strong and perfect, stems from the *vraisemblance* of the thing reported. This is the usual way accounts gain credibility, to which the first really reduces itself: when two accounts differ, we always choose the one that has more *probabilité*. The first means is tyrannical and may be rejected; the second wins us with mildness, stealing into the imagination of the listener and keeping him interested through its *convenance*. Of these two means, the first belongs to the historian, the second to the poet.[26]

Chapelain makes clear as well a point to which we shall return: if for the Augustans it is judgment to which literary probabilities submit themselves, for the Renaissance the faculty of literary probability is the imagination.

Even after the conflation of probability and verisimilitude, critics had of course to continue appeals to common opinion to justify past and continuing poetic use of superstitions, false religions, and known impossibilities. In his annotations to Pope's Homer, for instance, William Broome appeals to the ignorance of the Greek audience to excuse improbabilities in the *Odyssey* – though how this is to make Homer acceptable to an educated English audience he does not make clear.[27] When James Beattie comes to define literary probability in his *Essays: On Poetry and Music* (1776), similar arguments must provide criteria whereby "the fairies, ghosts, and witches of Shakespeare are admitted as probable beings":

Yet we neither expect nor desire, that every human invention, where the end is only to please, should be an exact transcript of real existence. It is enough, that the mind acquiesce in it as probable, or plausible, or such as we think might happen without any direct opposition to the laws of Nature: – or, to speak more accurately, it is enough, that it be consistent, either, first, with general experience; or, secondly, with popular opinion; or, thirdly, that it be consistent with itself, and connected with probable circumstances. (36–37)

But for Beattie's learned audience, appeal to common opinion is joined by precisely the sort of knowledge Renaissance writers exclude – knowledge of the "laws of nature." When Restoration writers such as Rymer began to translate *vraisemblance* as *probability*, they imported into criticism new standards of accuracy and conceptual apparatus (such as probable circumstances and signs) previously associated with probability's uses in other disciplines.

IV

The literary work as a hierarchy of probable signs

In fact, our words not only are the signs, but may be considered as the pictures of our thoughts. The same glow or faintness of colouring, the same consistency or incoherence, the same proportions of great and little, the same degrees of elevation, the same light and shade, that distinguish the one, will be found to characterise the other; and from such a character as Achilles or Othello we as naturally expect a bold, nervous, animated phraseology, as a manly voice and commanding gesture.

James Beattie, *Essays: On Poetry and Music* (1776)

"The signification of the word *sign*," claims Thomas Reid in his *Lectures on the Fine Arts*, "is so very well known that I need not attempt a definition of it. When two objects are so connected that the one leads us to knowledge of the other, the first is the sign of the last" (29). Speaking in the *Inquiry into the Human Mind* of such signate relations, Reid says, "The principles of all the fine arts, and of what we call *a fine taste*, may be resolved into connections of this kind" (67). The fine arts depend crucially on signs because they perform a function that we have already seen to be the distinctive capacity of signs: they mediate between body and mind, matter and spirit. Reid opens his *Lectures*:

All the objects of human knowledge may be divided into two kinds: those of body and those of mind. The arts and sciences may likewise be divided into two great branches, concerning things material & immaterial... But there is a third branch under which are comprehended music, poetry, painting, eloquence, dramatic representations, &c. They are in an intermediate state between the two... They are intended to operate on the mind, altho' the objects by which this is produced are material; their first principles then are neither to be sought from the sciences which relate to mind or body, but from the connection which subsists between them. (21)

In making the fine arts intermediaries between matter and spirit, Reid is not simply making the familiar point that poetry and eloquence, for instance, are made up of words, arbitrary signs that conventionally indicate ideas. He would of course agree that verbal discourse is only a set of signs for mental discourse – "the important fact," as Coleridge put it in the *Biographia*, "that besides the

84

language of words, there is a language of spirits (sermo interior) and that the former is only the vehicle of the latter."[1] He means more than this; "our words not only are the signs, but may be considered as the pictures of our thoughts."

The signate relations that characterize the arts depend for Reid not on artificial signs, but on natural ones:

It appears evident from what hath been said on the subject of language, that there are natural signs, as well as artificial; and particularly, that the thoughts, purposes, and dispositions of the mind have their natural signs in the features of the face, the modulations of the voice, and the motion and attitude of the body: that without a natural knowledge of the connection between these signs, and the things signified by them, language could never have been invented and established among men: and that the fine arts are all founded upon this connection, which we may call *the natural language of mankind*. (*Inquiry*, p. 65)

Painting, oratory, drama, and sometimes poetry, according to the *Lectures*, all attempt to recreate the "effects of passion," "to express the various passions of the mind in the face and gesture." Reid himself finds that the lexicon and syntax of this natural language was first codified "in the ancient doctrine of physiognomy" (31).

Poetry will use natural signs in more complex ways, marking effects that may not even be visual, but the nature of its signs is the same. Note how often in the passage quoted on page 84 Beattie describes such purely linguistic features as "elevation" and "consistency or incoherence" of language in visual terms ("glow or faintness of colouring," "light and shade"). Indeed, Reid claims in the *Lectures* that poetry and eloquence "aim more at the mind than any of" the other arts, that they have the greatest repertory of natural signs (21); poetry has the advantage over painting for reasons suggested by James Harris in his *Discourse on Music, Painting, and Poetry* (1744): it has at its disposal not only physiognomic signs, but also such signs as quality of speech and action.

As to that System of Qualities *peculiar* to *Aeneas* only, and which alone *properly constitutes his true and real Character*, this would still remain a Secret, and be no way discoverable. For how deduce it from the mere *Lineaments* of a Countenance? Or, if it were deducible, how few Spectators would there be found so sagacious? It is here, therefore, that Recourse must be had, not to *Painting*, but to *Poetry*. So *accurate* a Conception of Character can be gathered only from a *Succession of various, and yet consistent Actions*; a Succession, *enabling us to conjecture*, what the Person of the Drama will do in the *future*, from what already he has done in the *past*. (*Works*, I, 91)

Harris is using a vocabulary with which we are familiar: *sagacity* is the capacity for reading signs well, especially those outward signs that "discover" the "secret" of character; *conjecture* is the name for probable inference, here that prognostic inference made possible once we have read the diagnostic signs. Though Harris believes that the signs of poetry are more accurate in discovering character than those of painting, the kinds of signs involved are the same. Both are *natural* signs, because they mark a causal connection (it is this that distinguishes natural signs from artificial). Both kinds of signs are useful to art because they mediate mind and body – because they are the manifest signs caused by hidden qualities of character.

As a student of Reid, Beattie attempts to assimilate signs such as those mentioned by Harris to Reid's model of "the natural language of mankind." From the premiss that poetry is an imitation of nature, Beattie argues in the *Essays*, "it would seem to follow, that the *language of Poetry* must be an imitation of the *language of Nature*" (193). He proceeds to define this language, borrowing his formulation from unnamed "philosophers" who can only be Thomas Reid:

The term *Natural Language* has sometimes been used by philosophers to denote those tones of the human voice, attitudes of the body, and configurations of the features, which, being *naturally* expressive of certain emotions of the soul, are universal among mankind, and every where understood. Thus anger, fear, pity, adoration, joy, contempt, and almost every other passion, has a look, attitude, and tone of voice, peculiar to itself; which would seem to be the effect, not of men imitating one another, but of the soul operating upon the body; and which, when well expressed in a picture or statue, or when it appears in human behaviour, is understood by all mankind, as the external sign of that passion which it is for the most part observed to accompany. (193–94)

But, Beattie argues, naturalness in speech extends beyond mere matters of gesture and facial expression to all those features of discourse that may be understood as the causal products of character. "Would soft words, for example, be natural in the mouth of a very angry man?"[2] Naturalness, it turns out, is to be schematized through a pattern of sign-relations which embody the usual, typical, predictable ways in which internal states produce external manifestations. These are dependent in turn on the character of the speaker, his mood, age, occupation, rank, and other circumstances.

Circumstances in this sense are the familiar stuff of which decorum is made. Natural language, therefore, is that set of signs (effects) which arise from their causes according to the regularities of decorum. In short, it is decorous language. Beattie has thus succeeded in his attempt to assimilate "artificial" language (words) to Reid's notion of "the natural language of mankind"; he draws the conclusion himself:

May we not infer, from what has been said, that "Language is then according to nature, when it is suitable to the supposed condition of the speaker?" – meaning by the word *condition*, not only the outward circumstances of *fortune, rank, employment, sex, age,* and *nation,* but also the internal temperature of the *understanding* and the *passions,* as well as the peculiar nature of the *thoughts* that may happen to occupy his mind. (200)

A decorum is an inverse causal relation: just as natural signs are effects which lead the mind to infer to their causes, decorums are general rules stating typical lines of natural signification. (If anger causes shouting, then by this decorum shouting is an appropriate natural sign for portraying a character in anger.)

We are now in a position to understand Beattie's third ground of literary probability, that the work "be consistent with itself, and connected with probable circumstances" (36). Language (and action) must be appropriate to character, where appropriateness means observance of decorum; we know character not merely through language (and action), but also through the "outward circumstances" listed above. Circumstances are "probable" when they accord with the rest of what we know about a character – that is, when the signs of character which are language and action and the signs of character which are outward circumstances both point to the same character, yielding a consistent literary work. The outward circumstance of illiteracy, for example, would (at least in a print culture) be an improbable circumstance in a character who habitually uses elegant speech; elegant speech is a sign (effect) of literacy, but illiteracy is a circumstance usually productive of, and hence a usual sign of, its opposite. The example is an application of Beattie's own principles: "The *external circumstances* of the speaker, his rank and fortune, education and company, particularly the two last, have no little influence in characterizing his style" (198), where *characterize* carries the double sense of being a cause of, and hence also making a recognizable sign (effect) of, the style in question.

For language to be "natural," however, it must be consistent with both the internal and external circumstances of the speaker, as Beattie's analysis of the term *condition* makes clear. Further,

There are several particulars relating to the speaker which we must attend to, before we can judge, whether his expression be natural. – It is obvious, that his *temper* must be taken into account. From the fiery and passionate we can expect one sort of language, from the calm and moderate another... And as the temper of the same man is not always uniform, but is variously affected by youth and old age, and by the prevalence of present passions; so neither will that style which is most natural to him be always uniform, but may be energetic and languid, abrupt or equable, figurative or plain, according to the passions or sentiments that may happen to predominate in his mind. (197)

In this way especially, our words are "the pictures of our thoughts," and special decorums govern the expressive use of linguistic signs. For instance, "the passions that agitate the soul and rouse the fancy, are apt to vent themselves in tropes and figures" (247), so that through such external linguistic signs as these the passions may most successfully be "imitated" (245). Beattie's theory is once again an account of causes and effects: passion *causes* real speakers to use figurative language; therefore figures are appropriate (probable) *signs* (effects) of particular passions. Anger, for instance, gives rise to hyperbole, so that an angry character should give signs of his inward state by speaking hyperbolically (though excessive use of this figure "betokens" instead "absolute infatuation," 254). More permanent traits of character are to be signified in the same way: "From the fiery and passionate we expect one sort of language, from the calm and moderate another. That impetuosity which is natural in Achilles, would in Sarpedon or Ulysses be quite the contrary; as the melli-fluent copiousness of Nestor would ill become the blunt rusticity of Ajax" (197).

In all these cases, the expression of character or particular pass-ions is understood as the giving of specific signs to the audience: "expression" means the display or demonstration of signs that indicate state of mind. "But where the language of passion and enthusiasm is permitted to *display* itself, whatever raises any strong emotions, whether it be animated or inanimate, absent or present, sensible or intellectual, may *give rise to* the apostrophe" (261, my italics). Beattie draws an analogy between the expression (display by signs) of passion in poetry and expression in acting; Reid, too, equates *expression* with the evincing of signs, and cites acting:

Certain attitudes are expressive of certain passions as well as certain conforma-tions of the countenance... In dramatic performances, the beauty of the action lies in the expression. It is introduced as the sign or expression of the passions. (*Lectures*, 50, 51)

From the account of signs to be found in Reid and Beattie emerges a theory of the structure of literary works, and, because all theories of literary structure entail theories about how such structures are properly to be read, an account of interpretation as well. The literary work is a structure of signs organized in such a way as to lead the mind to their causes – a structure of what we have already come to understand as *probable* signs. Where the work is a fabric of signs, interpretation, the movement from formal features to meaning, will be a process of sign-inference. An example of the way signs are organized is through decorums: these are rules of natural significa-tion (i.e., of literary probability) that guide authors in making their works consistent, and guide readers (when circumstances are "probable") in their inference from signs to underlying meaning. Literary signs in general are "probable" to the degree that they point with adequate evidence to those causes (meanings) of which they are the most likely effects. Richard Hurd explains of the drama:

> For the *manners of men* only shew themselves, or shew themselves most usually, in *action*. It is this, which fetches out the latent strokes of *character*, and renders the inward *temper and disposition* the object of sense. *Probable circumstances* are then imagined, and a certain *train of action* contrived, to evidence the *internal qualities*. There is no *other*, or no *probable* way, but this, of bringing us acquainted with them. (*Works*, II, 38)

Hurd is more interested than either Reid or Beattie in large patterns of plot, less than they in fragmentary expressive effects or moments, but the theory of probable signs is the same. Probability in signs and circumstances guarantees that the literary work will possess that unity and consistency without which it will not be intelligible, that is, without which no clear probable inference will be possible from form (signs) to meaning.

The model of literary structure outlined here was not the invention of a few late-eighteenth-century theorists of signs. What follows will draw examples from the Restoration to the 1790s to show that the theory of the literary work as a structure of probable signs, of interpretation as a probabilistic process of sign-inference, of criticism as an attempt to formulate general rules of literary probability, and even of rhetoric and the theory of acting as formularies for the deployment of probable signs, was the property of the Augustan age as a whole. It was, in short, the Augustan theory of literature.

Reid and Beattie come late in the development of this theory. They are unusual, in fact, in stressing the "naturalness" more than the probability of signs, an emphasis which is the result of Reid's philosophic concerns in the *Inquiry* of 1764, the work which launched the Scottish philosophy of Common Sense and, as a later chapter will explain, gave a new direction to Augustan notions about how we make estimations of probability. Reid and Beattie further betray their status as latecomers to the Augustan model of literary structure by placing so much of their emphasis on local effects and on signs that reveal the intricate inner motions of character. In earlier Augustan theory, signs not only reveal character, but more importantly, they are the stuff of which plot is made. In the fully developed theory, narrative itself is a hierarchic structure of probable signs, signs which at once constitute narrative structure and reveal meaning. After about 1760, hierarchic models of literary structure give way to horizontal (sequential) ones; plot yields the stage to character; and probable signs and circumstances come gradually to lose their central place in literary theory.

(1) LANGUAGE AND SPECTACLE

Figurative speech, therefore, is indicative of a person's real feelings and state of mind, not by means of the words it consists of, considered as *signs of separate ideas*, and interpreted according to their common acceptation; but as *circumstances* naturally attending those feelings which compose any state of mind. Those figurative expressions, therefore, are scarce considered and attended to as *words*, but are viewed in the same light as *attitudes*, *gestures*, and *looks*, which are infinitely more *expressive* of *sentiments* and feelings than words can possibly be.

> Joseph Priestley, *A Course of Lectures on Oratory and Criticism* (1777)

The first function of the probable sign is to externalize the internal: to render mental qualities available to sense, by delineating their signate effects. In the arts, this means suggesting such internal workings as the passions through visual or verbal "images" of them, "imitations" of passions and other mental states that may include facial and bodily gesture, particular uses of language (such as figurative language), or, by extension of the use of the figure of prosopopoeia, the organization of signs into full-fledged allegorical figures, personifications of internal states complete with appropriate gesture, language, clothing, and other insignia. In all these cases of language and spectacle, the functioning of probable signs is essentially the same.

Richard Hurd gives an unusually clear analytical account of such signs, and of the process of interpreting them by inference from effect to cause, in the second and third "Dissertations" which he added in 1766 to his edition of Horace's *Ars poetica* (originally published 1751). In the third dissertation, "On Poetical Imitation," he distinguishes three aspects under which nature may be imitated in poetry:

> 1. The material world, or that vast compages of corporeal forms, of which this universe is compounded. 2. The internal workings and movements of his own mind, under which I comprehend the manners, sentiments, and passions. 3. Those internal operations, that are made objective to sense by the outward signs of gesture, attitude, and action. (*Works*, II, 116)

In the course of the essay, Hurd characterizes the "signs" of category three variously, as "sensible marks and symbols," "signatures of internal affection," "those *visible, external indications*, the sensible marks and signatures," "external marks or characters" – intentionally calling forth, it would seem, the whole vocabulary of probable signs.

As it turns out, nature under all three aspects is to be imitated only by signs; we may consider human nature first. Hurd calls such outward causal clues of inner motions "the visible effects of MIND"; often they are "the signs of ... passion, I mean, the visible effects in which it shews itself" (148, 149). As such they are natural signs:

regular and constant observation hath found such *external signs* consociated with the correspondent *internal workings*. A *heaven overhung with clouds*, the *tossing of waves*, and *intermingled flashes of lightning* are not surer indications of a *storm*, than the *gloomy face*, *distorted limb*, and *indignant eye* are of the outrage of conflicting *passion*. (161)

Hurd calls the use in poetry of such highly probable signs ("surer indications") "painting," and in the midst of his discussion of their use in the drama names what was one of the most influential recent treatments of them: "Le Brun's book of the Passions" (152).

The honor of "transforming the theory of signs from an epistemo-logical to an aesthetic doctrine" has been claimed for the Abbé Du Bos in his *Réflexions critiques sur la poésie et sur la peinture* (1719),[3] but the expressive use of signs is much older. Elizabeth Evans has shown in her study of *Physiognomics in the Ancient World*, for instance, how important a resource were physiognomic signs in ancient literature, even in works written before such signs became the subject of extensive treatment and warm recommend-ation by theorists such as Aristotle and Quintilian.[4] Late classical writers such as Galen and Nemesius (whose Galenic treatise *De Natura hominis* was reprinted and translated often in the seven-teenth century), too, extended the study, which passed in the Renaissance to such influential scientists as Giambattista della Porta (in his *De Humana physiognomia* of 1586, followed in 1603 by a *Coelestis physiognomoniae*), Levinus Lemnius (in *De Habitu et constitutione corporis* of 1561, translated by Thomas Newton in 1581 as *The Touchstone of Complexions*), as well as to rhetoricians, especially those concerned with rhetorical action. And though it ill accord with our notions of the "Enlightenment," we must admit that, given new scientific grounding, physiognomics received more attention in the Augustan age than ever before, and nowhere was it so assiduously pursued as under the patronage of the Académie des Arts in seventeenth-century France. Its most famous exponent was a student of Descartes, Charles Le Brun, whose *Conférence sur l'ex-pression* was delivered in 1688, later to be published as *L'Express-ion des passions*, with a set of illustrations still influential a century later, in England as well as France.

The *Conférence* announces itself as a treatise on "pathognomics" (the physical effects of the passions) rather than on physiognomics generally. Descartes, in the *Traité des passions de l'âme* (1649), had defined the passions as "emotions of the soul" (that is, "changes" in the soul which "powerfully agitate and disturb it") which are caused by movements in the bodily spirits and which in turn cause those spirits to move through the nerves (conceived as hollow tubes) to the muscles, thus mechanically causing the "external signs" of passion.[5] Le Brun applies in detail Descartes' physiological theory to the musculature, and hence expression, of the face, beginning with "simple" passions such as admiration, terror, and pity, moving on to "mixed" and "complex" passions; in each case, he shows how external events affect the body, which in turn affects brain and then mind, causing the passion; this effect in turn becomes a cause, producing bodily signs Le Brun illustrates.[6]

Le Brun's work was as influential in England as in France. Jonathan Richardson, who argues in his *Essay on the Theory of Painting* (1715) that "Painting is a kind of writing, it ought to be easily legible," knows the theory, as does William Hogarth, who devotes a section of *The Analysis of Beauty* (1753) to "the natural and unaffected movements of the muscles, caused by the passions of the mind," whereby "every man's character would in some measure be written in his face"; to learn this language of signs, Hogarth recommends "the common drawing-book, called, Le Brun's passions of the mind."[7] The theory penetrated not only painting, but the theory of acting and literary theory as well.[8] Its offspring in France include the work of Du Bos on signs and treatises to be found throughout the century with such titles as *Essai sur les signes inconditionnels dans l'art*. In England, Dryden remarks in his translation of Du Fresnoy's *De Arte graphica* (1695), "To express the passions which are seated in the heart by outward signs, is one great precept of painters, and very difficult to perform," adding that "In poetry, the same passions and motions of the mind are to be expressed; and in this consists the principal difficulty, as well as the excellency of that art" (*Essays*, II, 201). (Today, as art theorists grow more interested in the psychology of visual perception, Le Brun's work is enjoying something of a revival.)[9]

Richard Hurd likens the literary use of "such signatures as are most conspicuous in the operation of the leading *passion*" to the painting of "portraits of character," which "image" to us "not the *man* but the *passion*" (51), and many of his examples of literary signs are entirely visual, instances of what he calls "mute marks." Perhaps the clearest literary analogue to signs in the manner of Le Brun, however, is to be found in mid-eighteenth-century theories of poetical personification. Hurd's formula that "figurative language

... respects the pictures and images of things" calls to mind the work of contemporary poets such as Collins and Joseph Warton, replete with allegorical imagings of the passions. Personification was widely understood to be a natural linguistic effect of strong passion, as Kames, for instance, argues in the *Elements of Criticism*:

One thing is certain, that the mind is prone to bestow sensibility upon things inanimate, where that violent effect is necessary to gratify passion. This is one instance, among many, of the power of passion to adjust our opinions and belief to its gratification... Personification is a common figure in descriptive poetry, understood to be the language of the writer, and not of any of his personages in a fit of passion. (III, 55, 62)

In mid-century, personification came to have greater visual emphasis than ever before, and the term *allegory* itself came to mean any bodying forth of the unseen (through signs) in visual form.[10]

It is easy to liken mid-century taste for verse allegory to the popularity of allegorical history painting, but the model spreads far beyond these arts. Joseph Addison points out that "not only the Virtues, and the like imaginary persons, but all the heathen Divinites appear generally in the same Dress among the Poets that they wear in Medals," a phenomenon many writers were to notice, and, like John Ogilvie, to explain as a matter of maintaining a consistent system of probable signs: "We are ... naturally taught to distinguish properly the *insignia* of imaginary creatures. Thus Fear is always known by her bristled Hair, Admiration by his erected Eyes"; we recall that John Evelyn printed his essay on physiognomy as an appendix to his *Numismata*.[11]

Addison's remark finds exhaustive documentation in Joseph Spence's *Polymetis* (1747), whose full title continues: *An Enquiry concerning the Agreement between the Works of the Roman Poets, and the Remains of Ancient Artists*. Spence's aim in writing *Polymetis* is avowedly to induce consistency in both painterly and poetic allegory, by providing (reviving) a uniform vocabulary of signs; such uniformity will ease interpretation of allegory, for when signs are consistent, inference may with probability connect sign with meaning.

The ancients, Spence finds, used signs with far more probability than do the moderns: in ancient works, "All these marks are settled, and obvious; and most of them point to the character of the person they belong to, in a more easy and strong manner" than do the signs of modern works. Spence cites the *Faerie Queene* and Dryden's *Aeneid*: in these works ill-framed "machines or allegories" foil probable inference; signs are either inconsistent, or too many to permit easy inference to character. Thus Spenser is guilty of clusters of disparate signs "sometimes too complicated, or over-done," producing what the information theorists call interference; this for instance is the case in his "too complex way of characterizing Pride" (303–04). Other characters are "not well marked out" when signs are too difficult to read for other reasons; sometimes Spenser's signs are simply insufficiently probable: "Thus, in one Canto, Doubt is represented as walking with a staff, that shrinks under him," though such imagery hardly points univocally to the idea of doubt (306).

Whereas ancient uses of signs are habitually probable in their observance of "clearness," "propriety," and "simplicity," Spence generalizes, modern structures of signs fail in decorum, and hence also in probability, betraying "darkness," "impropriety," and "multiplicity." "Multiplicity" here is a complex allegation. Correlation of unity with simplicity, disunity with multiplicity is too common in Augustan criticism to require comment; Joshua Reynolds was to found a complex theory of the genres upon a scale of degrees of simplicity, and scores of writers can be found joining the terms, as does Shaftesbury for example in discussing the "just simplicity, and unity" required of painters setting out to illustrate Prodicus.[12] Multiplicity, a condition in which too many signs are pointing in too many different directions, not only foils correct reading but constitutes a failure to elaborate the allegory with probable circumstances so serious as to destroy the unity of the work. Probability, as we shall find again, is a guarantor of literary unity.

In his essay "On Poetical Personifications" (begun in 1783, but not published until 1811), John Aikin also discusses methods of portraying "a figure impressed with the external marks of its influence," especially when the figure requires additional probable circumstances in order to be understood:

This is often seen in painting, where the intended expression requires an interpreter to render it obvious to the spectator. In such cases, the association of a *type* or *emblem*, derived from some circumstance of cause or effect, is found of great use for illustration; and besides, such additions, even when necessary for that purpose, afford scope for the invention and ingenuity of the poet, and contribute to the decoration of his draughts.

Circumstances here are the crucial locus of signification, which is itself explicitly analyzed as the reverse of a causal relation; they provide probable signs which guide interpretation. Aikin's essay is heavily indebted to *Polymetis*; where Spence criticized the "multiplicity" besetting modern uses of signs, Aikin – renouncing the taste in the later eighteenth century for "minute circumstances" – criticizes the defect found even in the "greatest masters," wherein "the natural and artificial characteristics" (i.e., signs) of allegorical persons are "drawn out to minuteness," resulting in persons not strongly marked and hindrances to probable inference. Aikin differs from Spence only in his typically late Augustan emphasis on the distinction between "natural" and "artificial" ("emblematic," "symbolic") signs and marks, and for preferring modern writers for their fluent use of artificial signs; to Aikin, "The Passions of Le Brun, in which human faces are marked with vivid expressions of rage, terror, grief, &c., are merely *natural* personifications."[13]

Personifications thus embody in particularly concentrated form a number of expressive signate relations; according to some writers of the period, their invention by primitive man was itself the product of a reasoning from signs, a kind of primitive physico-theology.[14] Because these figures at once exist in speech (in the utterances of a poet) and may speak themselves, as well as make appropriate gestures and carry probable insignia, they represent the confluence of all the kinds of expressive signs, visual and verbal.

Thomas Twining makes explicit reference to Richard Hurd when in his essay on "Poetry as an Imitative Art" (1789), he classifies the methods of imitating internal states:

I mentioned also, description of *mental* objects; of the emotions, passions, and other internal movements and operations of the mind. Such objects may be described, either *immediately*, as they affect the mind, or through their *external* and *sensible effects*... The image carries us on forcibly to feeling of its internal cause.

But, Twining notes (as Hurd had as well), in descriptions mediated by signs, "the effects of a passion are of two kinds, *internal* and *external*"; the latter include gesture and spectacle of the sort we have been considering, while the former include signs of passion such as distinctive uses of speech, the effect produced by specific passions on language.[15]

In the same way, in his chapter on "External Signs of Emotions and Passions" in the *Elements of Criticism* (1762), Lord Kames, beginning with the observation that "So intimately connected are the soul and body, that there is not a single agitation in the former, but what produceth a visible effect upon the latter," treats together verbal and visual signs:

The external signs of passion are of two kinds, voluntary and involuntary. The voluntary signs are also of two kinds: some are arbitrary and some natural. Words are arbitrary signs, excepting a few simple sounds expressive of certain internal emotions... But though words are arbitrary, the manner of employing them is not altogether so; for each passion has by nature peculiar expressions and tones suited to it. (II, 117–20)[16]

In his *Lectures concerning Oratory* (1758), John Lawson, too, finds that

Nature hath so framed us, that all strong Passions stamp themselves upon the outward Form. They are visible in the Air of the Countenance, in every Gesture and Motion. The Use or final End of which Constitution is very evident; that our Passions may be communicated. These form a Kind of natural eloquence.

But by the same token, "Inward Emotion displaying itself as readily in the Language as in the Features," "Figures are the Language of Passion" and "Figurative Speech ... is a faithful Image of Nature"; in both language and gesture, a good speaker must be like a good stage actor.[17] For Bishop Lowth in his *Lectures on the Sacred Poetry of the Hebrews* (1753), poetry specifically is such a use of signs:

The language of poetry I have more than once described as the effect of mental emotion. Poetry itself is indebted for its origin, character, complexion, emphasis, and application, to the effects which are produced upon the mind and body, upon the imagination, the senses, the voice, and respiration by the agitation of passion. (1, 366)

Like other Augustan writers on rhetoric and poetics, Lowth adds to the ancient maxim that each emotion has its visual sign the view that each has also its characteristic linguistic sign: "Every impulse of the mind ... has not only a peculiar style and expression, but a certain tone of voice, and a certain gesture of the body adapted to it" (1, 75). The same account of visual and verbal signs will be found in Anthony Blackwall,[18] Alexander Gerard,[19] John Ward,[20] Thomas Gibbons,[21] John Ogilvie,[22] Sir William Jones,[23] George Campbell,[24] and Hugh Blair.[25] Even Edmund Burke, in the *Philosophical Enquiry* (1757), countenances that kind of "imitation" of the passions which proceeds by giving their signs:

Now, as there is a moving tone of voice, an impassioned countenance, an agitated gesture ... so there are words, and certain dispositions of words, which being peculiarly devoted to passionate subjects, are always used by those who are under the influence of any passion ... we take an extraordinary interest in the passions of others, and ... we are easily affected and brought into sympathy by any tokens which are shewn of them; and there are no tokens which can express all the circumstances of most passions so fully as words. (175, 173)

In an excellent chapter on "The Role of Feeling in Composition" in the Augustan age, P. W. K. Stone has catalogued and explained many of the causal sequences that link particular passion to specific verbal formulation; as he notes, the most commonly cited example of what Twining would call the "internal sign" of a passion is the figure of asyndeton, that abruptness of transition that critic after critic finds characteristic of high enthusiasm and so appropriate to the ode.[26] Other such correspondences include:

Joy, grief, and anger are most naturally expressed by exclamations, sudden starts and broken sentences...

The language of enthusiasm, and of all those passions that strongly agitate the soul, is naturally incoherent...

Admiration ... is frequently the efficient cause of sublimity. It produces ... language bold and elevated...

Passion naturally dwells on its object: the impassioned speaker always attempts to rise in expression; but when that is impracticable, he recurs to repetition and synonymy, and thereby in some measure produces the same effect.[27]

All these writers equate, as does Lowth, "the power of exciting and of imitating the passions," for passion is excited in an audience when "evidently demonstrated" by signs "calculated to display" it (I, 365, 321).[28] Just as Reid had argued that our knowledge of other minds arises from the signs of mental motion we perceive in other bodies, Lowth argues of the poet that "from what he feels and perceives in himself, he forms conjectures concerning others; and apprehends and describes the manners, affections, conceptions of others from his own" (I, 117). "Expression" thus consists in display of signs, and these signs are the more probable the more strongly they "mark" the speaker, that is, the more evidently they point to their cause.[29]

The same model guides contemporary theories of rhetorical and stage action. In his *Essay upon Acting* (1744), Garrick defines his art as "an entertainment of the stage, which by calling in aid the assistance of articulation, corporeal motion and ocular expression, imitates, assumes, or puts on the various mental and bodily emotions arising from the various humours, virtues and vices incident to human nature." The *Essay* ends with a promise of "a more complete and expanded treatise upon acting, with an accurate description of each humour and passion, their sources and effects"; this is the promise of an acting manual illustrated from Le Brun.[30] "Every passion has its peculiar and appropriate look," Thomas Wilkes reiterates the ancient maxim in his *General View of the Stage* (1759). The theory of acting as manipulation of signs has been traced to the Elizabethans,[31] but in the late seventeenth century the theory was put on a new scientific footing. Most writers adopted Le Brun's classifications and descriptions of the passions; some, like Aaron Hill in his *Essay on the Art of Acting* (1746), go farther: Hill not only believes with Le Brun that "there are only ten dramatic passions: – that is, passions which can be distinguished by their outward marks in acting," but proceeds to discuss the muscular origin and expression of each, drawing on recent advances in physiology.[32]

Hill's reduction of the repertory of "dramatic passions" to ten suggests a method in acting that modern research agrees to have been Augustan practice.

The traditional theory of patterned style prevailed when acting resumed after the restoration of Charles II. The spectator's enjoyment came from viewing the "passions" going through their paces, or being exquisitely delineated in a series of isolated actions and declamations, rather than from enjoying the development of a "whole" character, or the complications of a full plot. Set speeches were helpful, and soliloquies seemed made for exhibiting virtuosity. The star performer could declaim both, and rivet the attention on his individual performance.[33]

The very notion of passion inherited from Descartes through Le Brun was one of mental states in which the soul is passive, acted upon by the body and re-acting through it. As such, passions are not themselves motivations to further action; they are events rather than motives, and so lend themselves to piecemeal rather than connected portrayals of character. The actor's aim, as John Hill put it, borrowing a term from painting, is that of "keeping": making sure that portrayals of passion are kept well distinct.[34] Historians of the stage find a literary analogue to this procedure in the Augustan popularity of anthologies of "beauties" excerpted from longer works; that this was a habit of reading as well as of acting is suggested further by the episodic manner of reading which D. Nichol Smith finds Dryden applying to Shakespeare, and which John Butt finds embodied in the editorial procedures and decisions of Pope in his edition of Shakespeare (1725).[35]

The probable signs of the passions, in both writing and delivery, are local effects; they must be kept consistent, and so in that sense contribute in a negative way to the unity and larger structure of the work in which they appear, but make no positive contribution to the work that can justify our claim that for the Augustans the literary work is a structure (rather than simply an assemblage) of probable signs. John Ogilvie writes in his "Essay on the Lyric Poetry of the Ancients," "A Poet may even merit a great encomium who excels in painting the effects, and in copying the language of Passion, though the Disposition of his work be irregular and faulty."[36] To understand the structural significance of probable signs and circumstances, we must move beyond local matters of language and spectacle to larger concerns of character and action, where despite their more complex applications, the same procedures of relating effect to cause, of mediating body and spirit, obtain.

(2) SIGNS AND CIRCUMSTANCES OF THE WELL-MARKED CHARACTER

"I must confess (reply'd *Aurelian*) . . . I cannot help defending an opinion in which now I am more confirm'd, that probable conjectures may be made, from the fancy and choice of apparel."

"The humour I grant ye (said the lady) or constitution of the person whether melancholick or brisk; but I should hardly pass my censure on so slight an indication of wit; for there is your brisk fool as well as your brisk man of sense, and so of the melancholick ... "

William Congreve, *Incognita* (1691)[37]

"Character is that which distinguishes one object from another."[38] For the Augustans, the probable signs of character – of both the individual object or person as individual, and of the type or species (universal) character which the individual embodies – were most commonly known as "marks," and a strongly distinguished character was a "well-marked character." In the world of nature, John Aikin explains to his son in a letter "On Classification in Natural History," through accurate and attentive observation the natural philosopher will find "that marks are discovered sufficiently numerous and distinct to identify genus and species"; in the world of men, Richard Hurd speaks of "those peculiar *traits*, which distinguish the species ... in the characters of men" as "discriminating marks."[39] Those signs which most clearly point to the defining qualities of their objects are "characteristic marks"; thus to John Dennis, "Passion ... is the Characteristical Mark of Poetry," what distinguishes poetry from other forms of discourse (*Works*, I, 215). Such signals also reveal and discriminate human character, in literature and in life; thus Mrs. Barbauld can argue that "The most characteristic mark of a great mind is to choose some one important object, and pursue it through life," while Dennis can ask of the hero of Blackmore's *Prince Arthur*:

But where all this while is the Characteristical Mark of the Hero? Where is the Quality that distinguishes him from all other Heroes? *Aeneas* was pious and valiant, and was concern'd for his people; and so was *Godfrey* of *Bolloign* ... where is that Quality, that ought always to be seen in him to preserve the Unity of his Character, and which like an universal Soul, ought to run thro' the Poem, and to animate every part of it?[40]

Note that for both writers, characteristic marks are the effects of, and so signs that lead us to knowledge of, pattern and unity in a life. In this doctrine is a use of probable signs genuinely to structure works – one that mediates body and soul not merely locally, but gives form to all the parts of a whole. To learn the signs of local expressions of passion, Hurd recommended Le Brun; for more general signs of character, he calls upon Theophrastus (II, 52). A well-developed body of Augustan critical theory treats the legibility (probability) of the marking of character as necessary to literary unity, calling upon notions of decorum to organize and lend probability to the signs of character.

Dennis likens authorial marking of character to branding animals: he says of Blackmore's Arthur, "The Poet ought to have set his Mark upon him before he had turn'd him out upon the Common, that he might have been known to have been proper Goods, and might have been distinguish'd from the numerous Herd of Heroes" (1, 80). Such identification is the first step in coming to discover a character's unity and pattern of action, for

when they are well mark'd . . . the Discourse and the Actions of the Persons which are introduc'd, make us clearly and distinctly see their Inclinations and their Affections, such as they are, and make us judge by the Goodness or the Pravity of those Inclinations, what good or what evil Resolutions they are certain to take. (1, 72)

Later writers will extend the analysis to marks that reveal aspects of personality far more particularized than such universal moral qualities, but the logic of their appeal to signs will be the same. In the language of logic ("clear and distinct," "certain"), Dennis is making the point that signs of high probability make possible successful diagnosis, which in turn permits prognostic judgments of high probability. We have already found James Harris arguing this way (above, p. 85); Richard Hurd explains in his "Discourse on Poetical Imitation": "This is so true, that, from knowing the *general character*, that is intended to be kept up, we can guess, beforehand, how a person will act, or what sentiments he will entertain, on any occasion." Such probable knowledge of characters comes partly from what through signs the work has revealed of the characters in question, partly from our knowledge of character in general; Hurd continues: "And the critic even ventures to prescribe, by the authority of rule, the particular properties and attributes, required to sustain" character (II, 134). These rules of probability in character are decorums.

For the Augustans both the idea that character is to be understood through its signs, and the idea that these signs should fall into patterns (lines of natural signification) called decorums, obtain in literature first of all because they obtain in life. Dennis explains: "The proper delight which Poetry gives us, it gives us by Imitation. Now the Persons that it introduces are design'd for Imitations of Men; but they cannot be Imitations of Men, unless the Manners are clearly mark'd" (1, 72). Mrs. Barbauld (in a context not at all literary) makes the point in reverse, arguing that life is best when people are well-marked, that is, when they betray signs of high probability such as occur in the best literature:

It is the fault of the present age, owing to the freer commerce that different ranks and professions now enjoy with each other, that characters are not marked with sufficient strength... There is a cast of manners peculiar and becoming to each age, sex, and profession; one, therefore, should not throw out illiberal and commonplace censures against another. A woman as a woman: a tradesman as a tradesman. (II, 193–94)

Part of what Mrs. Barbauld is recommending here is *sincerity*, an integrity of character which does not attempt to mask or disguise itself through the conveying of false (misleading) signs; we shall encounter this idea again in the novel of sensibility. More important for us now, she casts her point that probable signs should structure society as they do literary works in the language of literary criticism, and envisages a well-ordered society as one whose members observe decorum. (We should nowadays perhaps call the passage an exercise in "dramaturgical sociology.")

The common term for that relatively stable aspect of character under which character is the cause of action – so that actions, in turn, express (signify) character – was *manners*. Thus to Dennis, "The Manners ... are Causes of Action" (I, 77). ("Cause" here includes the idea of ground of explanation: manners are revealed through language and action, but in another sense they comprise action.) Dryden defines manners in his "Grounds of Criticism in Tragedy" (1679), in what is actually a paraphrase of Le Bossu: "The manners in a poem are understood to be those inclinations, whether natural or acquired, which move and carry us to actions, good, bad, or indifferent, in a play; or which incline the persons to such or such actions."[41] (Once again, only moral aspects of personality are stressed.) In this sense, as Hurd argues, "misapplication of manners" in a character is "destructive of *probability*," for such misapplication destroys intelligibility in the relation between character and action (I, 43).

Notoriously, Dryden defined manners a second time, in his Preface to *Fables* (1700), and his second formulation is not consistent with his first. "Both [Ovid and Chaucer] understood the manners; under which name I comprehend the passions, and in a larger sense, the descriptions of persons, and their very habits" (*Essays*, II, 278). Whereas the earlier definition refers only to internal states ("inclinations"), the second includes descriptions of external appearances, even characters' clothes ("habits"). The second also refers to the passions; between 1679 and 1700, Dryden translated Du Fresnoy and wrote on the passions' external signs. His second definition of manners simply includes the external signs (effects) of the inward states mentioned in the first – a not unreasonable collocation for a critic whose first requirement of the manners of tragic characters is that they be "apparent," i.e., that the characters be well-marked. Dryden writes in the "Grounds," again paraphrasing Le Bossu: "first, [the manners] must be apparent; that is, in every character of the play, some inclinations of the person must appear; and these are shown in the action and discourse."[42] In life, some inward traits of character might remain forever inward and hidden – in insincere characters or hypocrites, for instance, though even here Renaissance theorists of signs thought the question debatable – but in literature, where all we know of a character comes through one or another outward sign of his inner state, no such final secrecy is possible.[43] For just this reason, a critic such as John Dennis can be found puzzling over whether and how hypocrites might appear in literary works, just as under the heading of action he must puzzle over how works can at once be probable and yet also contain scenes of "surprise."[44] We may see the practical effects of the demand that manners be apparent (that they be signified, and with high probability) in the way that Renaissance and Augustan stage hypocrites are careful to give themselves away to the audience, whereas more recent narrative works may reveal even the most essential elements of character only through the greatest indirection (we know with far greater probability the character of Wycherley's Horner than we do that of his namesake in John Barth's *The End of the Road*). In successive editions of *Clarissa*, Richardson felt compelled to explain in footnotes that various of his characters' actions indeed were consistent with and followed from what had already been revealed of them – in other words, to demonstrate that the characters were well-marked, and so that the narrative was probable.[45] As Hurd insists, manners must be "signified": "The *manners* of the several persons in the drama must, also, be signified, that the *action*, which in many cases will be determined by them, may appear to be carried on with *truth and probability*" (II, 33).

The signs of character must be probable: characters must be well-marked. But why should such markings follow in their lines of signification just those patterns known as decorums? The answer is of course that decorums are themselves accurate generalizations from the facts of human behavior. But to see how this is so – to see why the traditional decorums of age, sex, rank, etc., should indeed be considered *accurate* generalizations – we must look more deeply into Augustan concepts of character and its signs. We may begin by taking a hint from Alexander Pope's *Epistle to Cobham*.

The problem Pope poses in the epistle is a traditional one: how can we truly know others' characters when the signs from which we must judge are so seldom probable – when people are so rarely well enough marked to permit inference to their natures? The problem is most difficult in the attempt to "read" women: in the *Epistle to a Lady*, making free with the notion that the relation between soul and body is a relation between form and matter (i.e., a relation of formal causation), Pope finds that "Most Women have no Characters at all," because of the recalcitrant matter of which they are formed: "Matter too soft a lasting mark to bear." Hence they can be discriminated only by the grossest external signs, signs that do not really reveal character: "best distinguish'd by black, brown, or fair" (lines 2–4). (Since the soul as formal cause gives to life its proper "end," in achieving which a well-lived life is the means, Pope proceeds to argue that those of inconstant or perverse character are "Fair to no purpose, artful to no end": hence his habitual analogy of a well-lived life to a well-constructed work of art, one in which ends are adapted to means and, of course, characters are "strongly marked" – as they are in the *Epistle* itself.)

As writer after writer on the signs of character explains, actions are a more probable indicator of character than are such local signs as gesture and expression; in *Cobham*, in language rich with references to the theory of probable signs, Pope questions even this most certain of indicators. First of all, all men, like plants, are different one from another; since "marks" are signs of types (universals), they are unsuccessful indicators of specific characters:

> There's some Peculiar in each leaf and grain,
> Some unmark'd fibre, or some varying vein:
> Shall only Man be taken in the gross?
> Grant but as many sorts of Mind as Moss. (15–18)

Such signs of other minds as appear in ordinary life are too confused to permit inference to character:

> Our depths who fathoms, or our shallows finds,
> Quick whirls, and shifting eddies, of our minds?
> Life's stream for Observation will not stay,
> It hurries all too fast to mark their way. (29–32)

For the same reasons, even our own characters are not accessible to us through whatever signs we might glean by introspection; "the cause of most we do" is but "dim to our internal view" – Lockean terminology for the weakest probability. "Not always Actions show the man," so that even granting the maxim that "Actions best discover man," in only a handful of cases are the signs sufficiently probable for us to infer character ("The few that glare each character must mark"); for the rest, only the most improbable hypotheses can "save" the character, that is "save the phenomena" in a scientific sense (lines 61, 71, 72, 77). In sum, inference through signs cannot be made to character:

> In vain the Sage, with retrospective eye,
> Would from th' apparent What conclude the Why,
> Infer the Motive from the Deed, and show,
> That what we chanc'd was what we meant to do. (51–54)

Where such inference is impossible, action and character appear disconnected; as critics, too, explain of literary actions not adequately grounded in the signs of character, such disconnected actions can have no probability, but appear rather as the effects of "chance."

Yet, after such a skeptical proem, Pope begins at line 174 of the *Epistle* to do just what the first half of his poem would have us believe is impossible: to infer motive from action, to connect actions one to another in portraying the consistent character which gives rise to them – to "save the phenomena." He does so precisely by referring actions to an element of character knowledge of which the first half of the poem would seem to deny us: an organizing principle Pope calls the "ruling passion."

> Search then the Ruling Passion: There alone,
> The Wild are constant, and the Cunning known;
> The Fool consistent, and the False sincere;
> Priests, Princes, Women, no dissemblers here.
> This clue once found, unravels all the rest,
> The prospect clears, and Wharton stands confest. (174–79)

Given Pope's skeptical introduction, how are we to come to knowledge of this organizing "clue"?

Pope does not address this question directly, but we may hazard an answer to it: for Pope, there is independent evidence of the existence of something called a "ruling" or "leading" passion; in individual cases, we must save the phenomena by forming the most probable hypothesis about such a leading passion as we can (where probability is measured by the degree to which this central hypothetical clue "unravels all the rest"). We shall examine again the role of probable reasoning in Pope's thinking; now, we must consider the possibility that an idea such as that of a ruling passion could provide the Augustans with the specific guarantee that decorums are accurate generalizations about behavior, and hence provides the middle term we have been seeking between the decorous and the well-marked character.

The doctrine of the leading passion, as is well known, is a late version of the ancient view that each man's character is the result of a mixture in particular proportions of the four elemental humors. The Greek term for such a mixture was *krasis*, which in Latin became *temperamentum* (from *temperare*, to mix) – the source for English *temperament* as a particular character (a particular mix of humors), also called *temperature*. (*Intemperature* or *distemper* is a diseased state, the loss of one's ordinary balance of humors; because the diseased are so often fevered, and because the word could also refer to climatic conditions, *temperature* came in the seventeenth century to refer to hot and cold.) "The manners of the soule follow the temperature of the body," Thomas Wright translates the proverb *animi mores corporis temperamentum sequantur*, itself altered from the title of a work by Galen.[46] The temperament, in return, causes visible effects in the body – signs like those produced by the passions, but more permanent in nature, and so more trustworthy as indicators. Lemnius explains, "All the Complexion and temperament of mans bodye proceedeth from the powers of the Elementes"; such complexions appear as signs, effects that denote their causes, which may be detected in one's walk, voice, or other pattern of behavior.[47] Thus he describes those of melancholy humor: "As touching the notes and markes of their mindes, they are churlish, whyning, wayward and ill to please" (146r). Even in ancient times, physiognomic doctrine included signs of the humors; in the Renaissance, Ambroise Paré writes of the humors that "The signes of these Symptomes quickly shew themselves in the face: the heart, by reason of the thinnesse of the skin in that part, as it were painting forth the notes of the affections."[48] Such signs of character, furthermore, are only true "for the most part, or probably," as Jacques Ferrand writes in his dictionary-like work of 1612, *Erotomania, or A Treatise Discoursing of the Essence, Causes, Symptomes, Prognostics, and Cure of Love or Erotique Melancholy* (40). And just as the signs in a literary work may be too many, confused, or inconsistent to permit probable inference, so may be signs in life; Burton complains in the *Anatomy* that this is the result of the classification of melancholy into too many kinds: "in such obscurity, therefore, variety and confused mixture of symptoms, causes, how difficult a thing is it to treat of several kinds apart; to make any certainty or distinction among so many casualties, distractions, when seldom two men shall be like affected *per omnia*!"[49] The operations of temperament (or leading passion) are modified as well by such circumstances as age, education, or climate, causing them to express themselves in diversified ways.

This doctrine, rooted in ancient medicine, is Pope's independent evidence for the existence of a unified character beneath its all too confusing signs. To have a character *is* to have a ruling passion. Despite seventeenth-century attempts to replace humoral with mechanical physiology, it was largely the phenomena described by humoralism that mechanism was used to describe – and most early Augustan literary writers continued to accept the old doctrine, consciously rejecting its mechanical reformulation. Pope, then, could claim scientific support for his seeming leap of faith in the second part of the *Epistle to Cobham*. Already in the Renaissance, furthermore, doctrines of temperament had been conflated with ideas of decorum, as they are in Jonson: "manners, now call'd humors, feed the stage" proclaims *The Alchemist*.[50] Literary characters are well-marked because finally real characters are; through decorums, they translate scientific into literary fact. Thus for Hurd, "there is scarcely any mark or feature of the human mind, any peculiarity or disposition of *character*, which the artist does not set off and make appear at once, to the view, by some certain turn or conformation of the outward figure."[51] In discussing broader patterns of signification, Hurd can equate "common nature and just decorum" (II, 100).

In practice, the effects of such a theory are many. Since Hurd believes, for instance, that comedy demands more truth of character than does tragedy (and hence that comedy requires the "best-marked characters"), he can argue that "Comedy succeeds best when the scene is laid *at home*, tragedy for the most part abroad" (II, 53, 55). Such a principle is grounded in the fact that the signs of mental motions will be differently "diversified" (modified) in different circumstances (148); signs born of familiar circumstances will be easiest for an audience to read – a kind of reading most necessary in comedy, a genre whose very end is fulfilled only when "*manners in action* show us *character*" (38). Because he believes character so important to comedy, and because it is only known through probable signs, Hurd can summarize the difference between comedy and tragedy: "*probability* constitutes" merely the "*medium*" of tragedy (because tragedy focuses on action, requiring therefore characters less particularized than those of comedy), whereas it is "the very essence of comedy," whose aim is the instructive portrayal of the "specific differences" of characters through probable signs (I, 30, 44). (Probability is the "medium" of tragedy in the sense of that "through which tragedy is enabled most powerfully to affect us" – by being first understood, and then believed.) Because of the different aims of the two genres, finally, "tragedy does not require or permit the poet to draw together so many of those characteristic circumstances which shew the manners, as Comedy" (48).

Decorums are the laws of probability for all the genres: they provide rules for the probable linking of action and character, via their signs. Because such rules are grounded in truths of nature, they lend to works that credibility on which the all-important power of moving an audience – a work's life, or "operation," to use the Restoration word – depends.[52] The various lines of signification which are decorums are divisible into classes by their topics (age, rank, education, etc.); these topics are called *circumstances*. Circumstances, then, are classes of probable signs; in 1735 Thomas Blackwell makes the point in his *Enquiry into the Life and Writings of Homer*:

[Nature's] *Proportions* are just and invariable: Whoever paints her *true*, or any part of her that is full of Action; and applies that Action to *Times*, *Places*, *Persons*, and their *Signs*, will include those *Proportions*, and their *Measures*, without intending it, almost without knowing it, but never without some Perception of their Propriety and Truth. (314)

Circumstances can provide signs of character because they are also among the determinants of character (circumstances alter not only cases, but characters), and so too with actions. Hurd explains of a well-constructed work, "In all cases of this sort, the known *character*, in conjunction with the *circumstances* of the person described, determines the particular *action* or *employment*, for the most part, so absolutely, that it requires some industry to mistake it" (II, 158). Whenever in a work circumstances are organized in this way, the work is "natural": Hurd remarks of the elements of Vergil's narrative of Dido, "It need only be observed, that they are such, as almost necessarily spring up from the circumstances of her case, and which the reader, on first view, as agreeing to his own notices and observations, pronounces *natural*" (153).

Theorists of decorum present the same analysis. Decorums are of course of ancient vintage; we shall consider only that resurgence of theorizing about them that took place in the seventeenth century. According to René Bray, the term *bienséance* first appeared in French criticism in Jean Chapelain's *Traité de la poésie représentative* (1635); previously there had existed only the adjective *décore* and the term's Latin forms. In his *Poëtique* of 1639, La Mesnardière introduced the plural *bienséances* and spawned in France that proliferation of *convenances*, *propriétés*, and lesser decorums for which the century is justly famous.[53] Rapin comments on the origin and importance of these rules:

Beyond all those rules taken from the *Poetics* of Aristotle, there is yet another which Horace mentions, the most essential of all to which all the other rules must submit themselves: *bienséance*. Without this the other rules of poetry are false, because this is the most solid foundation of that *vraisemblance* so essential to poetry. It is only through *bienséance* that *vraisemblance* has its effect:

everything becomes verisimilar once decorum sustains its character through all circumstances.[54]

Decorums are the working out of probability in particular circumstances: from Rapin's time until both terms lost their allure, probability and decorum are found together, so that literary blunders are at once "improbable and unproper," in Rymer's phrase; theorists treat the two together, so that, for instance, d'Aubignac's *Whole Art of the Stage* contains a chapter titled "Of Probability and Decency."[55]

Rapin cites different sources among ancient critics for his notions of *vraisemblance* (Aristotle) and *bienséance* (Horace), yet he all but conflates the terms, as had Italian theorists before him: the Renaissance conflation of Horatian and Aristotelian principles followed quickly on the recovery of the *Poetics*, and many early critics even supposed the *Ars poetica* to have been a commentary on Aristotle.[56] Early support for finding a doctrine of decorum in the *Poetics* was discovered in Aristotle's oft-cited list in chapter 15 of the four requirements of character (*ethos*, later "manners"): character must be "good," "appropriate" (or "convenient"), "like" ("resembling" whatever real exemplars there may be), and "consistent."

The requirement that character be "apparent" is a later addition to the list, the product of an age which had far more difficulty than did Aristotle with relations such as that between mind and body, or character and action. As several modern commentators have noted, Aristotle appears to have believed *ethos* to be a concept inclusive in some sense of both character and action, one sometimes rendered simply as "character-in-action"; traces of the same combination of what we would distinguish as inner and outer events can be found in Scaliger, who, following Aristotle, can define "happiness" (internal state) as "perfect action" (external):

Since poetry is to be compared to that institution of state which leads us to happiness, and happiness is in effect nothing more than perfect action, a poem will not in any way lead to the development of character, but to the development of action.[57]

Poetry teaches us to be better citizens, but it does so for Scaliger according to a theory of action that is now nearly opaque, one that seventeenth-century philosophy – most famously that of Descartes – displaced. Mind and body come to be understood as different in essence; as their interrelation becomes problematic, the role of the sign in interpreting their interrelation becomes more pronounced. Stage characters must all the more pressingly be "well-marked," for in order to be moved or instructed, audiences must be able to read motive and character from action; what philosophers had sundered, critics became more and more aware, the playwright must reunite, lest dramatic action (and narrative generally) be fortuitous and uninstructive. Dennis explains, "for an Action instructing by its Causes, which Causes are the Manners, unless I can be certain, what the Principles of the Agents are, I can never deduce any certain Moral from the Action"; we are made certain of the manners through their signs, that is, when character is well-marked (I, 72).

Decorum and its signs have mainly to do with character, but because character itself is so bound up with the larger category of action, from the first any literary fault might be seen as a sin against both "the probability of actions" and "the decorum of persons"; as late as 1792 appear statements such as Henry Pye's that "necessity and probability should be as much considered in the manners, as in the action."[58] Considered only by themselves, decorum and the probable signs of character may be said to function in structuring a work only at a fairly local level; as Hurd says of the expression of "humour" in a work, "*humour*, though brought out by the *action*, is not the effect of the whole, but may be distinctly evidenced in a *single scene*." Other properties of works, such as "pathos," are "the result of the *entire action*: that is, of all the circumstances of the story taken together, and conspiring by a probable tendency to a completion in the *event*" (II, 45). Considered as the medium through which action occurs, decorum and the signs of character give structure to literary wholes. It is the role of action in the Augustan model of literary structure, then, which will finally prove that for the Augustans, the literary work is a hierarchy of probable signs.

(3) IMPROBABLE VILLAINS: EVIL AND THE STRUCTURE OF ACTION

God breaketh not all men's hearts alike.

Richard Baxter, *Reasons of the Christian Religion* (1655)

Generalizing from disputes about the possibility of Christian tragedy, Leopold Damrosch suggests that "The most untragic aspect of neoclassical theory is not so much that virtue is rewarded, as that evil – monstrous, unmitigated evil – is not permitted to exist."[59] That is, such evil is not permitted on the stage; whatever their final metaphysical commitments, few Augustans would agree with Benjamin Franklin's youthful claim that "Evil doth not exist."[60] Metaphysical commitments of a sort, however, do underpin Rymer, Dryden, and Dennis' notorious decorums for the representation of evil characters on stage.

Aristotle's first requirement of the manners, that they be good, had spawned a welter of divergent interpretations. To Castelvetro, the precept meant that a work's principal characters should be good; to Heinsius, that a work should on balance contain more good than evil characters. To Chapelain, the architect of *bienséance*, *bonnes moeurs* are simply manners appropriate to character, yet in practice his views are not very different from those of his student La Mesnardière, who argued that manners are good if they are exemplary, or of his opponent Corneille, who thought with his usual flair for intensification that *bonnes moeurs* are not only appropriate, but elevated (so that good characters must be very good, bad ones very bad). It was Le Bossu who finally and clearly distinguished the "poetical goodness" of manners from their moral goodness, arguing that Aristotle really meant that manners are good if they are properly revelatory of character, that is, when characters are well-marked.[61] Thus (calling on other decorums as well) Le Bossu gives his strictures on poetical footmen:

Without a doubt a foot-man cannot be a Master of that goodness, to which he has no right. He will then be *morally bad*, because he will be a dissembling, drunken, cheating Rascal, and he will be *Poetically good*, because these bad Inclinations will be exposed.[62]

English Restoration critics might appeal to any of these positions, but they continued the argument about how to present evil in a new way, a way they learned from Le Bossu. Le Bossu's *Traité du poème épique* (1675) was widely read in England before it was translated in 1695; to its common acclaim Dennis adds the praise that "none of the Moderns understood the Art of Heroick Poetry, who writ before *Bossu* took pains to unravel the Mystery" (i, 271–72). But what Rymer, Dryden, Dennis, and the Augustan age in general learned from Le Bossu was not merely a theory of the epic; they took from him a theory of literary structure applicable to all the narrative and dramatic kinds. Le Bossu's model became so pervasive in England that for a century different accounts of literary form had to be explained and justified as modifications of this one. It is an account of the literary work as a hierarchy of probable signs (see figure 1).

Le Bossu begins by interpreting Aristotle's treatment of plot (action), character, and expression in the time-honored way as the statement of a hierarchic interrelation. He adds to this hierarchy the prior requirement of a moral, which the fable "allegorizes." (For Le Bossu and his closest followers, such as Dennis, the poet chooses his moral even before designing his fable; other critics may not cede such *psychological* priority to the work's moral, but still allow it *logical* priority.)[63] The fable *simpliciter*, or "simple Action," may be identical in an Aesopic fable and an extended epic; in the latter case,

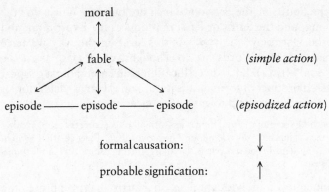

Figure 1

the poet must to greater degree *diversify* his fable with *episodes*, turning simple action into what Le Bossu calls "Episodized Action." The nature of these diversifications into episodes in turn dictates the poet's choice of character, expression, numbers, and spectacle. What Le Bossu's definitions unite to form is a hierarchy that proceeds by progressive diversification from moral through fable (simple action), episodized action, character, expression, and the rest.[64]

All the parts of a poem are interrelated as are the parts of a living body: in Dennis' words (in a passage explaining Le Bossu's views), "all the parts of the Poem, as parts of one and the same Body, may appear to have the same Nature and to be animated all with the same commanding Spirit" (1, 77). Specifically, the relation between moral and fable is one that Le Bossu likens to that between soul and body, while the parts of a diversified action are connected to one another as are the parts of one body.

The relation between body and soul, as we have seen, was in the Aristotelian tradition understood as one of *formal causation*. Thus, for instance, Spenser in the "Hymne to Beautie":

> For of the soule the bodie forme doth take:
> For soule is forme, and doth the bodie make. (132–33)

In this way, Le Bossu and his followers speak of the moral as the "Form" of a work, the fable as its "Matter." The same relation of formal causation (soul-to-body), furthermore, obtains at every step in the hierarchic structure of the work. Thus Dennis can speak of the "Fable" as "the Form or Soul of particular Poems" in relation to the episodes into which the fable is diversified (1, 216), which give that fable its "body." Further on in the model, "The Sentiments in Poetry create the Spirit, or the Passion, which are but two Words for the same thing; and the Spirit or Passion produces the Expression, and begets the Harmony" (1, 375). At this level, in the way we have examined before, "Words are to Thought, what Flesh is to the human Soul" (1, 44). Each diversification is an embodiment of spirit in matter, a product of formal causation; James Harris' definition of a formal cause may help to make this clear:

the Form and Exemplar of any Thing is its [formal] Cause; that is to say, in other Words, the Definition, the Detail or Narrative of its Essence (that which, characterizing it to be such a particular thing, distinguishes it from all things else). (*Works*, 1, 281)

This principle of individuation is, in Harris' happy phrase, the "narrative of its essence." Moral is the formal cause of fable, fable of its episodes, and so forth; the formal cause of a well-marked character is that internal state which an author attempts to suggest through appropriate marks and which serves a specific function within an action. (Well-marked characters exhibit "propriety" in the now almost lost sense of that word, in fully realizing the individual nature of a thing.)

It is through this relation of formal causation that each level in the hierarchy gains intelligibility: that it has a place in the systematic structure of the work, and that we come to realize its purpose in that structure. Zachary Mayne defines *form* in his "Dissertation concerning Sense" (1728), speaking of perceptions:

But, in the next place, to make appear the utter Incapacity of *Sense* for *Understanding*. I say therefore, that a corporeal Object of any kind whatsoever (and *Sense* perceiveth nothing else) is no otherwise intelligible, than from its Significancy, or as it means, imports, or denotes something that is intelligible... That which, in any sensible or corporeal Being, signifies or maketh it to signify, I shall beg leave to call in general *its Form*.

Interpretation, as we shall find, is the process of coming to understand such form; of any phenomenon new to us, says Mayne, we must ask

What does it signify and denote, or *what is its Meaning and Importance?* A plain indication, that the *Perception* of a corporeal Phenomenon is not the *Understanding* of it; and that it must be, as it were interpreted, before it can be understood; and that the *Knowledge* of it is nothing else but its *Interpretation.*

Mayne proceeds to apply his analysis to the interpretation of nature, and in particular to physico-theology; but before we can understand that this is the same process of interpretation which Augustan writers asked of their readers, we must further unfold their conception of the hierarchic structure of the work.[65]

With Le Bossu the doctrine of probable circumstances gains a new systemic importance. As was the case for Renaissance teachers of dialectic, in Le Bossu's process of diversification the movement is from general to particular, a particularizing according to probable circumstances. Of such circumstances Le Bossu writes:

I will maintain then that the Word *Episode* in the *Epick Poem* does not signifie an extraneous foreign Piece ... but that it signifies the whole Narration of the Poet, or a necessary and essential part of the Action and the proper Subject, extended and amplified by probable Circumstances. (64)

Traditionally, such circumstancing constitutes the difference between a general "thesis" (such as might be used in dialectic) and its particularization in a "hypothesis" (the material of rhetoric); one *locus classicus* for this distinction is the *Progymnasmata* of Aphthonius:

A *thesis* differs from a *hypothesis* in that the *hypothesis* deals with a particular circumstance but the *thesis* without complicating circumstances. The particular circumstances are persons, act, cause, and so on.[66]

It is in this way that Dennis can say, "I know no difference that there is, between one of *Aesop*'s Fables, and the Fable of an Epick Poem, as to their Natures, tho' there be many and great ones, as to their Circumstances" (II, 110): the two works have the same form, differently immersed in and diversified by matter. Le Bossu writes: an action "explain'd and amplified with all the Circumstances of Times, Places, and Persons, is not a simple and proper Action, but an *Episodiz'd Action*" (67); Dennis speaks of "the Incidents which compose those Episodes; or of those probable Circumstances which extend each part of the Action to the length of a just Episode" (I, 103). Circumstances are probable, Le Bossu explains, when through the places of circumstances events in a work are given a "Probable Connexion" with what surrounds them (57).

An action, then, "must be render'd *Probable* by the Circumstances of *Times, Places* and *Persons*" (14), but these particularizations must be only specifications of the fable and moral, not alterations of them: the poet must use "such Circumstances as alter nothing of the Essence either of the *Fable* or the *Moral*," the "*Ground-work* upon which all the rest is built" (17, 43). Episodes, for example, are not merely "added to the Action," but "constitute this Action and this Matter, as the Members of the Body constitute the Matter of it" (68); "The being adorn'd and loaded with Animate Things, will never make an Animal, but there must be a Soul added to it" (43). Episodes and incidents not "drawn from the very Essence of the Fable" are both improbable and disunifying, Le Bossu explains in his chapter "Of the Faults which corrupt the *Unity* of the *Action*" (76, 75). Following Le Bossu, English critics such as Dennis and Samuel Johnson also describe improbability as *corruption*, in the Latin sense of division into parts; any disunified work might be called corrupt in this sense, but improbabilities especially, in Dennis' words, "make the Poem episodick, and corrupt the Unity of the Action."[67]

Even the choice of a hero is a case of particularizing an action through probable circumstances. "The *Hero* is only design'd for the *Action*"; "the *Action* is not made for the *Hero*, since that ought to be feign'd and invented independently for him, and before the *Poet* thoughtˑof using his Name" (Le Bossu, 54). Naming itself is a further instance of this procedure: "The Names that are given to the Personages do first specifie a Fable" and "render the Action morȩ singular"; next comes "the Composition of the *Episodes*, which are made after the General Personages are singularized by the Imposition of Names" (16). Dennis uses the same term for naming (*imposition*): "the Action, at the bottom, is Universal and Allegorical, even after the Imposition of Names; and ... the Persons likewise, after they are made Singular by the Imposition of Names, remain at the bottom Universal and Allegorical" (so that inference will still be possible from particularized hero to general moral) (1, 68). The term comes from logic (Latin *impositio*, or sometimes *intentio*, from the Greek *thesis*), where it refers to the signate relation between a name or idea and the objects or class of objects to which the name refers (which it "intends").[68] Thus Le Bossu can speak of "the probable Circumstances of Places, Princes, and People" (63); naming the main character is an initial circumstancing that dictates what further circumstances will be probable. Sometimes he simply uses the phrase "Names and Circumstances" (63).

Because the relation between higher and lower levels in the hierarchy of moral, fable, action, etc., is one of formal *causation*, the relation of lower to higher levels is one of probable *signification*: lower levels are the signs of higher, just as bodily signs are expressions of the soul. Thus it is this model which makes possible throughout the literary work what we have seen to be the Augustan idea of literary interpretation: inference from signs, reasoning from effect to cause. It licenses, for instance, Rymer's procedure in giving nutshell formulations of the morals of plays, arrived at by inferring formal causes from signate effects. Each term in the hierarchy must be derived from the last by a diversification that is probable, as for example it is through probable circumstances that incidents are "amplified" and "singularized," so that readers may then infer with probability from episodes to fable, from fable to moral. Zachary Mayne explains interpretation:

And indeed all the several *Phenomena* in Nature, so far as they appear intelligible to us, are (as I may call them) so many natural *Hieroglyphicks*, each of which hath a certain Meaning and Importance; and the Discovery whereof is a sort of Interpretation; or the understanding them is the Knowledge of their several Meanings and Significations.

Mayne's procedure differs from the reader's only in that it seeks to unfold the meaning of divine rather than human art.[69]

Within this hierarchic model, then, judgments of probability are to be made wherever one term is related to another (see Figure 1): between moral and fable, between fable and its diversification into episodes, and between episodes themselves. Thus Dennis, following Le Bossu, gives three requirements for the constitution of episodes:

First, They are to be deriv'd from the first Plan of the Action. Secondly, They are to have a necessary or probable Dependance one upon another. Thirdly, Not one of them is to be an Action in it self, but onely a necessary Part of an Action extended by probable Circumstances. (1, 58)

To one or another of these requirements may be referred nearly all the specific judgments of probability to be found in Augustan criticism. Thus when Charles Gildon writes of heroic poetry, "the Decorum of Person, Time, and Place must be preserv'd. Without this Condition, an *Episode* is no longer *probable*," he is observing Dennis' third rule, that an episode be a probable unity in itself.[70] The familiar demand that, in Blair's words, a narrative should have "parts joined together with probability and due connexion" (*Lectures*, 1, 22), exemplifies Dennis' second rule, that, as many critics were to explain, episodes should "produce one another, as Causes do their Effects" (Dennis, 1, 61). In this sense one Italian critic can describe the unity of a narrative with the following list of intendedly synonymous expressions: "Tutta: Grande proportionamente: Una: Verisimile: Non Episodica."[71] Some writers pursue this rule so far as to claim, with d'Aubignac, that "it is impossible that an event should arise with probability from another which is not probable." Perhaps he means to invoke the old rule of argument that a conclusion can be no more probable than the least probable of its premises – as Abraham Tucker put it, "If our premises are uncertain, they can throw no stronger light upon the conclusion than they had themselves, or rather than belonged to the weaker, if they happen to differ in lustre." More likely, though, d'Aubignac means that incoherence, once introduced into a work, corrupts the unity of the whole.[72] It is Dennis' first rule that will help us to understand Augustan decorums for the presentation of evil in literature, and which will most clearly demonstrate the importance of the hierarchic model.

The last and most important interpretive inference which the Augustan reader was to make was that from fable to moral. Literature instructs, in this model, by presenting readers with signs structured so that a moral might with probability be inferred (enforcing that moral, of course, through the emotional appeal of the work). Actions must be designed, in other words, so that they "prove" their moral. Dennis explains, drawing an analogy to logical proofs:

> But here it will not be amiss to observe what has been all along hinted. That the Action is only fram'd for the Instruction; and that it is design'd for a proof of the Moral; that every part of that Action ought to be a gradual Progress in the proof; and that consequently all the Parts of it ought to be as dependant on one another, as the Propositions are of a Syllogism; and that to insert any thing between the Parts, which is foreign from the Action, that is, from the Argument, is to destroy, or at least to weaken that Argument; and is as absurdly impertinent, as a Parenthesis would be between the Propositions of a Categorical Syllogism. (I, 57–58)

Just as every matter has its form, every action has a moral by virtue of its form – a moral good or ill, whether the author intended it or not. Dennis explains, "no Author can form the Narration of any great and memorable Action, but some Moral will arise from it, whether the Writer intends it or not" (II, 110). Reading from fable to moral, then, is a reading of signs like that in physico-theology; in each case, readers of signs seek an organizing principle, a formal cause, in the matter before them. And just as some signs in nature might mislead the unwary natural theologian – some partial evils might not very obviously be assimilable to the universal good – an ill-constructed work will (intendedly or not) mislead audiences. As Richard Hurd explains of the ancient theater, when evil characters are painted in such "strong, vivid colours" that they please more than, and divert attention from, good characters, then a work is ill made; "Hence the sound philosophy of the chorus will be constantly wanting to rectify the wrong conclusions of the audience, and prevent the ill impressions that might otherwise be made upon it."[73]

Dryden writes of villains in the "Grounds of Criticism in Tragedy":

> a poet ought not to make the manners perfectly good in his best persons; but neither are they to be more wicked in any of his characters than necessity requires. To produce a villain, without other reason than a natural inclination to villainy, is, in poetry, to produce an effect without a cause; and to make him more a villain than he has just reason to be, is to make an effect which is stronger than the cause. (248)

The modern reader is likely to protest here that Dryden's principle is invalid, for there do exist some who simply *are* evil; such a reader (though he be otherwise quite correct) does not understand what sort of "cause" Dryden is appealing to, for he does not know the theoretical context from which the argument emerges – the hierarchic model of literary structure. Indeed, what Dryden says in this passage is again a paraphrase of Le Bossu. The original insight occurs in Le Bossu's chapter "Of the *Poetical Goodness* of the *Manners*"; Dryden's version is, characteristically, more lucid and scientifically accurate than his original.

'Tis necessity and probability that regulate these two contraries [virtue and vice]. And they regulate them so, that when they give to virtue all that is possible, yet they allow vice only that which cannot be cut off from the Poem without spoiling the Fable. Thus Aristotle censures the *Vicious Manners*, not because they are Vicious, but because they are so without any necessity for it. But he does not blame the obstinacy of *Achilles*, as unjust and unreasonable as it was, because it was necessary to the Fable.[74]

Rymer's well-known strictures on "Jago," whose crimes exceed the possibility of the stage to punish them, follow the pattern Dryden and Le Bossu outline, though in cruder form. Where all actions conspire to a moral merely by virtue of their form, failure to punish evil in just degree is to propound it. Where a good moral is intended, excessive or "uncaused" evil thus provides false signs to the audience. Rymer calls Jago a "monster" and a "prodigy," "a Rogue beyond what the Devil ever finish'd."[75] The opprobrium is familiar, but the terms also make a certain systematic sense in Rymer's larger argument. Monsters and prodigies were generally understood, along Aristotelian lines, to be exceptions to the regular workings of causation in nature; they are nature's teleological failures. (Scaliger remarks: "Indeed, not even nature herself is a perfectly reliable workman, for occasionally she is embarrassed and fails of her end, as when she produces a monstrosity, or brings forth defective bodies.")[76] The action of *Othello* is for Rymer such a defective body; as a moral monster, Jago is a surd in an otherwise intelligible order, and so a false sign of the nature of that order. Critics find monsters defensible in literary works (if at all) only when they are the products of providential intervention, wherewith they become trustworthy signs of a divine order. The devil is of course the paradigm of the moral *lusus naturae*, a surd even within the higher realm: he can be the source of no probable inference from effect to cause – from such a paradigm of unnaturalness to the nature of God; to suppose otherwise, one might say, would be to suppose that one had solved the problem of evil. Damrosch's observation about Augustan tragedy, then, is the joint product of Augustan theology and the hierarchic model of literary structure. In this way Dennis can call an ill-constructed action "a murmuring, as it were, at Providence," and can say of poetic justice: "Poetick Justice would be a Jest if it were not an Image of the Divine, and if it did not consequently suppose the Being of a God and Providence" (I, 21, 183).

Lest such exegesis appear overingenious, consider the statement with which Le Bossu opens his chapter "Of the *Causes* of the *Manners*": "God is the chief of all the *Causes* in general, we shall look upon him here in particular, as the most universal cause of the *Manners*. He is the Author of Nature, and disposes all things as he thinks fit" (161). Followed through, the structure of signs which comprises a literary work leads finally to God; "uncaused" evil, in obscuring poetic justice, misleads by licensing inferences to a less-than-perfect deity.

This image of the devil as the Great Anarch – paradigm of all breaches of decorum, because guilty of the greatest impropriety (falsehood to self, or role) – is a pervasively familiar one in Augustan literature, as is the kind of thinking from which the image comes. Pope, for example, teaches not only in the *Essay on Man* but throughout his work that individuals have their proper nature not only in themselves, but, most importantly, in relation to others. Failure to understand and to act on this knowledge – that between individuals, as Thomas Percival put it in a discussion of the *Essay on Man* in 1784, "the relation ... is reciprocal" – leads to an ironic return of evil upon the self which Pope likes in his verse to express through emblematic repetitions of verbs or nouns ("Sick of herself thro' very selfishness").[77]

Pride is the general name for the sin (at root a failure of self-knowledge) Pope is describing. The attempts of pride to shore up a self-sufficient self result, as Pope teaches, in fragmentation and division rather than unity (just as in the *Essay on Criticism*, pride is said to cause fragmenting readings of literary works, readings that attend only to parts); pride's attempts are in fact divisions of proper relations. Corruption, then, corrupts. This structure of ideas appeals even to the Augustan age's lesser lights; to Charles Gildon in *The Complete Art of Poetry*, for instance, the opposite of a "probable" literary event is one that is "affected" (I, 274, 278). Gildon's use of "affectation" is an extraordinary compression of the doctrines of pride and probability. The cognate function of pride to fragment in both literature and life – like the similarity between the Augustan ideas of interpretation and of physico-theology – may help us to see that Augustans conceived of literary works as hierarchies of probable signs because they believed that the world itself, what literature imitates, is such a hierarchy.

As sin fragments, so evil is a kind of fragmentation or multiplicity. Scaliger provides the reason concisely:

Of well-governed conduct there is, as it were, a definite form, which the philosophers call right reason (*ratio recta*). Is there any form of evil conduct? No, there is not.[78]

The lesson is widely applicable. Samuel Johnson notes of *Paradise Lost*, "Of the evil angels the characters are more diversified" than of the good; on the other hand, observes Pope, "Heroes are much the same."[79] On the difficulties of writing modern panegyric, Swift finds that

the Materials of Panegyric being very few in Number, have long since been exhausted: For, as Health is but one Thing, and has always been the same, whereas Diseases are by thousands, besides new and daily Additions; So, all the Virtues that have been ever in Mankind, are to be counted upon a few Fingers, but his Follies and Vices are innumerable, and Time adds hourly to the heap.

Defoe's Roxana agrees that there is an "infinity" of "Sorts of Fools."[80] Moving down Sir Joshua Reynolds' "scale" of painting, from heroic painting down to portraiture and still-life, details become more variously particularized. In general, as one moves from moral to fable down to expression, Augustan poetry by a decorum which Irvin Ehrenpreis has named "negative particularity" reserves concertedly particular detail for "vicious, low, or comic characters."[81] Such a decorum can exist because it is rooted in the truth that where evil is more diverse than good, so will be its signs; Lord Kames makes just this point about signs in the *Elements of Criticism*:

pleasant passions are, for the most part, expressed externally in one uniform manner; and . . . only the painful passions are distinguishable from each other by their external expressions. In the emotions accordingly raised by external signs of pleasant passions, there is little variety. They are pleasant or chearful, but we have not words to reach a more particular description. But the external signs of painful passions produce in the spectator emotions of different kinds: the emotions, for example, raised by external signs of grief, of remorse, of anger, of envy, of malice, are clearly distinguishable from each other. (II, 133)

Uncaused evil in literary works, in addition to traducing both God and authorial meaning by licensing inferences to an unintended moral, furthermore upsets through overdiversification sign-inferences at every level of the literary work. For Dennis, "the Improbability even of one Episode" will "ruine the Probability of the Poem, and destroy the Moral" (I, 61). (Where generic considerations require particularly good characters, the portrayal of evil's variousness is even further circumscribed; thus according to Jonathan Richardson, in an echo of the passage in *Paradise Lost* in which the serpent in Eden is struck dumb at his first sight of Eve's beauty [IX 464–66], "If a devil were to have his portrait made, he must be drawn as abstracted from his own evil, and stupidly good" [*Works*, 100].) We have already seen Spence complaining of the way such multiplicity is destructive of interpretive inference; it is through the judicious choice of probable circumstances that the poet avoids the disunifying and misleading effects of overdiversification as he particularizes his fable.

Contrasting the straight road to truth followed by science with the bypaths of imagination, Johnson remarks, "though rectitude is uniform and mixed, obliquity may be infinitely diversified," while Rymer feels compelled to answer those who fear that, because "*reason* is always principally to be consulted" in "the contrivance and *oeconomy* of a play," its "rules and restraints on the *Plot*" may conspire to "make all *Plays* alike and *uniform*."[82] There is of course no real issue here, since rectitude, though uniform, yet provides any number of morals for the poet to allegorize in action (unless we force Rymer to the counsel of perfection that the only perfectly constructed literary work is that structure of signs which is the world itself, of which there is only one – a position perhaps not far from James Thomson's in the *Seasons*). Immoral morals, however, pose an oddly ambiguous problem. Dennis stresses frequently both that all literary works have morals merely by virtue of their form, and that confusion and disorder cannot exist in reality, that they are "Nothing" (I, 202). Thus he is forced to argue that an ill moral is really no moral at all; the ill-made work is really not an exemplar of its intended kind, and is in fact "without any reasonable Meaning" (I, 61). For Dennis, Addison's *Cato* is such a work: "the Action of this Play is so far from carrying a Moral, that it carries a pernicious instruction with it" (II, 45). And to the extent that a play has an ill (or no) moral, it cannot be probable, for as we have seen, its parts cannot have the necessary hierarchic dependence on one another; for this reason too, it cannot be marvellous, because it cannot fully embody a proper framework of regularities from which marvels are real or seeming deviations. Thus Addison, says Dennis, "has found out the Secret, to make his Tragedy highly improbable, without making it wonderful, and to make some Parts of it highly incredible, without being in the least entertaining" (II, 49).

For the Augustans, to say that a narrative contains improbabilities and to say that it has an ill moral are different ways of saying the same thing. Improbabilities – failures of events to lead to one another in a probable way, failures of action and character to lead to and reveal one another with probability – are, according to the kind of interpretation licensed by the hierarchic model, probable signs of disorder, "murmurings at Providence." Conversely, an ill moral can be inferred with probability only from a work which contains such signs. In either case, events, actions, and the world itself appear to be ruled rather by *chance* than by a beneficent deity; to Dennis, for example, the opposite of poetic justice is just such an imputation against God: "The Good must never fail to prosper, and the Bad must always be punish'd: Otherwise the Incidents, and particularly the Catastrophe which is the grand Incident, are liable to be imputed rather to Chance, than to Almighty Conduct and to Sovereign Justice" (II, 6). Addison's famous rejection of such simple and direct poetic justice is not a rejection of the hierarchic model and the kinds of inferences it licenses (from signs), but only of what he conceives to be incorrect applications of it. Thus even *Spectator* 40, immediately after rejecting confined notions of poetic justice, condemns tragi-comedy, where signs are disorganized in such a way as (at least in Addison's opinion) to cloud probable inference from them; more tellingly, *Spectator* 548, returning to the subject, justifies the earlier opinion by referring to just that sort of inference from fable to moral which Dennis preaches. Here Addison argues that the good may with probability be made to suffer, for "The Poet may still find out some prevailing Passion or Indiscretion in his Character, and shew it in such a manner, as will sufficiently acquit the Gods of any injustice in his Sufferings"; Dennis could hardly disagree with Addison's remarks at the end of the essay:

I shall conclude with observing, that tho' the *Spectator* abovementioned [no. 40] is so far against the Rule of Poetical Justice as to affirm that good Men may meet with an unhappy Catastrophe in Tragedy, it does not say that ill Men may go off unpunish'd. The Reason for this Distinction is very plain, namely, because the best of Men are vicious enough to justifie Providence for any Misfortunes and Afflictions which may befall them, but there are many Men so Criminal that they can have no Claim or Pretence to Happiness. The best of Men may deserve Punishment, but the worst of Men cannot deserve Happiness.[83]

Where Dennis and Addison actually differ is in *how good* the heroes of literary works should be; Addison prefers flawed reflections of man's actual fallen state, Dennis, exemplars which exceed ordinary virtue. Both Addison and Dennis agree that "promiscuous Events call the Government of Providence into Question, and by Scepticks and Libertines are resolv'd into Chance" (Dennis, II, 7); to have believed otherwise would have been to give up the very means for interpreting literary works at all, the hierarchic model.

Until mid century, even those Augustans who disagreed most loudly with Le Bossu about the details of the theory of literary structure of which he, Dryden, and Dennis were the chief expositors, continue to believe firmly that literary works are composed of a hierarchy of levels unified by relations of formal causation, relations which license interpretation as reading from probable signs. Many, for instance, deny the psychological priority of moral over fable, but none rejects the logical connection between them or the general theory from which the connection emerges. What was ultimately to destroy the model was a shift that looked at first like nothing more than a rearrangement of the levels within it, giving character, rather than action, logical priority in the hierarchy.

A transitional work useful in understanding this shift is Henry Pemberton's *Observations on Poetry* of 1738, a defense of Glover's *Leonidas* which also attempts to revise prevailing critical commitments. Pemberton argues against Aristotle and Le Bossu that character, not action, is the poet's primary concern: "the primary intention of epic and dramatic poetry" is "the representation of the differing characters of men, and the effects of their several passions"; fable is to be judged only as it "consists in such a disposition of circumstances, whereby each character and passion may most fully, and most distinctly be set forth" (5, 26). Yet Pemberton makes this argument in a work organized in the time-honored fashion of Aristotle, as reinterpreted by Le Bossu: the *Observations* contains successive chapters entitled "Of the fable of epic and dramatic poems," "Of sentiments and character," "Of the language of poetry," "Of versification." Not only does his order of presentation embody the hierarchic model; his fundamental critical principles remain true to it as well.

Character is first of all to be presented and understood in the traditional way: poets present readers with "the natural effects of different tempers and actions," that readers may understand them by "making just deductions from the external appearances" and thereby learn the art of "prudence," the art of reading from outer to inner through signs (11–12). Because the "tempers and characters of men are made manifest in action," furthermore, that fable will best display character which is "a continued series of events dependent on each other, as may compose one well united course of action" (27); it must contain no such "perplexity of circumstances" as might hinder probable inference, but must be instead a "chain of events ... within the limits of probability" (38, 26); for consistent characters to emerge from it, the fable must be ruled by what Pemberton, quoting Milton, calls "verisimilitude and decorum" (9). Finally, although narratives may not be written with a moral in mind, or may even illustrate more than one moral, moral is still to be inferred from fable in the familiar way (17–18).

Despite such affinities with more orthodox statements of the model, we can see in the *Observations* too indications of the way in which a preference for character over action (i.e., a logical preference) was to put an end to the theory of the literary work as hierarchy, producing instead a model of the work as horizontal (sequential) structure of probable signs. The preference for character did this by undermining what had been the logical mainstay of the hierarchic model, the unity of action. As Dennis had said, an episode must not be "an Action it self"; once the unity of action fragments, local actions – episodes, parts of works – may embody hierarchy, but the work as a whole need not. Thus where Johnson took account in his discussions of Shakespeare of the complex requirements Shakespeare's plots made on the characters of his plays, Hazlitt can consider Shakespeare's characters in complete isolation from the actions in which they appear. The result is a new theory of literary structure and unity, and with this a new theory of the way literary works are to be read. It is not our purpose here to explain the new model in detail, but only to suggest the ways in which it grew from the older one.

So clearly had Dennis seen the older model to rest on unity of action that he insisted that a well-constructed work could, at the highest level, embody only one major moral maxim (1, 57); similarly, he placed such severe restrictions on consistency of character as a necessary part of that unity that within the hierarchic model any *change* of character appeared to be impossible.[84] The kind of fable that Pemberton describes – one that might illustrate any number of morals – need not have this kind of unity, and in his prescriptions for fables which best display character, we can see those pressures which, loosed later in the century, would result in new literary forms, horizontal rather than hierarchical in structure. Pemberton's advice that the poet "make it his chief endeavor to open the human mind, and bring forth the secret springs of action, the various passions and sentiments of men" (10) would not have ruffled Dryden, who can declare (and surely also follow his advice in practice), "'Tis not the admirable intrigue, the surprising events, the extraordinary incidents that make the beauty of a tragedy; 'tis the discourses when they are so natural and passionate" (*Essays*, 1, 220). But given the hierarchic model, it is through their unity of action that literary works gain intelligibility; unity of action will thus govern literary practice, however loosely, until the hierarchic model itself collapses. We will see in chapter VII that the hierarchic model depends upon certain widely held Augustan accounts of the psychological processes by which the mind infers from signs, and so of how parts join to form wholes; when these accounts are displaced by other theories of knowledge and inference, parts will join into wholes in new ways: there will emerge at once new literary forms and new procedures of interpretation.

We may find traces in Richard Hurd's thinking too which suggest what would happen to the hierarchic model. Hurd finds

there are *two ways* of evidencing the characteristic and predominant qualities of men, or, of producing *humour*, which require to be observed. The *one* is, when they are shewn in the perpetual course and tenor of the representation; that is, when the *humour* results from the *general* conduct of the person in the drama, and the discourse, which he holds in it. The *other* is, when by an happy and lively stroke, the characteristic quality is laid open and exposed *at once*. (II, 59)

Such "strokes of character" or "strokes of nature" had long been the staple of literary and dramatic criticism, but in mid-century they take on new importance as larger patterns of unity fragment.[85] As Isaac D'Israeli, that late eighteenth-century champion of small and fragmented literary forms, explains, "A well-chosen anecdote frequently reveals a character, more happily than an elaborate delineation, as a glance of lightning will sometimes discover what has escaped us in full light" (compare Hurd's "laid open and exposed *at once*").[86] E. N. Hooker has traced a shift in English theory of the epic from Le Bossu and Dennis' view of the place of "episodes" within the larger whole to the position of Trapp, that episodes might be mere embellishments, and that of the Richardsons, that episodes might, if good in themselves, be wholly "excrescences."[87]

As the new emphasis on character fragments the unity of action, a new particularity in the portrayal of the individual personality causes a shift in the doctrine of probable circumstances. Pemberton distinguishes "general" from "particular" character:

Again character is also either general or particular. By general characters or manners I mean the different cast of mind owing to difference of country, of age, sex, birth, and fortune. Character in particular denotes sentiment and general manners diversified according to the different temper and passions of each individual. (45)

Le Bossu and his followers were often content to discuss character only in Pemberton's first sense (with the important addition of *moral* character), diversification through the probable circumstances of country, age, sex, etc., providing enough particularization to form an individual literary character. Here Pemberton uses Le Bossu's own theoretic model (diversification through probable circumstances) to extend the model further; the usual name for those circumstances which produce this further particularization was, following the elevation of the particular by Joseph Warton in his influential *Essay on the Genius and Writings of Pope* (1756), "minute circumstances."[88]

According to John Ogilvie, the good painter of passions aims "to imitate nature in her most delicate signatures"; to Isaac D'Israeli, "Human nature, like a vast machine, is not to be understood by looking on its superficies, but by dwelling on its minute springs and little wheels."[89] Warton goes so far as to claim that "A minute and particular enumeration of circumstances judiciously selected, is what chiefly discriminates poetry from history, and renders the former, for that reason, a more close and faithful representation of nature" (1, 48). The second half of the eighteenth century teems with statements such as John Aikin's recommendation, "If you wish to feel the full force of the simple pathetic, raised by no other art than the selection of little circumstances which could only have suggested themselves to an exquisitely sensible heart," read the portrayal of "Mary" by Cowper.[90] To an earlier theorist of signs such as Spence, of course, such minuteness obstructs probable inference; he writes in *Polymetis*:

The third fault in the allegories of Spenser's own invention is, that they are sometimes stretched to such a degree, that they appear rather extravagant than great: and that he is sometimes so minute, in pointing out every particular of its vastness to you; that the object is in danger of becoming ridiculous, instead of being admirable. (304)

A critic such as Johnson might attempt to keep such criticism of minuteness alive, but the future lay with Warton.[91] We shall examine in chapter VIII a mid-century shift in the philosophical theory of probability which accompanies the appeal to minute circumstances and which underpins Aikin's appeal to the "sensible heart"; it will then be easier to understand why by the end of the century "probable circumstances" are scarcely mentioned by any but old-fashioned strict Aristotelians; in a work such as Archibald Alison's *Essays on the Nature and Principles of Taste* (1790), probable circumstances are mentioned only once, and in a sense that proponents of the earlier model would have found unrecognizable – to Alison, circumstances are probable when they do not wake readers from the "pleasing reverie" which is their experience of the literary work (107).

(4) POPE AND THE RULES: THE AUGUSTAN CRITIC AS PROBABILIST

> The *soule*, by *reason*, makes rules *general*,
> Of *things* particuler: but *sense* soth goe
> But to *particulers* material;
> The *soule* by th'*effect* the *cause* doth sho,
> But *sense* no more but bare *effectes* doth kno.
>
> Sir John Davies, *Nosce Teipsum* (1599)

> Geometry is employed only in demonstrations peculiar to itself: criticism deliberates between different degrees of probability.
>
> Edward Gibbon, *An Essay on the Study of Literature* (1764)

In 1782 William Hayley published his *Essay on Epic Poetry*, a vigorous attack on earlier Augustan critical methods. Its avowed aim is to "vindicate" Fancy against "Proud System," particularly against the "rules critics" who, mistaking "opinion's rule" for "reason's law," seek to constrain imagination within the bonds of principles essentially arbitrary. Chief among Hayley's villains is "grave Bossu," whose influence brought to England "System's studied laws" and in particular the hierarchic model of literary structure, wherein the poet supposedly

> First calmly settles on some moral text,
> Then creeps – from one division – to the next.[92]

Throughout the poem, Hayley contrasts imaginative "Freedom" to the rules of "vain system," "proud System," "systematic pride," and contrasts the true poet to the "Classic Bigot" like Le Bossu who, "with solid reason blest ... feel[s] that faculty above the rest."[93] The aim of poetic composition, in Hayley's view, is to engage feeling; the methods of such engagement are not available to mere reason:

> In vain would Reason those nice questions solve,
> Which the fine play of mental powers involve:
> In Bards of ancient time, with genius fraught,
> What mind can trace how thought engender'd thought,
> How little hints awak'd the large design,
> And subtle Fancy spun her variegated line? (I, 219–24)

The rationalist's rules, then, must if they aid poets in achieving their end at all do so by *chance* rather than rule:

> Yet of thy boundless power the dearest part
> Is firm possession of the feeling Heart:
> No progeny of Chance, by Labour taught,

No slow-form'd creature of scholastic thought,
The child of Passion thou! (1, 99–103)

Most modern readers of Augustan critical prose have agreed with Hayley. We value and praise (where we can) particular Augustan critical judgments, while minimizing or denigrating as machines for generating arbitrary rules the theories from which such judgments emerge. (While any number of modern writers have praised particular Augustans for their independence from "the rules," it is difficult to think of a single modern who has argued that adherence to these rules made any Augustan a better practical critic.) The rules are considered arbitrary in the sense of being prescriptions *a priori*, rather than descriptive generalizations about literature and response. In fact, however, nothing could be a grosser distortion of the structure of Augustan critical theory; particular prescriptions may of course always err, but the Augustans in general understood criticism as a fundamentally probabilistic affair.

Hayley himself accepts the same fundamental view of the structure of criticism that Pope does. After deploring the errors of "rules critics," Hayley turns to the question where *correct* rules may be found. Hayley's "true critic" studies the effects of literature's repertory of devices, that he may

With modest doubt assign each likely cause
But dare to dictate no decisive laws! (1, 155–56)

His antinomianism, then, is merely probabilism; criticism is still to be a formulary of rules, but of rules better grounded and more modestly propounded than previously. The critic reads from effect to cause, hoping to form likely generalizations about those methods of composition that have in practice proven most successful. This is precisely the argument Pope makes in the *Essay on Criticism*, a work that has only recently come to be understood to rest on a foundation of literary probabilism.[94]

Like the *Epistle to Cobham*, the *Essay on Criticism* depends crucially on ideas which Pope borrowed from and held about contemporary science; in the *Essay*, Pope argues not only that criticism is a probabilistic study and activity, but that it is so in the same way as natural philosophy. To see how his argument proceeds, we must review briefly some of the *Essay*'s guiding ideas (figure 2).

For Pope and his contemporaries, *art* retained its older meaning of any activity that proceeds according to rules: to be an art and to be governed by rules are the same. The foundation of all concepts of "art" until the eighteenth century – and a notion wholly unrelated to the "aesthetic" (literally, "the sensory") – this older sense of art

stems from the Socratic doctrine of *tekne*, a doctrine whose fundamental components are:

(a) a distinction between an end and the means to that end; (b) a distinction
between a preconceived idea or thought and the activity of imposing that form or
idea on some kind of matter; (c) an order where an end is conceived before the
means in thought but where the means are first in execution, so that the end is
attained through them; and (d) a hierarchical relation among the various arts or
crafts, where one art uses what another provides so that the matter or means of
one art is the finished product of another.[95]

(The third component explains the chronological as well as logical
priority of certain elements over others in the Augustan model of the
literary work, the fourth the verticality of the model.) Aristotle was
to add the proviso that all arts – medicine, chemistry, and physics, as
well as poetry and painting – are imitations of nature: all art is
nature's ape, as influential seventeenth-century writers such as
Bacon agreed.[96] Zeno the Stoic revised the Socratic definition of
tekne to "a set of percepts exercised together toward some end useful
in life": Cicero renders the formula into Latin, and later writers,
rejecting or failing to understand the materialist basis of Stoic
epistemology, substitute *praeceptio* for Cicero's *perceptio*, rules for
mental impressions, making *art* a synonym for *method*.[97]

Thus for Dennis, "The Rules of Poetry constitute the Art of it."[98]
And like all rules, the rules of art are statements of relations
between means and ends: the logical form of a rule is hypothetical:
to achieve x, do y. Such rules may be known only implicitly –
evidence for which being that they are followed in practice – or
they may be known explicitly, codified in an *art* or *method* for
some field, an explicit systematics for achieving ends. (Adam
Smith defines a *system* as "an imaginary machine invented to
connect together in the fancy those different movements and effects
which are already in reality performed.")[99] Where an agent
attempts to achieve some end inartistically – where in choosing his
means he depends neither on implicit nor explicit knowledge of any
rules (any means by which he may achieve his ends), he is in fact
abandoning his activity to chance.

Pope was of course no stranger to hypothetical reasoning. The
whole of the *Essay on Man* is a hypothetical argument resting on
the protasis introduced at the beginning of Epistle I: "Of Systems
possible, *if* 'tis confest" (I. 43).[100] The second half of the *Epistle to
Cobham* rests on a similar requirement: *if* we may believe the teachings of science about human character, *then* we may proceed to
formulate probable hypotheses based on the leading passion. In each
case, an end or effect is posited, and the poet proceeds to seek the

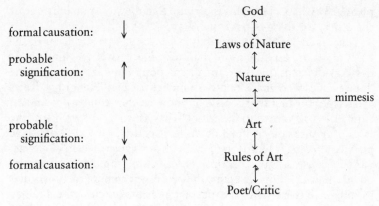

Figure 2

causes (means) that might with probability be supposed to have brought it about (diagnosis) as well as its other collateral effects (prognosis). Both poems also contrast the rule-governedness of art with *chance*: the *Essay on Man* in arguing that nature is God's art, so that all seeming chance is really "direction" (I. 289–90), *Cobham* in its opening lines.[101] The *Essay on Criticism* marks the same contrast: "True ease in Writing comes from Art, not Chance" (line 362).

Pope can contrast art and chance in composition because, like Dennis, he believes that the only difference between a practising poet and a critic is the implicitness or explicitness with which each may know the rules he follows: the poet may only know the rules of art implicitly (as evidenced by his composition of successful works, i.e., works wherein means conduce to ends), whereas the critic's task is to give the rules explicit formulation. Of the poet's genius and the critic's taste, the *Essay on Criticism* finds that "Both must alike from Heav'n derive their Light."[102] Pope describes such implicit knowledge early in the *Essay*:

> Yet if we look more closely, we shall find
> Most have the *Seeds* of Judgment in their Mind;
> Nature affords at least a *glimm'ring Light*... (19–21)

Implicit knowledge of rules, the innate ability to write or judge well, is the gift of grace ("Heav'n"). The poet's "ease" may be the result of rules only implicitly known, but this is grace, not chance. "In short," as Dennis puts it, "Poetry is either an Art, or Whimsy and Fanaticism"; "If they please not by Rules in Poetry, how must they please? By Chance! For this is certain, that they must do it by one or the other, for there is no Third Way" (1, 335).[103]

There is no third way precisely because to Pope and Dennis, the rules of art are nothing more than relations between means (poetic devices) and ends (pleasure and instruction); Pope says in the *Essay*: "Since Rules were made but to promote their End" (line 147). Rules are recipes for literary success; but how do they come to be known explicitly (i.e., known to the critic)? They are to be known just as the laws of nature come to be known to scientists, by a kind of poetic physico-theology: that is, by reading from signs (successful effects) to their causes. Thus are "Just *Precepts* ... from great *Examples* giv'n" (line 98); Pope explains the process of coming to know rules as inference from signs in a passage that makes clear the analogy between criticism and natural philosophy (or theology):

> First follow NATURE ...
> *Art* from that Fund each *just Supply* provides,
> Works *without Show*, and *without Pomp* presides:
> In some fair Body thus th' informing Soul
> With Spirits feeds, with Vigour fills the whole,
> Each Motion guides, and ev'ry Nerve sustains;
> *It self unseen*, but in th' *Effects*, remains. (68–79)

Just as by inference from probable signs the physiognomist reads character in outward expression and the scientist, God's ordering purpose in external nature, so the critic seeks the "unseen" rules which govern literary products, and so are visible only "in th' *Effects*." The rules observed by artists divine or human are thus arrived at not *a priori*, but by probable inference: where work x has been successful, the critic seeks the aspects of the work that have pleased, and attempts to read from signs what features of the work have given rise to these pleasing aspects (diagnosis); he then formulates a rule of art, stating that such-and-such feature will generally produce the same pleasing effect (prognosis).[104]

That Pope understands his rules as descriptive generalizations arrived at by probable inferences comes yet clearer in his account of how rules *change*, that is, how the body of rules explicitly propounded by criticism changes. The rules themselves, like the laws of nature, cannot alter; only our understanding of them can. This is so because the as-yet-unknown complete body of true rules of art must be one "*discover'd*, not *deviz'd*"; these rest in universal principles of human nature (those conditions of human psychology such that certain means universally give rise successfully to the ends an artist has chosen). Our critical canons, however, may change for two reasons: a new rule may be discovered, i.e., a probable means of achieving some effect may come to light; or previous formulations of a rule may be in error (for instance, because a critic has failed to identify correctly that feature of a successful work which caused the work to achieve its end). Pope describes the way new rules come to light:

> Some Beauties yet, no Precepts can declare,
> For there's a *Happiness* as well as *Care*.
> *Musick* resembles *Poetry*, in each
> Are *nameless Graces* which no Methods teach,
> And which a *Master-Hand* alone can reach. (141–45)

Such "graces" are as yet "nameless" precisely because they have not yet been formulated into precept (reduced to rule); we find their effects in the works of "genius," those artists who (like saints in theology) have the deepest and surest implicit grasp of natural law, and hence of the sometimes extraordinary means necessary to achieve their ends.[105]

> If, where the *Rules* not far enough extend,
> (Since Rules were made but to promote their End)
> Some Lucky LICENSE answers to the full
> Th' Intent propos'd, *that License is a Rule....*
> Great Wits sometimes may *gloriously offend*,
> And *rise* to *Faults* true Criticks *dare not mend*;
> From *vulgar Bounds* with *brave Disorder* part,
> And *snatch* a *Grace* beyond the Reach of Art,
> Which, without passing thro' the Judgment, gains,
> The *Heart*, and all its End *at once* attains. (146–57)

The "Grace beyond the reach of Art" is a *grace* both in its artistic success and its divine origin; it is "beyond the reach of *Art*" in that no rule has as yet been formulated to cover it. Such graces do not pass "thro' the Judgment" of readers, for readers as yet have no principles (rules) wherewith to judge them; they bypass the judgment of writers in the sense of not being the product of any yet formulated rule. (Only in this limited and temporary sense can Pope be said to defend any version of the so-called *je ne scais quoi*.) These are the "strokes of nature" that achieve their intended ends "*at once*."

John Dennis makes precisely this argument as well, finding in the "great Beauties" that may result from inspired rule-breaking a "certain Signal" that the old rules should be broken and new ones fitted to the new adaptation of means to ends.[106] In fact, Pope's probabilistic theory of the rules was common Augustan property. Hurd defines "rules" in his notes to Horace: "Rules themselves are indeed nothing else but an appeal to *experience*; conclusions drawn from wide and general observation of the aptness and efficacy of certain *means* to produce those *impressions*" (1, 390). In the manner of a philosopher of science, Hurd gives rules for the "establishing" and then the "confirmation" of these hypothetical generalizations.

Rules already established are then *confirmed*, when more *particulars* are referred to them. The invention of *new* rules implies, 1. A *collection* of various particulars, not yet regulated. 2. A *discovery* of those circumstances of *resemblance* or *agreement*, whereby they become capable of being regulated. And 3. A subsequent *regulation* of them, or arrangement into *one* class according to *such* circumstances of *agreement*. When this is done, the rule is completed. (1, 391)

"The *merit* of inventing *general rules* consists in reducing criticism to an *art*" (392): in this effort, even mere collections of uninterpreted beauties and blemishes may be useful, "just as collections of natural history, though no part of philosophy, may yet assist philosophical inquirers." "For such particular beauties and blemishes, as are barely collected, may yet serve as a foundation to future inquirers for making further discoveries" – like Baconian histories.[107]

If Hurd describes critical formulation of the rules as a process like investigation in natural science – his remarks could be Mill's on inductive generalization – Pope grounds his analogy between criticism and science in a larger theory that likens human to divine creation. The terms of this theory are arranged in Figure 2. God creates physical nature according to rules known to men as laws of nature; poets create successful works according to ordering principles known as rules of art. Just as natural scientists learn the laws of nature by reading the signs to be found in the external world, and natural theologians infer further to a divine orderer, critics infer from the signs to be found in successful works to the rules according to which the works are ordered. But in addition, art is an imitation of nature; thus the two orders of cause and signification are held together at the center, and the rules of art turn out to be formally the same as the laws of nature. John Dryden called this identity "the providence of wit." In "To My Honor'd Friend Sir Robert Howard" (1660), Dryden praises Howard's verse as the product of a genius which "excels art" (works by rules not yet formulated, line 6), and which is so "easy" that the search for the "hidden springs" of its successful effects is particularly difficult: "And yet no sign of toil, no sweat appear" (22, 18). But nor can such verse be the product of mere "fortune":

> ... this is a piece too fair
> To be the child of Chance, and not of Care.
> No Atoms casually together hurl'd
> Could e'er produce so beautifull a world.
> Nor dare I such a doctrine here admit,
> As would destroy the providence of wit. (29–34)

In the *Essay on Criticism*, failed literary works, like nature's teleological failures, are *"monstrous* and *mis-shap'd"* (171): recalcitrant matter has not successfully been impressed with its proper form or end. Because the rules of art are formally the same as the laws of nature, Pope can extend his analogy of a well-lived life not only to a well-constructed work of art, but to good criticism: "And make each Day a *Critick* on the last" (571). The whole of the second part of the poem is a set of instructions for "generous" reading, that morally and interpretively correct critical stance wherein the critic renounces self – that pride which in reading expresses itself as "a *Love to Parts*" (288) – in order to comprehend the literary work not *a priori*, but on its own terms, and as a whole. Pope's couplet at the end of *An Essay on Man* describing man's proper moral posture could as well be a description of proper critical reading by inference from signs:

> God loves from Whole to Parts: but human soul
> Must rise from Individual to the Whole. (IV, 361–62)

V

The role of probability in Augustan theories of imitation

... the imagination possesseth certaine unutterable properties, with which the same cleereth matters that cannot be expressed nor conceiued, neither is there found anie art to teach them. Wherethrough wee see a Physition enter to visit a patient, and by meanes of his sight, his hearing, his smelling, and his feeling, he knoweth things which seeme impossible. In sort, that if we demaund of the same Physition how he could come by so readie a knowledge, himselfe cannot tell the reason: for it is a grace which springeth from the fruitfulnesse of the imagination, which by another name is tearmed a readinesse of capacitie, which by common signes, and by uncertaine conjectures, and of small importance, in the twinckling of an eye knoweth a hundred differences of things, wherein the force of curing and prognosticating with certaintie consisteth.

Juan Huarte, *Examen de ingenios* (1575)[1]

In the Augustan period, as we have seen, the mental faculty that reads signs and makes probable inferences is judgment. In the Renaissance, however, testimony is not so clear. Some authors refer sign-reading to an "estimative power" of the soul, a faculty invented by Avicenna which passed from him through the Scholastics to innumerable theorists of a "vis cogitativa," "sensible reason," or "bodily wit." Others refer inference from signs directly to the imagination – conceived largely as a *physical* rather than a mental faculty (a "bodily wit") – of which "estimation" might be a component, or to "common sense," also a frequent component of imagination.[2] We have already found Jean Chapelain to refer probable inference to imagination (above, p. 83); George Puttenham does the same in his *Arte of English Poesie* (1589):

Even so is the phantasticall part of man (if it be not disordered) a representer of the best, most comely and bewtifull images or apparences of thinges to the soule and according to their very truth. If otherwise, then doth it breede *Chimeres* and monsters in mans imaginations, but also in all his ordinarie actions and life which ensues. Wherefore such persons as be illuminated with the brightest irradiations of knowledge and of the veritie and due proportion of things, they are called by the learned men not *phantastici* but *euphantasiote*, and of this sorte of phantasie are all good Poets, notable Captaines stratagematique, all cunning artificers and enginers, all Legislators Polititiens and Counsellours of estate, in whose exercises the inuentiue part is most employed and is to the sound and true judgment of man most needful. (35)

Such activities as military strategy, politics, jurisprudence, and medicine are all paradigmatic instances of those aspects of "ordinarie actions and life" in which inferences are only probable, and must be made through signs. (For Gianfrancesco Pico, similarly, because they lack the intuitive reason of angels, men must depend on signs, the faculty of judging which is imagination.)[3] Most Renaissance theorists add poetry to the list; some, like Huarte, try to refer to imagination all the sciences of signs and others besides:

From a good imagination spring all the Arts and Sciences, which consist in figure, correspondence, harmonie, and proportion; such are Poetrie, Eloquence, Musicke, and the skill of preaching: the practice of Physicke, the Mathematicals, Astrologie, and the governing of a Commonwealth: the art of Warfare, Painting, Drawing, Writing, Reading, to be a man gratious, pleasant, neat, wittie in managing, and all the engines and deuices which artificers make. (103)

Most of these are the fields which Balthasar Gracián referred to as the domain of "taste," a probable wisdom which does not stem from reason.[4] For many in the Renaissance, moreover, while *scientia* is the activity of reason, opinion – the probable – is the product of imagination. Charron defines "imagination" in *De la sagesse* (1601):

In this part and facultie of the Soul doth opinion lodge, which is a vaine, light, crude and imperfect judgment of things drawen from the outward senses, and common report, setling and arriving at the understanding, there to be examined, sifted and laboured, and to be made reason, which is a true, perfect solide judgment of things.

To this faculty Charron refers "Poetry" and "divination" (inference from signs).[5] As late as 1673, Obadiah Walker defines "Wit" (distinguished from "Judgment") in terms of capacities most Augustans would have ceded wholly to the latter:

Wit, the actions whereof are *fancy*, or *invention*, is in ordinary acceptation, *nothing else but a quicker apprehension of such notions, as do not usually enter into other men's imagination*. It consists (saith *Thesauro*) in 1. *perspicacity*, which is the consideration of all, even in the minutest, circumstances: and 2. *versability*, or speedy comparing them together; it conjoyns, divides, deduceth, augmenteth, diminisheth, and in summe puts one thing in stead of another, with like dexterity as a jugler does his balls. It differs very much from *judgment; that* is more perspicacious, *this more* profound; *that more* quick, *this more* stable; *that* chiefly considers appearances, *this* reality; *that* produceth admiration and popular applause, *this* profit and reall advantage. (122)

For the Renaissance, then, imagination is a faculty with intellective powers, one capable of reading probable signs and making probable inferences; it is also the faculty of artistic imitation. It was precisely imagination's intellective functions that made it capable of being the faculty of the arts of the probable and verisimilar. When, by the late seventeenth century, imagination had been stripped of its intellective functions – reduced to a faculty which recombines images nearly at random, or according to the rules of a mechanistic physiology – it could no longer serve as guiding faculty to the arts of the probable, including imitative arts. "Wit" must be supplemented and guided by "Judgment," the new faculty of probability, and in this way emerge not only new accounts of the practical arts but a new structure of thought in literary theory as well: a problematic that we recognize as Augustan criticism, fundamentally rooted in the opposition between wit and judgment, the lively and the just.

These are the contraries that every Augustan critic will argue must be mediated in imitation: works must balance the just and the lively; composition must be a poised balancing of judgment and fancy. The history of the changing interrelations of these terms is the history of Augustan criticism, one strand of which it is our task to trace here. Among the flaws in the internal logic of the Augustan problematic is one of its very mainstays, the new doctrine of judgment as faculty of probability. By mid-century, critics recognize this difficulty and devise a variety of theories to remedy it; at the end of the eighteenth century, a new problematic emerges, one which attempts a new solution to the role of probability in artistic imitation.

(1) PROBABILITY AS A TERM OF MEDIATION

A just *medium* reconciles the farthest extremes, and due preparation may give credit to the most unlikely fiction.

Thomas Rymer, Preface to Rapin (1674)

Imitation is the mesothesis of likeness and difference.

Coleridge, *Table Talk* (3 July 1833)

For verisimilitude short of truth, is the greatest virtue in poetry, but is the most dangerous of all qualities in philosophy connected with morals, unless kept within close bounds.

John Penn, Notes to *Ars poetica* (1797)

The unexampled vogue of *probability* in the critical lexicon of the Restoration and eighteenth century is to be explained not by an examination of the meaning of the word itself, but by determining what role the category played in literary theory. The term on its own may in the hands of any particular critic mean no more than "believable" or "natural," as it does in John Gay's lines: "Lest men suspect your tale untrue, / Keep probability in view."[6] We have already seen the concept of the probable functioning in more complex ways, however, especially in its embodiment in the theory of the probable sign. All these uses of probability follow a pattern, a pattern dictated by what for the Augustans was the central function of probability in the process of artistic imitation. For them, probability is preeminently a term of *mediation*. The term *probability* became important in English criticism when a theoretical context arose which made certain kinds of mediation pressingly necessary; it fell from favor (without ever wholly exiting the critic's lexicon) when it became clear that the concept could not do the job assigned to it.

That probability should be the term chosen to embrace a middle range between literary extremes is congruent with what we have seen to be its uses in other disciplines. In logic, the probable embraces a middle range between science and sophistic, between what is truly known and that of which some may merely be persuaded (mere "notion" said Augustan writers, for whom that word had particularly bad odor).[7] In theology, the probable helped forge a middle way between demands for infallible certainty and the rage of sectary opinion; the pattern of its use in seventeenth-century theological dispute helped shape its use in contemporary scientific argument.

We have already seen literary critics attempting to sharpen the boundaries of the artistically verisimilar, locating it on an epistemic scale between the merely possible and the philosophically probable. Through a judicious selection of "probable circumstances," furthermore, probability was to mediate between general and particular in the hierarchical structure of the literary work. Probability in a work guaranteed that formal identity between the rules of art and the laws of nature that constitutes "the providence of wit." Probability, then, was the quite natural term for Augustan critics to choose to "reconcile the farthest extremes."

What were these extremes, as Augustan critics understood them? Augustan literary theory, like much that preceded it, is an extended meditation on the nature of imitation: on what it is for a fictional work to imitate nature, on what imitative techniques most please while best fulfilling literature's instructive functions, on what play of mental faculties best conspires to produce such imitations. As such familiar formulations suggest, Augustan writers conceived the problem in terms of an interplay or balancing of contrary demands, opposites which the successful writer must mediate. Perhaps the favorite Augustan term for this balance was *poise* (or *equipoise*).[8]

Again, the most familiar Augustan truisms embody this pattern of mediation.

The probable mediates the falsehood of the fictional work and the truth of the reality it imitates (be that reality an ordinary or a heightened nature). "Rein n'est beau que le vrai": Boileau's maxim registers a critical commonplace to which the Augustans give unanimous, if differently qualified agreement; even in the wake of the "didactic shift," however, poetry trades most often in fictions.[9] Two passages from Richard Blackmore's "Essay upon Epick Poetry" make this mediation clear. To be an imitation of *nature*, a work (or its parts, in their manner of interrelation) must first of all be probable:

One inseparable Quality of Epick Poetry, is Probability. It has been already shewn, that the general Idea of this kind of Writing, which is common to it with all other Sorts, is Imitation, as its specifick Nature is constituted and distinguish'd by the Properties enumerated in the Definition: But in the first unrestrain'd Sense, as it is only a Representation of Nature, it is evident, that nothing unlikely should enter into it; for whatever is unlikely is unnatural, and for that Reason improbable.

On the other hand, to be an *imitation* of nature, the work must be no more than probable, as Blackmore explains in a formulation that looks backward to Aristotle's distinction between poetry and history, and forward to Coleridge's between an "imitation" and a "copy":

As the Narration ought to be probable, so it ought to be only probable, and not actually true; for since Poetry ... always strives to express some Object, it is very evident, that the Imitation must be formed by a devised Probability of Actions and Circumstances, and not by a relation of real Events; for otherwise it would not be an imitation of Nature, but Nature itself. Probability, as before asserted, is every where to be preserv'd; and as it should exhibit nothing inconsistent, monstrous, or unnatural, so it should relate nothing as real; for that would be a Transgression on the other Extream, and utterly destroys the essential Idea of a Poem. I admit that a true Fact or Event may enter into the Work, but then it must not be introduc'd as true, but only as it is likely, and bears a Resemblance to Truth.

Blackmore's painful logical groping with a problem not of his own devising – as witnessed especially by his final sentence – is a mediation on the verge of flying apart; what is important for us to note here is that he sees himself approaching the nature of imitation from two "extreams," falsehood and truth, which probability is to mediate.[10]

We shall examine later the tensions in accounts such as Blackmore's; it will be my argument that as soon as probability was put in the role of mediator, such tensions naturally arose. To see why this should have been so, however, we must look further at the kinds of mediation Augustan critics supposed literary works to embody. This, in turn, requires reviewing somewhat schematically some of those literary truisms mentioned above.

Time and Education begets experience; Experience begets memory; Memory begets Judgment and Fancy; Judgment begets the strength and structure, and Fancy begets the ornaments of a Poem. The Ancients therefore fabled not absurdly in making memory the Mother of the Muses.

Hobbes' allegory from his "Answer" to Davenant's Preface to *Gondibert* (1650), as is well known, stands commandingly behind a century and a half of criticism. His distinction between judgment and fancy corresponds to that between dialectic and rhetoric, of which Bacon said "the one [is] for judgment, the other for ornament."[11] Judgment, Hobbes' "severer Sister," inquires into "order, causes, uses, differences and resemblances" (although later inquiry in resemblance was more often, even by Hobbes himself, made the province of *wit*, which may encompass both judgment and fancy, or may comprehend only the latter). In doing so, judgment selects from ("bridles") fancy to produce the order of plot, or, as Rymer puts it, "the contrivance and oeconomy of a play." Fancy, which Hobbes finds responsible for "marvellous" inventions, supplies diversity, ornament, and liveliness: "For men more generally affect and admire Fancie than they do either Judgment, or Reason, or Memory, or any other intellectual Vertue; and for the pleasantness of it, give to it alone the name of Wit, accounting Reason and Judgment but for a dull entertainment."[12] As late as 1792, "fancy" is understood in the same way by Dugald Stewart, in his *Elements of the Philosophy of the Human Mind*: "its two qualities are liveliness and luxuriancy. The word *lively* refers to the quickness of one association. The word *rich* or *luxuriant*, to the variety of associated ideas" (*Works*, II, 282).

Judgment and fancy, then, are the faculties that severally produce what in Dryden's oft-repeated phrase is the "just and lively" in literature.[13] Hobbes relates the two faculties by saying that judgment provides the soul, fancy the body of a work.[14] Dryden's phrase, like Hobbes' distinctions, finds an infinity of uses; it is so much the Augustan recipe for literary composition that to advance an innovation in theory meant to alter the received formula: thus when Warton in the *Essay on Pope* attempts to elevate the status of literary particularity, he writes: "I have dwelt longer on this subject, because I think I can perceive many symptoms, even among writers of eminence, of departing from these *true* and *lively*, and *minute*, representations of Nature, and of dwelling in generalities" (II, 172).

In 1685, Robert Wolseley defines *wit* as a combination of judgment and fancy, and "a true and lively expression of Nature": "*true* this expression of Nature must be that it may gain our Reason, and *lively* that it may affect our Passions." What is just in a work instructs, what is lively pleases; further, the just is the decorous, and judgment the faculty that observes decorums. Wolseley explains as much, in squaring his definition of wit with Dryden's:

> *Wit*, says *Mr. Dryden, is a Propriety of Thoughts and Words* – Or *Thoughts and Words elegantly adapted to the Subject*. The judicious Reader will easily observe that this Definition, tho' it differ in sound, is much the same in sence with mine; what *Mr. Dryden* calls *Propriety*, I have call'd *true Expression*, and that *elegantly adapted* in the explication of his answers directly to what I intend by *lively* in mine.[15]

The same connection of judgment with decorum is made by Addison in his famous example of the dunghill in *Spectator* 418, where we find that our pleasure in the accurate representation of offensive objects "may be more properly called the Pleasure of the Understanding than of the Fancy" (III, 567); it is what informs John Aikin's scientific recasting of the just and lively as "congruity and animation."[16] Judgment, acting in application of decorums, mediates the diversity of fancy and the simplicity or generality of higher levels of meaning in the hierarchic structure of the literary work; it does so by careful attention to "probable circumstances."

All these terms are familiar to students of Augustan criticism, as is the demand that they be balanced in the literary work. Sir Thomas Pope Blount writes in 1694: "Without the Forces of *Wit*, all *Poetry* is flat and languishing; and without the Succours of *Judgment*, 'tis wild and extravagant. The true Wonder of *Poesie* is, that such Contraries must meet to compose it." Hurd's revealing variation on Dryden, "lively, *but* faithful," makes clear the difficulty of the mediation; too often, as Blount explains, "what is *admirable* fails in the *probability*; Or the *probability* is too plain and flat." Failure at mediation, intentional or otherwise, produces "that unnatural separation of DULCE ET UTILE" of which Hurd complains in his commentary on Horace.[17]

I have attempted this general review of terms in order not simply to show that Augustan criticism habitually understands successful imitation as mediation of contrary demands, but also to make clear that these various pairs of contraries are habitually *explained in terms of one another*. Without sifting examples further, we may list some of them schematically:

UTILE	DULCE
truth	fiction
dialectic	rhetoric

judgment	fancy
reason	passion
just	lively
structure	ornament
unity (simplicity)	diversity (multiplicity)[18]
design	"color"
soul	body
history	romance
probable	marvellous

In the broadest sense, probability fails as a mediator because, in the pattern of oppositions these lists embody, the term is understood and made to function in two contrary ways. We have seen how probability is to mediate truth and fiction, and how the resulting probable fictions are to unite the truths of plot with the variety of lively ornament (by diversification of the just into the lively through probable circumstances) – just as probable inference, reading by signs from effect to cause, unites for the mind soul and body. In this sense, probability stands between the two columns of the diagram. On the other hand, probability stands securely on the side of judgment and reason as another term for the accurate reflection of external truths – another occasion in which in critical formulations, fancy gives way to judgment. Because Augustan critics habitually explained the pairs of contraries we have listed *in terms of one another*, tension in the meaning of probability inevitably arose throughout the theory.

To put the point another way: Renaissance (scholastic) psychology referred probability to imagination, a faculty that mediated between sense and intellect; when it comes to be referred wholly to judgment, a part of the intellect, the system of mediations must break down.

Probability stands, again to speak schematically, at the point of splitting apart. In fact it did split apart. In his *Philosophy of Rhetoric*, George Campbell allegorizes the relations of judgment to fancy in what could only have been intended as a correction of Hobbes' account. Campbell splits what had been a unitary probability into two categories, *probability* and *plausibility*, terms meant to stand for the two schematic functions of probability. The first is related to judgment, the second to fancy:

These two qualities, therefore, PROBABILITY and PLAUSIBILITY, (if I may be indulged a little in the allegoric style), I shall call sister-graces, daughters of the same father *Experience*, who is the progeny of *Memory*, the first-born heir of *Sense*. These daughters *Experience* had by different mothers. The elder is the offspring of *Reason*, the younger is the child of *Fancy*. The elder, regular in her features, and majestic both in shape and mien, is admirably fitted for commanding esteem, and even a religious veneration: the younger, careless, blooming, sprightly, is entirely formed for captivating the heart, and engaging love... Sages seem to think that there is more instruction to be gotten from the just observations of the elder; almost all are agreed that there is more entertainment in the lively sallies of the younger. The principal companion and favourite of the first is *Truth*, but whether *Truth* or *Fiction* share most in the favour of the second it were often difficult to say... the younger, though perhaps not less capable of doing good, is more easily corrupted, and hath sometimes basely turned procuress to *Vice*. (85)

From mid-century on, increasing numbers of critics distinguish two kinds of probability, understood as Campbell does his two sisters. The commonest terminology was not Campbell's, however, but the more familiar language of probability *simpliciter* and "poetical" probability. Fumbling for terms, for instance, Thomas Twining distinguishes "poetical probability" from the ordinary kind, which he refers to as a more "general, and, if I may call it so, *possible* sort of *probability*." What Twining, Ogilvie, and Beattie were to call "poetical probability," John Penn calls "fictional probability"; Coleridge was to call it "dramatic probability," and John Hawkesworth, appealing to the distinction between moral and demonstrative certainty, calls it "moral" probability.[19] Other writers make the same distinction by speaking of different kinds of "truth." As the object of probability is truth, so the object of "poetical" probability is some kind of poetic truth. In his *Letters of Literature* (1785), for example, Robert Heron (John Pinkerton) distinguishes "truth of fact," the kind of truth the historian seeks to reproduce, from "truth of nature," which is "that represented and imitated by art" (216–18). Hurd also speaks of "poetical truth," and Coleridge of "dramatic truth."[20]

All these writers are making what is essentially the same distinction; what then is poetical probability? Modern commentators are agreed in supposing that ordinary probability is fidelity to fact (to the real world beyond the work), whereas poetical probability is fidelity to "the work itself" – inner consistency, which renders fictions such that we do not object to their falsity. These commentators mark what they suppose to have been the Augustan distinction with the terms "external" (or "natural") and "internal" (or "artificial") probability; M. H. Abrams, for example, sees the development of eighteenth-century criticism as a shift from external to internal standards of probability, from fidelity to the external world to an internal consistency that makes of the literary work a "microcosm," an autonomous world.[21]

Abrams' distinction seems to fit the facts. Campbell explains his "probability" as a relational term: "Probability results from evidence, and begets belief." Of "plausibility," on the other hand, we read that it is "a thing totally distinct from the former as having an effect upon the mind quite independent of faith or probability. It ariseth chiefly from the consistency of the narration, from its being what is commonly called natural or feasible" (82). Hawkesworth explains "moral probability" in speaking of the *Arabian Nights*:

But it is not perhaps the mere violation of truth or of probability that offends, but such a violation only as perpetually recurs. The mind is satisfied, if every event appears to have an adequate cause; and when the agency of Genii and Fairies is once admitted, no event which is deemed possible to such agents is rejected as incredible or absurd; the action of the story proceeds with regularity, the persons act upon rational principles, and such events take place as may naturally be expected from the interposition of superior intelligence and powers: so that though there is not a natural, there is at least a kind of moral probability preserved.[22]

According to Robert Heron, "There is no such thing as truth of fact, or historical truth, known to man"; upon realizing this skeptical doctrine, Raleigh burnt his historical manuscripts. But the artist's truth consists merely in "the propriety and consistence of event, of character, of sentiment, of language" – in consistency as measured by observance of decorum. For Heron, as for many critics, the character of Caliban is a test case: "A character may be drawn out of the usual progress of nature, and yet have truth; as the Caliban of Shakespeare... This singular character is *true* to itself, offends no idea of propriety, yet is not in nature."[23] Heron's reversal of Aristotle's (infinitely malleable) distinction between poetry and history is also what permits Robert Lowth to say that "The one [history] investigates causes through the uncertain medium of conjecture, the other [poetry] demonstrates them with clearness and certainty" – conjecture here carrying its usual probabilistic sense. (As historians and antiquaries, Heron and Lowth were well aware of the logical nature of their claims.)[24] As John Upton argued in his preface to the *Faerie Queene* (1758), finally – reversing the older view that, as we have seen, probability is what guarantees consistency in the literary work, by joining parts in the relation we have called probable signification – "A story will have probability, if it hangs well together, and is consistent" (I, xxv).

But simply to identify poetical probability with internal consistency is to mistake these critics' full meaning; it is to mistake what for them was a criterion of poetical probability for its definition. Upton is quite clear that consistency is simply a contributor to probability, just as Campbell says that plausibility "ariseth chiefly from the consistency of the narration" – not that it *is* such consistency. Probability is inevitably a relational term, a credibility based on evidence; even internal probability must be a fidelity to *something*. That even for Campbell poetical probability must have some object – some poetical truth which it takes as its evidence – is the result of the pressure of the structure of the concept of probability itself.

What then is the object of that poetical probability – the truth to nature Collins speaks of when he writes, "In scenes like these, which, daring to depart / From sober Truth, are still to Nature true?"[25] Heron suggests the answer when he speaks of poetical probability as "truth to nature," as does Campbell in describing plausibility as "captivating the heart, and engaging love." Beginning in mid-century, ordinary probability is usually thought to take its objects particularly from the mundane details of everyday social life; "poetical probability" is fidelity to deeper psychological truths, permanent truths of the heart and its emotions – what in the *Biographia* Coleridge was to call "the truth of passion" (II, 28). This is the "positive truth" to which according to Heron poetical probability refers (217). By mid-century, "nature" had in critical discourse come almost wholly to mean human nature, and especially passionate nature; at the same time, passion came more than ever to be considered the source and concern of all true poetry. Thus Lowth, following Warton, can contrast the "didactic" to the "truly poetical," and argue, as we have seen, that "Poetry itself is indebted for its origin, character, complexion, emphasis, and application, to the effects which are produced ... by the agitation of passion" (I, 98, 366). It was Warton who popularized at this time the term "pure poetry," used to mean passionate rather than didactic writing; Beattie defines the term in his *Essays*: "that which distinguishes *pure* poetry from other writing, is its aptitude, not to sway the judgment by reasoning, but to please the fancy, and move the passions" (267).

The terminology of external and internal probability, then, is if misguided at least fortunate. Like Twining (above, p. 95), Lowth distinguishes "internal" from "external" imitation: by the latter he means description of physical and social nature; the test of such imitation is "memory." Internal imitation is the attempt to express passion; it needs no test, Lowth argues, for "When a passion is expressed, the object is clear and distinct at once; the mind is immediately conscious of itself and its own emotions" (I, 368). Here, perhaps, we find the reason Campbell could say that plausibility has "an effect upon the mind independent of faith or probability," that does not "result from evidence."

Consistency was in fact a criterion of probability both internal and external and long had been so: mid-century critics hardly discovered the idea. To them, the important distinction was that between outward behavior and inward mental conditions, and the means of imitating each. This is the distinction Wordsworth was to draw in the first of his prefaces to the *Lyrical Ballads* when, having called on Aristotle's distinction between poetry and history, he says of poetry that "its object is truth, not individual and local, but general and operative; not standing upon *external testimony*, but carried alive into the heart by passion; truth which is its own testimony."[26] Here is the same association of the inner world of the passions with permanence, the external world with change; the first requires no external "testimony," whereas the second demands evidence in the conventional sense. Johnson had in mind the same divisions of both probability and testimony into internal and external when he wrote in his *Life of Butler*: "Of *Hudibras* the manners, being founded on opinions, are temporary and local, and therefore become every day less intelligible and less striking... Such manners as depend upon standing relations and general passions are co-extended with the race of man" (*Lives*, I, 213–14). The testimony on which external probability rests is "opinion," that on which internal probability rests, our knowledge of ourselves.

In the mid-eighteenth century, then, tensions within the structure of critical theory pressed the concept of probability to divide into distinct sub-concepts; the division did occur, producing external and internal, ordinary and poetical probability: fidelity to external nature and to the inward "truth of passion." To explain why this particular distinction should have been the issue of the tensions described schematically at the beginning of this discussion, we must examine more closely the content of the paired contraries listed on pp. 141–42; in particular, we must examine the mediations that failed.

(2) THE PROBABLE AND THE MARVELLOUS

The *admirable* is all that which is against the ordinary course of nature. The *probable* is whatever suits with common opinion.

Rapin, *Reflections* (1674)

Admiration is opposed to *probability*.

Le Bossu, *Treatise of the Epick* (1675)

It is of the last Importance to join this *admirable* and *probable* by a just Mixture of one with the other. For the Heroick Action ... must be render'd not only worthy of *Admiration*, but of *Credit*.

Gildon, *Complete Art of Poetry* (1743)

In practice, Augustan critics usually invoke poetical probability to cover the sorts of cases Gray had in mind when he remarked in 1751 – using the very term whose revival Campbell was to recommend – that by "good management" it is possible to render "*verisimile*" even "such absurd stories as the Tempest, the Witches in Macbeth, or the Fairies in the Midsummer Night's Dream."[27] Hence Heron's and others' repeated use of Caliban as an example. Dryden had been able to do no better with Caliban than to appeal to vulgar opinion: the fostering of a child "by an incubus upon a witch … is not wholly beyond the bounds of credibility, at least the vulgar still believe it."[28] But appeals to vulgar opinion were difficult to sustain in the new age that took as its audience the "wise." Because the logic of probability still required that the probable be grounded in some testimony, some opinion, Augustan critics had to revise their notions of probability lest one of the most important of critical mediations fail: that between the probable and the marvellous. Ordinary literary probability could hardly reconcile itself with its opposite.

This ancient distinction finds its source in the *Poetics*, particularly in chapter 24. There Aristotle enjoins the use of τὸ Θαυμαζόν (the surprising, astonishing, wonderful); distinguishes the marvellous from the wholly irrational or absurd (αλογος), which has more place in epic than tragedy, where it would displease when actually seen; and finds that a clever poet "can risk even a strong improbability" if he can "sweeten it" with "the other good things he has to offer." Aristotle concerns himself with the marvellous not for the reasons that German idealist aestheticians would impute to him, but for its provision of pleasure: "the astonishing does give pleasure."

Aristotle's discussion is difficult, and interpretations of it are no more in full accord today than they were in the seventeenth and eighteenth centuries. That the marvellous pleases, for example, easily became Edward Manwaring's sweeping principle that "The Miraculous is always agreeable."[29] We have seen that the presumptive opposite of the marvellous early became the dull and the mundane, as it is in Henry Pye's list of "things lamentable, terrible, great, or probable" – objects of pity, fear, sublime enthusiasm, or mere belief.[30] Under the heading of "the marvellous" the Augustans comprehended all machinery and persons supernatural, allegorical, and greatly admirable, though defenders of particular literary devices might argue that some favorite device was thereby misclassified; Kames, for instance, writes in the *Elements*:

personification, being the work of imagination, is descriptive only, and assumes not even an appearance of truth. This is very different from what is termed machinery, where deities, angels, devils, or other supernatural powers, are introduced as real personages, mixing in the action, and contributing to the catastrophe; and yet these two things are constantly jumbled together in reasoning. (III, 239)

Kames draws this distinction to save personification from the charge of improbability, which he freely levels at supernatural machines; but his protest betrays the commonness of the conflation, and his claim that personifications have "not even an appearance of truth" raises difficulties of its own. Joseph Trapp, like many others a vigorous defender of supernatural marvels, also defends his favored devices by arguing that they are not really improbable. Trapp manages this logical feat by a (misguided) appeal to Aristotle's distinction between Θαυμάσιος and αλογος: he identifies improbability wholly with the latter, and so can say:

The Moderns seem to mistake that Part of Epic and Tragedy which contains the τὸ Θαυμαζόν, or the *wonderful*, confounding the *wonderful* with the improbable, and using these two Words promiscuously. If it was really so, τὸ Θαυμαζόν would always be faulty; for that is always faulty, which is improbable.[31]

Again, the protest is heard far less often than the conflation it means to combat. Most writers understood the probable and the marvellous as contraries or opposites produced by and appealing to different mental faculties – judgment and fancy – and requiring somehow, like these faculties themselves, to be brought into balance in the finished work. William Belsham must have been rare in finding *Gondibert* dull mainly because of its lack of machines, but his judgment points to that mediation of interest and truth that the structure of Augustan critical theory at once demanded and made impossible.[32]

The Augustans essayed a number of different methods to reconcile truth with wonder. They inherited first of all the Italian and French debates on the Christian marvellous, which Boileau, for example, had opposed, but which a majority supported. In England, a young John Dennis took Boileau's part, but Dennis' later works constitute the most sophisticated theory of the Christian marvellous the age was to produce (see Appendix B). Englishmen, of course, could point to the example of Milton: Milton's gradual achievement of a successful mixture of what Henry Felton called "Truth and Wonders" in fact provided Samuel Johnson with the rhetorical structure in the critical part of his *Life of Milton*.[33] Of *Lycidas*, Johnson says "its inherent improbability always forces dissatisfaction on the mind"; of *Comus*, "The action is not probable," because there Milton allows to human agents the same behavior he does to supernatural ones. *Paradise Lost* Johnson introduces with the grand generalization that "Poetry is the art of uniting pleasure with truth, by calling imagination to the help of reason," and having thus set the terms of his discussion, comes to "the probable and the marvellous, two parts of a vulgar epick poem which immerge the critick in deep consideration." In *Paradise Lost*, Milton has finally found that just balance wherein "the probable therefore is marvellous, and the marvellous is probable." The later poems constitute a falling off: although "It was not to be supposed that the writer of *Paradise Lost* could ever write without great effusions of fancy and exalted precepts of wisdom," Johnson finds none of the later poems as powerful as Milton's initial success.[34]

Except in the hands of a brilliant theorist such as John Dennis, defenses of the Christian marvellous could not be made to extend to the gods of Homer or Aeschylus, or even to the surprises of a French romance. Extended beyond Christianity, the marvellous remains vulgar superstition. One author, for example, can justify the "miraculous" only by reference to vulgar opinion, "the usual propensity of mankind towards the marvellous," which, though all share in it, appears most markedly in "the gazing populace [who] receive greedily, without examination, whatever soothes superstition, and promotes wonder." This author is not a critic discussing literary works, but David Hume in the *Enquiries*.[35]

In fact, the language of critical discussion of the probable and the marvellous became, in the hands of Augustan philosophical probabilists, the language of debate on miracles. Hume's essay "Of Miracles," written for inclusion in the *Treatise of Human Nature* but not published until 1748, contains long passages that could easily find a place in his literary criticism. By a curious reversal, moreover, as soon as critics became aware that their vocabulary had been borrowed in this way, they took advantage of its added meaning. Hurd, for instance, begins his *Letters on Chivalry and Romance* (1762) by quoting Pope: "Nature once known, no prodigies remain"; a large part of his rhetorical strategy in his opening pages depends on frequent repetition of the word *prodigies*, so that finally he can deflate the term, showing that the prodigies of mediaeval romance "had their origin in the barbarous ages": "You see, then, my notion is, that Chivalry was no absurd and freakish institution, but the natural and even sober effect of the feudal society" (2, 3, 10).

In addition to the abuse it spawned, Hume's "Of Miracles" was responsible as well for Richard Whately's sparkling parody, *Historic Doubts Relative to Napoleon Buonaparte* (1819), a work which takes full advantage of the interanimation of literary and philosophical vocabularies for treating the probable. Whately, Archbishop of Dublin, was the author of several works on chance and a founder of Dublin's Statistical Society; in the *Historic Doubts*, he shows that Hume's arguments for disbelief in miracles, if consistently applied, lead as well to disbelief in the existence of Napoleon – a delightful extension of the usual purpose of the "historic doubts" genre, which had been to settle contested matters of historical detail, not to question the existence of famous – and recent – figures.

"The celebrated Hume has pointed out the readiness with which men believe, on very slight evidence, any story that pleases their imagination by its admirable and marvellous character" (19). Studied repetition of the word *extraordinary* ("this extraordinary personage"), like Hurd's use of *prodigies*, underlines for the reader the fact that, though Napoleon's life be an "extraordinary and romantic tale" full of "improbabilities" and of the "strange and marvellous," still we do accept the tale for true. Whately recounts the chief events of Napoleon's career twice; the first version is in the language of an epic catalogue of the acts of a hero, so that its author can later comment:

it carries an air of fiction and romance on the very face of it. All the events are great, and splendid, and marvellous ... everything upon that grand scale, so common in Epic Poetry, so rare in real life; and thus calculated to strike the imagination of the vulgar, and to remind the sober-thinking few of the Arabian Nights. (41)

After thus invoking the literary commonplaces that the marvellous is the product of and appeals to the imagination, especially that of the vulgar, Whately retells the story of Napoleon's career in a parody of the language of the King James Bible, commenting, and revealing the religious purpose of his satire: "Does any man believe all this, and yet refuse to believe a miracle?" (46)

Other Augustans look elsewhere for a purified, truthful marvellous: scientific writers suggest as source not religion but nature itself. John Aikin's *Essay on the Application of Natural History to Poetry* (1777) is a manifesto of the scientific marvellous: what has usually been noticed in the *Essay* is its long middle section criticizing a succession of poets for their infidelity to natural detail, but the piece begins and ends on quite another note. Properly used, Aikin finds, science may be a great source of literary novelty (1–6; novelty, the surprising, had of course a long history of connection with the marvellous). Proper observation of scientific marvels can lend to poetry the "congruity and animation of real life" (11), Aikin's scientific rephrasing of Dryden's "just and lively." After criticizing poetic mishandlings of natural history, Aikin ends the *Essay* with a list of natural phenomena that – as we come to realize in part through his use of the language of "prodigies" and "wonders" – combine scientific accuracy with the marvellous: the "prodigy" of birds in migration (a favorite topic of Aikin), the calabash tree ("What a more astonishing spectacle the prodigious mass of wood reard up in the *Calabash tree*, which sinks our noblest oaks into shrubs?" 147), giant serpents ("Mr. Adanson, however, furnishes some circumstances for a description of the enormous *gigantic serpent* of Africa, which a poet might employ with striking effect," 153).

In his "Alliance of Natural History with Poetry" (1784), Aikin's friend Thomas Percival concerns himself more explicitly with the probable and the marvellous, taking a more ecumenical line than does Aikin. Percival is content, for instance, that in "The Deserted Village," Goldsmith should place tigers in North America, to add to the "horrors of an American wilderness"; he also suggests ways to render the marvellous more scientifically accurate. He wishes, for instance, that Milton had known of electricity, that his angels' "flaming swords" might have burnt electrically.[36]

A few writers appeal directly to the passions to give probability to marvels – employing, in other words, what I have argued to be the real content of the concept of internal probability. Frank Sayers, inspired by Part v of Burke's *Enquiry* (on the non-mimetic status of verbal art), argues in 1793 that passages in which "no clear or connected ideas are raised, or in which ideas are even repugnant to sense or propriety" may yet, "merely from agreeable associations of the words," be "generally received as beautiful." Hume, too, had referred the "marvellous" to "eloquence," which "when at its highest pitch, leaves little room for reason or reflection."[37] The argument comes from Longinus, from whom for instance Boileau learned that a literary event may "pass for *vraisemblable* because it touches the passions"; in his translation, Longinus held that "things absurd in themselves may yet be *vraisemblable* if they move the passions."[38] But to the Augustan mind, such arguments remain incomplete: absurdity, no matter how passionately presented, still risks being seen for what it is. Thus Sayers, after citing examples to prove his principle, stipulates that once an absurdity is recognized as such the passage loses its beauty (33).

The difficulty here is, as always, that probability is a relational term: in literature as in life, to borrow a phrase from Johnson's *Life of Butler*, events are only "probable upon certain suppositions" (216). Among the most important of such suppositions is the previous knowledge of the audience; as Beattie explains, "in works of fiction, a like regard is to be had to probability; and no events are to be introduced, but such as, according to the general opinion of the people to whom they are addressed, may be supposed to happen."[39] And Beattie is quite clear that the audience in question is the modern one, the "wise" – the same audience Blackmore marked out when he wrote, "The devis'd Story must be related in a *probable* manner; without this all things will be *harsh*, *unnatural*, and *monstrous*; and consequently most *odious* and *offensive* to the *Judicious*."[40] In his *Principles of Taste* (1805), Richard Payne Knight makes clear just how difficult it was to square this principle with the canon of ancient masterpieces. He qualifies his discussion of literary probability by remarking, "I am of course supposing equal, or at least nearly equal degrees of knowledge in the persons to whom the events or circumstances are related or exhibited; there being no doubt that very ignorant persons may think even probable, what the learned know to be impossible." In contrast to many critics, Knight on these grounds finds Homer to have had more "judgment" than Vergil, but the kinds of examples open to him to use in support of his view are revealing. They are not the considerations of a Broome; rather, Knight claims, there is not in Homer "a single circumstance ever introduced, which the most scrupulous naturalist would not allow to be probable and consistent" – the mere details of an Aikin or a Percival.[41]

Because the opinions in which literary probabilities are grounded are in this period distinctly those of the educated, Augustan appeals to vulgar opinion are special pleading for particular literary effects, and it is far from clear how seriously such special pleading was taken. The same writers who make such appeals to vulgar opinion can also satirize them. Horace Walpole, whose works both literary and historical are filled with satirical play on the idea of probability, justifies the "air of the miraculous" which suffuses *The Castle of Otranto* on the grounds that "Belief in every kind of prodigy was so established in those dark ages." But neither this nor his amusingly peremptory, "Allow the possibility of the facts [e.g., the miraculous descent from heaven of a giant fragment of armor which flattens young Conrad], and all the actors comport themselves as persons would do in their situation" sounds like wholehearted literary theorizing, and it is hard to believe that the author of the *Hieroglyphic Tales* (1785) and *Nature will prevail* (1786) could have meant them so. This is the same Walpole who printed as the epigraph to the *Tales*, "Schah Banham ne comprenoit jamais bien que les choses absurdes et hors de toute vraisemblance," and who in the preface to the same work pokes fun at the ill-founded probabilistic arguments of antiquaries: "We might assign [the *Tales*] with great probability to Kemanrlegorpikos, son of Quat; but besides that we are not certain that any such person ever existed, it is not clear that he ever wrote any thing but a book of cookery, and that in heroic verse." Outside satire, in his *Historic Doubts on the Life and Reign of Richard III*, another work composed in the genre of those many French works whose titles begin, "De l'Incertitude de...," Walpole explains how, through lack of judgment and excess of imagination, improbabilities come to corrupt the historical record.[42]

In *Otranto* itself, Walpole pokes fun at the very populace whose beliefs (now seen to be credulity) were supposed to make his fiction credible. Of a very obscure oracle, the narrator comments, "Yet these mysteries, or contradictions, did not make the populace adhere less to their opinion," and later Walpole directly undermines the logic of justifying literary marvels through vulgar opinion, commenting of the "miracle of the helmet" that "The spectators" could arrive only at "senseless guesses" about its cause. Their "conjectures were as absurd and improbable, as the catastrophe was unprecedented" (16, 18). These are the remarks of a good probabilist but of an unconvinced theorist of the marvellous.

A modern reader of Walpole's romance very justly remarks, "*The Castle of Otranto* is a slight novel, curiously close to satire, yet never demonstrably self-conscious"; Walpole approaches self-consciousness most closely in his discussion of miracles and prodigies.[43] In the *Letters on Chivalry*, Hurd uses all the same arguments in defence of literary marvels, but undercuts them at a stroke: "We must distinguish between the *popular belief*, and *that of the reader*." With more serious consequences, he argues that marvels take greater hold of the imagination than of the judgment, so that "it is enough, if they can but bring you to *imagine* the possibility of them." It is to the imagination that his Gothic romances, like the higher kinds of poetry, are to appeal:

But the case is different with the more sublime and creative poetry. This species, addressing itself solely or principally to the Imagination; a young and credulous faculty, which loves to admire and to be deceived; has no need to observe those cautious rules of credibility so necessary to be followed by him, who would touch the affections and interest the heart. (85–90, 95)

The appeal via imagination to vulgar opinion, then – like Frank Sayers' passionate absurdities – ends by trivializing literary works. The appeal to vulgar opinion could only be reconciled with literature's present and high aims when, later in the century, the further argument was added that such old beliefs point the way to patterns of thought and feeling still buried in the modern mind; this new argument, however, supplies the marvellous with a new truth, what I have called internal probability.

Following Warton's sharp distinction in the *Essay on Pope* between the "two chief nerves of all genuine poesy," "the Sublime and the Pathetic" (I, x), furthermore, the distinction between senti-ment and fancy, the passions of the heart and the airy ideas of imagination, became a staple of late Augustan criticism. Thus in his *Letters on a Course of English Poetry*, John Aikin can say of Waller's verse, "in such cases, the fancy is gratified at the expense of the feeling, and fiction occupies the place of reality" (note the connec-tion of feeling with reality); of masques, "These pieces were almost solely addressed to the understanding and the imagination, and had scarcely any power of exciting the sympathetic feelings" (note the connection of imagination with understanding, both opposed to feeling); of a work by Tickell, that it has "that stamp of truth, which interests beyond the most brilliant creations of the imagination"; of Shenstone's "Schoolmistress," that "It touches upon the true path-etic, though mingled with the fanciful."[44] In terms of this discussion, Hugh Blair can claim in the *Lectures* that probability is more necessary in tragedy than in epic, because the "heart" is more upset by improbabilities than is the "imagination" (II, 480–81); such a distinction serves further to trivialize literature "addressing itself solely or principally to the Imagination."

Like many of his mid-century contemporaries (and like Words-worth after them), Hurd sought to isolate an element in poetry that would be "permanent," that would retain interest and value despite changes in taste and society. This is the sense of *universal* at use in his dissertation "On the Idea of Universal Poetry" (1766). To Hurd, the probable suggested a fidelity to local (and hence tem-porary) mundane detail typical of earlier Augustan satire and occasional verse. (As Johnson had explained in the *Life of Butler*, this impermanence comes from its probabilities being "founded on opinions.") Hurd singles out satire and the epistle, arguing indeed that the "DIDACTIC epistle was, in fact, the true and proper offspring of the SATIRE" (I, 17), as especially impermanent – the very charge that Warton had made in the *Essay on Pope*: "For WIT and SATIRE are transitory and perishable, but NATURE and PASSION are eternal" (I, 344). To endure, then, poetry must eschew such probabilities as John Cleland, for example, reviewing *Peregrine Pickle* in 1751, thought typical of "comic romance": "For as the matter in them is chiefly taken from nature, from adventures, real or imaginary, but familiar, practical, and probable to be met with in the course of common life ..."[45] Fleeing such local truth, literature gains only the triviality of an imagination divorced from both rationality and the heart; indulging (local) truth, it becomes impermanent. Thus for Hurd – one example among many, and an especially thoughtful one – does the system of mediations demanded by literary theory make itself felt. Only a more adequate account of internal probability could free him from his dilemma.

(3) ROMANTIC RECONCILIATIONS

Aubrey's authority, unsupported by circumstances or internal probability, is 1−1=0; and in this instance is of no weight against the fact that in the very next ℚ, that at 10 years old he was a Proficient in Latin, and a Page to a Person of Quality.

Coleridge, Marginalia to Aubrey's claim that Michael Drayton was son to a butcher (1807)

Let him work *physical* wonders only, and we will be content to *dream* with him for a while; but the first *moral* miracle which he attempts, he disgusts and awakens us.

Coleridge, Review of *The Monk* (1796)[46]

The seminal importance of Hobbes' statements on poetry was not a discovery of modern critics, but was well understood in the eighteenth century. In the *Letters on Chivalry*, we read:

Sir W. Davenant open'd the way to this new sort of criticism in a very elaborate preface to Gondibert; and his philosophic friend, Mr. Hobbes, lent his best assistance towards establishing the credit of it. These two fine Letters contain, indeed, the substance of whatever has since been written on the subject [of criticism]. Succeeding wits and critics did no more than echo their language. (81)

The critical remark of Hobbes which the Augustans most often quoted and paraphrased, even to the point of using it as a gloss on Aristotle, is his statement of the limits of "Poeticall Liberty":

For as truth is the bound of Historical, so the Resemblance of truth is the utmost limit of Poeticall Liberty... Beyond the actual works of nature a Poet may go; but beyond the conceived possibility of nature, never.[47]

Critics from Rymer to Coleridge can subscribe to this claim because its terms are elastic: Hobbes does not specify who is to do the conceiving, leaving open appeals to vulgar opinion; he does not specify what kind of "possibility" he means, leaving open its interpretation as the barest logical possibility, non-contradiction (consistency) – a requirement of poetry no critic, Augustan or Romantic, was willing to forego. More important, Hobbes does not examine the nature of his "conceiving"; that is, he does not specify the kind of belief poetry is to inspire.

The drama has always posed this question most directly, and on the matter of dramatic illusion Augustan opinion ranged from the demand of Castelvetro and Chapelain, that the audience suppose the fiction entirely real, to the view of Johnson (and many others), that "the spectators are always in their senses, and know, from the first act to the last, that the stage is only a stage, and that the players are only players."[48] Any theory of dramatic illusion entails ideas about what kinds of events will appear on stage, and such opposed theories of illusion would seem to entail differing accounts of probability. The history of controversies over the unities reveals, however, that both lines of argument could as easily avail themselves of probability in exactly the same sense, as Coleridge testifies in 1805:

> so many practical errors and false criticisms may arise, and indeed have arisen, either from reasoning on [stage illusion] as actual delusion (the strange notion on which the French critics built up their theory and French poets justify the construction of their tragedies), or from denying it altogether (which seems the butt of Dr. Johnson's reasoning, and which, as extremes meet, would lead to the very same consequences by excluding whatever would not be judged probable by us in our coolest stage of feeling with all our faculties in even balance).[49]

Coleridge argued further that we do not give to the words *probable* and *natural* the same meaning "in their application to the drama" as we do in life, precisely because the kind of belief that the dramatist seeks to inspire is not ordinary belief. His account remains the most widely held solution to the so-called "problem of belief"; it is also a direct outgrowth of the Augustan problematic.

We should note first that Coleridge often uses *probability* in its external sense. Even in discussing drama, he is capable of saying that the playwright depends on the "impassive slumber of our sense of probability."[50] He is also aware of and seeks again to refine the doctrine of "probable circumstances." Discussing the faults of Wordsworth's poetry in chapter 22 of the *Biographia*, Coleridge settles first on its "matter-of-factness," which he finds to be the product first of excessive minuteness, then of what Shawcross calls "irrelevant particularisation":

> *first*, a laborious minuteness and fidelity in the representation of objects, and their positions, as they appeared to the poet himself; *secondly*, the insertion of accidental circumstances, in order to the full explanation of his living characters, their dispositions and actions; which circumstances might be necessary to establish the probability of a statement in real life, where nothing is taken for granted by the hearer; but appear superfluous in poetry, where the reader is willing to believe for his own sake.[51]

Coleridge calls this second fault "a *biographical* attention to probability, and an anxiety of explanation and retrospect" of which "all the circumstances, which are feigned in order to make such incidents less improbable, divide and disquiet faith, rather than aid and

support it." The addition, then, of biographical (external) probability has an effect opposite from that for which probability and its
circumstantial signs were devised: they make fictions seem false, and
are a source of disunity rather than unity.[52] (In Colderidge, too,
probability has become not at all an affair of structure, but simply of
psychological belief; with the decline of the hierarchic model, probability is cut off from larger structures of meaning in works.)

The "accidentality" (101) of Wordsworth's biographically probable circumstances, furthermore, prevents his characters from
becoming sufficiently "catholic and abstract," in a sense any
Augustan would have understood: "The ideal consists in the happy
balance of the generic with the individual. The former makes the
character representative and symbolical, therefore instructive ...
The latter gives it *living* interest" (187). Coleridge returns to this
theme in chapter 23, in discussing the play called *Don Juan*:

> It is not the wickedness of *Don Juan*, therefore, which constitutes the character
> of an *abstraction*, and removes it from the rules of probability; but the rapid
> succession of the correspondent acts and incidents, his intellectual superiority,
> and the splendid accumulation of his gifts and desirable qualities, as co-existent
> with entire wickedness in one and the same person. (186)

To the extent that a character is instructive, he is abstract and
symbolic; to that extent, too (as Coleridge is saying here, while
allowing that a different reason must be given to justify the
improbabilities of *Don Juan*), biographical probability is unnecessary, even detrimental to his portrayal.

Opposed to biographical probability is that internal "dramatic
probability" Coleridge expounds so well in his notes to Shakespeare,
especially to *The Tempest*. Having remarked that we respond to
drama with an "impassive slumber of our sense of probability," he
yet finds that "there is a sort of improbability with which we are
shocked," and hence that "there must be rules respecting it."[53] It
turns out, of course, that these improbabilities are what disturb that
special kind of dramatic illusion (rather than *delusion*) which in
1805 Coleridge had called a "temporary half-faith" (178) and which
here he calls an "intermediate state" of belief (116). Where he had
earlier appealed, like his Augustan predecessors, to common
opinion ("old story") to justify action which follows "from the
assumption of a gross improbability" – as he justifies for instance
the first scene of *Lear*, which has an "improbable and nursery tale
character" – he can now redefine the dramatically improbable (33,
53, 50).

So far, however, Coleridge has considered only questions of
*im*probability and *dis*belief; he often puts the whole issue negatively,

calling poetic belief a kind of "negative belief."[54] The object of biographical probability is ordinary truth, but Coleridge has not explained the nature of that "dramatic truth" which is the object of "dramatic probability," and which judgment (still, in Coleridge, the faculty that weighs probabilities) will embrace.[55]

In *Don Juan*, it was not Juan's "character of an abstraction" that "removed it from the rules of probability," but rather his lively and passionate superiority. Coleridge explains that it is our desire for *power* – especially the power "of the mind" – to which Juan appeals; it is the same sense of power, he says, that allows us to "peruse with the liveliest interest the wildest tales of ghosts, wizards, genii and secret talismans," the standard fare of the marvellous. Marvels, appealing to our love of power, can woo us "into suspension of all our judgment";

On this propensity [desire for power], so deeply rooted in our nature, a specific *dramatic* probability may be raised by a true poet, if the whole of his work is in harmony: a *dramatic* probability, sufficient for dramatic pleasure, even when the component characters and incidents border on impossibility. The poet does not require us to be awake and believe; he solicits us only to yield ourselves to a dream. (189)

Here is internal probability fully worked out, and made fully consistent with Hobbes' strictures on "Poeticall Liberty." Here is Hobbes' requirement that the poet not stray beyond the "conceived possibility of nature," understood as non-contradiction (consistency); here is consistency ("harmony") related to probability, but only as a prerequisite, as an ingredient necessary in the imitation of a deeper truth. Here is the special psychology of literary belief, which can leave biographical probability behind, yet seems to save imaginative works from trivialization in the manner of Hurd. Here, finally, though judgment is only suspended, not courted, is an explanation of the truth to which dramatic (internal) probability approximates: strong passions permanent in our nature, appealed to and embodied in what may be the most marvellous characters and events. Here is the culmination of one strand of Augustan thinking about the role of probability in imitation.

With somewhat less clarity and rigor, Richard Payne Knight had reached the same conclusions in his *Principles of Taste* (1805). Knight defines "poetical probability" as what at first sight appears to be mere consistency:

Upon this principle, that sort of semblance of truth, which, for distinction's sake, we will call *poetical probability*, does not arise so much from the resemblance of fictions to real events, as from the consistence of the language with the sentiments, of the sentiments and actions with the characters, and of the different parts of the fable, with each other: for, if the mind be deeply interested; as it always will be by glowing sentiments and fervid passions happily expressed, and naturally arising out of the circumstances and incidents of a consistent fable, it will never turn aside to any extraneous matter for rules of comparison; but judge of the probability of the events merely by their connection with, and dependence upon each other. (274)

Whether or not we call on "extraneous matter" (Wordsworth's "external testimony") for comparison depends not on consistency (a mere *sine qua non*), but on the effective portrayal of passion. Revising once more Dryden's "just and lively," Knight finds of fictional characters that "we never stop to inquire whether they ever existed or not"; rather, we "consider the descriptions as embellished pictures of human nature, with the expression of which we sympathize, according to the degrees of truth and energy, with which the passions and affections are displayed" (269).

Knight's view of the ways passion should be portrayed differs from Coleridge's, with the result that he makes more use of probable circumstances; these are for him, as they were for John Aikin, details which convey "all the variety of passions," the "little expressions of nature and circumstances of truth, [in which] the mind discovers and feels the resemblance between fiction and reality" (284). Such guiding signs in the painting of passion properly deployed, "imagination, by a systematic elevation of language, is one of the most efficacious means of giving poetical probability; or making supernatural events appear credible" (282). It was as expression of passion that Jean Paul Richter could say in his *School for Aesthetics* (1804) that "All that is truly marvellous is poetic in itself," and that Coleridge could elaborate supernatural marvels in his contributions to the *Lyrical Ballads.*[56]

As I have suggested, there is nothing distinctively "Romantic" in these ideas. They are, however, only a partial solution to the problem of mediation set by Augustan critical theory. Must all representations of the "truth of passion" be clothed in marvels – must, to invert Richter's formula, the truly poetic be always marvellous? Can probability be reconciled not just with the marvellous, but with itself (internal and external)? Johnson had found in Shakespeare a poet who "approximates the remote, and familiarizes the wonderful"; at nearly the same time, James Grainger wrote of a poetry that defamiliarizes the ordinary:

> With you roses brighter bloom,
> Sweeter every sweet perfume,
> Purer every fountain flows
> Stronger every wilding grows.[57]

The project of defamiliarizing the ordinary which we associate with Romanticism (and with modern formalist criticism) is in fact part of the Augustan principle of *novelty*; yet a reimagined theoretical account of the familiarization of the wonderful and the defamiliarization of the ordinary – in the reconciliation of the marvellous with external probability – did accompany the new understanding of the relation of literary form to meaning, and of the faculties to one another in the process of composition, which is Romantic critical theory. Far more innovative (from a theoretical point of view) than Coleridge's contributions to the *Lyrical Ballads* are Wordsworth's.

"Imagination," Pope wrote to Swift in 1734, "has no limits, and that is a sphere in which you may move on to eternity; but where one is confined to Truth (or to speak more like a human creature, to the appearances of Truth) we soon find the shortness of our Tether."[58] Wordsworth's contributions to the *Lyrical Ballads* represent a new way of uniting imagination and truth, the probable and the marvellous – a reimagination of the old problems of mediation. The development of Gothic fiction provides an especially useful context in which to understand Wordsworth's achievement. Horace Walpole had explained his aim in the preface to the second edition of *Otranto* as that of unifying "ancient" and "modern romance": in the former, "all was imagination and improbability"; in the latter, fancy is "dammed up" by a "strict adherence to common life" (what "probability" had for many become). Finding Walpole to have failed in this aim, Clara Reeve raises the same hopes for her *Old English Baron* (1778):

This Story is the literary offspring of the *Castle of Otranto*, written upon the same plan, with a design to unite the most attractive and interesting circumstances of the ancient Romance and modern Novel... To attain this end, there is required a sufficient degree of the marvellous, to excite the attention; enough of the manners of real life, to give an air of probability to the work; and enough of the pathetic, to engage the heart in its behalf. (299)[59]

No wonder Walpole failed in his mediation: for Reeve as well the three demands – even those of the marvellous and the pathetic – remain baldly distinct.

Walpole had in fact attempted his union of the just and lively by distinguishing two different ranges of probability: an external probability of events, and an internal probability of characters' responses to those events. He claims that he retains the "stupendous Phenomena" of earlier romance – supernatural marvels required, according to Clara Reeve, "to excite the attention" – while at the same time seeking "to make [characters] think, speak, and act, as it might be supposed mere men and women would do in extraordinary positions." Here is the germ of a probability which takes human passions as its object, but it is alas a probability whose concrete manifestations are as often ludicrous as moving, as in a sequence of theatrical set-pieces characters and narrator must rummage the entire lexicon of amazement and horror to express what "mere men and women" would say and do "in extraordinary positions." Walpole's heavy reliance on dialogue is particularly unfortunate, even when he seems to justify his own comic effects by choosing as witnesses to his supernatural spectacles low characters such as servants; later practitioners of the Gothic would prefer natural description to dialogue as visible sign and conductor of feeling.

Walpole did not justify his deviations from "the appearances of Truth" by invoking a notion of internal probability, as very soon others would (to argue that marvels reveal passionate truth would hardly have been in his character); but neither did he finally give naturalistic explanations of them, as Mrs. Radcliffe was notoriously to do. To a Romantic such as Richter, who observed his German contemporaries making concessions to novelistic probability like Mrs. Radcliffe's, the explained marvellous was a kind of trivial "juggling."[60]

Fully Romantic Gothics, on the other hand, do invoke the theory of internal probability. Percy Shelley begins his preface to his wife's *Frankenstein* (1818) with a conventional defence of the work's external probability: "The event on which this fiction is founded has been supposed, by Dr. Darwin, and some of the physiological writers of Germany, as not of impossible occurrence." This said, however, Shelley turns immediately to a newer mode of argument:

I shall not be supposed as according the remotest degree of serious faith to such an imagination; yet, in assuming it as the basis of a work of fancy, I have not considered myself as merely weaving a series of supernatural terrors. The event on which the interest of the story depends is exempt from the disadvantages of a mere tale of spectres or enchantment. It was recommended by the novelty of the situations which it developes; and, however impossible as a physical fact, affords a point of view to the imagination for the delineating of human passions more comprehensive and commanding than any which the ordinary relations of existing events can yield. (6)[61]

It is of course also true that Frankenstein's monster is closer than many supernatural marvels to humanity, and that *Frankenstein* represents a domestication of the Gothic form.

The *Lyrical Ballads* had also advertised themselves as attempting "a natural delineation of human passions."[62] Coleridge, as a famous passage of the *Biographia* explains, took the route closer to the

Gothic (as well as to mid-eighteenth-century poetry in general), describing "incidents and agents . . . in part at least, supernatural" in order to interest "the affections by the dramatic truth of such emotions, as would naturally accompany such situations, supposing them real." Wordsworth had already experimented with Gothic tales in such early works as "The Three Graves" and *The Vale of Esthwaite*, rejected the form, and devised a revisionary union of the probable with the marvellous, a natural supernaturalism: according to Coleridge, his subjects were to come from "ordinary life," and his poems "to give the charm of novelty to things of every day, and to excite a feeling analogous to the supernatural, by awakening the mind's attention from the lethargy of custom."[63] The Gothic, Wordsworth came to believe, panders to the public's "degrading thirst after outrageous stimulation," for "gross and violent stimulants"; in its place he devised new ways of connecting the extraordinary and the everyday through such procedures as memory of landscape and of the sublime of terror.[64] In the process, he transformed the problem of unifying the marvellous and the probable – truth to imagination and truth to external nature – into that of explaining the interpenetration and interanimation of individual mind, the creative imagination, with the external world.

In the critical vocabulary of the eighteenth century, Wordsworth's accomplishment was the creation of a new kind of *allegory*. Described in this way, his contributions to *Lyrical Ballads* manifest yet deeper roots in earlier eighteenth-century poetics. Walpole's aim of uniting ancient and modern romance reflects a revisionary trend in mid-century literary history, a trend whose manifestations are as diverse as Collins' "Epistle to Hanmer," Hurd's *Letters on Chivalry*, and, in most detailed form, Thomas Warton's *History of English Poetry* (1774–81). As is well known, these writers elevate the Italian ancestry of English poetry at the expense of the French; the supposedly baneful influence of France infects England at the time of the Restoration, producing the "revolution" Hurd so memorably describes in the *Letters*:

What we have gotten by this revolution, you will say, is a great deal of good sense. What we have lost, is a world of fine fabling; the illusion of which is so grateful to the *charmed spirit*; that in spite of philosophy and fashion, *Faery* Spenser still ranks highest among the Poets; I mean with all those who are either come out of that house, or have any kindness for it. (120)

Spenser's importance to Hurd is as an allegorist; when the truly marvellous of the Gothic is no longer critically acceptable, the poet must have recourse to that way of relating form to meaning which is allegory:

Common sense being offended with these perversions of truth and nature (still accounted the more monstrous, as the antient manners, they pretended to copy after, were now disused, and of most men forgotten) the next step was to have recourse to *allegories* ... Milton, tho' he dropped the tales, he still kept to the allegories of Spenser. (118)

Elizabethan poetry, the product of an age capable of the precarious balance Thomas Warton called "civilized superstition," provided mid-century poets and critics with a standard against which to measure Augustan poetic achievement (as, in altered terms, Renaissance models were to serve the Romantics).[65] It was through a theory of allegorical personification as revelatory of the "marvellous of the mind," as Wallace Jackson has shown, that the mid-century tradition which made so many bows to Spenser was to achieve its own reconciliation of the probable and the marvellous.[66] To eighteenth-century notions of allegory, and to their importance to Wordsworth, we shall then briefly turn.

Eighteenth-century thinking about allegory falls into three stages. The emphasis of Le Bossu, Dennis, and their age was to find in those figures that Addison called "Tracks of Light in a Discourse" universalizable meaning as their characteristic mark. To Le Bossu, a work is an allegory when it has a moral, that is, when its moral is universal in reference. He distinguishes the components of a fable: "The one is *Truth*, which serves as a Foundation of it; and the other is *Fiction*, which Allegorically disguises this Truth, and gives the *Form of a Fable*."[67] Probability working itself out in a structure of probable signs is the guarantee of allegory in the whole, so that Addison can write in *Spectator* 315, "besides the hidden meaning of an Epic Allegory, the plain literal sense ought to appear probable" (III, 146). In this, the first Augustan sense of allegory, Aesop's fables and the Iliad are allegorical in the same sense: in their mediation of fiction with a (universal) truth.

Mid-century writers devised a way of understanding allegory as a descriptive procedure, as we have heard Kames explain (above, pp. 93, 146), and as is implied in such titles as Collins' *Odes on Several Descriptive and Allegorical Subjects* (1746) and Richard Shepherd's *Odes Descriptive and Allegorical* (1761). The mid-century allegorical figure, as we have seen, "bodies forth unsubstantial things, turns them to shape"; its objects are usually the passions, the "shadowy tribes of mind," objects which also give the figure allegorical universality (and hence permanence) in the earlier sense.[68] It was allegorical figures in this second Augustan sense that Johnson found so tedious in poetry; so did the translator of Lowth's *Sacred Poetry of the Hebrews*, producing an amusing running conflict between text and translator's notes.[69] Such figures, finally, are at once internally probable, because their object is universal passion, and marvellous, because externally improbable manifestations of what Dryden named "the Fairy kind of writing."

We have seen that mid-century criticism did not develop its theory of internal probability on the model of external sufficiently clearly that both could be understood as probability in the same sense (hence their being distinguished at all). While external probability was explicitly analyzed as a relation to evidence, a fidelity to truths outside the work, internal probability was thought to rest on another kind of testimony, one so different from the first as scarcely to deserve the name testimony at all. In this, of course, Augustan theorists were incorrect; both kinds of probability are relational terms, relations to evidence, and particularly to opinion; and as we have seen, the internal logic of the concept itself forced critics in practice, if not always in theory, to understand this. The Augustan error here resembles modern criticism's erroneous distinction between "internal" and "external" evidence of literary meaning; literary events do not "speak their own meaning," to borrow a phrase from the hermeneuticists, any more than real events do. From this error in modern criticism springs the misreading of Augustan internal probability as mere consistency; Abrams' distinction between internal and external probability, in other words, is a case of reading modern concerns into older critical formulations.

Blackmore's difficult passages on probability in epic are confusing because they appeal to conceptually distinct notions of the probable: the probable as what is like truth (but is not truth itself); as what is like truth in the sense of occurring most frequently (and which hence may be truth itself); as that which is credible; as that which is credible upon certain grounds. His demands that a work be probable and that it be only probable depend on different senses of the repeated term. Even within his sense of the probable as what is credible upon certain grounds, a further confusion arises; to explain what is wrong with events "inconsistent, monstrous, or unnatural," he appeals variously (as the terms themselves imply) to many different grounds of belief; when these conflict, he has no criteria for choosing among them. His predicament is typical of early Augustan uses of probability, uses which conflate a variety of meanings in what was thought to be a unitary notion.

Later writers were at pains to sort out these meanings, but often erred in their formulations. Campbell erred, for instance, in failing to make clear what he knew in practice, that both probability and plausibility are relations to evidence; he erred further in attempting to connect consistency directly with belief.[70] He is partly aware of the problem, as we have seen; he betrays his predicament in such admissions as that there "is a relation between these two" such that "the want of plausibility implies an internal improbability, which it will require the stronger external evidence to surmount." (This might happen, for instance, when a historical event related in a work is so unlikely that for an audience to accept it, they must know that it really occurred; Campbell's "external evidence" is again Wordsworth's "external testimony.") The difficulty with such a statement is of course that if implausibility implies improbability, *both* depend on a relation to evidence; and having distinguished plausibility from probability, Campbell has no middle ground left on which to explain what an "internal improbability" might be.[71]

Instead, then, of seeing that internal and external probability differ only in the aspects of nature each picks out for imitation, Augustan critics pursued internal probability from the direction of problems of belief, with the result that even theorists like Hurd, who advanced views both of poetical probability and of the special kind of belief we should have in poetry, could cede to marvels and allegories only an "air of probability," not probability itself. Internally probable marvels could still be condemned for their violation of (external) probability; because the same word might be used for probability both internal and external, two writers can hold seemingly opposed positions on the value of "probability" in a work and yet be in no disagreement.

That Augustan critics did not clearly realize that internal probability is also external results from what we have seen to be the literary psychology from which they began. The faculty that weighs probabilities is judgment; the faculties at use in producing and appreciating marvels are not judgment, but fancy (imagination) and, later, sensibility. In theory at least, unification of the internally and externally probable awaited a literary psychology that could reconcile fancy and judgment not merely by balancing them but through their actual fusion. In Augustan thought – not merely literary thought, but theorizing in all departments – no model for such fusion existed; to the Augustans, contraries are ineluctably contraries, and these can at best be mediated through the achievement of some kind of balance or "poise."[72]

That Romantic literary theory attempted just such a fusion of reason with imagination is too familiar a point to require elaboration. The fusion brought with it tentative suggestions of a new sense of the allegorical, that is, of a new relation of form to meaning. Wordsworth, for whom imagination was but "Reason in her most exalted mood," adumbrates an "allegorical spirit" productive of such fused relations:

Spenser, of a gentler nature, maintained his freedom by aid of his allegorical spirit, at one time inciting him to create persons out of abstractions; and, at another, by a superior effort of genius, to give the universality and permanence of abstractions to its human beings, by means of attributes and emblems that belong to the highest moral truths and purest sensations, – of which his character of Una is a glorious example.[73]

"The form of a character," wrote Richter, "is the general in the particular, allegorical or symbolic individuality" (158). Blake uses *allegory* in both the mid-century and the later, or third eighteenth-century sense. Speaking of mid-century allegory, he echoes Hobbes:

Fable or Allegory are a totally distinct & inferior kind of Poetry. Vision or Imagination is a Representation of what Eternally Exists, Really & Unchangibly. Fable or Allegory is Form'd by the daughters of Memory. Imagination is surrounded by the daughters of Inspiration.

Blake's "imagination" supplies the "permanence" of the mid-century critics' "heart"; as a partly intellective, partly emotive faculty, it can also create a new kind of allegory:

I consider it as the Grandest Poem that this World contains. Allegory addressed to the Intellectual powers, while it is altogether hidden from the Corpuscular Understanding, is My Definition of the most Sublime Poetry.

In the second passage, Blake is describing his own prophetic books.[74] (Despite the differences in their own poetry, furthermore, Blake and Wordsworth agree in their reasons for condemning mid-century allegory and personification.)

In the first of his prefaces to the *Lyrical Ballads*, Wordsworth eschews "personifications of abstract ideas" in the mid-century manner, desiring instead "to keep my Reader in the company of flesh and blood"; instead of adopting the "mechanical employment" of the poet who "describes and imitates passions" – what for the late Augustans was the chief sense in which poetry is "imitative" – he will write of "real and substantial action and suffering."[75] The appeal to drama brings with it the demand for probability. As is well known, Wordsworth's poetry and prose teem with examples wherein the writer professes to find marvels in commonplaces. He writes to Southey, in the dedicatory epistle to *Peter Bell*:

The Poem of Peter Bell, as the Prologue will shew, was composed under a belief that the Imagination not only does not require for its exercise the intervention of supernatural agency, but that, though such agency be excluded, the faculty may be called forth imperiously, and for kindred results of pleasure, by incidents, within the compass of poetic probability, in the humblest departments of daily life.[76]

Poetical probability is here more than the internal probability adumbrated by mid-century writers; it stands for a fusion not merely of the marvellous with the (internally) probable, but for a fusion of probability both internal and external. It was only within the new conceptual context of Romanticism – its new accounts of intellection and composition, of literary structure and interpretation, of fused relations, and of the relations of literary procedures to social life – that the new theory of internal probability as truth to passion could be made explicit; as a result, it was only within the new conceptual context also that Wordsworth's equation could be devised. Wordsworth has essayed that natural supernaturalism to which Dickens refers when he explains that in *Bleak House* he has "purposely dwelt upon the romantic side of familiar things," and when he claims in the first number of *Household Words* that "in all familiar things, even in those which are repellent on the surface, there is Romance enough, if we will find it out."[77]

PART III

Probability and the Meaning of Augustan Narrative

VI

Probability and literary form

But it will then be time to speak of what is probable ... when we come to the
Narration.

John Dennis, *Remarks on* Prince Arthur (1696)

The complex of ideas about probability and inference from probable
signs whose uses and effects we have traced in philosophy and
criticism inevitably makes itself felt as well in the ways in which
Augustan literary works are structured and conceived. But the
historian who seeks to demonstrate these connections faces an initial
difficulty: that of finding a suitable level of comparison between
thought and works – a level at which theory can intelligibly and
plausibly be expected to translate itself into practice, and at which
the literary embodiments of theory can be expected to change as the
theory itself undergoes alteration. When that theory is so multi-
fariously present and useful as we have seen ideas of probability to
be, the avenues of approach open to the historian are many; when
examining so foundational a category as probability, the most useful
and revealing results will come from tracing its effects at a similarly
foundational level in literary works.

In rare instances, of course, ideas of probability may form part of
the explicit thematics of a given work: thus, for instance, in "The
Odds Against Friday: Defoe, Bayes, and Inverse Probability," Paul
Alkon has attempted to extract from *Robinson Crusoe* a Christian
conception of the calculation of probabilities as a "Satanic subtlety"
of which the good man has no need, while in "Signs of Randomness
in *Roderick Random*," James Bunn seeks to find in Smollett's novel a
theory of the radical indeterminacy of temporal events. Neither
effort succeeds.[1] Wider knowledge of the historical development and
typical uses of probability in the Augustan period must precede an
understanding even of these isolated instances.

At a deeper level of analysis, it has been claimed that particular
genres were, at given times, understood probabilistically, that is, as
the natural forms in which to pursue probable rather than demonstrative argument, inductive inquiry rather than deductive exposi-

tion. Best known of such vehicles is of course the essay, a form popularized by French skeptics; here, we are told, opinion rather than science might find expression, and such opinions might be connected by inferential transitions weaker than those unifying treatises written *more geometrico*, or according to the strict *methodi* and *ordines* of the dialectician. Philosophers and scientists might write essays when not engaged in more rigorous exercises titled *Tractatus* or *Principia*.

But the very example of the scientific essay should make us wary of any easy assumption that in the Augustan period, choice of the essay form was an expression of probabilism. As a number of historians have shown, the dominant tradition in seventeenth-century natural philosophy was as concerned with certainty and demonstration as were its mediaeval forebears; only very late in the century do certain of the "new" scientists come to identify their methods and results as probabilistic. While Locke named his great work *Essay*, and even expressed doubt about natural philosophy being ever made a science, he betrayed no such doubt about the status of his own theories, which, he would have said, are the products of intuition and the comparison of ideas. In England, particularly after the mid-seventeenth century, the essay form indicates rather a choice of audience and hence of rhetorical pose than of philosophic commitment. The essay was a *popular* form, one not directed to the specialist. Considerations of a genteel and general audience govern its argumentative procedures.

The connection of essay with probabilism is far clearer in the Renaissance than in the period that follows, though even to Bacon the essay was first of all a popular form, and only secondarily, because popular writing for him entailed using probable inducements rather than his new demonstrative induction, a probabilistic one, the form "very properly applied to civil business and to those arts which rest in discourse and opinion."[2] Having demoted the "methods" of the humanist dialecticians to what Bacon saw as their only proper sphere – that of oratory and sophistic, of presentation rather than discovery – he found the methods of dialectic and rhetoric particularly suitable to his two favorite popular forms, parable and essay.[3]

Rhetoric, furthermore, "the doctrine concerning the illustration of Discourse" (IV, 454), is still to Bacon the toolbox of methods to be used when the learned are speaking to the vulgar. It is an "Imaginative or Insinuative Reason" (III, 383), in that it does not seek to persuade by argument or appeal to reason, but seeks rather to evade reason through persuasive appeals to imagination:

Rhetoric is subservient to the imagination, as Logic is to the understanding; and the duty and office of Rhetoric, if it be deeply looked into, is no other than to apply and recommend the dictates of reason to imagination, in order to excite the appetite and will. (IV, 455)

Among the tools of rhetoric, for instance, Bacon lists "*the popular signs* or *colours of apparent good and evil*": parting company with a long line of dialecticians, he finds that such signs, or popular judgments of value, are of use less "for probation than for affecting and moving" (IV, 458).

As we have noted before, it was because the faculty of imagination as understood in the Renaissance possessed cognitive (intellective) functions not allowed it by Augustan theories of mind that Augustan critics emphatically stress the need for literary works to balance judgment with fancy; it was this same intellective capacity of imagination that made imagination for Bacon the faculty of popular discourse. To Bacon, even inference from signs – for so he understands the "colours" of rhetoric – is the office of imagination; imagination judges of probability.

For Bacon, then, the methods of rhetoric and the old humanist dialectic are the tools of popularization. Bacon frequently justifies such figures as similitude, metaphor, and allegory as means for communicating with the vulgar (IV, 317, 452); such means persuade only with probability. The parables of *De Sapientia veterum*, for instance, use such figures by their very nature, and gain what probability they possess not from any argumentative appeal to reason, but through the close "fit" that Bacon preconstructs between his mythical vehicles and their philosophical tenor; such a means of persuasion can attain only to probability, for Bacon could as easily have devised any number of other interpretations to give his myths. The parables are only weakly probable signs of a sense their author must himself explicate. In both parable and essay, probable appeal to imagination – through rhetoric – follows from the choice of audience.

Probabilistic status and popular appeal remain the interconnected hallmarks of rhetorical figures throughout the seventeenth century, though the account of the faculties to which they appeal changes. Glanvill's account of the proper use of figurative language in sermons, for instance, is fully consistent with Sprat's proscription of such language (or rather, his rejection of its misuses) in his rhetorical programme for the Royal Society. According to Glanvill's *Essay concerning Preaching* (1678), the plain style is effective only for the wise; tropes and figures are "such schemes of speech as are apt to excite the affections of the most vulgar, and illiterate" (56). Of the probabilistic status of arguments from such figures, George Puttenham gives frequent testimony. He says of that form of "similitude" which is the "*paradigma*, or a resemblance by example," that it takes its force from its use in "matter of counsell or perswasion" to "compare the past with the present, gathering probabilitie of like successe to come in the things wee haue presently in hand: or if ye will draw the iudgements precedent and authorized by antiquitie as veritable. . . " Here are the familiar ingredients of Renaissance probability, induction and probable opinion (authority). Puttenham is clear that such figures provide only persuasion, never demonstration; he specifies their audience: "no one [method] preuaileth with all *ordinary iudgements* than perswasion by similitude." The point is rooted in a long tradition stemming from Aristotle, according to which rhetorical induction – argument from example – is an argument fitted only for the vulgar.[4]

As we saw in chapter III, the nexus of popular appeal and probability did not survive the seventeenth century, except in etiolated instances. With that nexus perishes as well any real ground for claiming a connection between choice of the essay form and probabilism. That the essay could become the vehicle for physicists as well as historians, politicians, and moralists is itself a product of the Augustan redirection of rhetoric from the vulgar to the learned – the learned now comprising an enlarged reading public interested to follow the reasonings of a Locke or a Boyle. At the same time, the repertory of literary devices open to the essayist widens. The most striking feature of the Augustan essay – aside from its broad appeal – is not probable argument but its endless variety and flexibility, its capacity to assimilate nearly all literary devices.

The organizing principles of the Augustan essay, finally, follow from consideration of its large, varied, learned (i.e., educated), and genteel audience. When for instance Henry Felton lards his *Dissertation on Reading the Classics* (1715) with reiterated disclaimers of any "method" of organization, claiming to present instead "some desultory Thoughts in their Native Order, as they rise in my Mind without being reduced to Rules, and marshalled according to Art," he explains his immethodical procedure as the result of his choice of audience: "Nor shall I need any Apology for the Style and Manner I have used... I was not writing to myself, nor to the grave and learned, but to a young Nobleman of sprightly Parts," and for the education of a wider public as well. The occasion demands the loose form of an essay, though Felton warns that his thinking is not immethodic: "I won't pretend to answer my Want of Method, perhaps I have observed it, tho' I seem to neglect it."[5]

Another genre supposed in itself and in its structure to have been understood as the vehicle of probable argument is dialogue. Both claims have been amply demonstrated for the revival of Ciceronian dialogue *in utramque partem* in the Renaissance, and the analysis has more recently been extended to the organizing procedures of Tudor drama.[6] Best known of Augustan dialogues in this mode is of course Dryden's *Of Dramatic Poesy: An Essay*, which Johnson himself described in his *Life of Dryden* as a "treatise ... artfully variegated with successive representations of opposite probabilities" (412). Dryden himself makes the point in his *Defense* of the *Essay* against criticisms by Howard (1668):

> He is here pleased to charge me with being magisterial, as he has done in many other places of his preface. Therefore, in vindication of myself, I must crave leave to say that my whole discourse was sceptical, according to that way of reasoning which was used by Socrates, Plato, and all the Academics of old, which Tully and the best of the Ancients followed, and which is imitated by the modest inquisitions of the Royal Society. That it is so, not only the name will shew, which is *An Essay*, but the frame and composition of the work. You see it is a dialogue sustained by persons of several opinions, all of them left doubtful, to be determined by the readers in general. (*Essays*, I, 123)

Among the few members of the Royal Society to write dialogues, Dryden may have had in mind Boyle, who explains his procedure in using a principal speaker in his *Sceptical Chymist* (1661): "it is enough ... if either of the proposed hypotheses be but as probable as that he calls in question" (5). In the "Proemial Essay" to *Certain Physiological Essays*, Boyle writes against "the systematical way of writing," promising instead to "speak so doubtingly, and use so often, *perhaps*, it *seems*, it *is not improbable*, and such other expressions, as argue a diffidence of the truth of the opinions I adhere to" (*Works*, I, 193, 198).

But even before the Augustan period, the connection of dialogue with probable inquiry is largely external and scarcely invariable. Phillip Harth has gone so far as to question Dryden's skeptical use of the form, arguing that for him the dialogue "is an excellent form in which to present not only an inquiry but an argument as well, for in the latter case it permits the author to air the possible objections to his proposition and to answer them fully."[7] Harth lists several such uninquisitive dialogues written by members of the Royal Society; the list should begin much earlier, and should include such unskeptical, anti-probabilist works as Bartholomeo Viotti's *De Demonstratione* (1560), Mersenne's *Vérité des sciences* (1625), *Rushworth's Dialogues* by Thomas White (1640), Descartes' *Recherche de la vérité* (?1641), Malebranche's *Conversations chrétiennes* (1676) and his volumes of *Entretiens* on metaphysics (1688), death (1696), and the existence of God (1708), and Lamy's *Entretiens sur les sciences* (1683). Dialogue could be a manner of concealing claims to certainty, as it was for Galileo. In the Augustan period, like the essay, it is a form used primarily for its popular appeal, as it is by Fontenelle in his dialogues on death (1683) and on the plurality of worlds (1686); it is so most clearly in the work of the form's master, Bishop Berkeley, who notoriously made it his pose to "think with the learned" but to "speak with the vulgar."[8] The same considerations of audience rather than epistemology surely governed Hobbes when late in life he cast his *Seven Philosophical Problems* as dialogues.[9]

Essay and dialogue are of course primarily nonfictional forms, or at least forms in which arguments are made explicitly rather than embodied in and dramatized by character and action. How did concepts of probability condition Augustan practice in other (or indeed, through the range of all) forms? To answer this question, we must look more closely where contemporary criticism points us: to the unifying procedures by which details of works are drawn together – to all those occasions on which the details of works stand in some inferential relation to one another; contemporary critics speak most often of the unifying procedures at use in the construction of character and action, and so our attention shall largely be on characterization and narration. These are practices at use in all periods, and so we shall be able to see them taking on a special Augustan shape under the influence of particular beliefs about probability and probable inference. Where the details of a work are to be related one to another, we can talk about the kinds of inference that authors expect of the readers of such structures. We must attend not merely to the epistemic status of persuasive arguments, but also to the kinds of inferential relations that hold works together and give them their character: to the way concepts of probability are implied and dramatized.

This after all was how Augustan criticism itself understood probability. We have already examined the theory that literary works are hierarchies of probable signs; the analyses of particular works that follow show in greater detail what literary form these organizations of signs take, and what interpretive procedures they require of their "implied readers."[10] At this most fundamental level, we shall find a crucial structural similarity – an isomorphism – among the following expressions of prevailing notions of probability: (1) the accounts given by philosophers and critics in their attempts to make explicit their beliefs about how the mind operates, especially about the nature and structure of probable inference; (2) the organization of probable signs in the literary work, what I call the work's "inferential structure"; and (3) those inferential procedures of interpretation required of readers if those readers are to identify and make sense of the particular inferential structures before them. In this isomorphism of theory of knowledge, literary structure, and implied procedures of interpretation we shall find the most fundamental level at which philosophic theory produces literary form.

We shall seek these interrelations in that literary kind wherein the Augustans demanded that probability be most strictly observed. Augustan critics fully understood the demand for probability to be mediated by considerations of genre: the demand is strongest in the higher kinds (epic, tragedy, comedy), less stringent in the lower. This was Johnson's point in the *Life of Butler*; his whole sentence reads, "Poetical action ought to be probable upon certain suppositions, and such probability as burlesque requires is here violated only by one incident." Johnson's "suppositions" are not, as Jean Hagstrum interprets them, the improbable premises from which a work may begin if only it follow them out consistently; they are considerations of genre.[11] In lower forms, and especially in mock-forms, improbabilities did not call for the kinds of special explanation they did in higher. Beattie speaks too of constraints on imitation as measured by what "the design of the piece will admit," arguing that works should contain "every probable ornament that can be devised, consistently with the design and genius of the work."[12]

Beattie speaks for his age in his ranking of the genres according to the probability each requires:

in some kinds of poetical invention a stricter probability is required than in others: – that, for instance, Comedy, whether Dramatic or Narrative, must seldom deviate from the ordinary course of human affairs . . . that the Tragic poet . . . may be allowed a wider range; but must never attempt the marvellous fictions of the Epic Muse . . . that the Epic Poem may claim still ampler privileges, because its fictions are not subject to the scrutiny of any outward sense, and because it conveys information in regard both to the highest human characters, and the most important and wonderful events . . . Nor would it be improper to observe, that the several species of Comic, of Tragic, of Epic composition, are not confined to the same degree of probability; for that Farce may be allowed to be less probable than the regular Comedy; the Masque, than the regular Tragedy; and the Mixed Epic, such as The Fairy Queen and Orlando Furioso, than the pure Epopee of Homer, Virgil, and Milton.[13]

Under "Narrative Comedy" Beattie lists "Fielding's *Tom Jones*, *Amelia*, and *Joseph Andrews*" (while admitting that "perhaps *the Comic Epopee* is a more proper term"). Fielding, of course, had used the commonplace procedure for elevating a favored form that Addison had before him used in treating ballad, that of making it a kind of epic; this brought with it all the considerations of probability he discusses in book VIII, chapter 1 of *Tom Jones*. Richardson similarly assimilated his narrative *Clarissa* to Christian tragedy, bringing with this identification all those considerations of poetic justice and probable signification of character we saw in his Post-script. We have also seen moreover that by mid-century the novel had become a touchstone for external probability; John Hawkes-worth writes of "The NOVEL," in comparison to epic and romance, "though it bears a nearer resemblance to truth, has yet less power of entertainment; for as it is confined within the narrower bounds of probability."[14] Thomas Twining, in distinguishing "poetical prob-ability" from that "more *possible* sort of *probability*," calls the latter "the probability of romance," explaining that he has in mind such works as *Clarissa* and *Cecilia* (rather than chivalric and Gothic tales).[15]

For the Augustans, then, comedy, and especially narrative comedy – the novel – requires in general the strictest observance of prob-ability. As a narrative form, the novel was quickly assimilated to the hierarchic model of literary structure, readily understood as a compages of probable signs. As a matter of historical fact, finally, the Augustan novel, usually cast in the form of an educational journey, frequently takes as its explicit subject the conditions of knowledge and learning, the need for the methods of cultivating probable inference. No form demonstrates more clearly the effects of proba-bilism on literary practice.

VII

The conditions of knowing in Augustan fiction

... works not raised upon principles demonstrative and scientific, but
appealing wholly to observation and experience...

Johnson, *Preface to Shakespeare* (1765)

In a much-quoted remark, Bishop Butler found that "probability is
the very guide of life"; in one of his best allegorical essays, Letter 38
of *The Citizen of the World* (1762), Oliver Goldsmith subjects
Butler's maxim to the favorite Augustan procedure of the literaliz-
ation of metaphor. Here probability is a personified guide, the
Genius of Probability, who vies with the Genius of Demonstration to
be the conductor of a youth seeking to travel from the Valley of
Ignorance to the Land of Certainty.[1]

Goldsmith's Valley of Ignorance is a version of the Happy Valley
of *Rasselas*; here, however, it is "wonder" – since the time of Plato
the initial motive to philosophy – that impels the youth to leave his
"sequestered vale," where nature is bountiful and the inhabitants, if
ignorant, are "happy in themselves, in each other." Reaching a
mountain peak, the youth sees in the distance a country "more
beautiful and alluring than even that he had just left behind":
Certainty. In language Dennis would have approved, Goldsmith
explains that "in that charming retreat, sentiment contributes to
refine every sensual banquet": in Certainty, the faculties have
regained their prelapsarian harmony.

"With a look of infinite modesty" the Genius of Demonstration
approaches and offers to conduct the youth to Certainty. But the
paths of Demonstration soon prove arduous and slow; another
Genius appears, one "who seem'd travelling the same way," offering
an easier passage. This is Probability, who wears "a countenance
that betrayed a confidence that the innocent might mistake for
sincerity"; our youth, inexpert in physiognomy as in epistemology,
yields to the new guide. Probability turns traitor, suggesting that an
easier goal than Certainty might be the Land of Confidence, whose
inhabitants "tasted almost as much satisfaction as if in the Land of
Certainty." To this suggestion, ignorance agrees; Probability calls
forth a new conductor, a hideous bird which, it turns out, is the

Demon of Error. Error flies the youth off across the Ocean of Doubts (which separates Ignorance from both Certainty and Confidence), drops him in, and the youth drowns.

Goldsmith's moral in this story is not fully clear. In undertaking his journey at all, the youth should have stuck to Demonstration; but Goldsmith never suggests that the journey is worth taking. Like Gray in the Eton College ode, he may see no vice in protracting one's stay in ignorance. This very ambiguity and the geography of Goldsmith's allegory form a pattern which, it might be argued, is an Augustan version of the similar but completed pattern that critics such as M. H. Abrams (in *Natural Supernaturalism*) have advanced as typical of Romantic poetry. In Goldsmith's Augustan version, the knowledge possessed by the inhabitants of Certainty is indeed moral and religious knowledge – Abrams' "apocalyptic knowledge" – but it is a knowledge not vouchsafed to mortals in their lifetime: Certainty is "a country where no mortal had ever been permitted to arrive." (Pope makes the same point to the curious in the cosmic survey with which he begins *An Essay on Man*: those who seek further enlightenment must "Wait the great teacher Death.")

In the original version of the essay, published in 1760 in the *Public Ledger*, the youth is seduced not by Probability but by the Genius of Presumption. Goldsmith may have had in mind such "presumptuous" applications of probable reasoning as Hume's in his recent essay "Of Miracles," or the probabilism of the more extreme and deistic of the physico-theologians; more likely, however, he was simply making the traditional point – not wholly consistently – that the truths of religion necessary for salvation are made clear with demonstrative certainty in revelation, and that the wages of attempting to substitute fallible human reason for divine wisdom is doubt and death. In any case, because of the allegory's religious bent, and because the goal of the youth's educational journey is not simply knowledge, but certainty, it would be a mistake to take the essay as evidence for Goldsmith's being, unlike the vast majority of his contemporaries, a defender of older canons of demonstrative science in the face of the pervasive new model of probable reasoning. In the same year the essay appeared in *The Citizen of the World*, Goldsmith showed himself an excellent probabilist and enemy of "credulity" in his contribution to the literature of the Cock-Lane ghost, "The Mystery Revealed."

Goldsmith's allegory might be the blueprint for any number of Augustan novels. Embodied in a narrative (fable) and diversified through probable circumstances – and made consistent with the demands of poetic justice – the story of Ignorance and Probability might suffer such names to be imposed on its hero as Ferdinand Count Fathom, Joseph Andrews, or Harley. Each of these characters appears in a didactic narrative – an educational journey – whose explicit subject is in large part the need for and constraints on probable inference, and whose underlying structure is that of an organization of probable signs. Each narrative pursues its didactic intentions by placing characters and readers in a world in which the conditions of knowledge are such as to render all knowing, all learning, a process of inference from signs; each does so, in fact, by a self-conscious procedure of making structure (probable signs) a part of subject (probable inference). (It is a characteristic of Augustan literature in general, as Irvin Ehrenpreis has noted, not only to pursue didactic ends but to provide readers with explicit explanations of those ends and of the procedures being used to achieve them: in no period since do authors so frequently or so fully explain themselves to their readers.)[2] Each, finally, is designed to teach certain capacities of judgment by dramatizing those capacities in action, that is, by creating inferential structures which to be read require the exercise of that very judgment which the author wishes to teach. Through such mapping of a preferred theory of judgment in a distinctive narrative structure, the novelist creates what Robert Uphaus has very aptly called "reading paradigms,"[3] invitations to exercise the mental capacities which the author is attempting to instill in his readers. Through the interpretive procedures each asks of readers, then, the educational journeys in which Goldsmith's youth finds himself convert the model of literary structure as a hierarchy of probable signs into didactic meaning. And as in the course of the Augustan period the understanding of probable inference changes, so will its paradigmatic expression in didactic narrative works.

(1) THE WORLD OF PROBABLE SIGNS: SMOLLETT

In like manner the Word *Judgment* is seldom in common Discourse confined to obvious and self-evident Truths. It rather signifies those Conjectures and Guesses that we form, in Cases which admit not of undoubted Certainty, and where we are left to determine by comparing the various Probabilities of Things. Thus a Man of Sagacity and Penetration, who sees far into the Humours and Passions of Mankind, and seldom mistakes in the Opinions he frames of Characters and Actions, is said to judge well or think judiciously.

William Duncan, *The Elements of Logick* (1748)

Lord Visage, we think particularly objectionable. He is a physiognomist, and in his character Lavater is satirized, or, to speak more accurately, burlesqued. A poet, who does not consider the moral effects of his satire, is, in our opinion, highly culpable. Any attempt to make men believe that the countenance of man does not bear visible signs of individual propensities, and of vicious habits, is immoral, because it is false.

Thomas Holcroft, Review of *False Colours* (1793)[4]

Modern readers find it easy to agree with Saintsbury's estimate of *Ferdinand Count Fathom* (1753) as Smollett's "least good novel," even as they come to understand it in new ways; they find the book disunified and overlong, and suggest that it would have profited from careful revision – a dangerous desideratum, since for most Augustan writers, revision meant lengthening, not shortening works. As Albrecht Strauss has pointed out, Smollett's portrayal of passion is here as throughout his novels monotonously formulaic; Strauss adds, however, that an artist's failures can be more revelatory of his technique than his successes.[5] Although I can hardly agree that *Fathom* is a failure, the novel is perhaps the most revelatory in Smollett's work of its author's views on probability, and of their effect on the construction of his narratives.

Hazlitt's criticism of Smollett sets Strauss' tone. To Hazlitt, Smollett is superficial: he "seldom probes to the quick beneath the surface"; his humor arises from "the situation of the persons or the peculiarity of their external appearance." To Strauss, Smollett gets at inner states only through their "external manifestations," a method which he finds to work only for comic effects; to him, "the physical reactions Smollett manipulates are so crude as to be incapable of doing justice to finer shades of feeling." "It is as though deep down Smollett feared sentiment," complains this champion of Henry James.[6]

What is most surprising about *Fathom*, however, is not so much that Smollett gets at inner states through their external physical manifestations (moving, via probable signs, from effect to cause) – for this is not the only way that he does so – but that he so frequently *says* that this is what he is doing. Characters in *Fathom*, when one loathes another, do not simply betray that loathing in action, leaving the reader to infer the cause; one does not say to another, "I loathe you" (even indirectly), nor does the narrator say "He loathed her." Rather, such characters are said to give "all the *signs* of loathing and abhorrence." Smollett uses the language of signs and probable inference with (to use one of his own favorite words) "incredible" frequency. Here is Ferdinand speaking to Monimia:

This *artful politician*, who rejoiced at the *effect* of her *penetration*, no sooner heard himself questioned on the subject, than he gave *tokens* of surprise and confusion, *signifying* his concern to find she had *discovered* what, for the honor of his friend, he wished had never *come to light*. His *behavior* on this occasion *confirmed* her fatal *conjecture*; and she conjured him, in the most pathetic manner, to tell her if he thought Renaldo's heart had contracted any new engagement. At this question, he started with *signs* of extreme agitation, and stifling an *artificial* sigh, "Sure, madam," said he, "you cannot *doubt* the Count's constancy – I am *confident* – he is *certainly* – I protest madam, I am so shocked."[7]

(Here of course Ferdinand is deliberately misleading Monimia by giving false signs: this is the sense in which Smollett so frequently describes his hero as "artful" and a "politician.")[8]

marks	38		
expressions/			
expressive	27		
tokens	17		
betoken	2		
signs	17	circumstances	86
signify	11	expect/	
signals	9	expectations	51
signalize	5	probability	35
symptoms	16	conjectures	26
presages	16	evidence/evince	13
proofs	11	penetration	11
demonstrations	11	discernment	9
testimonies	9	political/	
testimonials	1	politician	9
prognostics	8	plausible	5
omens	7	likelihood	4
denote	7	prudence	4
manifest	7	foresight	3
indications	7	construe	3
pledges	3	calculation	3
cues	2	certify	3
notices	2	verify	2
foretellings	2		
beacons	1		
flags	1		
portents	1		
prophecies	1		

Figure 3

This is a language we have heard before. To facilitate and render more persuasive the discussion to follow, I have tabulated the number of times certain of the most important terms of this vocabulary occur in *Fathom* (figure 3). In the first list, that of signs and its synonyms, very nearly all the uses noted are external signs (frequently so called) of inner states (frequently so called); most of these inner states are either motives or emotions. This is true even of what might seem the most unlikely signs:

her *heart* began to thaw, and her *face* to hang out the *flag* of capitulation. (1, 81)

This *adventure* fully answered all the purposes of our *politician*; it established the *opinion* of his fellow-laborer's virtue, beyond all the power of accident of information to shake, and set up a *false beacon* to *mislead* the sentiments of Medemoiselle, in case she should for the *future* meet with the *like* misfortune. (1, 64)

(In the second case, a false sign in the present provides for a misdiagnosis that in turn gives grounds for incorrect inductions, false inferences in future like cases.) Even the medical language of the novel is used to manifest inner states: thus four of the eight "prognostics" are explicitly medical, but only one of the "symptoms" is. The rest are present signs of future events, or manifest signs (again, frequently so called) of things hidden. Most of the signs of motives or emotions reside in the "face," "countenance," "aspect," "air," or "gesture," a few in tones of voice, and many in the general "circumstances" surrounding an event. These terms are also often qualified by others which mark the degree of their probability: "certain signs," "a certain omen," "an undoubted mark," "undoubted proofs."

The second list contains terms having to do with the reading or interpretation of these signs. Telling the reader what each character "expects," "suspects," or "conjectures" – and on what probability such conjectures are grounded – is Smollett's second principal method of conveying information about his characters' inner states. The faculty of reading signs is "sagacity," facility in its use "penetration" and "discernment"; facility in giving false signs is "art," "acting," "insinuation," and "policy." Inferences from signs are "conjectures," "expectations," "construings," and "calculations"; some of these inferences are "doubtful," others "probable," yet others "certain" and "infallible." Conjectures may be "confirmed," "verified," "certified," or "disappointed" by the event. The process of gleaning signs in circumstances, from which to conjecture, Smollett calls "reconnoitering":

Fathom had previously *reconnoitered* the ground, and discovered some *marks* of inflammability in Mademoiselle's constitution... she was of an age when the little loves and young desires take possession of the fancy; he therefore *concluded* that she had the more leisure to indulge these enticing images of pleasure that youth never fails to create. (1, 52)

But the *issue* of his last *adventure* had reinforced his caution; and, for the present, he found means to suppress the dictates of his avarice and ambition; resolving to employ his whole *penetration* in *reconnoitering* the ground, before he should venture to take the field again. (I, 191)

then our *adventurer*, approaching the bedside, *reconnoitered* the patient, examined the medicines which had been administered, and lifting up his *eyes* in *expressive* silence, detached the footman with a new order to the apothecary. (II, 130–31)

The reading of signs in ordinary conjecturing, then, is explicitly to be understood on the scientific model we examined in chapter II.

The information from which probable conjectures may be taken – the locus of signification that must be reconnoitered – is, according to the paradigm we have seen before, "circumstances" (facility in sorting out probable circumstances is "circumspection," while ineptitude is "credulity"). I cite a number of examples to demonstrate that this commonplace word does indeed bear such a burden of meaning:

The German paid implicit *faith* to every *circumstance* of his *story*, which indeed could not well be supposed to be invented extempore... [though Ferdinand has done so]. (I, 115)

for he soon *perceived* him to be a humorist, and, from that *circumstance, derived* an happy *presage* of his own success. (I, 162)

In a word, he rendered this *conjecture* so *plausible*, by wresting the *circumstances* of their *behavior* and retreat, that poor Elenor implicitly *believed* they were the thieves by whom she had suffered. (I, 250)

All these *circumstances* had been duly *weighed* by our *projector*. (I, 282)

Our *adventurer considered* all these *circumstances* with his wonted *sagacity*. (II, 112)

I could not have *believed* the human mind capable of such degeneracy, or that traitor endowed with such pernicious *cunning* and *dissimulation*, had not her *tale* been *congruous, consistent,* and *distinct,* and fraught with *circumstances* that left no room to *doubt* the least article. (II, 203)

Renaldo had no *reason* to *doubt* the truth of this *story*, every *circumstance* of which tended to *corroborate* the *intelligence* he had already received touching the character of Fathom. (II, 227)

and framed such a *plausible tale*, from the *circumstances* of your distress. (II, 279)

As narrator, Smollett feels free to tell the reader that the story he is telling is to be judged in the same way that the characters judge each other, and the stories they so frequently tell each other: "These *circumstances* being *premised*, the reader will not be surprised to find..." (I, 44). Further, although to Smollett the word *casuistry* has a bad odor, he is aware that casuistry is just such a weighing of circumstances as he so often describes and enjoins:

At every tea-table [Ferdinand's] name was occasionally put to the torture, with that of the vile creature whom he had seduced, though it was generally taken for granted by all those female *casuists* that she must have made the first advances, for it could not be supposed that any man would take much trouble in laying schemes for the ruin of a person whose attractions were so slender, especially considering the ill state of her health, a *circumstance* that seldom adds to a woman's beauty or good-humor. (II, 152)

(These women are casuists, of course, precisely in that their weighing of signs and circumstances is self-interested and faulty.) The description of the qualities of a probable story ("congruous, consistent, and distinct, and fraught with circumstances that left no room for doubt") is a prescription not only for trust in testimony, but as we have seen, for the construction of a probable and decorous literary work, a work "executed with propriety, probability" such as Smollett promises in his auto-dedication to *Fathom* (I, 3). In their uses in tales within the main tale, Smollett's probable circumstances combine the literary and the philosophic aims we have already observed: they are the units of literary construction while being also the data of probable judgment, judgment by both characters and reader.

Several modern readers of *Fathom* have noticed elements of this vocabulary and puzzled over its origin. In an argument heavily indebted to Strauss and to Brewster Rogerson, Thomas Preston suggests that Smollett's "marks" and "signs" of passion, which often arise in the novelist's passionate "tableau scenes," derive from the art of painting the passions as that art was expounded by theorists of the stage. As we have seen, many such writers discuss what Garrick called the actor's technique of putting "on the various mental and bodily Emotions arising from the Humors, Virtues and Vices, incident to human Nature," and many, like Aaron Hill, ground such technique in a "knowledge of those passions and a power to put on, at will, the marks and colours which distinguish them."[9]

By citing such sources, Preston tries, if not to obviate, at least to extenuate Strauss' criticism of Smollett's formulaic way of portraying passion, and to explain the interchangeability of many of these formulae as the reflection of the same failure of resolution to be found in the manuals of acting. Yet this account of Smollett's signs, while partly correct, leaves unexplained too much of what we have already seen going on in *Fathom*. First of all, Smollett does not use the language of signs and marks only to paint passions, nor do such signs appear more frequently in his tableau scenes than in the rest of the narrative (unless every opening of a character is to be considered a "tableau"); further, the theory of acting cannot explain why Smollett so consistently draws attention to his signs *as signs*, or why he so explicitly calls on the language of sign-inference. Like the theorists of acting, Smollett is drawing on and making special use of a theory whose implications reach far beyond stage passions.

"And it is well known to a number of cunning and astute persons; whose eyes dwell upon the faces and gestures of men, and make their own advantage of it, as being the most part of their ability and wisdom." This is not Smollett describing the sagacity of Ferdinand, but Francis Bacon in the *De Augmentis* on expertise in physiognomy (IV, 376). As we have seen, Bacon treats physiognomics in his section on "the doctrine concerning the League or Common Bond between the soul and body"; according to Bacon, physiognomics is an art, because it has rules; moreover, to Bacon as to Smollett, the faculty of reading physiognomic signs is *sagacity*:

Nor let any one imagine that a sagacity of this kind may be of use with respect to particular persons, but cannot fall under a general rule; for we all laugh and weep and frown and blush in nearly the same fashion; and so it is (for the most part) in the more subtle motions.[10]

Here we find also an explanation for Smollett's "monotonous" and "formulaic" portrayals of the marks of the mind: in the economy of nature, such "monotony" is uniformity and simplicity (i.e., governance by few and simple laws).

The characters and narrator of *Fathom* make explicit reference to physiognomics four times (I, 221; II, 11, 20, 79), but I do not mean to suggest that physiognomics is in any sense the "key" to the novel. Smollett was of course himself a physician, and it is no accident that for two long stretches of *Fathom*, Ferdinand sets up as a doctor. Not only has Smollett a specialist's knowledge of the field to bring to bear in a satire; medicine, a science rooted as we have seen in the observation and weighing of signs, typifies what Smollett consistently describes as the nature of Ferdinand's genius for conjecture. Physiognomics is but a prominent example of a science embodying the logical procedures that make up the fabric both of the novel and of medicine as Smollett knew it.

Smollett learned medicine at the hands of his friends John Armstrong and the Hunters, whose special interest was the nervous system, as understood through the mechanist physiology innovated by Descartes.[11] In *Fathom*, many of the passions' external signs are explained as products of stimulation of the nerves, as indeed are some occasions of failure to manifest such signs:

His nerves were too much overpowered by this sudden recognition, to manifest the sensation of his soul by external signs. (II, 268)

It is tempting to suppose that Smollett's last works contain fewer explicit uses of the language of signs and conjectures than do his first three novels because the author had by then given up the profession of medicine.[12] In any case, Smollett's notions of the economy of the physiological machine were popular among his contemporaries, as is testified in many titles such as Armstrong's own notorious *Economy of Love* (1736).

Critics from Alan McKillop onward have noticed Smollett's habit of explaining human response mechanically, and sometimes of likening men to animals. "Along with the animal symbols there may be symbols of mechanism; men become grotesque puppets or automata."[13] (In physiognomics, it should be noted, there long existed beside the study of human signs a related study of "theriologic" physiognomy, and Augustan criticism turns frequently to such signs as they appear in beast fables to explain the sense in which a narrative may be "allegorical.")[14] Augustan satire, of course, habitually likens its butts to animals and vermin, but to suppose that Smollett means such comparisons always as caricature or grotesque would be seriously to misread his intentions. More often, he means merely to make a point about the human make-up, an economy which is at base an "animal machine":

It was not from reason and reflection that I took these measures for my personal safety; but, in consequence of an involuntary instinct, that seems to operate in the animal machine, while the faculty of thinking is suspended. (*Fathom*, I, 217–18)

The context here is wholly serious, as it is when most of the signs of passion or effects of the nerves appear. References to mechanism are not, as is so often said, elements of Smollett's satiric arsenal, but much more often simple expressions of his theory of man. Unless most signification were mechanical, *Fathom*'s whole apparatus of signs and conjectures (as well as medicine itself) could not exist, nor could Ferdinand's "insinuating art" which works by feigning signs. Smollett himself distinguishes not only the fallibility and certainty of signs, but also the degree to which they are volitional:

So saying, he gently opened the door, and, at sight of the German and his wife, who, he well knew, waited for his exit, started back, and gave tokens of confusion, which was partly real and partly affected. (I, 114)

Further elements must be added to make involuntary (mechanical; natural) signs satiric; usually this involves either making the cause of the sign itself grotesque, or making it the occasion of some character's gross misconstruction.

Smollett's heroes characteristically are "sincere" in their manifestations even of volitional signs; his villains design and deceive by making artificial signs appear natural. Education, furthermore, teaches among other things the insincere use of voluntary signs, so that characters are the more noble as they combine education and sincerity. One of Smollett's greatest sources of fun is the sincerity of low characters; although modern readers have chosen not to take very seriously his defenses of low characters and situations, arguing that Smollett was merely trying to fend off the abuse which he knew would be (and was) heaped upon him for their use, yet from the point of view of his use of signs, we must give these defenses a hearing. In the Preface to *Roderick Random* (1748), he argues:

> though I foresee, that some people will be offended at the mean scenes in which he is involved, I persuade myself the judicious will not only perceive the necessity of describing those situations to which he must of course be confined, in his low estate; but also find entertainment in viewing those parts of life, where the humours and passions are undisguised by affectation, ceremony, or education; and the whimsical peculiarities of disposition appear as nature has implanted them. (xlv)

Sincerity accounts for the particular susceptibility of such characters to varying emotions, as it does for their not dissimulating the signs of such emotions; Smollett likes to demonstrate this in mass, as he does when Roderick recounts to Strap the history of his misfortunes:

> During the recital, my friend was strongly affected, according to the various situations described: He started with surprize, glowed with indignation, gaped with curiosity, smiled with pleasure, trembled with fear, and wept with sorrow, as the vicissitudes of my life inspired these different passions; and when my story was ended, signified his amazement on the whole, by lifting up his eyes and hands, and protesting, that tho' I was a young man, I had suffered more than all the blessed martyrs. (253)

More decorously, but to the same effect, Renaldo testifies to his good nature in *Fathom* by reacting similarly to Monimia's recital of her trials:

> While the young lady rehearsed the particulars of this detail, Renaldo sustained a strange vicissitude of different passions. Surprise, sorrow, fear, hope, and indignation raised a most tumultuous conflict in his bosom. (II, 206)

In part because of his education, Renaldo is farther from the "animal machine" than is Strap.

This understanding of sincerity as unimpeded natural signification (as well as the literary and philosophical presuppositions on which it rests) becomes increasingly important to Augustan fiction as the century progresses. Beattie argues in the *Essays* that literature flourishes best in cultural contexts not yet so developed that artifice masks natural signification, a context in which men most easily afford what we have come to understand as *signal examples* of generalizations: such a society is

one wherein men are raised above savage life, and considerably improved by arts, government, and conversation; but not advanced so high in the ascent towards politeness, as to have acquired a habit of disguising their thoughts and passions, and of reducing their behavior to the uniformity of mode.

In such a context, by Beattie's identification of nature with decorum, "the characters of particular men will approach to the nature of poetical or general ideas" (60). Especially signal in sentimental fiction are children; Beattie says of Joshua Reynolds that he "is particularly observant of children, whose looks and attitudes, being less under the control of art and local manners, are more character-istical of the species, than those of men and women" (58–59). Whereas in the earlier part of the century, Dennis might disqualify children from major dramatic roles on the grounds of their "inconsistent manners," and even Hogarth in the *Analysis of Beauty* finds that "There is little to be seen by childrens faces, more than that they are heavy or lively; and scarcely that unless they are in motion," later Augustan writers and artists value children, and for precisely these sorts of concerns; children provide not only easily legible indices of emotion, but are by extension truth-tellers in general.[15] In *Nature and Art* (1796), for example, Elizabeth Inchbald joins ideas about noble savagery with that of the child as natural signifier in the character of Henry, the "savage boy" whose years spent growing up apart from society make him an involuntary and irrepressible – hence also sincere – critic of English institutions. Smollett presents a type of such childlike sincerity in *Sir Launcelot Greaves*, in the person of Captain Crowe:

He was an excellent seaman, brave, active, friendly in his way, and scrupulously honest; but as little acquainted with the world as a suckling child; whimsical, impatient, and so impetuous, that he could not help breaking in upon the conversation, whatever it might be, that seemed to burst from him by involuntary impulse. (2)

Smollett does not use the child itself as natural signifier, however; his focus is on the genesis and interpretation of signs involuntary, voluntary and feigned, and on the relation of verbal to nonverbal expression. His emphases reflect a continuous, often painful, some-times tragic awareness that all we know of others we know by signs: all our knowledge is irremediably *mediate*.

Despite the sincere involuntary outbursts of characters in *Fathom*, despite the frequency with which characters give signs of their thoughts and feelings, despite even the great amount of talking that goes on in the novel, characters in Smollett's world are always at a distance from one another's thoughts: they are always isolated. They know one another only by signs and conjectures from signs, indications that all too often, because either of dissimulation or simple insagacity, lead astray. That "lack of access, one soul to another," which John Traugott finds to have been a "controlling fact of life for both Sterne and Locke," is, I suggest, typical of Augustan fiction.[16] As Smollett's emphatic dependence on the vocabulary of signs and probable inference makes clear, his is a world of Lockean minds severally embodied, knowing only their own sensations and reflections, observers and critics of the drama of ideas that unfolds before them. Locke and his contemporaries were unanimous in holding that our knowledge of other minds, let alone that of what others are thinking or saying, is through signs (inference from signs); all Smollett's characters' knowledge of the world and of each other is painfully and dangerously mediate, as the verbal devices and larger structural procedures of the novel (as well as its explicit statements) make us continually aware. The world of *Fathom* as it is visible to each character is a canvas in the manner of Le Brun: each is a spectator, and like the reader, he must make the best of the painting he can. (In the same way readers of *Humphry Clinker* must penetrate and weigh comparatively the divergent signs provided by letters which are frequently divergent commentaries on the same events.) What we are examining in *Fathom*, then, is the narrative representation of and response to the Lockean world of probable signs.

Language in such a world is as much a barrier as a bridge between characters. In physiognomics, rhetoric, and the theory of acting, the eyes had since ancient times been identified as our most expressive feature; in Augustan narrative, it is usually love, manifesting itself in a "speaking face" and especially in the eyes, that breaks free of the barriers separating characters one from another and provides privileged access to each other's thoughts. One thinks here of the glances that Anne Elliot and Captain Harville exchange at the end of *Persuasion*, just before Anne is reunited to Wentworth after years of isolation — glances that convey whole propositions and commands.[17] Characters such as Renaldo and Monimia also use this language:

She made no verbal reply; but answered by an emphatic glance, more eloquent than all the power of rhetoric and speech. This language, which is universal in the world of love, he perfectly well understood, and, in token of that faculty, sealed the assent which she had smiled, with a kiss imprinted on her polished forehead. (II, 260)

(What is most surprising about such a passage is not its use of nonverbal signs but its pausing to explain their logic.) But as Spenser's Una warns Redcrosse of the impediments to knowledge in the confused world of matter (the Wandering Wood), using textbook examples of sign-inference ("Oft fire is without smoke, / And perill without show"),[18] so in *Fathom* Ferdinand (like Archimago) is quite capable of simulating even loving glances, so that even these signs are dangerously fallible:

I speak the genuine, though imperfect, language of my heart [says Ferdinand convincingly to Monimia]. Words, even the most pathetic, cannot do justice to my love. (II, 92)

Our adventurer and the daughter had already exchanged their vows, by the expressive language of the eyes. (I, 78)

The novel's physiognomists are as often wrong as right in their conjectures; Don Diego boasts of his penetration in the midst of seriously misjudging Ferdinand:

I was at first sight prepossessed in your favor, for, notwithstanding the mistakes which men daily commit in judging from appearances, there is something in the physiognomy of a stranger from which one cannot help forming an opinion of his character and disposition. For once, my penetration hath not failed me; your behavior justifies my decision; you have treated me with that sympathy and respect which none but the generous will pay to the unfortunate. (I, 221)

Even that most certain of indicators, action, may be merely a false sign.

Language – both visual and verbal – is a barrier in the sense that it is not a certain communicator. And even when language has the most certain relation possible to the speaker's inner state – when sign most infallibly reveals signified – it may be also most meaningless. When it is merely the causal product of inner states, verbal language becomes simply a reflex, an action rather than a speech or communication. An extreme case of this is Random's outburst to Strap, on learning of Narcissa's attentions to a nobleman: "It set all my passions into a new ferment, I swore horrible oaths without meaning or application, I foamed at the mouth." In *Fathom*, expression often approaches this reflex state, often as the result of high passion or drunkenness:

This was so far from being an agreeable intimation to the jeweler, that he was struck dumb with astonishment and vexation, and it was not till after a long pause that he pronounced the word Sacrament! with an emphasis denoting the most mortifying surprise. (I, 108)

this stately declaration, which as the immediate effect of anger and ebreity... (I, 167)

Some of Fathom's silences are "expressive silences," but most are the products of a physical reaction such as the jeweler's, a paralysis of the nerves Smollett is particularly fond of describing.[19]

But language is even a barrier in its simple mediacy, a mediacy of which we are emphatically reminded by the particular formulae Smollett habitually uses to introduce speech. Whether two characters are sitting together conversing or one is imprisoned in a tower while the other is far below hoping the prisoner will give him some sign, Smollett describes their intercourse in the same terms:

Renaldo ... determined, as the last effort, to ride around the castle in the open day, on pretense of taking the air, when, peradventure, the Countess would see him from the place of her confinement, and favor him with some mark or token of her being alive. (II, 190)

"... wilt thou indulge this wretched youth with some kind signal of thy notice, with some token of thy approbation?" (II, 244)

Over and again, characters are not described as speaking to one another in direct or indirect discourse; they do not "tell" one another their thoughts, or "say" them or "declare" them; rather, the narrator tells us that one has "signified" a thought to another, or that he has "given an expression" of some feeling or idea. Conversations here, as Traugott remarks of *Tristram Shandy*, give the air of being "performed,"[20] and Smollett uses the same terminology whether the performance – the signs – are verbal or nonverbal. His use of *signify* shows the pattern most clearly:

he had signified his sentiments on that head to the Count. (II, 33)

when their commands were signified to him in a manner suited to his character... (II, 120)

Melvil, having signified his request... (II, 82)

Trebasi having intercepted a letter to her from Renaldo, signifying his intention to return to the empire... (II, 201)

Expression similarly comprehends both verbal and nonverbal signs:

Miss exhorted him to keep up his spirits, with many expressions of unreserved sympathy and regard. (I, 42)

... gave a loose to her sorrow in the most immoderate expressions of anguish and affliction.

The assimilation of verbal to nonverbal signs, clear through the frequent iteration of such uses of *signify* and *expression*, the more tellingly reveals the epistemic isolation of *Fathom*'s characters.[21] The same devices that isolate characters one from another, furthermore, isolate them as well from the reader: characters in *Fathom* do not introspect for us; seldom, except when narrating long stories, do they speak *in propria persona* and directly (the novel contains little dialogue); their thoughts are recorded in the very indirect form of indirect discourse which is the language of expressions and signs. It is primarily through the controlling narrator – especially in his manipulation of tone – that we do not suffer in relation to the characters the same fate they suffer in relation to each other; but of us the readers, as of its characters, the novel requires powers of probable conjecture and inference from signs.

The necessary epistemic response to such a world as this is that "sagacity" which is the ground both of Ferdinand's "penetration," his "faculty of discerning," and of his "art," his "gift of deceiving" (I, 69–70). "The Artist," writes the anonymous author of a dissertation on *The Polite Arts* (1749), "is essentially an Observer" (26); Ferdinand frequently is described as, and finds himself in the position of, a *spectator*:

he was often concerned in private concerts that were given in the hotels of noblemen; by which means he became more and more acquainted with the persons, manners, and characters of high life, which he *contemplated* with the most industrious *attention*, as a *spectator*, who, being altogether unconcerned in the performance, is at more liberty to *observe* and enjoy the particulars of the entertainment. (I, 109)

Attention we will see again to be the first requisite of the reader of signs; the greatest enemy to such attention and to correct sign-inference is passion.

how upright soever a man's intentions may be, he will, in the performance of such a task, be sometimes *misled* by his own *phantasy*, and represent objects, as they appeared to him, through the *mists of prejudice and passion*. (I, 5)

She, on the other hand, *misconceived* his sudden retreat; and now they *beheld* the actions of each other through the *false medium of prejudice and resentment*. (II, 58)

The passages might have been written by Crousaz or the author of the *Conduct of the Understanding*; imagination (the parent of prejudice and spur of passion) does not read signs, but clouds such ideas as appear to the mind – dims further the twilight of probability, obscuring inference from action to motive. Ferdinand himself, because he has no settled values, has no prejudices (save perhaps an excess of suspicion); and because he has no settled passions but avarice and lust, usually conjectures correctly. His misreadings of signs come (when at all) at those moments when he is most heatedly pursuing the objects of these passions; more often, his penetration is unobscured:

He seldom or never *erred* in his *observations* on the human *heart*. (I, 48)

He in a moment *saw through* all the characters of the party, and adapted himself to the humor of each individual. ... (I, 160)

It is such penetrating insight into the human heart that Smollett calls *sagacity*, an insight into character that makes possible Ferdinand's extraordinary "reflection and foresight" (I, 45), his ability to judge of the "probable consequences" of actions, and of "probable means" of success (I, 45, 110; II, 163).

howsoever unapt his understanding might be to receive and retain the usual culture of the schools, he was naturally a genius self-taught, in point of *sagacity* and invention. – He *dived into characters* of mankind, with a *penetration* peculiar to himself, and, had he been admitted as a pupil in any *political* academy, would certainly become one of the ablest statesmen in Europe. (I, 45)

He had *perceived* a perplexity and perturbation in the *countenance* of the Swiss, when he first entered the coffee-room; his blunt and precipitate way of accosting him seemed to *denote* confusion and compulsion; and, in the midst of his ferocity, this *accurate observer discerned* the trepidation of fear. By the help of these *signs*, his *sagacity* soon *comprehended* the nature of his schemes, and prepared accordingly a formal defiance. (I, 272)

This sagacity is what earns Ferdinand the name of "Fathom"; it is not only what makes him an excellent judge of the manifest signs and circumstances exhibited in the actions and narrations of others, but also what makes him a teller of convincing tales himself. As a literary probabilist, Ferdinand has a sure sense of audience that gains him the popular victory even, for example, in an argument about medicine, in which his opponent is a trained physician:

Secondly, in all disputes upon physic that happen betwixt a person who really understands the art, and an *illiterate* pretender, the arguments of the first will seem obscure and unintelligible to those who are unacquainted with the previous systems of which they are built; while the other's theory, derived from *common notions*, and *superficial observation*, will be more agreeable, because *better adapted to the comprehension of the hearers*. (I, 294–95)

Thus the learned (or those pretending to learning) persuade the vulgar; thus the philosophical probabilist rests his case on *notiones communes*. The reverse of Ferdinand's abilities appear in a character such as the much-misled Captain Minikin, whom Ferdinand meets in prison; for Smollett as for other Augustan satirists, the mark of an inattentive observer, and hence an unsagacious conjecturer, is a tendency to scatterbrained *digression*.[22]

Sagacity, penetration, and Ferdinand's spectatorial stance are a response to the conditions of knowing in a Lockean world in which knowing is a kind of seeing – so much so as to make commonplace analogies between the mind and a theater, mental processes and the unfolding of a drama, take on special meaning. Thomas Reid writes off-handedly in his *Inquiry into the Human Mind*, "The process of nature in perception by the senses, may therefore be conceived as a kind of drama, wherein some things are performed behind the scenes, others are represented to the mind in different scenes, one succeeding another." Reid even likens the rules that govern the sequence of our ideas to the "laws of the drama," those rules of probability which govern the way each "scene is ... succeeded by another," on stage as in the mind (213); hence Smollett's likening of Ferdinand's sagacity to that of a good interpreter of a drama.

Ferdinand's sagacious gift of conjecture is called a skill in *calculation*; it is what the information theorists call a gift for "uncertainty management." Typically, because what he must read are *probable* signs, Ferdinand is an expert gambler; gaming provides for Smollett a symbol of his probabilistic skill:

Fathom found some difficulty in concealing his joy at the mention of this last amusement, which had been one of his chief studies, and in which he could calculate all the chances with the utmost exactness and certainty. (1, 186)

Ferdinand's skill at cards is not cheating, but probabilism; when among other "adventurers" for whom the "arts" of gaming have been "carried to such a surprising pitch of finesse and dexterity, as discouraged him from building his schemes on that foundation" (1, 69), he exits the field; in London especially he finds that "the art of gaming is reduced into a regular system" and that gamblers ordinarily spend part of their day "in algebraical calculations" (1, 264). Ferdinand is not a mathematical probabilist but a genius self-taught, where "genius" means the capacity to read signs. (In the same way, Captain Booth, the inept conjecturer and sign-reader of Fielding's *Amelia*, typically loses in gambling.)

Chance and cheating are in the world of *Fathom* what make a sagacity such as Ferdinand's pressingly necessary. Not only may insincerity dissimulate (manifest false signs); as Paul-Gabriel Boucé writes, "Fathom's whole life is placed under the sign of chance, lucky or unlucky." Boucé catalogues at length the important turns in the novel's plot which result solely from chance.[23] In such a world, calculation is despite its occasional undependability a means of protection from uncertainty necessary to all. Ferdinand earns Boucé's characterization of him as a fine specimen of "literary teratology" – he is often called a "monster" – but it is not his skill in calculation and conjecture Smollett means to question, but merely the uses to which he puts his skills. The novel's earliest reviewers recognized that Smollett means equally to condemn, as Griffiths said in the *Monthly*, the "criminal credulity" of his virtuous characters – Renaldo, Don Diego, Monimia, and all the rest of Ferdinand's dupes and gulls.[24] Candor and a good heart require the supplement of calculation and a capacity for probable conjecture if they are to survive. This is Smollett's point in playing Ferdinand off against Renaldo and Monimia at all, and when seen in this light, *Fathom* appears less open to the criticism so often levelled at it, that its plot is unhappily bifurcated.[25] Even in the novel's last ten chapters, where Ferdinand does not appear until the very end, he still controls the action; *Fathom* ends as Renaldo, Monimia, and Don Diego come to understand his art and their own credulity.

Whether the present discussion assists in rescuing the reputation of a work which Robert Alter has called "as disastrous a failure of imagination as any novelist of stature has ever been guilty of" is far less important than that we understand the construction – the conditions of knowledge – of the novel's world.[26] If *Fathom* is an artistic failure, it is so not because of its disorganized plot – such a criterion would damn all Smollett's works – but simply because it is not as interesting in its details as works such as *Roderick Random*. *Fathom* lacks *Random*'s richness of historical detail; because more general, it is more repetitious. This repetitiveness at once condemns *Fathom* as an object of literary evaluation and renders it the more useful to literary interpretation.

The conditions of knowledge in this Lockean world penetrate *Fathom*'s verbal texture and inform its didactic meaning at every level. They govern the novel's fundamental structural procedures, organizing devices designed at once to provide characters with the data from which conjectures must be made and to invite readers to probable judgment. Aside from simple narration of events – rarely "pure" narration, but ironic commentary – Smollett habitually uses three main procedures in building his story, devices whose use can of course overlap: declarations and "expressions"; stories within the main story; and short, relatively detachable accounts of schemes, plots, plans, hopes, expectations, and conjectures, together with the judgment upon each which is its outcome. At every point, characters and reader are called upon to exert judgment: ironic commentary teaches readers to put events in their proper light by bringing to bear

information gleaned elsewhere (i.e., to discriminate relevantly probable circumstances). "Expressions" and recountings may mislead,
or be deliberate lies; conjectures are always to be confirmed or
overturned by the event:

Nevertheless, they were mistaken in both these conjectures. (I, 27)

... in such a manner, as confirmed their conjectures. (I, 36)

Here he was not disappointed in his conjecture. (I, 60)

With regard to his confederate, his conjecture was perfectly right. (I, 144)

in sundry subsequent attacks, by which his first conjecture was confirmed... (I,
177)

While I was thus undeceived in my conjecture touching his birth and quality... (I,
210)

His conjecture was verified the next morning by a visit from the chevalier. (I, 272)

At a variety of structural levels, then, the novel is composed of a
series of incidents and contexts each of which is built of conjecture
and its event, occasions for and invitations to probable judgment.

Intercalated tales are simply a special case of this didactic procedure of mapping meaning on structure. Characters in *Fathom* over
and again give narrative accounts of themselves; the novel teems
with tales within the main tale, the longest of which are the histories
of Don Diego, Monimia, and Ferdinand himself. Sometimes these
are histories of systematic misjudgment, sometimes (as in Ferdinand's case) of systematic attempts to mislead others' judgment;
always, they are occasions demanding acts of judgment from an
audience. The characters who listen to such tales, furthermore,
function in these cases not only as characters making judgments of
their own but as surrogate audiences to the reader, counterparts to
the judging reader who act as positive or negative guides –
trustworthy or unknowingly ironic guides – in the making of
probable inferences. (Perhaps the most extended use of this device in
Augustan fiction occurs in *Amelia*, where fully a sixth of the novel
consists of Booth's narration to Miss Matthews of his past history,
punctuated by her sometimes penetrating, sometimes misguided
inferences from what she hears, inferences like those the reader is
himself seeking to make about Booth, and which he must therefore
sift in the attempt to understand Booth's character.) Understood in
this way, the stories within Smollett's main story are continuous in
function with the simple declarations and "expressions": both are
organizations of signs which must be sifted by a process of inference,
didactic devices designed to aid in that rectification of judgment
which is the novel's theme and aim.

Smollett's narrative advances as much by his telling us what each character conjectures, hopes, expects, and plans as by his telling what at any given moment each actually does: contexts for and acts of judgment, not the simple retailing of events, are the substance from which *Fathom* is built. In this his narrative procedure is typical of the Augustan novel. Just as the interpolated tale is far more common in Augustan fiction than in that of any other period, the novel which dramatizes (in an effort to inculcate) probable judgment, through discrete structures of conjecture and expectation – probable signs – is a deeply Augustan phenomenon. It is a narrative response to a world understood to be composed of probable signs, and to the conditions of knowledge which such a world imposes.[27]

(2) TEACHING PROBABLE JUDGMENT: FIELDING

– What Place is not filled with austere Libertines?

Now that an austere Countenance is no Token of Purity of Heart, I readily concede. So far otherwise, it is perhaps rather a Symptom of the contrary. But the Satyrist surely never intended by these Words, which have grown into a Proverb, utterly to depreciate an Art on which so wise a Man as *Aristotle* hath thought proper to compose a Treatise.

The Truth is, we almost universally mistake the Symptoms which Nature kindly holds forth to us; and err as grossly as a Physician would, who should conclude that a very high Pulse is a certain Indication of Health... In the same Manner, I conceive, the Passions of Men do commonly imprint sufficient Marks on the Countenance; and it is owing chiefly to want of Skill in the Observer, that Physiognomy is of so little Use and Credit in the World.

Fielding, "An Essay on the Knowledge of the Characters of Men" (1743)[28]

Where more than metaphor licenses the assimilation of knowing to a process of vision, probable judgment may most usefully be likened to an attentive survey of visual signs. In *Emma*, Jane Austen reminds readers of Emma's errors of judgment (and of the reasons for them) in passages of the most contracted symbolism. In one such passage, Frank Churchill, repairing Mrs. Bates' spectacles, joins Emma and Jane Fairfax in conjecturing about who has given Jane her new piano; the gift has of course come from Frank himself, and his speech on this occasion should be a sign to Emma:

"Till I have a letter from Co. Campbell," said [Jane], in a voice of forced calmness, "I can imagine nothing with any confidence. It must all be conjecture."

"Conjecture – aye, sometimes one conjectures right, and sometimes one conjectures wrong. I wish I could conjecture how soon I shall make this rivet quite firm. What nonsense one talks, Miss Woodhouse, when hard at work, if one talks at all; – your real workmen, I suppose, hold their tongues; but we gentlemen labourers if we get hold of a word – Miss Fairfax said something about conjecturing. There, it is done. I have the pleasure, madam, (to Mrs. Bates,) of restoring your spectacles, healed for the present." (217–18)

"You have more circumspection than is wanted," cries Mrs. Primrose petulantly after Mr. Burchell in Goldsmith's *Vicar of Wakefield*, Burchell having suggested a careful scrutiny of the two "noble" ladies who have invited Olivia to London; by an ironic reversal typical of the story, on the next page Mrs. Primrose is found to cry, "The blockhead has been imposed upon, and should have known his company better," upon discovering that Moses has been hoodwinked by a rascal disguised as a scholar into selling the family horse for "a gross of green spectacles."[29] In Henry Fielding's *Joseph Andrews* (1742), though it may be how one behaves in the dark that most clearly reveals good or ill nature (Adams saving Fanny in a dark wood, Adams sleeping chastely with her in a dark house), it is how well one observes what is visible in daylight that is the test of prudence. More than any other novelist before Jane Austen, Fielding takes probable judgment as his theme and creates in his fiction structures which, to be interpreted correctly, demand an exercise of that same judgment.

(i)

... he no sooner perceived from his Father's Account, the Agreement of every Circumstance, of Person, Time, and Place, than he threw himself at his Feet, and embracing his Knees, with Tears begged his Blessing.

Joseph Andrews, bk. iv, ch. 15[30]

Joseph Andrews betrays in every chapter its author's controlling interest in education: the novel begins with an abstract discussion of the relative merits in teaching of precept and examples; Parson Adams, vain of his abilities as a schoolmaster, lectures Joseph on different methods of education, and on the role of travel in education (appropriately, in a novel itself cast as an educational journey); Mr. Wilson complains that in his years of youthful dissipation in London, he had neither father nor schoolmaster to guide him. Joseph writes to his sister, referring to Adams, "What fine things are good Advice and good examples!" (46); the novel closes as Joseph recovers a father and guide in Wilson himself. Throughout, Fielding's forceful narrative presence lectures, scolds, and cajoles readers, guiding the process of reading the novel in a manner intended to educate the reader's judgment.

Fielding's novel seeks to inculcate both specific moral ideas and, more generally, the capacity of a penetrating and probable judgment – a faculty which works by comparison and discrimination – primarily by inviting readers to exercise judgment in finding rela-

tions among the novel's parts. He understands these "parts" in turn
through the hierarchic model of literary structure. We may begin our
analysis at the level of the episode; in these discrete units of narrative, devices of narration and characterization function in two
primary ways. In Fielding's hands, the novel is essentially a repetitive
form which teaches through the structural procedures of repetition
with slight variation, and repetition with ironic reversal. The process
of recognizing and interpreting these didactic structures is the
process of judgment Fielding means the novel to teach.

Through a sequence of episodes embodying the first procedure,
for instance, *Joseph Andrews* comes progressively to define the
nature of charity, the virtue of which Adams tells Trulliber, "there is
no Command more express, no Duty more frequently enjoined"
(167). In Book I appears Mrs. Tow-wouse, whose motto is
"Common Charity, a F—t!" (56); only when she learns that Joseph
may be a gentleman – and so have money – does she offer him
hospitality. At the end of book III, to Adams' quotation from Isaac
Barrow defining charity as "a generous Disposition to relieve the
Distressed," Peter Pounce replies: "There is something in that
Definition . . . which I like well enough; it is, as you say, a Disposition
– and does not so much consist in the Act as in the Disposition to do
it" (274). From the speeches and actions of Mrs. Tow-wouse, we are
to infer that true charity is not self-interested; from those of Pounce,
that it is an active virtue. Other instances flesh out the concept
further. This technique of presenting a series of positive and negative
examples of the same values or views in a series of differing
situations designed so that readers may by degrees construct a
complete idea of each moral quality and of the ways each can be
expected to be practiced or perverted by different types of people is a
strategy central to both *Joseph Andrews* and *Tom Jones*; it is also the
strategy which in his Preface to *David Simple* Fielding finds to
govern his sister's novel, which, he writes, "chiefly turns on the
Perfection or Imperfection of Friendship; of which noble Passion,
from its highest Purity to its lowest Falsehoods, and Disguises, this
little Book is . . . the most exact Model."[31]

It is to prosecute a didactic structure of repetition with slight
variation that *Joseph Andrews* and *Tom Jones* are so full of inns:
Fielding uses the device of the inn not because he is writing "novels
of the road" – an explanation that is in any case circular – but
because through this device he can gather the same and new characters in a repetitive series of situations partly the same, partly
different, thus creating contexts in which judgment must penetrate
character and discriminate fine gradations of difference in circum-

stances generally similar. Both uses of judgment require the same mental operations we have so often before heard discussed as those at use in the weighing of probable signs and circumstances, because it is just such signs and circumstances with which Fielding self-consciously compounds his narrative.

These fictional journeys thus operate in generally the same manner as do many non-fictional Augustan works of travel. Travel literature was so popular a genre in this period in part because it dramatized the process of learning – of how the mind works – as understood by the prevailing empiricist philosophy. Its structures of repetition and discrimination embody a theory of the way the mind gathers and compares ideas in gaining knowledge; Obadiah Walker writes of this process of learning in *Of Education*:

> By the way it will not be amiss to take notice, that as there is *no new thing* under the Sun, so *neither any new action*; but the same are represented over again under varying circumstances; so that he, who intends to be a wise man, must endeavour to distinguish the Action (as Physicians do in judging diseases) from the circumstances; that he may be able to give a good judgment and prognostick; and afterwards to frame a *generall rule*, which may stand him in stead at other times and occasions. (175)

The metaphor of travel for the process of education became so common that Lord Chesterfield casts several of his most didactic letters to his son as stories of travel, and habitually speaks of education as a journey.[32]

In *Joseph Andrews* Fielding is explicit about the educative function of his travel narrative: about both the nature of the judgment he means to inculcate and the moral fruits which its exercise will bear. Judgment – or what he more often calls *prudence* – has for Fielding three stages. First is the act of *attention* (bluntly, seeing what is in front of us, taking the stance of a careful observer or spectator); second, *sagacity* (alternatively called *penetration* or *discernment*), seeing through what is presented – by a process of inference from signs – to its hidden cause; and third, judgment itself, or *discrimination*, the process of making comparative distinctions among the facts our sagacity has opened for us, and of framing these into general rules. (Compare Fielding's theory of the stages of judgment to that of Obadiah Walker, above, p. 63, where of course "circumspection" stands in place of Fielding's "attention," "solertia" for his "sagacity.")

At the beginning of I. 11, Fielding presents a comic rendering of the procedure:

> It is an Observation sometimes made, that to indicate our Idea of a simple Fellow, we say, *He is easily to be seen through*: Nor do I believe it a more

improper Denotation of a simple Book. Instead of applying this to any particular
Performance, we chuse rather to remark the contrary in this History, where the
Scene opens itself by small degrees, and he is a sagacious Reader who can see two
Chapters before him. (48)

The novel is to be read as is a complex personality. The entire process
of judgment is legible in a fine set-piece (a "reading paradigm") at
the end of II. 2. Adams has once again lost his companions on the
road and is sitting by himself.

He therefore resolved to proceed slowly forwards, not doubting but that he
should be shortly overtaken, and soon came to a large Water, which filling the
whole Road, he saw no Method of passing unless by wading through, which he
accordingly did up to his Middle; but was no sooner got to the other Side, than he
perceived, if he had looked over the Hedge, he would have found a Foot-Path
capable of conducting him without wetting his Shoes.

His Surprize at *Joseph's* not coming up grew now very troublesome: he began
to fear he knew not what, and as he determined, to move no farther; and, if he did
not shortly overtake him, to return back; he wished to find a House of publick
Entertainment where he might dry his Clothes and refresh himself with a Pint:
but seeing no such (for no other Reason than because he did not cast his Eyes a
hundred Yards forwards) he sat himself down on a Stile, and pulled out his
Aeschylus.

A Fellow passing presently by, *Adams* asked him, if he could direct him to an
Alehouse. The Fellow who had just left it, and perceived the House and Sign to be
within sight, thinking he had jeered him, and being of a morose Temper, bad him
follow his Nose and be d—n'd. Adams told him he was a *saucy Jackanapes*;
upon which the Fellow turned about angrily: but perceiving *Adams* clench his
Fist he thought proper to go on without taking any farther notice.

A Horseman following immediately after, and being asked the same Question,
answered, 'Friend, there is one within a Stone's-Throw; I believe you may see it
before you.' *Adams* lifting up his Eyes, cry'd 'I protest and so there is;' and
thanking his Informer proceeded directly to it. (96)

Adams' obliviousness to the foot-path and the alehouse are of course
failures of attention. His reading habits are another mark of inat-
tention, though on at least one emergent occasion Adams proves his
good nature by allowing in his haste to serve others the same book to
fall into the fire. Most remarkably in the passage, Fielding provides
Adams with not one but two passers-by whom he may ask about the
alehouse; to see him safely through the chapter, only one would have
been necessary. The differing speeches of each passer-by again follow
the pattern of repetition with variation; they do so to provide
invitations to judgment, to sagacity and discrimination. We must
notice his repetition, penetrate character and cause, and explain
Fielding's procedure. Typically, Fielding helps us along in the first
case, telling us the first passer-by's thoughts and explaining his
words as the result of a "morose Temper"; he leaves us to exercise

our own penetration on the second (to infer from his gentle words to his character), to discriminate this second temperament from the first, and to generalize about the moral and social effects of each.

Adams, of course, is conspicuously incompetent in all three phases of prudence. He is habitually inattentive to such matters as how much money may be left in his pocket to meet the reckoning at an inn. He lacks sagacity and penetration: Fielding tells us, and we see all too often, that he "never saw farther into People than they desired to let him" (144) and that hypocrites especially are "a sort of People whom Mr. *Adams* never saw through" (270). He lacks discrimination; this is part of Fielding's point in the repetition of scenes of loss, in which Adams counsels Joseph to a patient faith in Providence upon the abduction of Fanny but fails to exhibit such patience on hearing of the death of his own son. Adams' insagacity may be the product of good nature – Fielding reveals its cause at I. 3, explaining that "As he had never any Intention to deceive, so he never suspected such a Design in others" (23) – and such insagacity may thus become a moral yardstick, a light that finds out hypocrisy; but it is not a trait the novel condones. His view that "Knowledge of Men is only to be learnt from Books" and therefore that "the only way of travelling by which any Knowledge is to be aquired" is "in Books" constitutes an attack on the very values and habits of mind *Joseph Andrews* seeks to inculcate – on the very form of the novel, an educational journey embodying and proposing conventional Augustan theories about travel as a way of learning (176, 182). We know of course that Adams is as inept an educator as he is a traveller from his failure to teach charity to his own family, as witnessed by their reception of Fanny in Book IV.

Judgment of the sort outlined is what Fielding's victimized innocents – Adams, Joseph, and Fanny – must learn in order to survive in a world full of Roasting Squires and partial Justices; it is also what in *Tom Jones* Fielding warns us he expects of his reader:

Bestir thyself therefore on this Occasion; for, tho' we will always lend thee proper Assistance in difficult Places, as we do not, like some others, expect thee to use the Arts of Divination to discover our Meaning; yet we shall not indulge thy Laziness where Nothing but thy own Attention is required, for thou art highly mistaken if thou dost imagine that we intended, when we began this great Work, to leave thy Sagacity nothing to do, or that without sometimes exercising this Talent, thou wilt be able to travel through our Pages with any Pleasure or Profit to thyself. (614)

(The contrast between rational sign-reading and the arbitrary appeal to signs in divination is an ancient one.)[33] In *Joseph Andrews*, as is well known, Fielding reminds us that we, like his characters, are to learn judgment: he calls us travellers on the journey with Joseph and Adams, and calls himself our guide. Not only do the characters punctuate their travels at a series of inns; in opening book II, the novelist tells us that "those little Spaces between our Chapters may be looked upon as an Inn or Resting-Place," and warns the over-hasty and hence inattentive reader that he may not be engaging the work properly: he urges such a reader to

consider of what he hath seen in the Parts he hath already past through; a Consideration which I take the Liberty to recommend a little to the Reader: for however swift his Capacity may be, I would not advise him to travel through these Pages too fast: for if he doth, he may probably miss the seeing some curious Productions of Nature which will be observed by the slower and more accurate Reader. (89–90)

Fielding's authorial intrusions into his narrative, his self-conscious theatricality and artifice, also serve this larger didactic end. In reminding us that the book we read is only a book, the players merely players; in titling a chapter of *Tom Jones* "Chapter 1, Containing five Pages of Paper"; in using all the visual and theatrical devices learned in his career as writer for the stage, Fielding deliberately distances us from his characters: whereas some authors lead us to empathize or identify with their creations – to treat them, in short, as real psychological beings – Fielding forces us with all the power of artifice to stand off from them, the more freely to exercise judgment on what we see. (In the same way, Brecht might have characters in a play appear in whiteface, that the audience not fall into undesired habits of empathetic identification with them.)

Repetition with slight variation is part of what a speedy reader reader will overlook; each instance of such repetition is an invitation to attention (we must notice the iteration), to sagacity (we must penetrate to those underlying qualities that we are meant to compare), and to discrimination (we must sort out the distinction Fielding means us to draw, the moral point of the paired episodes). In short, such a reader will not interpret the work properly, that is, will not find relations among its parts. Fielding, never very round-about, cannot help giving clear signs that significant repetition is near. In book III, for instance, chapter 10 tells of a dialogue between a poet and a player, while chapter 11 retails Adams' counsel of patient resignation to the will of Providence; lest the unwary reader fail to see a connection between such disparate circumstances, Fielding ends chapter 10:

The Poet, whose Fury was now raised, had just attempted to answer, when they were interrupted, and an end put to their Discourse by an Accident; which, if the Reader is impatient to know, he must skip over the next Chapter, which is a sort of Counterpart to this, and contains some of the best and gravest Matters in the whole Book. (263–64)

Again, IV. 10 announces "The History of two Friends," the story of Paul and Leonard read by little Dick. The heading to the following chapter reads, "In which the History is continued," but in fact little Dick never reads any more about Paul and Leonard; in a straightforward sense, the history is *not* continued. Instead, chapter 11 stands in a more complex relation to chapter 10 – another explicit invitation to judgment, to find a relation between parts.

The history of Paul and Leonard is in fact the last of three long interpolated tales which appear symmetrically in the structure of *Joseph Andrews* and which serve the same function as do the interpolated tales of Smollett. The first is "The History of Leonora, or the Unfortunate Jilt" (II. 4, 6); the second, Mr. Wilson's story, the longest chapter in the novel (III. 3). Despite the signal Fielding gives by placing the tales symmetrically, some of his best readers have seen them as no more than needless excrescences added to fill out a shapeless narrative. Lest we conclude with such readers, we should heed a warning Fielding gives the reader of *Tom Jones* – significantly, it comes in a digression:

we warn thee not too hastily to condemn any of the Incidents in this our History, as impertinent and foreign to our main Design, because thou dost not immediately conceive in what Manner such Incident may conduce to that Design. This Work may, indeed, be considered as a great Creation of our own; and for a little Reptile of a Critic to presume to find Fault with any of its Parts, without knowing the Manner in which the Whole is connected ... is a most presumptuous Absurdity. (524–25)

In fact, the digressions are typical of and central to the procedures and meanings of *Joseph Andrews*; they function in the same way as any of the characters' ordinary speeches. Each of the interpolated tales concerns vanity and pride; in each, pride is overcome only by suffering, and eventual retirement.[34] Leonora and Bellarmine are vain of wealth and beauty; Wilson moralizes that "Vanity is the worst of Passions, and more apt to contaminate the Mind than any other" (214), after retailing instance after instance of such contamination; Leonard and his wife are tenaciously vain of being always in the right. Leonora suffers and retires; Wilson suffers and retires; the third tale breaks off. The story breaks because by now Fielding expects us, his readers, to have a sufficiently trained judgment to complete it for ourselves. The end of the story is for us to write – but Fielding cannot resist giving us hints. Little Dick reads the tale only at Lady Booby's instigation, so that Beau Didapper can make his addresses to Fanny; Didapper does so, gets from Joseph a box on the ear, and retreats (suffering and reform). Leonora's story is interrupted, too, just after Bellarmine and Horatio have joined in a duel; in the intervening chapter, Adams enters a mock-epic battle at an inn, only to be soused with pig's blood. Fielding leaves to his sagacious readers the task of discovering how this interruption "conduces to the main design."

In the repetitive structure of *Joseph Andrews*, more memorable than such repetitions with variation are Fielding's ironic juxtapositions, or repetitions with reversal. Adams preaches willing submission to Providence, but explodes with grief at the death of his son; the patriot preaches willingness to lay down one's life for his country, then is scared off from saving the distressed Fanny because her attacker may have a gun; the lady on the coach disclaims all familiarity with strong liquor, but thieves find brandy in her flask; Adams praises private education, but Fielding makes a point of telling us that the Roasting Squire was educated at home. Each such reversal is a clear sign of character, an unmasker of hypocrisy and affectation; often reversals are ostentatiously improbable events, mere chance. As has often been noticed, Fielding's wholesale dependence on chance events is part of a greater argument for providential design;[35] such benevolent coincidences are what in chapter II we called improbable signs of divine presence. Once again, Fielding is explicit about the structure of his story, and the didactic ends such structure serves. At the end of II. 15, just before a rash of adventitious turns of luck, he puts the point in capital letters:

Plato or *Aristotle*, or some body else hath said, THAT WHEN THE MOST EXQUISITE CUNNING FAILS, CHANCE OFTEN HITS THE MARK, AND THAT BY MEANS THE LEAST EXPECTED. (170)

It is here that we first meet the pedlar, that peculiar surrogate for Providence (like Burchell in *The Vicar of Wakefield*) who comes in and out of the story at the most opportune moments: it is he who happens by at the end of Book II to pay the bill at an inn; in book IV, he happens by again, just in time to save Adams' drowning child, and later to reveal the mystery of Fanny's parentage (for he happened years before to have met the gypsies who kidnapped her). Like all virtuous agents', his life is an imitation of Christ's; but more particularly, this secular redeemer sacrifices of his own small store to pay the debts of other men; he raises the dead; he sees into others' hearts, and knows their secret natures. In II. 16, again unable to meet the bill at an inn, Joseph cries, "all my Concern is, how we shall get out of the House; unless God sends another Pedlar to redeem us" (175). And in introducing the pedlar, Fielding deliberately piles coincidence upon coincidence:

There chanced (for *Adams* had not Cunning enough to contrive it) to be at that time in the Alehouse, a Fellow, who had been formerly a Drummer in an *Irish* Regiment, and now travelled the Country as a Pedlar. (170)

It is not enough that this instrument of Providence be a poor but charitable pedlar chancing by; he must be one who "had been formerly a Drummer in an *Irish* Regiment," and who now finds himself on the road from London to Somerset, just where our heroes happen also to be. Providence, as Smollett's Win Jenkins puts it in *Humphry Clinker*, is "God's grease" (219).[36] And in the world of *Joseph Andrews*, success at gambling is a sign not of expert probabilism but, like Harriet Hearty's lucky lottery ticket, of divine favor.

In all its deliberately improbable accidents, its chance "adventures" which intervene suddenly and seasonably for the relief of innocence, *Joseph Andrews* is structured as an argument from design: it requires of its reader that he be a natural theologian. Part of the reader's interpretive activity of finding relations among the novel's parts is that of coming to see the rationale of such relations, a rationale which becomes intelligible only if understood to reflect the workings of Providence in the practical world. Fielding of course makes clear throughout his works that in ordinary life the best are not always the most beautiful; the city is not less virtuous than the country (vice may "flourish as notably," he explains in *Tom Jones*, "in a country Church and Churchyard, as in a Drawing Room"); the virtuous are not always rewarded. In *Tom Jones* he is careful to remind his reader of such facts:

There are a Set of Religious, or rather Moral Writers, who teach that Virtue is the certain Road to Happiness, and Vice to Misery in this World. A very wholsome and comfortable Doctrine, and to which we have but one Objection, namely, That it is not true. (783)

Why then do such equations fill his novels, and why is virtue so obtrusively rewarded? The answer lies in Fielding's crucial phrase "*in this World*," and in his notion of *comedy*. *This world* (considered apart from the next) is not a comic world. It is only in a comic world, as Fielding warns in his Preface that *Joseph Andrews* will be, that vicious actions "never produce the intended Evil" (10). In the tragic world of Richardson's *Clarissa*, poetic justice is assured only through carefully staged visions wherein characters on their death-beds come to know – and with them the reader – what will be their fate in the afterlife. In Fielding's comic world, that same justice is meted out in this life ("in this World"). For Fielding, then, comedy is a literary form religious in its very nature, in its assumptions and implications – just as (Christian) tragedy is for Richardson: the two are in fact simply different glasses in which the same eschatology may be seen reflected.

Fielding's comic epics in prose require of their readers interpretive efforts resembling those of the natural theologian, but if my argument about the Augustan notion of literary structure is correct – if the literary work is indeed conceived as a hierarchy of probable signs – Fielding is not unusual in this respect. The idea of providential structure in Augustan fiction has recently come under suspicion;[37] but if these fictions are indeed hierarchies of probable signs, their providential structure and interpretation follows logically from the very notion of literary form as the Augustans conceived it. Fable conduces to moral by virtue of its form, providential interventions to a superintendent deity; as Pope explained, the literary reader must look from nature to nature's cause. *Mutatis mutandis*, the same interpretive procedures govern the Augustan georgic – the prospect poem, for instance – as the novel.

Joseph Andrews also marks a departure from earlier Augustan epic. In earlier ideals of heroism (such as Milton's), founded on the Book of Job, heroism resides in obedience and patient suffering, evil in the activity of a Satan or an Achitophel. Pope's advice in the *Essay on Man*, like Dryden's in *Absalom and Achitophel*, is "Submit." Epics are of course didactic works, designed to instruct a nation in its past and in its possibilities for heroism; in recalling Sarpedon's call to battle in her speech at the end of *The Rape of the Lock*, Clarissa argues that in a transformed world, the same noble ends are to be served by *forgoing* battle. *Joseph Andrews* is the first Augustan epic of activism. Adams may counsel submission to the will of Providence, but it is Joseph's moral striving – his active cooperation with that will – which constitutes a true understanding of it, and which secures the return (with divine assistance) of the abducted Fanny. To the Puritan and predestinarian Defoe, Robinson Crusoe's only hope of justification lies not in further (necessarily misguided) action – not in works – but in the gift of a grace which may rectify his obdurate will; Fielding's Pelagian hero earns his reward.

(ii)

From them [books] I learn what I asserted just now, that Nature generally imprints such a Portraiture of the Mind in the Countenance, that a skilful Physiognomist will rarely be deceived.

Joseph Andrews II. 27

"Did you ever see any thing look so modest and so innocent as that girl over the way? what pity it is such a creature should be in the way of ruin, as I am afraid she is, by her being alone with that rough fellow!" Now this lady was no bad physiognomist, for it was impossible to conceive a greater appearance of modesty, innocence, and simplicity, than what nature had displayed in the countenance of that girl; and yet, all appearances notwithstanding, I myself (remember, critic, it was in my youth) had a few mornings before seen that very identical picture of all those engaging qualities in her bed with a rake at a bagnio...

Amelia I. 6

Fielding's characteristically mixed allegiance to the science of signs known as physiognomics results in a double use of physiognomic signs in his fiction. On the one hand, physiognomics provides him, as it would also Smollett, with a paradigm of the processes of judgment by which we come to know character and penetrate the meaning of events (so too natural theologians, like prospect poets, read "the face of nature"); its fallibility and inept applications, on the other hand, serve equally well to mark the fallibility, precariousness, and mediacy of our knowledge. The "Essay on the Knowledge of the Characters of Men," first printed in Fielding's *Miscellanies* of 1743 and probably composed just before he began *Joseph Andrews*, begins like Pope's *Epistle to Cobham* with a warning that because men come in such an "immense Variety of Characters," "Those who predicate of Man in general, that he is an Animal of this or that Disposition, seem to me not sufficiently to have studied Human Nature," and proceeds to classify human dispositions and to explain how these are revealed by signs. These signs are not all facial, for Fielding allows that "the Actions of Men are the surest Evidence of their Character" (164); his point is in part that actions and faces must be interpreted through the same inferential procedures. Physiognomy is an art, because it has "rules," "those Diagnostics which Nature ... gives us of the Diseases of the Mind, seeing she takes such Pains to discover those of the Body" (156), though these rules are only probable: "these Rules are, I believe, none of them without some Exceptions; as they are of no Use but to an Observer of much Penetration" and "as a more subtle Hypocrisy will sometimes escape undiscovered from the highest Discernment" (162). Affectation in its guises of vanity and hypocrisy (failing to understand one's nature, and mounting false signs of character) is of course Fielding's announced targets in *Joseph Andrews*; unmasking these will be the fruit of a careful weighing of all the available signs. The "Essay," similarly, identifies "Deceit" and "Hypocrisy" as its principal targets, outlining a procedure of "Prudence" (or "Politics") wherewith observers may make just classifications of those they meet according to internal character. Unmasking irony is of course the most familiar literary vehicle of such knowledge; if penetration and discrimination are the later stages of such an interpretive procedure, the first is again attention:

> But however cunning the Disguise be which a Masquerader wears: however foreign to his Age, Degree, or Circumstance, yet if closely attended to, he very rarely escapes the Discovery of an accurate Observer; for Nature, which unwillingly submits to the Imposture, is ever endeavouring to peep forth and shew herself... In the same manner will those Disguises which are worn on the greater Stage, generally vanish ... if we employ sufficient Diligence and Attention in the Scrutiny. (155)

We have already examined the way in which for the Augustans having a character meant embodying the characteristics of a class or type. In *Joseph Andrews*, what licenses Fielding's use of Biblical namesakes for his heroes is his famous theory of the permanence of such character-types, and hence of certain moral classifications of character:

> I describe not Men, but Manners; not an Individual, but a Species... The Lawyer is not only alive, but hath been so these 4000 Years... Mrs. *Tow-wouse* is coeval with our Lawyer, and tho' perhaps during the Changes, which so long an Existence must have passed through, she may in her Turn have stood behind the Bar at an Inn, I will not scruple to affirm, she hath likewise in the Revolution of Ages sat on a Throne. (189–90)

Here again is the pattern of repetition with external variation ("Changes"). Such a scheme of moral classification cuts across history, universalizing Fielding's themes: it is well to recall that since the days of Ussher and Lightfoot, one commonly accepted date for the beginning of history itself was 4004 BC (the very word "prehistory" could be coined only a century after Fielding's death).[38] The scheme cuts across classifications by profession and social rank as well – barmaid to queen – across, that is, our natural and customary ways of classing people. Such moral reclassification is perhaps the most important kind of judgment Fielding's characters must learn, and which he means to teach readers. Thus he explains at the opening of I. 7:

> It is the Observation of some antient Sage, whose Name I have forgot, that Passions operate differently on the human Mind, as Diseases on the Body, in proportion to the Strength or Weakness, Soundness or Rottenness of the one and the other.
>
> We hope therefore, a judicious Reader will give himself some Pains to observe, what we have so greatly laboured to describe, the different Operations of this Passion of Love in the gentle and cultivated Mind of the Lady *Booby*, from those which it effected in the less polished and coarser Disposition of Mrs. *Slipslop*. (34)

The terms "gentle and polished," "less polished" are ironic; Fielding's point is that at root, these two women's minds are the same – or rather, their passions are the same, for both are ruled by the same love (and, the irony suggests, both, like Mrs. Slipslop, are ruled less by "mind" than simply by their "disposition"). Fielding has "laboured to describe" the same passion differently diversified through the probable circumstances of each character, that through attention, penetration, and discrimination the reader may infer from these presented signs and circumstances back to character. As James Slevin has argued very well, furthermore, the paired scenes in which these signs are organized embody as well two different genres – high comedy and low farce; just as for the Augustans the epic form was understood to comprehend all the literary kinds, part of the training Fielding means to give readers of his comic epic in prose comes through the application of comparative judgment to parts generically distinct. The entire procedure subserves that redemption of a divinely established social order, through the restoration of value in the various roles which comprise it, which the novel as a whole seeks to further.[39]

In *Amelia*, Fielding applies to his readers' judgment even more frequently than in *Joseph Andrews*.

That we may give the reader leisure to consider well the foregoing sentiment, we will here put an end to this chapter. (I, 96)

Some readers may, however, be able to make pretty pertinent conjectures by what I have said above, especially when they are told that Miss Matthews broke the silence by a sign. (I, 172)

We desire, therefore, the good-natured and candid reader will be pleased to weigh attentively the several unlucky circumstances which occurred so critically that Fortune seemed to have used her utmost endeavors to ensnare poor Booth's constancy. (I, 175)

What these were, the sagacious reader may probably suspect; but, if he should not, we may perhaps have occasion to open them in the sequel. (I, 274)

... there is no exercise of the mind of a sensible reader more pleasant than the tracing of the several small and almost imperceptible links in every chain of events by which all the great actions of the world are produced. (II, 292–93)

He does so because the judgments *Amelia* requires of readers are more complex and difficult than those of *Joseph Andrews* – a state of affairs that is at once a cause and an effect of *Amelia*'s being a less successful novel. Far more than the earlier novels does *Amelia* stress the mediacy of knowledge, and consequently the failures of judgment and the state of "suspicion" that this precarious mediacy engenders.

Eric Rothstein has written of *Amelia*, "More than ever before in his novels, Fielding returns to a theatrical mode in which all we know is what we can witness"; we see the characters through a "fog," for the "narrator of *Amelia* has retreated, and our attempts to deal with experience put us on the same level with the characters, who fumble blindly."[40] Fielding is quite serious when, for example, he heads II. 8, "In which our readers will probably be divided in their opinion of Mr. Booth's conduct" (I, 98). While in this novel Fielding does eventually make clear his intentions and thematic commitments, he defers far longer than ever before in his work clarification of what these are; the novel is no longer compounded of discrete episodes, inferential units arrayed in a repetitive form whose meaning emerges through patterns of repetition with variation and repetition with reversal. The result is more frequent comments such as, "Certain it is that the maid's speech communicated a suspicion to the mind of Amelia which the behavior of the sergeant did not tend to remove: what this is, the sagacious readers may likewise probably suggest to themselves; if not, they must wait our time for disclosing it" (II, 54). *Amelia* is an odd and troubling work because in it Fielding has attempted to join the structure of his earlier novels to a new narrative procedure.

The "fog" through which characters understand one another is in *Amelia* composed of the most uncertain signs and indicators. More often even than in the novels of such confirmed physiognomists as Thomas Holcroft and William Godwin are characters in this work described as knowing one another only through facial signs, their inferences about what underlies these signs described as mere "guess." Booth and Amelia especially are attentive to one another's faces, not because they have that privileged access to each other's thoughts through the signs of love but because they decisively lack such access. Only extended quotation can convey the claustrophobic quality of such an uncertain world.

During the first two hours the colonel scarce ever had his eyes off Amelia; for he was taken by surprise, and his heart was gone before he suspected himself to be in any danger. His mind, however, no sooner suggested a certain secret to him than it suggested some degree of prudence at the same time; and the knowledge that he had thoughts to conceal, and the care of concealing them, had birth at one and the same instant. During the residue of the day, therefore, he grew more circumspect, and contented himself with now and then stealing a look by chance, especially as the more than ordinary gravity of Booth made him fear that his former behavior had betrayed to Booth's observation the great and sudden liking he had conceived for his wife, even before he had observed it in himself.

Amelia continued the whole day in the highest spirits and highest good humor imaginable, never once remarking that appearance of discontent in her husband of which the colonel had taken notice; so much more quick-sighted, as we have somewhere else hinted, is guilt than innocence.

Whether Booth had in reality made any such observations on the colonel's behavior as he had suspected, we will not undertake to determine; yet so far may be material to say, as we can with sufficient certainty, that the change in Booth's behavior that day, from what was usual with him, was remarkable enough. None of his former vivacity appeared in his conversation; and his countenance was altered from being the picture of sweetness and good humor, not indeed to sourness or moroseness, but to gravity and melancholy.

Though the colonel's suspicion had the effect which we have mentioned on his behavior, yet it could not persuade him to depart. (I, 280–81)

In a world so thick with suspicion, *suspect* is appropriately Fielding's most frequent choice of terms to denote inference, the inferences both of characters and readers. [41]

Once again, however, narrative structure is the mapping of didactic function, and the claustrophobic, uncertain, suspicious world of *Amelia* is designed to be itself a sign of larger moral and religious truth. Chance events in the providential comedy of *Joseph Andrews* are probable signs of God's design; in *Amelia*, widespread failure of signification is in large part the result of – and hence also a sign of – Booth's misguided and irreligious devotion to Fortune rather than Providence, the error that makes Amelia suspect "that he was little better than an atheist."[42] It is as we have seen before chance which, expressing itself through such means as the recalcitrance of matter and of language, creates monsters and impedes the full and clear expression of causes in their signate effects; in *Amelia*, it is Booth's active belief in Fortune rather than an ordering God which throws out of proper relation to each other events and their consequences, internal states and their external expressions, causes and signs. *Amelia* remains a novel constructed on the principles of *Joseph Andrews* and *Tom Jones*; it deliberately calls upon and frustrates the inferential procedures invoked by those earlier works in order to dramatize the epistemology of unbelief. The reading of its signs is a physico-theology of derangement.

(3) THE RECTIFICATION OF EXPECTATIONS

Ye who listen with credulity to the whispers of fancy, and pursue with eagerness the phantoms of hope; who expect that age will perform the promises of youth, and that the deficiencies of the present day will be supplied by the morrow; attend to the history of Rasselas prince of Abyssinia.

Samuel Johnson, *Rasselas* (1759)

But should this brilliant faculty [imagination] be nurtured on the bosom of enthusiasm, or romantic expectation, or be left to revel in all its native wildness of combination, ... undiverted by the deductions of truth, or the sober realities of existence, it will too often prove the cause of acute misery, of melancholy, and even of distraction.

Nathan Drake, *Literary Hours* (1798)

The character who is an adept in the art of reading signs is not the peculiar property of Fielding and Smollett, or even of the eighteenth century; what is distinctive about the Augustan character is that he is a reader of *probable* signs and exercises his sagacity within a narrative whose very fabric is a structure of conjectures and expectations, probable inferences by which he judges others and by which he is himself judged. Will Barrett, the "sentient engineer" and amnesiac hero of *The Last Gentleman* (1966), by Walker Percy – a philosopher of language as well as a novelist – makes what way he can in the world by reading in others' faces and tones of voice meanings that lie behind their words – words he frequently does not attend to. But such twentieth-century proficiency in sign-inference, likened in the novel to the acute hearing of a man gone blind, comes not from probable judgment but by miraculous gift; its deliverances are not structured so as to teach character or reader anything about rational expectations or probable conjecture. They are the special faculty of a uniquely disordered soul, expressions of the same sensitivity to lost communal and religious values that drives Will to amnesia and informs the novel's title. Percy's implication is that in a better world, such roundabout ways of knowing would be unnecessary; all Percy's heroes are detectives, but they are so only because of the peculiar dislocations of modern life.

The world of *The Last Gentleman* is full of another kind of sign, however, to which Will and all the other characters are blind: the "signs and portents," as Percy calls them in Biblical language, of divine purpose in the creation. To such expressions of the spiritual in the temporal, Percy supposes his audience also to be blind; thus he never identifies these signs with precision nor permits readers to make any inferences from them: they are merely mentioned ominously. Percy's didactic emphasis is not on the art of reading signs, judging from them, and structuring one's life accordingly; rather, it is on the search for a lost ability to recognize signs at all, and on the kind of education needed simply to know that such signs might exist. In the course of each's education, Percy's heroes prosecute lives that take on providential and typological patterning, but such patterning is wholly unintended by them and remains unknown to them.

In Fielding as in the Augustan prospect poets, at the highest level of inference from fable to moral are probable signs of providential design. In the world of Fielding's comedies, the spiritual is immanently present in the temporal: this is what makes accidents signs of divine order and what guarantees that the good judgment of individuals will conduce to a harmonious (providentially and hierarchically ordered) social whole. The postulate that licenses correct interpretive inferences at the highest level in these novels is the view that, as Pope put it, nature is the world's body and God its soul. In such a world, signs are visible, and a sagacity or penetrating power can by reading signs lead to a religiously founded state of earthly bliss and justification.

As Mary Poovey has shown in a comparison of the religious outlooks of Fielding and Richardson, the spiritual and temporal realms are far less clearly connected – the first is far less immanent in the second – in the world of *Clarissa* than in that of *Tom Jones*.[43] As a result of such disconnection, signs of God's order and purpose are not so clearly visible in Richardson's world – least of all is traditional social hierarchy a repository of moral value; characters cannot read signs, and probable inference therefore cannot lead to a state of earthly justification or shore up a providentially ordered society. Instead, in Clarissa's world, action inevitably leads astray; whereas Fielding writes epics of heroic activism, in Richardson (as in Milton) heroism resides not in great action, but in patience, suffering, and passivity; will is a defiance of Providence, vice the ceaseless activity and plotting of a Lovelace. Intentional action cannot in Richardson have its intended shape, completeness, and significance; instead, all intentions are sunk in the ironic willy-nilly patterning of the characters' lives in a scheme of anagogic significance, a scheme in which completeness (like poetic justice) comes only after death. Richardson's world of Christian tragedy differs from Percy's, however, in that the reader of *Clarissa* can recognize the signs of such unintended patterning in the characters' lives; it is through recognition of the probable inference from these signs that Richardson means his novel to teach.

Through inducing recognition of the signate evidence in creation of divine design, both Fielding and Richardson attempt to lead their readers to infer to generalizations about the nature of that design and, further, to alter their lives accordingly. The alteration each has most clearly in mind is a rectification by readers of their ordinary hopes, plans, and behavior in attempting to achieve these, *through a rectification of the expectations* on which such behavior is built. Readers are to reshape their expectations that they may act in such a manner as may with probability lead to happiness (earthly justification) and salvation. This is, in the largest sense, the didactic procedure of the Augustan novel.

In attempting to induce a rectification of expectations, Augustan novelists are casting in secular form what had of course been for centuries a common theme of sermons and religious tracts. A long succession of such works enjoins attention to the ways of Providence and, accordingly, rearrangement of one's hopes and expectations. In the Augustan period, with the help of the doctrines of probable inference and probable signs, the rectification of expectations is the didactic end not only of works we have examined, but also of narratives as various as *Rasselas*, *Evelina*, Goldsmith's fable of probability and demonstration, and much of Jane Austen's fiction; in the Augustan period, it was the common subject as well of nonfictional works: Johnson's *Idler* 58, as well of course as his "Vanity of Human Wishes"; Mrs. Barbauld's essay "Against Inconsistency in our Expectations"; John Foster's essay *On the Application of the Epithet Romantic*. To repeat, what makes these works Augustan versions of such a timeless theme is their central use of the ideas and vocabulary of probability.

In Fanny Burney's *Evelina* (1778), the ideal of judgment is "that prudence and consideration, which, by foreseeing distant consequences, may rule and direct in present exigencies" (341). Mr. Villars, Evelina's guardian, writes to Lady Howard of what he hopes for his ward's education, laying heavy emphasis on the word *expect*:

Destined, in all probability, to possess a very moderate fortune, I wished to contract her views to something within it. The mind is but too naturally prone to pleasure, but too easily yielded to dissipation: it has been my study to guard her against their delusions, by preparing her to expect, – and to despise them.

He continues, preaching rectification of expectations:

A youthful mind is seldom totally free from ambition; to curb that, is the first step to contentment, since to diminish expectation, is to increase enjoyment. I apprehend nothing more than too much raising her hopes and her views, which the natural vivacity of her disposition would render but too easy to effect. (18)

Of Evelina's feelings after reading a letter from Lord Orville, he remarks, "Your disappointment has but been proportioned to your expectation" (267). "Too much raising of her hopes and views" is the substance of Emma Woodhouse's sin against Harriet Smith, a corruption of (among other things) Harriet's judgment and sense of probability. In both Burney and Austen, good characters are those who, like Edward Ferrars in *Sense and Sensibility*, are "most fearful of … wounding expectation," and like Fanny Price in *Mansfield Park*, are most critical of themselves on those occasions on which they have "deceived … expectations" (244, 319).

Mr. Villars' continual recommendation to Evelina is "circumspection and prudence," to the end of forming "rational expectations"

(164, 19). It is a prudence which in its operation requires considerable "sagacity," "discernment," and "penetration," virtues of
which Mr. Villars is himself a model. He attempts, for instance, to
"conjecture" the cause of Evelina's low spirits, deploying all his
armory of probability and prudence:

"At least let me try," answered he, mildly; "perhaps I may be a better diviner than
you imagine: if I guess every thing that is probable, surely I must approach near
the real reason." (264)

The same goal of rectifying expectation, and so of proportioning
assent (and hence also potential disappointment) to evidence and
probability is the explicit theme of John Foster's *On the Application of the Epithet Romantic* (1805), long sections of which read
like blueprints for novels such as *Evelina* and *Northanger Abbey*.
Foster's villain is the "romantic imagination," which, in the terms
of the familiar Augustan comparison between judgment and fancy,
"will throw its colours where the intellectual faculty ought to draw
its lines" (137). Foster singles out for special condemnation romances, "a kind of mental balloon, for mounting into the air from the
ground of ordinary experience":

One's indignation is excited at the immoral tendency of such lessons to young
readers, who are thus taught to undervalue and reject all sober regular plans for
compassing an object, and to muse on improbabilities till they become foolish
enough to expect them; thus betrayed, as an inevitable consequence, into one
folly more, that of being melancholy when they may expect them in vain.
(153–54)

Imagination itself, though its expression in romance satisfies an
endemic human "craving" (153), is for Foster as in the "imaginist"
Emma Woodhouse the enemy of probable inference:

it would seem an obvious principle of good sense, that an estimate moderately
correct of the value of each of our means according to those measures ... should
precede every application of them. Such an estimate has no place in a mind under
the ascendancy of imagination, which, therefore, by extravagantly magnifying
the virtue of its means, inflates its projects with hopes which may justly be called
romantic. The best corrective of such irrational expectation is an appeal to
experience... It is presumed, that truth must at length, through the indefatig-
able exertions of intellect, become generally victorious; and that all vice, being
the result of a mistaken judgment of the nature or means of happiness, must
therefore accompany the exit of error. (179, 163)

In an argument that resists easy summary, Foster concludes that
man's "visionary expectations" can find their best and least disappointing outlet in a rational Christianity; that religion provides a
set of probabilities on which our expectations, however lofty, may

justly be founded; and by extension, that the love of improbabilities that gives rise to romance may fruitfully be harnessed to the probability of a Christian marvellous (180–83). He writes, for instance, of prayer:

The most excellent of all human means must be that of which the effect is to obtain the exertion of divine power. The means which are to be employed in a direct immediate instrumentality toward the end, seem to bear such a measured proportion to their objects, as to assign and limit the probable effect. This regulated proportion exists no longer, and therefore the possible effects become too great for calculation, when that expedient is solemnly employed which is appointed as the mean of engaging the divine energy to act on the object. If the only mean by which Jehoshophat sought to overcome his superior enemy, had been his troops, horses, and arms, there would have been nearly an assignable proportion between these means and the end, and the probable result would have been a matter of ordinary calculation. (182)

"Regulated proportion" here means a mathematically calculable probability; what Foster has done, of course, is to borrow the argument of Pascal's wager.

In the final chapter of Charlotte Lennox's *Female Quixote* (1752), probably written by Samuel Johnson, part of the criticism of romance turns also on its corruption of that "Power of Prognostication" which "may, by Reading and Conversation, be extended beyond our own Knowledge":

We can judge of the Future only by the Past, and have therefore only Reason to fear or suspect, when we see the same Causes in Motion which have formerly produc'd Mischief, or the same Measures taken as have before been preparatory to a crime.

Thus, when the Sailor in Certain Latitudes sees the Clouds rise, Experience bids him expect a Storm. (372)

If literary works are to teach rather than corrupt, they must help to found in readers rational expectations, those founded on "prognostics" from the probabilities of real experience rather than of romance; this is of course the point of the satirical portions of *Northanger Abbey* (1818), where Henry Tilney remonstrates with Catherine Morland:

"And from these *circumstances*, he replied, (his quick eye fixed on her's) "You *infer* perhaps the *probability* of some negligence..."

"If I understand you rightly, you had formed a *surmise* of such horror as I have hardly words to – Dear Miss Morland, *consider* the dreadful nature of the *suspicions* you have entertained. What have you been *judging* from? Remember the country and the age in which we live. Remember that we are English, that we are Christians. Consult your own *understanding*, your own sense of the *probable*, your own *observation* of what is passing around you."[44]

What Henry is asking for is a survey of the probable circumstances of person, time, and place – the same probable circumstances that in her most self-conscious passages, Austen claims to have observed in constructing the novel itself:

The anxiety, which in this state of their attachment must have been the portion of Henry and Catherine, and of all who loved either, as to its final event, can hardly extend, I fear, to the bosom of my readers, who will see in the tell-tale compression of the pages before them, that we are all hastening together to perfect felicity. The means by which their early marriage was effected can be the only doubt; what probable circumstances could work upon a temper like the General's? The circumstance which chiefly availed, was the marriage of his daughter to a man of fortune and consequence. (250)

Writing just before the novel took a new direction in the works of Scott and Dickens, Jane Austen is the last and greatest novelist in the Augustan didactic tradition whose aim is the rectification of expectation through the education of probable judgment.[45] Several critics have noticed the importance of "probability" to her work and explained some of the means by which she invokes it in her effort to educate judgment.[46] Austen is a most precise epistemologist of the probable; we read in *Sense and Sensibility* (1811) that Elinor Dashwood

felt that Edward stood very high in her *opinion*. She *believed* the regard to be mutual; but she required *greater certainty* of it to make Marianne's *conviction* of their attachment agreeable to her. She *knew* that what Marianne and her mother *conjectured* one moment, they *believed* the next – that with them, to *wish* was to *hope*, and to *hope* was to *expect*.

... his marriage, which Mrs. Dashwood, from *foreseeing* at first as a *probable* event, had brought herself to *expect* as a *certain* one. (21, 213; my italics)

Mrs. Dashwood, who in Elinor's opinion lacks "common sense, common care, common prudence," complains: "Are no probabilities to be accepted, merely because they are not certainties?" (85, 79).

Austen not only conducts her novels in the Augustan vocabulary of probable inference, of sagacity in reading signs and circumstances; she builds them as didactic structures of conjecture and expectation, as judged by the event. There is once again more than playful irony in such claims from *Northanger Abbey* as:

Monday, Tuesday, Wednesday, Thursday, Friday and Saturday have now passed in review before the reader; the events of each day, its hopes and fears, mortifications and pleasures have been separately stated, and the pangs of Sunday only now remain to be described, and close the week. (97)

Emma (1815) is at once Austen's most complex study of probable judgment, and her narrative most completely built up from a fabric rather of accounts of what characters expect, conjecture, guess, and foresee than of what externally they do (see appendix C). Its parts are "open and frequent discussion of hopes and chances" (308):

While poor Mrs. Churchill lived, I *suppose* there could not have been a *hope*, a *chance*, a *possibility*. (361)

It must be her ardent *wish* that Harriet might be *disappointed*; and she *hoped*, that when able to see them together again, she might at least be able to *ascertain* what the *chances* for it were. (377)

Common sense would have directed her to tell Harriet ... that there were *five hundred chances to one* against his ever caring for her. (365)

The novel closes with a studied iteration of the vocabulary of inference, organized and confirmed to indicate the rewards of a virtuous probabilism:

But, in spite of these deficiencies, the wishes, the hopes, the confidence, the predictions of the small band of true friends who witnessed the ceremony, were fully answered in the perfect happiness of the union. (440)

In *Emma*, the enemy of probability is once again pride, but whereas earlier Augustans attacked that heroic kind of pride which lends itself to typological connection with Satanic evil, Austen is pre-eminently the moralist and epistemologist of that form of pride which is self-indulgence. Emma's imaginism, her supposed "genius for foretelling and guessing," her "talent for guessing" and for "speculation and foresight" (33, 363, 302), is a form of pride both in that it is self-serving and in its self-referring distortions of the processes of probable judgment. The novel conducts its analysis of the grounds of probable judgment in what is self-consciously the terminology of literary and philosophical probabilism:

Was it a new circumstance for a man of first-rate abilities to be captivated by very inferior powers? ... Was it new for any thing in this world to be unequal, inconsistent, incongruous – or for chance and circumstance (as second causes) to direct the human fate? (375)

How could she have been so deceived! ... She had taken up the idea, she supposed, and made every thing bend to it. His manners, however, must have been unmarked, wavering, dubious, or she could not have been so misled. (121)

VIII

Sentimental communion and probable inference: Mackenzie and Sterne

"Not a word of my wisdom," cries the doctor. "I have not a grain – I am not the least versed in the Chrematistic art, as an old friend of mine calls it. I know not how to get a shilling, or how to keep it in my pocket if I had it." "But you understand human nature to the bottom," answered Amelia; "and your mind is the treasury of all ancient and modern learning."

Fielding, *Amelia* XI. 5

In both its literary form and its philosophical presuppositions, the sentimental novel as it is practiced in England in the last third of the eighteenth century marks a departure from those didactic forms designed in the manner of *Joseph Andrews* and *Tom Jones* to teach probable judgment and to rectify expectation. The new form is also didactic, but it teaches a new doctrine, and employs new procedures of structure to train its implied readers. Once again structure is designed to teach by requiring inferential procedures of interpretation which embody the principles of that doctrine, i.e., by habituating readers to the kinds of inferential processes that the author means to inculcate. But these interpretive processes, and the general theory of inference that licenses them and that they dramatize, are products of the new philosophical outlook that came into being in England in the 1760s.

Narrative form continues overwhelmingly to be that of travel literature – novels tell of journeys – but the nature of travel as presented by Sterne and Mackenzie is not that of Fielding and Smollett. *The Man of Feeling* (1771) concerns itself as centrally as does *A Sentimental Journey* (1768) with proper modes of travel; both detail a new mode of travel, one informed by the theories of knowledge and learning developed by Thomas Reid and his followers.

The response to Hume known as the Scottish philosophy of Common Sense, begun by Reid and continued by such writers as Lord Kames, James Beattie, and Dugald Stewart, was fundamentally rooted in a new theory of knowledge and learning, one that brought with it revisions in the Augustan understanding of probability, inference, and signs. The components of Common-Sense philosophy cardinally important to literary sentimentalism are four: a new and programmatic emphasis on the "naturalness" of natural signs; the view that knowledge of many probable signs and of many of nature's patterns of probable signification is not learned through experience – not through processes of observation and judgment – but is innate; the view that much of probable inference, though it depend on probable signs, is an exercise not of the comparing power of judgment, but of mental processes at once unconscious and immediate; and, eventually, the positing of a new mental faculty whose office it is to read probable signs, especially those signs that reveal character.

It will be helpful to our understanding of sentimental narrative to begin by showing how these new philosophical commitments made themselves felt in late Augustan criticism, since that criticism is often our best guide to the way the Augustans themselves understood the meaning of their procedures of literary structure. I have chosen for particular consideration John Ogilvie's *Philosophical and Critical Observations* (1774), an undeservedly neglected work which is in fact one of the most insightful and far-reaching critical statements to be found in the period separating Pope from Wordsworth.

An initial word is in order about the choice of texts to represent "sentimentalism." Any attempt to discuss particular works as sentimental, and *a fortiori* any attempt to give even a partial definition of sentimentalism, must begin from an awareness that neither the intension nor the extension of the term has been agreed upon. Works taken by most as paradigmatic – those of Sterne and Mackenzie – are by others considered anti-sentimental. But since any discussion of a work as sentimental involves covert or overt reference to some definition of the label, we must either pursue the route of definition or abandon the term. My own account of sentimentalism as depending fundamentally on certain doctrines of probability and signs is such that "anti-sentimental" works, if they embody these doctrines, must also be considered sentimental; on the other hand, I do not believe my generalizations alter the traditional extension of the term so much as its intension. An example of the kind of revision in our definitions that I propose may be helpful.

The mid-century distinction between internal and external probability nowhere makes itself felt so clearly as in sentimental narrative. The sentimental villain is typically an adept like Count Fathom in "plots" and "schemes," in that Art of Thriving, Aristotle's "chrematistic art," mentioned by Dr. Harrison.[1] In characters such as the "prudent" and "pragmatical" Sir Thomas Sindall and the "scheming" Mr. Thornhill, novelists such as Mackenzie, Goldsmith,

Sterne, and Inchbald find a socially divisive evil, one rooted in a selfish narrowness of spirit. More important, these authors identify this worldly prudence with a facility in calculating probabilities, a kind of calculation that the sentimental hero typically eschews: "to calculate the chances of deception is too tedious a business for the life of man!" exclaims Mackenzie's man of feeling (53). As children, heroes like young Henry Norwynne in *Nature and Art* harbor desires that in their benevolence exceed rational probability; as adults their lives, conducted with more feeling than judgment, appear on examination to be an "improbable tale" (102).[2] Henry's beloved Rebecca comes painfully to this realization as she is subjected by her father to a quasi-judicial inquiry:

Questioned louder, and with more violence still, "How the child came there, wherefore her affection for it, and whose it was?" she felt the improbability of the truth still more forcibly than before, and dreaded some immediate peril from her father's rage, should she dare to relate an apparent lie – she paused to think upon a more probable tale than the real one. (96–97)

This is not an inquest in Fielding's manner: this Justice is impartial and a competent judge of probabilities; it is the defendant who, because judgment has not ruled her conduct, cannot under its scrutiny convince others of her innocence.

Instead of prudence (calculation), the sentimental novel celebrates the spiritual and social advantages of a quasi-intuitive communion with the thoughts and feelings of others. It is Rebecca's father's love that should be her justification. This communion, which the sentimental hero enjoys with a like-minded few, is also explicated as a kind of probabilism, but it is a probabilism of a different sort: not rooted in judgment, it is a special intuitive facility in reading probable signs, especially those signs that betray others' thoughts and feelings. In a famous passage, Sterne describes this as an ability to read nature's "*short hand*":

There is not a secret so aiding to the progress of sociality, as to get master of this *short hand*, and be quick in rendering the several turns of looks and limbs, with all their inflections and delineations, into plain words. For my own part, by long habitude, I do it so mechanically, that when I walk the streets of London, I go translating all the way; and have more than once stood behind in the circle, where not three words have been said, and have brought off twenty different dialogues with me, which I could have fairly wrote down and sworn to.[3]

Though translatable into the artificial language of words, such a shorthand is a system of natural signs revelatory of character; through probable inference from such signs, Yorick comes to achieve communion with others. Sterne's ideal is the same as Rousseau's dream of perfect, wordless communication, the transparency of one mind to another: "Que de choses sont dites sans ouvrir la bouche! Que d'ardents sentiments se sont communiqués sans la froide entremise de la parole! ... Quelle langue ose être ton interprète? Jamais ce qu'on dit à son ami peut-il valoir de qu'on sent à ces côtés."[4]

We have already seen the way in which Augustan critics came to understand external probability as a relation to evidence – hence a probability to be calculated, one available through the exercise of judgment – but found internal probability to rest on a kind of "testimony" so self-evidently present to the mind as to be a different kind of quality altogether, not a relation to evidence but something far more immediate – and as less mediate, available not through the conscious, comparing faculty of judgment but through some other mental operation. These two kinds of probability are dramatized in the sentimental novel: villains are typically external probabilists, heroes internal probabilists. The creators of these heroes modelled their alternative to the probability of judgment on the teachings of Reid and his school.

Late Augustan sentimentalists did not, of course, invent the contrast between selfish calculation and virtuous attention to the feelings of others. Rather, their innovation is in casting this distinction in terms of the two conceptions of probability – one the older, more familiar, Lockean kind, the other the new probability of Reid – and in designing their narratives not only to preach internal probabilism, but to teach it through the mental processes of interpretation called forth in the activity of reading. Much of that exercise of judgment which comprised the probabilism Fielding attempts to teach through his educational journeys is now cast aside as worldly prudence, selfish external probabilism. The sentimental indictment of judgment results in novels of anti-prudence and anti-probability; physiognomy and related arts of inferring from probable signs take on a new significance as they are understood to circumvent judgment so-called and lead instead to an immediate communion with others. As Fielding's model of judgment is rejected, so are his didactic structures (though vestiges of the earlier structural procedures remain, stripped of any function within the larger patterns of signification of the work, in novels such as *The Man of Feeling*). In place of earlier structural procedures, the most daring sentimental novelists attempt to construct new kinds of inferential structure to provide reading paradigms of *internally* probable inference.

(I) THE NEW FACULTY OF DISCERNMENT

That we should be conscious intuitively of a passion from its external expressions, is comfortable to the analogy of nature. The knowledge of this language is of too great importance to be left upon experience. To rest it upon a foundation so uncertain and precarious, would prove a great obstacle to the formation of societies. Wisely therefore is it ordered, and agreeably to the system of Providence, that we should have Nature for our instructor.

Kames, *Elements of Criticism* (II, 37) (1762)

The Common-Sense response to Hume is an attempt to shore up the many varieties of empirical (nondemonstrative) knowledge Hume's philosophy had endangered. Where Hume had found only the uncertainty of beliefs constructed by the mind – mere opinion – Reid and his followers found universally agreed upon knowledge they were unwilling to give up to the skeptic. Specifically, Reid's response to Hume is a revival of the idea of innate principles by reference to which "common-sense" knowledge may be explained and justified. These "first principles" arise from neither sensation nor reflection; they make themselves known through the universality of their application in certain "common-sense" perceptions; these perceptions, moreover, though they are inferences of a sort, are not the products of conscious judgment or reflection.[5]

Reid's most complete catalogue of innate first principles appears in his *Essays on the Intellectual Powers of Man* (1785); among the "First Principles of Contingent Truths" are these deliverances of common sense:

that there is life and intelligence in our fellow men with whom we converse. (633)

That certain features of the countenance, sounds of the voice, and gestures of the body, indicate certain thoughts and dispositions of mind. (635)

That there is a certain regard due to human testimony in matters of fact. (640)

Of the second of these principles, Reid says, "Nature seems to have given to men a faculty or sense, by which this connection is perceived" (we know this, for instance, because children are able antecedent to all experience to understand facial expressions); "the operation of this sense is very analogous to that of the external senses," that is, it does not operate through conscious processes of reasoning or judgment (638).

These and other first principles – all of which can be found somewhere in Reid's *Inquiry* of 1764 – are attempts to secure knowledge usually explained as the product of inference from probable signs. What justifies the claim that these are first principles is precisely that we make the inferences they license antecedently to any experience which could teach us to do so, or which could show us that the principles are justified. Reid writes in the *Inquiry* of what he distinguishes as the second of three classes of "natural signs":

A second class is that wherein the connection between the sign and the thing signified is not only established by nature, but discovered to us by a natural principle, without reasoning or experience. Of this kind are the natural signs of human thoughts, purposes, and desires, which have already been mentioned as the natural language of mankind... The principles of all the fine arts, and of what we call *a fine taste*, may be resolved into connections of this kind. (66–67)

The signs in the natural language of the human countenance and behavior, as well as the signs in our original perceptions, have the same signification in all climates and in all nations; and the skill of interpreting them is not acquired, but innate. (236)

In general, then, "There is no reasoning in perception... The belief which is implied in it, is the effect of instinct."[6] In such perception, the mind passes immediately and unconsciously from sign to thing signified:

They are natural signs, and the mind passes to the thing signified, without making the least reflection upon the sign, or observing that there was any such thing. (71)

When I see a garden in good order, containing a great variety of things of the best kinds, and in the most flourishing condition, I immediately conclude from these signs, the skill and industry of the gardener. (213)

Perception of this type is mediate only in the sense that it works through signs: "Although there is no reasoning in perception, yet there are certain means and instruments, which, by the appointment of nature, must intervene between the object and our perception of it" (214). On the other hand, it is immediate in the sense that it is "instantaneous" and operates "without our consciousness" (71, 216). Thus, to the question whether such perceptions deserve to be called *judgments*, Reid answers:

It is not worth while to dispute about names; but it is evident that my belief, both first and last, was produced rather by signs than by arguments; and that the mind proceeded to the conclusion in both cases by habit, and not by ratiocination. (226)

Thus for the first time signs are distinguished from arguments, in a way that no previous writer we have examined would have understood.

Because knowledge of this kind, even when only probable, comes to the mind through unconscious inference, Reid and his followers can at once believe that probability is a relation (a relation to evidence) and yet speak of "self-evident probabilities": in these cases, the evidence for a probable conclusion is its self-evidence to consciousness.[7] Here, then, is a philosophic theory of inference from probable signs capable of grounding the literary doctrine of internal probability.

Beattie never calls the capacity of making such unconscious inferences from probable signs anything but "common sense"; Reid himself sometimes calls it "Suggestion."[8] This is that "Good Sense" which Samuel Johnson defined in the *Life of Pope* as "a prompt and intuitive perception of consonance and propriety" (216); Joshua Reynolds called it a "sagacity" which "does not wait for the slow progress of deduction, but goes at once, by what appears a kind of intuition, to the conclusion."[9] For these and other writers of the later eighteenth century, the mental process Reid had outlined seemed so important as to deserve separate treatment and a special name. John Ogilvie is at some pains to erect this capacity into a distinct mental faculty, one for whose name he chooses the familiar term *discernment*:

That mental power which when exerted either in executing, or in judging of execution in the fields of composition takes the designation of discernment; in common life it is known by that of *sagacity*. In the last it is distinguished by a perception of the real character, and an *insight* (if we may thus term it) into the secret motives that influence conduct, no less justly than instantaneously conceived, from circumstances that escape a common observer.[10]

As Johnson's and Ogilvie's formulations make clear, it is the same mental power that infers to character from physiognomic and other signs, and infers from the probable signs of a literary work to their meaning; in a larger sense, it judges through signs of "consonance and propriety," and is the faculty that creates and reads those patterns of signs that are an organized literary structure. Discernment, finally, not judgment, has become the faculty of decorum.

Ogilvie's *Philosophical and Critical Observations on the Nature, Characters, and Various Species of Composition* is a detailed examination of the role of probable signs in literary composition, structure, and interpretation. Ogilvie lists four mental faculties – Understanding, Imagination, Discernment, and Memory – declaring his aim "to point out the spheres of the intellectual powers in this art, to mark the signatures by which each is discriminated" (1, 2). In the first volume, he unfolds the nature of each faculty, explains that "various Combinations" of each are required in and expressed through "the different Species of Composition" (including criticism), and shows how from the early "marks" and "indications" betrayed by children of those faculties they possess in highest degree, the preceptor may through carefully designed programs of literary education correct imbalances among these faculties, in order to produce that "equipoise of the powers" best suited to the production of all the literary kinds (1, 377).[11] In volume II, he shows how each of the various styles of composition – the Simple, Perspicuous, Elegant,

Nervous, Correct, and Sublime styles – "still continues to be marked by those radical signatures, in their full strength, which nature stamps as indelibly on the mind as on the countenance" (II, 80). In a series of particular analyses, he shows how specific methods of verbal expression are the effects of, and hence the "signs," "marks," "signatures," and "indications" of the balance of faculties, the "character or temper," of their author.[12] The whole of the *Observations*, then, is an endeavor to show how each of the literary styles and kinds (including procedures of structure) "may be most probably and completely effectuated" (II, 304).

Ogilvie begins his anatomy of the mind with the faculty of Understanding:

The understanding is that power of the mind which determines the relation of parts to each other in laying down the plan of a performance of any nature; which judgeth of its comprehension as suited to the subject; which, following the series of effects to their original, investigates a cause; and superintends the conduct of this procedure in such a manner as to make the expression bear the same relation to the sentiments of any performance which these last are required to do to each other. (I, 10–11)

Understanding, then, is in literature as in natural philosophy the faculty at play in "the discovery of a theory or hypothesis" (45); it is the power that Locke called *judgment*: "The task appropriated here particularly to the reasoning power, is that of adhering steadily to a general purpose, and of connecting a series of intermediate ideas, by whose intervention it is to be gained both with that end, and with each other" (65). In literary works, therefore, it is the power that maintains "that secret connection throughout; without which, a performance must cease immediately not only to be edifying, but intelligible" (63). It is, in familiar Augustan fashion, the faculty of structure: of probability.

"The Imagination, or the inventive faculty, is that which strikes out happy imitations, forms new and original assemblages of ideas" (10); it works far more quickly than Understanding, but "left to itself," it would produce no unified or intelligible imitation, but only "a resemblance of some scattered features" (302). So far, Ogilvie has only recast in late Augustan psychological terminology the familiar distinction between judgment and fancy; but he continues:

When we examine with close attention that combination of qualities greatly diversified, by which the characters of men are distinguished, reflection will point out to us the marks of one intellectual power different from both the former in its manner of operation; whose effects we shall endeavour to unfold more particularly, as it has not as far as we know been formerly distinguished from others. (I, 175)

This power is Discernment. Ogilvie explains Discernment as possessing the probabilistic functions of Understanding combined with the immediacy, the instantaneous speed, of Imagination: it "ariseth from judgment and imagination acting in vigorous concurrence" (131).

Discernment is an instantaneous power of unconscious inference, modelled on the theory of inference from first principles devised by Reid and his followers.[13] Those who are discerning, "As soon as the subject is laid down, and a few principal evidences laid before them ... take in the whole by a kind of intuitive perception; supplying the intermediate means so quickly, as to render particular representation inexpedient" (177). Thus Ogilvie has made of "sagacity" as Locke defined it a distinct faculty. It is a faculty "formed by the union of both judgment and fancy" (250), and thus performs in its operation the chief mediation required by Augustan criticism. But because Ogilvie lacks any Romantic theory wherein faculties may *fuse* – not merely work in "vigorous concurrence," but unite into one – the *Observations* must while claiming that Discernment is a distinct faculty always return to the point that it can be resolved into a balance of Understanding and Imagination.[14]

Whereas Understanding judges of probabilities slowly, Discernment does so instantly:

Penetration, as observing this fallacy immediately, though concealed by the most plausible representation, will render [the writer] qualified to enter with ease, as well as depth and compass into his subject; but reason alone, without this quick and almost intuitive perception, by its steady attention and gradual procedure, obtains its end at least as surely, though not so quickly as the former. (I, 367–68)

Discernment judges probabilities by reading signs; this may entail "reading in the countenance those sensations, however deeply concealed, that actuate the heart," or reading "the transitions particularly in poetic compositions," finding intelligible structure in passages "apparently negligent of methodical arrangement" (178, 203).

Children may be trained in Discernment – taught, that is, to "acquire an habit of tracing effects to their causes" – through the study of physico-theology: Ogilvie recommends assigning them to read works by Derham, Ray, and Wesley (421–22).

Because in life Discernment is the faculty that by reading signs "lays open ... the heart and the affections" – and which in observing the "signatures by which men are ... discriminated," permits us to classify them according to character (that is, according to their "ruling passion") – in composition, "true discernment is in nothing more conspicuous, than in combining the various principles of

action into some *original character*."[15] (Because of those rearrange-
ments of the hierarchic model of literary structure we examined in
chapter IV, late Augustan criticism reserves for the new faculty's
most important functions the creation, organization, and interpretation of character rather than action.) Operating in the creation of character as in its interpretation, Discernment is a
sympathetic power: a writer or reader is discerning if he is "capable
of placing himself, by an effort of imagination, in the circumstances
of him who is strongly actuated by a particular passion; and by
feeling (if we may thus express it) its temporary influence"
(215–16). Thus it is Discernment that makes possible a writer's
"throwing out those little strokes of nature, imperceptible to a
superficial eye, which command the immediate acknowledgment of
a feeling heart, not by language but by tears" (338). Ogilvie's
literary psychology is particularly important to us as he uses it to
explain how each faculty operates in the construction and interpretation of literary works; he is most suggestive in his discussion
of the novel.

Ogilvie divides the novels of his contemporaries into two classes;
of the first variety, which includes "the Tom Jones and Amelia of
Fielding, [and] the Roderick Random of Smollett," he finds that
"upon the whole, judgment is displayed in it more than imagination" (343–44). In these works, Ogilvie finds the kind of didactic
structure we have already examined; he writes, for instance, of the
arrangement of incidents in *Joseph Andrews*:

The judgment which rangeth these so justly as to employ the different persons
in such spheres of action as are best calculated to show their *peculiar qualities*
to advantage, must be uncommonly comprehensive and accurate. The Adams
of Fielding would have appeared to no advantage had he been wholly conversant with persons in very low life, or such as were entirely on a level with
himself. But the lady, the waiting maid, the hosts, the 'squires, the parsons, and
the justices, with whom he is alternately and most judiciously contrasted,
contribute separately to finish the character, until the figure is set before us
completely proportioned.
    Penetration likewise, as employed to develop the secret motives from which
the actions of men derive their origin, the ingenious novelist will display to
great advantage in the artful arrangement of his incidents ... in contrasting the
persons of his fable in such a manner as may most happily expose vice, detect
hypocrisy, and render presumption, affectation, or arrogance, the objects of
ridicule. (I, 345–46)

In this first kind of novel, "If we meet not in these with those
exquisite strokes of nature and passion which characterise the
[other], the defeat is, however, abundantly compensated by characters well supported, and happily discriminated" (344).

It is in the second kind of novel that Discernment rather than Understanding is the ruling faculty; in such works may most be felt

that instantaneous perception of certain attitudes, which discernment ultimately derives from imagination, that correspondence of which every man is sensible betwixt the action and the feeling giving rise to it in one heart, and excited in it by another... (I, 340)

"In this kind of fable Marivaux, Crebillon, and we may add, our own late countryman Sterne, in his Sentimental Journey, excel all other writers whatever."

The only theme we have mentioned in connection with sentimentalism's handling of the probable sign that Ogilvie does not explicitly pursue is the view that internally probable inference tends to the harmonizing of society. Through a number of didactic procedures – not least of which is the concluding of a happy marriage between members of different social classes, in the context of a work which has dramatized the causes and effects of class conflict – the narratives from Fielding to Austen whose aim is to rectify judgment attempt also, by harmonizing and healing breaches within it, to secure the values of a providentially ordered, hierarchical society. The sentimental novel, by contrast, attempts to further community by teaching the art of passionate communion with others. (In the process, it is often explicitly critical of the very notion of social hierarchy.) Reid had argued that the natural language of mankind must have existed as a basis from which men could go on to construct artificial languages, and form societies; Ogilvie finds the faculty of that natural language, Discernment, to be a principle that enables us to understand our fellows, but does not take the step from communion to community.

Scottish philosophy from Adam Smith to Adam Ferguson did take the step; the most famous presentation of the argument was of course Smith's *Theory of Moral Sentiments* (1759). In this work, Smith discusses not only the passions that socialize us (as had authors from Addison and Hutcheson to Burke), but also the external signs through which we know them:

Upon some occasions sympathy may seem to arise merely from the view of a certain emotion in another person. The passions, upon some occasions, may seem to be transfused from one man to another, instantaneously, and antecedent to any knowledge of what excited them in the person principally concerned. Grief and joy, for example, strongly expressed in the look and gestures of any one, at once affect the spectator with some degree of a like painful or agreeable emotion. (II)[16]

Of course Smith is more concerned with those actions that are the expressions of given passions than with facial expressions, but it is the general procedure of inference from probable signs that concerns us. Through God's ordering of our faculties, making certain "social passions" sources of pleasure and other antisocial passions sources of pain, the very constitution of the mind gives rise to actions productive of social harmony; the triggers of such action are the external signs of passion in others, signs which through a faculty of sympathetic unconscious inference we understand and act upon. "Generosity, humanity, kindness, compassion, mutual friendship and esteem, all the social and benevolent affections, when expressed in the countenance or behavior, even towards those who are not peculiarly connected with ourselves, please the indifferent spectator on almost every occasion" (38–39).

Late Augustan literary and social criticism teems with arguments about the ways in which inference from probable signs leads not only to communion, but to community. One especially ambitious attempt to harmonize Augustan ethical and aesthetic doctrines via the medium of the probable sign is John Donaldson's *Elements of Beauty; Also, Reflections on the Harmony of Sensibility and Reason* (1780), a work more famous in the history of criticism for its detailed associationist treatment of synaesthesia, which Donaldson calls "assimilation." Taking a cue from theories influential from Campanella to Du Bos, Donaldson argues that the true source of "beauty" is life itself, or "animation"; beautiful objects are those that display external signs of inner vitality, or external properties resembling or associated with such signs. Through our powers of sympathy, these signs in turn increase animation in the observer:

Qualities of objects, so far as they relate to beauty, are either such as most clearly excite *perception* or *life* in the senses; or they are composed of these, and somewhat *expressive* of *life* or *sensibility* ... Whatever most resembles the symptoms of sensibility in ourselves, we discern to have the greatest share of expression. That particular object is most agreeably distinguished, which either affects the senses by exciting the liveliest perceptions; or which, by means of what is delightful to sense, expresses the clearest sense of internal perception. (10, 50)

Because Donaldson's "animation," like Smith's "social passions," is providentially ordered to aid in the furtherance of community, its signs – the beautiful – also socialize:

And as it is the social or communicative principle which raises our enjoyments so far above the pleasures of other creatures, so it is the visible signs appropriated by nature to this principle, which render the human body superiorly beautiful ... The same power by which the nerves of the human body are internally agitated, affects their extremities, and induces an alteration in the external form. The pleasures of sensation are again reflected outwards, and again are perceived by the senses, communicating a new and social happiness. It is not till goodness be thus expressed, that it assumes the nature of beauty. (7, 50)

Thus does the new theory of Discernment and its functions transform the Cartesian physiology of a Le Brun into an ethical and social mechanism.

(2) THE USES OF DISCERNMENT

When the heart flies out before the understanding, it saves the judgment a world of pains.

Sterne, A Sentimental Journey (1768)

There was something predictive in his look! Perhaps it is foolish to remark it; but there are times and places when I am a child at those things.

Mackenzie, The Man of Feeling (1771)

For Sterne, as we have seen, human affairs are such a tissue of unpredictable improbabilities that rational calculation and conjecture are nearly impossible.[17] In his works both fictional and non-fictional, Sterne recurs to our ignorance of the internal constitution of things, an ignorance that baffles our attempts at prediction and control.

That in many and dark abstracted questions of mere speculation, we should err, – is not strange: we live among mysteries and riddles, and almost everything which comes in our way, in one light or another, may be said to baffle our understanding...

"But mark, madam, we live amongst riddles and mysteries – the most obvious things, which come in our way, have dark sides, which the quickest sight cannot penetrate into; and even the clearest and most exalted understandings amongst us find ourselves puzzled and at a loss in almost every cranny of nature's works."[18]

The understanding fails especially in its attempts to understand other minds, from which we are radically and painfully separated. In *A Sentimental Journey*, Yorick describes the way "nature has set up by her own unquestionable authority certain boundaries and fences to circumscribe the discontent of man":

'Tis true we are endued with an imperfect power of spreading our happiness beyond *her* limits, but 'tis so ordered, that from the want of languages, connections, and dependencies, and from the difference in education, customs and habits, we lie under so many impediments in communicating our sensations out of our own sphere, as often amounts to a total impossibility. (78)

Sterne does, of course, suggest one "language" capable of drawing us out of ourselves and into communion with others: a language of signs, available not to judgment but to discernment.

She repeated her instructions three times over to me with the same good natur'd patience the third time as the first; – and if *tones and manners* have a meaning, which certainly they have, unless to hearts which shut them out – she seem'd really interested, that I should not lose myself. (162)

This is nature's "short hand," described at length in Sterne's chapter titled "The Translation," what in *Tristram Shandy* he identifies as "a thousand unnoticed openings ... which let a penetrating eye at once into a man's soul" (497). *A Sentimental Journey* contains "looks" of such intricate significance "that all the languages of Babel set loose together could not express them – they are communicated and caught so instantaneously, that you can scarcely say which party is the infecter"; their meaning is available to "penetration," which looks into one's "very heart" (168–69). In his sermons, Sterne argues that such signification results from the human condition of being a composition of body and soul:

in the present state we are in, we find such a strong sympathy and union between our souls and bodies, that the one cannot be touched or sensibly affected, without producing some corresponding emotion in the other. – Nature has assigned a different look, tone of voice, gesture, peculiar to every passion and affection we are subject to; and, therefore, to argue against this strict correspondence which is held between our souls and bodies, – is disputing against the frame and mechanism of human nature.

"We are not angels, but men cloathed with bodies" – the dress of thought, its body, is of course language; "we have need of all these external helps which nature has made the interpreters of our thoughts."[19] The sentimental traveller achieves "sentimental commerce" with others through an exquisite discerning of signs (78). The *Journey* as a whole, as Martin Battestin has shown in the best reading of Sterne's tale to date, is a progress "from solipsism toward communion, from self-love toward a felt apprehension," an "immediate, intuitive apprehension of another's self."[20] Such apprehension comes through facility in reading probable signs, a non-rational discernment: as Sterne says of the book as a whole, "this is not a work of reasoning"; "there is no regular reasoning on the ebb and flows of our humours" (177, 70). The journey begins, of course, as Yorick "gives up an argument," deciding to travel instead – "I'll look into them" (65); it ends with "The Supper" and "The Grace."

Mackenzie shares the late Augustan commitment to a special, innate, non-rational faculty of reading probable signs; he writes, for example, of Burns, in *Lounger* 97: "With what uncommon penetration and sagacity this Heaven-taught plowman, from his humble and unlettered station, has looked upon men and manners" (Mackenzie was of course one of the chief disseminators of the myth of Burns' "natural genius"). *The Man of Feeling* is a curiously circumspect celebration of this faculty of "looking," explicitly framed as a travel narrative on the model of Sterne's literary success.

If travel is understood in the conventional sense, *The Man of Feeling* is a novel of anti-travel. The tale proper opens, like the *Sentimental Journey, in medias res* – in the midst indeed of a discussion about the advantages of travel to France. Since the journey of the sentimental traveller is an exploration rather of minds than of continents – physical places – the trip to France appropriately does not occur. To the proposition that "There is some rust about every man at the beginning" of his life, Mr. Silton (the very name suggests incrustation) and the narrator Edward Sedley (from *sedes?*) respond:

"Let them rub it off by travel," said the baronet's brother, who was a striking instance of excellent metal, shamefully rusted... "They should wear it off by travel." –Why, it is true," said I, "that will go far; but then it will often happen, that in the velocity of a modern tour, and amidst the materials through which it is commonly made, the friction is so violent, that not only the rust, but the metal too is lost in the progress." (7–8)

Thus later in the novel Sir George's son returns from his grand tour to add English seductions to the evil account he has learned to keep abroad (56–57). The "wise man" in London delivers the conventional attack on the pointlessness of most foreign travel. When Harley must leave the country for London, it is appropriately not his own choice, but financial need that makes him leave; upon his return,

his enjoyment was as great as if he had arrived from the tour of Europe, with a Swiss valet for his companion, and half a dozen snuff-boxes, with invisible hinges, in his pocket. But we take our ideas from the sounds which folly has invented; Fashion, Bonton, and Virtu, are the names of certain idols, to which we sacrifice the genuine pleasures of the soul: in this world of semblance, we are contented with personating happiness; to feel it, is an art beyond us. (100)

Such conventional travel is a mere attention to the "world of semblance" because, as Mountford tells Harley senior in the unhappy travel narrative with which *The Man of Feeling* ends, "The Pupil. A Fragment" (a journey whose itinerary, like Sterne's, has been France and Italy):

I travelled, because it is the fashion for young men of my fortune to travel ... But as to the higher part of education, Mr. Harley, the culture of the Mind; – let the feelings be awakened, let the heart be brought forth to its object, placed in the light in which nature would have it stand, and its decisions will ever be just. (118)

In rejecting travel, Mackenzie is rejecting the model of learning, education, and knowledge on which it rests – that slow accretion of Lockean ideas on which a conscious and comparing judgment may work; at the same time, he is rejecting the formal procedures of the novel in Fielding's manner, which through studied repetition with variation seeks to engage and train the power of (comparing) judgment.

It is penetration into character rather than prudence and judgment which this novel celebrates and teaches; in Mackenzie's world, even "wit" is suspect: "wits" are ill-natured deceivers, like the Italians Sedley meets; "wit" obstructs friendship and communion, as it does for the fortune-telling beggar; Miss Walton is valuable precisely because she lacks "wit."[21] Wit plays on the surfaces of things, while discernment penetrates. Typically in sentimental narratives, heroines are not only not witty, but also not conventionally beautiful; their beauty is a quality of mind, available only to the discerning hero, who can read it from the signs in her body:

Harley's notions of the καλον, or beautiful, were not always to be defined, nor indeed such as the world would always assent to, though we could define them. A blush, a phrase of affability to an inferior, a tear at a moving tale, were to him, like the Cestus of Cytherea, unequalled in conferring beauty. (14–15)

In the same way, Yorick's first French inamorata has a face "not critically handsome, but there was that in it ... which attached me much more to it" (93–94). In Inchbald's *Nature and Art*, Rebecca Rymer is "by far the least handsome daughter of four," but for Henry, "It was her mind, which beaming on her face, and actuating her every motion, had ever constituted all her charms"; this is a beauty that does not fade during all the years Henry spends abroad, seeking his father in America (60, 178). (By 1780, John Donaldson, who locates all beauty in the "external marks of sensibility," could write in *The Elements of Beauty* that "Even with regard to the human character, we do not find that virtue ever accompanies the fairest form" (96) – a conscious rejection of Renaissance physiognomics, in which the opposite view was normative.)

Mackenzie explicitly frames his novel's contrast between judgment and discernment as one between *prudence* and *physiognomy*. "The colder homilies of prudence," the "frigidity of a casuist," the "economy" of an aunt of "maiden coldness," the "grave and prudent friends" who advise Harley to curry favor with a rich old relation – all refer to that attention to "worldly interests" which Harley rejects, just as the narrator rejects those whose study is "the Complete Accomptant, or Young Man's best Pocket Companion" (53, 16, 113, 9–10). Mackenzie's treatment of prudence accords with the explication of it as a form of self-interest to be found in contemporary works of sensationalist ethics, such as *The Theory of Moral Sentiments*:

The care of the health, of the fortune, of the rank and reputation of the individual, the objects upon which his comfort and happiness in this life are supposed principally to depend, is considered as the proper business of that virtue which is commonly called Prudence. (213)

Smith's prudent man is "cautious in his actions" and "reserved in his speech"; "he is not always frank and open," and (like the casuists) "he does not always think himself bound to tell the whole truth." Though capable of friendship, he is not "distinguished by the most exquisite sensibility" and "not always much disposed to general sociality" (214). The sentimental hero is of course the opposite of such a man. In a discussion of poetry in chapter 33 of *The Man of Feeling*, though others accuse poetry of corrupting the judgment, Harley defends its power to "enlarge the heart" (lead to communion); he allows that "this is an argument with the prudent against it: they urge the danger of unfitness for the world," and finds that through modern methods of education, "Our boys are prudent too soon" (81–82). The condition of youth that Harley seeks to perpetuate is what in his sermons Sterne identifies as a stage of life that displays "the strongest marks of undisguised tenderness and distinct compassion"; youth for Sterne is "unsuspicious" and acts "without view to itself, or previous calculation either of the loss or profit which may accrue."[22]

As Mackenzie condemns worldly prudence, so he seeks to demote in the hierarchy of mental faculties the parent faculty of prudence, judgment. It is study of Newton's "conjectures" on comets that drives the mathematician to Bedlam (31); the novel glories in Harley's illogic:

By the time he had reached the Square ... he had brought his reasoning on the subject to such a point, that the conclusion, by every rule of logic, should have led him to a thorough indifference in his approaches to a fellow-mortal, whether that fellow mortal was possessed of six, or six thousand pounds a year. It is probable, however, that the premises had been improperly formed; for it is certain, that when he approached the great man's door, he felt his heart agitated by an unusual pulsation. (24)

Where the man of feeling acts well, he is described not as judging correctly but as being in effect the unthinking instrument of his own benevolence; he is less actor than one acted upon, a kind of robot of sympathy:

Harley had drawn a shilling from his pocket; but virtue bade him consider on whom he was going to bestow it. – Virtue held back his arm: – but a milder form, a younger sister of virtue's, not so severe as virtue, nor so serious as pity, smiled upon him: His fingers lost their compression; – nor did virtue offer to catch the money as it fell. (22–23)

Later, he draws Edwards' sword "with a convulsive sort of motion," again in an act of mechanical benevolence (91).

It is through the exercise of discernment – most frequently an internal probabilism that works by inference from physiognomic signs – that Harley makes such benevolent contacts with others. Mackenzie recurrently and centrally uses physiognomics to typify the power of discernment, but his use of physiognomics in the novel has not been properly understood. Harley's inferences from facial signs are at times resoundingly wrong, sometimes amusingly and expensively so; as a result, modern readers have found in Mackenzie's treatment of physiognomics either simple inconsistency, or, more subtly, a self-conscious ironic undercutting of the very theory of knowledge that the novel purports to embody. In fact, Mackenzie is neither inconsistent nor anti-sentimental; such readers should take a hint from the incident with which the novel opens. As a curate and the book's primary narrator are hunting, the narrator's dog makes "a false point" (misreading signs, makes both a false diagnosis and false prognosis); nonetheless, his owner immediately defends him as "an excellent dog": "the fault was none of his, the birds were gone" (3).

In chapter 25, "His skill in physiognomy," Mackenzie arranges events into what appears to be a conventional satiric scene of ironic juxtaposition. We are told that "physiognomy was one of Harley's foibles" as he mistakes a card sharp for an absent-minded and benevolent old man; Mackenzie omits no opportunity to make his hero look foolish. The old man has just told a beggar that he had no money about him, but suddenly finds in his pocket "ten shillings to serve as markers of his score" at cards; Harley misreads the sign rashly, and with unconscious irony:

"He had no change for the beggar," said Harley to himself; "but I can easily account for it: it is curious to observe the affection that inanimate things will create in us by a long acquaintance: if I may judge from my own feelings, the old man would not part with one of these counters for ten times its intrinsic value; it even got the better of his benevolence! I myself have a pair of old brass sleeve-buttons." (46–47)

The two even have a discussion of benevolence, in which the old man remarks that "We cannot easily distinguish" true from counterfeit objects of charity (45). The stage is carefully set for chapter 27, "His skill in physiognomy is doubted," in which Harley is told of his error, and which ends:

"Young gentleman," said his friend on the other side of the table, "let me advise you to be a little more cautious for the future; and as for faces – you may look into them to know, whether a man's nose be a long or a short one." (53)

In Fielding this would constitute an ironic juxtaposition, an invitation for the reader to judge (and condemn) physiognomic inference – but not here. Between these incidents, Harley meets a prostitute in the street, whose face convinces him that she is a worthy object of charity; his inference is overwhelmingly justified by the event, and as in chapter 33 Harley leaves London in a stage-coach, we read:

Though his inclination [to physiognomy] had met with some rubs in the metropolis, he had not yet lost his attachment to that science; he set himself therefore to examine, as usual, the countenances of his companions. Here indeed he was not long in doubt as to the preference; for besides that the elderly gentleman, who sat opposite to him, had features by nature more expressive of good dispositions, there was something in that periwig we mentioned peculiarly attractive of Harley's regard. (76)

Another benevolent-looking old gentleman; no better circumstances than a periwig; but once again, Harley's reading of signs proves correct, as it does throughout the remainder of the novel, especially in his discovery of old Edwards (85). What are we to make of Harley's varying success in an art about which the novel has so much to say, and in its most carefully wrought incidents seems at once to extol and condemn?

It is just after the advice about noses that Harley must decide whether or not to continue to aid the prostitute he has befriended; with that warning in mind, he weighs and rejects the "colder homilies of prudence," exclaiming: "Powers of mercy that surround me! ... do ye not smile upon deeds like these? To calculate the chances of deception is too tedious a business for the life of man!" (53). Mackenzie's point is simply that though physiognomic inference, and discernment generally, is only probable, not certain – it may fail to penetrate dissimulation – it *can* reveal distressed sincerity; more important, the spiritual openness to communion of the physiognomist is a good in itself. We should note that it is Harley's "*inclination* to physiognomy" which Mackenzie defends above, that state in which, as Sterne puts it, the heart does not "shut out" the signate expression of others.

The humor, even at his hero's expense, that so disquiets Mackenzie's modern readers is not an ironic undercutting of sentimental convention – Mackenzie does not mean to laugh us out of physiognomy – but is rather the product of a strain of moral realism which is seldom noticed but characteristic of sentimentalism, even in its

worst excesses. Mackenzie is no proponent of man's innate goodness; when in chapter 21 the "Misanthropist" argues that "In short,
man is an animal equally selfish and vain," Harley does not rise to
disagree. Rather, he concedes the truth of the observation, and
denies only that such reminders of our fallen state are generally
useful:

"This is a strange creature," said his friend to Harley. "I cannot say," answered
he, "that his remarks are of the pleasant kind: it is curious to observe how the
nature of truth may be changed by the garb it wears; softened to the admonition
of friendship, or soured into the severity of a reproof: yet this severity may be
useful to some tempers; it somewhat resembles a file; disagreeable in its
operation, but hard metals may be the brighter for it." (43)

To match this curious statement (which embodies in part the late
Augustan difficulty of reconciling sentiment with satire) can be
found other, more general affirmations of what might be called the
same perspectivism:

Though I am not of the opinion with some wise men, that the existence of objects
depends on idea; yet, I am convinced, that their appearance is not a little
influenced by it. The optics of some minds are in so unlucky a perspective, as to
throw a certain shade on every picture that is represented to them; while those of
others (of which number was Harley) like the mirrors of the ladies, have a
wonderful effect in bettering their complexions. Through such a medium
perhaps he was looking at his present companion. (25)

When Harley misjudged the card sharp, he was judging "from his
own feelings"; when his aunt – a woman whom "maiden coldness"
prevents from reading the signs that Harley and Miss Wilmot are in
love – argues against physiognomy, the narrator explains her
argument as again an expression of perspectivism, a projection
outwards of her own inner narrowness of spirit:

indeed physiognomy was one of Harley's foibles, for which he had been often
rebuked by his aunt in the country; who used to tell him, that when he was come
to her years and experience, he would know that all's not gold that glisters: and it
must be owned, that his aunt was a very sensible, harsh-looking, maiden-lady of
threescore and upwards. (44)

The generous outward projection of benevolence typical of the
sentimental physiognomist is a good not in its invariable correctness,
but in the spiritual condition of openness which it exemplifies. This
cultivation of communion, furthermore, is explicitly identified as the
instrument even of wider political community – what Smith called
"general sociality." Cursing the "narrow heart" of a landlord who
can tear down a schoolhouse to improve his "prospect," Harley
reminds the schoolmistress, now a keeper of orphans, "that we are

all relations"; a few pages later the same principle leads him to condemn British political intervention in India (95, 96, 102). The most famous treatment of this kind of progression outward of the social affections – of the movement from communion to community – is of course the *Theory of Moral Sentiments.*

The sentimental hero can consistently be a figure not only of fun but even of unmasking irony because the sentimentalist's claim is not that discernment and communion will reveal innate human *goodness* – Mackenzie does not accept such a doctrine any more than does Fielding or Smollett – but that it will reveal human *interrelatedness*, and in revealing this also further it. Virtue is simply a name for – a happy by-product of – this recognition and furtherance of community; the sentimentalist ethic, like that of Hume and Adam Smith, is naturalistic. Virtue is something to be achieved, to be realized in and through the furtherance of society – in Smith's words, "the immense fabric of society, that fabric which to raise and support seems in this world, if I may say so, to have been the peculiar and darling care of Nature" (86). Judgment might prescribe the formation of such a society, but it is our providentially ordered social instincts which in fact bring it about:

When by natural principles we are led to advance those ends, which a refined and enlightened reason would recommend to us, we are very apt to impute to that reason, as to their efficient cause, the sentiments and actions by which we advance those ends, and to imagine that to be the wisdom of man, which is in reality the wisdom of God. (87)

Arguments such as this are at the heart of the Scottish philosophers' belief, most forcefully stated by Adam Ferguson, that social order is the product of the unintended consequences of human action.[23] And as Mackenzie makes clear, those social instincts need not themselves be benevolent to be productive of socially good results; he comments just before a servant approaches Harley with "a meaning face of recital":

The desire of communicating knowledge or intelligence, is an argument with those who hold that man is naturally a social animal. It is indeed one of the earliest propensities we discover; but it may be doubted whether the pleasure (for pleasure there certainly is) arising from it be not often more selfish than social: for we frequently observe the tidings of Ill communicated as eagerly as the annunciation of Good. Is it that we delight in observing the effects of the stronger passions? for we are all philosophers in this respect; and it is perhaps amongst the spectators at Tyburn that the most genuine are to be found. (106)

In this way, too, we must make sense of the sexual humor of *A Sentimental Journey*, humor which disgusted Victorian readers and perplexes modern ones. Expecting Sterne to accept a doctrine of innate goodness, modern readers find Yorick's intrusive sexuality to be explicable only as an anti-sentimental undercurrent of irony in an otherwise paradigmatically sentimental book. But the sentimental hero can be the butt of humor and even unmasking irony precisely because his goodness is not something innate, but something to be achieved. The goal of the sentimental traveller "is an awareness of the unity and interrelatedness of all beings"; for Yorick, the "first approaches to that condition must be through a frank acceptance of his sexual nature."[24] Sexuality – in Smith's phrase, "the passion which unites the two sexes" (78) – has of course long been understood as a way out of self and toward communion with others; through the medium of the family, it is as well an unintended route to larger social arrangements, to community. In the completion of this state, Yorick feels a "divinity which stirs within," "generous joys and generous cares beyond myself," revealing the world to be unified as one "SENSORIUM."[25]

In fact, the philosophical realignment that made of discernment an independent faculty of unconscious inference solved a number of problems – especially moral problems – as these had arisen in mid-century narrative. It may be helpful before we proceed to examine the difficulties encountered by an emotivist ethic which does *not* have available this theory of an independent faculty of internal probability. These difficulties arise in works that stand uneasily between the novel of judgment and the novel of discernment, works such as Goldsmith's *Vicar of Wakefield* (1766).

In *The Vicar*, characters such as Squire Thornhill and Mrs. Primrose are repeatedly said to harbor "secret reasons" and "hidden motives"; they take "secret pleasures," give "secret instances" of affection, betray or successfully conceal "latent plots," and seek to further their schemes through "private conferences."[26] Like the language of plots and schemes, this vocabulary of internal and external – of things manifest and things kept hidden – always marks a moral distinction. Evil works through hypocrisy, the mounting of false and misleading signs; Goldsmith opposes to those who "counterfeit" natural signs (such as Jenkinson and Thornhill) others whose virtue consists in "candor" – a term which to Goldsmith meant generosity and good nature, but most of all frank openness. (Many late Augustan critics were to protest the extensions of the meaning of *candor* for goodness or intergrity to voluble sincerity.) All these virtues in fact resolve for Goldsmith into "sincerity," conceived as an integrity of character which naturally gives external, signate expression to what passes within – expression that because the product of natural signification is also of the highest probability.

Goodness may perhaps not open itself fully to strangers, but in such a case the fault is likely to be in the observer; even Mr. Burchell cannot avoid giving hints of his real identity.[27]

Because in the world of *The Vicar*, as in that of Fielding and Smollett, evil makes its way by forging natural signs, innocence must protect itself with a power to penetrate disguise: what Goldsmith calls "circumspection," a prudent "suspicion" of others. But such suspicion seems to savor of just the scheming which innocent good nature seeks to avoid; over and over, *The Vicar* raises the moral question: can circumspection coexist with candor? Can good nature be suspicious, and if it can, are the rewards of worldly prudence worth the risks? The book presents seemingly decisive evidence on both sides. According to Dr. Primrose (in his long speech on English politics), it is "sacred circumspection" (102) which keeps the "middle order of mankind" free; and we need hardly accept that oversubtle modern reading of Goldsmith's romance which finds irony throughout to agree that the work is full of instances of that familiar Augustan irony which is used to unmask, and so to teach judgment a healthy suspicion.

On the other hand, Moses elicits from a reformed Mr. Jenkinson the opposite view – in what might be an indictment of *The Vicar* itself:

"I suppose," cried my son, "that the narrative of such a life as yours must be extremely instructive and amusing."

"Not much of either," returned Mr. Jenkinson. "Those relations which describe the tricks and vices only of mankind, by increasing our suspicion in life, retard our success. The traveller that distrusts every person he meets, and turns back upon the appearances of every man that looks like a robber, seldom arrives in time to his journey's end." (147)

In short, Goldsmith is unable to distinguish a virtuous from a corrupt circumspection, a worthy exercise of judgment from an ill-natured suspicion. For him, discernment is still a capacity of judgment, not a distinct faculty of internal probability; when part of the exercise of judgment becomes suspect, there is no other faculty of circumspection to which Goldsmith can turn. Happily, his choice of the literary form of the comic romance saves him from having to settle his moral dilemma; in this story modelled on the Book of Job, "Our happiness ... is in the power of one who can bring it about a thousand unforeseen ways that mock our foresight" (133).[28] Unsuspicious innocence prospers – and *The Vicar* escapes the censures of a Jenkinson – because in its comic world of poetic justice, Providence finally rewards the sincere.

(3) DISCERNMENT AND FORM

It consists ov som eppisoddical adventures ov a *Man ov Feeling*: hware hiz sentiments ar occasionally exprest, and dhe features ov hiz mind devellopt, az dhe incidents draw dhem foarth.

Mackenzie, Letter to James Elphinston (23 July 1770)

Among these, I cannot but rank the author of Tristram Shandy, the Sentimental Journey, &c. In these most unclassical productions, we see all regard to connexion and arrangement thrown aside; the reader is frequently left to help himself to a meaning, or, if there is one, it is such as no two men understand alike.

George Gregory, *Letters on Literature* (1808)[29]

The sentimental indictment of judgment results not only in novels of anti-prudence and anti-probability, but also in the fragmentation of earlier narrative forms. Fielding's novels are repetitive forms, sequences of structurally similar contexts (like those encountered by a traveller) designed to invite comparative judgment. But as judgment was understood by the Augustans to be a conscious and comparing faculty, discernment was a power of unconscious inference used to penetrate in particular instances. The sentimental novel – the novel designed to embody and to exercise discernment – thus abandons earlier structures of repeated action, as well as the signs and cues of inferential relations among parts typical of the novel of judgment, and seeks a form of its own. As Sir Walter Scott observes of *The Man of Feeling*, "it is in fact no narrative, but a series of successive incidents, each rendered interesting by the mode in which they operate on the feelings of Harley."[30]

Mackenzie was aware of his departure from earlier narrative procedures. He writes to James Elphinston (using Elphinston's peculiar reformed spelling) that he adopted the fragmented form of *The Man of Feeling* "partly from wanting to' shun dhe common rote ov novvels," but he refers as well to "dhat logiscian, hoos figgure I hav chanced to bring into' my Introduccion," the curate who remarks of the manuscript tale of Harley, "I could never find the author in one strain for two chapters together: and I don't believe there's a single syllogism from beginning to end."[31] The curate finds – perhaps with an oblique reference to Fielding and Richardson – that "indeed it is no more a history than it is a sermon" (4). His hunting companion agrees, calling the work a "medley," "a bundle of little episodes, put together without art, and of no importance on the whole" (5); Harley's tale lacks "the intricacies of a novel," containing only "recitals of little adventures, in which the dispositions of a man, sensible to judge, and still more warm to feel, had room to unfold themselves" (125).

Thus Mackenzie gives his readers explicit warning of the new form with which they are engaged. Less explicitly, in a number of asides punctuating the narrative, he defines his own procedure by opposition to that of earlier writers:

In times not credulous of inspiration, we should account for this from some natural cause; but we do not mean to account for it at all; it were sufficient to describe its effects... (17)

From what impulse he did this, we do not mean to inquire; as it has ever been against our nature to search for motives where bad ones are to be found. (48–49)

It was frequently matter of discourse amongst the servants: perhaps her maiden coldness – but for those things we need not account. (113)

This method of coy and suggestive denial – probably learned from Sterne – serves a double function. It is a renunciation of more analytical narrative procedures, while of course being also a clear sign that a cause is indeed to be inferred from the presented effect. It is a cue that should activate the reader's discernment, while seeking at the same time to allay and disown judgment.

Where *The Man of Feeling* does employ the signs and structural procedures most typical of the novel of judgment, it does so either to renounce the kinds of interpretive inference such signs usually invite, or simply fails to give them any function in leading the mind to larger meanings. We have already observed the first of these alternatives in Harley's encounter with the card sharp; even after the structurally similar incident of deception in chapter 19, two chapters later the man of feeling again outrageously misreads signs that have been deliberately made clear to the reader, and again he suffers no ill consequences from his error. In similar fashion, when in chapter 28 Harley rushes off to keep his appointment with the prostitute, Mackenzie troubles to tell us that "two vibrations of a pendulum would have served him to lock his bureau; – but they could not be spared" (54). The reader of Fielding awaits a theft; such careful planting of details could not be without purpose; but Harley never suffers from his imprudence, and indeed we never hear of the bureau again. What would in another context have been a broad hint of events to come is here merely a sign of Harley's character – and an equally broad hint that we are not in Fielding's novelistic world.

Elsewhere, reminiscences of the structural procedures of the novel of judgment are mere vestigial formations: structures which help to fill out the narrative and give it shape, but which serve no inferential purpose. *The Man of Feeling* contains paired baronets, and paired scenes of characters who complain that the food served them is inedible before proceeding to devour it with relish (27, 38); in neither case is the repetition significant (the paired events do not comment on one another or provide contexts for discrimination). Harley makes three unsuccessful visits to the London baronet; none of these develops what occurs in any other, and after the third visit Harley misreads the baronet's motives (again mistaking selfishness for generosity) as he has often misread others' before, but without significant relation to these other similar incidents. To the reader of Fielding, these insignificant repetitions are adventitious circumstances; a modern reader might point to them in building a subversive interpretation of the novel; but they are merely vestiges of earlier procedures, without function in the new form.

It was from Sterne's argument that "a man would act wisely, if he could prevail upon himself, to live contented without foreign knowledge or foreign improvements"[32] that Mackenzie probably borrowed his censures on travel, as he did his devices of presenting chapters out of sequence and of giving commentary on events before they have actually occurred; he borrowed from Sterne the narrative procedure most characteristic of the new form, that of presenting events through disparate signate details organized into short, relatively detached scenes (often deliberate digressions). The most significant circumstances and signs so organized are usually deliberately small, seemingly trivial details, which to be understood require less to be related to one another than they do the reader's discerning penetration into character ("flying from my own head into his," as Tristram puts it, 630) – the kind of means to communion the form means to teach. In *Tristram Shandy*, "the penetrating reader" (106) replaces Fielding's "judicious reader" as recipient of authorial advice and cajollery; in *A Sentimental Journey*, participation in such didactic structure – penetrating reading – issues finally in self-knowledge: "It is sufficient for my reader, if he is a traveller himself,... to determine his own place and rank in the catalogue" of kinds of travellers (82–83).[33]

Sterne takes positive pleasure in frustrating and overwhelming probable judgment as called forth by the earlier form. *Tristram Shandy*, full of direct and oblique satire on the methods of Fielding,[34] repeatedly challenges its readers to find meaning and structure in its digressive fracturing of earlier narrative procedure:

Lay down the book, and I will allow you half a day to give a probable guess at the grounds of this procedure.

What these perplexities of my uncle *Toby* were, – 'tis impossible for you to guess; – if you could, – I should blush ... inasmuch as I set no small store by myself upon this very account, that my reader has never yet been able to guess at any thing. And in this, Sir, I am of so singular a humour, that if I thought you was able to form the least judgment or probable conjecture to yourself, of what was to come in the next page, – I would tear it out of my book.

... guess ten thousand guesses, multiplied into themselves – rack – torture your invention for ever, you're where you was – In short, I'll tell it in the next chapter.

How we disposed of our eggs and figs, I defy you, or the Devil himself, had he not been there ... to form the least probable conjecture.[35]

What larger structure *A Sentimental Journey* possesses – Yorick's progress from a désobligeant to chapters titled "The Supper" (a communion) and "The Grace," assisted along the way by the providential intervention of characters with such names as "Dessein" – is parasitic on earlier (sometimes perhaps inevitable) methods of narrative; its fabric, however, is composed of those very short episodes wherein, it is tempting to suggest, novel aspires to the condition of lyric (in a Palgrave sense):

As this is not a work of reasoning, I leave the solution as I found it, and content myself with the truth only of the remark, which is verified by every lane and by-lane of Paris. I was walking down that which leads from the Carousal to the Palais Royal... (177)

Sterne writes in *Tristram Shandy*: "I have constructed the main work and the adventitious parts of it with such intersections ... that the whole machine, in general, has been kept a-going" (81–82).

We may once again appeal to contemporary criticism to provide a rationale for fragmented forms as the special vehicles of the literature of discernment. As a procedure not of comparison but of penetration, discernment was widely recognized to be the justification not only for fragmented narrative structure, but also for those small forms, or fragment-wholes, in which late Augustan critics were increasingly interested. In such fragmented and (in their various ways) "unfinished" wholes as *Tristram Shandy, A Sentimental Journey*, and *The Man of Feeling*, the individual episode may as reading paradigm of penetration embody all the patterns of signification of the longer work in which it appears, itself an associative sequence of episodes. Each episode stands in a relation rather of synecdoche than of metonymy to the work in which it appears: whereas in the narrative of judgment, interpretation must proceed by attention to subordinate parts and then by inference to the whole, the pressure of the elevation of the faculty of discernment is toward works in which parts are themselves coordinate wholes.[36]

The attempts of a critic such as Isaac D'Israeli to elevate such small forms as anecdote, preface, textual commentary, marginalia, and even indices as in themselves literary genres susceptible of their own unity and structure; to elevate the status of such "poetical opuscula" as sonnet and epigram; and to treat forms such as the miscellany as fragment-wholes all depend on a commitment to discernment as the faculty of literary structure and interpretation.[37] According to D'Israeli, "A well-chosen anecdote frequently reveals a character, more happily than an elaborate delineation; as a glance of lightning will sometimes discover what had escaped us in a full light," for "A man of penetration sees relations in an anecdote, which are not immediately perceived by others."[38] It is in its minute particularity "that an anecdote, or a circumstance, which may appear inconsequential to a reader, may bear some remote or latent connection, which a mature reflection often discovers" (79).

Discernment is furthermore the faculty of synecdoche. Though in his *Dissertation on Anecdotes* D'Israeli is ostensibly committed to the familiar empiricist view that knowledge is the slow accretion of sensations and reflections, of attention and comparative judgment – "We gain our knowledge by the slow accession of multiplied facts; these our reflection combines, and thus combined, they form what we call experience" – he outlines as well another way of knowing whose typical embodiment is the fragment-whole, a form such as anecdote. This other way of knowing is an immediate and unconscious grasp of embodied universals (just what the earlier theory of knowledge had ceded only to judgment); "Of some extraordinary minds, it has been said, that their knowledge is attained by that sublime conception, which surveys at one glance the species, and becomes as it were by intuition, familiar with the individual" (26). Through discernment, the reader of anecdotes may infer from "these minute notices of human nature" directly to "the genius of an age or nation" (80, 9); "What perhaps [an artist] had in vain desired for half his life, is revealed to him by an anecdote" (65).

For the reader of discernment, D'Israeli notes in his essay "On Reading" (1796), it is not "always necessary ... to read every book entire" (he mentions Johnson's habit of reading only parts of books); "It may be unnecessary also, to read all the works of an author." According to this pattern of synecdoche, for instance, the discerning reader will find that "Of Lord Chesterfield's Letters, the third volume is the essential one, and concentrates the whole system."[39] Facility in this synecdochic reading of probable signs is "genius," a power not of "mechanical assiduity," but one which

seises, as if it were by the rapidity of inspiration, whatever it discovers in the works of others, which may enrich its own stores; which knows by a quick apprehension, what to examine and what to imbibe; and which receives an atom of intelligence, from the minds of others or it's own mind, as an accidental spark falling on a heap of nitre, is sufficient to raise a powerful blaze. (283–84)

That attention to "minute circumstances" and small details which we found in chapter IV to accompany the disjoining of character from action in the hierarchic structure of the literary work came easily to be assimilated to and justified by the new doctrine of discernment. According to George Gregory in the *Letters on Literature*, "The soul of poetry is particularizing and bringing to view the minute circumstances which give 'a local habitation and a name' to the subjects and animation to the picture"; "The soul of poetry is detail" which it requires "penetration" to observe (116, 103). It is genius, according to Duff's *Essay on Original Genius*, which is capable of "discerning those minute properties, or of relishing those particular and distinguishing beauties" (159); these are the bold "strokes of nature" which, William Gilpin argues in his essay "On Picturesque Beauty," the greatest artists command: "A stroke may be called *free*, when there is no appearance of constraint. It is *bold*, when a part is given for the whole, which it cannot fail of suggesting. This is the laconism of genius" (17).

We may take as a useful index of the transition from metonymic to synecdochic patterns of literary structure one more small example (recapitulated in larger ways throughout works) of the changing ways parts of works are related to others and so join into wholes: the device of the catalogue or list. In early Augustan literature the catalogue serves two central functions. It may function to suggest the divine order which underlies and informs nature's variety; in such uses, the catalogue usually consists of paired contraries understood to be in dynamic equipoise. This is a pattern we have often seen before; Pope gives a formula for it in his metaphysical principle that "All subsists by elemental strife," or, as Denham puts it in *Coopers Hill*, "While driness moysture, coldness heat resists, / All that we have, and that we are, subsists."[40] John Dyer presents a typical use of lists to suggest order in variety in "Grongar Hill" (1726):

> Below me trees unnumbered rise,
> Beautiful in various dyes:
> The gloomy pine, the poplar blue,
> The yellow beach, the sable yew,
> The slender fir that taper grows,
> The sturdy oak with broad-spread boughs...
>
> And see the rivers, how they run
> Through woods and meads, in shade and sun;
> Sometimes swift, sometimes slow,

Wave succeeding wave, they go
A various journey to the deep,
Like human life to endless sleep!
(57–62, 93–98)

These lists suggest "mutual dependence" among parts of a world harmoniously organized, but which finds its true meaning and completion only in the transcendent mind of its maker.[41] By substituting static opposition for dynamic equipoise, the catalogue may serve its second central function, that of suggesting the chaos or disorder which stems from the attempt to renounce proper relations of hierarchic interdependence (again, a pattern we have already seen at work in Pope's verse). The type for such lists is Milton's description of Hell in *Paradise Lost*: "Rocks, Caves, Lakes, Fens, Bogs, Dens, and shades of death" (II, 621), much imitated in the decades to follow: here not only harsh consonants, monosyllables, and spondaic interruption of a more various metrical pattern, but also the putting of such disparate items on a level are an emblem of Satan's pride, his work as leveller of God's order. The most famous echo of this line is of course Pope's "Puffs, Powders, Patches, Bibles, Billet-doux" in *The Rape of the Lock*; the poem contains as well more complex variants of the disorderly list, such as static opposition to suggest sterility, as in the "moving Toyshop" of the vain belle's heart:

Where Wigs with Wigs, Sword-knots with Sword-knots strive,
Beaus banish Beaus, and Coaches Coaches drive. (I, 101–02)

In these early Augustan examples, lists function metonymically, suggesting orderly or disorderly relations of parts. Romantic catalogues, by contrast, characteristically function by synecdoche; it is useful to compare Milton's line with Wordsworth's echo of it in *The Prelude*:

With temples crested, bridges, gondolas,
Rocks, dens, and groves of foliage taught to melt
Into each other.... (VIII, 87–89)

Here disorder is turned into harmonious union, but not in the Augustan manner of the poised balance of contraries: rather, elements *fuse* into Wordsworth's whole, just as lines once end-stopped now pointedly enjamb. The same shift from balance to fusion may be found by comparing Augustan prospect poems with such Romantic prospects as, for instance, Coleridge's in "Reflections on Having Left a Place of Retirement" (1795):

> But the time, when first
> From that low Dell, steep up the stony Mount
> I climb'd with perilous toil and reach'd the top,
> Oh! what a goodly scene! Here the bleak mount,
> The bare bleak mountain speckled thin with sheep;
> Grey clouds, that shadowing spot the sunny fields;
> And river, now with bushy rocks o'er-browed,
> Now winding bright and full, with naked banks;
> And seats, and lawns, the Abbey and the wood,
> And cots, and hamlets, and faint city-spire;
> The Channel there, the Islands and white sails,
> Dim coasts, and cloud-like hills, and shoreless Ocean –
> It seem'd like Omnipresence! God, methought,
> Had built him there a Temple: the whole World
> Seem'd *imag'd* in its vast circumference... (26–40)

Here what would in an Augustan poem remain distinct parts of a transcendently ordered whole are fused: sheep and clouds are equally spots against contrasting whiter or grayer backdrops (brought together in parallel at lines 30–31); the same speckling shows up, reflected in the river (line 32), in the gray islands and "white sails" seen at sea, and once again in "cloud-like hills" seen on "dim coasts" (lines 36–37). All these parts of the scene, in other words, are in some sense the same; each stands by synecdoche for the whole, "the whole World" which is itself by the same synecdoche "imag'd" here.

Late Augustan criticism stands midway in this transition. It is not uncommon in the 1780s and 1790s to hear complaints about uses of the catalogue, such as Frank Sayers' against "a long list of names of places, than which nothing can be more tedious in poetry."[42] Early Augustan catalogues had of course always been more than devices of amplification and magnificence: conveying the variety of nature, they embodied that literary ideal of variety which is the literary analogue of what in the world is God's plenitude; organizing this plenitude in specifiable ways (such as the balancing of contraries), these catalogues embody a view of the structure of the world. They invite discrimination – comparing judgment – to elicit these structuring principles, as even more do Augustan disorderly lists, which invite judgment to discover what is in fact an error of judgment (the indiscriminate heaping of Bibles with billet-doux). As the psychology of reading and composition rooted in judgment is displaced, so are its structural enactments. Moreover, as patterns of metonymy fragment, all lists seem chaotic, out of place in works possessing the strong unity critics such as Sayers require; but for narrators such as Sterne and Mackenzie, the whole of a novel may be a loose catalogue of discrete events, each of which functions by synecdoche. What Sterne called in *A Sentimental Journey* the "Novelty of my Vehicle" (82) is in this way an accurate reflection of what in *Tristram Shandy* he calls "this Fragment of Life" on a planet "made up of the shreds and clippings of the rest" (1, 8).

IX

Association, reverie, and the decline of hierarchy

The question still remains, what that process truly is, which the word *sagacity* is borrowed to denote, – whether the intermediate conceptions, that arise more readily, in certain minds, than in others, arise in consequence of any skill in discovering them, or any voluntary effort in producing them, or whether they do not arise in consequence of laws of suggestion, that are independent alike of our skill, and of any effort which that skill might direct?

Thomas Brown, *Lectures on the Philosophy of the Human Mind* (1820)

About probability explicitly so called, associationists from Hartley to Knight add little to what critics not also associationists have to say. As we should by now expect, it is not so much in its explicit definition of probability as in the role given it in a larger theoretical framework that association makes its contribution to our subject. On the associationist view, an improbability in a literary work is any incident or sentiment which breaks the mind's associative train; Kames describes the effect in the *Elements of Criticism*:

The improbability I talk of, is that of an irregular fact, contrary to the order and course of nature, and therefore unaccountable... an irregular fact always puzzles the judgment. Doubtful of its reality we immediately enter upon reflection, and discovering the cheat, lose all relish and concern. (I, 124)

Irregular facts rouse us from that "waking dream" which Kames calls "ideal presence."[1]

What makes this an *associationist* theory of probability is Kames' view, shared by such cobelievers as Campbell and Gerard, that "We find by experience, that objects are connected in the mind precisely as they are externally."[2] Yet it is also this associationist "hypothesis" (as Coleridge called it) "of an external world exactly correspondent to those images and modifications of our own being" that makes the associationist theory of probability so little different from others. More sophisticated thinkers, such as Hume and Abraham Tucker, who recognize both that in an empiricist framework experience could teach no such correspondence, and that associational ordering is wholly a mental product (that it provides, in Hume's words in the *Abstract*, "the only links that bind the parts of the universe together" for the mind), might have produced more radical and interesting accounts of probability.[3] That they did not stems of course from their rejection of any such subjectivism as this sort of account would entail.

Kames and Gerard, when they speak of probability explicitly so called, do so almost wholly in discussing *action*: the unity of action consists in an undisturbed associative train. "A play analyzed, is a chain of connected facts, of which each scene makes a link," Kames explains in a version of the doctrine of the *liaison des scènes* (III, 126). Although other associationists and indeed Kames himself define other kinds of literary unity than unity of action, none works out an explicit theory of probability to fit such new forms of unity. The reasons for this are several: the philosophical tradition, which treated probability mainly under the heading of cause and effect, exerted pressure to restrict probability to the realm of actions; as we have seen, internal probability, the obvious alternative, was not worked out on the model of external; and, finally, though the items in any associative train were understood to be signs – by the time of Thomas Brown's *Lectures*, Reid's "laws of suggestion" have come wholly to be identified with the laws of association – the probabilistic status of sign-inference was too familiar a point to warrant special notice.

But if associationism has little to tell us explicitly about probability in literary structure and interpretation, implicitly, through its theory of probable signs, it can tell us a great deal. Archibald Alison's influential *Essays on the Nature and Principles of Taste* (1790) develops in particularly interesting detail a theory of reading and composition as associative manipulation of probable signs.[4]

In the manner of all associationists since Hume, Alison's main concern is that principle of connection which gives structure and unity to works: this is "the great and fundamental Principle of Composition" and the criterion whereby "the excellence of poetical description is determined" (89, 92).

Ralph Cohen observes, "the associationist theory of unity," in literary works as elsewhere, is characterized by "its stressing relational unity and subtle transitions."[5] The unity Alison comes to define is a "unity of expression" constituted by a work all of whose parts are linked by easy transitions, linkages which Alison himself calls "associations or signs." Successful works are composed of what he calls "permanent signs" (128), i.e., those signs that, rooted in universal experience, bring about the same movements of thought in all readers at all times. Most important, association itself, acting according to its own rules, without the intervention of judgment (the

earlier Augustan faculty of structure), is productive of ordered
wholes. In Alison's theory, transitions, the connections of ideas that
constitute unity and convey meaning, cease to be objects of scrutiny
by reason and judgment; they must be "understood" by some other
faculty. His signs "lead" the *imagination*, the faculty to which
alone, he says, the fine arts are addressed (133, 1). Judgment only
impedes the process, both for writers and readers; thus it is within
the context of associationism that for the first time in history
appreciative reading is distinguished from criticism, and "criticism"
regarded as an inappropriate critical stance.

"Criticism" is an inappropriate stance because, like judgment in
Fielding's model, it involves as a first step the application of *attention*, which, Alison stresses again and again, is always to "minute
and solitary parts" (8). As an exercise of attention, criticism *fragments* the unity of the work: beauty is available to readers "only in
proportion to the degree in which they can relax this severity of
attention, and yield to the relation of resembling thought" (11–12).
As divisive, "the exercise of Criticism never fails to destroy, for the
time, our sensibility to the beauty of every composition," and habits
of criticism "generally end in destroying the sensibility of Taste"
(70). Thus attention, a faculty previously thought to be the first
requisite in revealing the unity and meaning of works, comes in
associationism to be the chief culprit in causing disunity and misunderstanding.[6]

Alison variously calls the state of mind of the receptive, as
opposed to the critical reader, a "pleasing reverie" or "romantic
dream" (3); it is in such a state that imagination prevails over
attention, and trains of ideas may be followed "without interruption" (90). A properly constructed work, according to this psychology of reception, is one made up of "such trains of imagery"
that "no labour of thought, or habits of attention, are required" in
reading it (14). The mental stance appropriate to literary response is
one wherein the mind is "vacant and unemployed," unconcerned
with the demands of appetite, interest, or will – a view which
though it entails a conscious rejection of judgment and attention
(thought to be exercises of will), has made Alison the subject of
particular study by modern philosophers seeking the roots of the
idea of aesthetics as an autonomous realm of experience distinguished by a specifically "aesthetic attitude," a peculiarly aesthetic
direction of the attention.[7] Alison himself gives a predictable class
analysis of those most able to follow out the associative links, the
relations of "signification" as he himself calls them, that constitute
works:

It is only in the higher stations accordingly, or in the liberal professions of life, that we expect to find men either of a delicate or comprehensive Taste. The inferior situations of life, by contracting the knowledge and the affections of men, within very narrow limits, produce insensibly a similar contraction in their notions of the beautiful or the sublime. (62)

For Alison, the poor and the scholarly both have minds too much given to strict reasoning to engage "in this powerless state of reverie, when we are carried on by our conceptions, not guiding them," wherein "the deepest emotions of beauty or sublimity are felt" (42); the minds of women are by contrast too much given to association to be guided by the signs of the work; it is only the "man of taste" who can be a literary reader. Moreover, "The business of life, in the greatest part of mankind, and the habits of more accurate thought, which are acquired by the few which reason and reflect, tend equally to produce in both, a stricter relation in the train of their thoughts, and a greater attention to the objects of their consideration," than occurs in *youth* (13): just as the child may serve the novelist as natural signifier, for Alison it is in youth that "the imagination is free and unembarrassed" (6).

From such a theory of reading and composition as a species of "reverie" follow predictable prescriptions for writers. Alison recommends to poets ideas that are "indistinct," for these will not tempt attention (32), and praises those that are "obscure." In the first Interlude in his *Loves of the Plants* (1789), Erasmus Darwin similarly recommends "indistinctness" in the presentation of allegorical figures, lest such figures tempt the attention, which is bound to find them improbable:

In poetry the personification or allegoric figure is generally indistinct and therefore does not strike us so forcibly as to make us attend to its improbability, but in painting the figures being all much more distinct, their improbability becomes apparent and seizes our attention to it... Whence I conclude that a certain degree of probability is necessary to prevent us from revolting with distaste from unnatural images unless we are otherwise so much interested in the contemplation of them as not to perceive their improbability. (1006–08)

A model work in prose on Alison's principles is William Beckford's travel narrative, *Dreams, Waking Thoughts, and Incidents* (1783), published (and suppressed) when its author was twenty-three. Beckford begins his first travel letter:

Shall I tell you my dreams? – To give an account of my time, is doing, I assure you, but little better. Never did there exist a more ideal being. A frequent mist hovers before my eyes, and, through its medium, I see objects so faint and hazy, that both their colors and forms are apt to delude me. This is a rare confession, say the wise, for a traveller to make; pretty accounts will such a one give of outlandish countries: his correspondents must reap great benefit, no doubt, from such purblind observations: – But stop, my good friends; patience a moment! – I really have not the vanity of pretending to make a single remark, during the whole of my journey: if — be contented with my visionary way of gazing, I am perfectly pleased... (53)

Beckford presents himself in the first leg of his journey asleep, waking only for a moment to catch a glimpse of an indistinct pastoral scene, which spurs a flood of associations. His accounts of the Low Countries are full of such admissions as "I neither heard ... nor noticed ... I closed my eyes upon the entire scene ... I know nothing more about it" (56). His most frequent narrative procedure is to present a single glimpse of a scene, usually in twilight – "I am very partial to seeing new objects by this dubious, visionary light" (58) – which then occasions a paragraph of vivid association; Beckford himself identifies his narrative procedure as "reverie."

Reading and composition are on this theory a sequential following-out of associative signs; Alison's "unity of expression" is available not to judgment but to the associating imagination. As such, it is embodied not in hierarchic structures (which require judgment to compose and interpret) but in horizontal ones: hierarchy gives way to the model of the literary work as a sequence of probable signs. In Alison, sign-inference is a dream-like process, a sequential activity of nearly unconscious structuring association; in the work of such contemporaries as Walter Whiter, whole new procedures of textual interpretation are devised which rest on a new understanding of probable inference as a wholly unconscious association of signs.[8] Alison's only mention of "probable circumstances" is a discussion of the way in which improbable circumstances, like Kames' "irregular facts," "wake" us from the mental state enjoined by and necessary for proper literary interpretation.

What kind of probability is it that sign-inference possesses once the work is understood as an unconscious sequence of probable signs? Once again, Common-Sense accounts of probable inference bear striking analogy to what critics such as Alison and Whiter describe as the processes of reading and composition. In his *Essay on Truth* (1770), Beattie distinguishes "common sense" from "reason" and "judgment"; common sense is "the energy of the understanding which perceives intuitive truth," or, more particularly,

that power of mind which perceives truth, or commands belief, not by progressive argumentation, but by an instantaneous and instinctive impulse; derived not from habit, but from nature; acting independently of our will, whenever its object is presented.[9]

Common sense is "permanent" in Alison's sense, as Beattie explains in a passage which uses a rhetorical device for contrasting unity and variety that we have seen before:

Common sense, or instinct, which prompts men to trust to their own feelings, hath in all ages continued the same: but the interests, pursuits, and abilities of philosophers, are susceptible of endless variety; and their theories vary accordingly. (43)

Again like Alison's sign-inference, Beattie's common sense acts in independence of interest or will – in independence also, therefore, of attention.

Beattie's discussion "Of Probable or Experimental Reasoning" occurs in his second chapter, which argues that "All evidence [is] ultimately intuitive" (31) and that all processes of consecutive reasoning have common-sense intuitive correlates capable of yielding the same knowledge otherwise arrived at through sequential reasoning. Taking as the paradigm of probabilistic inference reasoning from effect to cause, Beattie argues that if we have in mind like past cases of a relation, we can arrive from these cases without reasoning at certain knowledge of future events:

When this view is obtained, reasoning is no longer necessary; the mind, by its innate force, and in consequence of an irresistible and instinctive impulse, infers the future from the past, immediately, and without the intervention of any argument. (77)

Now it is evident, from what has already been said, that the degree of probability must be intuitively perceived, or the degree of assurance spontaneously and instinctively excited in the mind, upon the bare consideration of the instances on either side; and that without any medium of argument to connect the future event with past experience. Reasoning may be employed in bringing the instances into view; but when that is done, it is no longer necessary. (80)

Beattie's "irresistible and instinctive impulse" leads the mind "spontaneously" as do Alison's signs; his intuition acts in the absence of reason and judgment, as does Alison's sign-inference.

Alison explicates "unity of expression" as an emotional unity; parts blend into the passionate unity of Alison's literary wholes by their community of passion, by what I have called internal probability. Drawing, as had earlier critics, from the language of other arts, Alison characterizes the unity of literary works as "simplicity," by which he means to suggest an emotional unity achieved by easy transitions among parts; he contrasts such simplicity with mere "assemblage" (88). The requisite for such unity, as for maintaining the state of reverie, is strong passion, just as for Kames, "ideal presence depends on a lively impression" (I, 117) – "impression," since Hume, carrying the sense of passion. Various devices typical of earlier Augustan literature are destructive of this unity, which, in Alison's language, rather "pervades" than organizes the whole (54): it is at this period of shifting ideas about poetic unity that the lyric form is elevated to the highest position in the hierarchy of genres, and it is in a discussion of Horace's lyrics, for example – of that "connection of component parts, together with wholeness" which is "essential to the perfection of the ode" – that Frank Sayers voices his criticism of poetical uses of the catalogue or list. Even digression, once allotted only the most circumscribed place in the higher genres, comes to be thought not only acceptable but even beautiful in itself, so long as it does not violate but embodies and furthers the continuous play of mental faculties that literature is meant to engage. Thus Dugald Stewart distinguishes apt from unacceptable digression on the basis of a distinction between associations that all minds can naturally follow, and those which require a special effort of judgment to be followed:

It is owing to this distinction that transitions, which would be highly offensive in philosophical writing, are the most pleasing of any in poetry. In the former species of composition, we expect to see an author lay down a distinct plan or method, and observe it rigorously; without allowing himself to ramble into digressions suggested by accidental ideas or expressions which may occur to him in his progress. In that state of mind in which Poetry is read, such digressions are not only agreeable, but necessary to the effect; and an arrangement founded on the spontaneously and seemingly casual order of our thoughts, pleases more than one suggested by an accurate analysis of his subject.[10]

Thus Mackenzie writes in *The Man of the World*: "The reader will pardon the digression I have made; I would not, willingly, have led him out of his way, except into some path, where his feelings may be expanded, and his heart improved" (266–68).

The best literature may be digressive because (as Sterne testifies) so in a certain sense is the world; so certainly are the workings of the associating imagination, and moral training (like learning in general) proceeds first of all by a rectification of our patterns of association. Beckford's *Dreams, Waking Thoughts, and Incidents* is in various ways symptomatic of transitions found throughout the travel literature of the later eighteenth century. Mackenzie begins *The Man of the World* with a description of the narrator's return to a familiar landscape:

The remembrance of my infant days, like the fancied vibration of pleasant sounds in the ear, was still alive in my mind; and I flew to find out the marks by which even inanimate things were to be known, as the friends of my youth, not forgotten, though long unseen, nor lessened, in my estimation, from the pride of resentment, or the comparison of experience. (I, 3)

As discernment and unconscious inference supplant conscious and comparing judgment, travel literature comes more and more often to describe not the initial experience of a new landscape, but the psychological response to a landscape, and finally the psychological response of the traveller to a *re-experienced* landscape. Instances such as Wordsworth's "Tintern Abbey" come of course to mind; perhaps the most striking instance of this transformation of the travel genre is Browning's "Childe Roland": in this poem, designed as Robert Langbaum has argued to exhibit the form of an experience stripped of any particular content,[11] Roland reaches the goal of his journey not through geographical change of position but by suddenly seeing the landscape that surrounds him in a new way. The poem may usefully be understood as a work of travel literature, an educational journey constructed according to a new theory of knowledge and learning. Wordsworth's and Browning's poems incorporate past experience of the landscape which would in the narrative structure of a Fielding have been a separate incident to be repeated and judged; they incorporate such past experience into the present state of the traveller's mind (how rarely are characters in early Augustan fiction said to *remember* – this is the job of the reader); knowledge is achieved through an instantaneous illumination, an unconscious organizing inference which, though made possible by previously assimilated experience, is an exercise in the present not of judgment but of association and discernment.

The same transformation of the theory of probable inference which gave rise to new theories of reading, composition, and literary structure made itself felt in all the sciences of signs. In particular, as in literary interpretation, so in what we have throughout found to be an analogue of literary interpretation, the reading of nature's signs known as natural theology. Having put forth his doctrine of common sense, for instance, Reid was able to claim against Hume that we may infer design "with certainty, from the marks or signs in the effect."[12] Natural theology no longer has need of arguments such as those of Arbuthnot and Hutcheson which we examined in chapter II; the reader of nature, like the reader of literature, needs no guides such as Ray and Derham. Reid explains in the *Intellectual Powers of Man*:

I have met with one or two respectable authors who draw an argument from the doctrine of chances, to show how improbable it is that a regular arrangement of parts should be the effect of chance, or that it should not be the effect of design.

I do not object to this reasoning ... But the conclusion drawn from it has been held by all men from the beginning of the world. (665)

Concluding Theoretical Postscript

Perhaps the most important fruit of that movement in the philosophy of science which emerged in the second third of the twentieth century is the view, now commonplace, that, in Norwood Hanson's useful phrase, all observation is "theory-laden." Realization of the ineluctable interdependence of "fact" and theory altered our understanding of both individual scientific developments and the nature of scientific change. Emergence of this kind of understanding in literary studies has been slow, and is perhaps not yet complete. Where Hanson's insight has taken root, moreover, it has been taken as a license for critical stances which traduce the history of literature and the phenomena of response as much as do the stances they seek to replace.

The chief instrument of those who deny Hanson's insight has been the method of "close reading." Within that mid-twentieth-century movement in literary study known as the New Criticism, close reading came to be not only a pedagogical tool but also the model for literary interpretation generally. Under new guises it persists as the instrument of most formalist and deconstructive treatments of specific texts. Yet close reading has shown itself impotent to settle the most serious and interesting critical disputes, even where what is at issue is the meaning of a single text. This is so because, as several generations of critics have now demonstrated, close reading must be a fraud and a delusion if not deeply informed by what used to be called "external" evidence, that is, by historical knowledge, both of other texts than those under consideration and of materials not under the newer theories allowed to be "literary." This is true not merely in extreme cases, but in all instances of interpretation: the very construal of any configuration of marks on a page – the interpretation of these marks as representing a word, some particular word rather than another, with some particular meaning rather than another – is an act of historical inference impossible without considerable previous knowledge.[1] Much more so is any reading of a text which calls upon an interpretive judgment about the range of implication of any word or larger formulation.[2] In general, all interpretation begins from and depends on hypotheses which are constitutive of it, hypotheses concerning the nature and structure of works, of the relations of formal features to meaning, of the work and its procedures of structure to the genre and the period of which it is a member, of literary forms to social forms. The purist ideal of close reading is a recipe for ill-informed misreading.

Most notably, the procedure of close reading has depended in practice on certain stipulative definitions of the nature of "art" and "literature," definitions drawn not from the conceptual contexts from which works have in fact emerged and in which they have for centuries been understood, but from certain very recent theories which I have throughout this book labelled as "aesthetic." Formalist criticism has protected its procedures by giving privileged status to treatments of works "as art" (thus valuing interpretations, for instance, for their "richness" or other embodiment of "aesthetic" values), ruling out (or treating as peripheral) failures to read works "as literature" or in ways that do not acknowledge the primacy of its chosen aesthetic and conceptual norms. Since these definitions and norms have been in most cases the children of the late eighteenth and early nineteenth centuries and of the new category of the "aesthetic," most modern theoretical criticism can easily be shown to have its roots in Romantic critical theory.[3] The arbitrariness of such regulation of interpretation by stipulative definition has been amply demonstrated, but how many recent works of literary theory – particularly works of a structuralist tendency – continue to defend in their opening chapters purportedly timeless but in fact quite modern definitions of art, or poetry, or literature – or, more subtly, of "literariness," of what it is to be an instance of "literary" rather than "ordinary discourse," of what it is to be a "literary convention," or what it is for readers to possess "literary competence"?[4]

The emergence of "literary competence" as an object of study is in fact symptomatic of an opposed trend in critical theory, one which takes Hanson's insight very much to heart. On the one hand, we are told that the locus of meaning is not works but minds, that all meanings are meanings construed by someone, and so that the history of literature must be a history of response; on the other, that the intentions, conceptual frameworks, and value systems – and hence presumably also the responses – of past writers are inaccessible to us as modern readers, so that all construing is in fact constructing meanings, all reading misreading or (in M. H. Abrams' phrase) newreading, because we are necessarily cut off from the past. What is left when these two points of view converge is the theory that all reading and writing are techniques of more or less sophisticated self-examination and self-expression, all literary experiences fragments of an autobiography.[5]

If we cannot understand the past *wie es eigentlich gewesen* – because we inevitably distort past meanings through present conceptual frameworks – much less can we claim to know the past better than it knew itself: that is, if we cannot claim to know a past era through what it was itself aware of, nor can we claim to know it through those matters it repressed, ignored, rejected, or failed to bring to consciousness. Happily, however, this theory of the inaccessible past is a historical skepticism vitiated by the fact that any evidence for it turns out to be evidence against it: to show that any modern reading is a distortion of past meanings, we must possess as a standard of comparison that past meaning from which the modern reading is a deviation, knowledge which *ex hypothesi* is inaccessible. As is true of other forms of radical skepticism, evidence for such historical skepticism refutes itself.[6]

The other view, that texts have no stable meaning which it is the task of the interpreter to discover (though of course interpreters do more than this as well) – that there exists only a sequence of particular readings made by particular readers at particular times – constitutes in fact a denial of any distinction between correct and incorrect interpretation (though this implication of the theory is seldom made explicit). Most often, this kind of theory takes the guise of a belief that the meanings of literary works are the product of a "transaction" between reader and text. But it is far from clear what sense if any the metaphor of transaction makes, how it is to be cashed in at the literal level: it is far from clear in any critical study which takes this "transaction" as its object what contribution the text makes in the exchange (and the page before our eyes, we should remind ourselves, is after all no text but only one of its tokenings) – what if any norms the text is supposed to impose on its reader; it is even less clear what is to be the status of any historical or other previous knowledge which might be brought to the reading, knowledge which if different would yield a quite different interpretation. If texts impose on readers only those norms which, for whatever reasons, readers choose to impose on themselves; if no knowledge brought to bear in reading, no manner of applying this knowledge, has privilege over any other; then no distinction between reading and misreading (or "strong" reading, or strong-arm reading) can be sustained: interpretations can be judged only according to their fidelity to their own principles. That "autonomy" which was once thought to belong to the literary work is now transferred to the act of interpretation, and all attempts to mediate critical disputes which arise from the application in reading of different norms or different knowledge will be *eo ipso* misconceived. The predictable result in critical studies conducted according to these principles is that those who seek to illuminate works through an examination of the activity of reading them present in most cases the fruit only of application of quite modern procedures and principles of reading.[7] Those who are ignorant of the past – by genuine incapacity, or by willful design – are condemned not so much to repeat the *past* as endlessly to recapitulate fragments of the *present*.

This book has attempted to recapture some of the (changing) meanings for writers of the Augustan period of a various but interrelated vocabulary, including terms such as *probability, sign, circumstance, evidence, expression, conjecture, sagacity*, and *art*. To understand these terms and the range of their implications is to understand not something about Augustan verbal usage or philosophic outlook merely, but the very concepts for the Augustans of what it is to be a literary work, how such a work is structured (what are its parts and what is the nature of their interrelation in the formation of certain kinds of literary wholes), of what and how works mean, and how they mean in relation to other kinds of works. To understand these terms differently is to understand the age and its particular literary productions differently. And to understand the trajectory of their changes in meaning – the limits of that change, and the continuity of their meaning, 1660–1800 – is to understand something of the literary period constitutive of most of the works we have considered.

What is true of individual works (and of the structures of thought they bring with them) is true of larger patterns of discourse, including whole genres. In her ground-breaking study of *Paradise Regained*, for instance, Barbara Lewalski has demonstrated how generic reclassification of a work alters interpretation of that work at every level.[8] Nor do or can the motives for such reclassification come from "the work itself"; again, historical knowledge shapes both the process and the product of our inquiry. Kendall Walton provides an exemplary account of the logic of classification of works by genre and of the sorts of difference such classification makes to interpretation.[9] Our own discussions of *L'Art de penser* as a work of casuistry, of Dennis on the marvellous, and in general of the interanimation of the vocabularies of philosophic and literary debate are grounded in this logic. But Walton does not consider the nature of genre itself or the relation of genre to period: he cannot therefore account for the relation of specific structural procedures to genre in any but the most general way, nor does he consider the ways these connections change over time, or the way that, at a given time (in a given period), diverse genres are interrelated. It has been our claim, for instance, that many of the same structural procedures governing Augustan narrative forms (especially the novel) govern as well other forms as these appear in the same period, such as georgic, and in particular the prospect poem. Within a period norm, Ralph Cohen explains, diverse genres "are not merely interrelated, but ... their individual combinations reveal analogous or similar implications of construction."[10] As period norms develop, however, there will emerge *within* the larger context of continuity alterations in structural procedures and in the relation of formal features to meaning similar to those changes which, *outside* the same context of continuity, would define a change of periods.[11] Thus we have argued that in the transition from the novel of judgment to the novel of sensibility, certain formal features are parodied, others rejected; some are made to mean in new ways, while new structural procedures are also invented to serve the ends of the new form. At the same time, however, larger continuities connect the two kinds of novel, and relate them in similar ways to contemporary theories of probable inference. Chapters VII and VIII trace a variation within a larger literary period, while chapters VIII and IX suggest the kinds of innovation which were to characterize the shift in periods from Augustan to Romantic – a shift in the conceptual foundations constitutive of particular literary devices in themselves and as they combine to form diverse genres, and which is marked by new kinds of relations between literary and social forms – especially as this shift is illustrated in changing treatments of probability.

A complete literary history constructed according to this ideal model, even a complete history of probability, would of course be a vast undertaking, and only fragments of such an undertaking have been accomplished here. In relating concepts of probability to literary practice, I have been concerned especially to isolate a level of literary structure – what I have called the inferential structure of works – at which procedures of literary composition and philosophic inquiry may usefully and genuinely be seen to be related. It has been one purpose of this book to reconstruct the activity of reading certain Augustan works *wie es eigentlich gewesen*, and to argue by example that past procedures of interpretation can not only be recaptured, but that they are at once important products of and clues to the structure and meaning of literary works. The history of response is incomplete without study of the mental processes, the play of mental faculties – the principles and habits of reading –

constitutive of such response; these in turn cannot be understood apart from those procedures of literary structure which imply and invite, embody and dramatize, teach and are taught by such reading. Neither, finally, can these principles of reading and of structure be understood in isolation from those larger theories of how the mind operates and what constitutes the very nature of structure which obtain for any given writer or period. Thus we have attempted to examine for one period and in one body of works that isomorphism which obtains among Augustan theories about and practices of mental inference, literary (and other) structure, and literary (and other) interpretation. Our treatment of such varied materials has been at best fragmentary and incomplete. But any adequate literary history must take account of all of these, both in themselves and in their changing relations to one another. So, in the final analysis, must any interpretation of any literary work. All acts of interpretation make more or less implicit use of, depend more or less explicitly on, more or less informed commitments in each of these areas. This is so because literature – the activities of literary creation and response – is not divorced from the rest of human endeavor.

APPENDIX A

The Foucault–Hacking hypothesis

Despite occasional programmatic remarks that one reads from time to time, the early chapters of my own *Emergence of Probability* are perhaps the only detailed study in English of a changing style of rationality. Those chapters learned much from *The Order of Things*.

Ian Hacking, "Michel Foucault's Immature Science" (1979)

It would appear that the mathematical theory of probability came into being in only about 1660. Despite the inevitable success of the intellectual historian's search for precursors – he may turn up a promising paragraph on dice-games in Cardano's *Liber de ludo aleae* (written in 1526 but not published until 1663), or in Galileo's fragmentary *Sulla Scoptera dei dadi* (written sometime before 1642, but not published until 1718) – the decade of the 1660s remains a turning point in mathematical history. Mathematical probability requires only the most rudimentary arithmetic; its invention thus appears to be a conceptual development rather than simply an elaboration of formal methods. Why then did probability theory come into being so late in human history, and why in the mid-seventeenth century?

According to most historians of the subject, the concept of probability at use in the mathematical theory of chances differs so little from commonplace notions of likelihood that no very radical conceptual revolution is needed to explain its emergence: there had always existed a conceptual context into which mathematical probability could have fit. We might, with Nicholas Rescher, call their view of scientific progress in this area a "Geographic Exploration Model," one which assumes that the general shape of a terrain is known, and interprets progress as a better and better knowledge of its interior formations.[1] On this theory, the late emergence of mathematical probability is to be explained by reference to previous contingent impediments to its discovery, impediments which began to disappear only in the mid seventeenth century.

A varied list of such impediments has been proposed: previous lack of adequate technical tools (such as an easily manipulable arithmetic); the failure of ordinary life to suggest the possibility of such a theory (for instance because of a lack of dice well enough balanced to suggest the idea of a set of equiprobable outcomes to a randomizing process); previous external restraints (such as religious laws against gaming – what William Ames called "lusory lots"); conceptual restraints (disbelief in a true random, stemming either from scientific determinism, or an understanding of "chance" events as disguised acts of divine Providence). A number of writers have advanced each or several of these explanations.[2]

Yet none of these explanations convinces. Gaming has always existed, despite repeated attempts to eradicate it; the Romans and Egyptians made extremely well balanced dice, and even knew about loaded dice.[3] Simple theorems in probability require only the most rudimentary arithmetic, such as we know many mediaeval writers on gaming to have possessed.[4] Scientific determinism is too modern an invention to explain ancient and mediaeval silence on this subject. The argument from Providence is a powerful one, but even it cannot do the job assigned it. "Can any thing done by chance have all the marks of design?" asked Cicero in *De Divinatione*, as many Augustans were to ask as well; "Four dice may by chance turn up four aces; but do you think that four hundred dice, thrown up by chance, will turn up four hundred aces?"[5] Regularity of event implied to the Augustans an intelligent cause, as "chance" meant absence of an intelligent cause. The argument from Providence finds its most recent defender in Keith Thomas, who opposes providential to probabilistic ways of thinking in *Religion and the Decline of Magic*; Thomas notes that it was only in the late seventeenth century that *coincidence* came to mean a "juxtaposition of chance events," and concludes a brief discussion by saying of mathematical probability that "It was this nascent statistical sense, or awareness of patterns in apparently random behavior, which was to supersede much previous speculation about good or bad fortune."[6] The argument from Providence tries to have it both ways: irregularity implies absence of an intelligent cause; regularity implies absence of an intelligent cause. There is no evidence that it was the discovery of any previously unrecognized patterns in events that led the architects of mathematical probability to their conclusions, and we know that from its inception, the theory of chances could be viewed not merely as a fact of nature but as an expression of the divine will, yet another sign of God's beneficent presence.

Explanation of the late emergence of the mathematics of probability from particular impediments, then, may be correct but has not proved its case. Perhaps it has not because it rests on a false assumption: its model of gradual progress. Perhaps there did *not* always exist a conceptual context into which mathematical probability could have fitted. According to Michel Foucault and Ian Hacking, a development at once so far-reaching and fundamental as the invention of the probability calculus could only have been the result of deep-rooted conceptual change; because the invention was sudden, the conceptual shift must have been sudden as well. The mathematics of probability had to await a shift in what are nowadays popularly called "paradigms"; this new kind of explanation is particularly interesting because, among the sciences, mathematics has seemed least susceptible of such historical schematization, and very few explanations of changes in mathematics written in this manner exist.[7] Foucault, of course, propounds the view that succeeding ages are characterized by radically different underlying conceptual schemes, which he calls "epistemes"; fundamental conceptual novelty is to be explained only through the historical displacement of such epistemes: new categories arise when a place for them is opened, and places for such new concepts open only when a new episteme comes into being in which the concepts are already implicit.[8] The Geographical Exploration Model gives way to that of a historical atlas, in which all the maps outline different territories and are drawn according to different rules: with each age it is not only the objects of knowledge that are conceptualized in new ways; so is knowledge itself.

This radical theory of the origins of the mathematics of probability becomes important to us because of what it assumes about the non-mathematical, or ordinary idea of the probable. Foucault and Hacking agree that the mathematical theory embodies no great conceptual development from ordinary ideas; in arguing that deep-rooted conceptual shifts were necessary to bring the mathematical theory into being, therefore, they argue as well that *before about 1660 the ordinary idea of probability did not exist.* As Hacking puts it, "as a matter of historical fact epistemic probability did not emerge until people thought of measuring it" – a feat which, he finds, took place for the first time in history in the Port-Royal *Logic* of 1662.[9]

Hacking's detailed reconstruction of this innovation in his *Emergence of Probability* takes place within a theoretical context and on a historical timetable set up by Foucault in *The Order of Things*: his dating of the emergence of probability to "around 1660" (1) stems from Foucault's account of a "Classical period" in Europe whose chronological frontiers are "around 1660" and "around 1800–1810" (57). To understand Hacking's theory, we must first examine what for Foucault constitutes the transition from Renaissance to Classical in Western thought.

Foucault himself calls this transition a shift from "Interpretation" to "Order" (57). For Foucault's Renaissance, the world is a system of signs, a matrix of significant resemblances that exist apart from anyone's coming to know or interpret them; knowledge of nature – science – is thus a process of reading signs, as a paradigm of which Foucault cites the doctrine of signatures (25–30). The Classical period redefined the sign, with the result that resemblance ceased to be a primary category, yielding place to identity and difference (54); concomitantly, signs were no longer supposed to exist apart from thought. Science thus became not the finding but the making of order, an order which was to emerge not through any search for significant resemblances but through the Cartesian method of the agreement or disagreement of ideas.

Foucault's story is liable to numerous objections, which we should consider briefly. He argues that the Classical redefinition of the sign consisted in for the first time defining it "according to three variables": its certainty or mere probability; its naturalness or artificiality (conventionality); and its temporal copresence with or distance from the thing signified (58). We have already seen in detail, however, that none of these ways of classing signs was new to the seventeenth century: all of them were highly developed in ancient times, and all were commonly heard in the Renaissance.[10] Foucault claims, moreover, that Renaissance knowledge, because it was based on signs, could from the Classical perspective never achieve more than probability; when the Classical period reinterpreted the sign, opening the division between probability and certainty, knowledge had (again from the Classical perspective) its first chance for genuine certainty.

Such a claim rests on a deeply biased selection of evidence. The most remarkable part of Foucault's treatment of the Renaissance is his omission of all reference to the "high" sciences and to the theory of demonstrative knowledge that most thinkers of the time espoused: his entire account is built from the theory of signs as it was employed in the "low" sciences, particularly in medicine. (This is of course typical of the subjects Foucault has chosen to treat in separate studies such as *Madness and Civilization* and *The Birth of the Clinic*.) To represent the Classical period, on the other hand, he chooses the high road of the Cartesian programme. On the basis of such a selection of evidence he of course finds a transition from resemblance to identity and difference, from probability to certainty. Thus he can say that for the Renaissance, "Divination is not a rival form of knowledge; it is part of the main body of knowledge itself," whereas in the seventeenth century "knowledge breaks off its old kinship with *divinatio*."[11] Only in this way, too, can Foucault lend plausibility to his assertion that in the Classical period, resemblance ceased to be a fundamental category of thought.[12]

Whatever the merits of his account, Foucault did uncover a historical connnection which Hacking takes as the origin of his inquiry: the view that nondemonstrative inference – induction – grew from the understanding of the sign prevalent in the low sciences. Hacking is a more learned and circumspect writer than Foucault, one whose very lucidity is the tact of a modern Anglo-American philosopher of idealist leanings. He too believes that probability is a child of the mid-seventeenth century, but he traces its ancestry with more care; in outline, his theory is as follows. Until the Renaissance, "probability" *meant* backing by authority; no notion of evidence short of the demonstrative existed. In the low sciences of the Renaissance, however, the notion of testimony was extended to include not only human witnesses, but also that of inanimate nature, conceived as the incarnate Word of God (God's second book). This is testimony of the highest authority; the form in which it is encoded is the sign. From the Renaissance view of nature's signs as the signate utterance of God arose at once the concepts of nondemonstrative evidence and nondemonstrative inference: probability and induction were born together. Practical use of the sign-as-evidence characterizes Renaissance low science in general, but the schematization of the sign in probable inference – and the mathematical theory of probability – takes place only about 1660.

The trouble with this story is once again that it places in the Renaissance developments already under weigh in the ancient world. Hacking begins his story with a discussion of mediaeval Aristotelianism; he does not consider ancient medical theory, ancient skepticism, or the rebirth of skepticism in the Renaissance. He does not consider the traditions of rhetoric; only by restricting his attention to scholastic logic is he able plausibly to argue for the absence of a concept of probability in the Middle Ages. These omissions lead to startling errors of fact. According to Hacking, it was only when a concept of "internal evidence" arose – of the nondemonstrative testimony of things, as opposed to the "external" evidence of human witnesses – that probability could cease merely to mean authority and come to mean likelihood in a modern sense. He finds that "at the beginning of the Renaissance" no distinction between internal and external evidence existed (34); the "new distinction" appears first, he finds, in Hobbes and in the Port-Royal *Logic*: "In the *Logic* . . . there is a new and explicit statement of the distinction between internal and external evidence" (79). But as we have seen, the distinction can be found in Aristotle and Cicero; from the ancient rhetoricians it passes to dialecticians, logicians, and moral theologians – all long before the Renaissance. We have found that the theory of signs – indeed, the distinction between certain and probable signs – is crucial to the doctrines of the Hippocratics, Aristotle, and Sextus. All the materials Hacking cites as Renaissance innovations necessary for the final emergence of probability had been available since classical times: the timetable inherited from Foucault is in error by two thousand years.

Hacking gives a number of examples of what appear to be eighteenth-century uses of the word "probable" in what he regards as its pre-Classical sense – backing by authority – but once again, failure to examine literary and rhetorical contexts vitiates his argument. He cites the example of Thomas Church, writing in 1750 on miracles: Church finds himself arguing that "credibility" is a measure of the strength lent to any proposition by what we know to be the evidence for it, and so is at pains to account for other uses of the word, explaining

that in common discourse it is not unusual to call any thing credible or incredible, antecedent to our consideration of its proof. But if we examine our ideas, this will be found to be a loose unphilosophical way of expressing ourselves. All that can be meant is, that such a thing is possible or impossible, probable or improbable, or, at the farthest, happening very frequently or very seldom.

Church seems here to distinguish probability from credibility, possibility, and frequency of occurrence; to Hacking, all that can be left is probability as the testimony of authority. So too when Gibbon concludes a long entry in his journal for 24 October 1763, weighing the merits of Livy's account of Hannibal's march across the Alps against Polybius' differing story: "Let us conclude, then, though still with some remainder of scepticism, that although Livy's narrative has more of probability, yet that of Polybius has more of truth." Hacking reads this as saying that Livy is a greater *authority* than Polybius, but the passage is better read as testimony to Livy's literary skill in producing a plausible tale. The probability that both Church and Gibbon are invoking is in fact just that analogical probability "antecedent to our consideration of its proof" that Campbell was to name "plausibility"; in neither passage does "probability" mean backing by authority.[13]

Hacking does come to recognize something like Campbell's probability and plausibility: he distinguishes (using Peirce's terminology) induction from abduction, inference under uncertainty from the hypothesizing of theories, and says that each has a probability of its own. Abductive probability, he claims, emerges only in the nineteenth century, in the work of A. A. Cournot (1843; such a late date and choice of writers betrays a needless bias in favor of mathematics). Hacking does cite as an early example of the distinction a passage from Richard Price's presentation in 1764 to the Royal Society of the posthumous manuscripts of Thomas Bayes, arguing that "The inductive reasoning that Price has in mind was intended as a deliberate and conscious response to Hume":

Every judicious person will be sensible that the problem now mentioned is by no means merely a curious speculation in the doctrine of chances, but necessary to be solved in order to a sure foundation for all our reasonings concerning past facts, and what is likely to be hereafter... But it is certain that we cannot determine, at least not to any nicety, in what degree repeated experiments confirm a conclusion, without the particular discussion of the before mentioned problem; which, therefore, is necessary to be considered by any one who would give a clear account of the strength of *analogical* or *inductive* reasoning; concerning which at present, we seem to know little more than that it does sometimes in fact convince us, and at other times not. [14]

But Price's very language recalls Locke on the probability of fact, gotten at by reference to specific evidence, and the probability of matters of speculation (theory), gotten by analogy. Inductive and abductive probabilities were known to the Restoration, as is clear not only from Locke but also from Descartes, and from the many methodological discussions in the period on the nature of "probable hypotheses."[15] (The history of this distinction must once again be traced, as we have seen, to ancient rhetoric.)

Hacking's claim that before the mid-seventeenth century "probability" and its forms *meant* backing by authority gains what appearance of plausibility it has because he begins his account with scholastic logic: for many mediaeval Aristotelians did define the term this way, and more allowed that authority is the primary ground of probability. Such evidence can hardly be conclusive, however, that in the Middle Ages no *concept* of probability existed. Hacking's account of the genesis of ideas of likelihood from the idea of signs may be correct – but if so, it describes events that occurred among the pre-Socratics. Some effort of recovery did occur in the Renaissance, but it is not clear that the notion of likelihood was itself ever really lost.[16]

If the Foucault–Hacking hypothesis does not stand, two questions remain. Did the invention of a calculus of probabilities require so much conceptual innovation as to make an explanation of its emergence in the manner of Foucault and Hacking necessary? And if not, why did the mathematical theory emerge so late?

The very notion that mathematical probability embodies a concept of the probable different from other, philosophic or ordinary notions of likelihood may be questioned. The distinction between mathematical and ordinary probability is a modern one; it was very long in being drawn, so that instead of finding it in texts dating from the seventeenth century, we find Dugald Stewart complaining as late as 1828, in his *Philosophy of the Active and Moral Powers of Man*:

Under the general title of the doctrine of *Probabilities* two very different things are confounded together by Laplace, as well as by many other writers of an earlier date. The one is the purely mathematical theory of chances; the other the inductive anticipations of future events deduced from observations on the past course of nature. (*Works*, VII, 115)

Debate continues on how many and various are our notions of the probable, but whether, like Stewart, and most notably in our time, Rudolf Carnap, we discriminate these two senses, or whether, like J. L. Mackie, we find the concept susceptible of five, seven, or perhaps nine reasonable, mutually exclusive interpretations, we must remember that the Augustans did not draw these distinctions.[17] They saw no discontinuity between ordinary and mathematical probability; had they done so, they could never have found such wide application as they did for probabilistic argument, nor would there be such continuity in styles of argument at use in so many diverse departments of Augustan thought.

Why then did mathematical probability emerge as late as it did? Recently, a number of students of *The Emergence of Probability* have attempted to undermine the notion of a clear turning point in the 1660s, and to reinstate the Geographic Exploration Model. It appears first of all that the Port-Royal *Logic* is not the first work to quantify probability, though it may be the first to quantify *probability* (explicitly so called).[18] Scholars have turned up ancient and mediaeval appeals to ordinary probability, that is, to a notion of likelihood which admits of degrees and which does not rest solely on authorities.[19] Historians of mathematics have begun to note that seventeenth-century theorists of the doctrine of chances were aware and made explicit use of ancient skeptical writings, and have even begun to revive in more sophisticated form the argument from the specific impediment of gaming's disrepute.[20]

All must agree that the mid-seventeenth century remains, as Hacking has argued, a watershed in the growth of mathematical theory and, because of the widespread use of the calculus of probability, in the larger culture as well: Hacking is surely right that after about 1650 as never before, probability is on every pen. At issue is the extent of the conceptual revolution needed to bring this state of affairs about. Some years ago, Samuel Sambursky suggested that the Greeks never thought to measure probability because of certain (usually Aristotelian) views about the nature of chance: chance is "blind," by definition insusceptible of "scientific" treatment. This, the most subtle of arguments from previous impediments, remains in the hands of modern historians such as Ivo Schneider the most persuasive; to render it fully plausible, however, we should need in addition to a history of probability a history of the concept of *chance*.[21]

APPENDIX B

John Dennis and Christian marvels

The most subtle Augustan theorist of the Christian marvellous is John Dennis, particularly in his *Grounds of Criticism in Poetry* (1704) and, to a lesser extent, his *Advancement and Reformation of Poetry* (1701), but the argument of these essays has widely been misconstrued. At the center of modern misreadings is the famous example from the *Grounds* of poetical use of the image of the sun:

As for example, the Sun mention'd in ordinary Conversation, gives the Idea of a round flat shining Body, of about two foot diameter. But the Sun occurring to us in Meditation, gives the Idea of a vast and glorious Body, and the top of all the visible Creation, and the brightest material Image of the Divinity. (1, 339)

Dennis' "Meditation" has been taken to be a special mental process; his brief account of it (four sentences) and this, with a similar remark on thunder, his only illustration of the process, have led to comparisons with Wordsworth's discussion of emotion recollected in tranquillity and been used to explain what De Quincey called Wordsworth and Coleridge's "absurd 'craze' about" Dennis.[1] Martin Kallich finds in the example of the sun an early application of the doctrine of association of ideas; he is in fact following Samuel Holt Monk's suggestion that in the example "the author turns to association to explain aesthetic experience."[2]

It is highly unlikely that in 1704 Dennis could be appealing to association. The doctrine is commonly (and mistakenly) thought to have been popularized in England by Locke, but Locke's only treatment of association is chapter 33, book II of the *Essay*, a sharply critical account which first appeared in the fourth edition of 1700. For Locke, association is a kind of mental disease, akin to madness. Less critical accounts could be found in Hobbes or the Cartesians, but Dennis himself nowhere makes reference to the theory in any form.[3]

Monk's use of the term *aesthetic* should also give us pause. Monk, whose study of *The Sublime* is handicapped by a habit of reading all Augustan literary theory as teleologically aiming at Kant, finds evidence in the mention of "Meditation" that "Despite the obvious handicap of a lack of vocabulary ... Dennis has perceived the distinction between practical emotion and aesthetic emotion" (49), a distinction Dennis would not have understood, and of which he would certainly have disapproved.

Monk sows a far more important error in ascribing to Dennis' essays "the earliest theory of the sublime in England" (49). His classification of Dennis' aims in the essays has found universal acceptance, and interpretation has followed the classification. Kallich repeats the point, adding erroneously that in the *Grounds*, "Dennis' sublime is grounded entirely upon terror" (44). In fact, Dennis discusses both Admiration and Terror, and says that in the sequel (which he never produced), he will discuss the other four "Enthusiastic Passions," Horror, Grief, Joy, and Desire (1, 363). David Morris, a pupil of Monk, perpetuates this story in his study of *The Religious Sublime*, finding in Dennis a precursor of the Burkean and Wordsworthian sublime of terror. He cites, for instance, Dennis' list of the objects of Terror, "Gods, Daemons, Hell, Spirits and Souls of Men, Miracles, Prodigies, Enchantments, Witchcrafts" – without mentioning that Dennis also lists the objects of Admiration, and that the lists are in large part identical: "Demons, Apparitions of all sorts, and more particularly the Spirits of Men departed: then follow Prophecies, Visions, Miracles, Enchantments, Prodigies," etc. (361, 347). Again, the hint has come from Monk, who in his forward-looking way finds Dennis' "sublimity of terror is more interesting" than that of admiration.[4] But it is not at all clear that Dennis would have made the same valuation: in the manner of Descartes and Le Brun on the passions, Dennis treats Admiration first, and devotes nearly twice as much space to it as to Terror; in most respects, his characterizations of these and other passions follow received doctrine.

Finally, in *The Sublime Pleasures of Tragedy*, on the basis of Dennis' passage on Meditation and his claims that a reformed poetry will engage the whole man (claims that bear some resemblance to Coleridge's famous remarks in the *Biographia*), William Albrecht finds in the essays a unique Augustan account of the sublime, rooted in proto-Romantic opposition to the empiricists' distinction between reason and emotion (ch. 1).

All these readers are mistaken. The *Grounds* is most usefully understood in the light in which it appeared to Dennis himself: as an essay not on the sublime, but on the marvellous, indeed on what Dennis takes to be a new theory of the Christian marvellous. The distinction may at first appear tendentious: after all, Boileau titled his 1674 translation of Longinus *Traité du sublime ou du merveilleux dans le discours*; Augustan writers often use the words *sublime* and *marvellous* (or *admirable*) together, sometimes interchangeably; Dennis was in his own time satirized as Sir Tremendous Longinus for his views on enthusiasm; and the *Grounds* itself contains a long discussion of Longinus and the sublime.

We should note at once, however, that most writing on all these topics came after Dennis; the very diverse thing the sublime was to become – if we can class so many different notions under one rubric at all – bears slight resemblance to the particular theory that Dennis advances. In the *Grounds*, Dennis introduces Longinus not at the start of the work, nor at the beginning of his chapter "What the greater Poetry is, what

Enthusiasm is," but in the midst of both. Only after a discussion of Admiration does Longinus appear, and then almost exclusively in the treatment of Terror: "First Ideas producing Terror, contribute greatly to the Sublime. All the Examples that *Longinus* brings of the Loftiness of Thought, consist of terrible Ideas" (361). As Marjorie Nicolson notes, "The Longinian Sublime played some part in Dennis' criticism, but it was a minor part."[5]

Dennis introduces Admiration before even mentioning the sublime (345–55); his discussion comes, as we shall see, from Aristotle. Dennis himself says that he will appeal to Longinus (as well as to Aristotle and Hermogenes) "to prove by Authority, That the strongest Enthusiastic Passions in Poetry are only justly and reasonably to be rais'd by religious ideas" (340). This he of course does for the Enthusiastic Passion of Terror, but only after having done so in far more detail in those pages in which he "diversifies" Longinus by examining "Admiration alone, uncompounded with Terror" (341). We find indeed that all the Enthusiastic Passions are to be understood as variants of Admiration: Terror, for instance, is "a certain Admiration, mingled with Astonishment and Surprise" (350). In a broad sense, then, Dennis is (and sees himself as) *subsuming* Longinus and the sublime to his own more general argument: an argument about that category traditionally called the marvellous.

In his *Remarks* on *Prince Arthur* (1696), Dennis writes,

> I have often, indeed, wonder'd why I could never be pleased with the Machines in a Christian Poem. At length, I believe I have found out the reason. Poetry pleases by an imitation of Nature. Now the Christian machines are quite out of Nature, and consequently cannot Delight. The Heathen Machines are enough out of Nature to be admirable, and enough in Nature to delight. (I, 106)

Pagan machines thus perform that process of mediation which we have already seen Augustan imitation to require; they do so in a way Christian machines cannot: Dennis finds further that "to be instructed by Imitation, I must be a Judge of that Imitation, which I can never be, if I have not a clear and distinct Idea of its Object," which though we cannot wholly have of pagan deities, we lack entirely of Christian spirits. What in particular we lack is sensory detail upon which judgment, the faculty of probability, may operate. In the *Advancement*, however, Dennis argues that there is sufficient justification in the nature of religion and poetry themselves for the use of Christian machinery, and in the *Grounds* he devises a further theory to supply needed sensory concreteness to a Christian marvellous. (In Dennis, the marvellous or admirable is not sublimely obscure, but quite concrete; indeed, part of the reformation, or reharmonization, of the mind that Dennis hopes a reformed poetry can accomplish is a rectification of the senses.)

In both essays, Dennis' overarching argument is religious: a reformed poetry is to restore man to that harmony of mental faculties he possessed before the Fall, i.e., to bring sense and passion into proper relation to reason. Before the Fall, "the Eye of Man then saw the Majesty of God," and the passions of "Love, Admiration, Joy and Desire" (*not* Terror) "were all that he knew" (255–56). The first sin – that of "horribly diverting his affections from God to the Creatures" – is Dennis' emblem of that disorder among the faculties wherein sense and passion take as objects pleasures inappropriate to reason and religion; he stresses that at the Fall, the "Senses partook of the same disorder" as the passions (257). It is Christianity itself that is to provide a route to the much-needed reordering of the faculties: that is, the sensory content of *revealed* religion, with its angels, demons, and visions, is to do so; for, as Dennis argues in the *Grounds*, in contrast to "natural Religion," "all Reveal'd Religion, whether true or pretended, speaks to the Senses, brings the Wonders of another World more home to us, and so makes the Passions which it raises the greater" (364). In the *Advancement*, he had given a reconstruction of the history of Greek religion to show that it was the replacement in classical times of an older revealed religion, rich in sensory images, with a more intellectual natural religion that brought to an end the great age of Greek poetry.

Such then is the problem Dennis sets himself in the *Grounds*: to lay the foundation of a new marvellous, one that is sensory like the Greek machinery, but also true to Christianity. Dennis is facing a special version of the need to mediate the probable and the marvellous, through some form of probability: poetry, he writes, "is an Art, by which a Poet excites Passion (and for that very cause entertains Sense)," but "nothing but Truth can be long esteem'd" or can work man's reformation (336, 328). His new and purified Christian marvellous addresses itself, furthermore, not to the vulgar but to the wise: "But nothing but God, and what relates to God, is worthy to move the soul of a great and wise man" (345). Dennis' term for this marvellous is the "admirable," and he is quite consciously giving a new account of *to thaumazon*: "Religious Ideas are the most admirable, and what is most admirable, according to the doctrine of *Aristotle*, is most delightful" (360). Its objects are great ideas, those only which are capable of moving the greater, or Enthusiastic, Passions; these in turn are the stuff of the "greater Poetry," which "comprehends Epick, Tragick, and the greater Lyrick" (338).

Dennis' discussions of epic and tragedy, and the passions most appropriate to each, are studied revisions of Aristotle. The epic, following *Poetics* 24, is more "wonderful" than tragedy – Aristotle had said that it could partake more of the marvellous – because its hero is seen to be in the "concern of Heaven," and so "that which is admirable in the Action of the Hero, is heighten'd by Revelations, by Machines, and the Ministration of the Gods. For that Ministration, those Machines, and those Revelations are all Miraculous" (229). Admiration *per se*, then, is most fully the object of epic; Dennis introduces Terror as the passion, with piety, most proper to tragedy, again citing Aristotle (339). Nor is Terror poetically useful in itself, but only as it is conducive to pleasure, "by a secret intelligence that the Object is not real" (264) – a familiar explanation of the source of tragic pleasure. Dennis understands these passions, then, in a generally Aristotelian way, relating them to different genres. He gives in the *Advancement*, for instance, as a case of the marvellous of Terror in tragedy, the incident from *Poetics* 9 of "the Statue of *Mitys at Argos*, which fell upon his murderer" (230). It becomes clear that the marvellous of tragedy stems from the disguised intervention of Providence in what seem to be chance events; in this way the tragic marvellous finds its probability in poetic justice.

It is in the *Grounds*, however, that Dennis gives his most interesting arguments for a Christian probable marvellous, one indeed that can purify the machinery even of the pagan poets. This purification takes place through a process of metaphor, in light of which we must understand the controversial example of the sun. It is a process whose terms have already been set by Rymer:

Not to represent their Gods with face, and fingers, with actions, and passions, and other Modifications, after the fashions of men, were to say nothing ... Metaphor must be the language, when we travel in a Countrey beyond our Senses.[6]

Through this metaphorical process, the sensory basis of the marvellous, necessary if it is to move the passions, will be restored.

To the old query about how we are moved by marvels that are pagan, Dennis answers: "For that which moves us in effect in a false Religion, must be the Imagination of that which is true." By an act of mind, we Christianize pagan marvels:

As for example, in the above-mentioned Passage of the Wrath of *Neptune*, the anger of *Neptune* is Fiction, and so is the Stroke of his Trident; but that which moves us at the bottom of this Fiction is true, which is, that the Anger of a Deity, and the Effects of it, are very terrible. (396)

The psychological process at use here is not association. It is *selective attention*, i.e., what Augustan thinkers mean by *abstraction*.[7] Judgment abstracts from the pagan marvel that core of religious truth congruent with Christianity, ignoring all that is not so congruent; the pagan marvel thus becomes a mere sign, justified by the way in which at least parts of it point to Christian truths.

Before the onset of associationism, it was as such a process of abstraction that Augustan critics and writers understood the phenomenon of metaphor: to read a metaphor is to abstract relevantly similar qualities from juxtaposed objects, an abstraction guided by signs ("circumstances") and performed by judgment. This is a procedure different from that entailed by later theories of metaphor, and is I suggest responsible for many of those early Augustan comments on metaphor (by Bentley, for instance) that modern critics find troubling.

We are now in a position to understand "Meditation" and the example of the sun. Of the examples of the sun and thunder, it is important to note that they are brief and introduced offhandedly;

Dennis, who did not believe in using a good idea only once, never speaks of such "Meditation" again. As isolated instances, it would appear that we should read the examples and discussion of Meditation as brief illustrations of the larger argument of the essay, not as themselves foundations of any distinct theory, certainly not an "aesthetic" theory (application of the very category is anachronistic).

Dennis treats thunder in its familiar guise as the instrument of Providence, an image of the divine:

So Thunder mention'd in common Conversation, gives an Idea of a black Cloud, and a great Noise, which makes no great Impression on us. But the Idea of it occurring in Meditation, sets before us the most forcible, most resistless, and consequently the most dreadful Phaenomenon in Nature: So that this Idea must move a great deal of Terror in us, and 'tis this sort of Terror that I call Enthusiasm. (339)

Meditation, then, is a process of considering all the parts of a complex idea and abstracting out those relevant to the intended poetic effect, i.e., those that will make of the complex idea a sign of an object of Enthusiastic Passion. So much for the writer of poetry; for the reader, abstraction will be guided by surrounding signs in the poem, telling him which are the components of the complex idea the poet means him to attend to. Meditation is not a process of association. In fact, Dennis is describing one of the commonest structures of Augustan thought; understood explicitly as guided analogy, it is the structure of probable argument in all literary interpretation, and in the interpretation of nature as well. The following physico-theological passage from George Cheyne's *Philosophical Principles of Religion* provides a not unusually explicit example of the same procedure:

as the *Attraction* of the *Sun* on the *Planets*, makes them first move, and then describe regular *Orbits*, so this Divine *Attraction* in spiritual Beings, animates the Will, and actuates the Affections, and these do all the rest that is to be done in this present state: and as the discordant *Attraction* of some wandering *Comets* would certainly distract and disorder the *Harmony* of the Motions and Revolutions of the *Planets*, if they approach'd too near them; so gross irregular carnal Affections, earthy and sensual *Attractions* admitted too high, disturb and destroy the beautiful Progress of *Spiritual Beings*, towards the *Centre* and End of their Being.[8]

We recall that thunder appears in Dennis' list of the objects of "enthusiastick Terror" (361); the process I have described is that whereby it becomes so. "*This sort* of Terror" finds its commonest use in tragedy, and is hence mentioned after that sort typical of epic, the first of the three kinds of Greater Poetry. There, it is an image of divinity in its role of Providence, disguised as seeming chance – just the view of thunder we have already seen early theorists of probability attempting to eradicate from men's ordinary view of the world. The sun, too, by abstraction of certain of its properties from the sensory whole in which it is presented, provides by analogy attributes of divinity, and hence a "material Image of the Divinity"; here, however, such attributes are not in disguise, and Meditation on the sun produces not Terror, but "that Admiration I call Enthusiasm" (339).

Dennis ends the *Grounds* with a list of nine "Rules for employing Religion in Poetry" (369). The last three concern the need to give machinery full sensory content. The third demands that appeals to Enthusiastic Passion not obstruct a work's unity of action; it is a variant of Aristotle's strictures on the same subject – that the marvellous not disunify action – necessary to provide that ordering of signs which will guide readers in their procedures of "meditative" reading. The fourth and fifth rules are calls for Variety, what gives life and interest to a work, rouses the attention, and is the product of imagination (the source of the marvellous). The first two rules address matters of belief, or credibility. All these are topics habitually raised in Augustan discussion of the marvellous, the proper subject of Dennis' essay. (Even his distinction between Enthusiastic and "Vulgar" passions marks Dennis' concern to promulgate a marvellous that can satisfy the wise.)

In Dennis' procedure of guided abstraction (selective attention) from commonplace particulars might have been found a new way of accomplishing that "just Mixture" of the probable and the marvellous that contemporary critics enjoined. Theorists did not, however, adopt this procedure, much as it may have been used in practice. His insight would flourish in a later context in which association had replaced abstraction and judgment as the main faculty of sign-inference, misleading modern readers; but Dennis' own signs of divinity are products of a probable inference which, this book has argued, is typical of earlier Augustan habits of reading and composition.

APPENDIX C

The vocabulary of conjecture and expectation in *Emma*

hope	163	certainty	131
doubt	126	probability	56
wish	105	possibility	48
expect	101	likelihood	37
believe	96	plausibility	1
suspect	85		
suppose	84	chance	24
wonder	58	luck	23
convince	55	hazard	7
consider	46		
fancy	39	prove	49
guess	33	confirm	6
fear	25	certify	1
foresee	12	verify	1
trust	12		
conjecture	9	mistake	36
calculate	6	misunderstanding	8
estimate	6	misinterpret	2
look forward	6	misconceive	2
speculate	5	misjudge	2
surmise	5	misconstrue	1
anticipate	5	mislead	2
infer	4	blunder	15
foretell	2	error	14
predict	2	deception	11
detect	1	delusion	3
divine	1	dupe	2
fathom	1		
		surprise	73
circumstance	64	astonish	22
evidence	23	amaze	14
prospect	12	confidence	9
promise	10	sanguine	8
symptom	7	anxiety	21
denote	4	disappointment	43
testify	2	prudence	18
indicate	2	penetration	8
prophesy	2	discernment	7
token	1	caution	22
		sagacity	2
scheme	25		
plan	22		
project	5		

Notes

Preface

1 On the transition from *bonnes* to *belles lettres*, see E. D. Hirsch, *The Aims of Interpretation*, pp. 141–44. In his *Essay on Study* (1731), a work devoted to "the Support and Encouragement of good letters" (12), John Clarke provides a bibliography for those wishing to build a library which may give the modern reader some sense of the place of (what we would call) literature in the hierarchy of *bonae literae*. The disastrous results of the invention of the category of *belles lettres* (of the reclassification of literature as fundamentally "aesthetic" in purpose and effect), including especially the banishing of poetry from the center to the margins of our culture, have often been remarked upon; see most recently Christopher Clausen, *The Place of Poetry: Two Centuries of an Art in Crisis*.
2 Ralph Cohen, "Historical Knowledge and Literary Understanding," p. 227.
3 I use the term "Augustan" as nothing more than a label for the literary period 1660–1800. It is of course impossible even to read a single text without making some period distinctions, implicitly or explicitly; this study (as the logic of such argument requires) at once assumes and seeks to defend the coherence of a period whose *termini* fall in about 1660 and 1800, and which possesses a unity more fundamental than any division of the same span into an earlier "Augustan" age and a supposed later "Age of Sensibility."
4 See Trowbridge's essays on "The Place of Rules in Dryden's Criticism" (1946), "Edward Gibbon, Literary Critic" (1971), "Scattered Atoms of Probability" (1971), and "White of Selbourne: The Ethos of Probabilism" (1974), reprinted in *From Dryden to Jane Austen* (the passages cited here appear on p. 215).
5 See, e.g., Paul Korshin, "Probability and Character in the Eighteenth Century" (1979); Paul Alkon, "The Odds Against Friday" (1979); and James Bunn, "Signs of Randomness in *Roderick Random*" (1981).

I From rhetoric to science

1 See Warren Derry, *Dr. Parr*, pp. 180–84.
2 *Roxana*, p. 23 (cited in Hacking, *The Emergence of Probability*, p. 19). For *likely* in the sense indicated, see E. M. Forster, *Howards End* (1910), where Mrs. Munt asks her niece Margaret: "What do you think of the Wilcoxes? Are they our sort? Are they likely people?" (8). *Plausible* itself meant originally deserving of *applause*, as for instance Gracián defines "plausible employments" in his *Courtiers Manual* as "employments generally applauded"; with typical Renaissance conviction that virtuous action must be public, he explains, "I call that plausible, which is acted in view, and to the satisfaction of all people." The orator is to "prefer plausible

arguments," in the sense that he should please his auditors. (Courtiers
Manual Oracle, Maxim lxvii: "To prefer plausible employments," pp.
65–67.)
3 For "probabilism," see below, pp. 56–62; for "probable doctor" and
"probable opinion," p. 58.
4 For "probable demaund," see Ralph Lever, *The Arte of Reason,* p. 229; for
"probable witness," see Matthew Hale, quoted below, p. 8, and citations in
J. H. Wigmore, "Required Numbers of Witnesses," p. 89; for Hooker's
"probable voice," *The Laws of Ecclesiastical Polity,* p. 34.
    When Shakespeare's Phoebe says in *As You Like It,*

    'Tis pretty, sure, and very probable
    That eyes, that are the frail'st and softest things,
    Who shut their coward gates on atomies,
    Should be call'd tyrants, butchers, murtherers! (III. v. 11–14)

she is perhaps balancing ironic use of probability as credibility with an older
sense of sanction by authority (here, by poets). The phrase "pretty and
probable" was a common formula, with classical precedent: see Bacon's use
of it, quoted below, p. 12, and similar phrases in Cicero and Aulus Gellius
("jucundior et probabilior populo orator"; "eleganter et probabiliter hoc
dictum est").
5 *Prior Analytics* 11.26.70ᵃ; *Topics*1.1.100ᵇ; translated in *The Basic Works of
Aristotle,* pp. 105, 188. Nachum Rabinovitch summarizes Aristotle's sole
rule of probable inference as "Follow the Majority" (*Probability and
Statistical Inference in Ancient and Medieval Jewish Literature,* p. 154).
6 *Metalogicon,* pp. 79, 106; *Comm. Post. Anal.,* cited in Deferrari, *A Lexicon
of St. Thomas Aquinas,* art. *Probabilis; Summa theologiae,* VIII, 71; *Summa
totia logicae,* quoted in Ernest Moody, *The Logic of William of Ockham,* p.
211; Blundeville, *Art of Logike,* p. 146; Spencer, *Art of Logick,* p. 288; *De
Veritate,* p. 314. See also for similar definitions L. M. De Rijk, *Logica
Modernorum,* pp. 69, 275–76, 398, 400–01, 542–43. Julius Weinberg
traces some fourteenth-century attempts to redefine probability (which yet
begin from this Aristotelian account) in *Nicolaus of Autrecourt,* ch. 6.
7 Hooker, *Laws,* I, 33, 180; H. C. Porter, "Hooker, the Tudor Constitution,
and the *Via Media,*" p. 85. *Likelihood* in the last citation may be glossed as
similarity or likeness (to truth).
8 *Prose Works of Sir Thomas Browne,* p. 140.
9 See Gilby's remarks in *Summa theologiae,* I, 133, and for the relation of
authority to authorship, Foucault, "What is an Author?"; E. R. Curtius,
European Literature and the Latin Middle Ages, pp. 48–61; and Leonard
Krieger, "Authority," esp. 144–45.
10 Holdsworth, *A History of English Law,* IX, 126; quoted in Waldman,
"Origins of the Legal Doctrine of Reasonable Doubt," p. 308.
11 *De Laudibus legum Angliae,* quoted in Wigmore, "Required Numbers of
Witnesses," pp. 94–95.
12 See Foucault, *Discipline and Punish,* pp. 36–37, and Peter Gay, *Voltaire's
Politics,* p. 305. On these developments see also more generally John H.
Langbein, *Torture and the Law of Proof.*
13 Wigmore, "Required Numbers of Witnesses," pp. 87–93; according to
Wigmore, this view of the power of oath, originating in Teutonic law, was
influential in England "down into the 1700's" (89).

14 "Required Numbers of Witnesses," p. 90.

15 Shapiro, "Law and Science in Seventeenth-Century England," pp. 758, 760. Shapiro's fuller treatment of these ideas, entitled *Probability and Certainty in Seventeenth-Century England*, appeared too late to be taken account of here. (The reader should see ch. 5, on law, and especially Coke's doctrine of the *praesumptio probabilis*, cited on p. 178.) O. B. Sheynin lists a number of invocations of the probable in the history of jurisprudence in "On the Prehistory of the Theory of Probability," pp. 105–10.

16 *William of Sherwood's Introduction to Logic*, p. 69.

17 Locke, *Essay concerning Human Understanding*, 4. 15. 3; Watts, *Logick*, p. 176.

18 See, e.g., Aquinas, *Summa theologiae*, VIII, 108.

19 "In negotiis humanis non potest haberi demonstrativa probatio et infallibilis; sed sufficit aliqua coniecturalis probabilitas secundum quam rhetor persuadet" (*Summa theologiae*, XXIV, 288).

20 The Latin adjective *scientificus* (literally "productive of science") came in the sixth century to mean "pertaining to science" when an anonymous translator (perhaps Boethius) rendered Aristotle's *epistemonikai apodeixis* as *scientificae demonstrationes* (see Sydney Ross, "Scientist," p. 67).

   Aristotle distinguishes scientific, dialectical, and rhetorical induction, of which the second "is the ancestor of the modern notion of problematic induction" (see N. Jardine, "Galileo's Road to Truth," pp. 299–300). Scientific induction, as David Ross explains, is "a process not of reasoning but of direct insight" (*Aristotle*, p. 41) – a process which does not admit of analysis or degree, much less of codification in rules (such as Mill's). See also Hamlyn, "Aristotelian Epagoge," and Crombie, *Grosseteste*, p. 57; for rhetorical induction, see below, p. 319 n4.

21 *Posterior Analytics* I. 6. 75ᵃ35–36. On the question whether Aristotle himself believed that all demonstrative premisses be causes, see Barnes, *Aristotle's Posterior Analytics*, pp. 247–48.

22 *Post. Anal.* I. 8. 75ᵇ20–30. Thus John of Salisbury argues that while necessity is unchanging, "the reasons of probable things are subject to change"; "The method of demonstration is ... generally feeble and ineffective with regard to the facts of nature (I refer to corporeal and changeable things)" (105).

23 "That which is commensurately universal and true in all cases one cannot perceive, since it is not 'this' and it is not 'now' ... we clearly cannot obtain scientific knowledge from the act of perception" (*Post. Anal.* I. 8. 75ᵇ30–35). Crombie notes, "Even so empirical a natural philosopher as Adelard of Bath held that the senses, though necessary for investigating the particular and concrete, gave not truth but opinion (*Unde nec ex sensibus scientia, sed opinio oriri valet*), and when he castigated those who slavishly followed authority it was not to urge them to observe but to urge them to reason" (*Grosseteste*, p. 30).

24 *Grosseteste*, p. 58.

25 Anonymous Kentishman, c. 1590, quoted in Christopher Hill, *Milton*, p. 65; *Love's Labours Lost* V. i. 6; Walter Strickland, 1656, quoted in Hill, *Milton*, p. 223; Bossuet, cited in W. G. Moore, *La Rochefoucauld*, p. 2; Malebranche, *De la Recherche de la vérité*, I, 487.

26 Locke, *Essay*, I. 4. 23 (compare *Of the Conduct of the Understanding*, p. 70); Joseph Glanvill, *Vanity of Dogmatizing*, A2v.

27 Spencer, *Art*, p. 287. Aristotle defines commensurate universality at *Post. Anal.* I. 4. 73^{b}26–29; premisses are commensurately universal when the universal named in the predicate inheres always and only in the subject.
28 See Edmund Byrne, *Probability and Opinion*, p. 85.
29 Bacon, *Works*, IV, 42; *The Works of Thomas Nashe*, I, 371. Compare Fulke Greville in *A Treatie of Humane Learning*, stanzas 40–41:

> Nor is it in the Schooles alone where Arts
> Transform themselues to Craft, Knowledge to Sophistry,
> Truth into Rhetorike; since this wombe imparts,
> Through all the practice of humanity,
>   Corrupt, sophisticall, chymicall alwayes;
>   Which snare the subiect and the king betrayes.
>
> Though there most dangerous, where wit serveth Might,
> To shake diuine foundations and humane,
> By painting vices and by shadowing right,
> Which tincture of *probabile* prophane,
>   Vnder false colour giuing Truth such rates,
>   As Power may rule in chiefe through all estates.
>
> (Works, II, 21–22)

30 Butler, *Analogy*, p. 1; see also Weinberg, *Nicolaus of Autrecourt*, pp. 17–19.
31 "Certi humanis in rebus nihil esse, omnia probabilia, vitandam in omni re affirmandi arrogantiam" (quoted in Charles Trinkhaus, *In Our Image and Likeness*, I, 319, 455): "Philosophia tota opinionibus et conjecturis verisimilitudinis est innixa" (*Vivis opera omnia*, VI, 417).
32 John Monfasani, *George of Trebizond*, p. 305.
33 Linda Janik has explained cogently how Valla's use of terms such as "logic" and "philosophy" embodies a polemical stance devised to impugn the dogmatic views of his opponents, while Valla defends a skeptical probabilism of his own ("Lorenzo Valla," pp. 389–91).
34 Lisa Jardine, "Lorenzo Valla and the Intellectual Origins of Humanist Dialectic," p. 164.
35 G. E. R. Lloyd, *Magic, Reason and Experience*, p. 78.
36 See Clark Kubler, *The Argument from Probability in Early Attic Oratory*; George Kennedy, *Classical Rhetoric*, pp. 8–14.
37 See S. Sambursky, *The Physical World of the Greeks*, pp. 60–63, 177–81, and "On the Possible and the Probable in Ancient Greece" (the quotation from Simplicius appears on p. 37).
38 See Grote, *Aristotle*, pp. 269–71; J. D. G. Evans, *Aristotle's Concept of Dialectic*, pp. 77–79.
39 See McKeon, "Rhetoric in the Middle Ages," pp. 24–25 (Aristotle's use of *eikos* and *pithanos* is not consistent). In his commentary on the *Posterior Analytics*, Aquinas presents a schematization of the *ars logica*:

A. De necessitate	ars logica judicativa	ex forma syllogismi:
(cum		*Analytica Priora*
certitudine)		cum forma ex materia
		syllogismi:
		Analytica Posteriora

B. Frequentibus	ars logica inventiva	
1. In pluribus		
a. Cum probabilitate	dialectica	*Topica* (Dialectica)
b. Cum suspicione	rhetorica	*Rhetorica*
c. Cum existimatione	poetica	*Poetica*
2. In paucioribus	sophistica	*De Sophisticis Elenchis*

(From W. J. Ong, "The Province of Rhetoric and Poetic," p. 25.)

40 See Stough, *Greek Skepticism*, ch. 1. The account of Carneades which follows has recently been challenged in Myles Burnyeat, "Carneades Was No Probabilist."

41 *Academica* II. x. 32; *De Partitione oratoria* x. 34; Jardine, "Lorenzo Valla," pp. 151–52.

42 "Lorenzo Valla," p. 151. See also P. A. Meador, "Skeptic Theory of Perception: A Philosophical Antecedent of Ciceronian Probability," and Alain Michel, *Les Rapports de la rhétorique et de la philosophie dans l'oeuvre de Cicéron* and *Rhétorique et philosophie chez Cicéron*.

43 See Charles B. Schmitt, "The Recovery and Assimilation of Ancient Scepticism in the Renaissance," p. 365.

44 See Schmitt, *Cicero Scepticus*, ch. 1; David Marsh, *The Quattrocento Dialogue*, chs. 1–2. Augustine's *Contra Academicos* is, despite its rejection of the form, an argument *in utramque partem*, suggesting an ambiguity in Augustine's attitudes which neither Schmitt nor Marsh explores.

45 Quoted in Neal Gilbert, *Renaissance Concepts of Method*, pp. 153–54.

46 On the transition to humanist teaching of dialectic in Renaissance universities, see Terence Heath, "Logical Grammar, Grammatical Logic, and Humanism in Three German Universities"; Lisa Jardine, "The Place of Dialectic Teaching in Sixteenth-Century Cambridge" and "Humanism and the Sixteenth Century Cambridge Arts Course."

47 Thus Vives in the *De Tradendis* (I. 3. 3): "You, Aristotle, require necessary principles, namely those which cannot be otherwise. How and where can we know them? The universals are known to us only through an inference from the individuals which are almost infinite; and if one individual remains unknown the universal itself vanishes"; it was as a substitute for scientific induction that Renaissance logicians toiled to construct *regressus* arguments (see Jardine, "Galileo's Road to Truth").

48 *De Inventione dialectica*, p. 155.

49 *P. Rami Dialectica libro duo*, p. 1; Wilson, *Rule of Reason*, p. 8; compare Blundeville, *Art of Logike*, p. 1.

50 "Non ergo aliud est locus, quam communis quaedam rei nota, cuius admonitu quid in quaque re probabile sit, potest inveniri" (I. 2. 8); for similar definitions by Thomas Wilson and others see W. J. Ong, "Agricola's Place-Logic," ch. v of *Ramus, Method, and the Decay of Dialogue*.

51 See Jardine, "Lorenzo Valla," p. 159, and Carlos Noreña, *Juan Luis Vives*, pp. 279–80.

52 *On Education*, tr. Foster Watson, p. 43.

53 Armstrong, "The Dialectical Road to Truth: the Dialogue," p. 43; Marsh, *The Quattrocento Dialogue*, chs. 5–6.

54 For the humanist connection of rhetoric with law, see especially Noreña, *Vives*, pp. 267–68, and Jerrold Siegel, *Rhetoric and Philosophy in Renaissance Humanism*.

55 "Ramus and the Art of Judgment," p. 155.

56 See Noreña, *Vives*, pp. 249–59; Gilbert, *Renaissance Concepts of Method*, pp. 14–15, 155–57. (Gilbert notes that it is such common notions that Locke attacks in Book I of the *Essay*.)

57 Cited in Noreña, *Vives*, p. 251.

58 Noreña, *Vives*, p. 250; Malebranche, *De la Recherche de la vérité*, I, 25.

59 See especially Rule II: "Thus in accordance with the above maxim we reject all such merely probable knowledge [*omnes probabiles*] and make it a rule to trust only what is completely known and incapable of being doubted" (*Oeuvres de Descartes*, X, 362; see also John Morris, "Descartes and Probable Knowledge").

60 See articles by Benjamin Nelson cited in Bibliography, especially "The Early Modern Revolution in Science," and Nicholas Jardine, "The Forging of Modern Realism: Clavius and Kepler against the Sceptics." In the seventeenth-century phase of the dispute between the ancients and the moderns, it is the moderns who are certaintists; the ancients, children of Renaissance humanism, sought still a Ciceronian, probabilistic alternative to such doctrines.

61 *Summa theologiae*, I, 30; Edmund Byrne has given a careful reconstruction of Aquinas' system of ranking authorities in *Probability and Opinion*.

62 See especially pp. 102–06, which includes a table of the kinds of authorities.

63 *The Art of Logick*, pp. 163–64. (Coke's title to this work has recently been disputed; its author may be Henry Ainsworth. See J. S. Measell, "The Authorship of *The Art of Logick* (1654).")

64 See for a fuller discussion Grahame Castor, *Pléiade Poetics*, ch. 12.

65 See Richard Aaron, *John Locke*, pp. 247–48. The prevailing modern views about Locke's sources appear to be those outlined by Henry van Leeuwen in *The Problem of Certainty in English Thought 1630–1690*, which traces latitudinarian Anglican doctrine of the degrees of certainty from Chillingworth and Tillotson through such writers as Wilkins and Glanvill to its culmination in Newton and Locke.

66 *Essays on the Law of Nature*, pp. 62–63, 165, 177.

67 That this should be so is clear from the Jesuit Buffier's attack on Locke in his *Traité des premières vérités* (1724), a work which Thomas Reid identifies as the earliest ancestor of the Scottish philosophy of common sense (*Intellectual Powers*, pp. 687, 690). Locke's view that testimony loses force by growing older undercuts the Catholic doctrine, so important if tradition is to be a rule of faith, that within the Church a continuous and dependable tradition of scriptural interpretation and other knowledge exists; thus, in the manner of earlier Catholic polemicists, Buffier is concerned to prove as against Locke that "il est des opinions qui acquièrent des preuves en vieillissant" and that these opinions are not merely probable, but may attain to certainty (*Oeuvres*, p. 76). "Il me parait évident que l'*autorité*, prise de la sorte, n'est pas une simple *probabilité*, mais une véritable certitude," if only a "*certitude morale*" (64, 65). Buffier finds genuine difficulties in Locke's view that some probabilities may be so strong as to force assent as if they were certain, and, in attacking the priority Locke gives to our own testimony above that of others, recognizes the fundamental similarity of both: "je lui demanderais

volontiers pourquoi il admet pour certitude le témoignage des yeux et non pas le témoignage unanime de tous les hommes?" (64). At stake in both disputes is not merely an epistemological point, but a rule of faith; in Buffier's system, the truths of the Catholic faith receive new support from those first principles which to him are the deliverances of the "sens commun."

68 *A Treatise of Human Nature*, p. 145. After treating testimony Craig proceeds to a mathematical account of pleasure and pain, working from the assumption that the wise man will modify his actions according to the quantity of pleasure he may with probability expect to follow upon any course of action; this felicific calculus appears to have been the immediate source for Hutcheson's vector analysis of pain and pleasure in the *Inquiry* of 1725 (2. 3. 11–12) and so also of the social mathematics of Condorcet and Bentham (see Keith M. Baker, *Condorcet*, ch. 3). In the *Observations on Man* (1749), David Hartley presents an extended mathematics of testimony developed from Craig (1. 3. 2).

69 "Id nunc dicamus, quia volumus dialecticus esse, posse de quodlibet dicere probabiliter: probabile in disserendo non solum id esse, quod revera probabile est, hoc est, quemadmodum Aristoteles inquit, quod vel omnibus videtur, vel plurimus, vel sapientibus ... nobis erit probabile, quod aptae consentanaeque de re proposita dicetur" (*De Inventione dialectica*, p. 158).

70 See below, p. 141. Bacon was to impugn such probability when he complained that dialectical "invention does not discover principles and chief axioms, of which arts are composed, but only such things as appear to be consistent with them" (IV, 80–81).

71 See Lisa Jardine, *Francis Bacon: Discovery and the Art of Discourse*, p. 31.

72 See Linda Janik, "Lorenzo Valla: The Primacy of Rhetoric and the De-Moralization of History," and below, pp. 116ff. Janik finds of Facio's verisimilitude that "it functions not as a criterion for sifting evidence, but rather as a principle of selection"; "the use of evidence or testimony is distorted by expectations about who can be considered a reliable witness" (398, 397) – that is, as what we have found in jurisprudence to be an interest in admissibility rather than proof.

73 *Essay* 4. 12. 10; cf. *Some Thoughts concerning Education*, in *Educational Writings*, p. 301.

74 *Conduct*, p. 86; *Essay* 2. 29. 2 (cf. 4. 12. 1: "*Our Knowledge*, as in other things ... has great conformity with our Sight").

75 *Principles of Philosophy* I. xxx; *Rules for the Direction of the Mind*, IV, XII, IX; see also John Morris, "Descartes' Natural Light." In his well-known book on Ramus, Father Ong has argued that, as a result of the spatial understanding of the places in topical logic and mnemonics, Descartes conceived clarity and distinctness not only in visual but specifically spatial ("Euclidean") terms (see, e.g., p. 121). It is quite common, however, for Cartesian writers to contrast the false "dazzle" and "glare" of the visual with the truths "spoken" to us by reason or God; see for instance *De la Recherche de la vérité* I, 312, 354, 490. (Inspiration for such passages may come from Romans 10: 17: "So then faith cometh by hearing, and hearing by the word of God"; in mediaeval allegory, such as *The Pilgrimage of the Life of Man*, this becomes the requirement that the pilgrim's eyes actually be placed in his ears (see lines 5376–82; 6235–58).) On Locke's conception of both ideas and reasoning on visual models, see Robert McRae, "'Idea' as a Philosophical Term in the Seventeenth Century."

76 For later statements of Locke's notion of dim resemblance, see Watts, *Logick*, 1. 3. 4, and William Barron, *Lectures on Belles Lettres and Logic*, II, 372.

77 *The Remains of that Reverend and Learned Prelate, Dr. George Rust*, p. 23.

78 Boyle, *A Discourse of Things Above Reason*, in *Works*, IV, 30; Reid, *Intellectual Powers*, p. 619.

79 See Joseph Geyser, "Zur Einführung in das Problem der Evidenz in der Scholastik."

80 Johnson lists three definitions of *evidence*: (1) "The state of being evident; clearness; indubitable certainty; notoriety"; (2) "Testimony; proof"; (3) "Witnesses; one that gives evidence"; Bailey's more traditional account divides evidence into "formal," "objective," "physical," "metaphysical," "moral," and "legal" senses.

81 See R. A. Naulty, "Newman's Dispute with Locke," p. 456.

82 Seventeenth-century writers often distinguish the certainty of truth from that of knowledge in an effort to preserve the high degree of certainty supposed to be possessed by religious truth, while admitting that *we* may *know* religious truth with only a low degree of certainty. This distinction is usually an Anglican response to Catholic demands for infallibility in religious knowledge; Locke makes the distinction at 4. 6. 3, and applies it to revelation at 4. 16. 14. His procedure here is part of his larger argument for toleration (sketched at 4. 16. 4). George Tavard gives a useful survey of similar arguments at use in religious controversy in *The Seventeenth-Century Tradition: A Study in Recusant Thought*.

83 *Essay* 2. 21. 72; see Hacking, *Emergence of Probability*, p. 70. Pascal's *Pensées* were first published in 1670, and an early version of the wager appears at the end of the Port-Royal *Logic*.

84 Craig defines probability as "the appearance of agreement or of disagreement of two ideas through arguments whose conclusion is not fixed, or at least is not perceived to be so" (*Craig's Rules*, pp. 2–3).

II Probability and signs: reasoning from effect to cause

1 See H. R. Fox Bourne, *The Life of John Locke*, 1, 70, and, on the broader meanings of Locke's divisions of the sciences, K. L. Armstrong, "John Locke's 'Doctrine of Signs': A New Metaphysics."

2 According to Gassendi's great work on logic, the *Syntagma* (1658), all demonstration is sign-inference, because all middle terms are signs; see his *Selected Works*, pp. 367–69, and commentary in Hacking, *Emergence of Probability*, for which Gassendi is crucial (pp. 45–47). The best general commentary on Gassendi's signs is Olivier René Bloch, *La Philosophie de Gassendi*, pp. 26–28, 145–46.

3 See Bacon's *Preparatives Towards a Natural and Experimental History* (*Works*, IV, 249–64); Kenneth Dewhurst, *John Locke, Physician and Philosopher*; John Yolton, "The Science of Nature," p. 191; Dewhurst, *Dr. Thomas Sydenham*, p. 62ff.; Patrick Romanell, "Locke and Sydenham"; and especially François Duchesneau, *L'Empirisme de Locke*, pp. 66f. On contemporary systems of sign language devised for use by the deaf, see J. P. Siegel, "The Enlightenment and the Evolution of a Language of Signs."

4 J. L. Stocks, "Epicurean Induction," p. 203; Thomas A. Sebeok, *The Sign & Its Masters*, pp. 6–7, 259.

5 *Fundamenta*, pp. xi–xxiv. Comparing Hoffmann's work with the institutes of Lazar Riverius (1655) and Boerhaave (1708), King tabulates the following results (figures refer to percentages of total pages devoted to each topic):

	Riverius	Hoffmann	Boerhaave
Introductory	1	3	3
Physiology	14	24	63
Pathology	12	32	11
Semeiotics	33	14	8
Hygiene	15	7	2
Therapeutics	25	20	13

6 Lester King, "Signs and Symptoms," p. 1065.

7 *Physiologia*, p. 364. In the same chapter, Charleton expresses the "fear, that they [students of occult qualities] have not attained the happy shoar of verity, but remain upon the wide and fluctuating ocean of meer Verisimility"; he adds, somewhat disingenuously, "our Designe is only to explain sundry admired Effects, by such Reasons, as may appear not altogether Remote and Incongruous, but *Consentaneous* and *Affine* to Truth; that so no mans judgement may be impeached by embracing them for most Probable, untill the (in that respect, too slow) wheel of Time shall have brought up some more worthy Explorator, who shall wholly withdrawe that thick Curtain of obscurity, which yet hangs betwixt Natures Laboratory and Us, and enrich the Commonweal of Letters, by the discovery of Real Verity" (342). For attempts to reconstruct Charleton's changing views on probability and certainty in science, see Robert Hugh Kargon, *Atomism in England from Hariot to Newton*, Ch. 8, and Nina Rattner Gelbart, "The Intellectual Development of Walter Charleton."

For a "signal example," see Clarissa's remark to her correspondent Miss Howe expressing an awareness that she is being made an example of – a sign to others – by God: "Indeed, my dearest love permit me to be very serious, I am afraid I am singled out (either for my own faults, or for the faults of my family, or perhaps for the faults of both) to be a very unhappy creature! – *signally* unhappy! For see you not how irresistibly the waves of affliction come tumbling down upon me?" (*Clarissa*, 1, 419; cf. below, p. 305 n45).

8 See, e.g., Nathan Drake, *Literary Hours*, 1, 42–44.

9 Lodge, *Works*, IV, 20, 21; Defoe, *Journal of the Plague Year*; Dekker, "The Wonderfull Yeare," in *The Plague Pamphlets of Thomas Dekker*, ed. F. P. Wilson, pp. 1–62. Wilson suggests that the use of *token* to mean a mark of the plague comes from the marks' likeness to coins (224), but its use to mean sign long antedates this sense, which in fact is a product of the earlier meaning.

10 See, for instance, the critical account given by Crousaz in his *New Treatise of the Art of Thinking*: "The ancient Rhetoricians referred to the Class of Adjuncts a great many Relations, which did not belong to it: they placed in that Class, most of those Things which surround a Subject, when they contributed to the clearing of it. Such are *Signs*, for instance, which they defined thus: A Sign is *a Thing, which leads us to Knowledge of another*. Afterwards they divided them into many Orders, and among others, into *preceding, attending,* and *subsequent* Signs." (1, 428)

11 On Aristotle's conception of the enthymeme, see Edward Madden, "The Enthymeme" and "Aristotle's Treatment of Probability and Signs." Arthur Miller and John Bee speculate on etymological evidence for a physiological origin of the concept in "Enthymemes: Body and Soul."

12 See William Wallace, *Causality and Scientific Explanation*, I, 119–21, 140, 153, 234; and Nicholas Jardine, "Galileo's Road to Truth."

13 See Elizabeth Evans, *Physiognomics in the Ancient World*, and, for the best recent historical survey, Graeme Tytler, *Physiognomy in the European Novel*, pp. 35–48.

14 See E. H. Gombrich, "Moment and Movement in Art," and Jennifer Montagu, "Charles Le Brun's *Conférence sur l'expression*," Introduction.

15 See L. J. Rather, *Mind and Body in Eighteenth-Century Medicine*, p. 132.

16 *Oeuvres de François de La Mothe Le Vayer*, III, 848; Mersenne, *Vérité*, pp. 188–89. In the *Logike*, Ramus tells the story approvingly: "Heraclitus the Philosopher examyned the phisitions whiche came to heale hym, and because they were ignorant and could not aunswere to his interrogations he sent them away, and would receyve none of their Medicins: for (sayd he) yf ye can not shewe me the causes of my sickness, much lesse are ye able to take the cause awaye" (14).

For physiognomy as science of signs, see, e.g., Aristotle, *Physiognomicon*, and the discussion of reasoning "probabilibus signis" in Agrippa's "De Physiognomia" (*De Vanitate scientiarum*, p. 65); for meteorology, Lever, *Arte of Reason*, p. 191; astrology, e.g., Joseph Hall's satire in *Virgidemiae*, VII (1597; *Poems*, pp. 29–30); mineralogy, examples cited by Hacking, *Emergence of Probability*, pp. 35, 43.

17 For *specious* in the sense used here, cf. Owen Ruffhead, *The Life of Alexander Pope*, p. 427: "These reflections are specious, but, perhaps, on close examination, they will appear fallacious." White's strategy is typical of Roman Catholic attacks on Anglican writers of both "physicks and metaphysicks." Probability becomes "dirt" in comparison with the science of the learned according to comparisons invented by Zeno the Stoic between logic and rhetoric as the closed fist and the open hand – a comparison reinterpreted to mean that logic is the tool of learned thought and communication, rhetoric the method used by the learned in speaking to the vulgar. (For this image, see W. S. Howell, *Logic and Rhetoric in England*, pp. 3–4.)

18 Bernard Mandeville, *Treatise of the Hypocondriak Passions*, p. 38; *The Fable of the Bees*, II, 161–62.

19 In Dewhurst, *Dr. Thomas Sydenham*, p. 81. Authorship of the *De Arte medica* has been disputed: Fox Bourne and many others have attributed it to Locke, for it is in his handwriting; Dewhurst, remarking that we have many such works by Sydenham dating from Locke's tenure as his secretary, attributes the whole to Sydenham (p. 73). Duchesneau argues for joint authorship (*L'Empirisme de Locke*, p. 45).

20 *On the Study Methods of Our Time*, p. 8.

21 Scott Buchanan, *The Doctrine of Signatures*, pp. 42, xi; cf. Paracelsus himself: "*Siegwurz* root is wrappen in an envelope like armour; and this is a magic sign showing that like armour it gives protection against weapons. And the *Syderica* bears the image and form of a snake on each of its leaves, and thus, according to magic, it gives protection against any kind of poisoning" (*Selected Writings*, p. 161).

Buchanan's work is an attempt to revive the theory of signs in medicine; his banner has more recently been carried by a growing literature which seeks to revive medical signs by assimilating them to the modern theory called "semiotics" (see in Bibliography works by Barthes, Crookshank, Sebeok, Shands and Meltzer, and von Uexkull). Unhappily, most such attempts partake of the same sterility which besets "semiotics" generally. Part of the problem, of course, is that the student of semiotics casts his net too widely: as Jonathan Culler notes of "indices," by which he means any nonverbal indicative sign, "Indices are, from the semiologist's point of view, more worrying. If he places them within his domain, then he risks taking all human knowledge for his province; for any science which attempts to establish causal relations among phenomena could be seen as a study of indices and thus placed within semiology. Medicine, for example" (*Ferdinand de Saussure*, p. 105).

22 Like Paracelsus before him, and like Joseph Duchesne (Quercetanus) in his "De signaturis rerum internis seu specificis" (1603), Croll is concerned that iatrochemists attend not merely to the *external* (visible) signatures in things, but that they seek also the *internal* signatures revealed only by chemical analysis; on the distinction see Allen Debus, *The Chemical Philosophy*, I, 100, 122–23. According to John Webster, Adam could name all plants and animals appropriately because he "did understand both their internal and external signatures" (*Academarium Examen*, p. 29).

23 Owen Hannaway, *The Chemists and the Word*, pp. 67, 72; Hannaway's study is in part an attempt to find in the dispute between Croll and his Ramist critic Libavius evidence of Michel Foucault's model of the transition from Renaissance to Classical epistemes.

24 Hacking, *Emergence of Probability*, pp. 39–43 (see also Walter Pagel, *Paracelsus*, p. 224); Morris, "Descartes and Probable Knowledge," p. 304; Gay, *Voltaire's Politics*, p. 302; Lynn Thorndike, *History of Magic and Experimental Science*, VII, 353.

25 1st ed. 1597; from prefatory letter by "St. Bredwell Physition" in 1633 ed.

26 *Wisdom of God*, pp. 103–04; *Cambridge Catalogue*, tr. in Charles Raven, *John Ray Naturalist*, pp. 98–99. Like other "new philosophers" of the seventeenth century, Ray believed that "real essences" of things may exist, but that we cannot know them; for this reason, Ray believed also that plants may in fact possess signatures, but if so, we cannot know them: see Phillip R. Sloan, "John Locke, John Ray, and the Problem of Natural System," esp. p. 49.

27 Bacon, *Works*, IV, 164 (cf. 272); Jardine, *Francis Bacon*, pp. 198–99.

28 See J. E. McGuire, "Atoms and the 'Analogy of Nature'" and "Boyle's Conception of Nature," and, on the place of signs in the conception of occult and manifest levels of reality, Keith Hutchison, "What Happened to Occult Qualities in the Scientific Revolution?" These are of course very large issues which it is not our purpose to treat in detail here. The transition from Renaissance science (what has been called "Renaissance naturalism") to the corpuscular–mechanical philosophy of the seventeenth century brought with it, furthermore, changes in the conception of signs themselves; on this vexed matter, see below, p. 333 n12.

29 Power, *Experimental Philosophy*, Preface. See also Glanvill, *Vanity of Dogmatizing*, p. 3: "For since the most despicable and disregarded pieces of decay'd nature, are so curiously wrought, and adorned with such eminent *signatures* of *Divine wisdome*, as speak it their Author, and that after a curse brung upon a disorder'd Universe"; p. 199: "Now that this strange *power* of the *Imagination* is no Impossibility: the wonderful *signatures* in

the *Foetus* caused by the Imagination of the Mother, is no contemptible Item."

30 *Intellectual Powers*, p. 667; for Ogilvie and Duff, see below, pp. 223–32.

31 Hearne distinguishes two sorts of historical testimony, human and divine (145), and gives five rules for evaluating human testimony, much like those we have seen before (9–11). In most of history "we must necessarily be satisfied with Conjectures and Probabilities" (14), and so must depend on the evidence of signs. Some of these are actually certain, such as the "certain and demonstrable" arguments taken from records of eclipses ("Now since the Certainty which Eclipses give to History is infallible, we must account ourselves happy for the care Historians have taken to mention so great a number of them," p. 19); others, gleaned from analogy, are merely probable: Hearne argues, for instance, that the earth cannot have existed eternally, for if it had, arts and sciences would by now have been better developed, concluding: "there are many other visible Signs of its Infancy, which any Man of ordinary Capacity and Judgment will be sensible of" (2–3). It is antiquaries such as Hearne that Horace Walpole takes off in his satire on historical probabilism in *Hieroglyphic Tales* (see below, pp. 151–52).

32 Nicholas Jardine quotes Strebaeus on Cicero's *De Partitionibus*: "*argumenta coniecturalia* are either probable [*verisimilia*], or concerning the peculiar characteristics of things [*propriae rerum notae*], in Greek *eikota* or *tekmeria*. *Verisimilia* he defines as things which happen for the most part, such as youths having a tendency to unruliness. *Propriae notae* he calls signs and necessary arguments, which could not be otherwise, and they indicate what is certain, as smoke indicates fire; if these occur in a conjectural matter they resolve the dispute and controversy" ("Galileo's Road to Truth," p. 293).

33 *Works*, II, 172; III, 156.

34 *Sermons Preached upon Several Occasions*, I, 280.

35 Quoted in Gay, *Voltaire's Politics*, p. 306.

36 Several writers have recently described seventeenth-century hypotheticalism as "conjecturalism," but this is not a term known to the time. A. I. Sabra, for instance, calls Huyghens a proponent of such conjecturalism, but Huyghens himself calls his method one that proceeds by "preuves de vraisemblance"; Sabra has taken his terminology from Popper. See Sabra's *Theories of Light*, p. 182; see also A. Elzinga, "Huyghens' Theory of Research."

37 *The Vanity of Dogmatizing*, pp. 41–42, 180, 210, 6–7. See also the very useful essay by Keith Hutchison, "What Happened to Occult Qualities in the Scientific Revolution?"

38 Quoted in Wigmore, "Required Numbers of Witnesses," p. 89.

39 The sense of *propriety* at use here is explained by Bailey: "PROPRIETY (with *Logicians*) is the fourth of the Universal Ideas, and is when the Object is an Attribute, which in Effect belongs to the Essence of the Thing; but is not first considered in that Essence." Richard Sherry considers "circumstances" (which he conflates with "places") with signs as species of unartificial proofs (*A Treatise of Schemes and Tropes*, p. 79).

40 Keynes, *A Treatise of Probability*, p. 80.

41 "Tout ce que nous avons dit jusques icy, regarde les sciences humaines purement humaines, & les connoissances qui sont fondées sur l'evidence de la raison. Mais avant que de finir, il est bon de parler d'vne autre sorte de connoissance, qui souvent n'est pas moins certaine ny moins evidente en sa maniere, qui est celle que nous tirons de l'autorité" (355).

42 The distinction comes of course from Artistotle's between common and special *topoi* (*Rhet.* 1358ª2–32; *Top.* 119ª12–24); the Port-Royalists' distinction had already been framed as one between general and special *probability*, by literary critics such as Castelvetro and Chapelain (see René Bray, *La Formation de la doctrine classique*, p. 199). Thomas Rymer explains the distinction in 1677, revealing as well its source in Aristotle's *Poetics*: "many things are *probable* of *Antonius*, or of *Alexander*, and *particular* men, because they are *true*, which cannot be *generally probable*: and he that will be *feigning* persons, should confine his fancy to *general probability*" (*Critical Works*, p. 24).

43 "si elles ne sont point contrabalancées par d'autres circonstances particulieres, qui affoiblissent ou qui ruinent dans nostre esprit les motifs de credibilité qu'il tiroit de ces circonstances communes, nous avons raison de croire ces evenemens sinon certainement, au moins tres-probablement, ce qui nous suffit quand nous avons obligation d'en iuger. Car comme nous nous devons contenter d'vne certitude morale dans les choses qui ne sont pas susceptibles d'vne certitude metaphysique, lors aussi que nous ne pouvons pas avoir vne entiere certitude morale, le mieux que nous puissons faire quand nous sommes engagez à prendre parti, est d'embrasser le plus probable, puisque ce seroit vn renversement de la raison d'embrasser le moins probable" (376–77).

44 For the casuists' use of the distinction between intrinsic and extrinsic grounds of judgment – between evidence drawn from the nature of the case itself and the evidence of testimony – see Taylor, *Ductor*, p. 90; Kenneth Kirk, *Some Principles of Moral Theology*, pp. 194–95; Thomas Slater, *A Manual of Moral Theology*, I, 69.

45 *The Politician's Catechism for his Instruction in Divine Faith and Moral Honesty*, p. 19.

46 On the Catholic side, see Slater, *Manual*, bk. II, and J. M. Harty, "Probabilism," 442; on the Protestant side, Kirk, *Some Principles*. The most detailed general history of probabilism and its relatives is Th. Deman, "Probabilisme." A number of critics have examined the role of these moral–theological debates in shaping Renaissance and seventeenth-century devotional and other literature; see most recently Camille Slights, *The Casuistical Tradition*.

47 The point is obvious for Protestant vs. Catholic casuistry; for the issue of "droit et fait" in Jansenism, see Alexander Sedgwick, *Jansenism in Seventeenth-Century France*, ch. 5. Pascal addresses this issue obliquely in his fifth *Provinciale*: "Si le tesmoignage d'un tel homme est de grand poids pour nous assurer qu'une chose se soit passée par example à Rome; pourquoy ne le sera-t'il pas de mesme dans un doute de Morale?
    La plaisante comparaison, luy dis-je, des choses du monde a celles de la conscience!" (*Oeuvres*, IV, 311).

48 Tr. in Harty, "Probabilism," p. 442. The most careful reconstruction of the genesis of probabilism is J. de Blic, "Barthélémy de Medina et les origines du probabilisme." See also H. C. Lea, *A History of Auricular Confession*, ch. 21.

49 Tr. in Kirk, *Some Principles*, p. 196 (cf. Pascal, *Oeuvres*, IV, 310).

50 "Il n'y a presque rien que les Jésuites ne permettent aux Chrétiens, en réduisant toutes choses en probabilités, et enseignant qu'on peut quitter la plus probable opinion, que l'on croit vraie, pour suivre la moins probable; & soutenant ensuites, qu'une opinion est probable aussi-tôt que deux Docteurs

l'enseignent, voire même un seule." "La Théologie morale des Jésuites," p. 74.

51 *The Emergence of Probability*, p. 23.

52 Joseph Rickaby, *Moral Philosophy*, p. 157.

53 See especially p. 62: 'L'autorité humaine est appuyée sur ce que rapportent des hommes. Bien que tous en particulier soient fallibles, il est néanmoins des circonstances où l'on ne doit pas résister a leur témoignage... Il faut rechercher ces dernières circonstances pour faire l'analyse de cette sorte de première vérité qu'on appelle ordinairement *évidence morale*."

54 By Charles Trinkhaus, in "Italian Humanism and the Problem of 'Structures of Conscience.'" In general the same positions which emerge in Protestant and Catholic moral theology appear as well in Reformation debates over the assurance which an individual soul may have of its own election: the Reformers argue the possibility of complete certainty of salvation, their Catholic opponents (often castigated as "Papist Academics," i.e., probabilist skeptics) only probable knowledge and a theoretic faith (see Harold Skulsky, "Spenser's Despair Episode and the Theology of Doubt").

55 See works cited by Benjamin Nelson, especially "The Early Modern Revolution," p. 13; while Nelson's thesis is attractive, he has not demonstrated that in each pair theological and scientific views were in fact linked.

56 "La vraisemblance augmente, pour ainsi dire, et s'approche du vrai, par autant de degrés que les circonstances suivantes s'y rencontrent en plus grand nombre et d'une manière plus expresse" (71).

57 *Ductor*, pp. 91, 92; Johnson, *Lives of the English Poets*, I, 418.

58 Casuistry might be said to be an outline of a decorum of moral behavior, for instance, of lying: in his *New Art of Lying* (1621), Henry Mason defends "equivocation" "when circumstances of place, persons, etc., are such as that in reason, and in the judgment of sober men ... they may limit or restrain the speech to some special matter or subject, or otherwise alter the meaning of it from that which it would have, if it were in some other place or occasion." See George L. Mosse, *The Holy Pretence: A Study in Christianity and Reason of State from William Perkins to John Winthrop* (Mason is quoted pp. 45–46).

59 William Sharpe, *A Dissertation upon Genius*, p. 56; Locke, *Essay*, 4. 2. 3; 4. 17. 2 (compare *Conduct*, p. 34).

60 For sagacity as the physician's virtue, see also John Armstrong, "The Art of Preserving Health" (1744), I. 54, II. 139, and especially III. 225–26, where the "sagacious Muse" of medicine is said to trace "thro' nature's cunning labyrinths."

61 From MS quoted in J. R. Jacob, *Robert Boyle and the English Revolution*, p. 101.

62 Quoted in Jacob, *Robert Boyle*, p. 100.

63 Peter France reconstructs Descartes' views on rhetoric and literary scholarship in *Rhetoric and Truth in France*, ch. 2.

64 Spinoza, *Works*, II, 8.

65 On Descartes' influence in the Oratorian schools, see H. C. Barnard, *The French Tradition in Education*, ch. 5; on his educational views in general and in relation to Locke's, G. H. Bantock, *Studies in the History of Educational Theory*, pp. 215–27.

66 "nous ne voïons point de ce qu'elle est de l'interieur. Que peut donc faire un Phisicien, que de conjecturer?" (*Entretiens*, p. 259).

67 "Le moïen de s'assurer de la verité des Hipotheses qu'on fait, c'est-à-dire, si

les choses sont en éfet ce qu'on a pû supposer qu'elles sont selon les Loix de la Nature, c'est de tâcher de voir par les yeux du corps ce qu'on n'apercevoit que par des conjectures en raisonnant. Les Telescopes & les Microscopes servent à cela" (257).

68 "*Raisonnement exact, & demonstration*, est la même chose" (103); "Il ne s'agit donc que de régler ce qu'on apelle les operations de l'esprit, apercevoir, juger, raisonner, ranger nos pensées, nos jugemens & nos raisonnemens. C'est ce qu'enseigne la Logique quand elle est faite comme il faut. C'est donc par une bonne Logique qu'il faut commencer d'étudier" (65).

69 "Dieu a mis dans les Hommes des semences de doctrine, c'est à-dire, des veritez premieres, dont les autres coulent comme les ruisseaux de leurs sources. L'art d'apprendre ne consiste qu'à faire une attention particuliere a ces premiéres veritez, & à remarquer les consequences que l'on en peut tirer les unes aprés les autres" (63).

70 See Crousaz, *New Treatise of the Art of Thinking*, II, 216.

71 Quoted in *Study Methods*, p. xxiii.

72 *Study Methods*, pp. 15–19, 78; see also Ernesto Grassi, "Critical Philosophy or Topical Philosophy? Meditations on the *De nostri temporis studiorum ratione.*"

73 Yvon Belaval, "Vico and Anti-Cartesianism," p. 82.

74 *Essays* (1776), p. 71. As de Moivre explains, paying homage to the master in the dedication to the first edition (1718) of his *Doctrine of Chances*, it was the example of Newton more than that of any other natural philosopher which taught British "Philosophy how to collect, by a just Calculation, the Evidences of exquisite Wisdom and Design, which appear in the *Phenomena* of Nature throughout the Universe" (1756 ed., p. 329). See O. B. Sheynin, "Newton and the Classical Theory of Probability."

75 *Sermons of Mr. Yorick*, pt. I, 133, 132.

76 See Laurens Laudan, "Peirce and the Trivialization of the Self-Correcting Hypothesis."

77 Thus according to Dr. Bentley. "In the Atheistical Hypothesis of the World's production, Fortuitous and Mechanical must be the self-same thing" (*Isaac Newton's Papers and Letters*, p. 316). According to de Moivre, "chance" means action from an unknown cause; in any other sense it is "a mere word," as is "a *course of nature* in contradistinction to the *Divine energy*" (253). John Evelyn understands "chance" as absence of a designing mind in his *Essay on De Rerum Natura* (1656):

> Lucretius with a stork-like fate
> Born and translated in a State
> Comes to proclaim in English verse
> No Monarch rules the Universe.
> But chance and *Atomes* make this *All*
> In order Democraticall
> Without design, or Fate, or Force.

Dryden similarly contrasts "Chance" with "Care" in "To Sir Robert Howard," where the workings of mechanistic physiology (the *rete mirabile*, as opposed to rational thought consciously directed to the achievement of ends) are said to be occurrences of "chance" and "fortune" (lines 25–30).

78 See W. S. Howell, *Eighteenth-Century British Logic and Rhetoric*, pp. 288, 445, 493–95, 602.

79 See Lester M. Beattie, *John Arbuthnot: Mathematician and Satirist*, pp. 334–46.

80 In *The Economic Writings of Sir William Petty*, II, 352, 353; for evidence relating to authorship of the *Observations*, see I, xxxix-liv.

81 *Economic Writings*, I, 241; Peter Buck, "Seventeenth-Century Political Arithmetic: Civil Strife and Vital Statistics," p. 69.

82 See D. V. Glass, "The Population Controversy in Eighteenth-Century England."

83 *The Emergence of Probability*, p. 79.

III *Vraisemblance*, probability, and opinion

1 According to Baxter Hathaway, the opposition learned from Aristotle of the probable to the marvellous was "the hub around which the whole wheel of speculation turned" in Renaissance criticism (*Marvels and Commonplaces*, p. 53); see also William Nelson, *Fact or Fiction: The Dilemma of the Renaissance Storyteller*.

2 The terms come, of course, from *Poetics* 9. In his influential translation of 1570, Castelvetro renders Aristotle's phrase "verisimilitudine, ò la necessita" (*Poetica d'Aristotele*, p. 101b). Other versions of the *Poetics* translate more interpretively; the anonymous *Aristotelis De Poetica liber* of 1623 alternates "Verisimile, vel Necessarium" with "Necessario vel in Plurimis" (19, 16).

3 *Dialogue upon the Gardens... at Stowe* (1746), p. 6. For the epic content of an Augustan garden plan, see Kenneth Woodbridge, *Landscape and Antiquity: Aspects of English Culture at Stourhead*, and James Turner's argument that this garden imitates not Book VI but Book I of the *Aeneid*, "The Structure of Henry Hoare's Stourhead."

4 Phoebe's splendid response to a question about the play she is writing (whose subject is the Deluge) astutely parodies many of our concerns in chapters 3–5:

– Pray, madam, what is the subject?
– Oh! beyond everything. So adapted for the tragical machines! so proper to excite the passions! not in the least encumber'd with episodes! the vraysemblance and the miraculous are linkt together with such propriety. (192)

(Cf. p. 150: "Besides, it is form'd upon the vraysemblance: for I know you had a mummy and a crocodile to be brought home.")

5 "The Ancient Hypothesis of Fiction," p. 56.

6 *Marvels and Commonplaces*, p. 49.

7 René Bray, *La Formation de la doctrine classique en France*, p. 192.

8 Dryden's formula appears in "The Grounds of Criticism in Tragedy" (*Of Dramatic Poesy and Other Critical Essays*, I, 245).

9 *Formation de la doctrine classique*, p. 196.

10 The view is of course a Neoclassic commonplace; see, e.g., Robortello, quoted in Bernard Weinberg, "Robortello on the *Poetics*," p. 326. Chapelain's classic statement appeared in 1623: "ou la Creance manque, l'Attention manque aussi; mais ou l'Affection n'est point il n'y peut avoir d'Esmotion, et par conséquent de Purgation, ou d'amendement des moeurs des hommes, qui est le but de la Poésie" ("Lettere ... sur le Poeme d'Adonis," p. 28).

11 "Jugeant que la Verité des choses (supposé qu'elles dependissent du hazard)

nuisoit par leurs fortuits et incertains evenemens à leur intention si loüable, tous d'un accord on banny la verité de leur Parnasse" ("Lettere," p. 29).

12 "sans égard à la verité": Jean Chapelain, *Les Sentiments de l'Académie française sur la tragi-comédie du Cid*, p. 366. The idea of converting truth into verisimilitude was hardly new with Chapelain; compare Sperone Speroni (1596) on the poet's duty to remove the "material conditions" surrounding any real action, so that he can narrate it "as it should have or might have happened" (quoted in Bernard Weinberg, *A History of Literary Criticism in the Italian Renaissance*, II, 688).

13 "C'est une maxime très fausse qu'il faut que le sujet d'une tragédie soit vraisemblable" (Pierre Corneille, *Oeuvres*, I, 15, 14).

14 Thomas Twining, *Aristotle's Treatise on Poetry*, p. 130.

15 See Weinberg, "Robortello," and the similar ranking by Aquinas, above, p. 285 n39.

16 "Per opinione," "per sembianza di verità," "per composizion di senso diuiso": Lionardo Salviati, *Riposta all'Apologia di Torquato Tasso* (1585), quoted in Weinberg, *History*, II, 1018.

17 "Verisimile è una propositione probabile di maniera che per sapere la natura desso bisogna sapere quelle del probabile. probabili sono quelle cose le quali sono secondo l'oppenione di tutti o de piu saggi di maniera che la uerita in questo affare del uerisimile non adopera cosa nessuna.... stando adunque il uerisimile con loppenione degl huomini egli è al tutto di mestieri che secondo che esse si mutano si muti ancora il probabile" (quoted in Weinberg, *History*, I, 531).

18 "Non illud modo est verisimile, quod tale videtur sapientibus, aut omnibus, aut plurimis, aut maxime excellentibus, verum etiam quod vulgus tale judicat. Satis igitur est poeta" (*De Artis poeticae natura ac constitutione liber*, p. 15).

19 "La vraisemblance est tout ce qui est conforme à l'opinion du publique" (Rapin, *Réflexions sur la poétique d'Aristote*, p. 136); *Monsieur Bossu's Treatise of the Epick Poem*, pp. 133, 135 (I have replaced the "probability" of the translation with the "vraisemblance" used in the original). Eric Havelock suggests the ancient roots of the identification of poetry with *doxa* in "Poetry as Opinion," ch. 13 of his *Preface to Plato*.

20 See Wilbur S. Howell, *Logic and Rhetoric in England, 1500–1700*, pp. 364–65; and *Eighteenth-Century British Logic and Rhetoric*, p. 6.

21 *The Critical Works of Thomas Rymer*, p. 8; Rymer uses "probability" where Rapin has "vraisemblance."

As poetry came to be redefined as a probable, and not merely verisimilar, form of discourse – discourse whose audience is the wise rather than the vulgar – its logical status rose from the level of sophistic to that of dialectic (see Robortello's table, p. 80 above). Tasso argues against Mazzoni for such a reclassification in his *Discourses on the Heroic Poem* (1594), in a passage interesting because it represents a transitional stage in the shift we are examining:

I still would not concede that the sophist's art and the poet's are the same. I say, therefore, that poetry surely belongs under dialectic along with rhetoric, which, as Aristotle says, is the other child of the dialectical faculty, its function being to consider not the false but the probable. It therefore deals with the false, not in so far as it is false, but in so far as it is probable. The probable in so far as it is verisimilar belongs to the poet, because the poet uses proof less efficiently than the dialectician – indeed, imitation, example, and comparison are the weakest kinds of proof, as Boethius teaches in the *Topics*. But the sophist, according to Aristotle, again in his *Topics*, considers not the probable, but the seeming probable, that is, what is not truly probable, but seems probable to some. (29)

Tasso begins with a strong argument for reclassification – poetry takes as its object the probable – then weakens his case by admitting that, because poetry does not use the strict methods of logical proof, it must take as its object only those probabilities which are also verisimilar. Poetry is relapsing into sophistic, the disciplines of "what is not truly probable, but seems probable *to some*" (i.e., not to the many or to the wise). Tasso clearly needs to distinguish the logical status of *statements* in poetic discourse from that of the kinds of *arguments* poets, dialecticians, and sophists make. (On the *Discourses*, see Montgomery, *The Reader's Eye*, ch. 5.)

22 On Castelvetro's estimate of his audience and the relation of this estimate to his theory of probability, see Jones and Nicol, *Neo-Classical Dramatic Criticism*, pp. 27–33, and Robert Montgomery, *The Reader's Eye*, pp. 145–46.

23 Quoted in Weinberg, *History*, II, 944 (compare Vittori, quoted I, 466); insight into "the causes of things," of course, was the ideal of scientific knowledge.

24 Bray makes the point in *Doctrine classique*, p. 193.

25 See Weinberg, *History*, II, 861, 889, 683.

26

La Foy, en la signification que nous la prenons, c'est à dire une inclination de la fantaisie à croire qu'une chose soit plutost que de n'estre pas, s'acquiert par deux moyens: l'un imparfaict ou impuissant, par le simple rapport ou de l'Historien ou d'autre; et j'appelle celuy-là impuissant, pource que la sincerité des hommes est incognuë, et que le plus souvent on la revoque en doute, sur la moindre difficulté qui se presente. L'autre parfaict et puissant, par la vraysemblance de la chose rapportée, soit par l'Historien, soit par l'autre; qui est le moyen naturel efficace de s'acquerir de la foy, auquel le premier qui professe mesme la verité se reduict, s'il est vray que de deux Histoires contraires ou diversement racontées, on suit tousjours celle qui a le plus de probabilité; ce qui arrive pour ce que le premier estant Tyrannique, et sujet à estre rejetté, ce dernier-cy gaigne doucement, et empiete vigoureusement l'imaginative de celuy qui escoute, et par la convenance des choses contenues en son rapport se le rend bien veillant. Mais de ces deux comme l'un est propre de l'Historien, aussi faut-il sçavoir que l'autre est du Poëte. ("Lettere," p. 28)

27

And therefore those Episodes which are necessary, and make essential parts of the Poem, ought to be grounded upon human probability; now the Episodes of *Circe, Polyphemus*, the *Sirens, &c.* are necessary to the action of the Odyssey: But will any man say they are within the bounds of human probability? How then shall we solve the difficulty? *Homer* artificially has brought them within the degrees of it; he makes *Ulysses* relate them before a credulous and ignorant assembly; he lets us into the character of the *Phaecians*, by saying they are a very dull nation, in the sixth book.

Where never Science rear'd her laurel'd head.

It is thus the Poet gives probability to his fables, by reciting them to a people who believ'd them, and who thro' a laziness of life were fond of romantic stories: he adapts himself to his audience. (Pope, *Works*, IX, 336)

IV The literary work as a hierarchy of probable signs

1 (London, 1817), I, 279. Ian Hacking gives an excellent account of the notion from Hobbes to Berkeley of a mental discourse of ideas and its relation to verbal discourse in *Why Does Language Matter to Philosophy?*, pp. 15–53.

2 That both Reid and Beattie in listing and giving examples of the passions turn first to anger is probably the result of their reading of Seneca's *De Ira*; Seneca argues as well that of all the passions, anger produces the most marked external effects.

3 Among others, by V. A. Rudowski in his study of the distinction between natural and artificial signs in eighteenth-century aesthetics, "The Theory of Signs in the Eighteenth Century."

4 Aristotle, *Rhetoric*, III. 1. 7; Quintilian, *Institutes*, XI. 3. 61ff. Both authors consider – and, to a modern mind, would seem to confuse – verbal and physiognomic signs, the signs of language and of spectacle, what might appear on a page and what could only arise in an oral delivery. They do so, of course, because for them oratory is an oral form; that for centuries texts not only of rhetoric but more specifically of poetics included sections on *pronunciatio* (delivery) suggests that during those centuries poetry too continued to be conceived as an oral medium. (See Michael Murrin, *The Veil of Allegory*, chs. 1, 4.) Geoffrey of Vinsauf concludes his *Poetria Nova* with such a discussion, remarking: "In reciting aloud, let three tongues speak: let the first be that of the mouth, the second that of the speaker's countenance, and the third that of gesture" (90).

5 Descartes, *Oeuvres*, XI, 327ff. See also the excellent edition of Descartes' *Treatise of Man* by Thomas S. Hall, and Phillip R. Sloan, "Descartes, the Sceptics, and the Rejection of Vitalism in Seventeenth-Century Physiology."

6 See Jennifer Montagu, "Charles Le Brun's *Conférence sur l'expression*" (which also contains a new translation of the *Conférence* into English) and, for another instance of Cartesian physiognomy, Cureau de La Chambre, *Les Caractères des passions* (1648–59); see also "The legible body: Le Brun," ch. 2 of Norman Bryson, *Word and Image: French painting of the Ancien Régime*.

7 Richardson, *Works*, p. 40; Hogarth, *Analysis of Beauty*, pp. 126, 127. See also Alistair Smart, "Dramatic Gesture and Expression in the Age of Hogarth and Reynolds." According to Richardson, "That the face, the air, as well as our actions, indicate the mind is indisputable. It is seen by every body in the extreams of both sides. For example; let two men, the one a wise man, and the other a fool, be seen together dressed, or disguised as you please, one will not be mistaken for the other, but distinguished with the first glance of the eye; and if these characters are stamped upon the face, so as to be read by every one when in the utmost extreams, they are so proportionably when more or less removed from them, and legible accordingly, and in proportion to the skill of the reader" (51). What Richardson is describing here is the visual equivalent of the literary "well-marked character," and the high probability of such a character's signs.

8 See Brewster Rogerson, "The Art of Painting the Passions," and, more recently, Alan T. McKenzie, "'The Countenance You Show Me': Reading the Passions in the Eighteenth Century." This art, the kinds of inferences it licenses, and the psychological and physiological theory from which it

emerges, were so prevalent in England that it is hard to see how Patrick Crutwell can claim the opposite, that in Pope's age "'The inward service of the mind and soul' has become divorced from the body" ("Physiology and Psychology in Shakespeare's Age," p. 89).

9 See, e.g., Montagu's commentary, and E. H. Gombrich, "The Mask and the Face: the Perception of Physiognomic Likeness in Art," pp. 3, 5.

10 See Chester Chapin, *Personification in Eighteenth-Century English Poetry*, pt I.

11 "Dialogues upon ... Ancient Medals," in Addison, *Miscellaneous Works*, II, 298; Ogilvie, *Poems on Several Subjects*, I, cv.

12 In those papers written about 1712 and later published as *Second Characters* (ed. Benjamin Rand, p. 60).

13 "On Poetical Personifications," pp. 217, 242–43, 254. As Bacon had remarked of physiognomics, Aikin finds that whereas the ancients used as emblems only "quiescent signatures: such as elements of costume," modern poets and painters have "generally connected the symbol with the person by some kind of action" (254); cf. Beattie, *Essays*, where allegorical figures are discussed under the heading of personifications: "those that exhibit persons engaged in action, and adorned with visible *insignia*, give a brisker impulse to the faculties, than such as convey intellectual ideas only, or images taken from still life" (257).

14 See Beattie, *Essays*, p. 256: "Motion, too bears a close affinity to action, and affects our imagination in nearly the same manner; and we see a great part of nature in motion; and by their sensible effects are led to contemplate energies innumerable. These conduct the rational mind to the Great First Cause; and these, in times of ignorance, disposed the vulgar to believe in a variety of subordinate agents employed in producing those appearances that could not otherwise be accounted for. Hence ... Personification is natural to the human mind."

15 *Aristotle's Treatise on Poetry*, p. 16. Twining's essay was to make a deep impression on, among others, John Stuart Mill; see, for instance, Mill's distinction between "depiction" and "indication" (copied from Twining) in his essay, "What is Poetry?" (*Mill's Essays on Literature and Society*, p. 105).

16 Kames, like other rhetoricians, draws the analogy with acting: "Dramatic writers ought to be well acquainted with this natural manner of expressing passion. The chief talent of a fine writer, is a ready command of the expressions that nature dictates to every man when any vivid emotion struggles for utterance; and the chief talent of a fine reader, is a ready command of the tones suited to these expressions."

17 *Lectures*, pp. 171, 251. Lawson likens orators to actors in that both must be in such control that they do not actually feel the passions whose signs they manifest (256–57), and in that both must "perceive how the Audience is affected by visible Marks in their Countenance" (185).

18 Blackwall's rhetoric, printed as part II of his *Introduction to the Classics* (1719), is particularly interesting for its explicitly physiological account (ultimately Cartesian) of the origin of rhetorical and physiognomic signs; see, e.g., p. 183: "The Soul hath such a mighty Command over that curious Organ the human Body, that it can make all the Impressions upon it, (while it is in Health and Harmony) whereby all the different *Affections* and *Passions* are express'd. It can by its sovereign Pleasure so move and alter the Blood and Spirits, so contract or relax the Nerves, that in Sorrow, a

Deadness and Heaviness shall make the Countenance lowre: In Anger, a brutal Fierceness shall enflame the Eyes, and ruffle the Looks into Deformity... The Soul likewise tunes the *Organs* of Speech, and sets 'em to that *Key* which will most effectually express her present Sentiments. So that in Joy the Voice shall be tender, flowing, and rapturous; in Anger shrill, eager, and full of Breaks; in Fear, low, confused, and stammering."

19 In his *Essay on Genius* (1774), Gerard discusses "those effects, imitable in the particular art, by which each passion naturally shows itself" (357) and gives such specific examples of verbal signs of the passions as that "Every passion often occasions an abruptness of thought; different ideas being connected with the passion, in different respects, but with almost equal closeness, the passion introduces them all, or several of them at least, in alternate succession" (152).

20 John Ward, *A System of Oratory* (1759), II, 36–39, 64ff. On p. 39: "And as he finds them in life, from thence must he copy them; as a painter does the features of the countenance, and the several parts of the body; *Figures* being to [the orator] what lines and colors are to the other."

21 Thomas Gibbons, *Rhetoric, or, a View of its Principal Tropes and Figures, in their Origin and Powers* (1767), pp. 3, 122–25.

22 John Ogilvie, *Philosophical and Critical Observations on the Nature, Characters, and Various Species of Composition* (1774); for extended discussion of this work, see below, ch. VIII.

23 In his "On the Arts Commonly Called Imitative" (1772), Jones denies to expression through signs the title of "imitation," but his understanding of the procedure is the same as that outlined here. For him, "each artist will gain his end, not by imitating the works of nature, but by assuming her power and causing the same effect upon the imagination which her charms produce to the senses," i.e., reproduce not the objects but their signs; poetry is for Jones as for Lowth "the language of violent passions," and employs a language cognate with that of painting (pp. 880, 877, 879).

24 *Philosophy of Rhetoric*, pp. 4, 81–94, 340.

25 *Lectures on Rhetoric and Belles Lettres* (1783), II, 188–202 (on verbal signs of passion); II, 221–22 (on action and gesture).

26 See Stone's attempt to distinguish Augustan from Romantic poetics, *The Art of Poetry 1750–1820*, ch. 7.

27 *The Art of Poetry on a New Plan* (1762), pp. 39–40; Beattie, *Dissertations, Moral and Critical* (1783), p. 167 (cf. *Essays*, pp. 233–70); Lowth, *Lectures*, I, 377; Campbell, *Philosophy of Rhetoric*, p. 340. For Lowth, "enthusiasm" is "a style and expression directly prompted by nature itself, and *exhibiting* the true and express image of a mind violently agitated" (I, 79, my italics). Even the use of the future tense of a Hebrew verb may be a sign: "Now, if, as I have stated, this unusual form be the effect either of some sudden emotion in the speaker, or some new and extraordinary state of mind ... it will obviously follow, that it must more frequently occur in poetry than in prose, since it is particularly adapted to the nature, versatility, and variety of the former, and to be the expression of any violent passion" (I, 343). For Lowth, "the strongest indication of passion, and a perturbid mind" is "redundancy of expression" (I, 317).

28 In earlier theorists, according to Stone, the mind of reader or spectator is "naturally led" to the passion signified; later writers explain the power of signs to raise the passion itself through sympathy (*The Art of Poetry*, ch. 7). Thus according to John Ward, "to interrogate, exclaime, or admire, under

the influence of a passion, impresses the hearers ... There is a natural sympathy in mens minds, which disposes them to receive impressions from those, with whom they converse" (*A System of Oratory*, II, 38). Earl Wasserman discusses sympathy as the appropriate mode of "interpreting" the signs of acting in "The Sympathetic Imagination in Eighteenth-Century Theories of Acting."

In fact this theory was not new to the later eighteenth century: Descartes lays out the doctrine of sympathy in the early seventeenth century, and Malebranche (whose technical language Ward is calling on) treats the sympathetic imagination in detail in *De la Recherche de la vérité*, books II and V (on the imagination and the passions, respectively). According to the Cartesian Anthony Blackwall, rhetoric operates just as "Fire kindles Fire; Life and Heat in the Speaker, enliven and inspirit the reader" (*Introduction to the Classics*, p. 186).

29 Leibniz gives a particularly good analysis of this kind of expression in his account of *perception*, which he defines as the *expression* of some composite or manifold through something simpler. Thus for him "one thing *expresses* another (in my terminology) when there exists a constant and fixed relationship between what can be said of one and of the other"; "That is said to express a thing in which there are relations which correspond to the relations of the thing expressed." To say that x expresses y, then, is to say that x *maps* y: in this way, a blueprint is the expression of its object; a speech of thoughts; numerals of numbers; a map of a geographical area; an effect of a cause; actions of the soul. Leibniz calls such expressions "characters" rather than "signs," but he means by them what the scholastics meant by "natural signs." See Robert McRae, *Leibniz: Perception, Apperception, and Thought*, pp. 20–21. Leibniz' notion of expression is very close to that of formal causation discussed in sections 3 and 4 below.

30 Quoted in George Taylor, "'The Just Delineation of the Passions': Theories of Acting in the Age of Garrick," pp. 56–57. On stage action, see also G. W. Stone and G. M. Kahrl, *David Garrick: A Critical Biography*, ch. 2 ("Garrick and the Acting Tradition"); on rhetorical action, Michel Le Faucheur, *An Essay upon the Action of an Orator* (1702); John Walker, *Elements of Elocution* (1781); Thomas Sheridan, *Lectures in the Art of Reading* (1775).

31 See Alfred Harbage, "Elizabethan Acting," and B. L. Joseph, *Elizabethan Acting*, ch. 3.

32 See Taylor, "Theories of Acting," p. 64.

33 Stone and Kahrl, *David Garrick*, p. 31. In 1742, the *Gentleman's Magazine* praised Garrick in a manner that suggests how common was opposite behavior and so lends further evidence for Stone's description: "When three or four are on stage with him, he is attentive to whatever is spoke, and never drops his character when he has finished a speech, by either looking contemptibly on an inferior performer, unnecessarily spitting, or suffering his eyes to wander through the whole circle of spectators. His action corresponds with his voice, and both with the character he plays" (quoted in *Garrick*, p. 47).

34 "As in the landscape, so in the representation on the stage, things in their own place very remote, are obliged to be represented in small compass; the field is large that affords the view for the one, and the human mind, which is represented in the other is yet more extensive. Where so many things, so distinct in themselves, are to be thrown together, there requires great art to

shew that they are not joined to each other: in the scene, as well as in the picture, there is required what is called *keeping*; but as the painter's principle skill [*sic*] is to mark the distances, the player's is to shew the removes thro' which the transitions are made from one to the other: and great care is to be taken not to confound one with another, because they happen to succeed" (John Hill, *The Actor: a Treatise on the Art of Playing*, quoted in Taylor, "Theories of Acting," p. 62).

35 See Stone, in Stone and Kahrl, *David Garrick*, p. 32; D. Nichol Smith, *Shakespeare in the Eighteenth Century*; John Butt, *Pope's Taste in Shakespeare*. Stone cites among such anthologies Edward Bysshe's *Art of English Poetry* and William Dodd's *The Beauties of Shakespeare Regularly Selected from Each Play* (1752). E. N. Hooker has made the same point in his edition of Dennis' *Critical Works*: "the method of criticising by discovering 'beauties,' popular in English criticism from about 1675, involved the quoting of purple passages; and since accounts of action are commonly too extensive for brief quotation, the purple passages or 'beauties' exhibited were often descriptions. Consequently such anthologies of 'beauties' as Bysshe's *Art of English Poetry* and Gildon's *Complete Art of Poetry* were full of 'Allusions, Similies, Descriptions and Characters.' This admiration for, and emphasis upon, elements in poetry other than action, or fable, undoubtedly became a force tending to undermine strict Aristotelian regard for action as the essence of great poetry" (I, 465), on which transition, see below, section 4.

36 In *Poems on Several Subjects*, p. xlii.

37 P. 252. Some of the arguments in this section can (I think) be found woven into the dense and often incoherent texture of Alan Kennedy, *Meaning and Signs in Fiction*, a work which attempts to trace from the Renaissance to the present the changing relation that novelists have supposed to obtain between mind and body by examining changing uses of one "sign" of that relation, clothing.

38 John Donaldson, *The Elements of Beauty* (1780), p. 50.

39 John Aikin, *Letters from a Father to his Son*, p. 118; Hurd, *Works*, II, 57. On the use of "marks" in seventeenth- and eighteenth-century taxonomic biology generally, see Phillip R. Sloan, "John Locke, John Ray, and the Problem of Natural System."

40 *The Works of Anna Laetitia Barbauld*, II, 190; Dennis, *Critical Works*, I, 80. Ancient rhetoricians distinguished among the methods of delineating character *effictio* and *notatio*, to which the Middle Ages added the *blason*. Effictio (Greek χαρακτηρισμός), according to the *Rhetorica ad Herennium*, "consists in representing and depicting in words clearly enough for recognition the bodily form of some person," while notatio (Greek ηθοποιία), as its name implies, "consists in describing a person's character by the definite signs [*signis*] which, like distinctive marks [*notae*], are attributes of that character" (IV. xlix. 62–l.63). *Ad Herennium* spends several pages on *notatio*, only a few sentences on *effictio*, which, to be successful, must be *brief*; in his versification of this work, the *Poetria nova* (c. 1200), Geoffrey of Vinsauf demonstrates the same preference, pausing for only one sentence to explain *effictio* as that "whereby I depict or represent a corporeal appearance, *in so far as is requisite*" (62, my italics). *Notatio* has a larger function in constructing the meaning of a work; *effictio* is *mere* description, without greater literary interest than is possessed by any other form of *descriptio* – and Geoffrey goes so far as to class all

descriptio as nothing more than a species of *amplificatio* (36). (*Amplificatio* for Geoffrey is a condition of being richly wrought whose functions are more social than semantic: he likens its effect to "the splendour of dishes arriving in rich profusion and the leisured delay at the table," "festive signs" which serve a ceremonial function, 26.)

41 Dryden, *Essays*, I, 248; his source reads, in the translation of 1695: "Under the name of *Manners* we comprehend all the natural or acquired inclinations, which carry us on to good, bad, or indifferent actions" (159).

42 Dryden, *Essays*, I, 249; for his source, see *Monsieur Bossu's Treatise*, p. 180.

43 For the difficulties in accounting for hypocrisy encountered by those Renaissance theorists who believed that all internal states must express themselves externally (e.g., by appeals to the recalcitrance of matter to sigillation), see J. B. Bamborough, *The Little World of Man*, p. 140.

44 Dennis has difficulty with hypocrites because he believes that all characters "ought to have Manners: that is, their Discourse and their Actions ought to discover their Inclinations and their Affections, and what Resolutions they are certain to take" (I, 71); for this reason Stoics cannot make good dramatic characters (II, 50). Similarly, evil characters may speak impiously only if the audience knows from other signs that the character is evil (I, 35); because such revelation tends in the case of hypocrisy to be comic, Dennis finds that hypocrites belong in comedy rather than tragedy (II, 53).

On surprise, see I, 124 ("For since the Incidents ought naturally to produce one another, and the preceeding ought to be the necessary, or at least the probable Cause of the subsequent, I cannot imagine how any thing can be very surprizing to us, which has a necessary or probable Tendency to something which we are sure, must very suddenly happen"), and I, 201.

45 See also Richardson's Postscript, which argues against criticisms of the improbability of Clarissa's exemplary virtue that her upbringing was calculated to produce such a paragon (i.e., that she is indeed well-marked), and that to make Lovelace convert would be false to his character, hence improbable and ill-marked (IV, 564, 552–53; for the point that an inconsistent character is also ill-marked, see Dennis, II, 50). Richardson speaks here also of "probable circumstances" in letter-writing, and describes his method as one of providing readers with "hints ... by way of inference" (553, 560); he calls a good character's exemplary reward the making of her "signally happy" (558).

46 See Wright, *The Passions*, pp. 37–38; Rather, *Mind and Body*, p. 238; Evans, *Physiognomics*, p. 17; Bamborough, *Little World*, pp. 61–67.

47 From the pseudonymous Arcandam's *Most Excellent Profitable and pleasant book* (1552), J. B. Bamborough cites the following: "A weak voice betokeneth narrow arteries and want of spirit" (138); "when the man goeth lightly having al his body upright, it is a signe that hee will take in hand some enterprise... But if a man goe swiftly with his eyes looking downward and goe altogether crooked, it is a signe of a niggard, fearful and subtile" (137).

48 *The Works of that famous Chirurgeon Ambrose Parey*, p. 40.

49 Quoted in Bamborough, *Little World*, p. 101.

50 Prologue, line 9; see Bamborough, *Little World*, pp. 66, 104.

51 *Works*, II, 160; the terms *conformation* and *feature of the mind* suggest those likeness principles – cause must be like effect, sign resemble thing signified – that were widely part of the Aristotelian and Cartesian inheritances.

52 The popularity of this term in the Restoration is probably due to Bacon, who makes the point frequently that all knowledge is to be judged by its effectiveness in action; thus, for example, his "forms" are at once "contemplative" and "operative," because "that which in contemplation is the cause, in operation is the rule" (*Works*, IV, 47; cf. IV, 110, 146; III, 553–54). Bacon defines *operation* as the "production of Effects" (IV, 343), and uses interchangeably the terms "effecting or operation" (III, 230). Wordsworth was to revive the term in his first Preface to *Lyrical Ballads*, where he says of poetry that "its object is truth, not individual and local, but general, and operative" (*Prose Works*, I, 139).

53 *Doctrine classique*, pp. 219–20.

54 "Outre toutes ces règles prises de la Poétique d'Aristote, il y en a encore une dont Horace fait mention, à laquelle toutes les autres règles doivent s'assujettir comme à la plus essentielle, qui est la bienséance. Sans elle les autres règles de la poésie sont fausses, parce qu'elle est le fondement le plus solide de cette vraisemblance qui est si essentielle à cet art. Car ce n'est que par la bienséance que la vraisemblance a son effet: tout devient vraisemblable dès que la bienséance garde son caractère dans toutes les circonstances" (*Réflexions*, p. 156).

55 Rymer, *Works*, p. 42; compare d'Aubignac, *Whole Art*, I, 20, 25; II, 66; III, 60, and for "verisimilitude and decorum," Milton's Preface to *Samson Agonistes*, p. 209.

56 See Weinberg, *History*, I, 111–55, and Herrick, *The Fusion of Horatian and Aristotelian Literary Criticism 1531–1555*.

57 "Aristoteles it censuit: Quam poema conparatū fit ad eam ciuium institutionem, quae nos ducit ad beatitudinē: beatitude verò nihil aliud quàm perfecta sit actio: neutiquam ad mores cōsequencos deducet poema, sed ad facta ipsa" (*Poetices libri septem*, p. 348).

58 "Quod neque rerum probabilitatem viderit, neque personarum decorum obseruauerit" (G. A. Viperano, *De Poetica* [1579], quoted in Weinberg, *History*, II, 763); Pye, *A Commentary illustrating the Poetic of Aristotle*, p. 39.

59 Leopold Damrosch, Jr, *Samuel Johnson and the Tragic Sense*, p. 21.

60 Benjamin Franklin, *A Dissertation Upon Liberty and Necessity, Pleasure and Pain* (1725), p. 5.

61 Pye, who rejects Le Bossu's interpretation, writes in his *Commentary*: "The meaning of the word GOOD, as the first essential of tragic manners, has been a cause of much difference of opinion among the translators and commentators of the *Poetic*. If we consider χρησά here in its usual and obvious sense of morally good, the passage is neither reconcilable with Aristotle's definition of the proper tragic character in chapter XIII, nor with the practice of all the serious epic and dramatic writers, ancient and modern. To still greater impropriety shall we be driven, if we take up the opinion, originally I believe started by Bossu, and since followed by Dacier, Harris, and Metastasio; that Aristotle by χρησά meant manners well marked. So strongly expressed, as to shew clearly what the character is, whether good or bad. For such a quality, so far from being distinguished from the other three requisites, is essential to them all. Since, whether a character is to be drawn good, or proper, or like, or uniform, it certainly ought to be well drawn, and strongly marked" (310).

62 *Monsieur Bossu's Treatise*, p. 178; for Dennis' version of Le Bossu's argument, see *Critical Works*, I, 72.

63 Dennis accepts Le Bossu's view: "'Tis impossible for a Poet to form any Fable, unless the Moral be first in his Head" (II, 110); Addison and Blackmore deny such psychological priority, but do not comment on the logical point (*Spectator* 369; Blackmore, *Essays*, p. 71). See also p. 122 below. At no other level in the hierarchy does this issue arise: the Augustans remained within the model inherited in rhetoric and poetics, where *inventio* and *dispositio* differ both chronologically and logically. Writer after writer of works of poetics uses this fact to organize his presentation; here is Tasso in the *Discourses on the Heroic Poem*:

Three things, illustrious lord, whoever proposes to write a heroic poem must take into account: to choose matter fit to receive the most excellent form which the poet's art seeks to introduce into it; to give it such form; and finally to clothe it with those rarest ornaments appropriate to its nature... Beginning with the judgment the poet must show in choosing his material, I shall proceed to the art and invention required of him first in arranging and shaping it and then in clothing and adorning it. (22)

In this way Vida can advise in his *De Arte poetica* that the poet first draw up an outline (*simulacrum*) of the whole, thereby to fix the action with which the poem will be concerned ("to connect in order all the constituent parts"); only later need the poet address "the figures and embellishments of expression," which "may be added [*addita*] to material one wishes to ornament" (I. 75–79; III. 4–5). The initial outline is of course in prose: Vida writes, "I shall not give technical instructions here on the various meters and measures into which one arranges the verses he has drawn up in rough; this is the master's task and requires few pains" (I. 415–17).

Augustan critics typically consider works part by part – moral, fable, manners and character, sentiments, diction, versification – because it is thus by parts that authors compose, and it is out of such units that the meaningful structure of works is composed; the first condition is in fact the guarantee of the second. These are the poetic "parts" Pope catalogues in the second part of the *Essay on Criticism*, arguing that a just critic must "Survey the *Whole*" work (line 235) because literary excellence consists first in the merit of each part, but more in an appropriate integration of all parts into a whole:

> In Wit, as Nature, what affects our Hearts
> Is not th' Exactness of peculiar Parts;
> 'Tis not a *Lip*, or *Eye*, we beauty call,
> But the joint Force and full *Result* of all. (243–46)

In disputes over poetic merit, similarly, Augustan critics more often compare individual (cognate) parts of paired works, or the decorum with which these parts appear in their respective wholes, than they compare whole works with one another. (Thus in his famous comparison of Dryden and Pope in the *Life of Pope*, Johnson advances no estimate of the relative merits of whole poems by either author, but compares their address in each aspect of composition, i.e., in each of the artist's subordinate ends.) Other ways of conducting critical disputes emerge as does a new model of literary structure, a new understanding of what are the parts of which works are composed. In the Romantic period, *inventio* and *dispositio* are conflated (leading to the modern critical doctrine of the "heresy of paraphrase"), and the new model of literary unity implied in such a conflation necessitates new procedures for making comparative estimates of poetic merit.

64 Le Bossu sometimes calls this process *amplification* (see, e.g., below, p. 113). He and the other authors we are discussing would have learned this process early in their rhetorical education; students were often given "simple propositions" on which to practice *amplificatio*, which usually meant lengthening by selecting supporting material from a search of the relevant *loci*. The result was a dilated style that philosophers (particularly Cartesians) were to criticize as deviation from the ideal of plainness; see Peter France, *Rhetoric and Truth in France*, pp. 3–23.

65 Zachary Mayne, *Two Dissertations*, pp. 30–31; compare this notion of formal causation with Leibniz' concept of expression (above, n29).

66 R. E. Nadeau, "The *Progymnasmata* of Aphthonius," p. 281. The distinction was made popular by Boethius' *De Topicis differentiis*, and was thought to constitute the difference between dialectic (which considers "theses") and rhetoric ("hypotheses") (see translation of *De Topicis* by E. Stump, p. 35). In the same way Vives distinguishes *quaestiones* from *quaestiones definitae*: the latter "include determining circumstances" (*De Tradendis*, p. 185).

67 Dennis, *Critical Works*, I, 63–64. Cf. Johnson's comment in the *Life of Butler*: "Nor even though another Butler should arise, would another *Hudibras* obtain the same regard. Burlesque consists in a disproportion between the style and the sentiments, or between the adventitious sentiments and the fundamental subject. It therefore, like all bodies compounded of heterogeneous parts, contains in it a principle of corruption" (*Lives*, I, 218).

In the *Dictionary*, Johnson gives as one definition of *corrupt*, "The principle whereby bodies tend to the separation of their parts." Corrupt (disunified) literary works will die out, according to the Galenic maxim, for "whatever dies was not mixed equally" (John Jones, *Galens Bookes of Elements* (1574), p. 3v). Johnson, of course, puts the same argument into Rasselas' mouth in chapter 43 of *Rasselas*: that the soul being immaterial has no parts, and so must be indiscerptible and eternal. The argument is an ancient one; in the first *Critique* (where it was finally laid to rest), Kant calls it "the Achilles of Rationalist arguments" for the immortality of the soul, and under that title Ben Lazare Mijuskovic has written an excellent history of it (1974).

As the above quotation from the *Life of Butler* suggests, the opposite of a probable circumstance is an "accidental," or, more commonly "adventitious" one. The term *adventitious* had the authority of Bacon, who had called circumstances "Adventitious Conditions or Adjuncts of Essences" (see above, p. 55). Owen Ruffhead thus speaks in the *Life of Pope* of the "adventitious circumstances" that create reputation (3); in the *Philosophical Observations*, Ogilvie speaks of those "adventitious circumstances" which prevent poetical ideas from being "adapted with propriety to their objects" (II, 241); and in his *Dissertation upon Genius* (1755), William Sharpe finds the cause and nature of madness to reside in excessive attention to "adventitious and contingent circumstances" (26).

68 See, e.g., William and Martha Kneale, *The Development of Logic*, pp. 195, 229; Gordon Leff, *William of Ockham*, pp. 128–31, 159–60.

69 *Two Dissertations*, pp. 31–32. It is only through its form, according to Mayne, that an object can become intelligible to us: "any corporeal Object

or sensible Appearance is so far only intelligible, as it signifies or imports something," which something must itself be "intellectual" (35) and be, in fact, the end or purpose of the object: "under *Form*, I would comprehend every thing perceivable by our Senses that serves to signify and denote to us any Virtue, Power, or Capacity of such a Being, any Property or Quality belonging to it, or the End and Use it seems designed for" (32). Thus, for instance, "the *Form* of the Hand ... signifies and denotes that the Hand is an Instrument, or a Thing proper and commodious for managing, or grasping and wielding Bodies" (33). Form is thus that which gives meaning to the object in which it is embodied ("expressed"), where meaning is understood as purpose or function within a larger whole or intellectual system.

70 *The Complete Art of Poetry* (1743), I, 274.

71 Malacreta, from his *Considerationi sopra il Pastor Fido* (1600), quoted in Weinberg, *History*, II, 1096.

72 Tucker, *The Light of Nature Pursued*, I, 289. For a similar account drawn from the theory of painting that probability is necessary to give unity, and hence also intelligibility, to a work, see Michael Fried, *Absorption and Theatricality*, p. 83.

73 Hurd, *Works*, I, 147; compare Dennis, *Critical Works*, I, 35.

74 *Monsieur Bossu's Treatise*, p. 179; compare similar discussions in Dennis, *Critical Works*, I, 75, and Du Bos' account of tragic villains in the *Critical Reflections on Poetry, Painting, and Music* (1719), I, 96ff. In both Dryden and Le Bossu, this argument comes directly before a list of the four requirements of the manners. The closeness with which Dryden follows Le Bossu in the "Grounds" – which has not been fully recognized – as well as the intelligence of Dryden's interpretations of Le Bossu, provide evidence for Robert Hume's position (in contrast to George Watson's) that the "Grounds," not the "Heads of an Answer to Rymer," of which it may be an expansion, comes closer to representing the "true" Dryden. (See Robert Hume, *Dryden's Criticism*, pp. 118–19.)

75 Rymer, *Critical Works*, pp. 83, 135–36, 156, 163.

76 "Nam profectò ne ipsa natura quidem verus artifex videretur: quippe suo impedita fine nonnunquam aberrat: veluti cum aut monstra componit: aut defecta edit corpora" (*Poetices libri septem*, p. 2).

77 *Epistle to a Lady*, line 146; Thomas Percival, *Moral and Literary Dissertations*, p. 195.

78 "Studiosarum actionum quasi forma quaedã est ea, quam rectã rationem vocant Philosophi. Prauarũ verò an forma vlla est? nulla" (*Poetices libri septem*, p. 347).

79 *Life of Milton* (*Lives*, I, 173); *Essay on Man*, IV, 219. It is only in Nabokov's inverted world of Antiterra that, as we learn at the beginning of *Ada*, "All happy families are more or less dissimilar; all unhappy ones are more or less alike."

80 Swift, Preface to *A Tale of a Tub*, pp. 49–50; *Roxana*, p. 8.

81 Ehrenpreis, *Literary Meaning and Augustan Values*, pp. 45–47. Cf. Graeme Tytler's comments on eighteenth-century uses of the "grotesque portrait" to present "evil or eccentric characters" in *Physiognomy in the European Novel*, p. 131.

82 *Rambler* 121 (*Works*, VI, 278); Rymer, *Critical Works*, p. 20.

83 *The Spectator*, IV, 464, 465. Authorship of *Spectator* 548 has been disputed, and some have taken it to have come from the pen of Dennis himself;

Donald Bond argues for Addison's authorship, as a response to Dennis' letter "To the Spectator" (IV, 461).

84 Because, as Dennis summarizes Le Bossu, "It is not sufficient ... that the Manners be equal; there must besides be an Unity of Character, and the Hero must every-where appear to be animated with the same Spirit which inspir'd him at first" (I, 76), it appeared that character must not change; Hurd writes, "The mistake arose from imagining, that a character could no other way *consist* with itself, but by being *uniform*" (II, 123). In a more considered treatment, Dennis is willing to allow three causes of "inconstancy" in manners, i.e., alteration in character: if the character is a child; if he is passing from immaturity to maturity; or if he is influenced by "the Violence of an extraordinary Passion" (I, 97). In practice, however, Dennis reads character change as culpable inconsistency (see his treatment of *Cato*, II, 50f.).

85 See, e.g., Hurd, *Works*, II, 38; for the notion's importance in dramatic criticism, see Taylor, "Theories of Acting," pp. 60–62.

86 Isaac D'Israeli, *A Dissertation on Anecdotes* (1793), p. 16; see also below, pp. 246–48.

87 In Dennis, *Critical Works*, II, 384.

88 1782 ed., I, 43, 48, 131, 392; II, 37, 172; see also below, p. 248.

89 *Dissertation on Anecdotes*, p. 30.

90 Aikin, *Letters to a Young Lady on a Course of English Poetry* (1804), p. 294.

91 William Youngren presents however a revisionary treatment of this issue in "Dr. Johnson, Joseph Warton, and the 'Theory of Particularity.'"

92 Epistle I, lines 17–18, 32, 231, 237–38.

93 I, lines 278, 298, 284, 368, 330, 389, 312; for variants on "systematic pride," see also III, line 146; V, line 191.

94 The pioneer in showing Augustan critical methods to be self-consciously probabilistic was Hoyt Trowbridge, in "The Place of Rules in Dryden's Criticism"; see also more recently David Morris, "Civilized Reading: The Act of Judgment in *An Essay on Criticism*." The word *criticism* itself meant to the seventeenth century not literary criticism but the probabilistic arts of prudence: this for instance is the sense Gracián invokes in *El Criticon* (1653), translated in 1681 as *The Critick*, a work which nowhere makes reference to literary matters. According to René Wellek, *criticism* began to assume its predominantly literary meaning in England only in the 1670s, and it was Pope's *Essay on Criticism* which "established the term for good" ("A Historical Perspective," p. 298). Pope's understanding of the activity of the critic is however far broader than any current today, particularly in its ethical and social dimensions; it is well known that the poem, which attempts in its last third to teach "what Morals Criticks ought to show," chooses its terms for critical acumen from the language of courtly social behavior: good manners, good breeding, generosity, ease, graciousness, modesty – the same language in which Gracián understands criticism.

95 *Phaedrus* 271a–c and *Statesman* 281d–e, summarized by Lee Gibbs in his edition of William Ames' *Technometry* (pp. 18–19). The modern ("aesthetic") theory of art, which emerged sometime between the seventeenth-century coinage of terms such as *belles lettres* and *fine arts* (in which *arts* had at first its older sense) and Baumgarten's coinage of *aesthetics* in 1735, would appear to have been a product of the dispute between the ancients and the moderns; the consolidation of the new

category was in fact simultaneous with, and correlate to, the emergence of *science* in something like its modern, restricted sense. During that dispute were distinguished and consolidated two groups of human activities, those in which progress is possible and those which are non-progressive; these two became the arts and sciences in a modern sense at least by the time of William Hazlitt's fragment, "Why the Arts are Not Progressive" (1814) (see P. O. Kristeller, "The Modern System of the Arts," pp. 194–95).

Pope, Swift, and other "ancients" can thus fruitfully be seen as proponents of the view that the new division of the arts from the sciences is misguided: for Pope in *An Essay on Criticism*, the arts are as capable of progress as the sciences, because both share the same aim of imitating nature, and both share the logical structure analyzed in terms of means and ends. Understanding at least one phase of the Ancients–Moderns dispute this way, we may be justified in siding with the ancients: their loss of the debate was the creation of the new category of the aesthetic, the final splitting of the Renaissance ideal of a union of wisdom and eloquence, and the subsequent shift of the arts from the center to the margins of our culture. R. S. Crane has beautifully called up the intellectual landscape of the early eighteenth century, when the arts were continuous with the rest of intellectual endeavor, in *The Idea of the Humanities*, pp. 122–23; Alasdair MacIntyre provides a cogent analysis of the aftermath of the moderns' victory in *After Virtue*. Elaborating his maxim that "every philosophy presupposes a sociology," MacIntyre explains how there emerged in the Augustan period with the category of the aesthetic a new social type (the aesthete), as well as new forms of social behavior (such as private collecting and the formation of public museums); he calls this a new sociology of "aesthetic consumption": "where the notion of engagement was once socially central, the notion of aesthetic consumption now is, at least for the majority" (*After Virtue*, pp. 211–12).

Today complaints about the limitations of the category of the aesthetic and its attendant separation of eloquence from wisdom come less often from those from whom we might most expect them, literary scholars, for these are often the very beneficiaries of the new conceptual scheme; rather, they come from scholars generally considered the most marginally "literary," i.e. theorists of criticism and especially of rhetoric (see, e.g., James Murphy, *The Rhetorical Tradition*, pt. I).

96 Thus according to the *Novum Organon* the mechanisms of clocks "imitate the celestial orbs and their alternating and orderly motion," while the "heat of fire" used to hatch eggs "exactly imitates animal heat"; the alchemist in making gold seeks to imitate the natural processes whereby metals grow in the earth (see J. P. Zetterberg, "Echoes of Nature in Salomon's House"). Baconian "method" was to be a reasoned imitation of nature justified by the "works" in which it issued.

97 See Gilbert, *Renaissance Concepts of Method*, pp. 11–12; Gilbert points out that because *methodos* ("the way") had come to be associated with *tekne*, Aristotle never uses the phrase "scientific method," which would have been a contradiction (the phrase is introduced by Galen) (pp. 44–45).

98 Dennis, *Critical Works*, II, 197; cf. I, 229 ("Which may shew the Benefit of Art, that is, of Rules in Poetry"); I, 246 ("The Second Thing is Art, by which I mean, those Rules, and that Method, which capacitate us to manage every thing with the utmost dexterity").

99 *Essays on Philosophical Subjects*, p. 60; for the Renaissance origins of the

popularity of the word "system," see Gilbert, *Method*, p. 202, and W. J. Ong, "System, Space, and Intellect in Renaissance Symbolism."

100 See Douglas White, *Pope and the Context of Controversy*, pp. 11–13.

101 See lines 4 and 14. In the first Pope distinguishes knowledge gained through "gen'ral maxims" from being "right by chance," while in the second he argues that observation not guided by prudent theorizing is mere "Guess" (bad theorizing that leads to wrong theory-laden observation Pope here calls "Notions"; that better theorizing enjoined by the last half of the poem is, as we have argued before, that whereby "Nature well known, no prodigies remain, / Comets are regular, and Wharton plain," lines 208–09). Cf. Ben Jonson, from the Preface to *The English Grammar* (1640): "Experience breedeth Art: Lacke of Experience, Chance" (*Works*, VIII, 465).

102 Compare Vives, quoted above, p. 18; and Dennis, *Critical Works*, I, 201 (particularly in his collocation of "knowing or practicing").

103 The passage continues: "If it is an Art, it follows that it must propose an End to it self, and afterwards lay down proper Means for the attaining that End: For this is undeniable, that there are proper Means for the attaining of every End, and those proper Means in Poetry we call the Rules."

104 In Pope's criticism as in contemporary theology, certain truths are available to natural reason (demonstration), while others can be known only through testimony (revelation). As Robinson Crusoe learns in his efforts to convert Friday, reason alone can deduce the existence of a God, but only revelation can establish Christianity's more complex truths, especially those most needful for salvation; so too in art, reason alone can deduce from the very meanings of such terms as *art* and *end* that each literary kind has an end and so also rules, but the concrete content of these rules can be known only through the testimony of taste. Dryden draws this analogy between the structure of criticism and that of theology explicitly in *Of Dramatic Poesy* (*Essays*, I, 122).

105 "Genius" of course suggests that creative spirit given us by God and in respect of which we are created in His image (and can imitate His creativity) – as also in Dryden's "To Sir Robert Howard," it is "Genius" (line 35) which permits the human poet to create poems so lovely they appear to be works of art as perfectly formed as God's own (here, the songbirds). Later in the eighteenth century, *genius* will come explicitly to be defined as the ability to read probable signs well, a ready knowledge, as Daniel Webb explains in his *Inquiry into the Beauties of Painting* (1761), "of the human heart, its various affections, and the just measure of their influence in our looks and gestures" (151); see below, pp. 194, 248.

106 "Whereas the Rules are only Directions to an Epick or Dramatick Poet, for the Attainment of Sovereign Beauty; whenever it may happen, by very great Chance, that Sovereign Beauty can be better attain'd by suspending one of them for that Time ... In my humble Opinion, this ought to be the certain Signal for breaking thro' a Rule" (II, 198).

107 I, 391, 394. To describe the process of bringing some phenomenon under a rule of art Aristotle uses the verb τεχνολογέω (*Rhetoric* I. 1. 9, 12); it was Cicero who introduced the term *technologia* into Latin, orginally as a systematic treatment of grammar (*To Atticus*, 4. 16). Later, "technology" came to mean the rules or lexicon of any art (rules and vocabulary were the same, for "dictionaries" initially took it upon themselves "to explain not only the terms of art but the arts themselves"; see McKeon, "The Trans-

formation of the Liberal Arts in the Renaissance," pp. 176–80). The word *technology* did not take on its modern sense until the mid-nineteenth century.

V The role of probability in Augustan theories of imitation

1 Tr.R(ichard) C(arew) (1594), p. 180 (section on "Solertia").

2 See Bundy, *The Theory of the Imagination in Classical and Mediaeval Thought*, ch. 9, and Harvey, *The Inward Wits*, pp. 41–53. Charles Bouelles (Bovillus) distinguishes in his *Liber de sensu* (1510) between a mere presentative imagination (part of the physical body) and a judicative imagination (part of the immortal soul), while Pierre de La Primaudaye explains in *L'Academie françoise* (1577) that just as *souvenance* or *recordation* is the task of memory, so *considération*, a process of conjecture from signs, is that of imagination: "Les subtils et sages, par petites coniectures ou prinses de bien loin, apperçoivent ce qu'ils cherchent, et y parviennent. Il y en a des autres, qui sont de si grand esprit, qu'ils embrassent beauc[oup] de choses à la fois, et si voyant comme en vn iect d'oeil et en vn seul regard tout ce qui est à propos. En quoi il appert qu'ils ont l'imagination et la phantasie prompte, et vne memoire comme vn thresor tout ouvert, et la consideration prompte, et la souvenance entiere et vigoreuse. Car si l'imagination et la phantasie est lente et tardive, ou la memoire enserrée, ou si la consideration cesse, ou la recordation est debile, le discours sera tardif et rencontera bien mal" (Quoted in Grahame Castor, *Pléiade Poetics*, pp. 149–51).

The Renaissance connection of imagination with probability stems as well of course from traditional views of the nature of invention, which Cicero had defined as a power of "discovery and contrivance" which "investigates hidden secrets" ("illa vis quae tandem est, quae investigat occulta, quae inventio atque cogitatio dicitur": *Tusculan Disputations*, I. xxv. 61). Within rhetoric, more specifically, invention was understood as the faculty of finding probable arguments: "Inventio est excogitatio rerum verarum aut veri similium quae causam probabilem reddant" (*Rhetorica ad Herennium*, I. ii. 3). Invention in this sense became, for instance, the substance of Balthasar Gracián's "sixth sence," that faculty possessed by Egenio in *The Critick* and there defined as "that which gives life to Men, and awakens them to discourse, and searches out the most hidden secresie, contrives, invents remedies, gives us tongues, with confidence to speak, feet to run, and wings to fly, and a prophetick spirit to divine future accidents"; "it is witty, inventive, cautious, active, acute, and in a sence for its excellency hath preheminence over all the others" of the faculties (223, 244).

3 *On the Imagination* (1501), p. 63. Compare the nearly identical claims made for invention by Cicero and others, above, n2.

4 In *El Criticon*, first published serially in 1650–53, and the *Oracula Manual y arte de prudencia* (1653); on this aspect of Gracián's thought, see Addison, *Spectator* 409, and Thorpe, *The Aesthetic Theory of Thomas Hobbes*, pp. 63–64.

5 Pierre Charron, *Of Wisdom* (1601), pp. 67–68, 48–49. Cf. Ben Jonson in *Timber* (1641): "*Opinion* is a light, vaine, crude, and imperfect thing, settled in the Imagination" (*Works*, VIII, 564).

6 Fable 18, "The PAINTER who pleased No body and Every body," lines 1–2 (1727).

7 "Alass! a meer Chymerick Notion" says Swift in "The Beasts Confession to the Priest." This derogatory sense of *notion*, extremely common in the period, may have been a product of the term's use in scholastic philosophy. Tucker places "notion" in an epistemic scale in *The Light of Nature Pursued*: "There are various degrees of strength in judgments, from the lowest surmise to notion, opinion, persuasion, and the highest assurance, which we call certainty" (1, 289); more often the term is used in phrases such as Sprat's "Notionall Wars" or Glanvill's (defective) "notionall knowledge."

8 See, e.g., Ogilvie, *Philosophical Observations*: "the point of perfection lies in the equipoise of these faculties acting with perfect harmony" (1, 381); Robert Uphaus, "Johnson's Equipoise and the State of Man," ch. 6 of *The Impossible Observer*. According to Thomas Gordon, "this great Globe of Earth and Water" is "well put together, and so equally poiz'd" (*The Humourist* [1720], 1, 53); the rule of equipoise (like that of a balance of humors) is ultimately metaphysical in origin: see below, p. 248.

9 The phrase is R. S. Crane's; see his "Critical and Historical Principles of Literary History," in *The Idea of the Humanities*, 11, 85.

10 Richard Blackmore, *Essays on Several Subjects* (1716), pp. 24, 25–26. Blackmore is perhaps following Le Bossu's treatment of the same problem: "There is a great deal of Difference between *Fiction* and a downright *Lye*; and between a Thing's being *Probable*, and its being *no more than Probable*" (*Monsieur Bossu's Treatise*, p. 39).

11 Hobbes, "Answer," p. 59; Bacon, *Works*, IV, 288.

12 Hobbes, "Preface to Homer," p. 70.

13 The *locus classicus* is of course *Of Dramatic Poesy* (*Essays*, 1, 25).

14 See Hobbes, "Answer," p. 60.

15 Preface to Rochester's *Valentinian*, pp. 21–22.

16 John Aikin, *An Essay on the Application of Natural History to Poetry* (1777), p. 11.

17 Sir Thomas Pope Blount, *De Re Poetica* (1694), pp. 60, 50; Hurd, *Works*, 11, 98; 1, 267.

18 Or "variety," which in our period meant not so much variousness as (in Johnson's first definition) "Change; succession of one thing to another; intermixture of one thing with another." Thus, e.g., Louis Le Roy's work (translated by Richard Ashley), *Of the Interchangeable Course or Variety of Things in the Whole World* (1594); for other Renaissance and Augustan uses of *variety* to mean "change" or "vicissitude," see Kitty Scoular, *Natural Magic*, pp. 5–6.

19 Twining, *Aristotle's Treatise on Poetry*, pp. 277, 407; Ogilvie, *Philosophical Observations*, 1, 33; Penn, *Works* (1798), 11, 122–23; Hawkesworth, below, note 22.

20 Hurd, *Works*, 1, 252; Coleridge, quoted below, p. 157. Gordon McKenzie gives a conspectus of late Augustan ways of speaking of poetical probability and truth in *Critical Responsiveness*, ch. 7.

21 Abrams, *The Mirror and the Lamp*, pp. 271–84; for "artificial" and "natural" probability, see Weinberg, *History*.

22 *Adventurer* 4 (*The Adventurer*, 1, 22–23).

23 *Letters of Literature* (1785), pp. 215, 218; on Caliban, see also Twining, *Aristotle's Treatise*, p. 119: "Yet Shakespeare has made the character *appear probable*; not certainly to *reason*, but to *imagination*; that is, *we make no difficulty about the possibility of it*, in *reading*. Is not the *Lovelace* of

Richardson, in this view, more out of nature, more improbable than the *Caliban* of Shakespeare? The latter is, at least, consistent. I can *imagine* such a monster as Caliban: I could never imagine such a man as Lovelace."

24 See especially Lowth, *Lectures*, I, xx.

25 "An Ode on the Popular Superstitions of the Highlands of Scotland" (1749–50), lines 188–89.

26 *Prose Works*, I, 139 (my italics).

27 "Mr Gray's Remarks on the Letters Prefixed to Mason's Elfrida" (*Works*, IV, 3).

28 "Grounds of Criticism in Tragedy" (*Essays*, I, 253).

29 Edward Manwaring, *An Historical and Critical Account of the Most Eminent Classic Authors in Poetry and History* (1737), p. 341.

30 *A Commentary illustrating the Poetic of Aristotle*, p. 53.

31 Joseph Trapp, *Praelectiones Poeticae* (1711–19), tr. as *Lectures on Poetry* (1737), p. 341.

32 William Belsham, *Essays, Philosophical and Moral, Historical and Literary* (1799), II, 522.

33 The phrase comes from Henry Felton, *A Dissertation on Reading the Classics, And Forming a Just Style* (1715), p. 113.

34 *Lives*, I, 163, 168, 170, 174, 188.

35 *An Enquiry concerning Human Understanding* (1748) (*Enquiries*, pp. 119, 126).

36 Percival, *Moral and Literary Dissertations*, pp. 253, 247–48; on the arguments of both Aikin and Percival, see Jeffrey Plank, "John Aikin: The Scientist as Critic," pp. 34–68.

37 Frank Sayers, *Disquisitions Metaphysical and Literary* (1793), p. 29; Hume, *Enquiries*, p. 118. Cf. Priestley, *Lectures on Oratory*, p. 89: "Vivid ideas and strong emotions ... having been, through life, associated with reality, it is easy to imagine that, upon the perception of the proper feelings, the associated idea of reality will likewise occur."

38 Quoted in Jules Brody, *Boileau and Longinus*, pp. 110–11. As Brody points out, the Greek word Boileau renders as *vraisemblable* is *pithanos*; other translators render the Greek term with forms of *probability* (as for instance does Gabrielle della Pietra in his translation of Longinus into Latin of 1612).

39 *Dissertations, Moral and Critical* (1783), I, 223.

40 Preface to *Prince Arthur*, p. 328.

41 Knight, *An Analytical Inquiry into the Nature and Principles of Taste* (1805), pp. 268, 288.

42 *The Castle of Otranto*, p. 4; *Hieroglyphic Tales*, p. 5; *Historic Doubts* (1768), pp. 155, 158.

43 Mary Poovey, "The Novel as Imaginative Order," p. 50 (it is far from clear, however, that Walpole would have accepted the characterization of his tale as a *novel*).

44 *Letters to a Young Lady on a Course of English Poetry*, pp. 32, 120, 249–50, 261. The critical distinction between the sublime and pathetic appears at least as early as Trapp, who explains in his *Lectures on Poetry*, in terms learned from Dennis, that there "is one species of poetic *Pathos*, or Enthusiasm, viz., which consists in the Marvellous, and raises Admiration by impressing upon the Mind something great, unusual and portentious," while also "there are other kinds of it which excite Grief, Pity, Terror, and work upon the other Passions" (117–18).

45 *Monthly Review*, 4 (1751), 356.

46 *Marginalia I*, p. 55; *Coleridge's Miscellaneous Criticism*, p. 372.
47 Hobbes, "Answer," p. 62; for use of this passage as a gloss on Aristotle, see Twining, *Aristotle's Treatise*, p. 119.
48 *Preface to Shakespeare* (Johnson, *Works*, VII, 77).
49 *Shakespearean Criticism*, I, 179. The attack on the unities as leading to improbability became for Adam Müller a point in their defense; to Müller, the unities contribute to a desirable sense of artifice and unnaturalness in drama. (See René Wellek, *A History of Modern Criticism*, II, 294).
50 *Shakespearean Criticism*, I, 115.
51 *Biographia*, ed. Shawcross, II, 101, 289.
52 Coleridge finds "laborious minuteness" disunifying as well, and claims as a result that it is a case of the poet's failure to "paint to the imagination, not to the fancy," adding, "I know of no happier case to exemplify the distinction between these two faculties" (II, 102). *Imagination* here, as opposed to *fancy*, is a source of the same poetic unity that Wordsworth calls imagination's "inevitability" in the Prefaces to *Lyrical Ballads*.
53 *Shakespearean Criticism*, I, 115.
54 *Biographia*, II, 158.
55 Cf. *Shakespearean Criticism*, I, 155; "The old tragedy moved in an ideal world, the old comedy in a fantastic world. As the entertainment restrained the creative activity of both the fancy and imagination, it indemnified the understanding in appealing to the judgment for the probability of the scenes represented."
56 *The Horn of Oberon: Jean Paul Richter's School for Aesthetics*, pp. 25–26; cf. also note 59 below.
57 "Solitude. An Ode" (1753), lines 90–94.
58 Pope to Swift, 19 December 1734 (*The Correspondence of Alexander Pope*, III, 445).
59 Here and in the next two pages I closely follow Clifford Siskin, "Wordsworth's Gothic Endeavor."
60 Richter says of *Wilhelm Meister*: "One would gladly have spared Goethe from unlocking his cabinet of machinery and digging up the pipes which spouted the transparent, many-colored waterworks. A juggler is no poet, and even a juggler is only worthy and poetic as long as he does not destroy his marvels by resolving them" (*School for Aesthetics*, p. 25). Richter's favored wonders are to be found within: he calls them "inner marvels," and explains: "But the best is a third method. Here the poet neither destroys the marvel, as does the exegetical theologian, nor imprisons it unnaturally in the physical world, as does a juggler, but rather locates it in the soul, the only place where it can dwell next to God... *Meister*'s wondrous nature lies not in the wooden wheelworks ... but in Mignon's and the Harp Player's splendid spiritual profundity" (26).
61 Shelley proceeds to cite the familiar precedents for his procedure, and to argue in language reminiscent of Pope's *Essay on Criticism* that, properly grounded and explained, the licenses of Gothic fiction become rules: "I have thus endeavored to preserve the truth of the elementary principles of human nature, while I have not scrupled to innovate upon their combinations. The *Iliad*, the tragic poetry of Greece, – Shakespeare, in the *Tempest* and *Midsummer Night's Dream*, – and most especially Milton, in *Paradise Lost*, conform to this rule; and the most humble novelist, who seeks to confer or receive amusement from his labours, may, without presumption, apply to

prose fiction a license, or rather a rule, from the adoption of which so many exquisite combinations of human feeling have resulted in the highest specimens of poetry" (6–7).

62 In the "Advertisement": Wordsworth, *Prose Works*, I, 116.

63 *Biographia*, ed. Shawcross, II, 5.

64 Wordsworth, 1800 Preface to *Lyrical Ballads*, *Prose Works*, I, 128–30.

65 Thomas Warton, *History of English Poetry*, IV, 328; on Romantic use of the Elizabethans as a standard by which to measure the Augustans, see Upali Amarasinghe, *Dryden and Pope in the Early Nineteenth Century*, pp. 73–76, 85–92, 96–100.

66 Wallace Jackson, *The Probable and the Marvelous: Blake, Wordsworth, and the Eighteenth-Century Critical Tradition*, to which I am indebted for many suggestions about the nature of mid-century allegory.

67 Addison, *Spectator* 421 (III, 578); *Monsieur Bossu's Treatise*, p. 136. For similar suggestions by Dennis, see *Critical Works*, I, 56–58; II, 45. Among the most famous early proponents of this view was Tasso, who wrote in 1581: "Heroic poetry, like an animal in which two natures are conjoined, is composed of imitation and of allegory. With the former it attracts the mind and the ears of men to itself and delights them in a wonderful way; with the latter it instructs them in the virtues or in knowledge, or in both together" (quoted in Weinberg, *History*, I, 206; cf. 621). This is also, for instance, the sense of *allegory* to which Robbe-Grillet appeals when he writes in *In the Labyrinth*: "This narrative is not a true account, but fiction. It describes a reality not necessarily the same as the one the reader has experienced . . . the reality in question . . . is subject to no allegorical interpretation. The reader is therefore requested to see in it only objects, actions, works, and events which are described, without attempting to give them either more or less meaning than in his own life, or his own death" (*Two Novels*, p. 140).

68 Cf. Thomas Warton, *Observations on the Fairy Queen* (1762), II, 91, and Coleridge, *Biographia*, II, 98: "allegorically to body forth the inward state of the person speaking." It would appear that one central function of allegory to mid-century poets is to help them escape from the limiting demands of their own critical principles. Following Addison in the "Pleasures of the Imagination," they find "Our sight is the most perfect and most delightful of all our senses," and so that the highest function of art is to provide visual imagery (*Spectator* 411); allegorical poetry provides such imagery while at the same time avoiding the dangerous formalist tendency in Addison's theory, i.e., the tendency of a poet working on strictly Addisonian principles to do no more than describe the superficies of things.

69 "Every reader finds himself weary with this useless talk of an allegorical being": *Life of Cowley* (*Lives* I, 51; cf. 185); Lowth, *Lectures*, I, 107–09 and *passim*.

70 Campbell complicates the connection between consistency and belief by allowing that "fiction may be as plausible as truth. A narration may be possessed of this quality to the highest degree, which we not only regard as improbable, but know to be false" (82). Warton, more a rationalist, disagrees: "In the best-conducted fiction, some mark of improbability and incoherence will appear" (*Essay on Pope*, 1756 ed., p. 254).

71 In his very interesting doctoral dissertation of 1735, Alexander Baumgarten addresses many of the same issues as Campbell, but treats them with a surer intelligence. Baumgarten, a student of Leibniz and Wolff, gives a possible-

worlds analysis of literary probability, an analysis that depends on his distinction between "heterocosmic" and "utopian" fictions. Wellek has distorted the meanings of these terms by interpreting the first as probable fiction, the second as improbable (*History of Modern Criticism*, I, 145). What Baumgarten says is: "The objects of such representations are either possible or impossible in the real world. Let the latter be called *fictions* and the former *true fictions*... Objects (denoted by) fictions are impossible in either of two ways, in the real world or in all possible worlds. Those which are absolutely impossible we shall call *utopian*. The others we shall term *heterocosmic*... Only true and heterocosmic fictions are poetic" (*Reflections on Poetry*, p. 55). Utopian fictions, then, are not improbable, but impossible (in the Leibnizian sense of true in no possible world). In fact, for Baumgarten, probability is a property intrinsic neither to true nor to heterocosmic fictions, but is a relation to evidence. Baumgarten is clear, as Campbell is not, about the status of such evidence as comes from "the work itself": "More remote history is never so determinately known as the pen of the poet requires – as already demonstrated. What is narrated, therefore, has to be more fully determined. Determinations have to be added to the poem about those things concerning which history is silent. They can be discerned only by taking note of whatever must be presupposed for their literal truth. But since this does not fall within the limits of comprehension, they must be guessed at from very little and often insufficient evidence. In this respect the truth of poetic inventions is decidedly improbable; *that is, their nonexistence and their status among heterocosmic fictions is probable*" (59, my italics).

72 Cf. Ben Jonson in *Timber* (1641): "Contraries are not mixed" (*Works*, VIII, 563). Such a generalization is clearly too large adequately to be defended here; see also below, pp. 246–48. One striking exception to the generalization is Hume's argument about the conversion of one passion into another, contrary passion in his essay "Of Tragedy" (see Cohen, "The Transformation of Passion," the best modern reading of Hume's essay); in his own time, however, Hume's argument was rarely understood and still more rarely accepted, so that Hurd (who did understand it) can speak of it as an unintelligible appeal to fusion where mediation alone is conceivable, calling it "little less than a new kind of *Transubstantiation*" (*Works*, I, 119). An extremely instructive late eighteenth-century text on the transition from patterns of mediation to patterns of fusion is William Thomson, *An Enquiry into the Elementary Principles of Beauty* (1798); while speaking of the need to "educate" the senses, producing thereby such a "*rationally improved sense*" as a "learned and correct *Vision*" (24, 32), Thomson still argues of the mind that "those several powers or faculties, in a distinct and separate state, so as that each has its peculiar office, and performs its functions, independent of the rest ... the actions of the several faculties are thus necessarily in succession to each other" (10, 18).

73 *Prelude* 14, line 192; *Prose Works*, III, 35.

74 Blake, *Poetry and Prose*, pp. 1076, 828–29.

75 *Prose Works*, I, 130, 138; for an earlier judgment that it is chiefly through such "mechanical employments" that poetry is imitative, see Twining, quoted above, p. 95.

76 Wordsworth, *Poetical Works*, II, 331.

77 For extended commentary on both quotations, see Robert Newsom, *Dickens On the Romantic Side of Familiar Things*.

VI Probability and literary form

1 Alkon supports his contention that like God, Defoe's godly man has no use for probabilities, in part through the argument that it was only during and after Defoe's time that probability came to be applied to future events; this "shift from past to future orientation," from "retrodiction" to "prediction," Alkon finds to be "one of the major turning-points of Western thought during the eighteenth century" (32, 35, 45). In fact no such shift occurred. We have already seen that since ancient times judgments of probability were made not only in diagnosis but also in prognosis; Alkon's thesis depends in part on acceptance of the timetable of the Foucault–Hacking hypothesis (see appendix A).

   Bunn founds his case explicitly on Foucault and Hacking, from whom he learns that "Statistical inquiry and probability theory enter eighteenth-century epistemology at the same time as David Hume's philosophical quandary about personal identity" (457); Bunn finds that Hume therefore "provides an epistemological context by which to gloss *Roderick Random*" (458); but the disappointing result of bringing such heavy artillery to bear on Smollett is "that one will find no significant theory of chance in *Roderick Random*" (464).

2 "licet ad civilia et artes quae in sermone et opinione positae sunt" (*Works*, IV, 17). Rosalie Colie makes very suggestive remarks on Renaissance views of essay as a new and mixed form in *The Resources of Kind*, pp. 88–89.

3 See Lisa Jardine's excellent account of these terms in *Francis Bacon: Discovery and the Art of Discourse*.

4 George Puttenham, *The Arte of English Poesie* (1589), pp. 252, 247. Aristotle allows that "example" is one "kind of induction" in rhetoric (*Rhetoric* I. 2. 1357^b25), but has strong reservations about it as a form of persuasive argument (see, e.g., *Topics* 105^a10–18), and the tradition long persists. Thus for John of Salisbury, "We should deal with a learned man in one way, but with an illiterate person in another. The former is to be convinced by syllogisms, whereas the latter's assent must be won by inductive reasoning" (*Metalogicon*, p. 199); according to Ralph Lever, examples should be used "rather to perswade and leade the simple and the ignoraunt, then to force and overcome the wittie adversarie" (*Arte of Reason*, p. 196; cf. Blundeville, *Art of Logick*, pp. 149–50).

5 *A Dissertation on Reading the Classics, and Forming a Just Style* (1715), pp. ix–x, 58, 116.

6 See Joel Altman, *The Tudor Play of Mind: Rhetorical Inquiry and the Development of Elizabethan Drama* (1978).

7 *Contexts of Dryden's Thought*, p. 35.

8 Berkeley is following ancient advice. Ascham explains in the preface to *Toxophilus* (1545), "He that wyll wryte well in any tongue, must folowe thys councel of Aristotle, to speake as the common people do, to thinke as wise men do" ($a1^r$); Geoffrey of Vinsauf counsels, "Be of average, not lofty, eloquence. The precept of the ancients is clear: speak as the many, think as the few ... you can be at once elegant and easy in discourse" (*Poetria Nova*, p. 55).

9 *Pace* Miriam M. Reik, *The Golden Lands of Thomas Hobbes*, pp. 192–3.

10 The term is, of course, Wolfgang Iser's, from *The Implied Reader*; I do not in adopting it mean to adopt also Iser's too frequent practice of importing modern theories of reading into his analyses of older texts. For a conspectus

of recent theories about the kinds of readers which works imply, demand, invent, or manipulate, see Daniel Wilson, "Readers in Texts."

11 Hagstrum, *Samuel Johnson's Literary Criticism*, p. 59.

12 *Essays: On Poetry and Music*, pp. 58, 47.

13 *Essays*, pp. 42–43. There is of course nothing distinctively Augustan in this pattern of arguing from genre to probability; Coleridge says, for instance, of farce, in relation to comedy: "A proper farce is mainly distinguished from comedy by the license allowed, and even required, in the fable, in order to produce strange and laughable situations. The story need not be probable, it is enough that it is possible. A comedy would scarcely allow even the two Antipholuses; because... these are mere individual accidents, *casus ludentis naturae*, and the *verum* will not excuse the *inverisimile*. But farce dares add the two Dromios, and is justified in doing so by the laws of its own end and constitution" (*Shakespearean Criticism*, I, 89).

14 *The Adventurer*, I, 22.

15 Other critics, of course, turn the comparison to Fielding's advantage, as does the anonymous author of *An Essay on the New Species of Writing Founded by Mr. Fielding* (1751), who finds that the same desire for resemblance to truth "produced *Joseph Andrews*, which soon became a formidable rival to the *amazing* Class of Writers; since it was not a mere dry Narrative, but a lively Representative of real Life" (16). Twining's choice for comparison of a novel which, in Johnson's famous comparison to Fielding's truth of manners, is truer to the "heart," reflects the shift we have traced in preferred objects of imitation from those whose standard is external probability to events internally probable; it is through such dislocations alone that we can understand how in 1785 Edward Owen could nominate above all other Augustans Richardson as the one best able to carry on the tradition of Juvenalian satire (in his "Essay on Satire," in *Satires of Juvenal*, II, 260).

VII The conditions of knowing in Augustan fiction

1 Goldsmith, *Collected Works*, II, 156–61.

2 See Irvin Ehrenpreis, "Explicitness in Augustan Literature," in *Literary Meaning and Augustan Values*, pp. 1–48.

3 See Uphaus, *The Impossible Observer*.

4 Duncan, *Logick*, pp. 11–12; *Monthly Review*, 11 (1793), quoted in John Graham, "Lavater's *Physiognomy* in England," p. 569. Holcroft translated one of the most popular English editions of Lavater's *Essays on Physiognomy* (German ed., 1775–78). Lavater's system might be called, however, a Romantic rather than an Augustan system of signs. Instead of demanding that careful weighing of perhaps opposing signs required by all Augustan theorists of the probable, Lavater holds that "Every minute part has the nature and character of the whole... Each trait contains the whole character of man" ("Lavater's *Physiognomy*," p. 563). Such a view radically alters the process of sign-inference; it embodies a synecdochic view discussed below, pp. 246–51.

5 A. B. Strauss, "On Smollett's Language: A Paragraph in *Ferdinand Count Fathom*," p. 26. Strauss approvingly quotes Saintsbury's judgment of *Fathom*, as do Robert Spector (*Tobias Smollett*, p. 85) and Thomas R. Preston ("Disenchanting the Man of Feeling: Smollett's *Ferdinand Count Fathom*," p. 223).

6 William Hazlitt, *Lectures on the English Comic Writers*, p. 116; Strauss, "On Smollett's Language," pp. 28–34.

7 *The Adventures of Ferdinand Count Fathom*, II, 53. All italics in quotations from *Fathom* are mine. The discussion that follows does not consider the dramatic use of signs, but the author recognizes, as the anonymous author of *The Polite Arts* (1749) says, that "Tone and Gesture go directly to the Heart. Speech expresses Passions by naming them: if we say, I love you or I hate you, and don't join some Gesture and Tone to the Words, we rather express an Idea than a Sentiment" (51).

8 For the contrast between "art" and "nature" in *Fathom*, see M. A. Goldberg, *Smollett and the Scottish School*, ch. 4; on the background of Smollett's use of "policy," see Napoleone Orsini, "'Policy' or the Language of Elizabethan Machiavellism."

9 Quoted in Thomas R. Preston, "The 'Stage Passions' and Smollett's Characterization," p. 111; Preston takes the language of "tableau scenes" from Strauss, who in turn takes his analysis from McKillop's observation in *The Early Masters of English Fiction* (pp. 104–05) that in his Preface to *Fathom*, Smollett likens the method of his novel to that of composition in painting, and uses the word *group* in a painter's sense ("A novel is a large diffused picture, comprehending the characters of life, disposed in different groups, and exhibited in various attitudes for the puposes of an uniform plan": I, 31).

10 Bacon, *Works*, IV, 376. Compare the discussion of *sagacity* in *Sir Launcelot Greaves*, p. 274, and of the "art" of the "cunning man," who is able to "foresee" by "deciphering characters" and "hieroglyphics" (which are in fact "signs" and "indications": pp. 254–55).

11 Few modern readers have sought in Smollett's fiction any structural (as opposed to thematic) uses of the medical theory in which he was trained; exceptions are Donald Bruce's eccentric and sloppy, but nonetheless important, *Radical Doctor Smollett*, and several essays by G. S. Rousseau, newly collected in his *Tobias Smollett: Essays of Two Decades*.

12 See, however, the frequent "signs" and "marks" of *Humphry Clinker*, and particularly Smollett's revealing use of the phrase "tropes and figures" (pp. 52, 69, 100).

13 *Early Masters of English Fiction*, p. 153.

14 See, e.g., Evelyn, *Numismata*, p. 295; *The Polite Arts* (1749), pp. 12, 50.

15 Dennis, *Critical Works*, I, 97; Hogarth, *Analysis of Beauty*, p. 125.

16 John Traugott, *Tristram Shandy's World*, p. 8.

17 "Captain Harville ... looked at her with a smile, and a little motion of the head, which expressed, 'Come to me, I have something to say'"; "Captain Harville smiled, as much as to say, 'Do you claim that for your sex?' and she answered the question, smiling also, 'Yes ... '" (*Persuasion*, pp. 231, 232). Cf. Inchbald, *Nature and Art*, p. 28: "He walked into the room, not with a dictated obeisance, but with a hurrying step, a half pleased, yet a half frightened look, an instantaneous survey of every person present: not as demanding 'what they thought of him,' but expressing, almost as plainly as in direct words, 'what he thought of them.'"

18 *Faerie Queene* I. 1. 12; cf. Skulsky, "Spenser's Despair Episode," pp. 238–39.

19 For stupefaction, being struck dumb, and paralysis of the nerves, see Bruce, *Radical Doctor Smollett*, pp. 56–57.

20 *Tristram Shandy's World*, pp. 8–9.

21 See, e.g., I, 77, 78, 84, 98, 102, 108, 123, 130, 174, 194, 199, 202.

22 Cf. Captain Crowe in *Greaves*: "When he himself attempted to speak, he never finished his period; but made such a number of abrupt transitions, that his discourse seemed to be an unconnected series of unfinished sentences, the meaning of which it was not easy to decipher" (2); such digressiveness may also be a sign of simpleminded sincerity.

23 *The Novels of Tobias Smollett*, pp. 152–53.

24 *Monthly Review*, 8 (1753), 205.

25 Preston has worked out this interpretation in detail in "Disenchanting the Man of Feeling."

26 "The Picaroon as Fortune's Plaything," p. 150.

27 George Starr has described a variant of the phenomenon discussed here in his study of *Defoe and Casuistry*: according to Starr, casuistical procedures "dissolve" Defoe's narratives "into a series of discrete episodes" unified by considerations of the rights and wrongs of a given case, and by the verbal signs of such argument ("And ... But ... Yet ..."). Further, he finds that from casuistry's emphasis on motive in judging action "it is a very short step to the belief that characterization consists of the analysis of consciousness" (ix).

28 In *Miscellanies*, pp. 156–57.

29 Goldsmith, *Works*, IV, 66, 68.

30 *The History of the Adventures of Joseph Andrews*, p. 339. The account of *Joseph Andrews* which follows owes most to two treatments of the novel: Battestin's *Moral Basis of Fielding's Art*, and James Slevin, "Morals and Form: A Study of Tradition and Innovation in *Joseph Andrews*."

31 *The Criticism of Henry Fielding*, p. 266.

32 The best general treatment of the motives of Augustan travel remains George Parks, "Travel as Education"; the most interesting analyses of a work of travel for its epistemic assumptions and intentions have been of Johnson's *Journey to the Western Islands* (see especially Francis R. Hart, "Johnson as Philosophic Traveller"). See also Paul Fussell, *The Rhetorical World of Augustan Humanism*, ch. 11, and, more recently, Charles Batten Jr., *Pleasurable Instruction*. For Chesterfield's use of travel as metaphor for education, see his *Letters*, I, 136, 148, 155, 176–77, 184ff., 219.

33 Cicero draws the distinction in the *De Divinatione*, but it is already present in the Hippocratic corpus (see G. E. R. Lloyd, *Magic, Reason and Experience*, p. 45n195). Vives complains in *De Tradendis disciplinis* of those physicians who, "not satisfied with the art of healing ... also strive to reveal in themselves a power of divination" (224); cf. also John Evelyn, quoted on p. 42 above.

34 I owe this interpretation of the continuity of the interpolated tales to Irby Cauthen; see "Fielding's Digressions in *Joseph Andrews*."

35 See Aubrey Williams, "Interpositions of Providence and the Design of Fielding's Novels," Williams' most successful investigation of providential form in literature.

36 To understand the role of the pedlar in Fielding's providentially ordered world, it is useful to compare him to a cognate character in a world decidedly not so ordered. Especially after Scott, novels substitute historical process for providential patterning; historical process may take a variety of shapes (it may be progressive, or retrogressive), but in all cases it presumes a logic of events *internal* to those events, not externally imposed (by a superintendent deity). The world of Dickens' *Tale of Two Cities* (1859) is explicitly of the newer kind, and in Dr. Manette's role in the last third of the novel – in his

failed efforts to intervene to save Charles Darnay – Dickens consciously creates a failed version of that eighteenth-century novelistic type such as the pedlar or Goldsmith's Mr. Burchell, the character who acts as instrument of Providence. In creating such a figure, Dickens is consciously and publicly abjuring the earlier literary form, its theological underpinnings and typical characters.

In calling up the Revolution through natural imagery (imagery of storm, earthquake, rising seas, and lightning – the four elements), Dickens is at pains to make clear what he elsewhere makes explicit: that the Revolution is a natural growth of time, rather than a providentially appointed instance of moral vengeance: it is a "deluge rising from below, not falling from above, and with the windows of Heaven shut, not opened" (301). Darnay says of his own history that because the times are so disjoint – because evil is so pervasive – his story cannot be of that earlier kind wherein accounts are justly, happily, and fortuitously settled at the end: "Good could never come of such evil, a happier end was not *in nature* to so unhappy a beginning" (364, my italics). To paraphrase Rymer, the evils of the age exceed the possibility of the older literary form – of mere poetic justice – to punish them. Nor in this world do sudden and seasonable events unexpectedly but repeatedly intervene to save distressed innocence: here, genuine sacrifice alone works amelioration, and that not with certainty (with Carton dies an innocent young girl). Moreover, providential fictions end as social stations are newly filled with their most deserving aspirants; in the *Tale*, Dickens is at pains to show that "the new oppressors who have risen on the destruction of the old" (404), the revolutionaries who have replaced Monseigneur, resemble their hated forebears in injustice, cruelty, and even unfruitful management of the land. The victims have become victimizers, the hunted, hunters. Whenever Providence is mentioned explicitly, it is in a falsehood or a prediction which proves false, instances which are carefully crafted reversals of earlier belief and practice (pp. 59, 95).

It is in this world that Dr. Manette attempts to set up as an instrument of Providence, "a Spirit moving among mortals" (303), a pedlar or Burchell who will save his son-in-law from the prison of La Force. Manette's earlier suffering in the Bastille fuels his providential aspirations: "My old pain has given me a power"; "the Doctor felt, now, that his suffering was strength and power... 'It all tended to a good end, my friend; it was not mere waste and ruin ... by the aid of Heaven I will do it!'" (290, 300). This power is supposed to come because *in this world*, moral accounts are balanced; on condition that Lucie pledge her faith in her father (she is actually to repeat, "I trust in you"), she will find him able to "save," "redeem," and "deliver" Charles (300, 301, 304, 308, 316).

For a moment it appears that Manette's "promise was redeemed, he had saved Charles" (316); the passage in which it finally becomes clear that he has actually failed is richly ironic in its echoes of earlier scenes in which judgment is rendered by sudden reversal: "[Miss Pross and Mr. Cruncher] went out, leaving Lucie, and her husband, her father, and the child, by a bright fire. Mr. Lorry was expected back presently from the Banking House. Miss Pross had lighted the lamp, but had put it aside in a corner, that they might enjoy the fire-light undisturbed. Little Lucie sat by her grandfather with her hands clasped through his arm: and he, in a tone not rising much above a whisper, began to tell her a story of a great and powerful Fairy who had opened a prison-wall and let out a captive who had once done the Fairy a service. All was subdued and quiet, and Lucie was more at ease than she had been.

"'What was that?' she cried, all at once" (319).

Manette's fairy story is a self-satisfied rendering of his own service to Darnay; the sudden turn of events recalls innumerable reversals in *The Vicar of Wakefield* or *Joseph Andrews*, but here reversal is not a judgment *by* but *on* providential design. In Dr. Manette, Dickens says a public good-bye to earlier fictive forms.

(It is of course true that though Dickens has lost too much faith to believe the world to embody a providential promise – at least not for individuals – and so to write comedies embodying such design, his world is still *morally* ordered: evil reaps evil, and virtue alone may decide a battle. Modern readers are perhaps most troubled by this lingering faith when they learn why Miss Pross should overcome the experienced malice of Madame Defarge: "It was in vain for Madame Defarge to struggle and to strike; Miss Pross, with the vigorous tenacity of love, always so much stronger than hate" (397). It is as if Dickens expected the old machines to work even though he had turned the electricity off.)

37 See especially Melvyn New, "'The Grease of God': The Form of Eighteenth-Century English Fiction."

38 By Daniel Wilson, in his study of *The Archaeology and Prehistoric Annals of Scotland* (1851); see Glyn Daniel, *The Idea of Prehistory*, ch. 1.

39 See Slevin, "Morals and Form," and for the general theory of interrelations informing Slevin's argument, Ralph Cohen, "On the Interrelations of Eighteenth-Century Literary Forms" and "Pope's Meanings and the Strategies of Interrelation."

40 Eric Rothstein, *Systems of Order and Inquiry in Later Eighteenth-Century Fiction*, pp. 155, 164–65.

41 See, e.g., vol. II, 12, 13, 18, 19, 22, 23, 31, 34, 47, 52, 55, 89, 96, 109, 124, 128, 130, 144, 146, 147, 153, 219, 223, 293, 295, 296, 311.

42 *Amelia* X. 9 (II, 237). Maurice Johnson and Martin Battestin examine the role of Booth's adherence to Fortune rather than Providence in *Fielding's Art of Fiction* and "The Problem of *Amelia*."

43 Mary Poovey, "Journeys from this World to the Next: The Providential Promise in *Clarissa* and *Tom Jones*"; a more detailed analysis of *Clarissa* from the same point of view is Anthony Winner, "Richardson's Lovelace: Character and Prediction."

That in the world of Austen's novels moral and religious values are, as in Fielding, immanent in everyday reality is amply demonstrated by Alistair Duckworth in *The Improvement of the Estate*; one manifestation of this immanence which has not received the attention it deserves, however, is the recurrent pattern of characters' falling physically ill and proceeding to recuperate not merely physically but also morally (most notably, Tom Bertram in *Mansfield Park* and Louisa in *Persuasion*). The rationale for this pattern of illness and recovery is set for the novel by Defoe: Robinson Crusoe experiences "a Cure, both for Soul and Body" (93) after an illness sent by God to speed his conversion; we are to understand the person of Crusoe to be a combination of nature and grace, such that in his illness, while nature is in abeyance, the faint voice of grace becomes audible: "But now when I began to be sick, and a leisurely View of the Miseries of Death came to place itself before me; when my Spirits began to sink under the Burthen of a strong Distemper, and Nature was exhausted with the Violence of the Feaver;

Conscience that had slept so long, begun to awake, and I began to reproach my self with my past Life" (90). (One index of the differing distance between nature and grace in two novelists such as Defoe and Fielding is each's treatment of the comparatively new notion of kindness to animals: Defoe's Crusoe hunts and slaughters a lion in passages distasteful to many modern readers, while Fielding's Fanny weeps over a wounded dog: in Defoe's Puritan conception grace and nature are far more disparate than in Fielding's Pelagian world, where all nature – from the hierarchy of stations in society to that of beasts in the field – is infused by grace.)

Smollett provides an exemplary and extraordinary instance of such a double cure in *Sir Launcelot Greaves*, whose hero, throughout the novel described (often in clinical terms) as mad, is finally "cured" of his "disease" not by medical treatment but by *repentance*: "He could not conceive by whose means he had been immured in a madhouse; but he heartily repented of his knight-errantry, as a frolic which might have very serious consequences, with respect to his future life and fortune" (266). (The cure is carefully prepared for by Greaves' earlier stay in prison, where he learns to discriminate true from false objects of charity, and is immediately thereafter rewarded by the providential intervention of an "unexpected accident" which delivers him from the madhouse (276); the last chapters of the novel are a flurry of references to Providence, unexpectedly providing the occasions for Greaves' cure, rewarding each step in it, and reasserting its power and presence in the everyday moral world as Greaves returns to his proper social station and role.)

44 *Northanger Abbey*, pp. 196, 197; see also Mary Poovey's discussion of "probability" in Gothic fiction in "The Novel as Imaginative Order," pp. 57–58.

45 Irvin Ehrenpreis provides the clearest rationale to date for understanding Austen as an Augustan in *Acts of Implication*, ch. 4.

46 See Stuart Tave, *Some Words of Jane Austen*, pp. 53–54, and Hoyt Trowbridge, *From Dryden to Jane Austen*, pp. 214–15, 229–30.

VIII Sentimental communion and probable inference: Mackenzie and Sterne

1 See also Fielding's *Miscellanies*, p. 154, which identifies "This *Art of thriving*" as "the very Reverse of that Doctrine of the Stoics; by which Men were taught to consider themselves as Fellow-Citizens of the World, and to labour jointly for the common Good, without any private Distinction of their own"; this art "is the very Essence of that excellent Art, called *The Art of Politics*" (155; the term "chrematistic" art comes from Aristotle, *Politics*, I. 3. 10–20).

2 Cf. p. 126, of young Henry: "While a boy, he had frequently expressed these sentiments to both his uncle and his cousin: sometimes they apprised him of the total improbability of accomplishing his wishes."

3 *A Sentimental Journey Through France and Italy*, pp. 171–72.

4 Quoted by Peter France, *Rhetoric and Truth in France*, p. 237; according to France, Rousseau's ideal is one of "direct, uninterrupted communication (or communion) with others, through which he would appear in their consciousness as he knew himself to be. In his own words, 'Je voudrais pouvoir en quelque façon rendre mon âme transparente aux yeux

du lecteur'" (236). Jean Starobinski considers the ideal further in *Jean-Jacques Rousseau: la transparence et l'obstacle*.

5 Michael Morgan devotes ch. 5 of *Molyneux's Question: Vision, Touch and the Philosophy of Perception* to Reid's "new nativism."

6 Reid in fact distinguishes perceptions into "original" and "acquired," and into two degrees or kinds of "acquired" perception; our generalizations, however, are broadly true of all Reid's perceptions, and wholly true of those for which the language of probability and signs had been devised in previous centuries.

7 Thus, for instance, Reid lists under "the various sorts of *relation* which fall under our knowledge" the terms "*truth, certainty, probability, theorem, premises, conclusion*" (*Works*, V, 62). Reid can speak in the *Intellectual Powers* of "self-evident probabilities," however, even while making clear that probability is properly a relation, as when he writes, "There are many events depending upon the will of man, in which there is a self-evident probability, greater or less, according to circumstances" (597, 641). Similarly, in chapter 24 of the *Biographia*, Coleridge, arguing in defense of belief in the miracles of Christianity, is capable of saying that Christianity's "consistency with reason" and "The sense, the inward feeling, in the soul of each Believer of its exceeding *desireableness*" are together enough to give "a strong *a priori* probability" to the reality of miracles (II, 215–16).

   The effects of this kind of thinking may most clearly be seen in Knight. In the *Principles of Taste*, because even the laws of nature have only probable status within Knight's associationist scheme, judgments of "natural possibility" are themselves only probable; thus (natural) "possibility is only a degree of credibility" (268)! Whereas in the Restoration, credibility was founded on possibility, to Knight the terms are reversed; where once literary events were believable because readers thought they could actually happen, now they can happen because they are believed.

8 For Beattie's "Common Sense," see below, p. 256; for "Suggestion," see Reid, *Inquiry*, pp. 36–39 (esp. p. 38: "I beg leave to make use of the word *suggestion*, because I know not one more proper, to express a power of the mind, which seems entirely to have escaped the notice of philosophers, and to which we owe many of our simple notions which are neither impressions nor ideas, as well as many original principles of belief"), and Joseph Priestley, *An Examination of Dr. Reid's "Inquiry"* (1774), pp. 18f.

9 Discourse 13 (1786), in *Discourses*, p. 230. William Duff calls this faculty "taste," a third faculty of the mind after judgment and imagination, and that which in particular interprets for us the "signs of passion"; "We may define TASTE to be that internal sense, which, by its own exquisitely nice sensibility, without the assistance of the reasoning faculty, distinguishes and determines the various qualities of the objects submitted to its cognisance; pronouncing, by its own arbitrary verdict, that they are grand or mean ... decent or ridiculous" (*An Essay on Original Genius*, p. 11). Taste also goes under the names "perspicacity" and "discernment" (12).

10 *Philosophical and Critical Observations* I, 20. William Barron defines this faculty in his *Lectures on Belles Lettres* (1806): "Discernment is nothing more than prudent examination, previous to judgment, which leads to decide according to truth" (I, 466).

11 Ogilvie's idea of a "ballance of the intellectual powers" stems from his typically Augustan conception of the faculties as forming a hierarchy; Discernment mediates between higher and lower faculties (as imagination

itself had done in earlier theories). According to Duff's *Essay on Original Genius* (1767), "An exact equilibrium of the reasoning and inventive powers of the mind, is perhaps utterly incompatible with their very different natures; but though a perfect equipoise cannot subsist, yet they may be distributed in such a proportion, as to preserve nearly an equality of weight" (22), productive of the highest human endeavors.

12 Cf. Duff's similar enterprise of cataloguing the "indications" of genius in its various manifestations (through various "signs") in different fields.

13 Though Discernment is an "intuition" which "judges immediately ... without any tedious process of reflection" (I, 274), it is continuous with reason and Understanding: "When closely examined, I am persuaded that no philosopher ever meant to consider instinct (as it is termed) and reason as intellectual powers *really* distinct from, and independent of each other. This distinction however is *seemingly* made by those who define the reasoning faculty to be that by which the mind acquires the knowledge of truth, in consequence of progressionary evidence; and the instinctive or intuitive power is that which decides *instantaneously* of the truth or falsehood of certain propositions, and is termed a sense, from this quickness of perception" (I, 297). Ogilvie proceeds to identify this "intuition" with what other philosophers have called "common sense," finding that "we shall be convinced, with a little attention, that the power (whatever designation we apply to it) by which we deduce effects from a cause, or investigate a cause from its effects, is in no other respect different from that sense (as it is called) by which we perceive the truth of the simplest axiom, than as in the former instances it makes an exertion, which in the latter is unnecessary" (I, 298).

14 Duff's *Essay on Original Genius* is an especially good example of a work which cannot decide whether Discernment is a distinct faculty or merely the joint effort of other, simpler mental powers.

15 "It is the same sagacity by which, in the commerce of life, a man judgeth of the heart or intentions of another from openings that escape the greater number of mankind" (I, 270).

16 Imagination had long had this socializing function: see, for instance, Malebranche's treatment in Book II of *De la Recherche de la vérité*, and of course its function for Hume; what is new is the analysis of its workings in terms of natural *signs*. John P. Wright gives an excellent account of the origins and uses of Hume's doctrine of imagination (making clear its Cartesian and Malebranchean inspiration) in *The Sceptical Realism of David Hume*, sect. 7.

17 See above, pp. 69–70.

18 Sermon 19, "Felix's Behavior towards Paul, Examined" (*Sermons*, I, 312); *Tristram Shandy*, p. 350 (cf. p. 776).

19 Quoted by Stout in *Sentimental Journey*, pp. 162–63 (*Tristram Shandy*, pp. 431–32).

20 "*A Sentimental Journey* and the Syntax of Things," pp. 225, 230.

21 *The Man of Feeling*, pp. 50, 120, 21, 16. Stuart Tave puts this development in perspective in *The Amiable Humorist*; for the Victorian return to wit, see Robert Martin, *The Triumph of Wit*.

22 Sermon 7, "Vindication of Human Nature" (*Sermons*, I, 117, 118).

23 According to Ferguson, the social order is "indeed the result of human action, but not the execution of any human design" (*An Essay on the History of Civil Society* (1767), p. 187). It is generally true of the Scottish

philosophers that they use the same argumentative strategy to explain the origin in the unintended consequences of human action of such diverse social systems as language and money.

24 Battestin, "*A Sentimental Journey* and the Syntax of Things," p. 232.

25 *Sentimental Journey*, 277–78. Commentary on this passage has generally referred to Newton's famous reference in the *Opticks* to nature as the sensorium of God and so treated Sterne's use of the term as religious in the same way. But the passage makes no explicit reference to and does not immediately suggest the idea of divine presence. Rather, in this passage beginning "Dear sensibility!" Sterne means to suggest the *unity* of the world, likening this unity to that of the nervous system of the body. The "sensus communis," "sensorium" (see *Tristram Shandy*, p. 174), or "common sensory" was very much alive in the medical theory of Sterne's contemporaries (a body of theory of which he had a good amateur knowledge) as that place in the body where the nerves joined, and so which was also the seat of the soul; see, for instance, R. K. French's study of Sterne's contemporary, the speculative physician Robert Whytt (1714–66), *Robert Whytt, the Soul, and Medicine*. Sterne's reference in *A Sentimental Journey* is then not explicitly religious but *medical*; it is entirely consistent with the shift from mechanist to vitalist explanation going on in the medical theory of the 1750s and 1760s (a transition in which Whytt played a leading role).

26 Goldsmith, *Works*, IV, 22, 36, 37, 40, 58, 70, 81, 93.

27 For "counterfeit," see, e.g., pp. 106, 143; for the opposition between "apparent candour" and actually keeping a secret, p. 112. John Aikin complains in 1793 of the wide meaning given to *candour* in *Letters . . . to his Son*, p. 91. Cf. Davie, "An Episode in the History of Candor."

In Goldsmith's lexicon, *sincerity* carries its older sense of "integrity" (and so also dependability of signification); see, e.g., pp. 85, 86, 87, 91, 168, 175, 176, 179. The history of this term remains adequately to be written, though Leon Guilhamet makes a start in *The Sincere Ideal*; what is needed is a clearer explication of its earlier sense of integrity (such that, for instance, common Renaissance etymology explains *sincere* as originally meaning "without wax," in the sense that a well made statue requires no patching of crevices or flaws with wax).

28 On *The Vicar*'s relation to Job, see Battestin, *The Providence of Wit*, ch. 7.

29 *Forty Years' Correspondence between Geniusses of boath Sexes and James Elphinston*, I, 215; Gregory, *Lectures on Literature, Taste, and Composition*, I, 26 (note the clear connection of meaning with structure which Gregory posits).

30 Scott, *The Lives of the Novelists*, p. 298.

31 *Forty Years' Correspondence*, I, 163–64; *The Man of Feeling*, p. 5.

32 *A Sentimental Journey*, p. 84.

33 What we have identified as the faculty of discernment, Robert Uphaus (following Battestin in *The Providence of Wit*) calls Sterne's "sixth sense" (see *The Impossible Observer*, ch. 7 and 152n2). Similarly, in his essay on "*A Sentimental Journey* and the Syntax of Things," Battestin calls the faculty Sterne's "body language" (229).

34 Fielding's common formula, "*Plato* or *Aristotle*, or somebody else hath said" (see above, pp. 205, 209 becomes in *Tristram Shandy*: "'Tis either *Plato*, or *Plutarch*, or *Seneca*, or *Xenophon*, or *Epictetus*, or *Theophrastus*, or *Lucian* – or some one perhaps of later date – either *Cardan*, or *Budaeus*, or *Petrarch*, or *Stella* – or possibly it may be some divine or father of the church,

St. *Austin*, or St. *Cyprian*, or *Barnard*, who affirms that . . . – and *Seneca* (I'm positive) tell us somewhere, that . . ." (418).

35 *Tristram Shandy*, pp. 17, 89, 377, 647; cf. pp. 180, 456.

36 See Ralph Cohen, "The Augustan Mode," pp. 19, 31, and *The Unfolding of "The Seasons*," pp. 5, 52, 328. For an analysis of the earlier model of inference at use in the interpretation of metaphor, see below, pp. 278–79; Mackenzie typifies the later, synecdochic view in describing his method of unfolding the character of Harriet and her brother in *The Man of the World*: "A trifling incident, of which I find an account in one of their father's letters, will discriminate their characters better than a train of the most labored expression" (I, 36).

37 See D'Israeli, *A Dissertation on Anecdotes*, pp. 51, 53; *Miscellanies; or, Literary Recreations* (1796), pp. 2 ("Of Miscellanies"), 77 ("On Prefaces"), 148 ("On Poetical Opuscula"), 202 (marginalia), 327 (sonnets), 194–95 (indices).

38 *A Dissertation on Anecdotes*, 16, 74; cf. Ogilvie, *Philosophical and Critical Observations*, on the "sudden flashes of light" by which Discernment grasps its objects (I, 46). According to Duff, original genius "will at one glance, by a kind of intuition, distinguish and select the most proper, as well as most powerful topics of persuasion on every subject. . . . They will operate upon the mind by surprise; they will strike like lightning, and penetrate the heart at once" (*An Essay on Original Genius*, p. 206).

39 *Miscellanies*, pp. 194–95, 201, 197; cf. Sterne's synecdoche in *Tristram Shandy*, after having described "one accidental impression" from Tristram's boyhood: "This is to serve for parents and governors instead of a whole volume upon the subject" (131).

40 *Essay on Man*, I, 169; *The Poetical Works of Sir John Denham*, p. 79.

41 See Cohen's discussion of the prospect poem in "The Augustan Mode." A similar prospect opens Pope's "Windsor Forest"; here, to appreciate the quality of the compliment Pope pays Queen Anne in line 41 ("And Peace and Plenty tell, a STUART reigns"), we must realize that this climactic position in the prospect was usually reserved for praise of a divine rather than a human orderer. On the uses of the catalogue in general, see Leo Spitzer, *Linguistics and Literary History*, pp. 206–08, and (drawing on both Cohen and Spitzer) Claude Rawson's bravura performance in *Gulliver and the Gentle Reader*, chs. 4 and 5.

42 *Disquisitions Metaphysical and Literary* (1793), p. 145.

IX Association, reverie, and the decline of hierarchy

1 *Elements of Criticism*, I, 108; cf. Erasmus Darwin, in Interlude I of *The Loves of the Plants* (1789): "When by the art of the painter or poet a train of ideas is suggested to our imaginations which interests us so much by the pain or pleasure it affords that we cease to *attend* to the irritations of common external objects and cease also to use any voluntary efforts to *compare* these interesting trains of ideas with our previous knowledge of things, a complete *reverie* is produced, during which time, however short, if it be but for a moment, the objects themselves appear to exist before us. This, I think, has been called by an ingenious critic 'the ideal presence' of such objects" (1009, my italics). The phrase "waking dream" also became widely popular; see, e.g., William Cooke, *The Elements of Dramatic Criticism* (1775), p. 95.

Wallace Jackson has discussed the theory of ideal presence in his study of the critical concept of *Immediacy*, ch. 3.

2 Cf. Campbell, *Philosophy of Rhetoric*: "There is a variety of relations to be found in things, by which they are connected ... These we become acquainted with by experience; and prove, by means of association, the source of various combinations of ideas" (258).

3 Coleridge, *Biographia*, I, 92; Hume, *An Abstract of a Treatise of Human Nature*, p. 32.

4 On Alison's influence, see Martin Kallich, *The Association of Ideas*, pp. 428–29, and Coleridge, *Biographia*, II, 222, 306.

5 Cohen, "Association of Ideas and Poetic Unity," p. 467.

6 I hope in another study to trace the history in literary and philosophic psychology of the faculty of attention, changes in the understanding of which were crucial to the development of Augustan theories of reading.

Alison's view of criticism was of course soon contested; see, e.g., Thomas Brown, *Lectures on the Philosophy of the Human Mind* (1820): "That the feeling of beauty, which so readily arises when the mind is passive, and capable, therefore, of long trains of reverie, should not arise when the mind is busied with the objects of contemplation, – or even in any very high degree, when the mind is employed in contemplating the beautiful object itself, but in contemplating it, with a critical estimation of its merits and defects, – is not proof, as has been supposed [by Alison?], that trains of associate images are essential to the production of the emotion" (II, 352); Brown actually goes on to accuse Alison of supposing too much voluntary effort in the workings of imagination (363).

7 See, e.g., the usefulness of Alison to Jerome Stolnitz in his essay "On the Origins of 'Aesthetic Disinterestedness.'"

8 See Whiter's "Attempt to Explain and Illustrate Various Passages of Shakespeare, on a New Principle of Criticism, derived from Mr. Locke's Doctrine of the Association of Ideas," added to *A Specimen of a Commentary on Shakespeare* (1794).

9 *An Essay on the Nature and Immutability of Truth, in Opposition to Sophistry and Scepticism*, in *Essays* (1776), pp. 26–27.

10 *Works*, II, 263. In late Augustan literary and psychological theory digression comes in fact to be more and more difficult to define; ultimately, it comes to be distinguishable from more "methodical" connection only by reference to the mental faculties needed to follow its transitions. Poetry can only be digressive from the point of view of prose, or rather, of the prose treatise; thus T. J. Mathias defends the digressive structure of his *Pursuits of Literature* (1794–97) by arguing that it has the same "unity in the design" as does "Conversation": "It does not appear in the form of an Epistle, or a mock-epic, or a didactic poem; but as a conversation in which subjects are discussed as they arise naturally and easily; and the notes illustrate and enforce the general and particular doctrines. There is as much method and connection, as is consistent with what I state to be my plan, or *design*, if you like that word better. There is unity in the design. Conversation has its laws" ("An Introductory Letter," added to the edition of 1798).

11 See Robert Langbaum, *The Poetry of Experience*, pp. 192–99.

12 *Essays on the Intellectual Powers of Man*, p. 660; cf. *Inquiry into the Human Mind*, p. 213, quoted above, p. 225.

Concluding theoretical postscript

1 See for a version of this argument made in terms of the distinction between types and tokens of a text William Tolhurst and Samuel Wheeler, "On Textual Individuation."

2 See for a theory of implication applied to diverse texts from a given period Irvin Ehrenpreis, *Acts of Implication*.

3 The point is a familiar one, as is the effort to discover, for instance, a Kantian inspiration in various New-Critical manifestoes. A very useful study could be made of Bernard Bosanquet's *Three Lectures on Aesthetic* (1915) as a transitional stage between idealist/Romantic aesthetics and the work of modern formalist critics.

4 See for an especially clear instance Jonathan Culler, *Structuralist Poetics* (1975). Studies which begin with such prescriptions are doomed to fail precisely because the boundaries of the literary – and the meaning of the term "literature" itself – differ across periods.

5 See for such a consummation David Bleich, *Subjective Criticism* (1978).

6 As, for instance, do skeptical claims about translation such as those made by the Sapir–Whorf hypothesis, when the meaning of any supposedly untranslatable utterance from another language is demonstrated not to be captured in some proposed translation. See Hirsch, *The Aims of Interpretation*, ch. 3, and more recently, Hilary Putnam's compelling arguments against varied manifestations of relativist skepticism in *Reason, Truth and History* (1981), especially ch. 5.

7 In *The Act of Reading: A Theory of Aesthetic Response*, Wolfgang Iser baldly shapes his account of the reader's transaction with the text in terms of modern "aesthetic" norms (the same procedures, less obviously, govern also *The Implied Reader*). More baldly, Stanley Fish's "affective stylistics" assumes a stable ahistorical structure of affect – assumes, that is, that affect can exist in abstraction from the actual conditions of social (including literary) life. Varied authors whose opinions oppose some modern consensus (particularly some moral consensus) are especially prey to such revisionary reading: if it was the wearing of New-Critical blinders which created the ironical Defoe, it is something far more troubling (and less excusable) which has given us Sterne the phenomenologist or Richardson the student of the psychology of writing.

8 Barbara Lewalski, *Milton's Brief Epic: The Genre, Meaning, and Art of "Paradise Regained"* (1966); for related arguments, see Rosalie Colie, *The Resources of Kind*.

9 Kendall Walton, "Categories of Art." See for analyses of the importance of Walton's considerations in the interpretation of particular texts Irvin Ehrenpreis, "*Rasselas* and Some Meanings of Structure in Literary Criticism," and (on Swift's elegy on Marlborough) Timothy Keegan, *An Introduction to the Poems of Jonathan Swift*, ch. 3.

10 "Historical Knowledge and Literary Understanding," p. 237.

11 Cohen explains the logic of such alteration at the level of a change in period norms in "Some Thoughts on the Problems of Literary Change."

Appendix A The Foucault–Hacking hypothesis

1 See Rescher, *Peirce's Philosophy of Science*, pp. 25–30.

2 See F. N. David, *Gods, Games, and Gambling*; Kendall and Pearson,

Studies in the History of Statistics and Probability; S. Sambursky, *The Physical World of the Greeks*, pp. 176–81, 258, and "On the Possible and the Probable in Ancient Greece." William Ames protests the corruption of sortilege into a form of amusement ("lusory lots") in *Technometry*, p. 3.

3 It is true, however, that the earliest randomizers were not dice but *tali*, fragments of bone so irregularly shaped as not to permit an equiprobable set of alternative outcomes; that the earliest games played with cubical dice used three more often than one or two dice, making calculations of probability more difficult (though perhaps so many were used for this very reason); that in those games whose rules we know, those throws which are statistically rarest were not always the most valuable, nor the commonest the least valuable; and that many of these "games" were scarcely games at all, but complex exercises in divination. Nonetheless, and despite Hacking's claim that in ancient Rome "Somebody with only the most modest knowledge of probability could have won himself the whole of Gaul in a week" (*Emergence*, p. 3), most historians find ancient and mediaeval gamblers to have had an excellent practical grasp of the doctrine of chances; see Kendall, "The Beginnings of a Probability Calculus" (*Studies*, I, 19–21), and Sambursky, "On the Possible," p. 45.

4 See, for instance, the passages reproduced from such works as the *Chaunce of the Dyse* and the pseudo-Ovidian *De Vetula* in Kendall, "Beginnings," pp. 24–26.

5 As translated by Thomas Reid in *Essays on the Intellectual Powers*, p. 663; for the original, see *De Divinatione*, I. xii.

6 *Religion and the Decline of Magic*, pp. 655, 666.

7 See, for exceptional instances, Jacob Klein, *Greek Mathematical Thought and the Origin of Algebra*, and H. Freudenthal, "Y avait-il une crise des fondements des mathématiques dans l'antiquité?"

8 An episteme is thus a holistic unit implicitly containing its own determinations, with the result that conceptual development within the episteme need not be given a historical explanation that is causal; see, e.g., Hacking's argument that "Neither meanings nor intentions are to play any central role in the analysis" of the development of concepts ("Michel Foucault's Immature Science," p. 48). It is of course a common criticism of theories such as this that the more holistic the episteme becomes, the more difficult it is to explain (in any sense) the displacement of one episteme by another.

9 *The Emergence of Probability*, p. 73.

10 Foucault has taken his list of variables from a single source, the fourth chapter of Part I of the Port-Royal *Logic*, a chapter which first appeared in the revised edition of 1683.

11 What Foucault means by "divination" is far from clear, but to the extent that he means the making manifest of things hidden (occult), we have found the Classical period to be no less concerned with such revelation than its forebears. Indeed, to historians of science, inference from outer to inner, from manifest to hidden properties of things – what Maurice Mandelbaum calls "transdiction" and J. E. McGuire, in a slightly different sense, "transduction" – was the central philosophical problem of the "new" science of the seventeenth century. (See Mandelbaum, "Newton and Boyle and the Problem of Transdiction," in *Philosophy, Science, and*

Sense Perception, pp. 61–117; McGuire, "Atoms and the 'Analogy of Nature.'") To the extent that Foucault means by divination the supernatural art of foretelling, we have already found this criticized in antiquity; Lynn Thorndike writes of the seventeenth century: "As had previously been the case in the sixteenth century, most arts of divination were no longer living realities nor extensively practised, but possessed only an historical interest as relics of paganism or as classical antiquities" (*History of Magic*, VIII, 476). The non-supernatural art of foretelling by signs, of course, is typical of no age in particular.

12 We have already examined the role of resemblance in Locke's account of probability; it is hard to square Foucault's claim with what we know to be the category's importance to Berkeley, particularly in his central principle that ideas resemble only one another, not material objects, or to Descartes, whose seventeenth-century French critics made particular objection to his use of principles of resemblance, especially to his views that causes must be like their effects and the mind like what it knows (see R. A. Watson, *The Downfall of Cartesianism in France*). The category of resemblance really only begins to come under serious scrutiny in the late eighteenth century, when writers such as Reid object to assumptions made about it by theorists of ideas from Locke to Hume; it becomes an issue in itself only in the nineteenth century, especially in the context of idealism and its doctrine of internal relations. (See, e.g., F. H. Bradley "On Professor James' Doctrine of Simple Resemblance," a response to James' *Principles of Psychology* [1890] which originally appeared in three issues of *Mind* in 1893, and is reprinted in Bradley's *Collected Essays*, I, 287–302.)

A great deal has been made of Foucault's claim that the transition from Renaissance to Classical brought with it a change in the conception of the sign, such that where once signification was thought to be rooted in a relation of resemblance, it came to be rooted in identity. Some notion of resemblance would indeed seem to underpin the kinds of signs which made up the fabric of Renaissance science, or that tendency in it called "Renaissance naturalism" (e.g., by Richard Westfall, in *The Construction of Modern Science*); thus for instance Sir Thomas Browne finds the quincunx to be a nearly universal signature and ground of intelligibility of things (and even of the interrelations of literary genres: see Rosalie Colie, *The Resources of Kind*, pp. 84–85). In literature itself, scholars such as Ralph Cohen and Donald Benson have found in the seventeenth century a shift in "hieroglyphic" or "emblematic" poetic methods to more "sequential" and "expansive" procedures (see Benson, citations in bibliography, and Cohen, "Innovation and Variation," p. 5). But it might be argued just as well that Renaissance signs depend on a fundamental identity (or identity of essence) between sign and signified, Augustan signs only a resemblance of qualities; much closer attention to the philosophical presuppositions of the theory of signs in each age will be necessary to decide such an issue. Individual citations must without such analysis remain ambiguous: thus for instance Tasso writes in his *Discourses* on heroic poetry (1594): "the poet bases his work on some true action and considers it as verisimilar; hence his matter is the verisimilar, which may be true or false, but is generally closer to true. It would not be at all reasonable that the verisimilar should be closer to the false, from which it greatly differs. For where there is unlikeness, there cannot be identity, whereas things that resemble each other can be the same, if not in substance at least in quality" (28).

13 Thomas Church, *A Vindication of the Miraculous Powers which subsisted in the Three First Centuries of the Christian Church*; with Gibbon, quoted in Hacking, *Emergence*, pp. 19, 23. Hacking deals similarly with the following, a footnote to chapter 24 of Gibbon's *Decline and Fall*: "According to Rufinus, an immediate supply of provisions was stipulated by the treaty, and Theodoret affirms that the obligation was faithfully discharged by the Persians. Such a fact is probable, but undoubtedly false." Again, however, the more likely reading is not that it is Rufinus' authority which constitutes the claim's probability, but rather that the claim is analogically like what we should expect. (In fact, Gibbon's views on probability are very much those of his time: see Hoyt Trowbridge, "Edward Gibbon, Literary Critic," in *From Dryden to Jane Austen*, pp. 185–99.) Hacking is unfamiliar also with older senses of the word *evidence*: see, e.g., p. 83, where by misreading this term he has Bishop Wilkins arguing in *Of the Principles and Duties of Natural Religion* (1672) that God is no more than "an object of probable opinion."

14 Price, "An Essay towards solving a Problem in the Doctrine of Chances," pp. 371–72, partially quoted in *Emergence*, p. 76. On the relation of Price to Bayes, see D. O. Thomas, *The Honest Mind: The Thought and Work of Richard Price*, pp. 81–82, 128–35. In mentioning Hume, Hacking is perhaps thinking of that renewed interest in analogical and inductive reasoning among Hume's Common-Sense adversaries; see Richard Olson, *Scottish Philosophy and British Physics 1750–1880*, chs. 4–5.

15 On such discussions, see Morris, "Descartes and Probable Knowledge"; Laurens Laudan, "The Clock Metaphor and Probabilism: The Impact of Descartes on English Methodological Thought, 1650–1655," and "The Nature and Sources of Locke's View of Hypotheses"; McGuire, "Atoms and the 'Analogy of Nature'"; Jackson Cope, *Joseph Glanvill: Anglican Apologist*, pp. 61–63, 106–07, 130–42. (Laudan's study of Locke has been partially corrected by John Yolton in "The Science of Nature.")

16 Critics of Hacking who assemble such instances are Garber and Zabell ("On the Emergence of Probability," esp. pp. 20–21) and Ivo Schneider ("Why do We Find the Origin of a Calculus of Probabilities in the Seventeenth Century?" pp. 4–6); most commonly cited among mediaeval scientific thinkers who appeal to a (perhaps measurable) probability is Oresme.

17 See Carnap, *Logical Foundations of Probability*, ch. 2; J. L. Mackie, *Truth, Probability, and Paradox*, pp. 154–236.

18 Schneider cedes this honor to Huyghens, commenting of the Port-Royal *Logic* that "The only thing new here, in comparison with Huyghens' computation of expectation values, is the translation of ratios of chances in random decisions into a ratio of degrees of probability" ("Why do We Find the Origin of a Calculus of Probabilities," p. 10).

19 See especially Garber and Zabell, "On the Emergence of Probability."

20 On the awareness in the Renaissance of skeptical writings, see Schneider, "Why do We Find the Origin of a Calculus of Probabilities"; on gaming, see, in addition to Schneider, Garber and Zabell, "On the Emergence of Probability," and Ernest Coumet, "La Théorie du hasard est-elle née par hasard?" and "Le Problème des partis avant Pascal."

21 See Sambursky, *The Physical World of the Greeks*, pp. 176–81; D. M.

Balme, "Aristotle on Nature and Chance"; Coumet, "La Théorie du hasard"; and Schneider, "Why do We Find the Origin of a Calculus of Probabilities."

Appendix B John Dennis and Christian marvels

1 See James A. W. Heffernan, "Wordsworth and Dennis."
2 Kallich, *The Association of Ideas*, pp. 43–45; Monk, *The Sublime*, p. 49.
3 Most Augustans understood how critical Locke was in his treatment of association; Sterne writes in *Tristram Shandy*, for instance, of that "strange combination of ideas": "the sagacious *Locke*, who certainly understood the nature of these things better than most men, affirms [association] to have produced more wry actions than all other sources of prejudice whatsoever" (7). By the end of the century, however, it was commonplace to refer to the theory as "Mr. Locke's Doctrine" of association: see, e.g., Walter Whiter, cited above, p. 330 n8.
   It is seldom pointed out that Hobbes' treatment of association (which he calls an "unguided Trayne of Imaginations") at *Leviathan* I. 3 is really just as critical as Locke's. As unguided, association is distinguished from "the Discourse of the Mind, when it is governed by designe"; Hobbes defines this latter, guided train of ideas as "nothing but *Seeking*, or the faculty of Invention, which the Latines call *Sagacitas*, and *Solertia*." Applied to future contingencies, this use of mind "is called *Foresight*, and *Prudence*, or *Providence*; and sometimes *Wisedome*"; Hobbes says of this power of guessing that "the best guesser, [is] he that is most versed and studied in the matters he guesses at: for he hath most *Signes* to guess by," while admitting that "such conjecture, through the difficulty of observing all circumstances, be very fallacious." Hobbesian conjecture and probable inference, then, is *not* a process of association.
4 Morris, *The Religious Sublime*, p. 74; Monk, *The Sublime*, p. 52.
5 Nicolson, *Mountain Gloom and Mountain Glory*, p. 250.
6 Rymer, *Critical Works*, p. 108. What Rymer calls "Modification," we have called "diversification."
7 This is the universal definition of abstraction from Descartes and Locke to the end of the eighteenth century. See, e.g., Dugald Stewart, *Works*, II, 22: "The process of classification supposes a power of attending to some of the qualities, or circumstances of objects and events, and of withdrawing the attention from the rest. This power is called by the logicians Abstraction."
8 *Philosophical Principles of Religion: Natural and Revealed* (1715), Pt. I, 50. Cheyne's analogical equation of Newtonian attraction with divine love is of course typical; see, e.g., Desaguliers' "Newtonian System of the World."

Bibliography

My general procedure has been to omit works merely mentioned, without real comment on their contents, and works, especially poems and classical texts, available in many editions. In addition I have included works not mentioned in the text which I have found useful in preparing it.

Aaron, Richard I. *John Locke.* 2nd ed. Oxford: Clarendon Press, 1955.
Abrams, Meyer H. *The Mirror and the Lamp: Romantic Theory and the Critical Tradition.* New York: Oxford Univ. Press, 1953.
    Natural Supernaturalism: Tradition and Revolution in Romantic Literature. New York: Norton, 1971.
Addison, Joseph. *Miscellaneous Works in Verse and Prose.* Ed. A. C. Guthkelch. 2 vols. London: Bell, 1914.
Addison, Joseph, *et al. The Spectator.* Ed. Donald F. Bond. 5 vols. Oxford: Clarendon Press, 1965.
Agricola, Rudolphus. *De Inventione dialectica libri tres.* Cologne, 1528.
Agrippa von Nettesheim, Henry Cornelius. *De Incertitudine et vanitate scientiarum et artium.* 1531. Lugduni, 1580.
Aikin, John. *An Essay on the Application of Natural History to Poetry.* London, 1777.
    Letters from a Father to his Son, on Various Topics, Relative to Literature and the Conduct of Life. 1793. 3rd ed. London, 1796.
    Letters to a Young Lady on a Course of English Poetry. 1804. New York, 1806.
Albrecht, William F. *The Sublime Pleasures of Tragedy: A Study of Critical Theory from Dennis to Keats.* Lawrence: Univ. Press of Kansas, 1975.
Alison, Archibald. *Essays on the Nature and Principles of Taste.* Edinburgh, 1790.
Alkon, Paul K. "The Odds Against Friday: Defoe, Bayes, and Inverse Probability." In *Probability, Time, and Space in Eighteenth-Century Literature.* Ed. Paula R. Backscheider. New York: AMS Press, 1979, pp. 29–61.
Alter, Robert. "The Picaroon as Fortune's Plaything." In *Essays on the Eighteenth-Century Novel.* Ed. Robert D. Spector. Bloomington: Indiana Univ. Press, 1965, pp. 131–53.
Altman, Joel B. *The Tudor Play of Mind: Rhetorical Inquiry and the Development of Elizabethan Drama.* Berkeley: Univ. of California Press, 1978.
Amarasinghe, Upali. *Dryden and Pope in the Early Nineteenth Century: A Study of Changing Literary Taste 1800–1830.* Cambridge: Cambridge Univ. Press, 1962.
Ames, William. *Conscience with the Power and Cases Thereof.* N.p., 1639.
    Technometry. Ed. and tr. Lee W. Gibbs. Philadelphia: Univ. of Pennsylvania Press, 1979.
Arbuthnot, John. *Of the Laws of Chance, or, a Method of Calculation of the Hazards of Game.* London, 1692.

"An Argument for Divine Providence, taken from the Constant Regularity observ'd in the Births of Both Sexes." *Philosophical Transactions of the Royal Society of London*, 27 (1710), 186–90.

Aristotle. *Aristotelis De Poetica liber, Latinè conversus*. London, 1623.

The Basic Works of Aristotle. Ed. Richard McKeon. New York: Random House, 1941.

Armstrong, C. J. R. "The Dialectical Road to Truth: the Dialogue." In *French Renaissance Studies 1540–70: Humanism and the Encyclopedia*. Ed. Peter Sharratt. Edinburgh: Edinburgh Univ. Press, 1976, pp. 36–51.

Armstrong, John. *Miscellanies*. 2 vols. London, 1770.

Armstrong, K. L. "John Locke's 'Doctrine of Signs': A New Metaphysics." *Journal of the History of Ideas*, 26 (1965), 369–82.

Arnauld, Antoine, "La Théologie morale des Jésuites." 1644. In *Oeuvres de Messire Antoine Arnauld*. Paris, 1779, XXIX, 74–94.

Arnauld, Antoine and Nicole, Pierre. *La Logique, ou l'art de penser*. Paris, 1662.

Auroux, Sylvain. *La Sémiotique des encyclopédistes: essai d'épistémologie historique des sciences du langage*. Paris: Payot, 1979.

Austen, Jane. *Emma*. Ed. David Lodge and James Kinsley. London: Oxford Univ. Press, 1971.

The Novels of Jane Austen. Ed. R. W. Chapman. 5 vols. 3rd ed. London: Oxford Univ. Press, 1934.

Austin, Gilbert. *Chironomia, or, a Treatise on Rhetorical Delivery*. 1806. Facs. rpt. ed. Mary M. Rabb and Lester Thonssen. Carbondale: Southern Illinois Univ. Press, 1966.

Bacon, Francis. *The Works of Francis Bacon*. Ed. James Spedding, Robert L. Ellis, and Douglas D. Heath. 15 vols. London: Longmans, 1857.

Bailey, Nathan. *Dictionarium Britannicum: Or a more Complete Universal Etymological Dictionary than any Extant*. London, 1730.

Baker, Keith Michael. *Condorcet: From Natural Philosophy to Social Mathematics*. Chicago: Univ. of Chicago Press, 1975.

Balme, D. M. "Greek Science and Mechanism. I. Aristotle on Nature and Chance." *The Classical Quarterly*, 33 (1939), 129–38.

Bamborough, J. B. *The Little World of Man*. London: Longmans, 1952.

Bantock, G. H. *Studies in the History of Educational Theory. I: Artifice and Nature, 1350–1765*. London: Allen & Unwin, 1980.

Barbauld, Anna Laetitia. *The Works of Anna Laetitia Barbauld*. 2 vols. London, 1825.

Barnard, H. C. *The French Tradition in Education: Ramus to Mme Necker de Saussure*. Cambridge: Cambridge Univ. Press, 1922.

Barnes, Jonathan. *Aristotle's Posterior Analytics*. Oxford: Clarendon Press, 1975.

Barron, William. *Lectures on Belles Lettres and Logic*. 2 vols. London, 1806.

Barthes, Roland. "Sémiologie et médecine." In *Les Sciences de folie*. Ed. Roger Bastide. The Hague: Mouton, 1972, pp. 37–46.

Batten, Charles, Jr. *Pleasurable Instruction: Form and Convention in Eighteenth-Century Travel Literature*. Berkeley: Univ. of California Press, 1978.

Battestin, Martin C. *The Moral Basis of Fielding's Art: A Study of "Joseph Andrews."* Middletown: Wesleyan Univ. Press, 1959.

"The Problem of *Amelia*: Hume, Barrow, and the Conversion of Captain Booth." *ELH*, 41 (1974), 613–48.

Bibliography

The Providence of Wit: Aspects of Form in Augustan Literature and the Arts. Oxford: Clarendon Press, 1974.

"A Sentimental Journey and the Syntax of Things." In *Augustan Worlds: New Essays in Eighteenth-Century Literature.* Ed. J. C. Hilson *et al.* London: Leicester Univ. Press, 1978, pp. 223–39.

Battie, William. *A Treatise on Madness.* London, 1758.

Baumgarten, Alexander. *Reflections on Poetry.* 1735. Tr. Karl Aschenbrenner and W. B. Holther. Berkeley: Univ. of California Press, 1954.

Baxter, Richard. *The Reasons of the Christian Religion.* 1655. London, 1667.

Beattie, James. *Essays: On Poetry and Music, As They Affect the Mind.* 1776. 3rd ed. London, 1779.

Essays. Edinburgh, 1776.

Dissertations, Moral and Critical. 2 vols. London, 1783.

Beattie, Lester M. *John Arbuthnot, Mathematician and Satirist.* Cambridge, Mass.: Harvard Univ. Press, 1937.

Beckford, William. *Dreams, Waking Thoughts and Incidents.* Ed. Robert J. Gemmett. Rutherford, N.J.: Fairleigh Dickinson Univ. Press, 1971.

Belaval, Yvon. "Vico and Anti-Cartesianism." In *Giambattista Vico: An International Symposium.* Ed. Giorgio Tagliacozzo. Baltimore: The Johns Hopkins Univ. Press, 1969, pp. 77–91.

Belsham, William. *Essays, Philosophical and Moral, Historical and Literary.* 2 vols. London, 1799.

Benson, Donald R. "Platonism and Neoclassic Metaphor: Dryden's *Eleonora* and Donne's *Anniversaries.*" *Studies in Philology,* 68 (1971), 340–56.

"Dryden's *The Hind and the Panther*: Transubstantiation and Figurative Language." *Journal of the History of Ideas,* 43 (1982), 195–208.

Berkeley, George. *Berkeley's Philosophical Writings.* Ed. David M. Armstrong. London: Macmillan, 1965.

Bird, Otto. "The Tradition of the Logical Topics: Aristotle to Ockham." *Journal of the History of Ideas,* 23 (1962), 307–23.

Blackmore, Richard. Preface to *Prince Arthur.* 1695. In *Critical Essays of the Seventeenth Century.* Ed. J. E. Spingarn. Oxford: Clarendon Press, 1909, III, 227–41.

Essays on Several Subjects. London, 1716.

Blackwall, Anthony. *An Introduction to the Classics: With an Essay, on the Nature and Use of those Emphatical and Beautiful Figures which give Strength and Ornament to Writing.* 2nd ed. London, 1719.

Blackwell, Thomas. *An Enquiry into the Life and Writings of Homer.* London, 1735.

Blair, Hugh. *Lectures on Rhetoric and Belles Lettres.* 2 vols. London, 1783.

Blake, William. *Poetry and Prose.* Ed. Geoffrey Keynes. London: Nonesuch, 1927.

Blic, J. de. "Barthélémy de Medina et les origines du probabilisme." *Ephemerides Theologiae Lovanienses,* 7 (1930), 46–83, 264–91.

Bloch, Olivier René. *La Philosophie de Gassendi: nominalisme, matérialisme, et métaphysique.* The Hague: Martinus Nijhoff, 1971.

Blom, Siri. "Concerning a Controversy on the Meaning of Probability." *Theoria,* 21 (1955), 65–98.

Blount, Thomas Pope. *De Re Poetica: or, Remark's upon Poetry.* London, 1694.

Blundeville, Thomas. *The Art of Logike.* London, 1599.

Bodin, Jean. *Method for the Easy Comprehension of History.* 1566. Tr. Beatrice Reynolds. New York: Columbia Univ. Press, 1945.

Boethius. *De Topicis differentiis*. Ed. and tr. Eleonore Stump. Ithaca: Cornell Univ. Press, 1978.

Boucé, Paul-Gabriel. *The Novels of Tobias Smollett*. Tr. Antonia White. London: Longman Group, 1976.

Boyle, Robert. *The Sceptical Chymist*. 1661. Ed. E. A. Moelwyn-Hughes. London: Dent, 1964.

The Works of the Honourable Robert Boyle. Ed. Thomas Birch. 5 vols. London, 1772.

Bradley, Francis Herbert. *Collected Essays*. 2 vols. Oxford: Clarendon Press, 1935.

Bray, René. *La Formation de la doctrine classique en France*. 1927. Paris: Nizet, 1966.

Brody, Jules. *Boileau and Longinus*. Geneva: Droz, 1958.

Brown, Thomas. *Lectures on the Philosophy of the Human Mind*. 1820. 3 vols. Andover, 1822.

Browne, Thomas. *The Prose Works of Sir Thomas Browne*. Ed. Norman J. Endicott. New York: Doubleday, 1967.

Bruce, Donald. *Radical Doctor Smollett*. Boston: Houghton Mifflin, 1964.

Bryson, Norman. *Word and Image: French Painting of the Ancien Régime*. Cambridge: Cambridge Univ. Press, 1981.

Buchanan, Scott. *The Doctrine of Signatures: A Defense of Theory in Medicine*. New York: Harcourt, Brace, 1938.

Buck, Peter. "Seventeenth-Century Political Arithmetic: Civil Strife and Vital Statistics." *Isis*, 68 (1977), 67–84.

"People Who Counted: Political Arithmetic in the Eighteenth Century." *Isis*, 73 (1982), 28–45.

Buffier, Claude. *Oeuvres philosophiques du Père Buffier*. Ed. Francisque Bouillier. Paris: Charpentier, 1843.

Bulwer, John. *Chirologia: or, the natvrall langvage of the hand ... Whereunto is added Chironomia: or the art of manvall rhetoricke*. London, 1644.

Bundy, Murray Wright. *The Theory of the Imagination in Classical and Mediaeval Thought*. Univ. of Illinois Studies in Language and Literature, vol. 12, nos. 2–3. Urbana: Univ. of Illinois Press, 1927.

Bunn, James H. "Signs of Randomness in *Roderick Random*." *Eighteenth-Century Studies*, 14 (1981), 452–69.

Burke, Edmund. *A Philosophical Enquiry into the Origin of Our Ideas of the Sublime and the Beautiful*. 1757. Ed. J. T. Boulton. London: Routledge & Kegan Paul, 1958.

Burnet, Thomas. *The Sacred Theory of the Earth*. Ed. Basil Willey. Carbondale: Southern Illinois Univ. Press, 1965.

Burney, Frances. *Evelina, or the History of a Young Lady's Entrance into the World*. 1778. Ed. Edward A. Bloom. London: Oxford Univ. Press, 1968.

Butler, Joseph. *The Analogy of Religion, Natural and Revealed, to the Constitution and Course of Nature*. 1736. Ed. E. C. Mossner. New York: Ungar, 1961.

Butt, John. *Pope's Taste in Shakespeare*. London: Oxford Univ. Press, 1936.

Byrne, Edmund. *Probability and Opinion: a study in the medieval presuppositions of post-medieval theories of probability*. The Hague: Martinus Nijhoff, 1968.

Camden, Carroll. "The Mind's Construction in the Face." In *Renaissance Studies in Honor of Hardin Craig*. Ed. Baldwin Maxwell *et al*. Stanford: Stanford Univ. Press, 1941, pp. 208–20.

Campbell, George. *The Philosophy of Rhetoric*. 1776. London: William Tegg, 1850.

Carnap, Rudolf. *Logical Foundations of Probability*. Chicago: Univ. of Chicago Press, 1950.

Casaubon, Meric. *A Letter of Meric Casaubon ... to Peter du Moulin*. Cambridge, 1669.

Castellio, Sebastiano. *Concerning Heretics*. 1554. Tr. Roland Bainton. New York: Columbia Univ. Press, 1935.

Castelvetro, Ludovico. *Poetica d'Aristotele vulgarizzata et sposta*. Vienna, 1570.

Castor, Grahame. *Pléiade Poetics: A Study in Sixteenth-Century Thought and Terminology*. Cambridge: Cambridge Univ. Press, 1964.

Cauthen, Irby, Jr. "Fielding's Digressions in *Joseph Andrews*." *College English*, 17 (1956), 379–82.

Chapelain, Jean. "Lettere ... sur le Poeme d'Adonis du Chevalier Marino." 1623. In Giambattista Marino, *Adone*. Ed. Marzio Pieri. Rome: Laterza, 1975, I, 17–50.

Les Sentiments de l'Académie française sur la tragi-comédie du Cid. In *La Querelle du Cid*. Ed. Armand Gasté. 1898; facs. rpt. Geneva: Slatkine, 1970.

Chapin, Chester F. *Personification in Eighteenth-Century English Poetry*. New York: King's Crown Press, 1955.

Charleton, Walter. *Physiologia Epicuro-Gassendo-Charletoniana: or a Fabrick of Science Natural, upon the Hypothesis of Atoms*. London, 1654.

Charron, Pierre. *Of Wisdom*. 1601. Tr. Samson Lennard. 3 vols. London, 1607.

Chesterfield, Philip Dormer Stanhope, fourth Earl. *The Letters of Lord Chesterfield to his Son*. Ed. Charles Strachey and Annette Calthorp. 2 vols. London: Methuen, 1901.

Cheyne, George. *Philosophical Principles of Religion: Natural and Revealed*. In two parts. London, 1715.

Cicero. *Academica*. Tr. H. Rackham. Loeb Classical Library. London: William Heinemann, 1967.

De Oratore and *De Partitione oratoria*. Tr. H. Rackham. 2 vols. Loeb Classical Library. London: William Heinemann, 1977.

De Divinatione. Tr. William A. Falconer. Loeb Classical Library. London: William Heinemann, 1964.

Tusculan Disputations. Tr. J. E. King. Loeb Classical Library. London: William Heinemann, 1927.

Clausen, Christopher. *The Place of Poetry: Two Centuries of an Art in Crisis*. Lexington: Univ. Press of Kentucky, 1981.

Cohen, L. Jonathan. *The Probable and the Provable*. Oxford: Clarendon Press, 1977.

"Some Historical Reflections on the Baconian Concept of Probability." *Journal of the History of Ideas*, 41 (1980), 219–31.

"Bayesianism versus Baconianism in the Evaluation of Medical Diagnosis." *British Journal for the Philosophy of Science*, 31 (1980), 45–62.

Cohen, Ralph. "Association of Ideas and Poetic Unity." *Philological Quarterly*, 36 (1957), 465–74.

"The Transformation of Passion: A Study of Hume's Theories of Tragedy." *Philological Quarterly*, 41 (1962), 450–64.

"The Augustan Mode in English Poetry." *Eighteenth-Century Studies*, 1 (1967), 3–32.

The Unfolding of "The Seasons." Baltimore: The Johns Hopkins Univ. Press, 1970.

"On the Interrelations of Eighteenth-Century Literary Forms." In *New Approaches to Eighteenth-Century Literature.* English Institute Essays, 1974. Ed. Phillip Harth. New York: Columbia Univ. Press, 1974, pp. 33–78.

"Innovation and Variation: Literary Change and Georgic Poetry." In *Literature and History.* Los Angeles: William Andrews Clark Memorial Library, 1974, pp. 3–42.

"Pope's Meanings and the Strategies of Interrelation." In *English Literature in the Age of Disguise.* Ed. Maximillian Novak. Berkeley: Univ. of California Press, 1977, pp. 101–30.

"Historical Knowledge and Literary Understanding." *Papers on Language and Literature,* 14 (1978), 227–48.

"Some Thoughts on the Problems of Literary Change 1750–1800." *Dispositio,* 4 (1979), 145–62.

Coke, Zachary. *The Art of Logick; or the Entire Body of Logick in English.* London, 1654.

Coleridge, Samuel Taylor. *Biographia Literaria.* 2 vols. London, 1817.

Ed. John Shawcross. 2 vols. Oxford: Clarendon Press, 1907.

Coleridge's Miscellaneous Criticism. Ed. Thomas M. Raysor. Cambridge, Mass.: Harvard Univ. Press, 1936.

Marginalia I. Ed. George Whalley. Pt. 12: *The Collected Works of Samuel Taylor Coleridge.* Princeton: Princeton Univ. Press, 1980.

Shakespearean Criticism. Ed. Thomas M. Raysor. 2 vols. London: Dent, 1974.

Colie, Rosalie. *The Resources of Kind: Genre-Theory in the Renaissance.* Ed. Barbara K. Lewalski. Berkeley: Univ. of California Press, 1973.

Congreve, William. *Incognita: or, Love and Duty Reconcil'd. A Novel.* 1691. In *Shorter Novels: Jacobean and Restoration.* Ed. Philip Henderson. London: Dent, 1930, pp. 237–303.

Cooke, William. *The Elements of Dramatic Criticism.* London, 1775.

Cope, Jackson I. *Joseph Glanvill: Anglican Apologist.* St. Louis: Washington Univ. Press, 1956.

Corneille, Pierre. *Oeuvres de Pierre Corneille.* Ed. Charles Marty-Laveaux. 10 vols. Paris: Hachette, 1862.

Coumet, Ernest. "Le Problème des partis avant Pascal." *Archives Internationales d'histoire des sciences,* 18 (1965), 245–72.

"La Théorie du hasard est-elle née par hasard?" *Annales,* 25 (1970), 574–98.

[Coventry, Francis.] *An Essay on the New Species of Writing Founded by Mr. Fielding.* London, 1751.

Cowley, Abraham. *The Complete Works in Verse and Prose.* Ed. Alexander Grosart. 2 vols. Edinburgh: privately printed, 1881.

Craig, John. "A Calculation of the Credibility of Human Testimony." *Philosophical Transactions of the Royal Society of London,* 21 (1699), 359–65.

Theologiae Christianae Principia Mathematica. 1699. Partially rpt. and tr. as *Craig's Rules of Historical Evidence. History and Theory,* Beiheft 4 (1964).

Crane, Ronald S. *The Idea of the Humanities.* 2 vols. Chicago: Univ. of Chicago Press, 1967.

Croll, Oswald. *Basilica Chymica.* 1609. Tr. anon. London, 1670.

Crombie, Alistair C. *Grosseteste and Experimental Science.* Oxford: Clarendon Press, 1962.

"Contingent Expectation and Uncertain Choice: Historical Contexts of Arguments from Probabilities in the Biomedical Sciences." Unpublished MS.

Crookshank, F. G. "The Importance of a Theory of Signs and a Critique of Language in the Study of Medicine." In C. K. Ogden and I. A. Richards, *The Meaning of Meaning*. 1923. New York: Harcourt, Brace, 1938, pp. 337–55.

Crousaz, Jean Pierre de. *A New Treatise of the Art of Thinking: Or, A Compleat System of Reflections, Concerning the Conduct and Improvement of the Mind*. 1712. Tr. anon. 2 vols. London, 1724.

Crutwell, Patrick. "Physiology and Psychology in Shakespeare's Age." *Journal of the History of Ideas*, 12 (1951), 75–89.

Culler, Jonathan. *Ferdinand de Saussure*. Harmondsworth: Penguin, 1977.

Curtius, Ernst Robert. *European Literature and the Latin Middle Ages*. Tr. Willard Trask. Princeton: Princeton Univ. Press, 1953.

Damrosch, Leopold, Jr. *Samuel Johnson and the Tragic Sense*. Princeton: Princeton Univ. Press, 1972.

Daniel, Glyn. *The Idea of Prehistory*. Harmondsworth: Penguin, 1964.

Darwin, Erasmus. *The Loves of the Plants*. Interlude I. 1789. In *Eighteenth-Century Critical Essays*. Ed. Scott Elledge. Ithaca: Cornell Univ. Press, 1961, pp. 1005–10.

David, Florence Nightingale. *Gods, Games, and Gambling*. London: Charles Griffin, 1962.

David, M. *Le Débat sur les écritures et l'hiéroglyphe au XVIIe et XVIIIe siècle*. Paris: SEVPEN, 1965.

Debus, Allen G. *The Chemical Philosophy: Paracelsian Science and Medicine in the Sixteenth and Seventeenth Centuries*. 2 vols. New York: Science History Publications, 1977.

Deferrari, Roy J. *A Lexicon of St. Thomas Aquinas*. Washington, D.C.: Catholic Univ. Press, 1949.

Defoe, Daniel. *The Life and Strange Surprizing Adventures of Robinson Crusoe*. 1719. Ed. J. Donald Crowley. London: Oxford Univ. Press, 1972.

    A Journal of the Plague Year. 1721. Ed. J. H. Plumb. New York: New American Library, 1960.

    Roxana, The Fortunate Mistress. 1724. Ed. Jane Jack. London: Oxford Univ. Press, 1964.

Dekker, Thomas. *The Plague Pamphlets of Thomas Dekker*. Ed. F. P. Wilson. Oxford: Clarendon Press, 1925.

De Lacy, Phillip. "Ancient Rhetoric and Empirical Method." *Sophia*, 6 (1938), 523–30.

    "The Epicurean Analysis of Language." *American Journal of Philology*, 60 (1939), 85–92.

Deman, Th. "'Probabilis' au moyen age." *Revue des sciences philosophiques et théologiques*, 22 (1933), 260–90.

    "Probabilisme." *Dictionnaire de théologie Catholique*. 1936 ed. Vol. 13, Pt. 1, Cols. 417–619.

Demos, Raphael. *The Philosophy of Plato*. New York: Scribner's, 1939.

Dennis, John. *The Critical Works of John Dennis*. Ed. Edward Niles Hooker. 2 vols. Baltimore: The Johns Hopkins Univ. Press, 1939.

Derham, William. *Physico-Theology: or a Demonstration of the Being and Attributes of God from his Works of Creation*. London, 1712.

Bibliography

Derry, Warren. *Dr. Parr: A Portrait of the Whig Dr. Johnson*. Oxford: Clarendon Press, 1966.

Descartes, René. *Oeuvres philosophiques*. Ed. Charles Adam and Paul Tannery. 12 vols. Paris: Léopold Cerf, 1897–1913.

Treatise of Man. Ed. and tr. Thomas S. Hall. Cambridge, Mass.: Harvard Univ. Press, 1972.

Dewhurst, Kenneth. *John Locke, 1632–1704: Physician and Philosopher*. London: Wellcome Medical Historical Library, 1963.

Dr. Thomas Sydenham (1624–1689): His Life and Original Writings. Berkeley: Univ. of California Press, 1966.

Dickens, Charles. *A Tale of Two Cities*. 1859. Ed. George Woodcock. Harmondsworth: Penguin, 1970.

D'Israeli, Isaac. *A Dissertation on Anecdotes*. London, 1793.

An Essay on the Manners and Genius of the Literary Character. London, 1795.

Miscellanies; or, Literary Recreations. London, 1796.

Donaldson, John. *The Elements of Beauty. Also, Reflections on the Harmony of Sensibility and Reason*. Edinburgh, 1780.

Downame, John. *The Christian Warfare*. London, 1604.

Downer, Alan S. "Nature to Advantage Dressed: Eighteenth-Century Acting." *PMLA*, 58 (1943), 1002–37.

Drake, Nathan. *Literary Hours or Sketches Critical and Narrative*. 1798. 2nd ed. 2 vols. London, 1800.

Dryden, John. *Of Dramatic Poesy and Other Critical Essays*. Ed. George Watson. 2 vols. London: Dent, 1962.

Du Bos, Jean Baptiste. *Critical Reflections on Poetry, Painting, and Music*. 1719. Tr. Thomas Nugent. 3 vols. London, 1748.

Duchesneau, François. *L'Empirisme de Locke*. The Hague: Martinus Nijhoff, 1973.

La Physiologie des lumières: Empirisme, modèles et théories. The Hague: Martinus Nijhoff, 1982.

Duckworth, Alistair M. *The Improvement of the Estate: A Study of Jane Austen's Novels*. Baltimore: The Johns Hopkins Univ. Press, 1971.

Duff, William. *An Essay on Original Genius, and its Various Modes of Exertion in Philosophy and the Fine Arts*. London, 1767.

Duncan, William. *The Elements of Logick in Four Books*. London, 1748.

Ehrenpreis, Irvin. *Literary Meaning and Augustan Values*. Charlottesville: Univ. Press of Virginia, 1974.

Acts of Implication: Suggestion and Covert Meaning in the Works of Dryden, Swift, Pope and Austen. Berkeley: Univ. of California Press, 1980.

"*Rasselas* and Some Meanings of Structure in Literary Criticism." *Novel*, 14 (1981), 101–17.

Elphinston, James. *Forty Years' Correspondence between Geniusses of boath Sexes and James Elphinston*. 6 vols. London, 1791–94.

Evans, Elizabeth. *Physiognomics in the Ancient World*. Transactions of the American Philosophical Society. N.S. vol. 59, pt. 5. Philadelphia, 1969.

Evans, J. D. G. *Aristotle's Concept of Dialectic*. Cambridge: Cambridge Univ. Press, 1977.

Evelyn, John. *Numismata. A Discourse of Medals ... To Which is Added a Digression concerning Physiognomy*. London, 1697.

Fagot, Anne M. "Probabilities and Causes: On Life Tables, Causes of Death, and Etiological Diagnoses." In *Probabilistic Thinking, Thermodynamics and* the Interaction of the History and Philosophy of Science. Ed. J. Hintikka et al. Dordrecht: D. Reidel, 1981, II, 41–104.

Felton, Henry. A Dissertation on Reading the Classics, And Forming a Just Style. London, 1715.

Ferguson, Adam. An Essay on the History of Civil Society. Edinburgh, 1767.

Ferrand, Jacques. Erotomania, or a Treatise Discoursing of the Essence, Causes, Symptomes, Prognostics, and Cure of Love or Erotique Melancholy. 1612. Tr. Edmund Chilmead. London, 1640.

Fielding, Henry. The History of the Adventures of Joseph Andrews. 1742. Ed. Martin C. Battestin. Middletown: Wesleyan Univ. Press, 1967.

Miscellanies by Henry Fielding, Esq; Volume One. 1743. Ed. Henry Knight Miller. Oxford: Clarendon Press, 1972.

The History of Tom Jones, a Foundling. 1749. Ed. Martin C. Battestin and Fredson Bowers. 2 vols. Oxford: Clarendon Press, 1975.

The Criticism of Henry Fielding. Ed. Ioan Williams. New York: Barnes & Noble, 1970.

Forster, E. M. Howards End. 1910. New York: Random House, 1921.

Foster, John. On the Application of the Epithet Romantic. 1805. In Essays in a Series of Letters. London 1844, pp. 127–87.

Foucault, Michel. The Order of Things: An Archaeology of the Human Sciences. New York: Pantheon, 1970.

Discipline and Punish: The Birth of the Prison. Tr. Alan Sheridan. New York: Pantheon, 1977.

"What is an Author?" In Language, Counter-Memory, Practice. Ed. and tr. D. F. Bouchard and S. Simon. Ithaca: Cornell Univ. Press, 1977, pp. 113–38.

Fox Bourne, Henry Richard. The Life of John Locke. 2 vols. London: H. S. King, 1876.

France, Peter. Rhetoric and Truth in France: Descartes to Diderot. Oxford: Clarendon Press, 1972.

Franklin, Benjamin. A Dissertation Upon Liberty and Necessity, Pleasure and Pain. London, 1725.

Fraunce, Abraham. The Lawiers Logike, exemplifying the Precepts of Logike, by the Practise of the Common Lawe. London, 1588.

French, R. K. Robert Whytt, the Soul, and Medicine. London: Wellcome Institute, 1969.

Freudenthal, H. "Y avait-il une crise des fondements des mathématiques dans l'antiquité?" Bulletin de la Société Mathématique de Belgique, 18 (1966), 43–55.

Fried, Michael. Absorption and Theatricality: Painting and the Beholder in the Age of Diderot. Berkeley: Univ. of California Press, 1980.

Fussell, Paul. The Rhetorical World of Augustan Humanism: Ethics and Imagery from Swift to Burke. Oxford: Clarendon Press, 1965.

Gandillac, Maurice Patronner de. "De l'usage et de la valeur des arguments probables dans les questions du Cardinal Pierre d'Ailly sur le 'Livre des Sentences.'" Archives d'histoire doctrinale et littéraire du moyen age, 8 (1933), 43–91.

Garber, Daniel, and Zabell, Sandy. "On the Emergence of Probability." Technical Report No. 76. Departments of Philosophy and Statistics, University of Chicago, Nov. 1978.

Gardeil, A. "La 'Certitude Probable.'" Revue des sciences philosophiques et théologiques, 5 (1911), 237–66, 441–85.

"La Topicité." *Revue des sciences philosophiques et théologiques,* 5 (1911), 750–57.

Gassendi, Pierre. *The Selected Works of Pierre Gassendi.* Tr. Craig R. Brush. London: Johnson Reprint Corp., 1972.

Gay, Peter. *Voltaire's Politics: The Poet as Realist.* New York: Knopf, 1965.

Gelbart, Nina Rattner. "The Intellectual Development of Walter Charleton." *Ambix,* 18 (1971), 149–68.

Gentillet, Innocent. *Discours sur les moyens de bien gouverner ... un royaume.* Geneva, 1576.

Geoffrey of Vinsauf. *Poetria Nova.* Ed. and tr. Margaret F. Nims. Toronto: Pontifical Institute of Mediaeval Studies, 1967.

Gerando, Joseph Marie de, Baron. *Des Signes et de l'art de penser considerés dans leurs rapports mutuels.* 4 vols. Paris, 1800.

Gerard, Alexander. *An Essay on Taste.* 1759. 3rd ed. Edinburgh, 1780.

An Essay on Genius. London, 1774.

Gerarde, John. *The Herball, or General Historie of Plants.* 1597. London, 1633.

Geyser, Joseph. "Zur Einführung in das Problem der Evidenz in der Scholastik." *Beiträge zur Geschichte der Philosophie des Mittelalters,* Supplementband 2 (1923), 161–82.

Gibbon, Edward. *The Miscellaneous Works of Edward Gibbon.* Ed. John, Lord Sheffield. London, 1837.

Gibbons, Thomas. *Rhetoric, or, a View of its Principal Tropes and Figures, in their Origin and Powers.* London, 1767.

Gilbert, Neal W. *Renaissance Concepts of Method.* New York: Columbia Univ. Press, 1960.

Gildon, Charles. *The Complete Art of Poetry.* 2 vols. London, 1743.

Gilpin, William. *A Dialogue upon the Gardens ... at Stowe.* London, 1748.

Three Essays: on Picturesque Beauty; on Picturesque Travel; and on Sketching Landscape. 1791. 2nd ed. London, 1794.

Glanvill, Joseph. *The Vanity of Dogmatizing: or Confidence in Opinions Manifested in a Discourse of the Shortness and Uncertainty of our Knowledge.* London, 1661.

Essays on Several Important Subjects in Philosophy and Religion. London, 1676.

An Essay concerning Preaching. London, 1678.

Glass, D. V. "The Population Controversy in Eighteenth-Century England." *Population Studies,* 6 (1952), 69–91.

Numbering the People. Farnborough: Saxon House, 1973.

Goldberg, M. A. *Smollett and the Scottish School: Studies in Eighteenth-Century Thought.* Albuquerque: Univ. of New Mexico Press, 1959.

Goldsmith, Oliver. *The Collected Works of Oliver Goldsmith.* Ed. Arthur Friedman. 5 vols. Oxford: Clarendon Press, 1966.

Gombrich, Ernst H. "Moment and Movement in Art." *Journal of the Warburg and Courtauld Institutes,* 27 (1964), 293–306.

"The Mask and the Face: the Perception of Physiognomic Likeness in Art." In *Art, Perception, and Reality.* Ed. Maurice Mandelbaum. Baltimore: The Johns Hopkins Univ. Press, 1972, pp. 1–46.

Gordon, Thomas. *The Humourist: Being Essays upon Several Subjects.* 2 vols. London, 1725.

Gracián y Morales, Balthasar. *The Critick.* Tr. Paul Rycout. London, 1681.

The Courtiers Manual Oracle, or, The Art of Prudence. Tr. anon. London, 1685.

Bibliography

Graham, John. "Lavater's Physiognomy in England." *Journal of the History of Ideas*, 22 (1961), 561–72.

Grassi, Ernesto. "Critical Philosophy or Topical Philosophy? Meditations on the *De nostri temporis studiorum ratione*." In *Giambattista Vico: An International Symposium*. Ed. Giorgio Tagliacozzo. Baltimore: The Johns Hopkins Univ. Press, 1969, pp. 39–50.

Gray, Thomas. *The Works of Thomas Gray*. Ed. J. Mitford. 5 vols. London, 1835–47.

Gregory, George. *Letters on Literature, Taste, and Composition, Addressed to his Son*. 2 vols. London, 1808.

Greville, Fulke, Baron Brooke. *The Works in Verse and Prose*. Ed. Alexander B. Grosart. 4 vols. 1870. Facs. rpt. New York: AMS Press, 1966.

Grote, George. *Aristotle*. Ed. Alexander Bain and George Croom Robertson. London: J. Murray, 1883.

Guilhamet, Leon. *The Sincere Ideal: Studies on Sincerity in Eighteenth-Century English Literature*. Montreal: McGill-Queen's Univ. Press, 1974.

Gunn, J. A. W. *Politics and the Public Interest in the Seventeenth Century*. London: Routledge & Kegan Paul, 1969.

Hacking, Ian. *The Emergence of Probability: A Philosophical Study of Early Ideas about Probability, Induction, and Statistical Inference*. Cambridge: Cambridge Univ. Press, 1975.

——. *Why Does Language Matter to Philosophy?* Cambridge: Cambridge Univ. Press, 1975.

——. "Michel Foucault's Immature Science." *Noûs*, 13 (1979), 39–51.

——. "From the Emergence of Probability to the Emergence of Determinism." In *Probabilistic Thinking, Thermodynamics, and the Interaction of the History and Philosophy of Science*. Ed. J. Hintikka *et al.* Dordrecht: D. Reidel, 1981, II, 105–23.

Hagstrum, Jean. *Samuel Johnson's Literary Criticism*. 1952. Chicago: Univ. of Chicago Press, 1967.

Hall, Joseph. *The Poems of Joseph Hall, Bishop of Exeter and Norwich*. Ed. Arnold Davenport. Liverpool: Liverpool Univ. Press, 1949.

Hamlyn, D. W. "Aristotelian Epagoge." *Phronesis*, 21 (1976), 167–84.

Hannaway, Owen. *The Chemists and the Word: The Didactic Origins of Chemistry*. Baltimore: The Johns Hopkins Univ. Press, 1975.

Harbage, Alfred. "Elizabethan Acting." *PMLA*, 54 (1939), 685–708.

Hardison, O. B., Jr. *The Enduring Monument: A Study of the Idea of Praise in Renaissance Literary Theory and Practice*. Chapel Hill: Univ. of North Carolina Press, 1962.

Harris, James. *The Works of James Harris, Esq.* 5 vols. London, 1803.

Hart, Francis R. "Johnson as Philosophic Traveller: The Perfecting of an Idea." *ELH*, 36 (1969), 679–95.

Harth, Phillip. *Contexts of Dryden's Thought*. Chicago: Univ. of Chicago Press, 1968.

Hartley, David. *Observations on Man, His Frame, His Duty and His Expectations*. London, 1749.

Harty, J. M. "Probabilism." *Catholic Encyclopedia*. 1911 ed. Vol. 12, pp. 441–46.

Harvey, E. Ruth. *The Inward Wits: Psychological Theory in the Middle Ages and the Renaissance*. London: Warburg Institute, 1975.

Hathaway, Baxter. *Marvels and Commonplaces: Renaissance Literary Criticism*. New York: Random House, 1968.

Bibliography

Havelock, Eric A. *Preface to Plato*. Cambridge, Mass.: Harvard Univ. Press, 1963.

Hawkesworth, John. *The Adventurer*. 2 vols. London, 1753.

Hayley, William. *An Essay on Epic Poetry*. London, 1782.

Hazlitt, William. *Lectures on the English Comic Writers*. 1819. London: Dent, 1967.

Hearne, Thomas. *Ductor Historicus: or, a Short System of Universal History*. London, 1698.

Heath, Terence. "Logical Grammar, Grammatical Logic, and Humanism in Three German Universities." *Studies in the Renaissance*, 18 (1971), 9–64.

Hédelin, François, Abbé d'Aubignac. *La Pratique du théâtre*. 1657. Facs. rpt. Geneva: Slatkine, 1971.

The Whole Art of the Stage. Tr. anon. London, 1684.

Heffernan, James A. W. "Wordsworth and Dennis: The Discrimination of Feelings." *PMLA*, 82 (1967), 430–36.

Heinsius, Daniel. *De Tragoediae constitutione liber*. Leiden, 1611.

Herbert of Cherbury, Edward, Baron. *De Veritate, Prout distinguitur a Revelatione, a Verisimili, a Possibili, et a Falso*. 1624. 3rd ed., 1645. Tr. Meyrinck Carré. Bristol: Univ. of Bristol Press, 1937.

Heron, Robert (John Pinkerton). *Letters of Literature*. London, 1785.

Herrick, Marvin T. *The Fusion of Horatian and Aristotelian Literary Criticism 1531–1555*. Univ. of Illinois Studies in Language and Literature, vol. 32, no. 1. Urbana: Univ. of Illinois Press, 1946.

Hill, Christopher. *Milton and the English Revolution*. New York: Viking, 1977.

Hirsch, E. D., Jr. *The Aims of Interpretation*. Chicago: Univ. of Chicago Press, 1976.

Hobbes, Thomas. *Answer* to Davenant's Preface to *Gondibert*. 1650. In *Critical Essays of the Seventeenth Century*. Ed. J. E. Spingarn. Oxford: Clarendon Press, 1909, II, 54–67.

"To the Reader, concerning the Vertues of an Heroique Poem." 1675. In *Ibid.*, pp. 67–76.

Hoffmann, Friedrich. *Fundamenta Medicinae*. 1695. Tr. Lester S. King. Amsterdam: Elsevier, 1971.

Hogarth, William. *The Analysis of Beauty*. London, 1753.

Holdsworth, William. *A History of English Law*. 7th ed. 16 vols. London: Methuen, 1956.

Hooker, Richard. *Of the Laws of Ecclesiastical Polity I–IV*. Ed. Georges Edelin. Vol. 1: *The Folger Library Edition of the Works of Richard Hooker*. Ed. W. Speed Hill. Cambridge, Mass.: Harvard Univ. Press, 1977.

Howell, Wilbur S. *Logic and Rhetoric in England, 1500–1700*. Princeton: Princeton Univ. Press, 1956.

Eighteenth-Century British Logic and Rhetoric. Princeton: Princeton Univ. Press, 1971.

Huarte de San Juan, Juan de Dios. *Examen de Ingenios. The Examination of Mens Wits*. Tr. R(ichard) C(arew). London, 1594.

Hume, David. *A Treatise of Human Nature*. 1739. Ed. L. A. Selby-Bigge. Oxford: Clarendon Press, 1888.

An Abstract of a Treatise of Human Nature. 1740. Ed. J. M. Keynes and Pierre Sraffa. Cambridge: Cambridge Univ. Press, 1938.

Essays, Moral, Political, and Literary. London: Oxford Univ. Press, 1963.

Hume, Robert D. *Dryden's Criticism*. Ithaca: Cornell Univ. Press, 1970.

Hurd, Richard. *Letters on Chivalry and Romance*. London, 1762.

The Works of Richard Hurd. 8 vols. London, 1811.

Hutcheson, Francis. *An Inquiry into the Origin of our Ideas of Beauty and Virtue.* London, 1725; 2nd ed. London, 1726.

Hutchison, Keith. "What Happened to Occult Qualities in the Scientific Revolution?" *Isis,* 73 (1982), 233–53.

Inchbald, Elizabeth. *Nature and Art.* 1796. Ed. Janice Marie Cauwels. Diss. Univ. of Virginia, 1976.

Iser, Wolfgang. *The Implied Reader: Patterns of Communication in Prose Fiction from Bunyan to Beckett.* Baltimore: The Johns Hopkins Univ. Press, 1974.

The Act of Reading: A Theory of Aesthetic Response. Baltimore: The Johns Hopkins Univ. Press, 1978.

Jabre, Farid. *La Notion de la certitude selon Ghazali.* Paris: Vrin, 1958.

Jackson, Wallace. *Immediacy: The Development of a Critical Concept from Addison to Coleridge.* Amsterdam: Rodopi, 1973.

The Probable and the Marvelous: Blake, Wordsworth, and the Eighteenth-Century Critical Tradition. Athens: Univ. of Georgia Press, 1978.

Jackson, William. *Thirty Letters on Various Subjects.* 2nd ed. 2 vols. London, 1784.

Jacob, J. R. *Robert Boyle and the English Revolution: A Study in Social and Intellectual History.* New York: Bert Franklin, 1978.

Janik, Linda Gardiner. "Lorenzo Valla: The Primacy of Rhetoric and the De-Moralization of History." *History and Theory,* 12 (1973), 389–404.

Jardine, Lisa. *Francis Bacon: Discovery and the Art of Discourse.* Cambridge: Cambridge Univ. Press, 1974.

"The Place of Dialectic Teaching in Sixteenth-Century Cambridge." *Studies in the Renaissance,* 21 (1974), 31–62.

"Humanism and the Sixteenth Century Cambridge Arts Course." *History of Education,* 4 (1975), 16–31.

"Humanism and Dialectic in Sixteenth-Century Cambridge: A Preliminary Investigation." In *Classical Influence on European Culture A.D. 1500–1700.* Ed. R. R. Bolgar. Cambridge: Cambridge Univ. Press, 1976, pp. 141–54.

"Lorenzo Valla and the Intellectual Origins of Humanist Dialectic." *Journal of the History of Philosophy,* 15 (1977), 143–64.

Jardine, Nicholas. "Galileo's Road to Truth and the Demonstrative Regress." *Studies in the History and Philosophy of Science,* 7 (1976), 277–318.

"The Forging of Modern Realism: Clavius and Kepler against the Sceptics." *Studies in the History and Philosophy of Science,* 10 (1979), 141–71.

John of St. Thomas. *The Material Logic of John of St. Thomas.* Tr. Yves Simon *et al.* Chicago: Univ. of Chicago Press, 1955.

John of Salisbury. *The Metalogicon of John of Salisbury.* Tr. Daniel D. McGarry. Berkeley: Univ. of California Press, 1955.

Johnson, Maurice. *Fielding's Art of Fiction.* Philadelphia: Univ. of Pennsylvania Press, 1961.

Johnson, Samuel. *A Dictionary of the English Language.* 5th ed. London, 1773.

Lives of the English Poets. Ed. G. Birkbeck Hill. 3 vols. Oxford: Clarendon Press, 1905.

The Yale Edition of the Works of Samuel Johnson. New Haven: Yale Univ. Press, 1958 – .

Jones, John. *Galens Bookes of Elementes.* London, 1574.

Jones, Thora B., and Nicol, Bernard de Bear. *Neo-Classical Dramatic Criticism, 1560–1770.* Cambridge: Cambridge Univ. Press, 1976.

Jones, William. "On the Arts Commonly Called Imitative." 1772. In *Eighteenth-Century Critical Essays.* Ed. Scott Elledge. Ithaca: Cornell Univ. Press, 1961, pp. 872–81.

Jonson, Ben. *Ben Jonson.* Ed. C. H. Herford and Percy and Evelyn Simpson. 11 vols. Oxford: Clarendon Press, 1925–52.

Joseph, B. L. *Elizabethan Acting.* London: Oxford Univ. Press, 1951.

Kallich, Martin. *The Association of Ideas and Critical Theory in Eighteenth-Century England.* The Hague: Mouton, 1970.

Kames, Henry Home, Lord. *The Elements of Criticism.* 3 vols. Edinburgh, 1762.

Kargon, Robert Hugh. *Atomism in England from Hariot to Newton.* Oxford: Clarendon Press, 1966.

Keegan, Timothy L. *An Introduction to the Poems of Jonathan Swift.* Forthcoming.

Kendall, M. G., and Pearson, E. S. *Studies in the History of Statistics and Probability.* 2 vols. London: Charles Griffin, 1970.

Kennedy, Alan. *Meaning and Signs in Fiction.* London: Macmillan, 1979.

Kennedy, George A. *Classical Rhetoric and Its Christian and Secular Tradition from Ancient to Modern Times.* Chapel Hill: Univ. of North Carolina Press, 1980.

Keynes, John Maynard. *A Treatise of Probability.* 1921. London: Macmillan, 1948.

King, Lester S. "Signs and Symptoms." *JAMA,* 26 (1968), 1063–65.

Kirk, Kenneth E. *Some Principles of Moral Theology.* London: Longmans, 1920.

Klein, Jacob. *Greek Mathematical Thought and the Origin of Algebra.* Tr. Eva Braun. Cambridge, Mass.: M.I.T. Press, 1968.

Knapp, Lewis. *Tobias Smollett: Doctor of Men and Manners.* Princeton: Princeton Univ. Press, 1949.

Kneale, William and Martha. *The Development of Logic.* Oxford: Clarendon Press, 1962.

Knight, Richard Payne. *An Analytical Inquiry into the Nature and Principles of Taste.* 1805. London, 1808.

Korshin, Paul J. "Probability and Character in the Eighteenth Century." In *Probability, Time, and Space in Eighteenth-Century Literature.* Ed. Paula R. Backscheider. New York: AMS Press, 1979, pp. 63–77.

Krieger, Leonard. "Authority." *Dictionary of the History of Ideas.* 1973 ed. Vol. I, pp. 141–62.

Kristeller, P. O. "The Modern System of the Arts: A Study in the History of Aesthetics." In *Renaissance Thought II : Papers on Humanism and the Arts.* New York: Harper, Row, 1965, pp. 163–227.

Kubler, Clark George. *The Argument from Probability in Early Attic Oratory.* Chicago: Univ. of Chicago Press, 1944.

La Chambre, Cureau de. *Les Caractères des passions.* Paris, 1648–59.

Lambert, Johann Heinrich. *Cosmological Letters on the Arrangement of the World-Edifice.* 1761. Tr. and ed. Stanley L. Jaki. New York: Science History Publications, 1976.

  Neues Organon, oder Gedanken über die Erforschung und Bezeichnung des Wahren und dessen Unterscheidung von Irrtum und Schein. Leipzig, 1764.

La Mesnardière, Henri-Jules Pilet de. *La Poëtique.* Paris, 1540.

La Mothe le Vayer, François de. *Oeuvres.* 3 vols. Paris, 1662.

Lamy, Bernard. *Entretiens sur les sciences, dans lesquels on apprend comment l'on doit étudier les sciences, & s'en servir pour se faire l'esprit juste et le coeur droit.* 1683. Ed. François Girbal and Pierre Clair. Paris: Presses universitaires de France, 1966.

Landré-Beauvais, Augustin Jacob. *Séméiotique, ou, traité des signes des maladies.* Paris, 1809.

Langbaum, Robert. *The Poetry of Experience: The Dramatic Monologue in Modern Literary Tradition.* 1957. New York: Norton, 1963.

Laudan, Laurens. "The Clock Metaphor and Probabilism: The Impact of Descartes on English Methodological Thought, 1650–1655." *Annals of Science,* 22 (1966), 73–104.

"The Nature and Sources of Locke's View on Hypotheses." *Journal of the History of Ideas,* 28 (1967), 211–23.

"Peirce and the Trivialization of the Self-Correcting Hypothesis." In *Foundations of Scientific Method: The Nineteenth Century.* Ed. Ronald N. Giere and Richard S. Westfall. Bloomington: Indiana Univ. Press, 1973, pp. 275–306.

Law, William. *A Serious Call to a Devout and Holy Life.* 1728. London: Dent, 1967.

Lawson, John. *Lectures concerning Oratory,* Dublin, 1758.

Lea, Henry Charles. *A History of Auricular Confession and Indulgences in the Catholic Church.* 3 vols. Philadelphia: Lea Brothers, 1896.

Le Bossu, René. *Traité du poème épique.* Paris, 1675.

Monsieur Bossu's Treatise of the Epick Poem. Tr. W. J. London, 1695.

Le Clerc, Jean. *Reflections Upon what the World Commonly call Good-Luck and Ill-Luck, With Regard to Lotteries.* London, 1699.

Leeuwen, Henry van. *The Problem of Certainty in English Thought 1630–1690.* The Hague: Martinus Nijhoff, 1963.

Le Faucheur, Michel. *An Essay upon the Action of an Orator.* London, 1702.

Leff, Gordon. *William of Ockham: The Metamorphosis of Scholastic Discourse.* Manchester: Manchester Univ. Press, 1975.

Leibniz, Gottfried Wilhelm. *New Essays concerning Human Understanding.* Ed. and tr. Peter Remnant and Jonathan Bennett. Cambridge: Cambridge Univ. Press, 1981.

Lemnius, Levinus. *The Touchstone of Complexions.* 1561. Tr. Thomas Newton. London, 1581.

Lennox, Charlotte. *The Female Quixote, or the Adventures of Arabella.* 1752. Ed. Margaret Dalziel and Duncan Isles. London: Oxford Univ. Press, 1970.

Lenoble, Robert. *Mersenne, ou la naissance du mécanisme.* Paris: Vrin, 1943.

Lever, Ralph. *The Arte of Reason, rightly termed, Witcraft.* London, 1573.

Levine, Joseph M. "Ancients and Moderns Reconsidered." *Eighteenth-Century Studies,* 15 (1981), 72–89.

Lloyd, G. E. R. *Magic, Reason and Experience: Studies in the Origin and Development of Greek Science.* Cambridge: Cambridge Univ. Press, 1979.

Locke, John. *The Correspondence of John Locke.* Ed. E. S. de Beer. Oxford: Clarendon Press, 1976– .

The Educational Writings of John Locke. Ed. James L. Axtell. Cambridge: Cambridge Univ. Press, 1968.

An Essay concerning Human Understanding. Ed. Peter Nidditch. Oxford: Clarendon Press, 1975.

Essays on the Law of Nature. Ed. W. von Leyden. Oxford: Clarendon Press, 1954.

On the Conduct of the Understanding. Ed. Francis W. Garforth. New York: Columbia Univ. Teachers College Press, 1966.

Lodge, Thomas. *The Complete Works of Thomas Lodge.* 4 vols. Glasgow: Hunterian Club, 1883.

Loewenberg, Richard D. "The Significance of the Obvious: An Eighteenth-Century Controversy on Psychosomatic Principles." *Bulletin of the History of Medicine,* 10 (1941), 666–79.

Lowth, Robert. *Lectures on the Sacred Poetry of the Hebrews.* 1753. 2 vols. London, 1787.

McGuire, J. E. "Atoms and the 'Analogy of Nature': Newton's Third Rule of Philosophizing." *Studies in the History and Philosophy of Science,* 1 (1970), 3–58.

"Boyle's Conception of Nature." *Journal of the History of Ideas,* 33 (1972), 523–42.

MacIntyre, Alasdair. "Epistemological Crises, Dramatic Narrative, and the Philosophy of Science." In *Paradigms and Revolutions: Appraisals and Applications of Thomas Kuhn's Philosophy of Science.* Notre Dame: Univ. of Notre Dame Press, 1980, pp. 54–74.

After Virtue: A Study in Moral Theory. Notre Dame: Univ. of Notre Dame Press, 1981.

McKenzie, Alan T. "'The Countenance You Show Me': Reading the Passions in the Eighteenth Century." *Georgia Review,* 32 (1978), 758–73.

McKenzie, Gordon. *Critical Responsiveness: A Study of the Psychological Current in Later Eighteenth-Century Criticism.* Univ. of California Publications in English, Vol. 20. Berkeley: Univ. of California Press, 1949.

Mackenzie, Henry. *The Man of Feeling.* 1771. Ed. Brian Vickers. London: Oxford Univ. Press, 1970.

The Man of the World. 2 vols. London, 1773.

McKeon, Richard. "Rhetoric in the Middle Ages." *Speculum,* 17 (1942), 1–32.

"The Transformation of the Liberal Arts in the Renaissance." In *Developments in the Early Renaissance.* Ed. Bernard S. Levy. Albany: State Univ. of New York Press, 1972, pp. 158–206.

Mackie, J. L. *Truth, Probability, and Paradox: Studies in Philosophical Logic.* Oxford: Clarendon Press, 1973.

McKillop, Alan D. *The Early Masters of English Fiction.* 1956. Lawrence: Univ. of Kansas Press, 1968.

McRae, Robert. "'Idea' as a Philosophical Term in the Seventeenth Century." *Journal of the History of Ideas,* 26 (1965), 175–90.

Leibniz: Perception, Apperception, and Thought. Toronto: Univ. of Toronto Press, 1976.

Madden, Edward H. "Aristotle's Treatment of Probability and Signs." *Philosophy of Science,* 24 (1957), 167–72.

"The Enthymeme: Crossroads of Logic, Rhetoric, and Metaphysics." *Philosophical Review,* 61 (1962), 368–76.

Malebranche, Nicolas. *De la Recherche de la vérité.* 1674. Ed. Geneviève Rodis-Lewis. Vols. 1–3: *Oeuvres complètes de Malebranche.* Paris: Vrin, 1962.

Mandelbaum, Maurice. *Philosophy, Science, and Sense Perception: Historical and Critical Studies.* Baltimore: The Johns Hopkins Univ. Press, 1964.

Mandeville, Bernard. *The Fable of the Bees.* Ed. F. B. Kaye. 2 vols. Oxford: Clarendon Press, 1924.

A Treatise of the Hypocondriak and Hysterick Passions. 1711. London, 1730.

Bibliography

Manley, Lawrence. *Convention 1500–1700*. Cambridge, Mass.: Harvard Univ. Press, 1980.

Manwaring, Edward. *An Historical and Critical Account of the Most Eminent Classic Authors in Poetry and History*. London, 1737.

Marsh, David. *The Quattrocento Dialogue: Classical Tradition and Humanist Innovation*. Cambridge, Mass.: Harvard Univ. Press, 1980.

Martin, Robert B. *The Triumph of Wit: A Study in Victorian Comic Theory*. Oxford: Clarendon Press, 1974.

Mathias, Thomas James. *The Pursuits of Literature*. 1794. 8th ed. Dublin, 1798.

Mayne, Zachary. *Two Dissertations concerning Sense, and the Imagination. With an Essay on Consciousness*. London, 1728.

Meador, Prentice A., Jr. "Skeptic Theory of Perception: A Philosophical Antecedent of Ciceronian Probability." *Quarterly Journal of Speech*, 54 (1968), 340–51.

Measell, J. S. "The Authorship of *The Art of Logick* (1654)." *Journal of the History of Philosophy*, 15 (1977), 321–24.

Melanchthon, Philip. *Erotemata dialectices*. 1555. Wittenburg, 1562.

Menochio, Giacomo. *De Praesumptionibus, conjecturis, signis, et indicijs commentaria*. 2 vols. Venice, 1587–90.

Mersenne, Marin. *La Vérité des sciences, contre les sceptiques*. Paris, 1625.

Michel, Alain. *Les Rapports de la rhétorique et de la philosophie dans l'oeuvre de Cicéron*. Paris: Presses universitaires de France, 1960.

——— *Rhétorique et philosophie chez Cicéron: Essai sur les fondements philosophiques de l'art de persuader*. Paris: Presses universitaires de France, 1961.

Mijuskovic, Ben Lazare. *The Achilles of Rationalist Arguments*. The Hague: Martinus Nijhoff, 1974.

Mill, John Stuart. *Mill's Essays on Literature and Society*. Ed. J. B. Schneewind. New York: Macmillan, 1965.

Miller, Arthur B., and Bee, John D. "Enthymemes: Body and Soul." *Philosophy and Rhetoric*, 5 (1972), 201–14.

Milton, John. Preface to *Samson Agonistes*. 1671. In *Critical Essays of the Seventeenth Century*. Ed. J. E. Spingarn. Oxford: Clarendon Press, 1909, I, 207–09.

Minturno, Antonio. *L'Arte poetica*. Venice, 1564.

Moivre, Abraham de. *The Doctrine of Chances: or, a Method of Calculating the Probabilities of Events in Play*. 1718. 3rd ed. London, 1756.

Monfasani, John. *George of Trebizond: A Biography and a Study of his Rhetoric and Logic*. Leiden: E. J. Brill, 1976.

Monk, Samuel Holt. *The Sublime: A Study of Critical Theories in Eighteenth-Century England*. 1935. Ann Arbor: Univ. of Michigan Press, 1960.

Montagu, Jennifer. "Charles Le Brun's *Conférence sur l'expression*." Diss. Univ. of London, 1960.

Montgomery, Robert L. *The Reader's Eye: Studies in Didactic Literary Theory from Dante to Tasso*. Berkeley: Univ. of California Press, 1979.

Moody, Ernest A. *The Logic of William of Ockham*. New York: Sheed & Ward, 1935.

Moor, James. *Essays, Read to a Literary Society; at their Weekly Meetings, within the College, at Glasgow*. Glasgow, 1759.

Moore, W. G. *La Rochefoucauld: His Mind and Art*. Oxford: Clarendon Press, 1969.

Morgan, Michael J. *Molyneux's Question: Vision, Touch and the Philosophy of Perception*. Cambridge: Cambridge Univ. Press, 1977.

Bibliography

Morris, David B. *The Religious Sublime: Christian Poetry and Critical Tradition in Eighteenth-Century England*. Lexington: Univ. of Kentucky Press, 1972.

"Civilized Reading: The Act of Judgment in *An Essay on Criticism*." In *The Art of Alexander Pope*. Ed. Howard Erskine-Hill and Anne Smith. London: Vision Press, 1979, pp. 15–39.

Morris, John. "Descartes and Probable Knowledge." *Journal of the History of Philosophy*, 8 (1970), 303–12.

"Descartes' Natural Light." *Journal of the History of Philosophy*, 11 (1973), 169–87.

Mosse, George L. *The Holy Pretence. A Study in Christianity and Reason of State from William Perkins to John Winthrop*. New York: Howard Fertig, 1968.

Murphy, James J., ed. *The Rhetorical Tradition in Modern Writing*. New York: Modern Language Association, 1982.

Murrin, Michael. *The Veil of Allegory: Some Notes toward a Theory of Allegorical Rhetoric in the English Renaissance*. Chicago: Univ. of Chicago Press, 1969.

"The Rhetoric of Fairyland." In *The Rhetoric of Renaissance Poetry: From Wyatt to Milton*. Ed. Thomas O. Sloan and Raymond B. Waddington. Berkeley: Univ. of California Press, 1974, pp. 73–95.

Nadeau, Raymond E. "The *Progymnasmata* of Aphthonius." *Speech Monographs*, 19 (1952), 264–85.

Nashe, Thomas. *The Works of Thomas Nashe*. Ed. Ronald B. McKerrow. 5 vols. London: Sidgwick & Jackson, 1910.

Naulty, R. A. "Newman's Dispute with Locke." *Journal of the History of Philosophy*, 11 (1973), 452–57.

Nelson, Benjamin. "Comments by Benjamin Nelson." *Daedelus*, 91 (1962), 612–16.

"'Probabilists,' 'Anti-Probabilists,' and the Quest for Certitude in the 16th and 17th Centuries." *Proceedings of the Tenth International Congress of the History of Science*. Paris: Hermann, 1964, pp. 269–73.

"The Early Modern Revolution in Science and Philosophy: Fictionalism, Probabilism, Fideism, and Catholic 'Prophetism.'" *Boston Studies in the Philosophy of Science*, 3. Dordrecht: D. Reidel, 1967, pp. 1–40.

"Scholastic *Rationales* of 'Conscience', Early Modern Crises of Credibility, and the Scientific-Technological Revolutions of the 17th and 20th Centuries." *Journal for the Scientific Study of Religion*, 7 (1968), 157–77.

Nelson, William. *Fact or Fiction: the Dilemma of the Renaissance Storyteller*. Cambridge, Mass.: Harvard Univ. Press, 1974.

Nemesius of Emesa. *The Nature of Man. A Learned and Useful Tract ... Englished by Geo: Wither*. London, 1636.

New, Melvyn. "'The Grease of God': The Form of Eighteenth-Century English Fiction." *PMLA*, 91 (1976), 235–44.

[Newbery, John.] *The Art of Poetry on a New Plan*. London, 1762.

Newsom, Robert. *Dickens On the Romantic Side of Familiar Things: "Bleak House" and the Novel Tradition*. New York: Columbia Univ. Press, 1977.

Newton, Isaac. *Isaac Newton's Papers and Letters on Natural Philosophy*. Ed. I. B. Cohen. Cambridge, Mass.: Harvard Univ. Press, 1958.

Nicolson, Marjorie Hope. *Mountain Gloom and Mountain Glory: The Development of the Aesthetics of the Infinite*. Ithaca: Cornell Univ. Press, 1959.

Noreña, Carlos G. *Juan Luis Vives*. The Hague: Martinus Nijhoff, 1970.

Bibliography

Obortello, Luca. *John Locke e Port-Royal: Il problema della probabilità*. Trieste: Publicazioni dell'Istituto di Filosofia, 1964.

Ogilvie, John. *Poems on Several Subjects*. 2nd ed. London, 1769.

Philosophical and Critical Observations on the Nature, Characters, and Various Species of Composition. 2 vols. London, 1774.

Olson, Richard. *Scottish Philosophy and British Physics 1750–1880: A Study in the Foundations of the Victorian Scientific Style*. Princeton: Princeton Univ. Press, 1975.

Ong, Walter J. "The Province of Rhetoric and Poetic." *The Modern Schoolman*, 19 (1942), 24–27.

"System, Space, and Intellect in Renaissance Symbolism." In *The Barbarian Within and Other Fugitive Essays and Studies*. New York: Macmillan, 1954, pp. 68–87.

Ramus, Method, and the Decay of Dialogue. Cambridge, Mass.: Harvard Univ. Press, 1958.

Orr, Robert R. *Reason and Authority: The Thought of William Chillingworth*. Oxford: Clarendon Press, 1967.

Orsini, Napoleone. "'Policy' or the Language of Elizabethan Machiavellism." *Journal of the Warburg and Courtauld Institutes*, 9 (1946), 122–34.

Owen, Edward. *The Satires of Juvenal, translated into English Verse*. 2 vols. London, 1785.

Pagel, Walter. *Paracelsus: An Introduction to Philosophical Medicine in the Era of the Renaissance*. Basel: S. Karger, 1958.

Paracelsus, Theophrastus Bombastus von Hohenheim. *Selected Writings*. Ed. Jolande Jacobi, tr. Norbert Guterman. London: Routledge & Kegan Paul, 1951.

Paré, Ambroise. *The Works of that famous Chirurgeon Ambrose Parey*. Tr. Thomas Johnson. London, 1634.

Parks, George B. "Travel as Education." In *The Seventeenth Century: Studies in the History of English Thought and Literature from Bacon to Pope*. Stanford: Stanford Univ. Press, 1951, pp. 264–90.

Pascal, Blaise. *Oeuvres de Blaise Pascal*. Ed. Léon Brunschvicq, Pierre Boutroux, and Félix Gazier. 14 vols. Paris: Hachette, 1904–14.

Pemberton, Henry. *Observations on Poetry, Especially the Epic; Occasioned by the Late Poem upon Leonidas*. London, 1738.

Penn, John. *Critical, Poetical, and Dramatic Works*. 2 vols. London, 1797–98.

Percival, Thomas. *Moral and Literary Dissertations*. London, 1784.

Percy, Walker. *The Last Gentleman*. New York: Farrar, Strauss, Giroux, 1966.

Petty, William. *The Economic Writings of Sir William Petty*. Ed. C. H. Hull. 2 vols. 1899. Facs. rpt. New York: Augustus Kelley, 1963.

Pico, Gianfrancesco. *On the Imagination*. Tr. Harry Caplan. Cornell Studies in English, vol. 16. New Haven: Cornell Univ. Press, 1930.

Plank, Jeffrey Dennis. "John Aikin: The Scientist as Critic." Diss. Univ. of Virginia, 1975.

The Polite Arts, or, a Dissertation on Poetry, Painting, Musick, Architecture, and Eloquence. London, 1749.

Poovey, Mary Louise. "Journeys from this World to the Next: The Providential Promise in *Clarissa* and *Tom Jones*." *ELH*, 43 (1976), 300–15.

"The Novel as Imaginative Order." Diss. Univ. of Virginia, 1976.

Pope, Alexander. *The Correspondence of Alexander Pope*. Ed. George Sherburn. 5 vols. Oxford: Clarendon Press, 1956.

The Twickenham Edition of the Poems of Alexander Pope. Ed. John Butt *et al*. 11 vols. New Haven: Yale Univ. Press, 1961–69.

Pope, Alexander, Gay, John and Arbuthnot, John. *Three Hours After Marriage*. 1717. Facs. rpt. Los Angeles: Augustan Reprint Society, 1961.

Popkin, Richard H. *The History of Scepticism from Erasmus to Descartes*. New York: Humanities Press, 1964.

Popper, Karl R. *Conjectures and Refutations: The Growth of Scientific Knowledge*. New York: Basic Books, 1962.

Porter, H. C. "Hooker, the Tudor Constitution, and the *Via Media*." In *Studies in Richard Hooker: Essays Preliminary to an Edition of his Works*. Ed. W. Speed Hill. Cleveland: Case Western Reserve Univ. Press, 1972, pp. 77–116.

Power, Henry. *Experimental Philosophy ... With some Deductions, and Probable Hypotheses, raised from them, in Avouchment and Illustration of the now famous Atomical Hypothesis*. London, 1664.

Prentice, W. P. *The Indicative and Admonative Signs of Sextus Empiricus*. Gottingen, 1858.

Preston, John. *The Created Self: The Reader's Role in Eighteenth-century Fiction*. London: William Heinemann, 1970.

Preston, Thomas R. "Disenchanting the Man of Feeling: Smollett's *Ferdinand Count Fathom*." In *Quick Springs of Sense: Studies in the Eighteenth Century*. Ed. Larry S. Champion. Athens: Univ. of Georgia Press, 1974, pp. 223–39.

"The 'Stage Passions' and Smollett's Characterization." *Studies in Philology*, 71 (1974), 105–25.

Price, Richard. "An Essay towards solving a problem in the Doctrine of Chances." *Philosophical Transactions of the Royal Society of London*, 53 (1764), 370–418.

Priestley, Joseph. *An Examination of Dr. Reid's "Inquiry," Dr. Beattie's "Essays," and Dr. Oswald's "Appeal to Common Sense in Behalf of Religion."* London, 1774.

A Course of Lectures on Oratory and Criticism. London, 1777.

Puttenham, George. *The Arte of English Poesie*. London, 1589.

Pye, Henry James. *A Commentary illustrating the Poetic of Aristotle*. London, 1792.

Quintilian. *The "Institutio Oratoria" of Quintilian with an English Translation by H. E. Butler*. Loeb Classical Library. 4 vols. London: William Heinemann, 1921.

Rabinovitch, Nachum L. *Probability and Statistical Inference in Ancient and Medieval Jewish Literature*. Toronto: Univ. of Toronto Press, 1973.

Ramus (Pierre de la Ramée). *The Logicke of the Moste Excellent Philosopher P. Ramus Martyr*. London, 1574.

Rapin, René. *Réflexions sur la poétique d'Aristote*. Paris, 1674.

Reflections on Aristotle's Treatise of Poesy. Tr. Thomas Rymer. In *The Continental Model: Selected French Critical Essays of the Seventeenth Century*. Ed. Scott Elledge and Donald Schier. 1960. Ithaca: Cornell Univ. Press, 1970, pp. 279–306.

Rather, L. J. *Mind and Body in Eighteenth-Century Medicine: A Study Based on Jerome Gaub's "De regimine mentis."* Berkeley: Univ. of California Press, 1965.

Raven, Charles E. *John Ray Naturalist: His Life and Work*. Cambridge: Cambridge Univ. Press, 1942.

Rawson, C. J. *Gulliver and the Gentle Reader: Studies in Swift and our Time.* London: Routledge & Kegan Paul, 1973.

Ray, John. *The Wisdom of God manifested in the Works of the Creation,* 1691. Glasgow, 1744.

Reeve, Clara. "Preface" to *The Old English Baron.* 1778. In *Novel and Romance 1700–1800: A Documentary Record.* Ed. Ioan Williams. New York: Barnes & Noble, 1970, pp. 298–300.

Regis, L. M. *L'Opinion selon Aristote.* Paris: Vrin, 1935.

Reid, Thomas. *An Inquiry into the Human Mind.* 1764. Ed. Timothy Duggan. Chicago: Univ. of Chicago Press, 1970.

Thomas Reid's Lectures on the Fine Arts. 1774. Ed. Peter Kivy. The Hague: Martinus Nijhoff, 1973.

Essays on the Intellectual Powers of Man. 1785. Ed. Baruch Brody. Cambridge, Mass.: M.I.T. Press, 1969.

Reik, Miriam M. *The Golden Lands of Thomas Hobbes.* Detroit: Wayne State Univ. Press, 1977.

Rescher, Nicholas. *Peirce's Philosophy of Science: Critical Studies in his Theory of Induction and Scientific Method.* Notre Dame: Univ. of Notre Dame Press, 1978.

Reynolds, Joshua. *Discourses on Art.* Ed. Robert R. Wark. New Haven: Yale Univ. Press, 1975.

Rhetorica ad C. Herennium. Tr. Harry Caplan. Loeb Classical Library. London: William Heinemann, 1977.

Richardson, J. *Thoughts upon Thinking, or, A New Theory of the Human Mind.* London, 1773.

Richardson, Jonathan. *The Works of Mr. Jonathan Richardson.* London, 1773.

Richardson, Samuel. *Clarissa.* 4 vols. London: Dent, 1976.

Richter, Jean Paul. *The Horn of Oberon: Jean Paul Richter's School for Aesthetics.* Tr. Margaret R. Hale. Detroit: Wayne State Univ. Press, 1973.

Rickaby, Joseph. *Moral Philosophy: Ethics, Deontology and Natural Law.* London: Longmans, 1923.

Rijk, L. M. De. *Logica Modernorum: A Contribution to the Early History of Terminist Logic.* Assen: Van Gorcum, 1962.

Robbe-Grillet, Alain. *Two Novels by Robbe-Grillet.* Tr. Richard Howard. New York: Grove Press, 1965.

Rogerson, Brewster. "The Art of Painting the Passions." *Journal of the History of Ideas,* 14 (1953), 68–94.

Romanell, Patrick. "Locke and Sydenham: A Fragment on Small-pox." *Bulletin of the History of Medicine,* 32 (1958), 292–321.

Rose, Eliot. *Cases of Conscience: Alternatives open to Recusants and Puritans under Elizabeth I and James I.* Cambridge: Cambridge Univ. Press, 1975.

Rose, Paul Lawrence. *The Italian Renaissance of Mathematics: Studies on Humanists and Mathematicians from Petrarch to Galileo.* Geneva: Droz, 1975.

Ross, David. *Aristotle.* 1923. London: Methuen, 1974.

Ross, Sydney. " 'Scientist': The Story of a Word." *Annals of Science,* 18 (1962), 65–85.

Rossky, William. "Imagination in the English Renaissance: Psychology and Poetic." *Studies in the Renaissance,* 5 (1958), 49–73.

Rothstein, Eric. *Systems of Order and Inquiry in Later Eighteenth-Century Fiction.* Berkeley: Univ. of California Press, 1975.

Rousseau, G. S. *Tobias Smollett: Essays of Two Decades*. Edinburgh: T. & T. Clark, 1982.

Rudowski, Victor Anthony. "The Theory of Signs in the Eighteenth Century." *Journal of the History of Ideas*, 35 (1974), 683–90.

Ruffhead, Owen. *The Life of Alexander Pope, Esq*. London, 1769.

Rust, George. *The Remains of that Reverend and Learned Prelate, Dr. George Rust*. London, 1686.

Rymer, Thomas. *The Critical Works of Thomas Rymer*. Ed. Curt A. Zimansky. New Haven: Yale Univ. Press, 1956.

Sabra, A. I. *Theories of Light from Descartes to Newton*. London: Oldbourne, 1967.

Sambursky, S. "On the Possible and the Probable in Ancient Greece." *Osiris*, 12 (1956), 35–48.

The Physical World of the Greeks. London: Routledge & Kegan Paul, 1956.

Sayers, Frank. *Disquisitions, Metaphysical and Literary*. London, 1793.

Scaliger, Julius Caesar. *Poetices libri septem*. Lyons, 1561.

Schmitt, Charles B. "Experience and Experiment: A Comparison of Zabarella's View with Galileo's in *De motu*." *Studies in the Renaissance*, 16 (1969), 80–138.

Cicero Scepticus: A Study of the Influence of the Academica *in the Renaissance*. The Hague: Mouton, 1972.

"The Recovery and Assimilation of Ancient Scepticism in the Renaissance." *Rivista critica di storia della filosofia*, 27 (1972), 363–84.

Schneider, Ivo. "Wahrscheinlichkeit und Zufall bei Kepler." *Philosophia Naturalis*, 16 (1976), 40–63.

"Why do We Find the Origin of a Calculus of Probability in the Seventeenth Century?" In *Probabilistic Thinking, Thermodynamics and the Interaction of the History and Philosophy of Science*. Ed. J. Hintikka *et al.* Dordrecht: D. Reidel, 1981, II, 3–24.

Scott, Walter. *The Lives of the Novelists*. London: Dent, 1910.

Scoular, Kitty. *Natural Magic: Studies in the Presentation of Nature in English Poetry from Spenser to Marvell*. Oxford: Clarendon Press, 1965.

Sebeok, Thomas A. *The Sign & Its Masters*. Austin: Univ. of Texas Press, 1979.

Sedgwick, Alexander. *Jansensim in Seventeenth-Century France: Voices from the Wilderness*. Charlottesville: Univ. Press of Virginia, 1977.

Shaftesbury, Anthony Ashley Cooper, third Earl. *Second Characters or the Language of Forms*. Ed. Benjamin Rand. Cambridge: Cambridge Univ. Press, 1914.

Shands, Harley C., and Meltzer, James D. "Clinical Semiotics." *Language Studies*, 38 (1975), 21–24.

"Unexpected Semiotic Implications of Medical Inquiry." In *A Perfusion of Signs*. Ed. Thomas A. Sebeok. Bloomington: Indiana Univ. Press, 1977, pp. 73–89.

Shapiro, Barbara J. "Law and Science in Seventeenth-Century England." *Stanford Law Review*, 21 (1969), 727–66.

Probability and Certainty in Seventeenth-Century England: A Study of the Relationship between Natural Science, History, Law, and Literature. Princeton: Princeton Univ. Press, 1983.

Sharpe, William. *A Dissertation upon Genius; Or, an Attempt to shew, That the Several Instances of Distinction, and Degrees of Superiority in the human Genius are not, fundamentally, the Result of Nature, but the Effect of Acquisition*. London, 1755.

Shell, E. D. "S. Pepys, I. Newton and Probability." *The American Statistician*, 17 (1960), 27–30.

Shelley, Mary. *Frankenstein, or, the Modern Prometheus*. 1818. Indianapolis: Bobbs-Merrill, 1974.

Sherlock, William. *A Discourse concerning the Divine Providence*. London, 1694.

Sherry, Richard. *A Treatise of Schemes and Tropes*. London, 1550.

Sheynin, O. B. "Newton and the Classical Theory of Probability." *Archive for History of Exact Sciences*, 7 (1971), 217–43.

"On the Prehistory of the Theory of Probability." *Archive for History of Exact Sciences*, 12 (1974), 97–141.

"Early History of the Theory of Probability." *Archive for History of Exact Sciences*, 17 (1977), 201–59.

"On the History of the Statistical Method in Biology." *Archive for History of Exact Sciences*, 22 (1980), 323–71.

Siegel, Jerrold E. "'Civic Humanism' or Ciceronian Rhetoric? The Culture of Petrarch and Bruni." *Past and Present*, no. 34 (July 1966), 3–48.

Rhetoric and Philosophy in Renaissance Humanism: The Union of Eloquence and Wisdom, Petrarch to Valla. Princeton: Princeton Univ. Press, 1968.

Siegel, Jules Paul. "The Enlightenment and the Evolution of a Language of Signs in France and England." *Journal of the History of Ideas*, 30 (1969), 96–115.

Siskin, Clifford. "Wordsworth's Gothic Endeavor: From *Esthwaite* to the Great Decade." *The Wordsworth Circle*, 10 (1979), 161–73.

Skulsky, Harold. "Spenser's Despair Episode and the Theology of Doubt." *Modern Philology*, 78 (1981), 227–42.

Slater, Thomas. *A Manual of Moral Theology for English-Speaking Countries*. 2 vols. New York: Benziger Brothers, 1908.

Slevin, James F. "Morals and Form: A Study of Tradition and Innovation in *Joseph Andrews*." Diss. Univ. of Virginia. 1975.

Slights, Camille Wells. *The Casuistical Tradition in Shakespeare, Donne, Herbert, and Milton*. Princeton: Princeton Univ. Press, 1981.

Sloan, Phillip R. "John Locke, John Ray, and the Problem of Natural System." *Journal of the History of Biology*, 5 (1972), 1–53.

"Descartes, the Sceptics, and the Rejection of Vitalism in Seventeenth-Century Physiology." *Studies in the History and Philosophy of Science*, 8 (1977), 1–28.

Smart, Alistair. "Dramatic Gesture and Expression in the Age of Hogarth and Reynolds." *Apollo*, 82 (1965), 90–97.

Smith, Adam. *The Theory of Moral Sentiments*. 1759. Ed. D. D. Raphael and A. L. Macfie. Oxford: Clarendon Press, 1976.

Essays on Philosophical Subjects. Dublin, 1795.

Smith, David Nichol. *Shakespeare in the Eighteenth Century*. Oxford: Clarendon Press, 1928.

Smollett, Tobias. *The Adventures of Roderick Random*. 1748. Ed. Paul-Gabriel Boucé. London: Oxford Univ. Press, 1979.

The Adventures of Ferdinand Count Fathom. 1753. In two parts. New York: Brown, Bigelow, n.d.

The Adventures of Sir Launcelot Greaves. 1762. Vol. 6: *The Works of Tobias Smollett*. Ed. James Browne. London: Bickers, 1872.

The Expedition of Humphry Clinker. 1771. Ed. André Parreaux. Boston: Houghton Mifflin, 1968.

South, Robert. *Sermons Preached upon Several Occasions.* 6 vols. London, 1737.

Spector, Robert. *Tobias Smollett.* New York: Twayne, 1959.

Spence, Joseph. *Polymetis: or, an Enquiry concerning the Agreement between the Works of the Roman Poets, and the Remains of Ancient Artists.* London, 1747.

Spencer, Thomas. *The Art of Logick.* London, 1628.

Spinoza, Benedict. "On the Improvement of the Understanding." *The Chief Works of Benedict de Spinoza.* Tr. R. H. M. Elwes. London, Bell, 1883, 1, 1–41.

Spitzer, Leo. *Linguistics and Literary History: Essays in Stylistics.* Princeton: Princeton Univ. Press, 1948.

Starobinski, Jean. *Jean-Jacques Rousseau: la transparence et l'obstacle.* Paris: Gallimard, 1971.

Starr, George A. *Defoe and Casuistry.* Princeton: Princeton Univ. Press, 1971.

Stephens, James. *Francis Bacon and the Style of Science.* Chicago: Univ. of Chicago Press, 1975.

Sterne, Laurence. *Letters of Laurence Sterne.* Ed. Lewis Perry Curtis. Oxford: Clarendon Press, 1935.

The Life and Opinions of Tristram Shandy, Gentleman. Ed. Melvyn New. 2 vols. Gainesville: Univ. of Florida Press, 1978.

A Sentimental Journey through France and Italy. Ed. Gardiner Stout, Jr. Berkeley: Univ. of California Press, 1967.

Sermons of Mr. Yorick. Vol. 5: *The Complete Works and Life of Laurence Sterne.* In two parts. Ed. Wilbur L. Cross. New York: AMS Press, 1970.

Stewart, Dugald. *The Collected Works of Dugald Stewart.* Ed. Sir William Hamilton. 11 vols. Edinburgh: Constable, 1854.

Stockdale, Percival. *An Inquiry into the Nature, and Genuine Laws of Poetry.* London, 1778.

Stocks, J. L. "Epicurean Induction." *Mind,* 34 (1925), 185–203.

Stolnitz, Jerome. "On the Origins of Aesthetic Disinterestedness." *Journal of Aesthetics and Art Criticism,* 20 (1961), 131–43.

Stone, George Winchester, Jr., and Kahrl, George M. *David Garrick: A Critical Biography.* Carbondale: Southern Illinois Univ. Press, 1979.

Stone, P. W. K. *The Art of Poetry 1750–1820: Theories of poetic composition and style in the late Neo-Classic and early Romantic periods.* New York: Barnes & Noble, 1967.

Stough, Charlotte L. *Greek Skepticism: A Study in Epistemology.* Berkeley: Univ. of California Press, 1969.

Strauss, Albrecht B. "On Smollett's Language: A Paragraph in *Ferdinand Count Fathom.*" In *Style in Prose Fiction.* English Institute Essays, 1958. Ed. H. L. Martin. New York: Columbia Univ. Press, 1958, pp. 25–54.

Stubbs, Henry. *Legends no Histories: or, a Specimen of some Animadversions upon the History of the Royal Society.* London, 1670.

Swift, Jonathan. *The Poems of Jonathan Swift.* Ed. Harold Williams. 2nd ed. 3 vols. Oxford: Clarendon Press, 1958.

A Tale of a Tub. Ed. A. C. Guthkelch and D. Nichol Smith. Oxford: Clarendon Press, 1958.

Talbot, Peter. *The Politician's Catechism for his Instruction in Divine Faith and Moral Honesty.* Antwerp, 1658.

Tasso, Torquato. *Discourses on the Heroic Poem.* 1594. Tr. Mariella Cavalchini and Irene Samuel. Oxford: Clarendon Press, 1973.

Tavard, George H. *The Seventeenth-Century Tradition: A Study in Recusant Thought*. Leiden: E. J. Brill, 1978.

Tave, Stuart. *The Amiable Humorist: A Study in the Comic Theory and Criticism of the Eighteenth and Early Nineteenth Centuries*. Chicago: Univ. of Chicago Press, 1960.

Some Words of Jane Austen. Chicago: Univ. of Chicago Press, 1973.

Taylor, George. "'The Just Delineation of the Passions': Theories of Acting in the Age of Garrick." In *The Eighteenth-Century English Stage*. Ed. K. Richards and P. Thomson. London: Methuen, 1972, pp. 51–72.

Taylor, Jeremy. *Ductor Dubitantium: or, The Rule of Conscience*. 1660. 4th ed. London. 1696.

Thomas Aquinas, St. *Summa theologiae*. Ed. Thomas Gilby. 60 vols. London: Blackfriars, 1964.

Thomas, D. O. *The Honest Mind: The Thought and Work of Richard Price*. Oxford: Clarendon Press, 1977.

Thomas, Keith. *Religion and the Decline of Magic*. New York: Scribner's, 1971.

Thompson, W. N. *Aristotle's Deduction and Induction*. Amsterdam: Rodopi, 1975.

Thomson, William. *An Enquiry into the Elementary Principles of Beauty*. London, 1798.

Thorndike, Lynn. *A History of Magic and Experimental Science*. 8 vols. New York: Columbia Univ. Press, 1958.

Thorpe, Clarence De Witt. *The Aesthetic Theory of Thomas Hobbes*. Ann Arbor: Univ. of Michigan Press, 1940.

Todhunter, Isaac. *A History of the Mathematical Theory of Probability from the Time of Pascal to that of Laplace*. Cambridge and London: Macmillan, 1865.

Tolhurst, William E., and Wheeler, Samuel C., III. "On Textual Individuation." *Philosophical Studies*, 35 (1979), 187–97.

Trapp, Joseph. *Lectures on Poetry*. 1711–19. London, 1742.

Traugott, John. *Tristram Shandy's World: Sterne's Philosophical Rhetoric*. Berkeley: Univ. of California Press, 1954.

Treadwell, T. O. "The Two Worlds of *Ferdinand Count Fathom*." In *Tobias Smollett: Bicentennial Essays Presented to Lewis M. Knapp*. Ed. G. S. Rousseau and Paul-Gabriel Boucé. New York: Oxford Univ. Press, 1971, pp. 131–53.

Trimpi, Wesley. "The Ancient Hypothesis of Fiction." *Traditio*, 27 (1971), 1–78.

"The Quality of Fiction." *Traditio*, 30 (1874), 6–40.

Trinkhaus, Charles. *In Our Image and Likeness: Humanity and Divinity in Italian Renaissance Thought*. 2 vols. Chicago: Univ. of Chicago Press, 1970.

"Italian Humanism and the Problem of 'Structures of Conscience.'" *Journal of Medieval and Renaissance Studies*, 2 (1972), 19–33.

Trowbridge, Hoyt. *From Dryden to Jane Austen: Essays on English Critics and Writers, 1660–1818*. Albuquerque: Univ. of New Mexico Press, 1977.

Tucker, Abraham. *The Light of Nature Pursued*. 1768. Ed. Sir H. P. St. John Mildmay. 7 vols. London, 1805.

Turnbull, John M. "The Prototype of Walter Shandy's *Tristrapaedia*." *Review of English Studies*, 2 (1926), 212–15.

Turner, James. "The Structure of Henry Hoare's Stourhead." *Art Bulletin*, 61 (1979), 68–77.

Twining, Thomas. *Aristotle's Treatise on Poetry*. London, 1789.

Bibliography

Tytler, Graeme. *Physiognomy in the European Novel: Faces and Fortunes.* Princeton: Princeton Univ. Press, 1982.

Uexkull, Thura von. "Terminological Problems in Medical Semiotics." In *Semiotik 3: Zeichentypologie.* Ed. Tasso Borbé. Munich: W. Fink, 1978.

Uphaus, Robert W. *The Impossible Observer: Reason and the Reader in 18th-Century Prose.* Lexington: Univ. Press of Kentucky, 1979.

Upton, John. *Spenser's Faerie Queene.* 2 vols. London, 1758.

Vico, Giambattista. *On the Study Methods of our Time.* Tr. Elio Gianturco. Indianapolis: Bobbs-Merrill, 1965.

Vida, Marco Girolamo. *The "De Arte Poetica" of Marco Girolamo Vida.* Ed. and tr. Ralph G. Williams. New York: Columbia Univ. Press, 1976.

Vives, Juan Luis. *J. L. Vivis opera omnia.* Ed. Gregorio Mayans y Siscar. 8 vols. Valencia, 1782.

    On Education. A Translation of the "De Tradendis Disciplinis" of Juan Luis Vives. Tr. Foster Watson. 1913. Totowa: Rowman & Littlefield, 1971.

Voltaire (François Marie Arouet). *Essai sur les probabilités en fait de justice.* 1772. *Oeuvres complètes de Voltaire.* Ed. A. J. Beuchot *et al.* Paris: Garnier, 1879, XXVIII, 495–516.

Vossius, Geraldus. *De Artis poeticae natura ac consitutione liber.* Amsterdam, 1647.

Waldman, Theodore. "Origins of the Legal Doctrine of Reasonable Doubt." *Journal of the History of Ideas,* 20 (1959), 299–316.

Walker, John. *Elements of Elocution, being the Substance of a Course of Lectures on the Art of Reading.* 2 vols. London, 1781.

Walker, Obadiah. *Of Education, Especially of Young Gentlemen.* Oxford, 1673.

Wallace, William. *Causality and Scientific Explanation.* 2 vols. Ann Arbor: Univ. of Michigan Press, 1972.

Walpole, Horace. *The Castle of Otranto.* 1764. Ed. Wilmarth S. Lewis. London: Oxford Univ. Press, 1969.

    Historic Doubts on the Life and Reign of Richard III. 1768. In *Richard III: The Great Debate.* Ed. Paul Murray Kendall. New York: Folio Society, 1965, pp. 153–239.

    Hieroglyphic Tales. 1785. London: Elkin Mathews, 1926.

Walton, Craig. "Ramus and the Art of Judgment." *Philosophy and Rhetoric,* 3 (1970), 152–64.

Walton, Kendall. "Categories of Art." *Philosophical Review,* 79 (1970), 334–67.

Ward, John. *A System of Oratory.* 2 vols. London, 1759.

Warton, Joseph. *An Essay on the Genius and Writings of Pope.* Vol. 1. London, 1756.

    4th ed. 2 vols. London, 1782.

Warton, Thomas. *Observations on the Fairy Queen of Spenser.* 2 vols. London, 1762.

    A History of English Poetry. 1774–81. 4 vols. London, 1824.

Wasserman, Earl. "The Sympathetic Imagination in Eighteenth-Century Theories of Acting." *Journal of English and Germanic Philology,* 46 (1947), 264–72.

Watson, Richard A. *The Downfall of Cartesianism in France 1673–1712.* The Hague: Martinus Nijhoff, 1966.

Watts, Isaac. *Logick; or, the Right Use of Reason in the Enquiry after Truth.* 1725. London, 1786.

Webb, Daniel. *An Inquiry into the Beauties of Painting.* London, 1761.
 Remarks on the Beauties of Poetry. London, 1762.
 Observations on the Correspondence between Poetry and Music. London, 1769.
Webster, John. *Academarium Examen, or the Examination of Academies.* London, 1653.
Weinberg, Bernard. "Robortello on the *Poetics.*" In *Critics and Criticism: Ancient and Modern.* Ed. R. S. Crane. Chicago: Univ. of Chicago Press, 1952, pp. 319–48.
 A History of Literary Criticism in the Italian Renaissance. 2 vols. Chicago: Univ. of Chicago Press, 1961.
Weinberg, Julius R. *Nicolaus of Autrecourt: A Study in 14th Century Thought.* Princeton: Princeton Univ. Press, 1948.
Wellek, René. *A History of Modern Criticism, 1750–1950.* 5 vols. New Haven: Yale Univ. Press, 1955– .
 "Appendix: A Historical Perspective: Literary Criticism." In *What is Criticism?* Ed. Paul Hernadi. Bloomington: Indiana Univ. Press, 1981, pp. 297–321.
Wendorf, Richard. *William Collins and Eighteenth-Century English Poetry.* Minneapolis: Univ. of Minnesota Press, 1981.
Westfall, Richard S. *The Construction of Modern Science: Mechanisms and Mechanics.* New York: John Wiley, 1971.
Westman, Robert S. "Kepler's Theory of Hypothesis and the 'Realist Dilemma.'" *Studies in the History and Philosophy of Science,* 3 (1972), 233–64.
 "The Melanchthon Circle, Rheticus and the Wittenberg Interpretation of the Copernican Theory." *Isis,* 66 (1975), 165–93.
Whately, Richard. *Historic Doubts Relative to Napoleon Buonaparte.* 1819. New York: Carter, 1856.
White, Douglas H. *Pope and the Context of Controversy: The Manipulation of Ideas in "An Essay on Man."* Chicago: Univ. of Chicago Press, 1970.
White, Thomas. *Controversy-Logicke. Or the Methode to come to Truth in Debates of Religion.* London, 1659.
 Peripateticall Institutions in the Way of that eminent Person and excellent Philosopher Kenelm Digby. London, 1661.
 An Exclusion of Scepticks From all Title to Dispute: Being an Answer to the Vanity of Dogmatizing. London, 1665.
Whiter, Walter. *A Specimen of a Commentary on Shakespeare.* London, 1794.
Wigmore, John H. "Required Numbers of Witnesses; a Brief History of the Mathematical System in England." *Harvard Law Review,* 15 (1901), 83–108.
Wilkins, John. *The Mathematical and Philosophical Works.* 2 vols. London, 1802.
William of Sherwood. *William of Sherwood's Introduction to Logic.* Tr. Norman Kretzmann. Minneapolis: Univ. of Minnesota Press, 1966.
Williams, Aubrey. "Interpositions of Providence and the Design of Fielding's Novels." *South Atlantic Quarterly,* 70 (1971), 265–86.
Wilson, Daniel. "Readers in Texts." *PMLA,* 96 (1981), 848–63.
Wilson, Thomas. *The Rule of Reason Conteinyng the Arte of Logique.* 1551. 2nd ed. 1553. Northridge: San Fernando State Teachers College, 1972.
 The Arte of Rhetorique. 1553. 2nd ed. 1560. Facs. rpt. London: Oxford Univ. Press, 1909.

Bibliography

Winner, Anthony. "Richardson's Lovelace: Character and Prediction." *Texas Studies in Language and Literature*, 14 (1972), 53–75.

Wolseley, Robert. Preface to Rochester's *Valentinian*. 1685. In *Critical Essays of the Seventeenth Century*. Ed. J. E. Spingarn. Oxford: Clarendon Press, 1909, III, 1–31.

Wood, Thomas. *English Casuistical Divinity During the Seventeenth Century With Special Reference to Jeremy Taylor*. London: S.P.C.K., 1952.

Woodbridge, Kenneth. *Landscape and Antiquity: Aspects of English Culture at Stourhead*. London: Oxford Univ. Press, 1970.

Wordsworth, William. *The Poetical Works of William Wordsworth*. Ed. Ernest de Selincourt. 5 vols. Oxford: Clarendon Press, 1940–49.

The Prose Works of William Wordsworth. Ed. W. J. B. Owen and J. W. Snyder. 3 vols. Oxford: Clarendon Press, 1974.

Wright, John P. *The Sceptical Realism of David Hume*. Manchester: Manchester Univ. Press, 1983.

Wright, Thomas. *The Passions of the Minde in Generall*. 1601. London, 1604.

Yolton, John. "The Science of Nature." In *John Locke: Problems and Perspectives*. Cambridge: Cambridge Univ. Press, 1969, pp. 183–93.

Youngren, William. "Dr. Johnson, Joseph Warton, and the 'Theory of Particularity.'" *Dispositio*, 4 (1979), 163–88.

Zetterberg, J. Peter. "Echoes of Nature in Salomon's House." *Journal of the History of Ideas*, 43 (1982), 179–93.

ADDENDA

Ascham, Roger. *Toxophilus*. London, 1545.

Burnyeat, Myles. "Carneades Was No Probabilist." In *Riverside Studies in Ancient Skepticism*. Ed. D. K. Glidden. Forthcoming.

Clarke, John. *An Essay on Study*. London, 1731.

Davie, Donald. "An Episode in the History of Candor." *Dissentient Voice: The Ward-Phillips Lectures for 1980 with some Related Pieces*. Notre Dame: Notre Dame Univ. Press, 1982, pp. 83–93.

Elzinga, Aant. "Huyghens' Theory of Research and Descartes' Theory of Knowledge." *Zeitschrift für Allgemeine Wissenschaft*, 2 (1971), 174–94; 3 (1972), 9–25.

Langbein, John H. *Torture and the Law of Proof: Europe and England in the Ancien Régime*. Chicago: Univ. of Chicago Press, 1977.

Lydgate, John. *The Pilgrimage of the Life of Man*. Ed. F. J. Furnivall. London: Early English Text Society, 1899, 1901, 1904.

Pearson, Karl. *The History of Statistics in the 17th and 18th Centuries against the Changing Background of Intellectual, Scientific and Religious Thought*. London: Charles Griffin, 1978.

Putnam, Hilary. *Reason, Truth and History*. Cambridge: Cambridge Univ. Press, 1981.

Index

Index

verisimilitude *cont.*
 distinguished from probability,
  77–83; *verisimile*, 16, 18, 77, 115,
  146, 320 n13; *vraisemblance*, 23,
  25, 29, 59, 64, 77–83, 150
vestigium, 40
Vico, Giambattista, 45, 46, 65–67
Vida, Marco Girolamo, 307 n63
Viotti, Bartholomeo, 17, 173
Viperano, G. A., 306 n58
visual metaphors, 29–31, 85, 194,
  197–98, 288 n75, 317 n68
Vives, Juan Luis, 13, 18–19, 62, 63, 286
  n47, 308 n66, 312 n102, 322 n33
Voltaire, 7–8, 48
Vossius, Geraldus, 81
vraisemblance, see verisimilitude

Waldman, Theodore, 6
Walker, John, 303 n30
Walker, Obadiah, 62–66, 135, 200
Wallace, William, 291 n12
Wallis, John, 33
Walpole, Horace, 151–52, 159–60, 161,
  293 n31
Walton, Craig, 18
Walton, Kendall, 263
Ward, John, 96, 302 n28
Warton, Joseph, 93, 125, 139, 144, 153,
  317 n70
Warton, Thomas, 161, 162, 317 n68
Wasserman, Earl, 303 n28
Watson, George, 309 n74
Watson, R. A., 333 n12
Watts, Isaac, 9, 32, 47, 58, 289 n76
Webb, Daniel, 312 n105
Webster, John, 292 n22
Weinberg, Bernard, 297 n10, 306 n56,
  314 n21
Weinberg, Julius, 283 n6, 285 n30
Wellek, René, 310 n94, 316 n49, 318
  n71
Wesley, John, 228
Westfall, R. S., 333 n12

Whately, Richard, 74, 148–49
White, Douglas, 312 n100
White, Thomas, 43, 173
Whiter, Walter, 256, 335 n3
Whytt, Robert, 328 n25
Wigmore, J. H., 8, 283 nn4, 13
Wilkes, Thomas, 97
Wilkins, John, 37, 287 n65, 334 n13
will, 32, 41, 95, 171, 186, 188, 207, 214,
  252, 254, 257, 329 n1, 330 n6
William of Sherwood, 8–9, 20
Williams, Aubrey, 322 n35
Wilson, Daniel (1851), 324 n38
Wilson, Daniel (1981), 320 n10
Wilson, F. P., 290 n9
Wilson, Thomas, 12, 17, 25–26, 40, 51,
  62
Winner, Anthony, 324 n43
wit, 132, 135, 137, 139–40, 153, 235;
  "bodily wit," 134
witness (*see also* testimony), 21, 32, 269,
  288 n72; "probable," 4, 8; in law,
  6–8
Wolff, Christian, 317 n71
Wolseley, Robert, 140
wonder, 120, 146–47, 148, 150, 158,
  177
Woodbridge, Kenneth, 297 n3
Wordsworth, William, 145, 153,
  155–56, 158, 159–66, 221, 249,
  259, 274, 306 n52
Wright, John P., 327 n16
Wright, Thomas, 35, 41, 42, 50, 51, 105
Wycherley, William, 102

Xenophanes, 14

Yolton, John, 289 n3, 334 n15
Youngren, William, 310 n91

Zabell, Sandy, 334 nn16, 19, 20
Zeno, 128, 291 n17
Zetterberg, J. P., 311 n96

The Definition of Good

THE DEFINITION
OF GOOD

By

A. C. EWING

M.A., D.Phil. (Oxon); M.A., Litt.D. (Cantab).
Fellow of the British Academy
Lecturer in Moral Science in the University of Cambridge

New York

THE MACMILLAN COMPANY

1947

Preface

The question *What is the definition of goodness* must be distinguished from the question *What things are good;* and it is the former, not the latter, question which I discuss in this book. This question, while less immediately and obviously practical, is more fundamental, since it raises the issue whether ethics is explicable wholly in terms of something else, for example, human psychology, and it certainly ought to be answered before we decide either on the place value is to occupy in our conception of reality or on the ultimate characteristics which make one action right and another wrong.

I shall not attempt to give a list of those to whom I am indebted, because such a list would probably embrace all the main works on ethics which I have read and most of the people who have discussed with me, orally, the fundamental concepts of ethics. I must express my gratitude to my mother for her valued help in proofreading. I also have to thank the editors of *Mind* and *Philosophy* for having allowed me to use articles I had previously published in these periodicals.

A. C. EWING

TRINITY HALL
  CAMBRIDGE
  ENGLAND

November, 1946

Contents

CHAPTER I

Subjectivism

One class of answer to the question how "good" is to be defined is given by the subjectivists. But, before we consider this type of answer, we must try to make clear to ourselves what could be meant by the "objectivity" of ethical judgements or of value judgements in general. It obviously does not mean that they ascribe value properties to physical objects. These clearly do not possess ethical qualities. It might indeed be held that they possessed the property of beauty and therefore the property of intrinsic goodness quite independently of being perceived. This view does not seem to me obviously false, but it is plain that most philosophers who have asserted the objectivity of value judgements did not wish to commit themselves to it, still less to maintain that all value judgements were objective in precisely the same sense as that in which judgements about physical objects are. We can therefore rule out at once the sense of "objective" as referring to what exists independently of being experienced. What then does "objective" mean when used in reference to ethics?

1. It may mean "claiming to be true." Obviously in this sense judgements about psychological events and dispositions are objective, though they do not refer to what exists independently of experience, and in this sense ethical judgements may be objective. To say they are is indeed to say no more than that they are judgements and not merely something else which we have confused with judgements. But even this much is denied by some who maintain that so-called ethical judgements are only exclamations, commands, or wishes.

I

2. However, a person who admitted the occurrence of ethical judgements, but denied that they were ever in fact true or that we could ever have any justification for believing them to be true, would not usually be described as holding an objective view of ethics. So "objective" here may be taken as implying that ethical judgements in particular and value judgements in general are sometimes true and can be sometimes known or at least justifiably believed to be true. An objective view involves the rejection of scepticism in ethics.

3. But this would not by itself be sufficient to satisfy the holders of the view that ethical judgements are objective. Suppose "A is good" simply meant "I have a certain feeling about A." It would then be a judgement and could perfectly well be true and known to be true, yet anybody who maintained such a position would be said to be holding a subjective and not an objective view of ethics. The proposition that ethical judgements are objective, therefore, besides asserting that they are judgements, asserts of them a certain independence of the feelings or attitude of the person judging. They are not merely judgements about his feelings, or for that matter his thoughts. Even if partly based on feeling, they are not about the feeling itself but about something to which the feeling points, and something which cannot adequately be described in terms merely of the man's own psychology.

The view that "ethical judgements are objective" therefore excludes the following views: (a) that they are not really judgements at all, (b) that they are all false or that we are never justified in thinking them true, (c) that they are merely judgements about one's own psychological state or dispositions. Any of these three alternative views may be called "subjective." [1] The "objective" view is also commonly understood as excluding any view which holds them to be analysable

---

[1] My use of this term is quite different from the use made of it by Ross in *Foundations of Ethics*, Chap. 7.

exclusively in terms of human psychology, but here a distinction is required between "naturalism" and "subjectivism." A person who opposes naturalist theories of ethics in general is often spoken of rather loosely as defending the objectivity of ethics, but a naturalist theory need not be, though it may be, subjective.[2] A typical example of naturalist ethics would be the theory that to say some action is right or some experience good merely means that most men, or most men in a certain group, tend to have a particular kind of feeling about it or that it tends to the satisfaction of most men's desires. Now on such a theory "good" and "right" still stand for objective facts quite independent of the attitude towards them of the person who makes the ethical judgement in question; that is, they stand for facts about a class of people, or people in general. They would still be as objective as the judgement that many Germans admired Hitler or that generally a man is distressed by the death of his parents. These forms of naturalist ethics differ from non-naturalist forms not in denying the objectivity of ethics, for judgements of psychology are objective, but in making ethics a branch of an empirical science, and will therefore be discussed not in the present chapter but in the following one.

Perhaps the most striking feature of present-day ethics is the frequent occurrence of theories of a frankly naturalist or subjectivist type. For this there are several obvious causes. Firstly, the success of the natural sciences as compared with philosophy and the failure of obscurantist opposition in the name of religion have made people reluctant to admit anything which cannot be subjected to the methods of empirical science. Secondly, the decline in the influence of organized Christianity and the widespread doubts as to the justification of its central

---

[2] Of the three types of subjective theory above I should call (c) both naturalist and subjective; (a) and (b) could not claim that ethical propositions are part of a natural science, and therefore I should hesitate to call them naturalist.

theological beliefs have contributed to the rise of scepticism about ethics. This must specially be the case with those who thought that ethics was essentially bound up with religion but have lost their faith in religion. Thirdly, the radical divergence in ethical views between different people and different civilizations has been realized as never before (and, I think, exaggerated). Fourthly, since the war of 1914–18 there has been a world-wide reaction against rationalism in all spheres, so that there is a consequent tendency to regard any *a priori* element in ethics with great suspicion and to connect "value judgements" closely with feeling, even sometimes to the extent of saying that they are not judgements at all but only expressions of feeling. We must not, however, exaggerate the prevalence of such opinions. When I reviewed the ethical literature published in 1937 and 1938 in order to write a manual for the *Institut International de Collaboration Philosophique* [3] I found that on the continent of Europe naturalist or subjectivist ethics was decidedly the exception among philosophers. I even noted an assertion in an article by Professor Urban [4] that the objectivity of value can now be regarded as one of the things "we know" in axiology, in the sense that among critical opinion there is a large measure of assent on this point even in America and more markedly in Europe. It is too early to say how the situation will be affected by the war.

The simplest form of the subjectivist view is that according to which ethical judgements, though genuine judgements, assert only that the person who makes the judgement has or tends to have certain feelings. "This is good" or "right" on such a view becomes "I have [or tend to have] an emotion of approval on considering this." A number of incredibly para-

---

[3] This was unfortunately never published, owing to the German occupation of Paris.

[4] *Journal of Philosophy*, 1937, p. 588 ff.

doxical consequences would follow from the adoption of this view. Firstly, the judgements could not be false unless the person judging had made a mistake about his own psychology. Secondly, two different people would never mean the same thing when they made such a judgement, since each would mean "This is approved by *me*." Indeed the same person would never mean the same by it on two different occasions, because each time he would mean "I *now* feel [or tend to feel] approval of this."

Thirdly, if I judge something to be good and you judge it to be bad, our judgements would never be logically incompatible with each other. It is not a sufficient reply to point out that they can still be incompatible with each other in some different sense, for example in the sense that they express attitudes which are in conflict with each other or lead to incompatible policies. For we do not see merely that A's judgement "This is good" and B's judgement "This is bad" (in the corresponding sense of the word) lead to or express incompatible policies like A's judgement "I desire to further X" and B's judgement "I desire to oppose X." We see that the two judgements logically contradict each other so that it is logically impossible that they could both be true. No doubt, since "good" and "bad" can each be used in different senses, "this is bad" may not always contradict "this is good," because, for example, "good" may mean "instrumentally good" and "bad" may mean "intrinsically bad"; but at any rate they sometimes do so, and on the view under discussion they could, when asserted by different people, never do so. Fourthly, no argument or rational discussion, nor indeed any citation of empirical facts, could be in any degree relevant to supporting or casting doubt on any ethical judgement unless it could be directed to showing that the person who makes the judgement has made a mistake about his own feelings or tendencies to have feelings. It is true that argument or fresh knowledge about the circumstances and likely consequences of an act might lead me to have different feelings about it and so judge it right while I had judged it wrong before, or vice versa; but it would not in any way indicate that my previous judgement was false.[5] The judgements would be different; but since they referred only to my feelings at different times they would not contradict each other any more than "I was ill on January 1" contradicts "I was well on February 1." Yet it is clear that argument can really cast doubt on propositions in ethics.

Fifthly, I could not, while asserting an ethical belief, conceive that I might possibly be wrong in this belief and yet be certain that I now feel (or tend to feel) disapproval. Since it is quite clear that I can conceive this in some cases at least, this argument provides another *reductio ad absurdum* of the theory. To think that an ethical belief now expressed by me may possibly be wrong is not the same as thinking that I may come in the future to have different feelings, for I think that the present judgement may be wrong and not a future one. To put the objection in another way, it would follow from the theory that to say "If I feel approval of A, A is always right [good]" is to utter a tautology. But it is not, it is a piece of gross conceit, if made in any ordinary context. Even if it were true that, if I feel approval of A, I shall always at the time judge A to be right (good), this is quite a different statement. I need not always be certain that my judgements are correct (unless judgement is so defined as to cover only cases of *knowledge*).

---

[5] I am therefore quite unmoved by the elaborate discussion by C. L. Stevenson in *Ethics and Language* as to how argument can be relevant to ethical disagreements on a subjectivist view. It does not show it to be relevant in the sense in which we really see it to be relevant, but in some other sense. The book is no doubt a very able exposition of subjectivism for those who are already convinced, but it does not, as far as I can see, bring any real argument for it or avoid any of the objections that I have mentioned against it.

Sixthly, it would follow from the theory under discussion that, when I judge that Hitler was bad or acted wrongly, I am not really talking about Hitler at all but about my own psychology.

To me the consequences that I have mentioned are all quite incredible and constitute a fully sufficient *reductio ad absurdum* of the theory from which they are deduced. They hold whether it is applied both to "good" and to "right" or only to one of them. I do not, however, see how the theory could be applied to "right" without being also applied to "good"; but it might be held that it applied only to "good" and that "right" was to be defined as "a means to the state of affairs for which (of those producible in the context) I felt, at the time I made the judgement, most approval on the whole." This would be a naturalist non-subjectivist theory of "right" combined with a subjectivist theory of "good." However, it is clear that this cannot be the meaning of "right," for if my emotions were ill adjusted a quite wrong action might be, and be believed by me to be, the most effective means to the state of affairs for which I felt most approval. I should probably in that case not judge it to be wrong at the time (though I might even do this if I distinguished between what I really thought good and my emotional feeling of approval); but I might quite well judge afterwards not only that it was wrong but that my earlier judgement that it was right was mistaken, while admitting that the act was the most effective means to the state towards which at the time I made the first judgement I felt most approval. Nor can we define a right act as "means, etc., to the state of affairs towards which I should always or ultimately feel most approval," for that would make it a prophecy about my future emotions. It clearly would not necessarily invalidate my present judgement that some particular act is right if it should turn out that my emotional disposition changed later in my life in such a way that I no longer felt approval of the state of affairs to which the action was an efficient means. It is true that I should in that case be disposed later to contradict my present judgement, but it certainly would not mean that my present judgement as to the rightness of the act was necessarily false.

Finally, if I ask somebody for advice on a question of practical ethics, I do not merely want to be brought into a certain emotional state about the proposed act or be persuaded that it is the best means to what will produce such an emotional state in me (or in other people, for that matter). Or at least, if that is all I want (which I suppose is the case with some people's requests for advice), it would be agreed that I am not asking in the right spirit, that is, I do not really want to know what is right but only to feel comfortable about the act advised. When I am asking for ethical advice I am asking, if I am genuine, whether a proposed act has an objective characteristic and not merely about its relation to my own emotions. And likewise when I am making up my own mind I do not regard my feeling of approval as a proof, even for myself, that a certain act is right but only as an indication. Because emotions are conservative, a man may easily have the feeling of disapproval towards something he thinks right if he formerly thought it wrong or towards something which offends his taste but which he believes is ethically neutral. But there are cases where I clearly see that something is good or bad, right and obligatory or wrong, and this insight has often been confused with the feeling which usually accompanies it.

Practically the same objections apply whether the subjectivist takes ethical judgements to be about the speaker's feelings or about his thought or about an attitude of mind including feeling, thought, and conation alike. Further, if we introduce the notion of thinking into the definition, an additional objection arises. For, if "this is good or right" means or includes in its meaning "I think it good or right," it may be objected that "I think this good or right" would become "I think that I think it good or right," so that we have either a vicious circle or an infinite regress.

It should however be noted that I have not included in the objections the argument sometimes used that from the subjectivist view it would follow that the same act may be both right when I speak about it, that is, approved by me, and wrong when you speak about it, that is, disapproved by you. For on any view the same act might be both right and not right (wrong) in different senses of "right." Even on the subjectivist view it need not be both right and not right in the same sense of "right." It is, however, very hard to believe that "good" or "right" means something different every time the word is used by a different speaker, and this is a furthur objection.

We should note an ambiguity in the terms "approval" and "disapproval." As used in recent philosophical discussion they have commonly stood for emotions, but in ordinary speech they usually express a judgement. "I approve of A" is then identical with "I judge A good," "I disapprove of A" with "I judge A bad" (in some respect at least). All ethical judgements express approval or disapproval in this sense, as all judgements without exception express the thoughts of the person who makes them. But if I therefore went on to say that I meant by "A is good" that I approve of A, I should be saying that I meant by "A is good" that I judge that A is good. This as a definition is obviously circular.

None of the objections I have given are avoided by substituting for "feelings" "tendencies to have feelings," as the subjectivist must indeed do if he is to avoid the different objection that I may make a true ethical judgement without actually feeling an emotion of approval or disapproval at the time I make the judgement or just before. It is indeed less difficult to suppose that, when a man makes a wrong ethical judgement (other than one which turns merely on a question of means), he is always mistaken about his unconscious tendencies to have feelings than that he is always mistaken about the present feelings he has; but it still seems perfectly obvious that "A was wrong in judging p right or good" does not entail "A was mistaken as to his own psychological tendencies to have feelings about p." Perhaps he could not in fact change his opinion and recognise himself to have been mistaken without a change in (not a mistake about) the tendencies in question, but this is quite a different point. The remaining objections are still less affected by this amendment.

It may still be true that the agent is often, though by no means always, the only person capable of judging with adequate assurance that it is right for him to do A rather than B. For he alone knows his own nature and state of mind, and these are often data highly relevant to the rightness or wrongness of an act. But this does not prove that his thinking the act right is the sole circumstance which makes it right, unless the fact that I am the only person who can remember what I felt like on a certain occasion a month ago proves that my feelings at that time were caused by my remembering them now.

Thwarted in their attempts to make "ethical judgements" merely autobiographical, subjectivists have commonly taken to maintaining that they are really commands, wishes, or exclamations. In that case they are neither true nor false and so are not judgements at all, though for the sake of convenience in terminology I shall use the phrase "ethical judgements" in inverted commas to cover such a view, meaning by "judgements" here real or apparent judgements. To say that "ethical judgements" are exclamations is to say that they are expressions of emotion, but this is distinguished from saying that they are judgements about the speaker's emotions. To say

"Alas!" is not, it may be contended, to assert, though it is to
suggest, that I am in distress. This solution has been rightly
challenged on the ground that it must be admitted at any rate
that ethical expressions are sentences deliberately constructed
by the speaker to express his feelings, and voluntarily and deliberately to employ a form of language intended to express
the fact that I have a particular kind of feeling can hardly
be distinguished from asserting that I have the feeling in
question.[6]

The criticism could be met only if it were held that all
ethical expressions were merely involuntary exclamations like
"Ou!" But it is certain that many ethical expressions, so far
from being mere involuntary cries, are made only after careful deliberation and with the conscious purpose of conveying
something believed to be true. These cases at any rate are not
covered by the theory in question, even if there are some other
cases which it does cover. I should indeed maintain that the
theory was not true of any ethical expressions, for I do not
see how mere involuntary exclamations could be regarded as
ethical expressions even if they included words like "good"
or "right." As Professor Broad has just pointed out,[7] there
is more than a verbal difference between saying "I have an
emotion" and merely exclaiming because I have it, but there
is not between saying that I have an emotion and deliberately
exclaiming with the purpose of telling people that I have it.
No doubt, when I exclaim with this purpose, I may have in
mind something other than the mere communication of a
truth about my emotions, but so I may if I state, for example,
that I am sorry about so-and-so.

If this argument is justified the exclamational view of such
judgements is indistinguishable from the autobiographical
view; that is, the view that ethical judgements are judgements

6 E. F. Carritt, *Philosophy*, Vol. XIII, No. 50, p. 133.
7 *Philosophy*, Vol. XXI, No. 79, p. 101.

about the speaker's feelings, and falls before the objections which we have just brought against that type of view, so that it is perhaps not really worth while discussing it by itself. But, even if this argument were invalid and the two views could be distinguished, we could urge against the exclamational view most of the objections brought against the other. We could still object that, if I say something is bad and you say it is good, we are sometimes contradicting each other. We could point out that it is incompatible with the place which argument and citation of empirical facts have in ethics. We could urge that for me to make a moral judgement about, for example, Hitler is not merely to express my own psychological state. We could insist that, when I ask for advice on an ethical point, all that I am wanting or should want is not just to have my emotions affected. That the view would make it impossible for an "ethical judgement" to be true or false at all is a more fundamental objection which does not apply to the autobiographical view. If "ethical judgements" are neither true nor false, not only would such "judgements" not be strictly provable (which may be admitted in any case), but nothing whatever could be said in their support. For to say something in their support would be to say something which makes their truth more likely, but they can no more be true according to this view than a blow can be true. Now that in making "ethical judgements" we are at least claiming to assert what is true is surely obvious from a consideration of our psychological attitude when we make them. When I try to decide what I ought to do in a given case I am conscious of trying *to find out something*, not merely of feeling in a certain way, or resolving, or wanting to do something, or trying to produce a certain state of mind in myself, and "to try to find something out" is to try to discover what is true. There is commonly an emotive aspect to ethical judgements, that is, they express feelings as well as make an objective truth claim; but they cannot be confined to the former function. The only case of which I can think where this aspect is almost the sole one is when a man uses terms of abuse in sheer anger without the least consideration whether they are justified or not but calls somebody names without really meaning what he says. In such an instance he might equally well have said "Damn him!" as "He is a cad," but it is obvious that there is a great difference between these cases and a genuine ethical judgement. Again, we can hardly avoid admitting that "All acts done out of a desire to give pain as such are wrong" entails the judgement "If this act is done out of such a desire, it is wrong," and how could this be so if they were not propositions, and therefore true or false, instead of being mere commands, wishes, or explanations? Nor do I see how either form of the subjectivist theory could be reconciled satisfactorily with the important part played by reasoning and consistency in ethics when we are, for example, deciding what is just and what is not. Though it goes too far, the coherence theory of ethics has, as we shall see, shown that ethics has more affinity to logic than subjectivists could allow.

The same type of objections seems to me valid against the view that "moral judgements" really express wishes. The view that they are commands or exhortations is in some respects in a different position. For, firstly, a command or exhortation deliberately expressed in language can be distinguished from a statement that I have or tend to have certain feelings. Secondly, the view is not open to the objection that no two people would then ever mean the same thing by an "ethical judgement," since two persons can issue the same command in a sense in which they could not be said to have the same feelings or the same wish. But the view would still imply that no "ethical judgements" claim to be either true or false. Some people do not find this as incredible as I do; but I can only say that, when I look seriously at what I am doing when I make

what is ordinarily called an ethical judgement, it is as plain to
me that I am asserting what I think to be true, and not merely
wishing, commanding, or exclaiming, as it is when I assert that
"two plus two is four" or "there is a table in this room."
Since we are talking at present about what sentences with
ethical terms in them commonly mean I do not see how I can
possibly go behind this introspective evidence. To mean is to
intend to assert, and if I do not know when I intend to assert
something and when I do not nobody else can. It is theoretically possible that I may be peculiar in my moral experience;
but I do not think that I shall be taking any undue risks if I
assume that the mode of experience known as "moral judgement" is not fundamentally and generically different in me
from what it is in other people, though their theories about it
may be in some cases very different from my own. In speaking of the view that "moral judgements" are commands or
exhortations I mean here commands or exhortations of the
person making the "judgement"; if it is held that they are
commands of society or of God, we have different (though
still objectionable) views which leave them the status of
propositions that claim objectivity and that can be true. To
command is not to assert a proposition, but that somebody has
in fact issued a command is a proposition which can be true
or false, so the two last views mentioned, though they are
liable to other objections, are not open to the charge of subjectivism.

There are plenty of other objections to the command
theory besides the objection that it would make "ethical
judgements" neither true nor false. There is nothing specifically moral about a command. I may command something
which I know or believe to be wrong, and I may quite well
think you ought to do something which I should not dream of
commanding you to do, for example, punish me. Nor is there
anything moral about obeying a person just because he issues a

command. If we obey him for a moral reason, for example, because we have given a promise, it is a reason over and above the command. So "You ought to do" cannot mean "I command or exhort you to do," because this would put you under no obligation. Even while I was giving the command, I should be aware that I must back it up by some additional reason which rendered obedience in this instance a duty or at least a matter of prudence. The knowledge that you ought to do something is sufficient in so far as you are moral to make you do it, the knowledge that I command you is not. If it were said in reply that a "moral judgement" is not a command to others but to oneself, then every resolution of mine to do anything would be a judgement that I ought to do it, which is clearly not the case, since I may resolve with great fervour to do something which I believe to be wrong. We could only develop the command theory in this way if we made a distinction between moral and non-moral or immoral resolves and begged the question by calling only the former commands. The command view is also open to the objection, brought against other subjective views, that it would entail the conclusion that, when one person asserts an action to be right and another asserts it to be wrong, what they say is not logically incompatible.

If it is maintained, as by Professor Stevenson in his recent book, *Ethics and Language*, that "ethical judgements" are partly judgements about the speaker's psychology claiming to be true and partly the expressions of emotive attitudes, including under this some kind of command or exhortation, the force of my objections is not diminished. The objections to the autobiographical view are objections which, if they show anything, show that the element in "ethical judgements" which is capable of being true or false is not merely autobiographical, and therefore they will not be removed by the theory that there is another element in "ethical judgements" which is not true or false at all. The element capable of being true or false, let us call it the "propositional element," cannot be merely autobiographical, because it may be false without the person judging having made a mistake about his own psychology, because it may be either the same as or logically incompatible with the propositional element in another person's judgement, when he condemns or approves the same thing, because arguments which are not relevant to conclusions about my psychology are relevant to the truth of this propositional element, because I might be uncertain whether the propositional element in my ethical judgement was true and yet certain that the autobiographical proposition to which it was claimed to reduce it was true, because it is clear that when I, for instance, judge that Hitler was a bad man or acted wrongly, I am asserting a proposition about Hitler and not merely about myself, though I am no doubt also expressing myself. So my objections are totally unaffected by the question whether or not there is another element in "ethical judgements" besides the propositional.[8]

At least two recent writers, Professor Kraft [9] and Professor Stace,[10] have attempted, while retaining the command theory, to secure a kind of universality for ethics by attributing to the commands expressed in "ethical judgements" a dependence on universal human desires such that to obey the command is a means to the attainment of what none of us can help desiring. Stace, at least at the time he wrote the book in question, held that the sentence "You ought to do this" is indistinguishable from the command "Do this," but added that the validity of the command for a person depends on the action commanded being an essential means or the most effective means to the

---

[8] For reply that it means "I should have done so but for irrelevant motives" v. below, p. 61.

[9] *Die Grundlagen einer wissenschaftlichen Wertlehre*, Springer, Vienna, 1937.

[10] *The Concept of Morals*, Macmillan, New York, 1937.

fulfilment of his desires. He then derives moral laws binding on all human beings from a consideration of the fact that human beings all desire happiness, which he thinks experience shows can best be attained by acting unselfishly. (He sharply distinguishes happiness from pleasure.) Similarly, Kraft says [11] that the imperatives which are commonly called value judgements, though not, strictly speaking, true or false, and therefore not judgements in the ordinary sense, yet may be universal and necessary in the ethical sense if (a) the action commanded is a causally necessary means for the satisfaction of a need or desire, (b) this need or desire is universal in human beings, (c) men are determined to have the need satisfied or the desire fulfilled. He is, I think, more logical than Stace in recognising that universality is in that case a matter of degree, because we can never be sure that there are no men who constitute exceptions to any psychological generalisation about human beings.

Such views come very near to analysing "ought to be done" as "is the best means to satisfy desire." A distinction is indeed made between truth and validity, and it is contended that a command cannot be true or false, but only "valid." But I do not see what the statement that a command is valid can mean except that it is legally or morally obligatory to carry it out, which does not take us much further. If commands cannot be true and to say "A ought to do so-and-so" is just a command, it cannot ever be true that anybody ought to do anything. However, since it is admitted that we are under no obligation to obey commands unless they are valid and they are held not to be valid unless obedience to them is a necessary means to the fulfilment of desires, this practically amounts to analysing judgements which assert an "ought" as simply judgements about the right means to the production of what is desired. Such a view would be naturalist, but not subjectivist, unless

---

[11] Op. cit., pp. 192–3.

it were held, as by Stace, that the desires on which the validity of the commands depends are only one's own desires, and not the desires of men in general. This seems to me a particularly unplausible form of subjectivism, since moral obligation presents itself so obviously as independent of the agent's own desires except in so far as the latter happen to be an indirect indication that the action is likely to produce good results, and since it would commit us to a theory of complete ethical egoism. The desire theory is discussed in the next chapter in its general non-subjectivist form.[12]

So far I have been discussing what sentences appearing to make ethical statements mean. But I should not have gained much by refuting the subjectivist views as to this if it could be shown that there are conclusive arguments, if not for a subjectivist analysis, at any rate against the view that ethical propositions could be reasonably held to be true of anything. I should then indeed be worse off than the person who accepted a subjectivist analysis, since I should have to hold that all our ethical judgements were false or at least quite unjustified, while he may say that they still quite properly fulfil the function for which they are really intended, that is, to express the speaker's state of mind, or even, on one form of the theory, that they are true—that is, of the speaker's psychology. So let us now examine the case against the objectivity of ethical judgements. If it is conclusive we shall have to be subjectivists in the sense that we shall have to admit the impossibility of making any true or at least any justified ethical judgements, even if we do not admit that ethical judgements are of such a nature that they could not conceivably be true at all or true of anything but the mental state or dispositions of the speaker.

One argument is based on the striking differences in ethical views between different people. But the differences between the views of savages and those of modern scientists about

---

[12] V. below, pp. 62 ff.

eclipses, or between the views of different politicians as to the causes and likely effects of contemporary events, are as great as the differences between the views of savages and of Christians, or the views of democrats and of Nazis, as to ethics. Are we to conclude from this that the scientists are no more right than the savages or that the political events about which the disputes turn have not objectively any causes or effects? If we do not draw this conclusion here, why draw the corresponding conclusion about ethics? There are also various ways of explaining the differences of view that exist without casting doubt on the objectivity of ethics. In the first place, acts which bear the same name may be very different acts in different states of society, because the circumstances and the psychology of the people concerned are very different. So it might be the case that, for example, slavery or polygamy was right, as the course which involved least evil, in certain more primitive societies and wrong in ours. This is quite compatible with the objectivity of ethical judgements. The proposition that slavery was right in ancient Egypt would not contradict the proposition that it was wrong in the United States in 1850 A.D. Both we and the ancient Egyptians may be right in our ethical judgements. Let us, however, take cases where one party is wrong. Now it is important to note that differences in ethical beliefs are often due to differences of opinion as to matters of fact. If A and B differ as to the likely consequences of an action, they may well differ as to whether the action is right or wrong, and this is perhaps the most fertile source of disputes as to what is right. But it is not an ethical difference at all; it is a difference such as arises between rival scientific predictions based on inductive evidence. Differences or apparent differences of opinion of these two kinds obviously constitute no possible argument against the objectivity of ethics.

But there are also genuine ethical differences—that is, differences as to our judgements not of fact but of value. These may sometimes be explained by differences in people's experience of life. If I never experience A, I cannot realize the intrinsic goodness of A and may therefore wrongly subordinate it to something less good. And we must remember that what is intrinsically good is not a physical thing or a physical act, but the experience or state of mind associated with it. Even a long study of philosophical books would not qualify a person to pass a judgement on the intrinsic value of philosophy if he were hopelessly bad at the subject, because then, however many books he read, he would not have a genuinely philosophical experience. Two persons who differ as to the aesthetic value of a picture may really be judging about different things, their several experiences of it. Or at least their judgements will be based on different data. Other differences of view may be due to the misapplication of principles previously accepted, or to genuine intellectual confusions such as the philosopher or even the man of common sense who is not a philosopher could remove. For instance a man may confuse badness and wrongness and conclude or assume, for example, that, because he really sees lying to be always bad (an evil), he sees it to be always wrong, while it may be a case of choosing the lesser evil rather than the greater. Often a man will think that he knows intuitively P to be R when he really only sees it to be Q but confuses Q with R.

Or the judgement that something is good or bad on the whole may have been due to concentrating attention on one side of it while ignoring or underestimating the other sides, as, for instance, militarists concentrate their attention on the unselfish heroism which war brings out in men and forget or underestimate war's evils. Lesser degrees of such onesidedness it is impossible to avoid, and yet they may detrimentally influence ethical judgements. To decide what is right in a particular case is often a difficult matter of balancing the good or evil likely to be produced by one proposed act against that likely to be produced by others. For, even if we do not hold the view that the rightness of an act depends solely on its consequences, we cannot in any case deny that such balancing of the consequences should play the predominant part in at least many ethical decisions. Perhaps, if we foresaw all the consequences clearly as they would be in their factual character and could keep our attention fixed equally on them all, we should always be in agreement as to the degree in which they were good or evil as compared with the consequences of other possible acts. But, apart from the difficulty of estimating what the consequences of an act will be, it is practically impossible in cases which are at all complex to keep our attention sufficiently fixed at the same time on all the foreseeable consequences likely to be seriously relevant for good or evil, and so we are likely through lack of attention to underestimate the value or disvalue of some as compared to that of others.

The lack of attention I have mentioned is in some degree inevitable, but it is greatly enhanced by the influence of desire and prejudice. It is a commonplace that ethical mistakes are often due to non-intellectual factors. Whether these act only through affecting the attention or whether they can lead to mistaken valuations even in the presence of full attention to the object valued we need not discuss. Their influence is certainly not confined to ethical mistakes; we may note the different conclusions as to the factual consequences of a policy which members of different political parties may draw from the same evidence. There is in any case a large class of errors for which some form of "psychoanalysis" (I do not say necessarily the Freudian) is required rather than argument, and another (probably much larger) of which it can be said only that the person in question fell into error because he did not steadfastly will to seek the truth and therefore did not fix his attention on points which displeased him. The convictions of some people as to the objectivity of ethics appear to have been shaken by the fact that enthusiastic Nazis seem to have believed that it was their duty to do things which we are convinced are completely wrong, such as ill-treating the Jews; but is there any reason to think that these Nazis really wanted to arrive at the truth regarding the question whether it was right or wrong to send Jews to concentration camps? If not, we need not be so surprised that they did not attain the truth which they did not seek.

So it may well be the case that all differences in people's judgements whether certain actions are right or wrong or certain things good or bad are due to factors other than an irreducible difference in ethical intuition. But, even if they should not be, we must remember that ethical intuition, like our other capacities, is presumably a developing factor and therefore may be capable of error. But in any case we have said enough to show that great differences of opinion as to ethics are quite compatible with the objectivity of ethical judgements.

Differences between philosophers about the general theory of ethics are remarkably great; but experience shows that very wide philosophical differences are quite compatible with striking agreement as regards the kind of action judged right or wrong, just as radical differences between philosophers in their theory of perception and of physical objects are quite compatible with complete agreement in ordinary life as to what particular physical objects are in a particular place at a particular time. The differences between philosophers are differences not mainly as to their ethical judgements in concrete ethical situations, but as to the general theory explaining these. We may add that the differences between different peoples and different civilisations as to concrete ethical judgements are commonly exaggerated. David Livingstone says that nowhere had he need to teach the African savages at any rate the ethical, as opposed to the religious, portion of the Decalogue. But there is of course a great inconsistency (not only among savages) in confining to a limited group rules which demand universal extension.

Another argument is that ethical beliefs can be explained psychologically as having originated from non-ethical factors such as fear of punishment. Now there must be a psychological history of the origin of any beliefs, and there must have been a time when no ethical ideas or beliefs yet existed, both in the history of the individual and in the history of the race. But this does not prove that ethical beliefs originated solely from the pre-existing ideas through a sort of confusion and were not due to a genuine cognition of properties really present. There was also a time when there were no logical or mathematical ideas, but nobody would entertain a similar argument against logic or mathematics.

Further, to be sceptical about ethics on the strength of a theory as to the origin of ethical ideas would be to give up the more for the far less certain, indeed the extremely uncertain. For such a sceptical theory would rest on the psychology of children if applied to individual development, and the psychology of savages if applied to the evolutionary development of the race. But, owing to the impossibility of obtaining reliable introspective evidence, the psychology of children and savages, at least when we consider their higher mental processes or the beginnings of such, is speculative in the extreme. To quote from Broad, "Of all branches of empirical psychology that which is concerned with what goes on in the minds of babies must, from the nature of the case, be one of the most precarious. Babies, whilst they remain such, cannot tell us what their experiences are; and all statements made by grown persons about their own infantile experiences on the basis of ostensible memory are certainly inadequate and probably distorted. The whole of this part of psychology therefore is, and will always remain, a mere mass of speculations about infantile mental processes, put forward to explain certain features in the lives of grown persons and incapable in principle of any independent check or verification. Such speculations are of the weakest kind known to science." [13] The psychology of primitive savages is in an equally or almost equally weak position. Some of our ethical judgements, on the other hand, I should insist, are quite or almost as certain as any judgement, and, even if the reader is not prepared to go so far, he must admit that they are at any rate far more certain than could be any theory founded on the psychology of children and savages which explained them away. The same uncertainty must attach to any theory of ethics or analysis of ethical terms based on the way in which children learn the use of the terms. Such a theory is irrelevant unless it is based on a study of what children exactly have in mind and what their mental processes are when they use the words, and how can we possibly have a well founded idea of that when they cannot introspect or adequately report introspections?

Westermarck contends that objectivity is disproved by the fact that ethical judgements are based on emotion; [14] but he does not even try, as far as I can see, to disprove the view that emotions only provide a psychological condition in the absence of which we should not have been in a fit state ever to intuit the characteristic of goodness or the relation of obligation. I certainly should not admit that the emotion was normally or originally prior to at least a confused apprehension of good or evil, rightness or wrongness; but even if I, like some even among the objectivists and non-naturalists, admitted this and made the feeling of the emotion a necessary prior condition of the apprehension, Westermarck's conclu-

---

[13] *Mind*, Vol. LIII, No. 212, p. 354.
[14] *Ethical Relativity*, p. 60.

sion would not follow. The making of an ethical judgement will in any case presuppose various psychological conditions, but it does not follow that the judgement must be about these conditions. Nobody would argue that ethical judgements must all really be about breathing because breathing is a necessary condition without which we could not have made the judgements. Professor Brandt [15] argues that the laws governing changes in our ethical judgements are derivative from the laws of emotional phenomena in general, but he succeeds only in showing that emotional conditions lead to many errors and non-rational changes of opinion in ethics. It may be urged that ethical terms must at any rate have some connection with emotions and emotional dispositions, and this I am not prepared altogether to deny; but the connection I envisage and of which I shall speak later is certainly not one which supports any form of subjectivism.

Westermarck has another argument against the objectivity of ethical judgements, which seems to be due to a downright confusion. He argues that moral judgements cannot be true because there are degrees of goodness, badness, etc., but there are no degrees of truth.[16] But, if this argument were valid, it would surely prove equally that there could be no true judgements about the size or temperature of an object. He seems to have confused the assertion that it is true that something has a property in a greater or lesser degree with the assertion that truth itself has degrees. He is not even consistent, for, being himself a naturalist rather than a subjectivist, he does ascribe truth to ethical judgements as assertions about the usual feelings of people, although feelings vary in degree.

But probably the principal reason which makes people inclined to deny the objectivity of ethics is the fact that in ethical argument we are very soon brought to a point where

[15] *Ethics*, Vol. LII, p. 65.
[16] *Ethical Relativity*, p. 218.

we have to fall back on intuition, so that disputants are placed in a situation where there are just two conflicting intuitions between which there seem to be no means of deciding. However, it is not only ethics but all reasoning which presupposes intuition. I cannot argue A, ∴ B, ∴ C without seeing that A entails B and B entails C, and this must either be seen immediately or require a further argument. If it is seen immediately, it is a case of intuition; [17] if it has to be established by a further argument, this means that another term, D, must be interpolated between A and B such that A entails D and D entails B, and similarly with B and C, but then the same question arises about A entailing D, so that sooner or later we must come to something which we see intuitively to be true, as the process of interpolation cannot go on *ad infinitum*. We cannot therefore, whatever we do, get rid of intuition if we are to have any valid inference at all. It may, however, be said that in subjects other than ethics people at any rate agree in their intuitions. But outside mathematics or formal logic this is by no means universally true. There is frequent disagreement about matters of fact as to what has happened or will happen or concerning the causes of something, and when we have exhausted the arguments on a given point in these matters there still remains a difference between the ways in which these arguments are regarded by the disputants. In any science where you cannot prove your conclusions but only make them more or less probable there will be different estimates as to the balance of probability. As in ethics you have to balance different values against each other in order to decide what you ought to do, so here you have to balance different probable arguments, and in order to do this you must rely at some point or other on an estimate of their

---

[17] This proposition is not convertible: I include under "intuition" cases where some mediation is required but insight goes beyond anything that could be strictly proved by the mediation.

strength which cannot itself be further justified by mediate reasoning. Yet, when everything has been said in the way of argument, people may not all agree. Some will attribute more weight to one consideration, others to another, as they do in ethical questions about what is the right action in a given case. Our decision as to which of two probable arguments is the stronger may be influenced by other arguments in turn; but in order to deal with the situation rationally we must also estimate the weight of these other arguments, so that in the last resort it is a matter of insight into their nature which cannot be settled by other arguments *ad infinitum*. Just as in a demonstrative argument you must see intuitively how each step follows from the preceding one, so in the case of a probable argument you must rely on estimates of the degree of probability given by the argument as compared to that given by arguments on the other side, and these estimates, unless the degree of probability can be mathematically calculated, must either be themselves intuitive or be deduced from other estimates which are intuitive. I do not wish to maintain that reasoning in these matters is altogether analogous to that which occurs in dealing with ethical questions, but at any rate it is the case here that, as in ethics, we are often confronted with a situation in which we either see or do not see, and cannot logically prove, that what we seem to see is true. Yet we cannot surely therefore conclude that the scientific or historical propositions under discussion are really only propositions about the state of mind of the people who assert them, or that they are neither true nor false, or that we have no justification whatever for believing any of them!

We must therefore have intuition, and in a subject where infallibility is not attainable intuitions will sometimes disagree. Some philosophers indeed prefer not to call them intuitions when they are wrong, but then the problem will be to distinguish real from ostensible intuitions, since people certainly sometimes think they see intuitively what is not true. Now Earl Russell says: "Since no way can be even imagined for deciding a difference as to values, the conclusion is forced upon us that the difference is one of tastes, not one as to any objective truth"; [18] but what I have said shows that we can imagine plenty of ways. I have indicated that errors as to judgements of value may arise (a) from lack of the requisite experience, (b) from intellectual confusions of some sort, (c) from failure to attend adequately to certain aspects of the situation or of the consequences, or (d) from psychological causes such as those with which the psychoanalyst deals. Therefore to remove errors we may (a) supply the lacking experience, or failing this, if possible, describe it in a way which will make its nature clear to the other party; we may (b) dispel intellectual confusions by making adequate distinctions or exposing actual fallacies such as make a person think he has seen that A is C when he has really only seen that A is B and mistakenly identified B with C; we may (c) suggest the direction of attention to the neglected points, or we may (d) use psychological methods. And we shall, if we are wise, also look out to see whether we ourselves have tripped up in any of these ways. Further, even when inference cannot completely prove or disprove, we may use it to confirm or cast doubt on ostensible intuition. The large class of errors which result mainly from an unwillingness really to seek for the truth can hardly be used as an argument against objectivity, since they are due to the moral fault of the persons who are in error and could have been removed if the latter had tried. In these cases the trouble is not that there are no means of deciding but that the means are not used.

The methods I have suggested will not always be successful, but then is there any sphere in which human efforts always do succeed? Even the methodology of physical science cannot

---

[18] *Religion and Science*, p. 250.

lay down rules which will guarantee that any scientist can make discoveries or show him in detail in advance how to prove to others the truth of the discoveries when made. I am not claiming that it is possible in practice to remove all ethical differences, but how do we know that it could not be done if there were a will on each side to listen to what the other had to say and an intelligence to discern the best methods to adopt in order to facilitate a decision? A person cannot be brought into agreement even with the established truths of science if he will not listen to what the scientist says, and there is no reason to think even with ethical intuition that there are not describable processes by which any cause of error can on principle be removed. I insert the words "on principle" simply because it will still often be the case that none of the disputants thinks of the right way of removing the error or that the person in error will not or cannot take it, as also occurs in disputes about questions of fact outside ethics.

Where the intuitive belief is due to non-intellectual factors of a kind which vitiate it, there seem to be two possibilities of cure. First, the person concerned may lose all tendency to hold the intuitive conviction when its alleged cause is clearly pointed out to him. The alleged cause is then in his case probably at least an essential part of the real cause. If, on the other hand, the intuitive belief remains unimpaired, and the man does not react to the causal explanation in a way which suggests that it has really touched a sore point, this is presumptive evidence that the explanation is mistaken. But, secondly, the cure from a false belief due to non-intellectual factors is more likely to arise because the man has been induced to approach the subject in a new spirit than merely because the true causation of the belief has been suggested to him. After all it is impossible to prove even to an unprejudiced person that such a causal theory as to the origin of a person's belief is really correct. How to induce a person to make such a new approach is a question not of logical argument but of practical psychology.

We must not think of intuition as something quite by itself, uninfluenced by inference; it is helped by inference but sees beyond what could be proved by inference. And, when intuitive ethical views differ, use may be made of inference to support one or other of the clashing views, especially by showing that it fits well into a coherent ethical system. This will not settle the question absolutely conclusively, but it can help toward settlement. Perhaps as the result of the inference one of the parties to the dispute may realize that he does not see by intuition what he claimed to see, but something rather different. It would thus be a great mistake to say that, when two men disagree on an ethical question, there is nothing to be done about it or that there is no scope in ethics for inference. No argument is available which could prove the subjectivity or fallaciousness of all ethics without establishing a similar conclusion about all other branches of study except mathematics and formal logic.

This leaves the sceptical view still unrefuted; but we have removed the main motives for its acceptance, and there remains just the gratuitous possibility that our ethical judgements may all be mistaken. We may reply by asking whether it is even a possibility. Do we not *know* that some (not of course all) of our ethical judgements are true? Do I not *know* that it would be wrong of me to go into the street and torture the first person I met even if I happened to be so constituted that I should enjoy watching his sufferings? And if we must admit absolutely certain knowledge of even one ethical proposition, have we not disposed of the sceptic? If we must admit at least almost certain knowledge, is it not almost certain that we have disposed of the sceptic? I think this answer is quite right, but the sceptic will not take it. He will say: "However certain you are in your ethical judgements you may be wrong, and I cannot therefore accept them till you have proved them to be true." Now I just cannot believe that our ethical judgements are all mistaken, and I suspect that nobody really does believe it when they are concerned with practical issues. But I cannot prove by any formal logic that I am right in my view. An opponent may admit that the naturalist and subjectivist accounts do not give any adequate analysis of ethical judgements and yet maintain that these judgements, in so far as they assert anything more than is given in such an analysis, are false, or that at least there is no justification for believing them to be true. On the other hand, he cannot possibly prove that I am wrong, and now that the positive arguments for subjectivism have been removed I think that the *onus probandi* is on him.

This brings us to a fundamental cleavage in philosophy, a great parting of the ways. There are a number of different kinds of field where we have from the commonsense point of view what anybody would ordinarily call knowledge and yet are quite unable to give arguments which *prove* it really to be so. This occurs in the case of memory, in the case of minds other than one's own, in the case of induction, and in the case of ethics. In all these cases the philosophers have despite repeated efforts not succeeded in giving a proof which provides anything like general satisfaction, so if we are determined to be sceptical we can without logical absurdity decline to believe any and every proposition that falls within the field in question. This course is consistent, but it is very difficult to find a philosopher who has taken it throughout and it would be still more difficult to find one who really thought like this in daily life. Some philosophers have indeed tried to make the best of both worlds by maintaining that the propositions in question were true but analysing them in such a way as to satisfy the sceptic. For instance, it has been said that propositions about other minds are true but are merely about one's own sense data, and it has been said that ethical propositions are true but are only statements about one's own feelings. A view like this seems to me to be still more incredible, since it not only maintains the sceptical position in effect, though not in words, but makes out that the plain man is himself a sceptic. No doubt it is a little less incredible to most people in some of these fields than in others, for example, subjectivist ethics is not so incredible as solipsism, but either seems to me to be the sort of thing one could not seriously believe for an hour in the emergencies of daily life. And I demand of a philosophy that it should be in accord with what we cannot possibly help believing in ordinary life. No doubt it may criticise our commonsense beliefs in detail and improve the concepts involved by clarification, but if it throws them overboard altogether it is destroying its own basis and condemning itself to vacuity. For a philosopher cannot in his epistemology have any basis but the cases of knowledge and reasonable belief in ordinary life. He can deny the truth of these only on the strength of philosophical arguments which will hardly be as certain as the propositions which they are used to deny. Even Earl Russell admitted that "all knowledge must be built up upon our instinctive beliefs, and if these are rejected, nothing is left." [19] But certainly our instinctive beliefs include ethical ones.

The position of the absolute ethical sceptic is analogous to that of the absolute theoretical sceptic. The theoretical sceptic cannot be refuted, unless we admit that it is a refutation to point to propositions which we cannot possibly help believing but cannot prove by argument; and of course he may talk if he likes, but he cannot without inconsistency claim that any of his statements are rationally justified. Similarly, the complete sceptic as to values cannot be refuted, except by pointing

---

[19] *Problems of Philosophy*, p. 39. I should not, however, commit myself to his terminology.

to value propositions which we cannot help believing but cannot prove by argument, a kind of refutation which, though I think it valid, he would never admit. Further, just as the theoretical sceptic can still talk, so the ethical sceptic can still act in accordance with his desires, but he cannot consistently claim that there is any justification for any of his acts, that any one is more rational than any other. If it is retorted that, even if we grant an objective "ought," we might be equally said to require a reason why we should do what we ought, the reply is that the ought is itself a reason so that there is no further room for question left, just as there is no sense in asking why we should believe what is shown to be true. People who ask why they should do what they ought either are confused, or they are really asking what it is about the particular act in question which makes it the act they ought to do, or they are wanting to know what good they will obtain for themselves by doing it. The last question brings in a different kind of reason from the moral reason, namely a prudential reason, but (though not such a satisfactory reason as an answer to the problem of obligation) it is still a reason founded on the notion of good.

Some people forget that not only specifically moral acts but even mere acts of ordinary prudence in furtherance of one's own interests presuppose the abandonment of the sceptic's position. The sceptic as to values is not entitled to believe even the proposition that it is more reasonable to wash his hands in water than in sulphuric acid, for this presupposes at any rate that pain is evil. So he has no real ground for not washing his hands in sulphuric acid. To say that he does not like to do so is to give a psychological cause and not a reason, unless we assume that it is *good* to do what one likes or that our desires ought to be satisfied. It is not possible to prove even that our own pain is evil; and if we admit even this judgement to be self-evidently true, there are other judgements as to values, such as that we are under some obligation to further the good of others, which are as evidently true, so that it is inconsistent to accept the first and reject the second. If we trust our intuitive awareness of values in the one case we are equally justified in trusting it in the others; if we were to reject it in the one case we should have no less call to reject it in the others. And if the sceptic demands for judgements in ethics a logical proof as we have in mathematics, or an empirical inductive proof as we have in natural science, he is condemning ethics because ethical cognition is not like other kinds of cognition but has its own distinctive nature, which is like condemning empirical evidence because it is not mathematical or mathematical proof because it is not empirical. As Aristotle says, it is a mark of lack of intelligence to demand in a given subject arguments of a kind which that subject does not admit. It is not a question of meeting the sceptic by metaphysical or epistemological arguments which fall outside ethics or by considerations of general probability, but of returning to one's conviction in concrete ethical cases. If we attend to actual concrete ethical problems we cannot at the time of attention be sceptics, and what we see when actually considering ethical problems is the first consideration in framing a theory of ethics. Even professed subjectivists in ethics regard some acts as unreasonable in the sense of imprudent and express strong *moral* opinions against others.

Such is the reluctance of serious thinkers to adopt a position of ethical scepticism that those who held that we have no right to claim truth for any ethical propositions which are anything more than psychological propositions about human desires or feelings have generally maintained, not that all ethical propositions are false, but that they are in fact merely propositions about human psychology. Rather than argue "They go beyond this, therefore they are false," they argued "They are true, therefore they cannot go beyond this." So they have adopted what, since Moore's *Principia Ethica*, has been called a "naturalist" analysis of ethical propositions. With this we shall deal in the next chapter, except in so far as some naturalist views have already been handled under the heading of sub-jectivism.

CHAPTER II

Naturalism

Let us now turn to naturalist views of ethics which are not subjectivist. Without dwelling on the intricacies of the definition of "natural" or "non-natural" as the terms appear in Moore's *Principia Ethica*, I think we may understand a naturalist view of ethics as one which, while admitting that ethical propositions are sometimes true, analyses ethical concepts solely in terms of the concepts of a natural science. This must involve making ethics potentially a mere branch of the science, though this latter point is not always realized. The science in question is usually psychology, but we must not identify a naturalist definition with a psychological definition. If anybody were silly enough to define "good" in terms of the concepts of physics or geology, it would still be a naturalist definition. But the only at all plausible naturalist definitions have been in terms of psychology, though there have also been attempts made at biological definitions. All definitions of ethical concepts in non-ethical terms are not, however, naturalist. A theological definition would not be, since God is not a concept of a natural science. The same applies to any metaphysical definition.

Denial of the possibility of a naturalist definition does not commit one to saying that value properties in other than an instrumental sense belong to anything but experiences, states of minds, or persons; but to say they belong only to psychological entities is not to say they are themselves psychological properties which we can discover by empirical introspection

36

or analysable completely in terms of such properties. Nor need a non-naturalist hold that there are no senses of words such as "good" and "ought" in respect of which a naturalist definition is allowable. All he need hold is that there are some senses which cannot be defined in such a way, especially the sense of "good" in which the word stands for "intrinsically good."

A naturalist view, as I said earlier, need not be subjectivist. If ethical propositions are regarded as propositions asserting only that most people, or people of a particular class, have certain feelings, or that certain things will satisfy them, they are still objective in the sense in which psychological generalisations of a non-ethical kind about human beings are objective. They do not depend for their validity on the subjective state of the person who asserts them. Non-subjective naturalist views are therefore exposed to a somewhat different type of criticism from that to which subjectivist theories are open. The alternative to a naturalist view is the view that, besides any elements which could be analysed in psychological terms or other terms appertaining to a natural science, ethical propositions include at least one concept which cannot be thus analysed. Since we are here talking of the analysis of propositions and not of the question whether they are true, it does not straightway follow that this "non-natural" concept applies to anything. It is logically possible to maintain that the concepts expressed by "good" and "ought" in the ethical sense are "non-natural" and yet that nothing is really good or really obligatory in this sense but only in a naturalist sense. In that case all our statements which use the terms "good" or "ought" in their ethical sense will be false in the most essential respect. Or, if the sceptic does not go so far, he may say that, though it is possible for anything we can tell that these non-natural properties really belong to something, we are not justified in asserting that they do. Thus a non-naturalist analysis may be combined with a subjectivist view in the sense in which the latter term stands for the position of the moral sceptic. This is a position that cannot be refuted either by a formal logical proof or by an appeal to introspection, since introspection by itself can only reveal what we have in mind and not what is true. But anyone who like myself finds it impossible to deny that there are some ethical propositions which we have a right to hold true will, if he rejects any naturalist analysis of ethical propositions, have to admit that there are experiences and actions which really have properties (goodness and obligatoriness) that cannot be reduced to psychological terms.

This is the importance of the question of the analysis of commonsense propositions. It does seem as if we know the truth of certain commonsense propositions; and, if so, when we have given their analysis we shall have also determined what is true of the objectively real. I have already towards the end of the last chapter said something about the position of the ethical sceptic. Though this sceptical position cannot be refuted logically, most people find it hard to accept it, and some have thought that they could avoid it and yet escape the admission of non-natural ethical concepts by giving a naturalist analysis of ethical propositions. If they can be convinced that such an analysis is impossible, they may, rather than become moral sceptics, admit the real existence of non-natural properties. So the interest of the question does not lie merely in determining what people think when they use ethical terms, but has a bearing on what is objectively true.

It is worth noting that, if someone both held that ethical propositions could not be analysed without introducing a non-natural concept and yet held that this non-natural concept, though present in our minds, did not apply to anything, he would have to admit that the human mind can create an idea of something which is neither itself given in any sort of experience nor composed of elements given in experience. Now, if my type of view is correct, though we must admit that ethical concepts are non-empirical in the sense of not being derived from sensation, we may still hold that we are immediately aware of the properties of goodness and obligatoriness as belonging to certain states of minds and actions, so that they are given in experience in a wider sense of that word. But they cannot be given in experience at all if they are not really properties or relations of anything, even of ourselves or of our own mental states. The notion of goodness in the intrinsic sense is in that case the notion of a property which does not belong to anything and the notion of obligation the notion of a relation which does not relate anything, yet we have ideas of intrinsic goodness and of obligation. If it turns out that they cannot be analysed in empirical, or any non-ethical terms, they are not compound ideas formed by putting together other ideas given in experience, nor can they, on the sceptical view, be the fruit of an intuitive insight into the real. But to have to admit that the human mind can thus form a new idea "off its own bat" is repugnant to most philosophers, and in a special degree to the type of empiricist philosopher who is inclined to deny the objectivity of ethics. It is an axiom for such thinkers that "the mind cannot create a new simple idea." The case is all the stronger because what is in question is not a determinate quality or relation under some determinable of which instances have already been experienced, but a new determinable of a quite unique kind. And in any case, if we have an idea of a relation or quality and it is irreducible, surely the most plausible explanation is that the relation or quality is given in some experience and is therefore really present in something if only in an experience (though this does not hinder us, when we have really found it present on some occasions, from thinking wrongly for some reason, for example, a false analogy, that it is present in others when it is really absent). How is the sceptic to explain our alleged mistake about obligation? He cannot well

hold that it is a concept which has a right application somewhere but is misapplied in being applied to ethics. The suggestion has been made to me [1] that relative obligation plainly
occurs in experience, since we find by experience that, if we
want to attain certain ends, we are obliged to behave in a
certain way, and that we may have formed from this by a
confusion the idea of absolute obligation which we apply in
ethics, just as we confusedly thought, till we knew better,
that there was an absolute and not only a relative "down."
This explanation is, however, inadequate because the idea of
moral obligation is radically different from that of "relative
obligation" thus understood. For the latter only contains the
notion of means to an end and is quite compatible with the end
being known to be ethically evil. For instance, we can say that
in this sense of "ought" Hitler "ought" to have invaded Britain
after Dunkirk or that a murderer "ought" to have killed not
only A but B to escape exposure, however evil we think such
a deed would have been. From this the idea of ethical obligation does not differ merely in respect of the absence of a
relation but in respect of the presence of a totally new feature,
the distinctive characteristic of the moral "ought." Anybody
who disagrees with me in this must be referred to the arguments of the present chapter by which I try to disprove the
view that "ought" is to be analysed in terms of conduciveness
to objects of desire.

Two, as I think, fatal objections to any naturalist analysis
are stated by Broad and Moore respectively. Broad points out
that the logical consequence of a view which defines ethical
concepts in psychological terms is "not (as with subjectivism)
that in disputes on moral questions there comes a point beyond
which we can only say 'De gustibus non est disputandum.'"
On the contrary "the logical consequence is that all such disputes *could* be settled, and that the way to settle them is to

---

[1] By R. Robinson.

collect statistics of how people do feel. And to me this kind
of answer seems utterly irrelevant to this kind of question." [2]
This objection, brought by Broad against the particular view
of Hume, would apply to all forms of psychological naturalism. For all such views would equate ethical propositions with
propositions about the psychology of men in general or of
some class of men and therefore with propositions the truth
of which is capable of being determined in this way. We might
put the argument even more strongly and say that such a view
would make ethical propositions identical with vaguely
expressed propositions about statistics. For the difference between vagueness and definiteness is the only difference
between saying "most" and saying "882 out of 1024." Yet
ethical propositions, whatever they are, are surely not just
vague propositions about statistics. Any biological definition
would, I have no doubt, be open to the same objection. If, for
example, we defined ethical conduct as what makes for survival
we should have to mean by commending a practice ethically
that the rate of increase of population was greater among
those who adopted such a line of conduct than among those
who did not.

Secondly, Moore objected to all naturalist definitions of
"good" that, no matter what the alleged definition is, we can
always see that it is quite sensible to ask whether something
which has the property put forward in the definition is or is
not good, and that therefore the definition is wrong. For, if
it were right, to say that something which had the defining
property was good would be to utter a tautology, and to
question whether it was good would be to ask whether what
is good is good.[3] This, I think, expresses a valid objection,

[2] C. D. Broad, *Five Types of Ethical Theory*, p. 115.
[3] *Principia Ethica*, § 13. When I quote from Moore I am not trying to
give his present view, nor should I defend his detailed statement any more
than he now would.

but one that must be used with care. Obviously, till we have made up our minds whether a particular definition of "good" is correct or not, it may still be a question the answer to which can seriously be doubted whether something which has the defining property is correctly called "good," and naturalists have thought that they could meet Moore's objection by raising this point. But surely the trouble with the naturalist definitions is that, when we consider them and ask if what has the defining property is always good, we are clearly conscious that we are asking, not a question about what a term means, but the question whether everything which has the defining property has also a different property, signified by "good." It is not merely that it is an undecided question of definition, but that it is not a question of definition at all. The naturalist says that "good" means "desired" or "such that men feel approval" or "such as ultimately to satisfy men"; but it presents itself to us as, at least partly, a contingent question of empirical fact whether what is approved or desired or will ultimately satisfy us is also good. Perhaps men are so constituted that in fact they only desire or only feel approval of what is in some way good (provided they know what it is like), and perhaps they are so constituted that the good and only the good will ultimately satisfy them. But at least whether they are so constituted is a doubtful question the answer to which we could not know without enormously extensive and indeed unobtainable empirical information, and not one an affirmative answer to which follows from the very meaning of "good." We never, with any of the definitions which have been proposed, reach the stage at which it seems at all plausible (at least except for extraneous and, I think, wrong reasons) to hold that to say a thing is good is at all the same as to say that it has the defining property in question. But before we are entitled to accept a definition (in Moore's sense of the word) that stage must be reached.

As far as I can see, it is never possible to prove strictly that an analysis of a given concept is correct, though it may be possible to prove that one is incorrect. For, however clear it may be that AB always accompanies C and vice versa, somebody who nevertheless maintains that he can apprehend the property C as something distinct from AB can never be logically refuted, however unreasonable his attitude may be in a given instance. We can only ask ourselves carefully whether we do have this property C in mind as distinct from AB when we use the words. So in dealing with attempts at analysis we are in the last resort forced to fall back on our consciousness that a proposed analysis does or does not express what we mean. For, even if a philosophical analysis expresses something more than what we mean, it must at least include approximately all that we mean. It is true that an analysis may sometimes express what I mean when I think it does not, but I can never be justified in positively accepting an analysis as an expression of my meaning until I have reached the stage at which I can say: "Well, this is what I meant all along, although I did not put it so clearly." Now, in the case of naturalist definitions of "good," so far from my seeing this I see quite definitely the contrary. I see that propositions about what is good in some senses of "good" are propositions which cannot be analysed adequately in psychological terms; I see it almost as clearly as I see that they cannot be analysed adequately in terms of physics or mathematics. It is not merely that I have been unable to think of any naturalist definition which satisfied me but am prepared to leave it an open question whether somebody may not in the future think of one which would satisfy me. On the contrary I see that "good," "right," "duty," "ought," "morality" are just not the sort of concepts which can ever be analysed completely in terms of psychology, as I can see that sights cannot be analysed in terms of sounds (however many correlations we may establish between sights and sounds). This awareness is immediate, but it is a sort of immediate awareness which even a sceptically minded philosopher cannot rule out. For even such philosophers will admit the possibility of some introspection. "What I mean" is, in the case of propositions, "what I intend to assert," and I surely can sometimes be immediately aware of my own intentions. Merely to use the words on the right occasions is not to understand their meaning, unless we are prepared to adopt a purely behaviouristic account of human thought. There may be senses in which it is sometimes true to say that a man does not know what he means, but I could not use words intelligently if I were not, sometimes at least, immediately aware of my meaning. And if I am quite clear in my mind what I mean, I do not know how anybody else can get behind this and prove to me that I mean something else. For we are discussing at present not whether anything has a property of goodness that is not naturalistically definable but whether we are thinking of such a property when we assert ethical propositions.

Now, while it is theoretically possible that I may be peculiar in this respect and have a quite different kind of moral consciousness from other people, this supposition is in the highest degree unlikely, so that what I find when I investigate my own experiences is also evidence in regard to the experience of others. As a matter of fact the philosophers who give naturalist definitions of ethical terms do not, despite their predilection for empiricism, commend their conclusions as the direct result of a plain empirical investigation of our moral experience, but put these forward on the assumption that if they can find a hypothesis which will rid them of any concept different from those of the natural sciences they ought to accept it whether or not it seems introspectively plausible. This *a priori* assumption I can see no reason to make.

What arguments could be brought to show that I do not

mean what I think I mean? The most plausible perhaps is that, if goodness were, as Moore claimed, a simple property, it is strange that nobody had discovered this till the time of Sidgwick. If we are aware of such a simple property or concept, must we not know that we are aware of it? Now, as we shall see later on, I do not agree that goodness is simple and indefinable. All non-natural concepts need not be indefinable, provided they are definable in terms of some other non-natural concept. What I do maintain is that "goodness" cannot be defined wholly in non-ethical terms. The argument is indeed relevant to my position, since I am committed to holding that there is at least one indefinable ethical term. But, if "good" is really definable in any way, this would be an adequate reply to the argument about "good"; and while it is a matter of doubt whether many people have had an idea of the indefinable goodness, it is quite certain that people have for ages had a definite idea at least of an "ought" which was to them *prima facie* distinct from desire, fear, emotion, or any other psychological terms, thus giving at least one indefinable concept of ethics. We are not dealing with a property that only a few modern philosophers claim to discover but with one that is present in the thoughts of almost every man, so that the naturalist cannot possibly bring it forward as a positive argument for his view that people were not aware of the property in question till quite recently. And if there are difficulties in seeing how there could be all this dispute about a concept which is simple and can be recognised by immediate inspection, there are also difficulties in seeing how, if all ethical terms are definable non-ethically, there can be such wide divergencies of opinion as to what the definition is or whether there is a definition. Of the naturalists themselves two are rarely agreed on the same definition. A correct definition should give us what we mean by "good" or "ought," and how is it that there should be such widely different beliefs not only as to what is true but as to what we mean? If philosophers did not till recently commit themselves to the view that some ethical concept is simple and unanalysable, neither did they till recently, except in rare cases, commit themselves to a naturalist analysis of all ethical concepts. As a matter of fact the same sort of puzzle arises about any fundamental conception in regard to which there are philosophical disputes, and is not peculiar to ethics.

However, I think the disagreement in the case of ethics may be accounted for largely by the following circumstances:

(1) The naturalists, either because they have a general philosophical outlook which makes them unwilling to admit the existence of any characteristics which cannot be reduced to empirical terms, or for some other reason, think that we could never be justified in asserting that anything was good or bad, right or wrong, if we meant anything more by these statements than what could be analysed in psychological terms. They are therefore forced to hold either that our ethical judgements are analysable in such a fashion, or that these judgements are all mistaken or unjustified—and they prefer the first alternative. I doubt whether anybody would be inclined to analyse ethical judgements naturalistically if he considered merely his state of mind as it seemed to him in making such judgements, and was not influenced by other, epistemological considerations.

(2) Some writers have apparently confused the highly plausible view that value predicates in their basic senses are only applicable to psychological entities; that is, minds and their states, with the view that they are reducible to psychological properties empirically discoverable.

(3) There are some senses of "good" in which "good" might well be defined naturalistically. For example, "strawberries are good" may well equal "I like strawberries" or "I find the taste of strawberries pleasant." "This is a good knife" seems

to mean only that it is useful for certain purposes, which may be bad or indifferent; I should still call it a good knife even if it had not been used for anything except committing murders. Philosophers in the past have usually not paid sufficient attention to the multiplicity of senses in which the same word is used, so those who defined "good" naturalistically may easily have confused different senses of "good," though this is more likely to be the case with earlier than with contemporary naturalists, since more attention is now being paid to differences of meaning.

(4) Just as there are some senses of "good" which require a naturalist definition, so perhaps there are some senses of "definition" in which we might have a naturalist definition of every sense of "good." Colours could be said to be definable in terms of wave-lengths because they are correlated with them, but this would not commit one to saying that the colour as seen was just the wave-length which occurred in its definition or the property of being accompanied by such a wave-length. People knew what yellow was long before they knew anything about the wave-length. Similarly it might be possible in a sense to define "good" in terms of a characteristic which always accompanied goodness without holding that goodness just was the characteristic in question. I do not wish to commit myself to the view that such a universally accompanying characteristic could be found, but at least the view that there is such a characteristic is in some of its forms less unplausible than the view that this characteristic is identical with goodness. We must remember that the fact, if it be a fact, that A and BC go together is no proof that BC is identical with A. Suppose a future physiologist were, as is logically possible, to discover a specific modification of the brain which accompanied every good experience and action and never occurred without being accompanied by a good experience or action. The brain-modification would then be an infallible sign of

goodness, but it still certainly would not follow that "good" just *meant* "accompanied by this brain-modification" or that goodness *was identical with* the property of being accompanied by it. Till recently the different senses of "definition" have not been clearly distinguished, at least with reference to ethics, and even now the most prominent school of naturalist philosophers, the verificationists, regard as unanswerable, or at any rate take no interest in answering, the question what we mean by a word in any sense in which this can be distinguished from the empirical criteria on account of which the word is applied. It is therefore fair to say that there has been a great deal of confusion about the matter, and that it is highly probable that most people who put forward naturalist definitions of "good" either never meant at all by "definition" what Moore meant in *Principia Ethica*, or at least confused it with other senses of "definition."

(5) It seems very unsatisfactory to conclude a long ethical discussion with the tame remark that the central concept which we have been discussing cannot be defined. But it is important to realize that to say this is not necessarily to exclude the possibility of being able to say more about it, but only to exclude the possibility of reducing the central concepts of ethics to non-ethical terms. It may be perhaps that, when we have said that they cannot be thus reduced, we shall still be able to say other things of a more positive kind about them, such as that what is good is always the fulfilment of a teleological tendency, or would be desired by all men if they really knew what it was like, or that God commands us to do what we ought. All I am denying is that such statements could exhaust the meaning of the terms "good" or "ought." Even if they are correct descriptions, they are not definitions, at least in the sense under discussion. In that sense some terms must be indefinable, for analysis implies the unanalysable. Those who say that everything can be defined must either be

using "define" in a different sense or be muddled, for every concept could not be reduced without residuum to others. If so, there would be no concepts left at all. But to say that a term is indefinable is not to say that we do not know what it means. It is only to say that the concept for which it stands, with which we may still be perfectly familiar, is too ultimate and unique to be analysed in terms of anything else. I do not indeed hold that "good" is indefinable, for Moore's arguments only support the view that "good" cannot be defined adequately by means of non-ethical terms. But the remarks here will still be relevant to my position, for even if "good" is defined by means of ethical terms, this will still presuppose the indefinability of some ethical term.

(6) Even philosophers who have insisted on analysis have rarely clearly committed themselves to the view that, when they put forward an analysis, they are just giving an account of what people mean in the ordinary sense of "meaning." What they seem often to be doing is rather giving that element in the meaning of a general statement which they take to be true, while rejecting the rest as false, ungrounded, or confused, or, alternatively, stating a proposition which they think has the same implications as the original one. We need not, therefore, be very surprised at the disagreement between the naturalists and the non-naturalists, since the people who disagree with each other are generally trying to do different things. And prior to this century the question whether a naturalist definition was possible or not was hardly ever clearly raised, so that we need not be surprised that it obtained no clear answer.

(7) I do not, indeed, altogether rule out the possibility of a failure to see what might have been discovered by careful attention to what we mean. A circumstance that makes it easier for people to overlook the specifically ethical element which cannot be analysed in terms of psychology is that the

times when we actually have first-hand ethical experience and the times when we discuss philosophically the analysis of good do not usually coincide. It is perhaps even impossible to engage in the two activities exactly simultaneously, so that we are dependent for our ethical experiences on memory when we are philosophizing. For we do not have first-hand ethical experience all the time we do what is right and every time we make a judgement about the good, especially when we take the judgements only as examples for a philosophical argument. Some of our judgements as to good and evil, right and wrong are almost parrotlike; some are mere applications of a general rule the truth of which is not intuited, at least at the time, but taken for granted; some involve an insight into the particular case as regards means but presuppose prior judgements as to ends. It is therefore easier than might be expected to go wrong when we investigate these matters philosophically, because we have not before us at the time a genuine ethical experience, and at the very moment when we have such an experience we are too much concerned with it as a practical issue to philosophize about it. This perhaps explains why good and intelligent men could sometimes put forward quite preposterous ethical theories, for example, egoistic hedonism. In any case whether the naturalist or the non-naturalist is right, we must admit error on one side or the other as to what we mean.

Naturalists and subjectivists usually pride themselves on being empiricists, so one would expect them to base their views mainly on a direct observation of the ethical experience. That this is not their method is to my mind highly significant and should give pause to any would-be converts to their views. Their method is rather to assume on epistemological grounds that any non-naturalist account is almost certainly wrong, and then to try to devise a theory which will come only as close to accepting the empirical evidence as can be done without contradicting this assumption. I prefer to base my account primarily on an examination of my psychological attitude when I consider actual concrete ethical questions. For it is this attitude of which we should be giving an account when we analyse commonsense ethical propositions.

Let us now examine critically the objections to the view that the fundamental concept (or concepts) of ethics is (are) indefinable. Some people are dissatisfied with the view that "good" is indefinable because they want to be able to say more about it than this, and they would probably be dissatisfied for the same reason if "ought" were declared to be indefinable; but we must distinguish between saying more about ethical concepts and reducing all ethical concepts to non-ethical. The indefinability theory need only be a statement that the latter reduction cannot be achieved, leaving it open to make whatever other positive statements about ethical terms we think to be true. Again, Moore's comparison of good and yellow has given rise to misunderstandings. Moore says that good is like yellow in being simple, unanalysable, and discoverable by immediate awareness; he does not suggest that it is like yellow in any other respect. Yellowness is a sensible quality, or rather a class of slightly varying sensible qualities, good a categorial property, but they still might have the features mentioned in common.

Field [4] objected to Moore's account that, whereas it is admittedly an essential feature of goodness that it is capable of moving us to action, the alleged simple indefinable quality has no necessary connection with desire, and cognition without desire cannot move to action. But no doubt Moore would reply that we can see no *reason* in the nature of anything why it arouses desire, but must accept this as an empirical fact, as with all the other inductive generalizations we make, and if

---

[4] *Moral Theory*, pp. 56 ff. I think Field would now admit that his argument referred to a different sense of "definition" from that used by Moore.

so we need not be troubled because we cannot see *a priori* why goodness does stimulate desire.

Then there is the general objection to any concepts supposed not to be derived from mere empirical observation. It is a common assumption that there cannot be any such, but I do not see any conceivable way in which the truth of the assumption might be proved. Indeed I cannot think of any attempt at a proof, unless we are to regard as one the vicious circle of Hume. The latter first concludes that there are, with what he dismisses as an insignificant exception, no ideas derived from impressions, simply because we cannot cite any examples of such.[5] Since he, and not his opponents, wrote the *Treatise*, no examples are of course cited in this passage; but some chapters later when he comes to discuss substance and objective causal connection, which were generally cited as cases of ideas not derived from impressions, he dogmatically denies that we have any such ideas on the ground that they cannot be derived from impressions, a generalization which was only established by ignoring these cases. Any proof that there were no such ideas would in fact already presuppose that there was at least one. For, if the proof were valid, its premises would have to entail its conclusion, and this idea of entailment or necessary logical connection is one that could not be given in mere observation. Whatever non-empirical ideas we may get rid of, we cannot get rid of entailment if we are to have any inference at all. We must therefore decide in each case on its own merits whether an idea is non-empirical or not, since we cannot disprove the possibility of non-empirical ideas by a general argument, and have to admit at least one.

No doubt in one sense ethical ideas are empirical, because even in Moore's theory we could not have any idea what good was if we had never had the experience of apprehending the

---

[5] *Treatise of Human Nature*, I, I, I.

property of goodness; but the idea may still be called non-empirical if by this is meant that it is not apprehended by sense perception or by introspection,[6] as I can discover by introspection whether I am angry or feel hot. The same applies to obligation. That they are not apprehended in such a way is surely shown by the fact that, when we see that something is intrinsically good or some act morally obligatory, we also see that it must be so—its factual properties being what they are. Goodness, badness, obligatoriness and wrongness are not properties that could possibly be removed from an experience or action without the experience or action being in other ways different, and this impossibility is not merely the effect of causal laws. Hitler could not have done the actions which had the factual properties his actions towards the Jews possessed and yet have prevented the actions having the additional properties of badness and wrongness. It is not that we generalize from experience that he could not do this, but that the very suggestion is absurd. On the other hand, what we learn by observation might always have been different, at least for anything we can see. This of itself is a strong argument against any view which analyses ethical concepts in terms of the attitude of the person or persons judging. For it is quite conceivable that the attitude of the latter towards the same action might in a particular case have been different from what it actually was so that they disapproved of the action instead of approving of it or vice versa, yet granted that the action had the factual characteristics which it did have it could not

---

[6] This may seem indeed to contradict what I said earlier when I repeatedly based my account on introspection of my ethical attitudes, but it does not really do so. There is no more contradiction in saying that I can discover by introspection that I have an ethical concept which is not itself derived from introspection than there is in saying that I can discover by introspection that I have concepts of physical objects. The apprehension that this concept applied to something would not be itself an act of introspection, but it might still be observable by introspection, as are many psychological phenomena which are not themselves introspections.

have had different ethical characteristics. "Good" cannot mean, for example, "approved," for anything which is good could not, being what it was in other respects, have failed to be good, but it might well, the psychology of the person or persons who make the judgement having been different, a quite contingent circumstance, have not been approved.

I am not suggesting that the fundamental concepts of ethics are innate in any other sense except that we have an innate capacity to apprehend them, and that is only a tautology since whatever we do apprehend we must have a capacity to apprehend. If the characteristics of obligatoriness or goodness belong to any actions or experiences, they and their opposites may be apprehended directly as belonging to the real, for our actions and experiences are just as real as physical objects; and in that case "good" and "ought" are no more innate ideas than are the qualities we discover in sense perception. We could not perceive even the latter if we had not an innate capacity for sense perception. Having apprehended the ethical properties in some actual instances we have the idea of them and may apply it hypothetically even to what is not in existence, since we can see it to follow from the nature of certain things that if they existed they would be good (or, in other cases, bad).

But probably the chief motive which leads people to give a naturalist analysis of ethical propositions is the belief that, if they adopted any other analysis, it would make it impossible to hold any justifiable ethical beliefs, just as the chief motive for adopting a phenomenalist analysis of physical object propositions is the belief that only in this sense can physical object propositions be justified. In both cases it is thought incredible that our commonsense judgements could be quite unjustified, in both it is held that they would be unjustified if interpreted in the *prima facie* more plausible way, and it is therefore concluded that they must be interpreted in another way. Now there might be something in the contention if there were some

other positive argument which showed that ethical judgements, if non-naturalistically interpreted, could not be true;
but we have seen that such arguments are not available. The
worst we could say is that there is a lack of positive justification for non-naturalist ethical propositions, and if so it can
be shown that the above argument can provide no support for
its conclusion. For there are two premises: one (a) is that, if
our ethical propositions are to be interpreted non-naturalistically, we can have no justification for asserting any of them
to be true; the other (b) is that we are justified in asserting
some ethical propositions to be true. Obviously (b) is needed
if (a) is to provide a reason for giving a naturalist analysis
of the propositions. By itself, (a) would lead to the conclusion,
not that our ethical judgements are to be naturalistically interpreted, but only that, if and in so far as they assert anything
which cannot be naturalistically interpreted, we are not
justified in saying they are true. But either (b) can be known
or rationally believed without first presupposing that the
ethical propositions are to be analysed naturalistically or it
cannot. If it can (a) is false; if it cannot, there is a vicious
circle, because then the second premise presupposes the conclusion. This does not prove that the naturalist analysis is
wrong, but it does seem to remove what has been probably
the most strongly felt argument for such an analysis.

Another influential type of argument for naturalism is that
we can explain the origin of ethical ideas and beliefs psychologically from the non-ethical. But, even if they originated
from non-ethical factors such as, for example, the fear of
punishment, this would not prove that they now contained
nothing beyond these. If the psychological theory of the
origin of ethical ideas merely tells us what experiences preceded their formation, it is innocuous; but if it claims to analyse
the ideas in terms of these non-ethical experiences it is open
to the objections which I have brought against naturalism.

Further, we are less likely to be wrong about what we mean now than we are to be about the psychological history of the origin of the ideas in children and savages, and we must not reject the more certain for the sake of the less certain. The impossibility of obtaining reliable introspective information must make the psychology of children and savages, at least when we are concerned with anything but simple sense perceptions, highly speculative. The same remark applies to any theory of ethics based on a study of the way in which children learn the use of ethical words.

What is it that is missing from any naturalist or subjectivist account of ethics? Well, I should not like to say the only missing element, but at any rate the most important one is represented by the term "ought." "Good" in its non-natural sense or senses carries with it the notion that the good thing *ought* not to be wantonly sacrificed but, other things being equal, pursued. Now to say that I wish for something or that I have a certain kind of emotional feeling about it, or to exclaim in a way which expresses these psychological states, if that can be distinguished from saying I have them, does not entail that I am under any obligation whatever to produce the objects of this wish or emotion even if I am quite able to and there is no objection to doing so. Nor does the notion of being commanded (or of commanding myself) involve in any way that of being under an obligation unless we presuppose such propositions as that the person who commands has a special claim on me such that I ought to obey him, or that the action commanded is on its own account my duty apart from the fact of its being commanded, and to presuppose these propositions is already to assume the fact of obligation. Similarly, that everybody or most people or some group of people will feel an emotion of approval towards me if I do x may make me more inclined to do x because I like this result, but it is quite incapable of putting me under an obligation to do x. As Kant insisted, we can see that the "ought" is quite distinct from the "is," and this is fatal to all naturalist definitions. "Ought" is what subjectivist and naturalist theories leave out, and to have an ethics without "ought" is like playing Hamlet without the Prince of Denmark. The stand against naturalism has usually been made in relation to the notion of "good," but to make it in relation to "ought" would have been to take up an even securer line of defence. Only, if once it is granted that we cannot give a naturalist or subjectivist account of "ought," it is then in any case unreasonable to try to give one of all senses of "good." For it is plain that at least some meanings of good, for example, morally good, include a reference to the non-naturalist ought.

Of course a naturalist might claim to analyse moral obligation in terms of approval or desire, but it is even more plain that to say to A that he ought not to cheat B is not merely to make a statement about his or other people's psychology than is the corresponding proposition in the case of "good" or "bad." There is surely some concept there quite different from that of any psychological feeling or empirical tendency? The concept carries with it a unique authority which does not belong to any other feeling or desire as such and is quite irrespective of whether it happens to be in accord with the keenest or most widespread feeling or the strongest or most widely influential desire. "That principle by which we survey, and either approve or disapprove our own heart, temper, and actions, is not only to be considered as what is in its turn to have some influence, which may be said of every passion, of the lowest appetites; but likewise as being superior, as from its very nature manifestly claiming superiority over all others, insomuch that you cannot form a notion of this faculty conscience, without taking in judgement, direction, superintendency . . . Had it strength as it has right, had it power as it has manifest authority, it would absolutely govern the world." [7]

It will be noticed that I have so far not tried to refute the particular naturalist theories one by one but have claimed that we can see at once that any naturalist theory must be wrong.[8] That we should be able to perceive such a truth as that "good" and "ought" are not definable in purely psychological terms need not occasion surprise any more than the fact that we can perceive it to be true that sights cannot be reduced to sounds. Even a naturalist would presumably admit that he can see that goodness or obligation is not analysable in terms of numbers and would not say, "Well, I have tried various definitions of 'good' in terms of numbers, $3 + 4$, $5 + 7$, $6 + 9$ etc., and have not found any which would fit, but perhaps somebody will some day find one which does." No, he would see that it was ridiculous to suppose this could ever happen, because numbers and ethical properties are fundamentally discrepant in their natures so that one can never be reduced to the other. I should claim that, if we once grasp the issue clearly and keep it steadily before our minds, we can see the same about psychological definitions of ethical concepts or definitions of them in terms of any other science. I do not therefore think it necessary to consider separately the various naturalist definitions that have been proposed, but perhaps if I do so briefly it will bring out my points still more clearly.

The view that "good" means "approved by me" I have already considered under the heading of subjectivism, but it has sometimes been held that "good" or "right" means "approved by most people" or "approved by the society in which I live." The theory might also be expressed by saying that

---

[7] Butler, *Sermon* II, § 19.

[8] I think we can perceive directly that good is not analysable in psychological terms, but not that it is simple.

"goodness" means "the power to arouse the emotion of approval." I do not see how such a view is to escape the obvious criticism that a conscientious objector or a martyr might without contradicting himself hold both that something was bad or wrong and that it was approved by most people in his society or in the world. Whether he judged rightly in the particular case or not is irrelevant: right or wrong, he is certainly not committing a verbal contradiction. Again, if we defined "good" or "right" as "approved by people in general," and not only in a particular society, an insuperable difficulty would arise about what constituted a majority. If we took into account everybody who ever lived—and I do not see where we can consistently stop short of this—we should arrive at some queer results for, taking into account all past ages, very crude and savage far outnumber even partially civilized men. If, on the other hand, we redress the balance by including all the men who ever will live, it becomes quite impossible to decide what the majority will approve. If we say that "good" or "right" means "approved by the social group of the speaker," we shall have to admit that the Nazis spoke truly when they said that it was right to ill-treat the Jews. It might be suggested that "good" or "right" always meant "approved by some group which the speaker had in mind," but that the group might vary with the context and speaker. But this would make the meaning of ethical statements shift in an impossible fashion. The Nazi who said it was right to send Jews to concentration camps would on that view still be saying what was true, for most members of the social group he had in mind felt approval for the action. In saying it was wrong I should also be speaking the truth; but that is not good enough. When I say it is wrong I am claiming that the Nazi is mistaken even if the social group he had in mind felt approval of the action; I am not merely saying that, though in his sense of the word he was right, in mine he was wrong.

On this view there would be no sense in saying any group was right rather than any other, unless it was merely meant that the group of the speaker felt more approval for that group than for the other. And if I could only influence my group so as to change their feelings and make them approve, anything I did would be right, whatever it was. It should also be noted that most of the ethical judgements we make are about particular actions, states of mind, characters, which are not generally known, so that on the approval theory the judgement "This is good" or "right" must mean, not that a majority actually approve this, but that they would approve it if they knew about it. This seems to me to make the view still less plausible. Surely ethical judgements about what has been actually done claim to assert an actual fact, not what only would be a fact if something else happened which we know will never happen, that is, if most people were to know of the particular actions or states of mind in myself, perhaps secret, perhaps known just to a few people, which I approve or condemn. And surely ethical judgements are judgements about the action etc. named in them, not about something quite different, that is, the feelings of other people, still less about something that does not exist, that is, the feelings most people would have if they knew of the action, which they do not.

Again, as I have pointed out earlier, it is plain that whether something is good or right is not a question that could be settled straight off merely by disclosing a set of statistics, if we had them, about people's feelings. For instance, if it were discovered that the feeling of approval of most people towards something was always in strict proportion to the amount of pleasure they thought it produced and depended solely on that, it would by no means follow necessarily that hedonism was the true theory of ethics. We should not alter our ethical opinions as to the goodness or badness of something or the rightness or wrongness of some act straightway as a matter of course just because we found that the majority of people had different feelings from ourselves about it. Such a discovery would indeed be liable to influence us, but it would be ridiculous to say that it would necessarily be or ought to be the only deciding factor, as should be the case on the approval view. Again, the degree of approval or disapproval felt varies in proportion to circumstances which are admittedly irrelevant to the ethical quality of its object. For instance, men tend to feel more approval for the acts of close friends than for those of enemies or even strangers. It is difficult to see how the impartiality necessary for ethics is to be given a place in such a theory. The objection might be met by analysing "A is right" or "A is good" as meaning "most men feel approval of A in so far as they are not affected by irrelevant circumstances," but I do not see how "irrelevant" could be defined without circularity. It can only mean "what is irrelevant to the rightness or goodness of A." It will not do to define "influenced by irrelevant circumstances" as meaning "feeling in a way in which you would not feel if you were not personally affected," for example, because it is *you* whose interests have been injured, for this does not cover all cases of irrelevancy. If I felt more disapproval of a man's deeds just because he was a Jew I should be affected by irrelevant circumstances, even where his acts did not concern me personally at all. The majority of men are less inclined to feel approval of the actions of somebody if the latter is unattractive in appearance and in superficial matters unconventional. Does it follow that physically unattractive and unconventional men are morally worse than others? Further, the belief that other people approve or disapprove what I propose to do owes more than half its effect on me to the belief that their emotions would be objectively justified, that there are qualities in my proposed action which would make it fitting to approve or disapprove it.

Finally, the notion of obligation is neither contained in the notion of general approval nor deducible from it. On the contrary it is an essential feature of the moral consciousness that I realize that, if I ought to do something, I ought to do it whether others feel approval of it or not. Obligation need not, indeed, conflict with the approval of others, and their approval may even be one of the factors in helping to determine what I am under an obligation to do, since—other things being equal—I am more likely to do good by doing what is generally approved than by doing what is not so approved. But if "what ought to be done" means "what is generally approved," general approval would have to be the only factor which ultimately counted in deciding what we ought to do, and this it certainly is not. We can even say that indifference to approval is an essential part of the notion of obligation, because once we grant that something is our duty it follows that we ought to do it irrespective of whether others feel approval or not. Their approval is a contingent accident. This point may be made clearer still by considerations such as the following: It is obvious that we ought to seek what is good and/or right as the only end in itself. But it certainly is not the case that we ought to seek what other people approve as the only end-in-itself or even a main end-in-itself just because they feel approval of it. And I cannot see what point there could possibly be in doing what other people would approve *if* they knew what I have done when in fact they do not know it, unless there is some other reason besides the approval; yet, if something is my duty, I clearly ought to do it whether other people know of it or not. The good man will not value approval except as a sign of something objectively right or good. Views that ethical predicates are to be defined in terms of the commands of society or combinations of this with approval theories are open to similar objections.

Perhaps a little less unplausible are the naturalist theories which try to define "good" in terms of desire. It might be held that "good" meant either what somebody desires or what the speaker desires or what most people desire. These views might also be expressed by saying that "goodness" equals "the power to arouse desire." It has been objected that you can desire only what is absent, while the good may be present. But I think this objection could be met, without fundamentally altering what the holders of these theories maintain, by substituting "desired or liked" for "desired." Desire and liking are, I think, fundamentally the same attitude except that desire has for its object what is absent and liking what is present. If "good" is defined in terms of desire or liking, "the right action" or "the action we ought to do" will probably be defined as the one most efficient as a means to the fulfilment of desires or to the production of what is liked. The objection that it is not by any means self-contradictory to say that an action is not the most efficient means to this and yet that we ought to do it seems to me adequate to refute this view of "right," whichever form of the desire theory we take. For instance, Kant or Ross would say that we ought to keep certain promises even if we were convinced that alternative actions more efficient as means towards the fulfilment of desires or the production of what was liked were open to us, and nobody has claimed that their view is self-contradictory, though many have said it was false. Somebody might also combine a desire theory of good with an approval theory of right, but this would subject him both to the objections against approval theories and the objections against desire theories, and so it need not be discussed. I cannot see what other naturalist theory of "right" could be plausibly combined with the desire theory of good, and the objections to these theories of "right" are therefore for me objections against the desire theory of good.

The first form of the desire theory, that "good" means "desired by somebody," is adopted by R. B. Perry, except that he substitutes for desire the term "interest," which also covers liking. Now is this view not obviously false, since people desire and like bad things? It will be retorted that, if something is desired or liked, it must be in one aspect good, and will be desired for that aspect, though it may still be wrong to seek it, because that aspect is outweighed by its bad aspects or by the evil means necessary to obtain it. But it is not easy to apply this to people who desire the torture of others or even to less desperately wicked desires "to have one's own back," for what seems to be desired here is the pain of the other man, and not only, or perhaps at all, the advantages which the pain is conceived to bring. To reply that it is not his pain but one's own pleasure in the pain that is desired seems to me to be a case of the hedonistic fallacy. A man would not take pleasure in revenge if he did not desire revenge as an end-in-itself and not merely as a means. Further, it would certainly not be self-contradictory to say both that somebody desires A and that A is intrinsically and wholly evil, whether such a thing ever occurs in fact or not. In the second place, if "good" means desired, what does "better" mean? Could it in that case possibly mean anything else but "more desired" or "desired by more people"? This would commit one to the view that not only are desire, liking, and interest always directed to what is good, but that desire, liking, and interest are in exact proportion to the goodness of their objects, if not in the individual, at any rate when we take into account the desires of different people. This is surely a fantastic hypothesis which has no ground whatever. If we are considering the desires of people in general, it is obvious that on the whole (though with considerable exceptions) riches and what they bring, for instance, have been desired and liked in excess of their real value. Further, as with all these other naturalist definitions, even if the proposition that things were desired or liked in proportion to their real value were true, it would express not a tautology but a contingent fact or at the most a universal causal law of psychology.

The second view, that "good" means "desired (or liked) by the speaker," falls under the heading of subjectivist views, but the criticisms which I have just brought against a corresponding naturalist view in the last paragraph can be turned also against it, besides the special objection that it would commit us to a completely egoist view of good.

The view that "good" means "what most people desire (or like)" is open to similar objections. Most people desire and like happiness more than great virtue, yet it does not therefore necessarily follow that the former is better. And, if we could count heads, we should no doubt find that the majority of people who have hitherto lived, which would of course include a great preponderance of the "uncivilized," desired revenge on those who they thought had wronged them and did not desire to forgive these. Is revenge therefore good and forgiveness bad? In any case it is surely obvious that no collection of statistics as to people's desires would of itself completely settle the question what is good. Still less could a vague statement about such statistics, for example, that more than fifty per cent (or eighty per cent) of people desired or liked so-and-so, be possibly regarded as equivalent to the statement that so-and-so was good. All three theories would encounter extreme difficulties in defining "better" in terms of "desired or liked more." Even if action be the criterion of desire, it is certainly not, in view of the frequency of wrong and bad actions, the criterion of rightness or goodness. The definition of "better" could not be in terms of felt intensity of desire, because this varies according to many quite irrelevant circumstances, for example, mood or proximity in time of expected satisfaction, to say nothing of bad desires. If, on the other hand, we say either that the measure of the strength of a desire, at least for this purpose, should be taken to be not its felt strength as a desire but the degree of satisfaction which will accrue when it is fulfilled, or frankly define "good" as "satisfaction of desire" or "what satisfies desire," this is equally difficult to measure, even apart from the difficulty of making predictions about it.[9] If the measure is to be felt intensity and duration of satisfaction we are virtually committed to a hedonistic theory of ethics, and hedonism as a definition of "good" is even less plausible than hedonism as a theory of what things are good. Permanence of satisfaction is often suggested as a criterion, but it is just as inadequate to measure only the duration, and ignore the intensity, as vice versa. Or, it is said, good is what satisfies the whole man. But this is not true if by "satisfying the whole man" is meant "satisfying all his desires." It does not satisfy his wrong desires, and since no man can live a good life without sacrificing even some satisfactions innocent in themselves it will not satisfy even all his good and justified desires. If we say that the unsatisfied desires will eventually disappear and that the whole man will then be satisfied, we are open to the objection that many of the better desires, if unsatisfied, would likewise disappear, perhaps more quickly. It is a commonplace that one of the evil effects of persistently following the lower rather than the higher is that it destroys desire for the higher. This might happen, not only in an individual, but in a whole race who neglected culture and liberal education. We cannot meet this objection simply by arguing that such an individual or race would enjoy less pleasure and suffer more pain, because this is just to fall back on hedonism. We could only meet it by drawing a distinction as regards importance and quality between the different parts of one's nature sacrificed or their satisfaction, and I do not see how this could be worked out except on the basis of the belief that some factors in our nature or experience were qualitatively better than others in a non-

---

[9] On this subject v. W. D. Ross, *International Journal of Ethics*, XXXVII, p. 117 ff.

natural sense of "better." To define "good" as "that which satisfies the more important parts of our nature," or as "what we desire in so far as we are influenced only by relevant considerations," is to commit a vicious circle, since "more important" here can only mean "intrinsically or instrumentally better," and "relevant" can only mean "such as to affect its goodness."

All forms of the desire theory are clearly open to the fundamental objections which hold against any naturalist view of good. (1) To say that what is desired, whether by anyone or by oneself or by most people, or what satisfies desires in the long run, is good is not to assert a verbal proposition which cannot be denied without self-contradiction. (2) No collection of statistics as to people's desires or their satisfactions could settle the question what was good. (3) You cannot derive obligation from desire. Indeed it seems to me that to obtain what one desires is good only because of the specific quality of the object desired, or because pleasure in general is good and the fulfilment of desire brings pleasure. If the reference is to one's own desires, it seems plain that, so far from obligation being derivable from these, we are conscious of obligation primarily in independence from or even opposition to what we most keenly desire. If it is meant that we ought to do what will satisfy people's desires in general and not only our own, I do not see what *locus standi* the naturalist who holds this position can have against the person who asks, "Why ever should I bother about other people's desires (except in so far as to do so is a means to satisfying my own)?" This question could be answered only by admitting that it is obligatory for us to try to satisfy them, in some sense of "obligatory" which does not itself mean merely "conducive to the satisfaction of desire." If the naturalist then admits this and gives some other naturalist definition of "obligatory," for example, in terms of approval, the question may be asked again: "Why on earth should a man bother about gaining the approval of most people unless he wants to do so more than he wants to perform an action which would forfeit their approval?" The naturalist view to my mind takes all the point away from morality.

A slightly different view would be that to call anything "good" is to say that it is the object of some "pro attitude" on the part of most people. Following Ross I use "pro attitude" to cover desiring, liking, seeking, choosing, approving, admiring, etc. These attitudes obviously have something in common which is suitably indicated by the prefix *pro-*. Such a view would be more elastic and has a considerable affinity to the definition which I shall finally adopt, but it is obviously still exposed to the main objections brought against the approval and desire theories. It is perfectly sensible to say that something is bad or wrong though most people have a pro attitude to it, and the pro attitude of others carries with it no obligation on me except in so far as I already presuppose that it is good for them that their desires should be fulfilled. In fact if the reader cared to run through the last few pages again he would find that the theory in question was liable to most of the objections brought against either the approval or the desire theory. It should be noted that in working the theory out we can only include "approve" under the pro attitudes in the uncommon sense in which it signifies "have a certain emotion towards," not in the sense in which it signifies "think right" (or "good"). If we defined "right" or "good" in terms of "approve" in the latter sense, we should be defining it in terms of itself.

In view of the fact that people desire many things which they would not desire if they knew what they really involved, it has been suggested that "good" means, not what is actually desired, but what all men would desire if they knew its true nature; but such a view is open to many objections. It is still naturalist in character and therefore open to the general objections which we have brought against all naturalist views, besides some peculiar to itself. The terms used in the definition are purely psychological, and the fact that the property identified with goodness is hypothetical and not categorical does not make any essential difference. We still cannot derive an ought from mere psychological facts about desire, or if we could it would certainly be a synthetic and not an analytic proposition, so that we should still have at least one ethical concept irreducible to psychological terms, namely, the concept signified by "ought." That all men would desire whatever is good in proportion to its goodness if only they knew its true nature is a highly doubtful proposition, so far from being merely verbal, and I see no means of proving it or even showing it to be at all probable. For us to desire the good of all other men fully as much as an equivalent amount of good for ourselves or those closest to us it would be necessary not only that we should know all the circumstances including the state of their feelings, but that our emotional nature should be completely altered. And, if we imagine our emotional nature thus completely and superhumanly or inhumanly altered, we can no longer have any foundation for saying what we should desire under the circumstances. In any case it is surely obvious that to call anything good is not to say what would happen if some quite impossible psychological revolution were effected in our nature. But, even if it were a fact that we are so built that we should desire what was good in proportion to its goodness if we knew its true nature, it would be a quite contingent fact, for we still might well have been built differently. Further, we are sometimes immediately aware that something is good or bad, but hypothetical facts about what would happen if our situation and nature were quite different from what it is are not facts that any philosopher in any other context has ever suggested could be known immediately. How could we know by intuition the truth of such extraordinary prophecies?

Some would-be naturalists admit that we can see any naturalist analysis to be incomplete, but attempt to meet the objection by calling in subjectivism as an ally and contending that naturalist definitions leave out something, but only the emotional or hortatory element. In that case an "ethical judgement" is really a psychological judgement plus an exclamation, wish, or command. "You are acting wrongly" becomes, for example, "You are interfering with the fulfilment of other people's desires, damn you!" or "You are deceiving people; stop doing this." But this is to make the worst of both worlds. For the position is liable to the main criticisms already brought against subjectivist modes of analysis, since it involves a subjectivist view not indeed of the whole judgement but of the only specifically ethical part. And it does not in any case escape the main objections against naturalism, for it is just as obvious that the element in "ethical judgements" which is capable of being true or false includes more than can be given in any naturalist analysis as it is that the "judgement" as a whole does so. The view I am criticizing tries to avoid the objections to subjectivism by admitting an assertive element in "ethical judgements" but denying that it is non-naturalistic, and the objections to naturalism by admitting an element which is not merely an assertion about human psychology but denying that it is assertive at all. I reply that my objections, if valid, show that there is an *assertive* element in ethical judgements which is *non-naturalistic*, and I can therefore claim them to be just as valid against this combination of subjectivism and naturalism as against either view undiluted by the other.

Again, some naturalists try to escape objections by shifting the meaning of "good." When objections to a particular view of "good" are pointed out, they say that, while this view applies to some uses of "good," in the cases where objection is taken "good" is being used in a different sense, though one that is still naturalist or subjectivist. If objections are brought against this second sense, they can then say in any case where the objections are insuperable that "good" is being used not in this second sense but in the first or in a third sense. They may thus hope that, whatever particular objection is brought, they can always find some sense of "good" which will avoid this particular objection, and that the other objections to which the new definition may be liable will apply only in cases where they could claim that "good" was being used in another sense without exposing themselves to worse objections. For example, if "good" or "right" is defined as that of which most men feel approval and it is then pointed out that a moral reformer or conscientious objector may, without contradicting himself, assert that something is bad or wrong while admitting that most people feel approval of it, the naturalist may try to avoid the difficulty by saying that "good" or "right" as used by him in this context means not "what most men approve" but "what I, the speaker, approve." If then it is objected, for example, that in that case two men do not contradict each other when one asserts that A is bad and the other that A is good, he may retort that, in cases where they do really contradict each other, they are using "good" not in the second sense but in the first or in some third sense, for instance, as meaning what will satisfy most men's desires in the long run. But it seems plain to me that the main objections I feel about any exclusively naturalist or subjectivist analysis apply to all such attempts at analysis and cannot therefore be avoided by putting forward one analysis in one case and another in another case. I have admitted [10] that there are some senses of "good"—not ethical ones—which have to be analysed naturalistically; but I claim to have given adequate reason for

[10] V. above, p. 46.

thinking that there are some others which cannot be analysed in any naturalist or subjectivist way at all, not only that each of the particular attempts made at such analysis fails to do justice to some of the senses of "good." When I use a sentence such as commonly expresses an "ethical judgement," not parrotlike but sincerely and with clear consciousness of what I am doing, it is quite clear to me that I am asserting something which may be either true or false (except in so far as I think I see it to be certainly true and therefore cannot entertain the idea of its being false), and which is not merely about my state of mind or disposition, thus excluding any subjectivist analysis. It is also quite clear to me that I am asserting something which goes beyond any statement about people's psychology, thus excluding naturalism. The chief objections that I have brought against subjectivist modes of analysis apply equally to any or all of them, and the chief objections that I have brought against naturalism apply equally to all forms of naturalism. The same insight shows the falsity of all; and it seems perfectly clear to me that, if other people mean at all the same sort of thing when they use ethical words as I do (which assumption, though not strictly provable, is most unlikely to be wrong), no subjectivist or naturalist can possibly give an adequate analysis of what they mean. No doubt there are some objections applying only to particular forms of either theory which might be avoided by shifting the meaning. But each time the naturalist has to save himself by postulating a shift of meaning where there is no other reason for supposing this except to bolster up naturalism, the plausibility of his case is lessened, and he will have to do it very often. No doubt "good" and "ought" are used in various different senses, but this does not justify us in assuming a different sense just to fit in with a preconceived theory in cases where we should otherwise never have supposed such a thing. If in defining a term we are to be allowed, whenever our theory of its definition does not fit, to say "Oh, the speaker must be using the term in a different sense"—and then do the same again about the second sense, we shall be able to defend some very odd definitions. In defining we surely must not suppose a difference of usage unless there is evidence for it to be found in a direct study of the proposition asserted and its context, and not do so merely in order to save a general theory about the definition. Such a theory should be based on a study of general usage taking into account its differences and not serve as a premise for inferring differences which would otherwise never have occurred to us.

Merely biological definitions of fundamental ethical concepts would be still harder to defend.[11] "Good" or "right" cannot just mean "what tends to further human survival," for in ethics we aim at the good life as well as at mere life, and though some virtues and vices are likely to affect the duration of life or the number of descendants produced this is not the case with most. If the view mentioned were adopted it would follow logically that one of the worst crimes was to remain a childless bachelor, and that it did not matter how miserable one made anybody else provided the misery did not actually shorten his life or diminish the chance of his having many descendants! If we try a sociological definition and substitute for mere survival the survival of the existing type of society, this would rule out all very radical reforms as necessarily unethical. If we say that "good or right is what furthers the evolution of society," we are faced with the difficulty of defining evolution and distinguishing it from other kinds of change without already presupposing the notion of goodness. There can be no chance of defining "good" in terms of evolution, unless, as is often the case, we mean by "evolution"

---

[11] For criticism of a biological view of ethics that has come to the front lately, that is, that of C. H. Waddington, see Ewing in *Proceedings of Aristotelian Soc.*, XLII, 68 ff and Broad, *id.*, pp. 100 A ff.

"good change," and that would constitute a vicious circle. For all development is not necessarily good, whether "development" just means change or whether it is defined in terms of increased complexity. It is not even an obviously true, let alone verbal, proposition that change going further in the same direction as that which it has predominantly followed in the past is good. There are times when it is best to make a sharp turn and, having developed a certain mode of action up to a point, adopt a quite different one, and this may be true of the race as well as of the individual. For instance one of the features of change in the past has been that people have shown more and more efficiency in destroying each other in war. Does it follow that it would be good for this process to continue? If it is said in reply that this is not a fundamental enough development to figure in the criterion, it becomes a matter quite impossible to settle what is and what is not fundamental enough to do so. Besides, we shall then be left with nothing but one or two generalizations far too vague to be capable of application. Finally, the fact that change has developed in a certain way in the past cannot possibly itself entail any proposition about what ought to be done. There is nothing logically absurd about the supposition that the whole evolutionary process was harmful and that it would have been better if life had never developed beyond its first stage, or any intermediate stage we might happen to fancy.

The main objections against naturalist theories of ethics may be summed up as follows:

1. It is clear that ethical propositions cannot be established merely by giving statistics of people's psychological reactions, and still clearer, if possible, that they are not themselves propositions about statistics, as they would have to be if they asserted merely "Most people feel . . ."

2. Whatever empirical property is put forward as a definition of "good" or "obligatory," it is clear that the question

whether everything that is good (or obligatory) has that property or vice versa is not merely a question of definition.

3. If something has the property of goodness or obligatoriness at all, we can see that it must have that property in the degree in which it has it, provided only its factual properties are what they are. Yet it is always conceivable to us that the attitude of people to it, or its relation to their desires, in terms of which "good" or "obligatoriness" has been naturalistically defined might have been different, its other factual properties being what they were. Therefore goodness or obligatoriness cannot be identified with being the object of a certain attitude or standing in a certain relation to desire.

4. The naturalist definitions leave out the essential nature of obligation. If they constituted a full account of the meaning of "ought" and "good" there would be no point in my trying to do what I ought rather than anything else which I happened to desire.

5. When we make ethical judgements about an action or state of mind, we are clearly talking primarily about this action or state of mind, not about other states of mind, still less, states which are purely hypothetical, that is, the feelings or attitudes most people would have towards the action or state of mind if they knew about it, which they usually do not.

6. We can after careful reflection see that ethical concepts are generically different from, and therefore incapable of reduction to, the concepts of psychology or any other empirical science.

It is clear that in none of these cases can the missing element be supplied by subjectivism, that is, by admitting that naturalism cannot give a complete account of ethical propositions but maintaining that what is left out is not something which could be objectively true, but only the expression of an emotion or a command. For, if we look at any of these arguments again, we can see that they show, not merely that any naturalist analysis is incomplete in respect of not including the emotional overtones, but that such an analysis does not do justice to the objective element in the judgement itself, namely that for which truth is claimed. Ethical judgements assert truths which go beyond any psychological or biological statistics; to apply ethical properties to whatever has any psychological or biological property is to make a (not merely verbal) objective assertion and not only to add injunctions or expressions of emotion. The ethical properties ascribed to something, if they belong to it at all, *must* so belong, its intrinsic nature being what it is, whereas the emotional attitude of the speaker as well as of others is contingent. If I am to be under any obligation, it must be objectively true that I am under the obligation, and therefore, if there is no adequate naturalist definition of obligation, the deficiency cannot be supplied by emotions or desires which do not claim truth. Ethical judgements are expressions of belief about what we call their objects, and not merely either expressions of something other than belief or expressions of belief about something else, such as people's states of approval, or both together. Ethical concepts are generically different from the merely psychological concepts which either on the subjectivist or on the naturalist view make up the only elements of which they could be composed. In short, the arguments for the view that a naturalist analysis of ethical judgements must be inadequate are at the same time arguments for the view that such an analysis cannot do justice even to the objective element in these judgements.

If we have thus to admit that "good" and "ought" in their ethical senses stand for non-natural concepts, it is still logically possible to avoid admitting that the non-natural properties thus conceived belong to anything. We may admit that most human beings believe in the truth of ethical propositions in a sense in which these cannot be analysed naturalistically, and yet we may hold that they are mistaken in doing so and that these propositions are true of nothing, or at least that we are not justified in thinking them true of anything. This is the position of the moral sceptic, which I earlier classed as a variety of subjectivism. But I cannot believe that all our ethical beliefs are false or unjustified, and therefore I accept the view that the non-natural properties or relations for which the terms "good" and "ought" stand in some of their usages really belong to some selves, experiences, or actions. It, further, seems to be the case that people have analysed ethical propositions naturalistically or subjectively chiefly because they thought that they could then and only then still go on saying that the ethical propositions were true. If people who think like this realize that no naturalist or subjectivist analysis of ethical propositions can be adequate, it may be that they will prefer to admit the real existence of non-natural ethical properties rather than take up a position of ethical scepticism. This ought to be the case especially with those philosophers who take the view in general that commonsense propositions are true and that it is the business of philosophers to analyse them, for ethical propositions are certainly propositions of common sense. Hence the importance of the question of analysis discussed in this chapter. Those who accept views like mine as to the analysis of ethical propositions but doubt whether these propositions are true of anything are referred to what I said in the first chapter.[12] Those who are influenced by what I say but still think that there is an important element of truth in naturalism are asked to wait till Chapter V, when I shall say what I think that to be.

---

[12] V. above, p. 30 ff.

The Coherence Theory of Ethics, and Some Other Non-naturalist Definitions of the Fundamental Ethical Terms

If we reject the naturalist and subjectivist views of ethics, is there any alternative to admitting that the fundamental ethical concept is just indefinable and can be grasped by intuition but not further described? Many find this a very unsatisfactory view. But it may be retorted with point that some concepts *must* be indefinable in the sense of "unanalysable," since you cannot reduce everything by analysis to something else without a vicious circle or infinite regress; and it is surely clear that, if all ethical concepts are analysable completely in terms of non-ethical, this will reduce ethics to something else and destroy its distinctive nature altogether. If, however, ethical terms are not all to be defined (analysed) in terms of non-ethical, since they cannot all be defined in terms of each other, at least one ethical concept must be indefinable. This does not imply that its nature cannot be known—it may be very distinctly known—only that it cannot be reduced to anything else. Nor need it imply that nothing more can be said about it. It may perhaps turn out possible to say a great deal more about it; only what is said will never exhaust its nature without residuum. When he denied that "good" was definable, Moore [1] was using "definition" to cover only definition by analysis. We may use "define

---

[1] In speaking of Moore's views I shall refer to those maintained in *Principia Ethica* and *Ethics*, and not to his present views, which in the absence of fresh published works on Ethics are not known.

78

A" to mean "give properties which accompany A and constitute a distinguishing mark of the presence of A" or "fix the place of A in the system of concepts"; and in these senses it might be possible to define "good," though the term was in Moore's sense indefinable. Again, it may turn out that "good" can be defined, even in Moore's sense, in terms of other ethical concepts or partly of ethical and partly of psychological concepts; but in any case that would still leave some fundamental ethical term, such as "ought," which could not be thus defined. About the fundamental ethical term we naturally want to be able to say something more than that we know what it means but cannot explain it; yet it is important to insist that it stands for a quite distinctive quality or relation which cannot just be identified with any mere object of psychological introspection or any concept derived merely from the latter source.

Now if we keep strictly to Moore's sense of definition, it seems clear to me that a definition exclusively in metaphysical or logical terms would explain away the distinctive character of ethics just as much as would a definition in terms of psychology. When I say this, however, I do not mean to rule out of court the view that everything which we call good has, besides the attribute of goodness, other attributes which are correlated or perhaps inseparably connected with goodness, and that we may make important philosophical generalizations about the attributes in question. Bearing this in mind let us consider the theory which seeks to define goodness in terms of coherence. We shall, first, consider briefly whether such a definition can be regarded as giving a fully adequate equivalent of goodness; that is, as a definition in Moore's sense. Then, if we answer the first question in the negative, we shall ask whether such a theory, if it does not do this, can still provide a definition in some other sense or at least give us important information about ethical matters.

The most elaborate account of the coherence theory of

ethics that I know is given in Professor Paton's book, *The Good Will*, which puts forward the view that to be good is to be coherently willed. Now if this were taken in the way in which the author did not mean it to be taken, that is, as a definition in Moore's sense, it would certainly be very open to criticism. I have indeed heard his view wrongly interpreted as giving one of the naturalist definitions which I have rejected —the definition of "good" as meaning "what will ultimately satisfy us"—on the ground that this alone could be consistently willed, since all wrong doing is due to a search for satisfaction, which yet cannot be obtained by wrong doing.[2] Or, if the egoism implied in such an account is rejected, as I should reject it, and the view is interpreted in terms of general satisfaction, we still have to note that the definition of "good" as what will give satisfaction to somebody (whether oneself or another), or to people in general, is a definition in purely psychological terms and therefore an example of the naturalist error. This is still the case even if we qualify "satisfaction" by a word like "real" or "ultimate," unless we thereby covertly introduce into the definition a non-psychological content.

On the other hand, as Paton maintains while repudiating the view that a thing is made good merely by being willed or desired, it seems at least plausible to say that nothing could be good unless it could satisfy some kind of desire or will. The character and value of the view thus depends on the nature of the predicate introduced to distinguish good willing from the other kinds of willing. Now coherence is certainly a logical and not a psychological concept, and still less is it an object of sense perception. The coherence theory might therefore be less unfairly accused of reducing ethics, not to psychological, but to logical terms, or to a combination of the two. This would exempt it from the charge of naturalism, for the pres-

---

[2] Bosanquet and Bradley both "define" good as "what satisfies," but I cannot think they were then using "define" in the sense of the naturalist.

ence of some naturalist elements in a definition does not make the definition naturalist, unless there are no other elements in it except the naturalist ones. But, if it is intended to give a definition of "good" or "right" in Moore's sense, the coherence theory can in any case fairly be accused of committing the same sort of error as naturalism; that is, of trying to reduce ethics without residuum to the non-ethical. For it is as impossible to get ethical content out of the merely logical as out of the merely psychological, or out of a combination of logical and psychological terms as out of either taken in isolation.

"Coherence" might also be identified with a kind of harmony of different wills together with an internal harmony within the individual's life, such harmony being analogous to, though different from, logical consistency. This brings one nearer to Paton's view, and, if we are to deduce all ethical judgements from a single principle, this is perhaps the most plausible line of derivation; but, if this is intended as a definition in Moore's sense, it will still be naturalist, unless we have already covertly included goodness in the conception of "harmony." "Good" cannot be defined as harmony, at least in Moore's sense, for there is no *verbal* contradiction in saying even that war is intrinsically better, though less harmonious, than peace. Such a definition would confuse the questions what goodness is and what things are good. The considerations that I have brought forward would apply equally to a coherence definition of "right" or "obligation," if one of these terms was taken as fundamental in ethics instead of "good." The same objections hold also against the view that "good" applied to the will means just "aimed at harmony." There is no *verbal* contradiction in saying that a good will might be aimed at lessening harmony instead of increasing it.

But, while these objections may apply to some people who have accepted the coherence theory of ethics, I do not think they would apply to its more distinguished exponents. Professor Paton, for instance, makes it quite clear that he is not providing a definition in Moore's sense of the term. Yet he is not content to say that he is merely giving an account of a quality, coherence, which all good things have over and above the quality of goodness. He admits that to be good and to be coherently willed are not just the same thing; but he insists that the only alternative to saying this is not to say that they are "just two different things each of which is and is knowable in entire isolation from the other." [3] Moore himself does not, however, hold that goodness is separable from the other properties of something good in the sense that goodness could ever fail to be present, the other properties being what they are. He admits that we can rightly make synthetic *a priori* judgements to the effect that, if something has certain qualities, it is necessarily in so far good. But this does not content Paton, who "cannot believe that it is possible to understand thinking on the supposition that some judgements are just analytical and others just synthetic." Paton cannot see how there can be synthetic *a priori* judgements connecting other properties with goodness, if goodness is just simple and quite intelligible apart from its relations; and I for my part am inclined to agree that this is difficult to understand. I do not wish to discuss the question whether Paton has given an adequate interpretation of Moore, but the latter's account certainly does seem to imply that once we have apprehended goodness by a kind of intuition we have apprehended all there is in it!

The holders of the coherence theory do not mean to maintain that all *a priori* propositions are analytic in the sense of verbal. Indeed there is no view more opposed to their conception of the *a priori* than that one; but they would say that, where what is called a synthetic *a priori* proposition con-

---

[3] *The Good Will*, p. 52.

necting A and B is true, neither A nor B could be understood without reference to the other, so that each would have no complete nature by itself, whether definable or indefinable, independently of the other.

We might, I think, combine the essential truth in both views, if we realize that it may be the case that a property is not just reducible to other properties and yet that it may be intrinsically impossible to see what it is like apart from them. "Four" does not just mean two plus two, since it also is six minus two, and the square root of sixteen, etc.; but we cannot know or describe the nature of four adequately without presupposing the whole numerical system and therefore all these relations. I do not think we need deny that there are simple and unanalysable properties, on the contrary I cannot get away from the logical argument that the complex presupposes the simple. That there should be any synthetic *a priori* propositions connecting a simple property with other properties does seem incompatible, not indeed with its irreducibility by analysis, but with the notion that its full internal nature could be grasped apart from its relations to the other properties which are entailed by it, as Moore seemed to hold. May it not be that there are cases of properties which are indefinable in themselves and yet incapable of being understood apart from each other? Shape and size seem to be indefinable in the sense that no analysis could be produced which would make clear what they were to anybody who had not experienced them, or (if that were possible) had only experienced one and not the other, yet each entails the other and could not be understood without reference to it. Again, a term is something over and above its relations, otherwise the relations would not relate anything, but it does not follow that a term is always intelligible apart from its relations. Granted that a concept is simple and unanalysable, the correct point of view may be to look upon it not as for that reason intelligible in itself, but rather as being too much of an abstraction to stand by itself. This it may be just because it is simple.

Now I find it difficult to maintain that I can understand what goodness is quite apart from my knowledge of the nature of things which are good, or what moral obligation is quite apart from my knowledge of the kind of acts which are obligatory. This is not necessarily to deny that there is some indefinable flavour about the notion of goodness (or of obligation) itself which just cannot be reduced to any other properties or relations; but it does not seem to me that you can have a clear idea of this quality or relation without others, and not only without some other qualities or relations, but without some specific kinds of qualities or relations. It is unfortunate that Moore in his account of good took yellow as an illustration of another simple indefinable quality, because goodness and yellowness are such very different kinds of properties, but as a matter of fact even yellow is an example of what I have been saying. For it is not just a single quality but a class of shades, and nobody could grasp what "yellow" meant without being acquainted with several of these shades. Indeed I should go further and say that the notion of yellow was unintelligible apart from that of light (not in the sense in which "light" is used in physical science), and perhaps apart from that of colours other than yellow. However it is still less plausible to hold the view which Paton is attacking in regard to good. Goodness is rather of the nature of a categorial property, a very abstract universal, and, whatever may be the case with yellow, it is more than doubtful whether the nature of categorial properties can be grasped apart from the scheme or system of entities subject to the category. This is not the same as saying that we could not grasp the nature of goodness without knowing every good thing that has ever existed, but we must know some.

Now, if Paton is right, any coherent will, and (I suppose

in a different sense of "good") everything which is coherently willed, is good. The connection is not on his view contingent but necessary; and Moore would agree that anything which was good at all was so necessarily because of its other qualities. But if to be a case of coherent willing is necessarily to be good and vice versa, even though this may not give the *meaning* of good, it is difficult to see how the nature of the one concept could be grasped in complete abstraction from the nature of the other; and so, if Paton is right, we may both grant Moore's point that good cannot be defined in the sense of analysed, and yet insist with Paton that we cannot understand goodness except in relation to coherent willing. (Paton admits that his doctrine could be stated in terms of Moore's view.[4]) Goodness and a certain kind of coherence might be two different irreducible [5] and yet inseparable aspects of the same thing. Let us now consider whether they are inseparable.

It seems to me that there are different respects, not always distinguished, in which ethical principles might be said to be coherent:

(1) The coherence of ethical principles might be interpreted to mean simply formal logical consistency both internally and with each other. They undoubtedly must have this characteristic, otherwise they could not be true; and it cannot be disputed that consistency is a valuable test both for practical decisions and for a general theory of ethics. But unless we can show that there is a logical self-contradiction involved in denying the validity of ethics and can thus prove *a priori* some ethical propositions without already presupposing the truth of any other such propositions, we cannot make coherence in this sense the sole criterion and basis of

---

[4] Op. cit., p. 224.
[5] I do not mean to imply that coherence is unanalysable, only that it is not reducible to goodness, though perhaps necessarily connected with the latter. Indeed, as we shall see later, I do not hold that goodness is itself unanalysable.

ethics. Nobody has shown such a contradiction in the strict logical sense to be involved in refusing to assent to any particular ethical proposition, and it is certainly against any modern views of logic to suppose that it ever could be shown.

(2) There is, however, another kind of inconsistency, to which Kant makes reference, that is at least a frequent feature and a valuable criterion of wrong action. Kant does not claim that, for instance, to tell a particular lie is self-contradictory, but he holds that there would be a sort of self-contradiction in asserting or at least in trying to carry out the universal principle that everybody should tell lies whenever it suited them. For the principle would be self-defeating. What the liar wants is by no means that lying in general should be regarded as justified. He does not want other people to lie to him. Hitler showed no lack of ability to appreciate the badness of breaches of faith when he himself was the victim of one; for example, at the hands of Badoglio. What the liar wants is to make an exception in his own case. Now it may be said that this course of action is fundamentally inconsistent unless there are special circumstances relevant to the situation other than the fact that it is he himself (or somebody specially connected with him) who is concerned. If there is no relevant difference between two cases it is inconsistent to do A in the one and B in the other.

We may in fact distinguish two different kinds of inconsistency:

(a) There is the kind which consists in seeking A and then doing something which prevents or hinders my attainment of A; for example, going to somebody to come to an agreement with him and then wrecking or diminishing the prospects of agreement by an outburst of anger. We may admit that very much wrong action is inconsistent in this sense. It has even been contended that all wrong action is, on the ground that we desire ultimate satisfaction and that only right action will lead to this. But this inconsistency is certainly not the only circumstance which makes it wrong, otherwise an act would be right simply because it led to the agent's own satisfaction. It is more plausible to say that what makes an act right is that it tends ultimately to produce general satisfaction; but, apart from the hedonist and naturalist character of this view, which in my opinion lays it open to objection, it would not show that there was any inconsistency in wrong action. For it certainly cannot be maintained that everybody always desires the greatest satisfaction of people in general even when it conflicts with his own, and therefore to show that an action does not lead to this may be to show that it is wrong, but certainly is not to show that it is inconsistent or self-defeating.

But (b) there is a second kind of inconsistency, the kind which consists in doing or approving A on one occasion and B on another when there is no relevant difference between the set of circumstances on the two occasions to justify this distinction. This is the sort of inconsistency shown by the man who makes an unjustifiable profit himself, yet rails against profiteers in other articles which he wants to buy, or in its extreme form by a savage who, when asked whether he knew the difference between right and wrong, is reputed to have said: "Yes, if another man takes my wife, it is wrong; if I take another man's wife, it is right." There is a corresponding distinction in the realm of logic: a man may be inconsistent either in the sense of asserting or implying both p and not-p or in the sense of asserting in some cases a conclusion as following from evidence which in other cases he would never admit could lead to such a conclusion. In practical action inconsistency in the first sense is appropriately called imprudence or irrationality; in the second sense it is usually called unfairness.

It is this second kind of inconsistency to which Kant is

referring. When he insists that all lying is wrong because of its effects if universalized, he is not arguing that a particular lie is wrong because it will eventually harm the man who tells it. He is contending that it appertains to the nature of a rational being not to make exceptions in his own favour but only to adopt principles of action which he could consistently universalize. Why cannot we consistently universalize the principle that we should lie whenever it suits our interests? Because this principle would be self-defeating. The motive for lying is to further one's own interests, but, if everybody lied, our own interests would thereby be not furthered but defeated. Therefore, if we are to lie we must be inconsistent in the sense of claiming for ourselves what we could not allow to others. We must be inconsistent in the second sense because, if our policy were universally adopted, it would be inconsistent in the first. The fundamental injustice of the attitude of the man who profits by others obeying the law while he himself violates it is at any rate a reason against lying, even if it does not, as Kant thought, prove all lies without exception wrong. And it is very interesting to note that even a utilitarian like Hume finds himself forced to admit that there are cases where we ought to perform an action which by itself will do harm rather than good, on the ground that it is one of a class of acts which, taken together, do good rather than harm.[6]

A good instance of this is the case of paying taxes. Suppose a man to urge that he will miss the sum he has to pay much more than it would be missed by society. The absence of the few pounds which he has to pay will not, he may urge, make any perceptible difference whatever to the public funds, but it will make a very perceptible difference to himself, therefore to force him to pay it will do more harm than good; and it will be difficult to answer him if we consider the partic-

---

[6] *An Enquiry Concerning the Principles of Morals*, Appendix III.

ular act by itself. But the real answer surely is that he still ought to pay it, because this argument, if admitted at all, would apply to practically everybody, and it would therefore be unfair of him to benefit by other people's taxes while not paying his own share. (The unfairness would not arise if he had strong special grounds for exemption which did not apply to everybody.) It is a difficult question how far and under what circumstances we are to apply Kant's principle that we must not do what we could not will universalized, but it certainly supplies a valuable practical criterion in many cases where the utilitarian criterion as applied to the particular act would lead us wrong or be very uncertain.

This is not to say that it would be logically inconsistent for me, for instance, to lie in these cases. There is no logical inconsistency in doing what I believe to be wrong. But it would be logically inconsistent for me to maintain that I was doing right and yet that other people who lied under similar conditions were doing wrong. Nor is it to say that there are no possible exceptional cases in which I should be justified in doing what it would be wrong for most people under similar external circumstances to do. But in that case there would be an argument based on my psychology in favour of the action, which would not apply to people who had a different psychology. What would be inconsistent would be for me to try to justify my action by any argument which, if valid at all, would apply to everybody.

A somewhat similar distinction arises even in regard to purely prudential considerations: it is prudent for an undergraduate to work sufficiently to pass his examination, yet it may well be the case that in regard to any particular hour he can truly say that to spend this hour differently would give him more pleasure [7] and would not by itself jeopardise his chances

---

[7] The pleasure might even be qualitatively better; for example, its aesthetic value might be greater than the intrinsic intellectual value of an hour's study.

of passing, yet if he says that about every period of an hour
and acts accordingly, he will certainly fail. Here, however,
the question of neglect to perform the action being unfair to
others by whose performance of the action we have benefited
does not enter directly.

There are thus a good many acts which, as far as one can
tell, do more harm than good, and yet are obligatory for the
reason given, for example, paying taxes where the individual
taxpayer misses the money much more than, if his particular contribution were not forthcoming, it would be missed
by the community. I am not satisfied that this is the only reason
why we ought not to tell lies or act unjustly—another reason,
I hold, is that these activities are intrinsically evil—but at any
rate it is one reason. We must note further that it can be
applied only in cases where there is no ethically relevant
difference between my case and the case of others. There
might be special circumstances which made it right for me
to be exempted from taxes, while other people paid them;
all we can say is that, if this diversity of treatment is to be
defended, I must be able to cite some special difference in my
circumstances. The principle does not really therefore tell
one much, but it does at any rate show that strict utilitarianism
is not the true theory of ethics; and it is an important illustration of the part rational coherence plays in ethics. If an action
is to be right, it must also be right for everybody in similar
circumstances to act in the same way. It is not, however, the
case that all duties can be deduced from this principle. To
use the principle we must indeed know independently of it
whether it would be right or wrong for everybody to act in
this way. And the principle cannot by itself prove the intrinsic goodness or badness of anything.

(3) Logical "coherence," however, in the sense in which
the term is used by holders of the "coherence" theory of truth
does not mean mere consistency; it means that true proposi-

tions are supposed to form a system such that they are not divisible into logically independent groups but help to confirm one another's truth, and that none of them could be false while all the others (or perhaps even any of the others) remained true. I do not think it is worth while discussing whether coherence in this sense is the definition of "good" in at least Moore's sense of "definition," for I am not sure whether anybody has ever really meant to maintain this, and it is quite obviously false. But it may be maintained rather more plausibly that the criterion of the truth of an ethical judgement, whether we are thinking of one which expresses a general ethical theory or of a particular decision in practical life, is whether the judgement coheres with our other ethical judgements in a way which brings us nearer to such a system than we should be if we believed it false. This is at least one interpretation which might be given of the view. The coherence theory is indeed put forward as an ideal; it does not claim that we have already established such a coherent system either in ethics or in the realm of truth generally, but it does claim that the criterion of truth is the degree in which the propositions we assert to be true show a more or less feeble and inadequate approximation towards this coherence, and this would have to be understood as applying to true ethical judgements as well as to true judgements about anything else. Further, it is held that it is this coherence which makes them true. But this theory, in at least its unqualified form, seems to me again quite untenable, because it is not mere coherence with any sort of judgements, but at the most coherence with true judgements, which makes a judgement itself true.[8] The advocates of the coherence theory of truth have therefore commonly been forced to say that it is not mere coherence, but coherence plus comprehensiveness, or coherence with experience, which is, for us at least, the criterion; and a similar view, it seems,

[8] On this v. Ross in *Arist. Soc. Supp.*, Vol. X, pp. 61 ff.

would have to be taken in regard to ethical judgements. Suppose the judgement that A is good coheres with the judgements that B and C are good. This surely cannot be either what makes A good or a ground for affirming A to be good, unless we assume that B and C really are good? If they are not, coherence with the judgement that they are good is an argument against, rather than for, the truth of the judgement that A is good. And therefore, just as the coherence test will not work in regard to theoretical judgements unless we admit that there are truths based on sense experience with which the judgements have to cohere, so it will not work in ethics unless there are ethical truths apprehended intuitively with which other ethical judgements may be expected to cohere. The only way of replying to this would be if it could be maintained that there is one, and only one, coherent system of ethical propositions conceivable, but I do not know how this could be shown.

No doubt, granted some ethical propositions which we know by other means, coherence in the sense described above is a useful test. It is not only that, if we know some ethical propositions, any others inconsistent with these must be false; this will be true on any theory. It may be the case that some ethical judgements which we are inclined to make are not actually inconsistent with any others known to be true, but are of such a kind that they cannot be fitted into any systematic ethical theory. They cannot then be deduced from or rendered probable by any more general judgements which have their application also in other parts of ethics. If so, I should regard this as an argument against them as far as it goes. (The retributive theory of punishment I should take as an example.) The argument is not conclusive: after all, even if all true ethical judgements make up a completely coherent system, we cannot expect to be in a position to see the coherence in all cases, and we may be able to know by intuition the truth of certain ethical judgements which do not stand in any relation of entailment to others that we thus know. Further, if we do know the truth of an ethical judgement intuitively, any further test by coherence will be superfluous. But the value of the test is to be found in cases where we are not certain of the truth of an ethical judgement, but are inclined to believe it intuitively. Then, if it coheres positively in a system and is not merely logically compatible (non-contradictory) with other ethical judgements that we are inclined to believe, the different ethical judgements within the system will help to confirm each other. Thus intuition and coherence may help each other out as tests in cases where the intuition does not amount to knowledge. If there is no other justification whatever for thinking either p or q true, the fact that they cohere does not provide a ground; and if they are already known to be true, their coherence is not needed as a further ground for accepting them. But, if we are doubtful whether we can see them to be true or not, we may be thankful for coherence as an additional ground, which at least strengthens the probability of the various judgements which cohere with each other. For, if there is some probability both that p is true and that q is true, the fact that p and q are interrelated so that the one entails the other, or at least strengthens its probability, will increase the probability of both, since any grounds for the one will now support the other also.

The application of this test will be discussed later in the book, but I have said here sufficient to show that coherence in this sense is not the sole basis of goodness. That coherence or system is an important characteristic of the class of ethical propositions is in practice admitted by almost all writers on ethics. For they aim at systematizing their ethical data as far as they can, thus presupposing that the more they can do this the nearer they will be, *ceteris paribus*, to the truth; and a similar assumption is made in physical science. This is not to say that ethical propositions could necessarily ever fulfil the ideal of a completely coherent system; but it is clear that no philosopher believes that they cannot be brought into any sort of system, though opinions may differ very much as to the looseness or simplicity of the system. Nobody believes that every single ethical judgement is unique in such a way that we can never argue from one to another.

(4) But "coherence" as applied in ethics may mean something different from "coherence" in logic, because it may be held, as it is, for example, by Paton, that it is coherence in willing, or between different acts of will, which constitutes ethical goodness.[9] This relation of coherence between wills could obviously only be analogous to and not the same as the relation of coherence between propositions. Ethical goodness on that view consists in willing in such a way that one's different purposes will help, and not frustrate, each other, and that they bear the same relation of cooperation and mutual usefulness to the purposes of other men. Now it is clear that any fully adequate ideal includes a due development of all the different sides of life, so that they will not conflict with, but rather supplement and further each other. This ideal in its completeness is, short of immortality, quite unattainable, for the mere fact that time is limited, to speak of nothing else, makes it necessary to sacrifice one end worth pursuing to another. But it is one of the marks of a satisfactory as opposed to an unsatisfactory life that it is much nearer attaining this ideal. A bad life will either be much less integrated or much narrower than a good life. It will either be spoiled by a constant oscillation between conflicting ends, or be harnessed to the service of an end which impoverishes life by suppressing many of the real needs of our nature, for among these we must include the more altruistic side of man as well as the

---

[9] This is given by Paton as an account of what goodness is, not as its criterion (*The Good Will*, p. 368).

egoistic. Unfortunately an ethically good life may itself suffer from grave impoverishment owing to circumstances and may include the continuous struggle against and suppression of strong and normal desires involving a whole important side of a man's nature; but that this has to occur is admittedly an evil, though the person to whom it occurs may not deserve blame and may even deserve high praise for voluntarily sacrificing his potentialities for the sake of other men. If we look at the question from the point of view of humanity as a whole, we may think of ethical conduct as that conduct which is conducive to the cooperation of all in such a way that each man satisfies his own needs best by contributing to the common weal (though, since we are so far removed from this ideal good, the right thing to do may under present conditions very often be to deny one's own nature for the sake of others' good). But this again cannot be put forward as a definition of "good." That would constitute a vicious circle, for by "need" we must understand not any and every desire, but a desire which it is good should be fulfilled. If a man desires sadistic pleasures, it is not good that his desire should be attained, yet it is a real desire, and we only refuse to call it a real "need" because we judge that it is bad both for himself and others that the desire should be fulfilled. Have those who put forward this ideal then said anything more than that it is best that a man's actions should give him what is really good for himself and others what is really good for themselves? Yes, they have. For, besides its hortatory value in relation to certain political notions, what has been said calls attention to the important fact that the different goods (or, if this is preferred, the different *prima facie* duties) are so related to each other that on the whole the furtherance or performance of one helps the furtherance or performance of others and that their furtherance or performance in the case of one man helps their furtherance or performance in the case of other men. To say

this is not a tautology; antecedently to a specific consideration of the nature of what is good it might conceivably, for
anything we could know, have turned out to be the case that
the good was like a store of food on a desert island, which
could not be increased by cooperation and of which one individual could only have more at the expense of others, and it
might have also turned out to be the case that there was no
connection between the different kinds of good such that the
attainment of one ever facilitated the attainment of others.
That this is not the case is seen to follow, not from the abstract
concept of good, but from the examination of the specific
nature of goods.

We may think that this characteristic is bound up with the
fundamental nature of good, but we obviously cannot say
that what makes a thing good is always that it tends to contribute to the production of other goods. Still less could we
make this a definition of "good." But it may be held that this
is a characteristic which always necessarily accompanies goodness, though it could not have been discovered without considering not just the abstract nature of goodness, but the
specific nature of the things which are good, and though it
is not true without limitations except in the sense that, other
things being equal, one good will *tend* to facilitate another.
(That sometimes we have to sacrifice one good for the sake
of another is obvious, and we can only say that it is not the
essential tendency of good to demand this ultimate sacrifice.)
In any case, to ask whether it contributes towards such a
system in which all sides of life will be developed and harmo-
nized and each man will work for the good of all and all for
the good of each is no doubt a very useful question to ask
about proposed actions and may serve as a criterion of their
value. The world would have been a much better place if
politicians had had this ideal more frequently present to their
minds.

(5) But the coherence theory has also been interpreted as expressing the view that goodness consists in coherence with the realization of as many desires and the fulfilment of as many potentialities as possible. If this is taken as a definition of "good," the view is difficult to distinguish from the naturalist one that "good" means what satisfies desire, a doctrine that has been criticised in the previous chapter. But, if not a definition, is this at least an adequate description of a property essentially bound up with goodness? Now I think we must make a distinction here. It does seem that, if something is to be good, it must give satisfaction; but that it will satisfy in proportion to its goodness, even if it is known as it is, seems much more doubtful to me. It may be, as has often been suggested, that if we knew the good as it really was we should always desire it in proportion to its goodness; but how are we to know that we should? Conceivably, if Hitler had known at the time exactly what it felt like to be ill-treated, he would not have desired in any way to ill-treat the Jews; but I do not know how this could be proved. Still less do I see how we could establish the proposition that, if we knew fully what anything was like, our desire for it would correspond exactly to the degree of its goodness. It is an obvious fact that it does not always so correspond. Few people, if any, do not desire their own or their family's good more than the much greater good of a total stranger, even when they do not act on the desire. Few people would really rather have violent toothache than suffer a very slight deterioration of character, yet they would usually admit that the second was worse than the first. And in the absence of the complete knowledge referred to I do not know what empirical evidence there could possibly be for the view that, if we had it, this discrepancy would always be completely removed. But even supposing that it would be thus removed, this would still strike me as a quite contingent fact. I cannot see that it follows necessarily from the nature

of goodness: we may be built that way, and again we may not. As for the "fulfilment of potentialities," I cannot see that this is good at all unless we first know that the potentialities are good potentialities. We cannot even say that right action or a good life fulfils more potentialities than does the reverse, since for each potentiality for good there must be at least one potentiality for evil (in fact many, since where you can do what is right in one way you can always deviate from it in many). On the other hand, it is important to insist that the good does satisfy, and that on the whole (though with many exceptions in human life) the greater good will ultimately give the fuller satisfaction.

(6) "Coherence" may be used loosely to mean any sort of harmony. It is certainly a mark of right action and good living on the whole that it conduces to harmony both within the self and between different persons; but it is not so clear that harmony is the sole criterion of goodness or the sole characteristic which makes anything good. For (a) an increase in goodness may result in a loss of harmony. A man who consistently cheats without compunction is in a more harmonious state of mind than he would be if he had improved sufficiently to hesitate, upbraid himself, and struggle against the temptation, but not sufficiently in most cases to overcome it; and a good man will be less in harmony with a bad society, such as Nazi Germany, than a bad man would. (b) One of the greatest goods is the heroic struggle against difficulties, which can hardly be described as a case of harmony. (c) Harmony cannot be the only good, if once it is admitted that a harmony involving richer content is preferable to the harmony of a very unintelligent and limited mind with few moral ideas. A fortiori, "good" cannot be defined as harmony. This would also be open to the objections to a naturalist definition, unless ethical content was already smuggled into the notion of harmony, thus involving a vicious circle in the definition; and

it would involve a confusion between the notion of goodness and the notion of what is good. Harmony is good, but it is not goodness, nor is it the only characteristic which makes what possesses it good.

The present discussion should have made it clear that the same applies to all the different interpretations of "coherence" discussed. None of them can be regarded as giving either the analysis or the sole ground of goodness, but they do all bring out important features of the good life. Important features of ethical action are that it is not self-defeating, that it can be universalized, that it can be fitted into a coherent plan of life, that it finds one's own good in serving that of others, that it is internally harmonious and subserves harmonious relations with other men. But these properties are at the most necessarily connected, and not identical, with the quality of good.

Paton does not use "definition" either in Moore's sense or in the sense merely of exclusive description, but still in some sense of "definition" which admits necessary connection and even substantial, though not absolute, identity between *definiendum* and *definiens*. In this sense he defines "good" as "aimed at by a rational will," or, as applied to human beings, that will itself. Now to me a "rational will" means "a will which wills what it ought," but this would still be a definition of "good" in ethical terms, and one which is like the definition that I shall give later. Only this of course is not all that Paton meant by the phrase. On the other hand he did not mean merely either a will which takes the steps most adapted to securing its own satisfaction or a logically coherent will. Coherence in action is for him analogous to coherence in thought but not identical with it. His definition then seems to amount to asserting that good is a quality of the will or (in a different sense) of objects of the will, and that it is analogous to logical coherence in a very important way. This statement seems somewhat jejune, but it acquires concrete filling and interest by the admirable way in which the analogy is brought out in the actual content of the book. That, in one sense of the word, "good" is a quality which can only apply to the will and in another only to objects of the will I admit, and I have also pointed out its connection with coherence. But I should prefer not to call this a definition of "good" as attribute of the will but rather an account of it which brings out its analogy to logical coherence. Possibly he may have even shown that goodness is, on one side of its nature, a species of coherence, logical coherence being another species. By saying "one side of its nature" I wish to exclude the view that goodness of will is just a species of coherence in the sense in which yellow is just a species of colour and to avoid committing myself to the denial of the possibility that it might be equally appropriately made also a species of some other genus. I should certainly not wish to say that "good" in any ordinary sense just meant "coherence in willing."

Let us turn to other non-naturalist definitions of "good."

Prof. Broad once suggested in his lectures a new type of analysis of "good," not indeed as his own theory, but as a view worth discussion. He suggested that "A is good" might mean "there is one and only one characteristic or set of characteristics whose presence in any object that I contemplate is necessary to cause an emotion of approval in me, and A has that characteristic." What the characteristic is in itself we do not know, but only its effects on our emotions. This view does not therefore make "good" equivalent to the property of causing an emotion, but to the unknown characteristic which causes the emotion. Since this characteristic may for anything we can tell be either naturalist or non-naturalist, it is impossible to apply either term to this theory, the "descriptive theory," as Broad called it, of "good." As he pointed out, it might be the case that a character which was itself non-naturalist could only be conceived by us as the character which was related to our experience in a certain way, and in that case it would without being itself given in experience answer to a description in which all the terms were naturalist. In that case "good" would be indefinable, by us at least, in Moore's sense, since we could not reduce it to anything else to which it was exactly equivalent, but definable in the sense that we could give an exclusive, though not exhaustive, description of it. The description would not give the nature of goodness, but it would provide relations by which to identify it. And the only evidence for something being good would still consist of empirical facts. This is not a view which Broad himself holds, but it is a conceivable alternative that is worth a short discussion at any rate.

Broad works the theory out in terms of the relation of goodness to the emotions of the speaker, but it might also be worked out in relation to the emotions of most people. Or again it might be worked out in terms not of the emotion of approval but of desire, and it might be said that goodness was that characteristic whose presence in anything, x, is necessary to enable x to satisfy human desires. In fact for every naturalist theory (not every subjectivist theory) of "good" we might have a "descriptive" theory of "good." And a similar treatment might be applied to any naturalist definition of "right"— for example as that characteristic whose presence in any action is necessary if that action is to be commended by society— though of course some of these descriptive theories would be less plausible than others.

At any rate the suggested theory seems to me to be open in all cases to serious objections. In the first place, we sometimes know, it would seem indeed with absolute, but at the very least with almost complete, certainty, that something is good or bad. But we could never know or even have a right to be confident of this if the descriptive theory were true. As Broad admitted: "If the descriptive theory is correct, then every judgement of the form 'x is good' that I have ever made has been false unless there is one and only one characteristic or set of characteristics whose presence in any object that I can contemplate is necessary to make me contemplate it with approval." Now if, as admitted, we have no idea what the characteristic in question is like, I do not see how we could ever be justified in being very confident, let alone know, that the same characteristic or set of characteristics was present in everything of which we felt approval and was a necessary condition of our having the feeling. The feeling might well be due to different characteristics on different occasions, and no one of these might be a necessary condition of its occurrence; or it might be the case that the only characteristic which was a necessary condition of our feeling of approval was present also in things of which we had no tendency to feel approval and which were not good.

Could the theory be amended to meet this objection? I doubt it. It would not do to define "good" as *any* characteristic of the several whose presence may be necessary if something is to arouse the emotion of approval, because if there were several conditions and one or more were missing the thing in question might well be the reverse of good. For instance, it is plausibly held that being a conscious state of some mind is a characteristic necessarily present in anything which is intrinsically good or gives rise to approval, but it is certainly also a characteristic of many things which are bad or indifferent. Nor would it do to define "good" as a characteristic which constitutes a sufficient condition for exciting the emotion of approval. For the sufficient condition would in any case include a great complexity of circumstances many of which could not possibly be called good-in-themselves, including, for example, certain physical conditions in the observer without which he could not feel the emotion. Nor again could we define "good" as any characteristic which *tends* to excite an emotion of approval, for the characteristic of being a painful experience of a hated person does, yet that does not prove the characteristic to be good. It may be objected that the approval in this case is not the moral emotion of approval, but if A really hates B there is at least a *tendency* in A to feel the emotion of moral approval of the sufferings of B under the belief or "rationalization" that they are a just punishment for his sins. (No doubt it is not "moral" in the sense of right, but the descriptive theory was not meant to define "good" as that towards which it was right to feel an emotion of approval— otherwise it would come much closer to the theory I propose in a later chapter to defend—and there is no psychological distinction between an emotion of approval felt on a right occasion and one felt on a wrong one.) Moreover practically all men have a tendency to feel more disapproval at wrong acts directed against their friends than at similar acts directed against strangers, yet it does not follow that the former are therefore worse acts. If, on the other hand, we merely say that "A is good" means "A has some qualities or other which make most men approve it," we have said hardly anything more than if we had just said that it means "most men approve it." If most men approve it, it must have some qualities or other which make most men approve it.

In any case goodness is surely a property the presence of which we know directly sometimes, at least in our own experiences, and not one which we hypothetically suppose to account for a similarity in our emotions. It seems to me quite impossible to make the question whether something is good turn on whether there is some unknown characteristic which is a necessary causal condition of our approval. It is logically conceivable that physiologists might sometime discover that the production of a certain physical modification of the brain was a condition which was fulfilled in all cases when something caused the emotion of approval in a person and on no other occasions, but would that justify them in identifying the property of goodness with this modification or the capacity of producing it? This illustration shows it to be at least logically possible that a characteristic other than goodness may be a necessary condition of approval, therefore being good cannot be identical with being a necessary condition of approval. We are extremely interested for itself in whether things are good; we are not interested for itself in the question whether there is one and the same unknown property present in all of them.

Nor does the theory seem to escape at least most of the objections which I have directed against naturalism. It is admitted that, on the descriptive theory, the only evidence for the truth of an ethical judgement lies in empirical facts about people's emotions. Now, as Broad himself very rightly objected in criticizing Hume, "the logical consequence of his theory . . . is that the way to settle ethical disputes is to collect statistics of how people in fact do feel. And to me this kind of answer seems utterly irrelevant to this kind of question. If I am right in this, Hume's theory must be false." [10] But surely the same objection might now be applied to the descriptive theory? And I do not see how we can judge that this notion of an unknown condition behind our emotions of approval carries with it the notion of obligation any more than the mere fact that we have a certain feeling could. Since we do not on that view know what the quality goodness is, we cannot say that the contemplation of it either directly excites our approval or puts us under an obligation, for we cannot contemplate goodness at all.

Another definition of "good," which might be regarded either as naturalist or as logical or even as metaphysical, is in terms of the notion of a good (typical or characteristic) speci-

---

[10] *Five Types of Ethical Theory*, p. 115.

men of a class. (It should be noted that this attempt at definition, unlike any of the others discussed, takes as the primary sense of "good" that in which it is applied to an individual as a whole, not to a single experience.) No doubt if "typical" means "like most other members of its class," such a view would not be worth the least consideration. An advocate of the definition would rather regard goodness as consisting in fulfilling the characteristic function of the species not with average but with specially great effectiveness. And he would distinguish what functions of the species are characteristic by asking what it is that members of the species can do which members of other species cannot do at all or cannot do so efficiently. The definition may be viewed either as logical because it depends on the logical relation between member and class, or as naturalist because it defines the ethical wholly in non-ethical terms that might occur in other sciences. It may even be viewed as metaphysical if its upholder goes on to say that, just as goodness relative to one's species consists in the fulfilment of the tendency characteristic of that species, so goodness in an absolute sense consists in what makes for the fulfilment of the tendency characteristic of reality as a whole. In that way it can be connected either with evolutionary or with theological ethics. For the sciences which study the evolutionary process may be regarded as disclosing empirically the leading tendencies in the real world; and theology is bound up with the conviction that the fundamental nature of reality is in accord with the highest ethical ideals that can be conceived, so that to act well is to act in a way which is in harmony with the ultimate purpose of the universe and the ultimate nature of things.

In criticism of any such definition we may urge that it would not be self-contradictory to say that something was good (in almost all senses of the word) and yet to deny that it was a typical specimen of its class. The sense in which we can speak of a "good burglar" is clearly a special and paradoxical sense of "good." We can also be certain that something is good and yet extremely doubtful whether it is typical of its class. To fulfil the function of one's class efficiently is not to be good, unless it is good that this particular function should be fulfilled, a question which could only be decided by examining it on its own merits. It seems to me that the kind of view under discussion would turn out to be exposed either to the objections which I have already brought against naturalist theories, or to the objections which I shall bring directly against theological theories, or to both together. The notion of doing efficiently what one's class normally does is not one from which obligation can be derived. Why *ought* I to act like typical members of my class? If it is said that goodness consists in the fulfilment of the function which I was designed to fulfil, the reply may be made that this cannot carry with it an obligation unless we assume that the designer is good, and in order to be entitled to maintain this we must already presuppose independent ethical ideas. We cannot arrive at an ethical conception of God without already having an idea of what goodness is. Consideration of this brings one to theological views of ethics.

A theological definition of ethical terms is the commonest and most intelligible type of metaphysical definition, and the natural form it would assume would be that "A ought to be done" is to be analysed as "A is commanded by God." At first sight it seems as if such a theory were refuted at once by the mere fact that an atheist or agnostic can judge that something ought to be done; but it might be said that what even the atheist really has in his mind when he thinks of moral obligation is some confused idea of a command, and that a command implies a commander and an ethically valid command a perfectly good commander on whose mind the whole moral law depends. In that case the atheist would be inconsistent in denying or even doubting the existence of God and yet insisting on the validity of the moral law, which he could justify only by assuming what he doubted or denied. But there is an important distinction to be made. I do not intend to discuss here whether such an argument, or any argument based on ethics, for the existence of God is valid; but I must insist that to say that ethical concepts properly thought out can provide an argument for or even logically entail the existence of God would not be the same as to say that a reference to God is included in their definition. To take an analogous case, anybody who believes in the argument from design argues to the existence of God from certain features of animal bodies, but it would never occur to him to say that our concepts of these purely biological features must therefore be analysed in such a way as already to include the notion of God. His biology would still be like anyone else's and would not be based on concepts referring to God. This would still be true even if he accepted the cosmological proof and so held that the existence of this world entailed and did not merely provide evidence for the existence of God. If God exists he is the *ratio essendi* of the beings from whom we argue to God, but he is not for us their *ratio cognoscendi* since we cannot deduce their nature from his. And even if it be the case that the whole moral law depends on God, this is not to say that in order to reach moral conceptions we have first to form a conception of God. A theist holds that trees or stones could not exist without God; but he will not therefore insist that all our commonsense propositions about trees and stones have to be analysed in such a way as to include the notion of God.

To a theological definition of the fundamental ethical concepts there seem to me to be fatal objections, though these objections must not be taken as excluding the possibility that we might be able to argue from ethical premises to the existence of God, as was indeed held by Kant, the strongest defender of the autonomy of ethics from other studies including theology. In the first place, if "obligatory" just means "commanded by God," God cannot command an act because it is right, and there is no reason whatever for his commands, which therefore become purely arbitrary. It would follow that God might just as rationally will that our whole duty should consist in cheating, torturing, and killing people to the best of our ability, and that then it would be our duty to act in that fashion. I am assuming that "good" is defined in the same kind of way as "obligatory." Otherwise it might be held that God commanded acts because they produced good, but in that case we should not have given a theological definition of all the fundamental ethical concepts, and we should be either falling back on an indefinable "good" or adopting one of the definitions of it that I have already criticised.

Secondly, why obey God's commands? Because I ought to do so? Since "I ought to do A" is held to mean "God commands me to do A," this can only mean that I am commanded by God to obey God's commands, which supplies no further reason. Because I love God? But this involves the assumptions that I ought to obey the commands of God if I love him, and that I ought to love God. So it again presupposes ethical propositions which cannot without a vicious circle be validated by referring once more to God's commands. Because God is good? This could on the view under discussion only mean that God carries out his own commands. Because God will punish me if I do not obey? This might be a very good reason from the prudential point of view, but these considerations of self-interest cannot be an adequate basis for ethics. Even if there is some affinity between command and obligation, a mere command, however powerful the being who issues it, cannot of itself create obligation. Without a prior conception of God being good or his commands being right God would have no more claim on our obedience than Hitler except that he would have more power than even Hitler ever had to make things uncomfortable for those who disobeyed him. It is only because the notion of God (for Christians at least, not to mention other religions) already includes the notion of perfect goodness that we are inclined to think it self-evident that we ought to obey God. And even if it were self-evident, without presupposing this, that we ought to obey God's commands, the proposed analysis of "ought" still could not be accepted. It is plain that the sentence "We ought to obey God's commands" does not just mean "We are commanded by God to obey his commands." But in any case it is obvious that doing what one ought could not be equated with obeying the commands of any sort of God but only with obeying those of a *good* God.

It should be noted that there is a certain similarity between the theological view I have criticised and naturalism. For, as we could find no necessary relation between goodness and obligation on the one hand and the alleged naturalist definitions on the other, so we can find no necessary relation between being commanded by God and being obligatory, unless we already assume the goodness of God, thus exposing ourselves to a vicious circle, for we should in that case have both defined God in terms of goodness and goodness in terms of God. Just as it was a fatal objection to the naturalist definitions of "good" that they did not provide any ground for obligation or reason for doing any one thing rather than any other, so the theological definition is open to the objection that a command cannot in itself be a moral reason for action. Like naturalist definitions the theological definition would destroy what Kant calls the autonomy of ethics by refusing to recognise the uniqueness of its fundamental concepts and trying to make it a mere branch of another study, in this case not a natural science but theology. Both types of view overlook the gulf between the "ought" and the "is" so far as to think that you can reduce propositions about the former to mere statements as to what actually is the case. The theological view is more ethical than the naturalist only in so far as it covertly reintroduces the concept of obligation which it had verbally tried to explain away by equating it with a mere command. Except in so far as it smuggles the concept in again it makes the fulfilment of duty consist just in obeying the stronger, for if you once exclude the specifically ethical element from the concept of the deity God has no claim on us except that of mere power. Similar objections, besides others, can, I think, be turned against any one who, whether or not he defines ethical concepts in theological terms, claims that ethics is somehow to be derived from theology. But they do not necessarily hold against the view that you can derive theological conclusions, partly or wholly, from ethical premises.

Some thinkers have tried to provide a metaphysical definition of "good" in terms not of God but of our "real self." We may even accuse Kant of having sometimes come at least perilously near to this, inconsistent as it is with his main attitude to ethics. Theories of the real self are particularly difficult to discuss owing to their obscurity, which is partly no doubt the fault of their authors, but partly also due to the real difficulty of the subject. In one form the theory of the "real self" is a species of naturalism, amounting to the assertion that "good" means what would satisfy us ultimately or would satisfy us if we knew its true nature. In another form it is a type of theological ethics, God being regarded as immanent instead of transcendent, and the notion that something is good because it or the striving for it is commanded being superseded by the notion that it is good because it satisfies our "true" nature which is somehow bound up with that of all other selves. But that it will satisfy me is no reason for seeking anything unless I assume that my satisfaction is good, and the addition of the word "true" does not alter this, unless "true" is being used to mean "good," in which case the definition is obviously useless. The theory is, further, open to the objection that it would lead to an egoistic view of ethics unless *myself* is used in such a wide sense as to include all other selves, in which case the meaning of the term and therefore the point of the definition is destroyed. But I think upholders of such theories had usually no intention of defining "good" in Moore's sense of "definition." They may or may not have succeeded in discovering important truths about goodness, good things, and the nature of the real, but they certainly did not succeed in showing and probably did not in most cases intend to show that ethical concepts are reducible to non-ethical.

The main upshot of all the discussion in this book so far is the defence of the view that we must recognise that ethics is a branch of study of its own which cannot be reduced to or derived from any other. Good, right, obligation are not at all like non-ethical concepts and cannot be reduced to them. This is not necessarily to deny that they are intimately related to some non-ethical concepts, but it is to assert that they cannot just be identified with any combination of such concepts. It is now for us to go on to the more positive task of considering the relations between the different non-natural concepts of ethics itself.

CHAPTER IV

Different Meanings of "Good" and "Ought"

We shall pass in due course to another definition of "good" which is not open to the same objections as the definitions which I have discussed, but since "good" and "ought" are very ambiguous words it will be wise first to distinguish various senses in which they are used, and the present chapter will be devoted to this essential preliminary.

In the first place I must remind the reader (1) that, whether a naturalist view of ethics be right or not, it is certainly true that "good" is sometimes used in a purely naturalist, psychological sense to mean "pleasant." When I say "This pudding is good" I do not think I mean anything more than that I like it or find it pleasant, with the possible implication that most other people would do so too.

Similarly, (2), when I talk of somebody's good, I may only mean what will satisfy his desires.[1]

But I may also mean what is "really to his good," as when I say that it is not to a man's good to have everything that he wants, and the two meanings shade into each other so that it is often difficult to tell which is intended. This is because it is usually assumed that to have one's desires satisfied is for one's real good, provided they are not positively immoral desires. To say that something is for a man's good is to say that it will directly or indirectly result in a part of his life being better in some way (not necessarily hedonistically) than would

---

[1] V. Carritt, *An Ambiguity of the Word "Good."*

otherwise be the case without a counterbalancing loss some-where else in his life. If "better" is being used naturalistically, this will probably mean only that his desires will be more fully satisfied; but the word may also be used differently, and then it will fall under one of the other senses of "good" to be enumerated later.

It is clear also that "good" is very often, perhaps most often, used in an instrumental sense to signify "good as a means," which sense has, almost from time immemorial, been dis-tinguished from "good-in-itself." But the term "instrumentally good" or "good as a means" is itself ambiguous. It may mean —and this gives another naturalist sense of "good"—(3) ca-pable of doing a particular kind of thing efficiently, whether that thing be itself good, bad, or indifferent. A knife might still be a "good knife" even if it were never used for anything but the most atrocious murders.

(4) *"Good as a means"* may also mean "productive of some-thing intrinsically good." In this sense we speak of pure water as good and impure water as bad. Pure water, while more efficient as a means of maintaining health than impure water, is far less efficient as a means of producing typhoid fever; but we look on typhoid fever as evil or necessarily accompanied by intrinsic evils, while we look on health, which is main-tained by pure water, as intrinsically good, or necessarily or probably accompanied by what is intrinsically good, and there-fore we speak of pure water as good and impure water as bad. The distinction between (3) and (4) is still clearer in the case of "bad." We may call somebody or something bad just because it is inefficient, or we may call it bad because it is all too efficient in producing intrinsically bad effects. For exam-ple, diseases and hurricanes are called in this sense bad, though not themselves intrinsically bad.

(5) "Good" may mean not "efficient in producing effects" but rather "efficiently produced." I think this is the most usual

meaning of a "good book," a "good stroke at cricket," etc.

(6) It is obvious, however, that these senses (at least 4 and 5) presuppose a further, more primary sense of "good." This sense is commonly expressed by the terms "intrinsically good," "good-in-itself," "good as an end." There would be no point in being efficient if we could not thereby produce something that was good as an end and not only as a means.

But there is a point I wish to mention here. By calling a thing "intrinsically good" or "good-in-itself" I do not mean to commit myself to the view that it would necessarily be good in all contexts or could still be good if everything else in the universe were different. "Good-in-itself" has been used in this sense; but it need not imply this, as far as I can see. What I mean by "good-in-itself" is simply "good itself," in opposition to good as a means; that is, I mean that the thing called good really has the characteristic goodness in its primary sense, and is not merely called good because it produces something else which has the quality in question. As far as I can see, something might really have the characteristic goodness in some contexts and yet not have it in others, or have it only in a lower degree, as a poker is really hot when placed near the fire and not hot or not so hot when placed elsewhere.

Again, there is nothing to exclude a thing being both good in itself and good as a means in any ordinary sense of the latter term. The things that are intrinsically best themselves are also most likely to produce intrinsically good effects.

(7) Moore makes a distinction between "ultimately" and "intrinsically good." [2] Anything is intrinsically good, provided it contains elements which are good for their own sake, even if it also contains elements which are quite indifferent, provided only the other elements do not actually counteract the value of the good part. Such a thing would still be good

---

[2] *Ethics*, pp. 73–5.

even if it existed alone, he says, and he therefore calls it intrinsically good; but he will call something ultimately good only if it has no parts which are not themselves intrinsically good, so this gives a seventh sense of "good," ultimately good. In the sixth sense a successful life or a long holiday might be described as good, but it could hardly be called good in the seventh sense because the best holiday and, still more, the best life will contain stretches which are indifferent in respect of value, or at any rate stretches which are unpleasant rather than pleasant and in which there are no other values realised adequate to counteract this unpleasantness.

It is not clear whether it is the sixth or the seventh sense of "good" which should in preference be regarded as indefinable. In the passage mentioned Moore defines the seventh in terms of the sixth sense—what is "ultimately good" is something intrinsically good which either has no parts or has parts which are all intrinsically good—so presumably he regarded the sixth sense as primary. It might be argued that it would be better to take the reverse course on the ground that it is the ultimately good parts belonging to it which make anything intrinsically good, but this does not agree with Moore's principle of organic unities according to which something in itself indifferent or even bad might increase the intrinsic goodness of the whole to which it belonged. Usually no distinction has been made between these two senses, but I think the term "intrinsically good" has generally been used to express the seventh rather than the sixth sense of good.

"Good" is also often used to mean "either instrumentally or intrinsically or ultimately good," where the speaker believes something is good in one of these senses but has not thought it necessary to ask which (as indeed it often is not for purposes of practice). But we should swell our list of meanings so far as to exhaust the patience of the reader if we assigned a separate heading for each such unprecise usage of "good."

(8) "Good" in sense (6) or sense (7) is not properly applied to characteristics. When "good" is applied to a characteristic of something it signifies not that the characteristic is intrinsically good itself, but that things which have the characteristic are in so far intrinsically good. Thus we get an eighth sense of "good," in which "good" means good-making, to use Broad's terminology. In this sense "good" is applied to qualities to signify that the quality in question makes the things which have it good in sense 6 or sense 7. For example, the statement that pleasure is good means that the quality of pleasantness makes what has it good.

(9) "Good" often means morally good. Obviously moral goodness is not the only kind of intrinsic goodness, and it may possibly be denied that it is a case of intrinsic goodness at all, yet the people who deny this would still use of it the term "good." But this must be a matter for further discussion. In the sense of "morally good," the term is applied both to men and to actions, but it can hardly be applied to both in the same sense, so we now get both a ninth sense, "good" means "morally good" as applied to actions, and a tenth, "good" means "morally good" as applied to persons. No doubt "good" as applied to persons may also mean merely "efficient" (sense 3), for example, when we speak of a man as a good cricketer or a good philosopher, but it obviously sometimes stands for a more specifically moral quality.

Laird also introduces the concept of "dominant good" as of fundamental importance, meaning by this a good "which, irradiating its surroundings, dignifies whatever it touches"; [3] but I am not sure that this is not better regarded as a description of a particular species of good thing than as a different sense of "good." Moore also points out that "good" is sometimes used to mean "adding to the value of many intrinsically good wholes." [4]

---

[3] *A Study in Moral Theory*, p. 46.
[4] *Ethics*, p. 250.

Another sense of "good" which is sometimes admitted is "typical of its species," [5] but I think this is reducible to some of the other senses mentioned above. A thing is most commonly called a good specimen of its class because it is more efficient than the average member of the class in fulfilling certain ends, namely, those characteristic of the class or those for which that class of thing was made. It may also be called "a good specimen of the class" because it is a useful sample for the purposes of research. And, finally, it may be called a good specimen because it provides a certain aesthetic satisfaction, that is, something good in senses 6 and 7, for aesthetic satisfactions should be regarded as intrinsically valuable and not valuable merely in a naturalist sense.

Corresponding to the ten senses of "good" there are ten senses of "bad." "Bad" may mean (1) unpleasant; (2) contrary to what we desire; (3) inefficient in fulfilling certain purposes, whether these are themselves good, bad or indifferent; (4) productive of something intrinsically evil; (5) inefficiently made; (6) intrinsically bad, in Moore's sense as applied to particulars; (7) ultimately bad as applied to particulars; (8) as applied to qualities, such as to make what has it bad in the sixth or seventh sense; (9) morally bad as applied to actions; (10) morally bad as applied to persons. "Evil" is synonymous with "bad," except that it is not customarily used unless the degree of badness is very serious, and it could not, I think, correctly be applied to what was considered bad only in senses 1,2,3, or 5, except as a piece of "slang." It has therefore, unlike "bad," no purely naturalist sense at all.

The terms "good" and "bad" are thus extremely ambiguous, and in ethical discussion it is therefore most important to be clear in which sense we are using them. It is obvious, however, that sense 6 or sense 7 is fundamental and is of very special importance for philosophers. We have now come to the con-

---

[5] For the attempt to make this the main definition of good v. above, pp. 104-6.

clusion that in these senses at any rate "good" cannot be naturalistically defined. Of the other senses some are definable in terms of (6) or (7), others may be naturalistically defined. Senses 9 and 10 at least seem definable in terms of another non-naturalist ethical concept, ought. I shall now turn to the terms "ought," "right," "duty." It is obvious that these have a close relation to each other and that their chief application is to actions. They are not such ambiguous words as "good"; but there are at least three different usages of them in ethics which it is very important for the philosopher to distinguish. I shall explain the three different usages in the case of "ought." [6]

1. "The action we ought to do" may mean that action which is really preferable, taking everything into account. This would be the action which an omniscient and perfectly wise being would advise us to perform; but it is impossible for us to take everything into account, and it may even be doubted whether any action that ought to be done in this sense has ever in the whole of history been performed by a human being. For, whatever benefits I may produce by a certain expenditure of time or money, it seems in the highest degree likely that a being who knew all the circumstances and foresaw all the consequences could suggest some expenditure still more beneficial. For example, such a being would know the cure for cancer and would know how to prove to the medical profession that it was a cure. Now obviously to inform medical experts of the right cure and persuade them to adopt it, if I could do this, would be a more beneficial action than any which I am likely to perform during my life in the normal course and would be an action that ought to be carried out immediately to save life and suffering, so that whatever I

---

[6] In *Philosophy*, Vol. XXI, No. 79, pp. 110–11, Professor Broad distinguishes three senses of "right." The first and third respectively correspond to my first and second, but Broad's second ("formally right") does not correspond to my third.

do now such a being could advise me of something more beneficial to do instead; that is, take steps to bring about the adoption of the method of cure. It may be retorted that at any rate I know that I ought to pay my debts and this could not be altered even by the information of an omniscient being, but "pays a debt" is an incomplete description of an act. I am under an obligation to pay my debts; but I am not under an obligation to pay them this very moment, especially where there is some other pressing obligation, and hardly anybody would expect me to keep an appointment if, as in this case, the lives of many people depended on my missing it. Besides, even in the case of paying debts, such a being could probably suggest something in my manner of doing it which would have better effects than my present manner of doing it,[7] and could certainly suggest some mental state in repaying the debt preferable to the one actually experienced by me. It is highly doubtful whether the mental state of any human being is ever completely and absolutely ideal even for a moment. It seems to me therefore objectionable to take the present as the main sense of "ought," "right" or "duty," as is done, for example, by Moore in his *Ethics*,[8] at least when we are applying "ought" to actions regarded as a whole. It is surely desirable to use the word in a sense in which we can be confident that there are actions to which it applies. It is unsatisfactory to choose a meaning for the word which makes it necessary to say that probably no human being in the whole course of history has ever acted as he ought. On the other hand, there is plenty of scope for this sense of "ought" when not applied to actions regarded as a whole. We can use it of what have been called *prima facie* duties, and say that in the absence of a conflicting

---

[7] I am not assuming that the consequences are the only factor in determining whether one action is preferable to another, but only that they are at least highly relevant to this question.

[8] P. 190 ff.

obligation we ought always to keep a promise in this sense of "ought." We can also say in this sense that we ought to prefer certain ends to certain others, for example that we ought to value justice rather than money, and that certain emotional attitudes are fitting or unfitting towards certain kinds of objects, for example, we ought to dislike cruelty, we ought to love good parents. For here the complications about consequences do not arise, it being rather a question of the intrinsic value of something, so that if we had made any mistake in such judgements it would be a mistake of value and not of fact. We are rightly so confident of the truth of many such judgements that we use the term "know" rather than "believe," and the objection that probably no human being has ever done as he ought is certainly not applicable here. I am convinced that I ought to dislike the unnecessary infliction of pain, and not only that relatively to the available evidence I ought to do so; and this is not contradicted by the fact that it might under certain circumstances be the least undesirable course for me to choose to do something which gave much pain, and even which by an unfortunate concatenation of circumstances encouraged people to take pleasure in the pain; for example, if I take steps to secure the punishment of a criminal.

2. "Ought," both in philosophy and in ordinary discussion, is also used in a sense in which not to do what one ought, or to do what one ought not to do, is always morally blameworthy. To say that I ought to do A in this sense is indeed not the same as saying that I believe I ought to do A, for the proposition that I ought to do what I believe I ought to do is synthetic, but it is, I think, synthetic *a priori*. This sense of the word is extremely important, but it obviously presupposes another sense. That is made clear by considering the principle that we always ought to do what we believe we ought. We may believe, for example, that the soldiers who fight

against us in a war are acting wrongly in fighting, yet every
reasonable person will admit that, as long as they really think
they ought to fight, they ought "to obey their consciences"
and fight. In general, it is clear that a person may make a
mistake and decide that he ought to do A, though A is really
wrong. In that case he clearly ought to do A, therefore he
ought to do what is wrong, that is, what he ought not to do.
Self-contradiction can only be avoided if we suppose that
"ought" is being used in two different senses here. Again, if
there is no sense of "ought" in which it is false to say that we
always ought to do what we think we ought, we could discover what we ought to do by mere introspection without
considering anything else whatever. These paradoxes can only
be met by recognising another sense of "ought" besides the
sense in which not to do what one "ought" is always morally
blameworthy, and we have seen that the first sense is not
adequate. So a third sense is required.

3. "The action which I ought to perform" may mean the
action which it is, humanly speaking, preferable to choose,
though it may not in fact necessarily turn out best. It seems
to me that this is the sense in which the term "ought" is most
commonly employed. We should not usually say that a man
had not done what he ought just because some unforeseeable
accident had changed the consequences from good to bad. It
would be a very unusual use of language to say that I had
done something which I ought not to have done because a
man whom I had invited to tea was run over and killed on his
way to my house; and if I saw somebody about to drink a
glass of prussic acid and refrained from warning him, it would
hardly be said that I had done what I ought because it was a
new variety of prussic acid just discovered which was harmless or the man had such an abnormal physiology that he could
drink prussic acid with impunity, if I had no knowledge of
this circumstance but believed that the drink would bring

about his death. Likewise no one would say that I had acted wrongly or had not done my duty in the first case, or that I had acted rightly or had done my duty in the second. We rarely employ these terms in our first sense, but we do employ them in our third sense very frequently. A good example of the difficulties which arise from not making the distinction between the first sense and the third sense is provided by Professor Prichard in his paper on *Duty and Ignorance of Fact*.

We may explain the third sense further by saying that in this sense we ought to perform an act if in the light of the available evidence it seems the preferable act to choose. By "available evidence" I mean evidence which the agent either possesses already or could obtain without more trouble than is practicable or worth while, everything considered. The phrase is vague, but so is the common usage of words, especially words like "ought," and though it is difficult in borderline cases to say how much the agent could have been expected to foresee, it is easy enough to distinguish between some consequences which he could have been expected to foresee and some which he could not, and clear enough that he would be accused of not having done what he ought on account of the former but not on account of the latter. The definition is not intended to exclude cases where the only evidence of which he could be expected to take account is evidence which he actually had in mind when the emergency came or could obtain in the course of a very short time, for example in meeting a sudden attack, because immediate action of some sort was necessary.

I have not in all this attempted to give a definition of the different senses of "ought," but a rough explanation sufficient to distinguish them. The phrase I have used to explain the third sense of "ought," and perhaps also those used to explain the first and second senses, if taken as defining "ought," would be circular. For "preferable to choose" here really only means that the action is the one the agent *ought* to choose in preference to others. The first and the third alike depend directly on the same indefinable notion, as we shall see; with the second usage the question is a little more complicated.

A person who fails to do what he ought in the third sense is not necessarily morally to blame for this, since he may be honestly mistaken in the conclusions he drew from the evidence; but he will be either morally or intellectually to blame or both, that is he will have either willed more or less badly or reasoned more or less badly (including under this the omission of relevant points), or both. The difference between the three senses of "ought" may be illustrated in this way: If a motor knocks down and kills a man it is plain that the motorist ought not to have done what he did in the first sense of "ought," since it had unfortunate consequences (unless we argue that perhaps the death was a blessing in disguise); but it would be a matter for a court to decide whether he ought not to have done it in the third sense, with a view to determining whether damages were payable, while the question whether he did what he ought in the second sense would be considered by the court if it were a question of murder or manslaughter.

Corresponding to the three different senses of "ought" there are three different senses of "duty," "right," "wrong," which can easily be derived from the different senses of "ought," *mutatis mutandis*. Nor is the difference between the usage of the terms "ought," "right," "duty" of much philosophical importance. It does not at any rate point to a difference of fundamental concept at all. "The right action" is synonymous with the action which ought to be done, except that we should speak of God as doing what was right but should not apply to God the terms "duty" and "ought." This is because we do not admit the possibility of God's doing wrong. But "right" without the definite article has a wider significance. While an action which I ought to do or which it is my duty to do is always right, in the sense corresponding to the one of the three senses in which "ought" is being used in the given context, the converse does not hold. It is, for example, a right action to hand, with appropriate motives, a five-pound note to somebody to whom I owe five pounds, if I am not thereby violating any still more important obligation; but I cannot say that I ought to do this or that it is my duty to do this, because I should still be acting rightly if I handed him five pound notes instead, and two incompatible actions cannot both be duties. So we should say that I ought to pay the debt, but not that I ought to hand him a five-pound note. An act is thus right but not a duty, nor an act which we ought to do, where it is one of a number of alternative acts which are such that one ought to be done but there is no reason for preferring any one to any other of them. "Right," I think, means the same as "not wrong." We do not indeed usually use the term, "right," of indifferent acts because we are not interested in these; but we should, if asked whether these were right or not right, admit that they were right. Ross, though he notes the distinction between "right" and "what ought to be done," in *The Right and the Good* [9] purposely chooses to use "right" as the adjective corresponding to "something that ought to be done"; but I do not intend to follow him in this, which, as he admits, is not the normal usage.

A "duty" is generally equivalent to an action or class of actions which ought to be done. But the term is not applied if (1) the main direct reason in favour of the action is its

___

[9] Pp. 3–4. In *Foundations of Ethics* (p. 44) he expresses the view that according to the normal usage of "right" any right act must be "a fulfilment of at least one claim upon us." But suppose somebody asks—Is it morally right to read a particular, harmless novel on Sunday? Anybody but a fanatical sabbatarian would surely answer—Yes, it is right, though no one would hold that there was a moral claim on us to read the novel.

conduciveness to the agent's own pleasure, and if (2) the action is in accord with the inclinations and present mood of the agent. If one of these two conditions is fulfilled but not the other, the action may, I think, still be called a duty. In general, however, the term is reserved for occasions on which we wish very specially to emphasize the moral aspect of an act. We are reluctant to describe acts of slight importance too readily as duties, thus cheapening the notion. It would not, however, be correct to say that "duty" was limited to the second sense of "ought," since we certainly admit that it is possible to make a mistake about one's duty.

In so far as the rightness or obligatoriness of an action depends on its consequences at all, whether we ought to perform an action in the first sense of "ought" will depend on the actual consequences, whether we ought to do it in the second sense on the consequences we judge likely, whether we ought to do it in the third sense neither on the actual consequences, nor on the consequences we judge likely, but on the consequences that relatively to our data really are likely. For to say that something is likely or probable is not merely to make a statement about my own or anybody else's subjective state. It has often been supposed that it is,[10] because I may truly say that something is improbable and yet it may really happen, or again I may judge something to be probable at one time and improbable at another and yet neither of the judgements may be wrong. If a person in July, 1940, judged that Germany would probably win the war, he is not proved to have been wrong by the fact that she did not do so. But judgements of probability cannot really be judgements about the subjective state of the person judging, for they are not reached by introspection but by considering the objective situation,

[10] See Prichard in *Duty and Ignorance of Fact*. Prichard's difficulties in this pamphlet seem to me to arise mainly from (a) ignoring the third sense of "right," (b) assuming that probability cannot be objective.

and I may make mistakes about estimating probability that are not mistakes about my subjective condition at all. If judgements of probability are judgements about one's own subjective state, it may be asked what they assert. They cannot be merely assertions about the degree of confidence with which the assertor entertains a proposition, if by "confidence" is meant confident feeling, because it is quite obvious that somebody, for example a sanguine gambler, may judge A to be less probable than B and yet feel more confident about A's happening than B, and it is still more obvious that he may feel a high degree of confidence concerning an event which he is quite wrong in judging probable at all. Nor can judgements of probability be merely assertions as to whether the assertor thinks something to be probable. The vicious circle is perfectly plain, and it is equally plain that a person may be mistaken in judging something probable and yet that it may be perfectly true that he thought it probable, indeed this must be true if he is even to make a mistake in judging the event probable. To be mistaken in judging it probable he must really judge it probable. Nor on a subjective view of probability do I see what possible sense could be given to statements attributing to an event a more or less definite degree of numerical probability. Some people have asserted that, when we judge an event probable, what we are really judging is that we shall act as if the event were going to occur; but owing to human folly or immorality people do not always act in accordance with their beliefs as to what is probable and, when I judge an event probable, I need not even anticipate that I will act in accord with my belief that it is probable. If I do anticipate this, it will only be because I have first concluded that the event is probable. After all it is surely quite clear that an event is not made probable, in any ordinary sense of the term, because we feel confident about it or think that it will happen or act as if it will.

Another objection is that, if we take a subjective view of probability, we shall have to say that all or most judgements of physical science or human history, since they are believed, or ought to be believed, by the person who makes them not to be quite certain but only probable, are or ought to be merely judgements about his state of mind at the time he makes them. Some philosophers have indeed held that all judgements, outside mathematics and formal logic, except those about one's own present state are uncertain; but surely they would not therefore be committed to saying that all these judgements are only about their own state of mind. That would commit them to solipsism. And if we do not go so far as these philosophers and admit that some judgements about physical objects and other human beings are certain, we still surely cannot say that, while the judgement that King George VI of England is alive at a particular date is about King George, the judgement that one of the Roman emperors was alive at a particular date, because it is only probable, only asserts that the man who makes it is in a certain state of mind now.

I therefore hold probability [11] to be an objective relation, whether definable or indefinable I need not discuss. This seems to me the only satisfactory way of reconciling (a), the fact that some events may truly be said, at different times, to be both probable and improbable, with (b), the fact that we can make mistakes about probability. The statement that A is probable is an incomplete statement like the statement that A is to the north or to the right, and there is no more difficulty in seeing how the statement that A is probable may be true in one case and false in another of the same event A than there is in seeing how the statement "Cambridge is to the north" may be true in London and false in Edinburgh. Nobody doubts on this ground that "Cambridge is to the north" can

---

[11] At least in the sense under discussion here.

describe an objective fact. "A is probable" makes no sense unless it is understood in relation to certain data, namely those available at the time the judgement is made, and therefore it may be true at one time and false at another according to differences in the data. It is obvious that in the light of probabilities we can determine with relative ease and even sometimes with fair certainty what we ought to do in the third sense of "ought" where it would be quite impossible to determine what we ought to do in the first, and that this goes far to explain the confidence which we often feel in ethical judgements, despite the multiplicity of possible consequences.

I must add, however, that, while I generally prefer to use "ought" in my third sense rather than in my first sense, what I "ought" to do in my first sense is still highly relevant to ethics. For it is only because, if I find out what is right in my third sense and act accordingly, I am more likely to approximate to what is right in my first sense, that I ought to do what is right in my third sense at all. We only consider what we ought to do in the third sense as a means to this approximation. We may compare the case of most theoretical knowledge. Outside mathematics, formal logic, and simple observations and memories, we have in theoretical knowledge to content ourselves with finding out what is probably, not what is certainly, true, yet the value of finding out what is probably true only lies in the fact that it is the best way of approximating to the objectively true, which is not itself probable or improbable but actual. In the theoretical sphere, if we accept what is really most probable relatively to our data rather than rush to conclusions without due consideration, we may err but at any rate we are likely to get nearer the truth than if we do not act in this reasonable way. We can be confident at least that we shall be far more often right, and that, where we err, we are likely to be less badly wrong and almost certain in most cases to have included some substantial

morally bound to do it. Some philosophers have spoken as if
the only proper sense of "ought" were the specifically moral
sense.[12] But I do not know what the criterion of "proper"
usage can be except the way in which educated people use a
term, and it is quite certain that "ought" is very widely and
constantly used in a sense which does not necessarily presuppose that it is morally wrong not to do what we ought. Indeed
it seems to me that in ordinary conversation it is more commonly used in such a way than in the specifically moral sense,
largely because people are shy of commenting to somebody
else about his morals. "You ought to have seen this film,"
"You ought to have moved your queen," even "Hitler ought
to have invaded England immediately after Dunkirk," are perfectly good English, and may be quite true statements even
though it is not considered a moral duty to see a film, to make
the right move in chess, and still less (by an Englishman) for
Hitler to invade England. The third sense of "ought" cannot,
however, be strictly described as a non-moral sense, nor for
that matter can the first sense of "ought." For to say that A
"ought" to do so-and-so in either of these senses entails that
under certain (factual) conditions he ought to do it in the
specifically moral sense of "ought." The proposition that a
man "ought" to do n in the first sense entails that he will do n
if he is adequately informed, wise and moral, and the proposition that a man "ought to do n" in the third sense entails
that he will do n if he is wise and moral. Similarly the proposition that he ought not (in the third sense) to have done what
he has done entails that he either has been unwise or has immorally neglected his duty. For I may fail to do what I
"ought" in that sense for two reasons, (a) because of a defect
of intelligence, (b) because of a defect of will. To say A

---

[12] Ross seems to take this view about "ought," though he admits that
"right" may legitimately be used in both senses (*Foundations of Ethics*, p.
55).

ought in that sense of "ought" to have done something which he did not do is to say that his action was inadequate or harmful through a defect in him, but to leave open (as we very often must in judging others) the question whether the defect was one of intelligence or of will. It implies that he either acted immorally or made a mistake. We are using "ought" in a completely non-moral sense only where we do not attach moral significance to the act at all, as in a game, or where we are considering not whether the act is right or wrong on the whole, but only whether it is so as means to a given end, which, as in the Hitler example, may be bad.

This brings out the point that "ought" really covers two different concepts, the concept of fittingness [13] and the concept of moral obligation. If I ought to do something there must be a certain relation between the action and its environment such that the action is fitting, appropriate, suitable, and its omission unfitting, inappropriate, unsuitable. This in itself is, however, a different concept from the concept of a moral obligation which we must fulfil or be guilty of sin, yet the latter concept must always be based on the former. Sin cannot occur unless our act is inappropriate in some way to the situation or at least we believe it to be so. This is obviously true, though we generally express it by using some stronger word than "unfitting" or "inappropriate." Nobody would in ordinary conversation describe a brutal murder as "unfitting"; the murder would no doubt be unfitting, but the word is not felt to be strong enough. It is, however, very convenient for philosophical purposes to have a single word which covers all degrees, so I shall follow Broad in using "fitting" for this purpose, as a physicist in defiance of ordinary usage employs the word "heat" to cover temperatures far below zero. But this concept of fittingness by no means exhausts the significance

---

[13] This term is borrowed from Professor Broad.

of "ought." There is the further concept of strictly moral obligation. We feel that we are under binding laws which we cannot break without being ourselves evil in a more serious and quite different way from that in which pain is evil. We feel that it is not merely an interesting fact that A is an unfitting action in circumstances B, C, D, but one which has a claim to authority over us. This is not to define "moral obligation," but to clarify the distinction between it and mere fittingness. Even if it is held that we are morally obliged to do what is most fitting, it must be admitted that the two concepts are distinct. But it is not the case that we are always morally obliged to do what is most fitting. For, although A is really the most fitting action relatively to all the circumstances, or even to those which are known to the agent, he may through ignorance or misjudgement not be aware of this, and in that case he will not be under a moral obligation to do A. Further, we can apply the term "fitting" in regard to matters which are not subject to volition, while we cannot apply the term "morally obligatory" in that way. Finally, certain actions are fitting simply because they are conducive to the agent's happiness, yet it may at least be doubted whether this is a sufficient ground to make them morally obligatory, which at any rate proves the two concepts not to be identical, even if we should finally reject the doubt and decide that they are morally obligatory after all. "Fittingness" stands for a relation between an action and its environment, moral obligation is something analogous to an imperative on the agent. So we have at least three different and apparently fundamental ethical concepts —goodness, fittingness, and moral obligation—the relations of which to explore.

It may be objected that the concept of moral obligation in so far as it goes beyond fittingness is theological, as has often been said to be the case with the allied concept of sin, and that therefore as long as we are dealing simply with ethics apart

from any theological assumptions we ought not to in roduce
it. But it is certainly a part of the moral consciousness, f anything is, that we are under binding obligations, and if w took
the notion away from ethics there would be little le t of
ethics. If this concept does necessarily involve theology, hen
we can argue from ethics to the existence of God. As I h ve
tried to make clear earlier, we must in any case not reverse t he
argument and say that we must first believe in theology befo e
we can rightly believe that we are under moral obligation:
We are directly and certainly conscious of moral obligation,
and if that is disputed there can be little ground for a theology
which would re-establish ethics. If belief in a good God—and
a God that was not good would assuredly provide no basis
for ethics—is to be established by argument, the argument
must already presuppose ethical concepts and propositions.
On the other hand, if it is claimed that we can be immediately
aware without argument of such a being independently of
the ethical consciousness and deduce our ethics from the nature of the being thus intuited, we are basing the more certain
on the less certain, since we are appealing to an intuition
which is, at the best, less, not more, certain than are our clearest
ethical intuitions. Even if belief in God were based exclusively not on our reason or intuition at all but on the revelation
of Christ, we may reply that there would be little ground
indeed for believing in the revelation if we did not assume at
least that Christ was good, and we could not assume this
without trusting to our own power of ethical discrimination.
Even if theology be the *ratio essendi* of ethics, it is certainly
not its *ratio cognoscendi*. In order to be aware that we are
under moral obligations we need not first come to know or
believe anything about God, even that there is a God. This
will be the case even if it should turn out that some of the
concepts of ethics—we have seen above [14] that this cannot be

---

[14] V. pp. 106 ff.

the case with all—cannot be analysed or at least grasped adequately without a reference to God.

My first and third senses of "ought" express fittingness, not merely fittingness for a particular end (as with Kant's "hypothetical imperatives"), though I do not deny that "ought" is also used in that sense, but fittingness in regard to the situation as a whole. But with the first sense the situation is viewed in abstraction from any imperfections in the agent's knowledge and beliefs, and with the third sense the situation is viewed in abstraction, not from all such imperfections, but from those due to his mistakes, negligence, or prejudice. The first and third senses give the act which of those possible is the most fitting if we take into account everything except the above circumstances. The second sense gives the action which is fitting in relation to the situation as the agent views it and at the same time the action which is morally obligatory. I think it to be a true synthetic *a priori* proposition that it is morally obligatory for an agent to do A where he thinks A the most fitting action in his power and where it is both possible for him to do and also possible for him not to do A. There would be serious difficulties and disputes about the definition of "possible," but these are beyond the scope of this book; and even the determinist would admit some sense of "possible" in which it is possible for a man to act differently from the way in which he actually does act. In order to decide which action is most fitting the agent cannot first take into account his belief as to which is most fitting, for this is not yet formed, therefore he must be asking himself which action he ought to do in my third sense of "ought," not in my second sense which already presupposes that he has made up his mind as to which act is the fitting one to do. Now suppose he is mistaken and acts according to his false belief. He can be said to have done what he morally ought to do, but he cannot be said to have done what he ought in the sense of what is most fitting to the situation. It might be argued that he has still done the most fitting, or the least unfitting, act in his power, for if l e had done the act which was externally the most fitting, he wc ild have done it from a bad motive or in a bad state of mind, and it therefore would not have been really the most fitting actic n. In such a situation, since there is no absolutely fitting act, in which he could do, the question is which is the least unfitt. ig. But, bad as it is to do what one believes to be wrong, it may be on occasion less inappropriate to the situation that some body should do this than that he should do a terribly harmful act which he erroneously thinks right. To make this clear by in example, let us suppose that on September 1, 1939, Hitk really thought it his duty to order the invasion of Poland. I, would still have been less inappropriate to the situation that Hitler should have neglected to obey his conscience on this occasion, even through bad motives such as laziness or coward-ice, than that he should have obeyed it with all the terrible effects in suffering and moral evil that the war brought in its wake. We cannot therefore say that it is always most fitting to do what one thinks most fitting, but one may still be able to say that it is always morally obligatory to do so. To keep the peace, even believing this to be wrong, would have been less unfitting than to break the peace believing it to be right. Yet the latter, and not the former, was Hitler's duty in my second sense of "duty," if he held that belief, though no doubt he violated his duty in all senses in getting into a state in which it was possible for him to hold (if he ever did hold) the belief. I think, therefore, that the second sense of "ought" differs from the other two in that to say something ought to be done in this sense is to make no statement about the real, as opposed to the believed, fittingness of the action. It also differs in that it can be applied only to actions. The first and third can also be applied to emotions or opinions, whereas it cannot be said that a person "ought" in my second sense to have an emotion

ence there would be between choosing to act on one and choosing to act on the other except that I should feel differently, and it is generally admitted, as Ross urges, that my feelings cannot be changed immediately by an act of will but require for their alteration a longer process.

In order to deal with this question I think the best course is to ask: What then ought I to do if I believe that n is the right act but the state of my desires is such as to make me inclined to do n from a wrong motive? Clearly I ought to take special care in deciding whether n really is the right act, since there will be a great danger of my desires prejudicing me in the matter, and it may even for that reason be best to postpone acting. On these grounds Plato laid down the rule that we ought to avoid punishing somebody while we are angry. But postponement of a decision may sometimes be disastrous. Suppose I am convinced after adequate consideration that n is right and that it would be foolish to wait longer before doing n, but suppose also that the bad motive is more clearly present in my mind than the good. (It cannot be alone present, otherwise I should not seriously ask the question what I ought to do at all.) Clearly it is now my duty to do n, and it will not be possible for me to prevent myself feeling a certain satisfaction at this for wrong reasons, but I can at least direct my attention to the aspects of the question which make the action my duty rather than to those which give me illicit satisfaction. Modern psychology has shown that it is best to recognise frankly that the less desirable tendency is present, but it is clearly also true that I ought not to rest in the enjoyment of this but recognise it as something to be fought against. At any rate it is clear that, although we cannot alter our desires at a moment's notice, we can control our attention and therefore our present state of mind to some extent, so that there seems to me to be no adequate ground for saying that it can only be my duty to act, not to act in a certain state of mind. A state of mind in which I will to punish A but attend mainly to the pleasure I obtain from doing so or to the harm A has done *me* is radically different from a state of mind in which I will to punish A but direct my attention to the good reasons for doing so, even if I cannot now help feeling the pleasure (whatever I might have done earlier to avoid getting into this malevolent frame of mind). The morally important thing is, not how I feel, but how my will is directed. If it be objected that some time, however little, will elapse between my willing to attend and my actually attending, it may equally be said that some time will elapse between my willing to perform and my actually performing a physical act. If, as in Prichard's *Duty and Ignorance of Fact* and Ross's *Foundations of Ethics*, what a man ought to do is held to be simply to "set himself" to effect a certain change, this is already to admit that his duty is to change his state of mind in a certain way. So why not also admit a duty to change it in the way I suggest, since he would thereby, as Ross and Prichard both admit, make his action intrinsically better than it would otherwise be?

So the answer to the question whether it is our duty only to do something or to do it from a particular motive seems to depend on whether we mean by "motive" (1) a desire causing action or (2) circumstances relevant to the action on which our attention is fixed at the time of action. In the former case we perhaps cannot say that it is our duty at the time of action to act from one motive rather than another, for, since a cause must lie in the past, that would be saying that it was our duty to alter the past. But we can say that it is our duty to deflect our attention in such a way as to weaken the desire by attending to circumstances which would discourage rather than encourage it. In the latter case we can say that it is our duty at the time to act from a certain motive, as truly as we can say that it is our duty to act, or set ourselves to act, at all. It may be contended in regard to acting and acting from a given motive alike that they are duties which never refer to the present but always only to the (very) immediate future, since all causation takes time. The recognition that the exhortation to act from good motives is an exhortation not so much to cultivate certain feelings directly as to attend to certain features of the act and of its consequences in preference to others also enables one to reconcile the duty to act from good motives with a new line of argument introduced by Ross in *Foundations of Ethics*.[18] He says there: "When we ask what it is that makes an act my duty we are asking what is the *distinctive* feature of that act that makes it and not some other to be my duty. Now, *whichever* of two or more acts I decide to be my duty, I shall do it (if I carry out my intention) from the sense of duty. The motive will be the same whichever I do; the motive therefore can be no part of that which makes the one act my duty while the others are not, since the same motive will be the motive of whichever act I do. . . . What is it to which we in fact find ourselves attending when we are trying to discover our duty in some situation? Is it not clear that what we attend to is the nature of the possible acts, considered apart from the motive from which we should do them —their tendency to affect the welfare of other people in this way or in that, their quality as fulfilments of promise or breaches of promise, and the like?" I certainly agree that, except for some indirect reason, consideration of my motives as desires does not help me to find out what is my duty. On the whole the objective features of an action are what we should consider, and the duty to act from a good motive, in so far as it can be contrasted with the duty of acting as such, seems to lie in attending to some of these rather than to others.

Ross also argues that, if it is my duty to do act A from the sense of duty, we must admit that it is my duty to do A from

[18] P. 123.

the sense that it is my duty to do A from the sense that it is my duty to do A and so on *ad infinitum*, thus involving a vicious infinite regress.[19] However, it seems to me that in the sentence "It is my duty to do A from a sense of duty" "duty" is usually being used in two different ways. Where it occurs first in the sentence, it is used in my second sense, that is, to mean that it is morally obligatory to act in a certain way; where it occurs for the second time, it is used in my third sense. The sentence then will mean that it is a moral obligation to do A because you believe A to be objectively fitting relatively to the available data, and therefore there will be no contradiction in saying that it is my duty to do A from the sense of duty, even though we mean by the latter the sense that it is our duty to do it *simpliciter* (not from a sense of duty), because "duty" means something different in the two cases. But even if it were held that I ought to act from a sense that it was morally obligatory (not merely from a sense that it was fitting) to act in this way, it would not necessarily follow that I ought to act from a sense that it was morally obligatory to act from a sense that it was morally obligatory to act in this way, still less from a sense that it was morally obligatory to act from a sense that it was morally obligatory to act from a sense that it was morally obligatory to act in this way. It may be doubted whether anybody has such a sense at all, and certainly nobody will have it but a philosopher! These conclusions, it seems to me, would only follow if we assumed that it was my duty always to do whatever I did from a sense of duty, and this Ross himself does not hold. If it is only my duty to do some of the things that I do from a sense of duty, it may well be my duty to do A from a sense of duty without its being also my duty to have this motive itself from a sense of duty and so on *ad infinitum*.

---

[19] *The Right and the Good*, p. 5; *Foundations of Ethics*, pp. 116 ff.

Ross's argument seems to depend also on supposing that there is a contradiction between saying that it is my duty to do A *simpliciter* and saying that it is my duty to do A from a sense of duty. But doing A is a genus of which the various species are doing A from the various kinds of possible motive, and if it is my duty to do an action which falls in one of the species it is *ipso facto* my duty to do an action which falls in the genus. The latter assertion, so far from contradicting the former, is entailed by it. There can be no contradiction in saying that I ought to do an action of genus A from the sense that it is my duty to do an action of this genus. It might after all be true both that I ought to pay a particular debt and that I ought to pay it from certain motives rather than from others. That the statement that I ought to pay the debt does not give a complete description of what I ought to do in this matter does not prevent it from being a true statement as far as it goes. However, as what I have said before suggests, the truth probably is, not that we ought to act from a sense of duty in the sense of our act being determined by the desire to do our duty, but in the sense that we ought to act with our attention directed to those characteristics of the act which make it a duty rather than to others. For example, in paying our debts we ought to attend rather to the fact that we owe the money than to the fact that we shall be summoned if we do not pay them, or shall make it easier for ourselves to obtain improper favours from our creditors if we do.

It follows that in all the senses of "ought" discussed what we ought to do is not merely to act, but to act in a certain state of mind or with a certain direction of attention. I therefore cannot agree with Ross's view in *The Right and the Good* [20] that what ought to be done is never morally good. It is morally good to act in the fitting way with my attention

---

[20] P. 4.

directed towards the right aspects of the act, especially where there is a temptation to do the opposite. And to do so is both fitting and, if I believe it to be the fitting course, obligatory. An immoral action, on the other hand, is from the nature of the case one not done with a right direction of attention, and so even if it turned out by accident to be in its external features the most beneficial act possible it would not be right. As regards mistakes I should say that if I mistakenly believe that *a* is my duty (in my first or my third sense), when *a* is really wrong, it is impossible for me to perform the right (fitting) action (in the sense in question), though it is possible for me to perform the morally obligatory act (second sense of "duty" or "right"). For if I do the act which I think right, it will for external reasons be unfitting, and if I perform the act which is really externally right I shall be performing it in a state of mind which is unfitting.

CHAPTER V

An Analysis of Good in Terms of Ought

Having distinguished the different senses of "good" and "ought" as far as necessary, we can now consider whether it is possible to define the one ethical concept in terms of the other. What Moore was attacking when he insisted that "good" could not be defined was any attempt to define it in purely non-ethical terms. The objections to such attempts are not valid against an attempt to define it by means of other ethical concepts or to give it a mixed definition consisting partly of ethical and partly of psychological terms. This proceeding would not be open to the charge of explaining away or destroying the specific character of ethical ideas; and it is such a definition that I propose now to attempt. I have indeed insisted that at least one ethical concept must be unanalysable, but that concept may perhaps not be the concept of good. Now the only other ethical term besides "good" which could be plausibly claimed to be fundamental is "ought." We have, however, seen that this term expresses two different fundamental concepts, fittingness and moral obligation. Let us try first whether we can define "good" in terms of "ought" as standing for the former, and then consider the notion of moral obligation afterwards. I do not indeed see any prospect of defining "good" in terms of fittingness alone—that could only be done if goodness and fittingness were simply synonymous—but it might be definable in terms of fittingness together with some psychological concept.

The question at issue between naturalist and non-naturalist is not whether "good" is ever used in a non-natural.st sense, but whether it is always so used. Now the sense of "good" which is usually being considered when we ask whether "good" is or is not analysable is that usually disting ished from others by the use of the phrases "intrinsically g ood," "good as an end," "good-in-itself." It is this sense of "good" that we shall discuss. When we have arrived a a definition, we can try to derive from it definitions of a ly other non-naturalist senses of "good." The term "intrins - cally good" may be technical, but in so far as there is no poin in anything being good as a means unless something is good as an end it is presupposed in all commonsense talk about what is good.

The definition I shall suggest will be partly in ethical and partly in psychological terms. Provided irreducible ethical terms are introduced at all, even if they do not make up the whole of the definition, this will save it from the charge of being naturalist. I do not claim orginality for the defini- tion; [1] if I show any originality at all, it will be in the con- sequences that I deduce from it. Now, strange to say, the definition is one actually suggested by Moore himself. For he suggests that we might take as a synonym for "good" as applied to an experience the phrase "worth having for its own sake." [2] To say this is not necessarily inconsistent with the view that good is indefinable, for there might be various phrases which could be properly used as verbal synonyms in order to help people to see more clearly what is meant by a term without being themselves eligible as definitions of the term. It might be the case that "worth" in "worth having for its own sake" could itself only be defined in terms of "good," so that the phrase would be quite useless as a definition of

---

[1] V., for example, Osborne, *The Philosophy of Value*, pp. 93 ff.
[2] Proceedings of Arist. Soc., Supp. Vol. XI, pp. 122 ff.

the latter, and yet it might be appropriately used to help some people to become clear as to what they meant by "good," and especially to distinguish the sense under discussion from other senses of "good." However I think that in fact "worth having for its own sake" can be analysed in a way which does not make it a vicious circle to use the phrase as a definition of "good"; but, before I propound my analysis, I should like the reader to consider carefully whether the phrase "an intrinsically good experience" is or is not the exact equivalent of "an experience worth having for its own sake." In this definition, unlike the naturalist definitions, it seems clear both that the *definiens* and the *definiendum* are coextensive, and that this is necessarily so. It seems clear that there could not be an experience which was intrinsically good that was yet not worth having for its own sake, nor an experience which was worth having for its own sake that was not intrinsically good. This seems to me not merely a contingent fact but a logical necessity. Now it may well be the case that, say, A B entails and is entailed by C, and yet that A B is not a definition of C; consequently it is impossible strictly to prove that anything is a definition of anything else. So in the present case it is open to anybody to maintain that besides the characteristic expressed by the words "worth having for its own sake" there is another, indefinable characteristic, goodness. He should maintain this, if he thinks he can discern such a characteristic which always necessarily accompanies, but is different from, the characteristic of being worth having for its own sake. But I am not clear that I can discern any such characteristic, and I should point to the fact that, when in ordinary conversation we wish to convey exactly the meaning of the term "intrinsically good" to a person not familiar with it, we should most naturally use the phrase in question. "Worth having for its own sake" seems to be in fact just the phrase which the man in the street, when he is talking about experiences, would use to express what the philosopher calls "intrinsically" as distinct from "instrumentally good."

But, while "worth having for its own sake" is equivalent to "intrinsically good" when applied to an experience, there is an objection to taking it as equivalent to "intrinsically good" without qualification. It is this: though it is often held that experiences are the only things which can be intrinsically good, we must not define "intrinsically good" in a way which would make it a verbal contradiction to say of anything but an experience that it was intrinsically good. To say that the State is good-in-itself or to say that beautiful things are good-in-themselves may be wrong but is not verbally self-contradictory. Now on the definition of "intrinsically good" suggested it would be verbally self-contradictory or meaningless, because experiences are the only kind of things that we can be said to "have" in this sense of "have," [3] though there are other senses of "have" in which it is possible to have, for example, beautiful objects. But this does not prevent the definition from being adequate when we are talking of a person's experiences as such. What is an experience which is worth having for its own sake? It is one that it is reasonable to choose for its own sake, or that a man ought, other things being equal, to bring into existence for its own sake. Now these phrases themselves are not by the very meaning of the words limited to experiences. So, if we are looking for a definition which will not be confined to experiences, we might define "intrinsically good" as "worth choosing or producing for its own sake." However, though this definition will mostly serve, there may be cases where it cannot well be applied, and it is difficult to find a single form of words which is always applicable. But we might adopt a technical term and define "good" as what ought to be the object of a pro

---

[3] As Moore points out, id., p. 124.

attitude (to use Ross's word). "Pro attitude" is intended to cover any favourable attitude to something. It covers, for instance, choice, desire, liking, pursuit, approval, admiration. The variety of these attitudes would go far to explain how it is that "good" may be used in so many different senses. "Worth having" as applied to experiences seems to mean that the experience in itself is a suitable one to choose for one's own or to give to somebody else, and to entail that it should be welcomed and not avoided or deplored. It may be reasonable to renounce or avoid it on account of some bad consequences which it may have or for the sake of obtaining something still better, but as an experience it is not only desired but desirable in the absence of any positive reason against it. So we have obtained a definition of "intrinsically good" in terms of "ought," and while the phrase "worth having for its own sake" can without verbal contradiction be applied only to experiences, the definition now given can be applied more widely, if there are indeed things other than experiences which are good in the sense under discussion. When something is intrinsically good, it is (other things being equal) something that on its own account we ought to welcome, rejoice in if it exists, seek to produce if it does not exist.[4] We ought to approve its attainment, count its loss a deprivation, hope for and not dread its coming if this is likely, avoid what hinders its production, etc. A definition of this sort is indicated by the very common tendency to take "desirable" as a synonym for "good" in ordinary speech. I do not think myself that in most cases where "good" is used it is best defined in terms of desire, but it may well be that it is best defined in terms of some similar attitude. We must, however, unlike Mill, remember that "desirable" signifies what "ought to be desired," not just "what is desired"; and this same point will apply, what-

---

[4] I think it to be a synthetic *a priori* proposition that we ought to welcome what is worth producing for its own sake, etc.

ever mental attitude we select for our definition in preference to desire. It need not always be the same attitude. When we call something good, we may be thinking sometimes rather of the fact that we ought to welcome it, sometimes rather of the fact that we ought to seek it, etc. But we can see various attitudes I have mentioned to have something in common that is opposed to the common element in condemning, shunning, fearing, regretting, etc., which would supply the corresponding definition of "bad." The former may be called pro attitudes, the latter anti attitudes. The former are positive and favourable to their objects, the latter negative and hostile.

But what is the sense of "ought" when we say we ought to have a pro attitude to what is good and an anti attitude to what is bad? In the last chapter I have distinguished the concept of fittingness from the concept of moral obligation. It is clearly the former which is involved here, not the latter, though there may be other senses of "good" in which the latter comes to the fore. When we are saying that something is worth pursuing for its own sake, we are not saying that one morally ought to pursue it. That may be impossible for a particular person and therefore not morally obligatory. Nor are we necessarily even saying that a man morally ought to pursue it if he can and if there is no positive objection to his doing so. Most [5] pleasant experiences are worth having for their own sake, but, if the experience is merely a pleasure of an innocent but not very elevated kind, most people would hold that I should not be morally to blame for deliberately neglecting to obtain that experience for myself. Now this, whether a right judgement or not, is certainly not verbally inconsistent with saying that pleasure is intrinsically good. As I have pointed out, the word "ought" (without its strictly moral implications) is constantly used in such cases, for

---

[5] Not all, for example, not drunkenness or sadism.

example, "You ought to have seen that film." It does seem
clear that, when I say that such a pleasant experience is intrinsically good, I am asserting that it is preferable to have it
rather than not, or that, other things being equal, I ought to
choose it in my first or third sense of "ought." Whether I
should be morally to blame or not for declining to choose to
have it when I could do so without corresponding harm, at
any rate it would be fitting, rational, desirable for me to
choose the experience in question. If we mean by "good"
what ought to be desired, approved, or admired, it seems still
more obvious to me that we are thinking of "ought" in the
sense in which it signifies fittingness rather than moral obligation. For I cannot by an act of will desire, approve, or admire
something. Yet it is perfectly plain that there is a sense in
which it can be said that I ought to have these emotional attitudes to certain things—and not merely that I ought to cultivate them as far as I can. "Ought" here signifies that these
emotional attitudes are fitting. It is more appropriate, or fitting,
to feel disgust than pleasure at cruelty, more appropriate to
desire reconciliation than revenge, to admire fidelity than
clever cheating, to feel aesthetic emotions on contemplating
great works of art than not to do so. When we say this, I do
not think we are directly considering whether the person who
has the appropriate or inappropriate feelings has done what
he morally ought or not. His feelings are still unfitting even
if he was so badly brought up that he could not be expected
to see their wrongness or try to improve his feelings. He may
not be to blame for them, but that does not make them fitting.
If it did, the fact that he had been badly brought up would
not be so deplorable; indeed if his bringing up did not produce
unfitting feelings and actions he could not be said to have
been "badly brought up." Similarly an action may be condemned as unfitting in the circumstances under which it is
done even if the person who does it has not the intelligence

to foresee the likelihood of the consequences which make it unfitting, provided only these consequences were humanly foreseeable.

So we are in the definition of "good" using "ought," not in the second sense, earlier distinguished,[6] to signify moral obligation, but to signify fittingness. We may therefore define "good" as "fitting object of a pro attitude," either without qualification (my first sense of "ought"), or as qualified by the terms "so far as is in the light of the available evidence foreseeable" (my third sense of "ought"). (While we could never be confident that any complete action we did was one we ought to do in the first sense, we can be confident or even know that we ought to treat certain objects as ends-in-themselves, have certain mental attitudes, and feel certain emotions in this sense of "ought.") When I say this I think I am giving a strict definition of what "good" means, or at least approximating as closely as a philosophical analysis ever could to an exact definition of a commonsense term. I am not merely saying what being good entails, still less amending the commonsense meaning so as to fit in with my philosophy. The position is complicated by the variety of the different senses of "good"; but I think it is a strong point of my definition that all the different senses can be brought under it or at least closely related to it. In its primary sense as intrinsically good, "good," I think, usually means "worth producing or pursuing for its own sake, other things being equal." To apply "good" to something is to say of this that it is fitting, other things being equal, to bring it into existence. That, as we have seen, is shown by the naturalness of the equation of "good" with "worth having" when applied to experiences. It has been several times proposed to define "good" as "desirable," meaning by this word not, as Mill apparently did in a famous (or notorious?) passage,

---

[6] V. above, pp. 120–21.

"actual object of desire" but "fitting object of desire." But, if "desire" means a certain uneasy emotion, it is not true that we ought to feel desire towards whatever is intrinsically good. The less we feel this emotion towards what we cannot obtain, or in any degree bring about, however good that object may be, the better on the whole. For such desire will only make us less happy and distract us from our other activities without doing any good. On the other hand, if desire means something more than an uneasy emotion, it becomes a striving to pursue and bring about the existence of its object, and if so the definition in terms of desire merges into the definition in terms of pursuit. This is in fact, I think, what we almost always mean when we say that something is desirable; we do not mean that we ought to feel a certain emotion towards it, but that the object is worth producing or pursuing. It is therefore better to say this frankly in our definition than to use a word which is more ambiguous. There may well be cases in which "good" is used to signify rather "what it is fitting to desire" than "what it is fitting to produce or pursue," but I think they will be rare. I am in this objecting to "desirable" as the standard definition; but "fitting object of pursuit," though a great improvement as a definition, cannot itself be substituted for "good" in all cases even of what is pronounced intrinsically good.

Among the things which are spoken of as "intrinsically good" are actions. Now in this case I do not think that people are generally using the term in the same sense as when they use it, for example, of pleasant experiences. We regard, for example, a particular act of self-sacrifice as intrinsically good. Do we mean to say that it is fitting that the person who makes the sacrifice should choose, produce, or pursue it for its own sake quite apart from consequences? Surely not. That would lead to irrational asceticism. To sacrifice himself when it does no good to anyone is not something which a man ought to choose

to do. The self-sacrificing action does not seem to be intrinsically good in the sense in which, for example, innocent
pleasures, aesthetic experiences, personal affection, intellectual
activity are held to be so. If it were, ought we not to spend
most of our time torturing ourselves in order to realize the
value of self-sacrifice, since moral values are generally admitted
to be higher than happiness and their absence in beings capable
of them a worse evil than pain? But intrinsic goodness as
applied to actions may still be analysed in terms of fittingness
provided the psychological term of the analysis is different.
Now we certainly regard righteous acts of self-sacrifice as
admirable in themselves even if they fail to achieve the desired result. So I suggest that we usually mean by "good
actions" simply actions that it is fitting to admire or approve.
This is certainly not the usual meaning of "intrinsically good"
in the earlier cases. A pleasure, however innocent, is not something to be admired, though it is something to be liked and,
other things being equal, pursued.

But we must add a qualification and say "morally admired"
or "morally approved." For we may also admire or approve a
cleverness which does not display moral qualities, though
our admiration even for the cleverness in itself is lessened if it
displays immoral ones. Nor must we use "admired" or "approved" here to stand for "judged good," since in that case
we should be guilty of a vicious circle. The word must, in the
analysis given, stand for an emotion or a state of mind tinged
with emotional qualities. I do not wish to discuss the psychological question whether moral emotion is a single emotion
or a class or blend of emotions; but it does seem to me that
there is something specific about this kind of admiration which
distinguishes it from other kinds. And it is quite clear that
there are certain actions to which this kind of feeling is the
appropriate reaction, as sympathy is to suffering and certain
aesthetic experiences to a great drama. There is, however, a

curious point here to note in passing: with persons other than the agent himself the appropriate reaction is admiration, but with the agent himself it is not. A man should not admire himself. Such a difference between the emotion appropriate to a quality in another person and that appropriate to the same quality in oneself is, however, not unparalleled; sympathy and pity are appropriate emotions when directed towards another's pain, but one should try to avoid self-pity, and it is doubtful whether there is any sense in talking about feeling sympathy with oneself. Moral disapproval or condemnation is, on the other hand, a fitting emotion for both the agent and others when directed towards morally evil actions, but most moral disapproval of oneself feels so very different from most moral disapproval of others that it is appropriately designated by a different word, "shame." (We may indeed feel shame for the actions of another person; but it is clear that this feeling is derivative from the feeling one has for one's own wrong acts and moral defects, and only arises because through sympathy we put ourselves in the place of the person who has done wrong.)

If we are not willing to regard moral admiration as a specific emotion, we can still retain the principle of the definition by defining "good actions" in the moral sense as actions more or less admirable on account of certain volitional characteristics. They will be those actions that show a direction of the will to right ends and a persistence in face of temptation in doing what is thought right. In that case moral admiration and other kinds of admiration will be distinguished, not by the way they feel but by their objects. Clever or beautiful pieces of work would also be fitting objects of admiration but for a different reason, not so connected with the will, and we should therefore not speak of moral admiration of them. In any case the term "admirable" is wider than "morally admirable," so this already gives us two different senses of "good," one wider, one narrower, "admirable" and "morally admirable," besides the previous sense discussed in which it stands for an object which it is fitting to pursue, promote, or choose for its own sake.

These three different senses will have two very important points in common: (a) they define "good" in terms of fittingness together with a psychological factor, (b) the latter is a "pro attitude," though the pro attitude is different. The attitudes are, in a very definite sense, favourable to the object towards which they are directed. That "intrinsically good" should be used in different senses not clearly distinguished is, when the senses have so much in common, not very surprising. My view here bears a certain similarity to that of Ross, though it was reached independently before I knew that he had also made the distinction in question. Ross distinguishes two senses of "good": in one sense the term applies to certain moral dispositions and actions, and intellectual and aesthetic activities, and in the other to pleasure. In the former sense the term "may be paraphrased by saying that they are fine or admirable activities of the human spirit, and by adding that they are good in such a way that any one who has them or does them is to that extent being good himself. Pleasure is never good in this, which I should call the most proper sense of 'good.' But the pleasures of others (except those which are immoral) are good in a secondary sense, viz. that they are morally worthy or suitable objects of satisfaction." [7] The differences between us are, however, greater than appear at first sight.

(1) Ross holds that his first sense of "good," though capable of being "paraphrased" in the way given, is indefinable, while I have put forward "fitting object of admiration" as a definition of this sense of "good." I do not know how to decide

---

[7] *Foundations of Ethics*, p. 283.

between the two views except by asking myself whether I can form a distinct idea of a characteristic, goodness, common to morally admirable actions over and above the characteristic of being a fitting object of moral admiration, and I do not think I can. It may be retorted that, if an action is to be worthy of moral admiration, this must be because of something in the action itself. But this, though true, need not imply that there must be a single quality, goodness, over and above both the psychological qualities which make the action morally admirable and the non-natural characteristics of being an action which ought to be admired and one which ought to be done. There are various psychological characteristics, for example the direction of the will to a certain end, and there are the non-natural characteristics, based on these, of being an action which ought to be done [8] and of being a fitting object of admiration, but besides these there is no further quality of goodness which I can detect. Ross says that "admiration" is "an emotion accompanied by the thought that that which is admired is good," and concludes that it would therefore be a vicious circle to say that anything was good if we meant by this only that it was worthy of admiration. We admire something only because we first think it good, and therefore, he holds, we cannot base the definition of "good" on the concept of admiration. Now we certainly may sometimes admire something because we first think it good, but this is not incompatible with my definition. If we define "good" as "worthy of admiration," the sentence will still make sense, for I might well admire something just because I thought it worthy to be admired. But this is not the only proper ground of admiration. We must guard against a confusion here: the reason why it is proper to admire anything must be constituted by the qualities which make the object of admiration

---

[8] At least in my second sense of "ought."

good, but it does not follow that the thought that it is good must, if the admiration is to be justifiable, intervene between the perception of the factual qualities admired and the feeling of admiration. Again it is clear that we cannot properly admire anything which is not good in that respect for which we admire it; but this would obviously be true on my definition also, indeed it would be a tautology. And we can certainly distinguish between our attitude of mind when we admire something spontaneously because its qualities directly call forth this emotion and our attitude when we admire it because we have first come to the conclusion that it ought to be admired, for example if I am at first prejudiced against somebody but realise that he is displaying qualities which I should greatly admire in somebody against whom I was not prejudiced. Of the two kinds of admiration the latter, so far from being preferable, is a feeble substitute for the former, unless and until it merges itself in the former. On the other hand, once the question of fittingness is raised at all, it is not easy for the emotion of admiration to attain much strength if we do not think that it is also fitting to feel it. But this is not to say that we need think its object good in a sense of "good" other than that in which the word expresses fitness to be admired. The emotion of admiration is different from the judgement that its object is one which it is fitting to admire, though the two are very closely connected.

(2) Ross, in view of (1), cannot say in general that to call something "good" means just that it is a fitting object of a pro attitude, though he does admit that in one of its primary senses "good" does stand for "fit object of satisfaction." [9] But in the other, as we have just seen, "good" is for him indefinable. He admits that, when we call something "good," we are always expressing a pro attitude towards it,[10] but he distinguishes

---

[9] Id., p. 279.
[10] Id., p. 254–5.

what is expressed from what is meant. The former must from the nature of the case be a psychological attitude of the speaker, but this need not apply to the latter. I should make the same distinction between expressing and meaning, and agree that, while ethical statements, like any others, *expressed* a state of mind of the speaker, they might *mean* something quite different. Even on my view "this ought to be admired" is different from "I feel admiration for this." The distinction is quite compatible with the view that what an ethical statement means is always that it is fitting to have some pro attitude.

(3) Ross prefers to define "good" in the sense other than "admirable" in terms of satisfaction rather than in terms of pursuit or choice.[11] No doubt whatever is a fit object of choice or pursuit for its own sake is a fit object of satisfaction, but serious difficulties arise when we consider degrees of goodness. It seems to me far from evident that it is fitting always to feel satisfaction in something in proportion to its goodness. It is by no means unfitting to feel more satisfaction in the happiness of my mother than in that of a total stranger, yet the two are equally valuable (at least if the stranger is equally deserving).[12] This is true even in cases where it is my duty to pursue the good of the stranger at the time rather than that of my mother.

(4) I have rather in mind the sense of "ought" or "right" in which these words express fittingness, Ross rather the specifically moral sense, though I do not see how his view could be worked out if we excluded the former sense. For instance, if we say that morally good acts are admirable, we must mean that it is fitting to admire them, not that we morally ought to admire them, unless we think that it is a moral duty to have (and not merely to cultivate) certain feelings, a view

---

[11] Id., p. 279.
[12] For the difficulties that such considerations present to my own theory, which seem to me not insuperable, v. below, pp. 192-93.

cases are usually very trivial, and we rightly do not use the solemn word "duty" on trifling occasions, and partly because we have a strong natural inclination to seek our own pleasure even to excess. It is thought unlikely that we shall fail to seek it where we ought except through mistakes of judgement, which are not in themselves moral faults, or through passions the yielding to which is already wrong on other grounds. But if I ask whether it would be my duty to be as cheerful as I could, even if it made no difference whatever to anybody else's happiness or to the fulfilment of any other duties whether I was cheerful or not, I must answer that it would. Apart from such temptations as gluttony or passions like anger which injure others as well as oneself and indulgence in which, at least beyond a very limited degree, is intrinsically evil, why do people neglect to do what will be conducive to their own pleasure? If they do so, as often, through a genuine mistake of judgement, we must not say that they are morally to blame, but neither can we say so if they fail to further the pleasure of others as much as they might through an honest error of judgement. But I might know or believe that some action was conducive to my own pleasure and that there was no moral objection to it, and yet I might not do it. Why not? I do not see how this could occur except through a desire for something else which, though less productive of pleasure for me, was more immediately obtainable or otherwise attractive, or through laziness. The two cases may indeed both be brought under the former heading, since laziness is due to a desire to avoid present trouble. Now it does seem to me that it must be in some slight degree morally wrong to let oneself be swayed against reason by a present desire. Knowingly to act against reason must be in some degree morally blameworthy, even if what reason tells us is only that such and such a course will be most conducive to our own pleasure. But, as I have said, blameworthiness is usually slight in cases where only our own pleasure is at stake, and therefore we are apt not to apply the term "duty" in such cases, reserving it for more serious matters and thinking that, since most people already seek their own pleasure much too much, it is better not to encourage them in this by saying that it is a duty to seek it. However we do blame people morally if they eat to excess of kinds of food which they know are liable to give them severe indigestion or are grossly extravagant or give way excessively to moods of depression, and it would be far-fetched to explain this entirely by the effect either on other people or their own character. Part of the reason why such conduct is blameworthy is the direct one that it involves wantonly sacrificing one's own happiness through slackness or from a devotion to trivial goods. We should add, as Ross himself did at a time when he still believed it to be a *prima facie* duty to produce pleasure for oneself, that "it is only if we think of our own pleasure not as simply our own pleasure, but as an objective good, something that an impartial spectator would approve, that we can think of the getting it as a duty; and we do not habitually think of it in this way." [13] No doubt to think too much of one's own pleasure is both wrong and likely to defeat its own object, but on the other hand there is no doubt a vast loss of pleasure through people neglecting to take desirable precautions or making the efforts needed to secure it.

If I had not decided that it was a duty *ceteris paribus* to further one's own pleasure, I should have been forced to deny either that my own pleasure is a good or that it is a moral duty to pursue the good as far as we can. To my mind this is a strong argument for my conclusion about pleasure, since I have a strong inclination to think both these propositions self-evidently true. But, even if we decide that we have no moral

---

[13] Ross, *The Right and the Good*, p. 26.

obligation to pursue our own pleasure, we surely cannot deny that it is fitting (in my sense) to pursue it and unfitting to neglect it, so that it will still remain a good. We shall then escape dilemmas like that of Ross who has to hold that the same thing, namely a pleasant experience, is good from the point of view of a man who has not the experience but not good from the point of view of a man who has. I admit that his view is the logical consequence of his definition of "good," in the sense with which we are concerned here, as a morally suitable object of satisfaction, since there is a moral suitability about feeling sympathetic satisfaction in the happiness of others which does not arise in our own case.[14] But this seems to be an objection to his definition, since it makes the same thing both good and indifferent and forces him to contradict the proposition that my own pleasure is good, which seems to me an obvious truism.

The case of vicious pleasures may be cited against me. I should reply that we must distinguish their pleasantness from the characteristics which make them vicious. If it be objected that on my view we should at least be under a *prima facie* duty to pursue them because they are pleasant, I should reply that the objection is innocuous if we realise what is the only sense in which this would follow. It would only follow if it means that, provided we could obtain the same amount of pleasure in ways which were not immoral, we ought *ceteris paribus* to take action to obtain it, or that the fact that they have the universal characteristic of pleasantness (as opposed to being pleasant in the particular, evil way in which they are pleasant) is, as far as it goes, a reason why we ought to pursue them, though it is completely outweighed by others. This is, I think, quite compatible with the particular kind of pleasure felt being so bound up with the character of the experience as

---

[14] V. *Foundations of Ethics*, p. 282.

a whole that, the greater the pleasure, the worse the state of mind of, for example, one who enjoys cruelty.

It is certainly not true that, when we speak of a moral action as "good," we are never using "good" to mean "fitting object of choice"; but in the majority of cases I think it is impossible to distinguish "intrinsically good" as thus applied from "morally admirable." For "fitting object of choice" as applied to actions one would rather say "right." I also think that, when we speak of a man's character or life as good, we usually mean "worthy of moral admiration or approval"; though we should grant that it can also be good in the sense of being the kind of character or kind of life which it would be fitting to choose to have. A good character or a morally good life is assuredly a fitting object of pursuit, and is so not merely on account of any hedonistic advantages it may have for oneself or for others. But I do not believe that we are usually thinking of this when we appraise a character or life as good, and still less so when we thus appraise particular actions. We are rather thinking of their admirableness; and, as I have said earlier, there are cases of actions that we rightly admire which certainly ought not to be done for their own sake but only for their consequences. Certain aesthetic and intellectual activities will be, like many moral dispositions and actions, good in both senses, that is, fitting objects in themselves both of choice or pursuit and of admiration, though not in this case of moral admiration. In fact, I think everything that is good in the sense of being admirable will be good in the other sense, except some (not all) moral actions. The exception is made because some moral actions ought to be done only for their consequences and not for their own sake.

While I recognise that aesthetic and intellectual, as well as moral, activities are good in the sense of being fitting objects of admiration, I admit that there is an easily recognisable psychological difference between the kind of admiration that it is fitting to feel towards such objects and the kind that it is fitting to feel towards what is morally good. It has been contended, for example, by Hume, that the feelings with which we contemplate different kinds of moral virtue also differ, and this may well be the case. It certainly is so with the opposite emotions towards different kinds of morally evil actions. For instance, the kind of feeling with which it is appropriate to regard cheating is clearly different from the kind with which it is appropriate to regard cruelty, and this is not merely a difference in the degree but in the felt quality of the emotion. But we need not let these differences lead us, as they did Hume, to slur over or even repudiate the distinction between moral and other approval. For at any rate our feelings towards the display of different moral virtues have, despite their minor differences, something in common which they do not share with the feelings of admiration we have towards intellectual and aesthetic productions, though the latter feelings still belong to the same genus, admiration. The same applies even more clearly to the feelings of disapproval we have towards the display of different vices as compared with those we have towards the display of intellectual and aesthetic deficiencies.

It is irrelevant to object to my account on the ground that we cannot alter our emotions at a moment's notice and therefore cannot be told that we ought to feel a certain emotion but only that we ought to cultivate it. Perhaps "ought" in the sense in which it asserts moral obligation is applicable only where what it is said we ought to do could be brought about by an act of will on our part at the time; but we can certainly speak of the emotions a man "ought" to have in the sense of "the suitable emotions for him to have." It remains a fact that they are the suitable emotions whether he can feel them or not. We should use his inability for feeling them as a ground for denying that he ought to feel them in this sense of "ought" only if we held that he was by his constitution unalterably cut off from any emotions of that kind, as an animal is cut off from delight in philosophy.

The proposed definition of "good" as "fitting object of a pro attitude" can be applied to others of the senses of this word. If my definition is right, it will in fact explain why the word is used in so many different senses. For the sense will vary according to the particular pro attitude or attitudes the fittingness of which we intend to assert. This is to my mind both an argument for the definition and a reply to the naturalist who wants to know how it is that a word which in one sense stands for a simple indefinable quality should stand for something so different in other contexts. "Good" may, as I have pointed out earlier,[15] mean (1) pleasant or liked, (2) capable of satisfying desire, (3) efficient, (4) productive of something intrinsically good, (5) efficiently produced, (6) intrinsically good, (7) ultimately good, (8) as applied to characteristics, good-making, (9) morally good as applied to actions, (10) morally good as applied to persons. I have defined sense (6) as signifying what is a fitting object of welcome, choice, or pursuit for its own sake, and sense (7) can be defined in terms of sense (6), or vice versa if this is preferred. Sense (8) is obviously definable in terms of other senses, since "good-making" presupposes "good." Sense (9) I have defined as usually signifying "object of moral admiration," though it may also be used to mean "object of moral choice." Sense (10) seems also usually to mean "morally admirable," but here as applied to a person. Senses (2), (3), (4), and (5) signify that the object called "good" is a fitting object of approval or admiration in certain non-moral respects, or of choice if one desires to attain certain ends. (1) asserts rather that what is pronounced good is actually an object of a pro attitude than that it ought to be one; but we need not be

---

[15] V. above, pp. 112 ff.

surprised if common usage, which cannot be expected to make subtle distinctions, sometimes employs to signify "actual object of a pro attitude" a word which usually means "fitting object of such." The two senses are in such cases very closely connected because, if I regard something as capable of satisfying desire, I *ipso facto* regard it as in so far and subject to certain assumptions a fitting object of pursuit, though it may be open to objection in other respects so that it is on the whole not desirable to pursue it. With similar reservations, what is pleasant is regarded as a fitting object of liking. For a person with my sense of taste it is after all appropriate to like strawberries. So even where "good" means the object of an *actual* pro attitude, it stands for what is also at the same time regarded as a *fitting* object of such.

There are no doubt many different shades of meaning attached to the word "good" which neither I nor anybody else has distinguished in our classifications, but a place is left for these in my definition, though not in any narrower one. For in thinking of the good as a fitting object of a pro attitude we may sometimes have more in mind one of the numerous pro attitudes, sometimes another. We may sometimes think of it rather as a fitting object of desire, sometimes rather as a fitting object of satisfaction or choice or pursuit or approval, etc., thus giving scope for a great variety of minor differences of meaning within the definition that I have provided. In view of the vagueness of ordinary usage I cannot help regarding this as a point in favour of my definition.

I have defined one of the ethical concepts often taken as ultimate, namely good, in terms of another, fittingness. My definition of "good" also enables me to analyse another ethical notion which would otherwise have had to be taken as indefinable, namely, the notion of badness, and this I regard as one advantage of my view. The fewer unanalysed ethical concepts we have the better, provided we do not explain away facts. Now, if "good" is taken as unanalysable, "bad" will also have to be so taken, for it certainly is a positive notion and not merely equivalent to "not good." But if we analyse good as "fitting object of a pro attitude," it will be easy enough to analyse bad as "fitting object of an anti attitude," this term covering dislike, disapproval, avoidance, etc. The more specific meaning of the term will vary according to which of the different possible anti attitudes we have in view. To say that a man is bad is certainly not to say that we ought to take all the possible anti attitudes against him, including, for example, hate, but only the specific one of moral disapproval.

But there still remain two undefined concepts in ethics, though they are both expressed by the same word, "ought," namely (1) fittingness, (2) moral obligation.[16] Could we analyse either in terms of the other? I do not see how we could analyse fittingness in terms of moral obligation. Indeed I think that any such attempt would involve a vicious circle, for it is only because we first think an act fitting that we are under a moral obligation to perform it. There remains a possible way of defining "moral obligation" in terms of fittingness together with some psychological concept or concepts, as I defined "good." We might say that "A morally ought to do this" means (1) it would be fitting for A to do this, and (2) if he does not do it, it is fitting that he should be in that respect an object of the emotion of moral disapproval, or perhaps simply (2) without (1). This too sounds like a vicious circle, but it is not really one if we mean by "moral disapproval" either some specific emotion indefinable but introspectively recognisable and distinguishable from other kinds of disapproval, or else just disapproval felt for a person in respect of a certain kind of qualities of the will as distinct from, for example, qualities of the intellect or qualities of the

---

[16] V. above, pp. 130 ff.

body. "To be a fitting object of disapproval" is equivalent to "deserving blame," "blame" being the expression of disapproval. I think it preferable to define moral obligation in this way rather than in terms of moral admiration. For there are many morally obligatory actions which we should not admire a man for performing, though we should blame him for not performing them. I do not deserve moral admiration because I pay my ordinary debts since I have no real temptation not to pay them, but I should certainly deserve moral disapproval if I failed to pay them. One might say that I deserve at any rate approval for paying them and then define moral obligatoriness in terms of moral approval, but the appropriate approval in these cases would be so tepid, since the merit incurred by me is so slight, as to make it unsuitable to use this in defining a concept so connected with marked emotions as is that of moral obligation. Further, the consciousness of obligation seems to be more closely connected with the notions of shame and disapproval as fitting "sanctions" if we do not do what we ought than with the notion of approval if we do. Good is more connected with the positive side, obligation with the negative side, of ethics.

This definition has the advantage of providing the minimum non-naturalist theory of ethics, by which I mean the non-naturalist theory which a converted naturalist could accept with least divergence from his previous views. For it admits only one unanalysable concept, and it is more difficult to deny that there is a relation of fittingness not analysable in purely psychological terms than to deny that there is a quality, goodness, which is not thus analysable. In these days when naturalist tendencies are so strong, it is more than ever worth while for a non-naturalist to ask "What is the maximum of concessions I can make to the naturalist without destroying my whole view of ethics," and for a naturalist to ask "Have I refuted all forms of non-naturalist ethics or only some?"

There still remains a radical difference between doing something because I think that I shall be an actual object of disapproval if I do not do it and doing it because I think I shall be a fitting object of disapproval (*deserve* blame). The view suggested would not, however, necessarily imply that even the latter is the usual motive of moral action. The main motive should normally be derived directly from an apprehension of the nature of the proposed act and its consequences, and so of its objective fittingness, not from the hypothetical fact that I should deserve blame if I acted differently. It is obvious that the latter consideration does often play a part, but it is better for a man to tell the truth because he hates lies than because he would deserve to be blamed if he told lies.

It may be doubted, however, whether the analysis given brings out the full specific nature of the ethical ought. If not, we may have to admit a second indefinable concept in ethics, moral obligation, as distinct from fittingness. There is another possibility. It is arguable that the concept of fittingness is all we can have in an ethics without a theology, and that anything additional in the content of moral concepts is really supplied by the notion of a personal God, or at any rate by the idea of sin as going against the fundamental nature of reality so that we are fighting against the main stream of the universe when we act wrongly. If this further concept is a necessary part of our ethical thinking, we shall then have an argument from ethics to the existence of God or to other metaphysical conclusions.

What is in a person's mind when he recognises something to be his moral duty? There is (a) the consciousness that it is fitting for him to do it; (b) the consciousness that, if he does not do it, he will deserve condemnation; (c) the concept that there is in some sense a law binding him to do it, which law, while it does not compel in the sense of taking away his liberty to disobey it, yet has authority in another meaning of the term, so that morality consists in acting as if he were compelled by it. It may be that the third element is a theological concept, or one which, if adequately analysed, would have to be developed into such. Is it clear that there is anything more in the concept of duty besides these three concepts? I doubt it.

Among the things to which the relational property of being fitting can belong are of course included actions, and one of the meanings of "rightness" as applied to an action is "fittingness in relation to the situation." If by this is understood fittingness in relation to the situation as a whole you have my first sense of "rightness," if fittingness in relation to the situation as apparent to reasonable human beings my third, if fittingness in relation to the situation as apparent to the agent my second sense of rightness (except in so far as this sense of rightness includes in addition the notion of moral obligation). To say that an action is right is not the same as to say that it is good, for to call it "good" would mean that not necessarily it but some pro attitude relative to it was fitting; but no doubt all right actions are good in some sense, for in relation to them some pro attitude is fitting, if only the pro attitude of doing them, and we do say that it is always good to do what is right. On the other hand a right action is not necessarily good if by "good" is meant "fitting object of admiration," hence the distinction made by many philosophers. It was right of me to pay my bus fare home, but I do not deserve to be admired for it. Nor, as I have pointed out, are all fitting actions actions which we ought to do in the sense of being morally obliged to do them. Sometimes the fitting action is one which we cannot do or do not think of doing, and then we are not morally obliged to do it. In such cases we may or may not be morally to blame for previous action or neglect to act which prevented us from being able to do it or think of doing it.

To return from the analysis of obligation to that of good,

I think that one of the chief reasons why my analysis is liable to appear unsatisfactory is simply due to a misunderstanding. It will be objected against me that it is only fitting to approve, or have a pro attitude towards, what is good because we first know or believe it to be good and that, if we did not believe it to be good, there would be no ground for such an attitude, so that the attitude would not be fitting. The answer is that the ground lies not in some other ethical concept, goodness, but in the concrete, factual characteristics of what we pronounce good. Certain characteristics are such that the fitting response to what possesses them is a pro attitude, and that is all there is to it. We shall not be any better off if we interpolate an indefinable characteristic of goodness besides, for it is no easier to see that it follows directly from the nature of things that they are good than it is to see that it follows directly from their nature that they are fitting objects of a pro attitude. We see directly that pleasant experiences as such, natural beauty, unselfish love, are fitting objects of pro attitudes. That they are follows necessarily from their specific nature, as Moore held that it followed that they had the simple property of goodness. If we ask why we should admire so-and-so the answer is to recite his good deeds, not just specify that he is good without explaining further how he is good.

In the case of moral, and perhaps in some other cases, of goodness the situation is, however, a little more complicated than these remarks would suggest. For the fittingness of adopting an attitude of moral admiration toward an action depends on the rightness of the action (that is, its fittingness in certain respects), that is, on another non-naturalist value fact, itself in turn dependent on the natural, factual characteristics of the action. This may be so also in the case of the goodness of an aesthetic experience. That may depend, not merely on the factual characteristics of its object, but on a certain quality which would have to be likewise understood in terms of a non-naturalist fittingness. In a great work of art the different parts fit together harmoniously and they are a fitting representation of reality, or at least human life, not in the copying sense but in some deeper sense, and these may be regarded as non-natural characteristics which condition the work being aesthetically admirable, as rightness in some sense is a necessary condition of an action being morally admirable. It is difficult to see how a merely naturalist analysis could do justice to aesthetic fittingness. And that would explain the inclination to say that a work of art is admirable only because it is first good in some other sense, though "right" or "harmonious" would perhaps be a better word. Again it may be said that knowledge is a fitting object of pursuit or approval only because it has the non-natural characteristic of being true. I should not, however, call this a value fact or value property. Knowing what is true may be valuable, but not truth itself as a property of propositions.

We may now explain how it is that the connection between "good" and "ought" seems synthetic and not analytic. We often think of "ought" as expressing not only fittingness but moral obligation; and to say that we are under a moral obligation, where we can, to produce what it is fitting to choose for its own sake is a synthetic proposition. It will moreover remain so even if "we morally ought" has to be analysed as equivalent to "we should be fitting objects of moral disapproval if we did not do so." Propositions as to what kinds of things it is fitting to approve or disapprove are obviously synthetic. In this case, however, the character of the transaction is liable to be concealed by the use of the same word, "ought," in two different senses. At the same time the fact that fittingness carries with it a moral obligation, where we can do what is fitting, explains why the same word, "ought," is used to cover both concepts.

Moore now thinks there is equally good reason for rejecting

the view that "intrinsically good" is definable in terms of "ought" and for rejecting the view that "ought" is definable in terms of "intrinsically good," [17] the reason being in each case that we can think of the *definiendum* without thinking of the alleged *definiens;* [18] and Rashdall maintains that it is quite consistent to hold both that "good" is indefinable in Moore's sense and that "we can only bring out the real meaning of the idea by the use of words which equally imply the notion of 'ought.' " [19] So it may be questioned whether I should not, instead of defining "good" in the way in which I did, have just admitted that "good" and "ought" are correlative and left it at that. Or it may be asked why I defined "good" in terms of "ought" when I might equally well have defined "ought" in terms of "good" by saying that "I ought to do A" meant "of the actions that were in my power at the moment A was that one which would be most effective as a means for the production of good." Now if, as seems to be the case, Rashdall and Moore were thinking of "ought" as including moral obligation in its meaning, I should contend that "good" is not definable in terms of "ought" thus understood; but it does not follow that it is not definable in terms of "ought" understood only as asserting fittingness. I defined "good" in terms of "ought" rather than "ought" in terms of "good," because I found that I could not form a clear concept of intrinsic goodness without including in it the concept of ought, but that I could form a clear concept of ought without including in it the concept of good. Ought is also a wider concept in extension, for there are mental attitudes which we can describe as fitting and which are yet not directed towards the good. There are also fitting mental attitudes possible

---

[17] *The Philosophy of G. E. Moore* (Library of Living Philosophers), p. 610.

[18] Id., p. 599.

[19] *Theory of Good and Evil*, Vol. 1, pp. 135–6 n.

towards evil things, the anti attitudes, and even a fitting attitude towards indifferent things, the attitude of ignoring them.

It has been said that, if there is nothing intrinsically good, only an "ought," this takes the value out of life. Clearly, if my view did "take the value out of life," the view would be false, because it purports to be an analysis of what is meant by saying that people find value in life. But the objection in question is due to forgetting that we are only analysing what is meant by goodness and not giving an account of what things are good. A statement of the abstract distinguishing feature which belongs to all good things or our relations to these must from the nature of the case be jejune and colourless, because it has abstracted from all the concrete content which belongs to such things. If we admitted an indefinable intrinsic goodness besides the "ought," this intrinsic goodness would still not be itself valuable. What would be of value would be the experiences which had it; and these will be of value in any case. The intrinsic goodness of an experience, whether definable or indefinable, is not an additional value which we enjoy; to appreciate the experience is to appreciate its goodness. Life is of intrinsic value in so far as it consists of experiences which are worth having for their own sake and comprises qualities which are worth admiring for their own sake: you cannot ask for more value than that. And the value of these experiences and qualities cannot possibly be diminished by coming to the conclusion that what is meant by saying they have value is that it is fitting to have a favourable attitude towards them. They will be just as good as before.

It has been objected that my view is excessively indirect on the ground that it involves saying that, when we judge something to be good, we are really judging not it but our attitude towards it. But we must remember that fittingness as a relation has two terms, so that to judge what attitude is fitting to A is at the same time to judge A. The judgement is no more about ourselves, who constitute one term of the relation, than it is about A. To say it is fitting to approve A is to say that A is of such a nature as to call for our approval. We can only see whether we ought to have a pro attitude towards something by seeing what the nature of that something is, and the right pro attitude is dictated by its nature. We do not first learn what attitudes towards A are fitting and then decide that A is good; on the contrary to learn that certain attitudes towards A are fitting is to learn that A is good.

It has also been objected that my view involves a vicious infinite regress on the ground that, if to judge something good is to judge that it is fitting to approve it, this amounts to saying that to judge it good is to approve my approval and so on *ad infinitum*. But the infinite regress would arise only if we meant by "fitting" just "good" and therefore were defining "good" in terms of itself. In that case to judge A good would be to judge that it was good to approve A, and therefore it would be to judge that it was good to approve of approving A and so on *ad infinitum*. But, because "good" and "fitting" are different terms, the regress need not be carried beyond its second step. I did not say that "it is fitting to approve A" meant "it is fitting to approve my approval of A," but only that "A is good" meant "it is fitting to approve A." "Fitting" must not be itself defined in terms of another fittingness or of anything else whatever. "It is fitting to approve," I suppose, entails "it is fitting to approve of approving A," and so on *ad infinitum;* but it is no objection to the truth of a proposition that it would entail the truth of an infinite number of propositions, unless it entailed that we could not assert the first proposition intelligently without having already grasped all these infinite other propositions. It is no objection to our knowing the truth of the proposition that "London is the capital of England" to say that it entails that it is true that it is true that London is the capital of England and so on *ad infinitum*. It would be an objection only if it were the case that we could not be justified in asserting that London was the capital of England without having first recognised the truth of this infinite number of propositions.

It has also been made an objection against my view that it makes all value judgements ultimately hypothetical. To say that "A is a fitting object of a certain pro attitude" would seem to mean either that, if any one adopts the attitude, he will be doing what is fitting, or that if any one is confronted with or thinks of A he ought to adopt the attitude. To this I should reply: (1) We have to admit in any case that the very important class of ethical judgements which assert that an action ought to be done are hypothetical unless and until the action to which they refer has been done.[20] If I ask what I ought to do next I am asking which of the alternative actions possible will have the attribute of fulfilling my obligations if it is done. It would not therefore be so paradoxical if we had to admit that judgements involving good are also hypothetical. (2) If there is nobody to have an attitude of approval towards them, "good" may still be viewed as a positive characteristic in whatever is good, namely, that of requiring approval. (3) In an actual case when I say "A is good," I am feeling approval of A myself, and therefore A is always the object of an actually existing pro attitude of a kind deemed fitting by me. True, my judgement does not confine itself to asserting that my attitude to A is fitting, but lays it down also that the attitude would be the fitting one for anybody else to have whether anybody is actually having it or not, so it may be contended that it is still partly hypothetical. But at any rate it has a categorical core, and this will explain why we are inclined to think all such propositions categorical not hypothetical in character.

---

[20] This is not to say that they are all hypothetical imperatives in Kant's sense, for their obligatoriness still does not depend merely on our desires.

A view like mine is for various reasons in a particularly strong position as against naturalism. In the first place, naturalism is commonly supported by doubts as to whether we can really be aware of an indefinable quality, goodness, but it is impossible to doubt at any rate that we are aware of some relation signified by the term "ought" and *prima facie* different from any purely psychological relation. As long as the only alternative to some form of naturalism or subjectivism seems to be the view that good is just a simple quality, it seems open to doubt whether naturalism or subjectivism is not true. It has been asked whether anybody besides a few philosophers has thought they could perceive such a simple quality. But it cannot be doubted that practically everybody is aware of the relations of fittingness and moral obligation, which are lumped together under the term "ought," though they may not always distinguish them clearly. The difficulty arose, on my view, through looking for the indefinable where it could not be found. We are not clearly aware of an indefinable non-natural goodness, but we are of fittingness and obligation. Now on my view the reason why a naturalist definition of "good" is unsatisfactory is, not because good is indefinable, but because these relations are included in the notion of good. A principal objection made by me against naturalist definitions of "good" was just that, if "good" were defined naturalistically, it would be no more rational, right, fitting to pursue the good than the bad and that good would carry with it no moral obligation to pursue the good.

Secondly, the most popular naturalist modes of analysis of good are in terms of various pro attitudes, such as interest or approval. Now I have defined "good" as what ought to be the object of a pro attitude. So, if the view I have suggested is true, what the naturalists are doing is to take the concrete, more distinctly perceptible element in goodness but omit the relational element. Therefore, although people feel as if something had been left out, they, misled partly by the fact that "good" is grammatically an adjective, look for some other quality and, being unable to find it, become more and more inclined to adopt a naturalist view. My theory explains the connection between emotional attitudes and judgements about goodness or badness, which connection is often taken as an argument for naturalism. In general, if a judgement about the goodness of something is simply a judgement to the effect that we ought to have a certain attitude, we can easily see how it is that people have taken it to be a judgement about the attitude actually adopted. The only other element in my analysis besides the purely psychological ones is a relation, and it is a well known historical fact that philosophers have been apt to overlook the importance of relations. We are not conscious of relations with the same vividness and distinctness as we are of qualities, and they are harder to abstract from the rest of our experience and thought. We do not have a distinct idea of what it is like to perceive between-ness or with-ness, in the sense in which we have a distinct idea of what it is like to see blue or to feel fear. And what I have said applies most of all to formal, very general relations like the one in question. Even the vitally important relation of logically necessary connection or entailment is hardly noticed as a special relation by anybody but philosophers, though it must be apprehended in particular instances by everybody who can argue at all. It is no more difficult to admit the relation of fittingness than to admit, the relations of similarity or consistency, or even the relations expressed by "of" or "towards" in "approve of" or "feel emotions towards," relations which even the naturalist must admit in his account of ethics. None of these relations can really be said to be given in sensation.

So we can see how those already disposed not to admit any non-naturalist element in knowledge could persuade themselves that they had given an adequate analysis of ethical concepts when, fastening on the only concrete non-relational elements in the concept, they had analysed good in terms of the same psychological factors that I admit in my analysis but had left out the relation or relations signified by "ought." I thus admit an important element of truth in naturalism. It is in any case difficult to believe that we could have formed the idea of good if we had never had any pro attitudes and this is used as an argument for naturalism. My view gives an explanation alternative to naturalism.

It is also easier to understand how the subjectivist theory that "good" is relative to the person judging could grow up, for "good" is relative to some person or other in the sense that it means that towards which it is fitting for a person to have a pro attitude. This being so, it is easy to fall into confusion and regard it as relative in some other sense. We may agree that it would be senseless to speak of anything as good if nobody could conceivably ever desire or appreciate it; but the view does not require that it should be actually desired or appreciated by anybody. It may well be the case that it is fitting to desire and appreciate something which men are not yet developed enough to desire or appreciate. I make good and evil relative to all rational beings, not only to human beings, and this in two respects: (1) If it is fitting for somebody to have a pro attitude towards *a*, the judgement that it is thus fitting for him will be true, whoever makes it, whether man, Martian, angel, or God. (2) If it is fitting for any being to have a pro attitude towards *a* as such in a given respect, it will be fitting for any other being who knows what *a* is factually like also to have a pro attitude.[21] This will apply even if

---

[21] The pro attitude will, however, not necessarily always be the same. It may be fitting for A to admire B without its being fitting for B to admire himself. Or it may be fitting for A to be grateful to B, who has rendered him great services, without its being fitting for C to be grateful to B where C knows of B's services to A but has himself received no such benefits from B. But it will be fitting for everybody to adopt some pro attitude in all cases

a is only judged good as a means to something else, since the causal laws which make it a good means are not dependent on the subjective characteristics of the person who judges whether or not they hold, but it is more important to see that it is true of intrinsic goodness. This is not to say that all rational beings will be able to appreciate *a* in all cases where *a* is good; but if not they will not be able to take a fitting attitude towards *a*. A tone-deaf man cannot take a fitting attitude towards Beethoven's music as such, because he does not know what it is like, though he may of course take a fitting attitude towards the situation created by his own deficiencies. Usually the inability to appreciate *a* will occur because the person in question cannot obtain the experience requisite to find out what *a* is like factually, but it may be due to lack of the requisite emotional capacity. This is not of course the same as to say that all rational beings who know *a* ought morally to have a pro attitude towards *a*. If they do not have it, they are lacking in some respect, but they are not necessarily morally to blame for this.

Actions, it may be urged, present an exception to the rule I have laid down, since in the same objective situation a particular action may well be right for me and wrong for you. But the whole situation relevant to the rightness of the action includes subjective as well as objective factors; and, if these are taken into account, the action as done by me would not be the same as the action as done by you, and it would be quite consistent to approve of one action and disapprove of the other. If the action as done by me is really good it is fitting that all rational beings who know of it should feel approval, and unfitting that they should not; and this is true even

where the admiration or gratefulness of A is justified. B should not admire himself, but he should realise that to do what he was doing was in certain respects preferable to different courses, otherwise there would be little merit in his doing it, and, without being grateful to B, C should approve B's action *qua* beneficial to A.

where they are of such a nature that for them it would have been quite wrong to do what I did. Even a person of very ordinary intelligence is quite capable of making this distinction and approving of, for example, the marriage of A to B, while realising quite well that it would not have been at all appropriate for himself to marry B, even if it had been possible for him to do so. I think it is implied by the notion of goodness that anything which we rightly regard as intrinsically good will be a fitting object of a pro attitude on the part of any beings who know what it is like, though whether and how it can be attained will depend on conditions which are not necessarily the same for all rational beings but might vary widely as between us and, for example, the inhabitants, if any, of Mars or Venus. It is very difficult to see how we could ever be justified in saying something was good if no human being, even if he knew what it was, were capable of appreciating it; but some propositions are no doubt true which we could never be justified in asserting, and there is certainly no self-contradiction in the suggestion that there are such non-human goods. I think it is likely that there are; the universe is rich. It would be rash of a canine philosopher to say that nothing was good which could not be appreciated by a dog.

My analysis would also explain how it is that the application of "good" and "bad" are in the first instance learned through noticing and imitating the emotional attitudes of others. As these circumstances are often regarded as constituting a strong argument for naturalism, this may be of some importance. A young child seems to learn the application and even the meaning of the words "good" and "bad" by hearing them spoken in tones or with gestures that indicate approval or disapproval, and this is taken as evidence that "bad" *means* "disapproved," and that "good" means "approved." But clearly, if "bad" does not mean just "what is disapproved" (either by the speaker or by people generally) but "what ought to be disapproved," this will also explain why the expression of approval or disapproval is the natural and normal way of teaching a child both what is meant by "good" or "bad" and to what things he should apply the terms. For, in so far as "good" means that towards which you ought to feel approval and "bad" that towards which you ought to feel disapproval, it follows that in order to teach a child the meaning and application of the terms you must express to it the attitudes of approval and disapproval on suitable occasions. In so far as "good" means "what we ought to pursue" and "bad" "what we ought to avoid," ethical education will consist in inducing the child by example and precept to pursue and avoid what it is suitable to pursue or to avoid. If to call something "good" only signifies that it is a fitting object of certain attitudes, it is easy to see why the attitudes should figure predominantly in learning the use of the word. The attitudes are expressed by others as a means to inducing the child to take them himself. Now we learn best to do the right things by doing them ourselves, and therefore in order to learn when it is fitting to take certain attitudes the child must be encouraged to take them himself.

My definition also has the advantage over any other I know, whether naturalist or non-naturalist, of explaining how it is that "good" is used in so many different senses, a fact which has for many minds been a serious obstacle to taking the view that it ever stands for a simple indefinable quality intuitively perceived. On my view it naturally will stand for various different senses according to the pro attitude in question. Further, if goodness is, as I have suggested, a relational property, this makes it easier to maintain that it is a non-natural concept, for all other plausible cases of such concepts are, I think, cases not of qualities but of relational properties.

A criticism which some will direct against me is that I have already surrendered the fort, because the only non-natural concept retained by me in ethics is not one that is specifically ethical at all, but one that belongs even to purely prudential action. However even purely prudential action presupposes value judgements, if only that one's own pain is bad and one's own pleasure good. What is wrong with egoistic hedonism is not that it does not presuppose a goodness which if it is to serve the purpose even of the egoistic hedonist could not be equated with an empirical property, but that it is unduly limited in its view as to what things are good and what things we ought to pursue. It may, however, be argued that, while I admit value judgements, I do not do justice to those judgements which are specifically ethical. But it may be that the distinction between specifically ethical and other value judgements is not that the former admit new simple concepts not included in the latter but that they admit a new class of things as having value. I am not indeed prepared to commit myself to the view that there is no irreducible non-naturalistic value concept except fittingness, since I am not fully satisfied with the proposed analysis of moral obligation in terms of fittingness; but in any case fittingness, as understood by me, is not to be equated with the characteristic of being an effective means to the production of something. That fittingness is not to be thus identified is shown by the fact that it is often fitting to do something or aim at something for its own sake and not merely as a means. Further, even where we perform some act merely as a means to something else, its fittingness as a means could not be a ground why it was morally obligatory or even prudent to do it, unless it was also fitting to treat its results or some of them as ends-in-themselves. Nor, when I say that it is fitting to admire morally good actions, do I mean merely that our admiration is a useful means to something else. In none of these three cases could "fitting" possibly be translated as just "efficient as a means."

Why did I make fittingness rather than moral obligation the fundamental concept of ethics? Might I not have analysed the fittingness of doing A in terms of the moral obligation to do A if we could? My reasons for not adopting this course were as follows: (a) It is clear that for me to be under a moral obligation to do A I must first believe that it is fitting for me to do A. Therefore the concept of moral obligation presupposes the concept of fittingness and not vice versa. (b) There is no verbal contradiction in saying both that my own pleasure is a good and that I am never under a *moral* obligation to pursue it as such, or in saying that I am under no moral obligation to sacrifice somebody else's lesser good for the sake of my own greater good. Therefore we cannot use "ought" in the moral obligation sense when defining "good." (c) As we have seen, "good" does not always mean only what ought to be chosen; it sometimes means what ought to be admired, or be the object of other pro attitudes such as desire or liking, and we cannot say that we are under a moral obligation to admire, desire, or like something, but we can say that we ought, in the fittingness sense, to have these feelings towards it.

CHAPTER VI

Consequences of the Analysis for a General Theory of Ethics

What bearing has my analysis on the question of the general criteria for determining what is right? Here the chief controversy in recent years has perhaps been between the "ideal utilitarians," who make the right depend solely on the good, and the adherents of a view like that of Ross, who maintains that we have *"prima facie"* duties not explicable simply by reference to the amount of good produced or likely to be produced. The "ideal utilitarian," while not restricting good to pleasure as the hedonistic utilitarian does, insists that the ultimate ground which makes an action right must always be its conduciveness to the production of good. Others have maintained in opposition that there is no necessary connection between good and ought and that it may quite well be our duty, for example, to keep a promise even though there is every reason to think that we could do more good by breaking it. In this connection Sir David Ross introduced the conception of *"prima facie* duties,"* by which he means obligations which hold not absolutely but only in the absence of a stronger obligation.[1] To say we have a *prima facie* duty to do a certain kind of thing is thus to say that we ought to do it on its own account, *other things being equal.* To do what will produce the greatest good is held by him in this sense to be a *prima*

---

[1] Ross, *The Right and the Good*, Chap. II.

facie duty,[2] but not the only one. Thus we have also, for example, a *prima facie* duty to keep promises or to make reparation for wrongs we have done, that is, the fact that I have, for example, made a promise is always an *independent* reason why I should keep it; and if these obligations conflict with the obligation to produce the greatest good, they will not necessarily give way to it. They may do so or may not, but no general rule can be laid down for deciding which obligation should be regarded as more binding.

There is no doubt that Ross's view represents better than utilitarianism the way in which we actually think, but it still may be held that the latter gives a better account of the ultimate reason why acts are obligatory. Now I think we must admit with Ross that the obligation, for example, to keep promises, is not to be explained solely by the consequences of doing so; but the utilitarian, if he is not also a hedonist, may meet this by maintaining that the practice of keeping promises is good-in-itself, or at least that the action of breaking a promise is intrinsically bad. In that case the obligation would not be explained entirely by the consequences, actual or likely, of the act, and yet it would be derivable from the obligation to produce the greatest good, as the utilitarian maintains. For in the good produced by an action must be included not only the good lying in its consequences but also any intrinsic goodness that belongs to the action itself in its own right. This intrinsic good might indeed be outweighed by the badness of its consequences, so that the ideal utilitarian must admit the possibility of circumstances arising which would make it a duty to break a promise or violate other laws which are generally morally binding. But in this he would be in agreement with Ross, who holds that two *prima facie* duties may clash and that one will then have to give way to the other.

---

[2] With certain modifications of detail which we need not discuss here.

Now, if the utilitarian takes the line indicated, it seems impossible to refute his theory at the usual level at which the controversy is conducted. But suppose we define "good" as "what ought to be chosen, produced, or pursued." Then to say that something is "intrinsically good" will be to say that one ought to choose, produce, or pursue it on its own account, not indeed under all circumstances, because its production or pursuit might involve the sacrifice of something better, but at any rate other things being equal. But this is to say that we have a *prima facie* duty to choose, produce, or pursue it. So to give a list of our different *prima facie* duties will be to give a list of the different kinds of things (including actions) which are intrinsically good.[3] What would then be meant by "the greatest good"? Presumably that which we ought to pursue, produce, or choose above all other alternatives. This might seem to make utilitarianism a tautology, but it would at any rate be a Pyrrhic victory for the latter. The utilitarian principle is that what we ought to do is derivable from the good, while the reverse is true if my analysis is correct. The utilitarian would be guilty of a vicious circle if he insisted on deriving the "ought" from the "good" and then accepted an analysis which made "good" itself definable in terms of "ought." That it makes the principle that we ought always to produce the greatest good in our power necessarily true seems to me the chief argument for utilitarianism against Ross's view, for it is hard to believe that it could ever be a duty deliberately to produce less good when we could produce more; but, if the analysis I have given were adopted, this principle would be accepted in a form which did not contradict the contentions of Ross, for to say that we ought to produce the greatest good in our power would then only be to say that we ought to act

---

[3] I have pointed out that "intrinsically good" may be applied to actions both in this sense and in the different sense of "being fitting objects of admiration." I am not here talking about the latter sense.

in the way which was preferable above all others; that is, the way which ought to be chosen. The antithesis between a view which based the "ought" on the "good" and a view which based it on *prima facie* duties would thus disappear. There would disappear also the duality between two kinds of moral criteria, conduciveness to the production of good and fulfilment of obligations independent of the good produced, which must be present in any non-utilitarian view that does not disregard consequences altogether. This is surely in so far a gain. There would still be an antithesis between a view according to which what we ought to do depended entirely on consequences and a view according to which it depended partly on the intrinsic nature of the action; but the former view seems to me very unreasonable, for surely we must take account of the intrinsic nature of an action before we decide whether to do it or not. There would also be an antithesis between a view like that of the Hebrews which emphasized more the ought of moral obligation and a view like the Greek which emphasized more the ought of fittingness and the attractive nature of concrete ends. But the particular antithesis under discussion between Ross and the utilitarians would have gone.

Ross might indeed reply that he did not mean by a *"prima facie* duty" what one ought to do in the fittingness sense of "ought," which was the sense in which "ought" occurred in my definition of "good," but in the moral-obligation sense of "ought." But it is clear that for an action to be one which I ought to do in the latter sense it must also be one which I believe I ought to do in the former. It can hardly be my moral duty to do something which I do not believe to be the most fitting thing in the circumstances to do. Therefore of the two senses of "ought" the fittingness sense must be basic, in that I cannot determine what I ought to do in the other sense without first considering what I ought to do in the "fittingness" sense of "ought." This is so even if the moral-obligation sense is not analysable in terms of the fittingness sense, as I suggested it might possibly be. And therefore it is fittingness which we must consider in discussing the ultimate reasons which put us under a moral obligation to do some things rather than others. For it is not on the question whether we morally ought to do what is fitting that the utilitarians and Ross are at variance, but on the question what actions are fitting and why they are so. To the former question both sides would give an affirmative answer.

I distinguished earlier the sense of "good" in which it means "fitting object of choice or pursuit" from the sense in which it means "worthy of admiration," and if good was analysed in the latter way it would not carry with it the consequences I have suggested, for it is a synthetic proposition that it is always fitting to produce the state of affairs which is most worthy of admiration (and not, I think, a true one). But this cannot be the sense of "good" under discussion in the utilitarian controversy, since this dispute is about what we ought to do, and therefore we are in it directly concerned with fitting choices and not with fitting admiration or other emotional attitudes. Again, it is certain that pleasure is not "admirable" (worthy of admiration), and yet it is reasonable to say in the sense under discussion between Ross and the utilitarians that pleasure is good.

It may be objected that there seem clearly to be cases where it is at least arguable that the act which I ought to perform is not, as far as we can tell, the act which is likely to produce the greatest good, for example the case of stealing from a rich miser in order to give to a deserving poor man. It seems a perfectly intelligible and not self-contradictory position to admit both on the one hand that I should do more good if I stole the money and gave it to the poor man and on the other that I still ought to refrain from stealing it. But I suggest that the distinction here is really between (a) what I ought to prefer in abstraction from the only available means of producing it, (b) what I ought to choose to produce with the means at my disposal. Thus I ought to prefer in the abstract that A who is poor should have £100 rather than B who is rich, but I ought not to choose that he should have it through my stealing. We think it a greater good, that is a state of affairs which it is more fitting to produce, in itself, that A should have the hundred pounds, and other things being equal I ought to bring this about if I have the chance. But other things are not equal, since I can only bring it about by stealing, and it may still be better that B should have the hundred pounds, and not A, than that A should have the hundred pounds obtained by stealing.

A similar objection is that, if "the greatest good" means "that which we ought to choose in preference to any other," it would seem to follow that it was a tautology to say that I ought, apart from ulterior consequences, always to choose my own greater good in preference to somebody else's lesser good, or the greater good of a total stranger in preference to my mother's lesser good. But these statements are not tautologies. They would be hotly disputed, and to dispute them is certainly not equivalent to the self-contradiction of asserting that the greater good is not greater. Therefore it may be objected that my theory is mistaken since it makes into a tautology what is plainly a synthetic proposition. To this objection we may reply in the same way as we did to the previous one. What I am choosing in cases like this is not just my mother's good but my mother's good as produced by myself. (I cannot indeed, strictly speaking, choose the former in abstraction from the latter.) Now the production of my mother's good by myself is a different thing from the production of my mother's good by a stranger, and therefore it might easily be the case that I ought to choose the production of my mother's good by myself in preference to the production of a stranger's equal good by myself, and yet that the stranger's son ought to choose the production of his parent's good by himself in preference to the production of my parent's good by himself. To speak of the good of the parents as equal means that, other things being equal, neither has more claim to pursuit than the other; but, if I have a special relation involving obligation to one person which I have not to the other, other things are not equal. It does not follow, because the good of A and that of B are equally worth pursuit *per se,* that therefore the whole—good of A plus the pursuit and attainment of A's good by me—will have a value equal to the other whole—good of B plus the pursuit and attainment of B's good by me. Similarly, production of my own good by myself is lacking in a value possessed by the action of producing somebody else's good, or, to put it in other words, it is sometimes fitting to choose to produce another's good rather than my own, just because it is his, not mine. The reverse may also be true; it would not be right of me to sacrifice my own moral good by, for instance, dishonesty on the ground that if I did not take an opportunity of stealing somebody else would and that I was therefore unselfishly sacrificing my good in order to save his.

The objection would be stronger if I gave "ought to be desired" as an analysis of good. To say that I ought to desire the good of a stranger as much as the good of my mother is quite obviously false. Nor can my desire for the good of my mother be reduced to the desire that I should produce her good, for it is fitting that I should desire her good more than the equal good of a stranger even in cases where it is not in my power to produce it, or where for special reasons, for instance because I have made a promise, it is my duty to further the stranger's good rather than hers. The same applies to Ross's definition of "good" as "worthy or fit object of satisfaction," [4] since it is also fitting that her good should give me more satisfaction. If and when such an analysis of "good" gives the true meaning of the word, we must admit that what is good relatively to me is not always equally good relatively to you.[5] We could then call the goods of two different people equal only in relation to a third observer who had no special relations of affection or obligation to either of the parties. I think this a reason for defining "good" in most usages in terms of some pro attitude other than desire or satisfaction.

Were then the people who disputed as to whether the utilitarian principle was or was not true merely getting excited about a tautology? Surely there was a real issue? But we must remember that to say that, if certain propositions are analysed in a certain way, they become tautologies is not the same as to say that the proposition that they are to be analysed in that way is itself a tautology. Further, the controversy is certainly mixed up with questions which cannot be settled simply by accepting my analysis. There is in the first place the question whether the rightness (fittingness) of an action depends solely on its consequences, actual or likely. Of this question my analysis certainly does not dispose, for it is possible compatibly with this analysis either to include actions among the things which ought to be chosen on their own account or not. The question is not indeed identical with the question whether utilitarianism is true, for one might return a negative answer to it, while remaining a utilitarian, by including in the good produced a goodness belonging to the action itself as such. But it may be contended that utilitarians have not paid enough attention to this possibility, while non-utilitarians have not paid sufficient attention to the consequences.

Further, even if we grant that we ought always to choose

---

[4] *Foundations of Ethics*, pp. 275, 279.
[5] Ross makes this admission, id., p. 282.

the greatest good in the sense in which "ought" signifies "fit-tingness," it may still be contended that it does not follow that we are always under a moral obligation to choose the greatest good; and this might still be made an object of dispute, especially as Ross meant by *prima facie* duty not merely what is fitting but what is, other things being equal, morally oblig-atory. Most people would admit that their own pleasure was good and a fitting object of pursuit, but would deny that they were under a moral obligation to pursue it. I think it is clearly self-evident that we cannot be under a moral obligation to do anything unless we think this the most fitting course available, but the converse proposition that whatever course we think most fitting is morally obligatory on us is somewhat less cer-tain (chiefly owing to the doubts about the obligatoriness of pursuing one's own pleasure), though I have a strong inclina-tion to believe it true *a priori*.

The conception of *prima facie* duties has sometimes been criticised on the ground that it is clearly secondary and pre-supposes the conception of absolute rightness, and some justification for this criticism is provided by Ross's suggestion that they are to be viewed as *tendencies* to be absolute duties.[6] But to say that something is a *prima facie* duty is surely al-ready to say not merely that there is a tendency for it to be fitting that we should adopt a certain attitude to it, but that it is absolutely fitting that we should do so, and also absolutely obligatory on us as far as it is in our power to take up the attitude at all. The attitude in question is not necessarily that of performing the act; this will be fitting only if certain other conditions are fulfilled. But it is categorically, not merely hypothetically, fitting that we should take the attitude of ap-proving the proposed act in the respect under consideration (even if it would be wrong on the whole), of considering its

---

[6] *The Right and the Good*, pp. 28–9; *Foundations of Ethics*, p. 86.

performance favourably in this respect, of deploring and trying to make up for the omission if we cannot fulfil the *prima
facie* duty without violating another more important, of
mitigating our condemnation of the act in so far as it has this
feature in its favour, etc. As a matter of fact, even in the exceptional cases where it is our duty, for example, to break a
promise, we shall never, if we act rightly, let our attitude and
hardly ever our behaviour be quite unaffected by the fact that
we have promised. We shall, for instance, explain ourselves to
the promisee and offer to make it up to him in some other
way.[7] We shall at least regret the breach of faith. We shall
look about for ways of avoiding it. We shall probably ask
for release from the promise, if we can communicate with the
promisee in time, rather than just break it. In general we shall
adopt a pro attitude towards the act *qua* keeping a promise,
though perhaps an anti attitude towards it in other respects,
for instance, *qua* greatly hurting somebody. That we have
made a promise must always be a factor to be taken into
account, and to take anything into account is a positive attitude even if it does not lead to action in accord with the
promise being taken, but it is hardly conceivable that the
ideally right way of performing whatever action is performed
would not be appreciably affected by the fact that we have
promised. Still more obvious is it that, when we refer to a
whole class of acts and describe promise-keeping as a *prima
facie* duty, we are enjoining a very important positive attitude
towards a large part of conduct. The primary ethical intuition,
I think, is not that any action as a whole is fitting or unfitting,
but that it is fitting or unfitting in certain respects. It is indeed
often the case that we are entitled to conclude that an action

---

[7] The obligation to do this is most doubtful in cases where the promise
has been extracted from us by violence or fraud, but in such cases it is
doubtful whether there is even any *prima facie* fittingness about keeping it.
If there is, it is certainly appropriate to regret breaking it.

is unfitting as a whole from having seen only its unfittingness in one particular respect, but this is because in such cases there is obviously no other aspect that we can see to counterbalance this or because the action seems to be done from a motive which would make the action immoral even if it happened by some accident to have good consequences, as when a man squanders on his own pleasures money without which it will be impossible for him to pay his debts.

Some of the difficulties in ethics no doubt arise because of the different senses in which "good" is used; that is, the different pro attitudes which people have in mind when they call something "good," or are at least aggravated by these differences. For instance, it is contended on the one hand that all goods must be commensurable because we have to decide between them in order to act, and on the other hand that it can never be morally right to sacrifice moral good for the sake of any other kind of good. In dealing with this question I should first ask in what sense "good" was being used. If we mean by "good" what ought to be admired, it is obvious that pleasure is not good and moral virtue is. If we mean by "good" what it is fitting to welcome or take satisfaction in, it seems to me that it would be unreasonable asceticism to insist that it is fitting to welcome less or take less satisfaction in the happiness of millions than in a slight moral advance by one man. If "good" means "desirable," it seems to me still clearer that it is fitting to desire the former more than the latter. If "good" means what ought to be pursued or chosen, the answer seems to me similar except for one reservation. Suppose I had to choose between causing a slight moral advance in myself or somebody else and giving a great deal of pleasure to millions and could not do both. Suppose in that case I believed it was my moral duty to do the latter. Then for that very reason I should be sacrificing moral good as well as pleasure if I did not do it, for I should then be doing the morally worse action.

There is then a sense in which it could never be my moral duty to sacrifice my present moral good for any amount of pleasure (or, for that matter, moral good) of anybody else. For suppose it were my duty to sacrifice it. In that case I should be doing my duty and therefore not sacrificing my present moral good, so the supposition is a self-contradictory one. But it might well be my duty to sacrifice some future moral good. For example it might be my duty for various reasons to accept a post although it seemed likely to me that the post would have in some degree bad effects on my character. A situation like this must very commonly arise. It is a well founded psychological generalization that a post carrying with it a great deal of money and power is more likely to be bad than good for the character of most people who have the chance of obtaining it, yet it is certainly often their duty to accept it and incur this risk for the sake of the good they may do.

Another difficulty for the ideal utilitarian, and indeed for other writers on ethics, is this. An infinite amount is obviously greater than any finite amount. Therefore it seems to follow that, however much higher in the scale of values virtue is than pleasure, provided the two are commensurable at all, any finite amount of virtue or higher good, however large, would be less good than an infinite amount of pleasure. In that case there would be more good in the life of a single being which enjoyed itself continually without achieving any other goods except pleasure, provided that being lived for ever, than there would be in the lives of any finite number of beings who lived for only a finite time, however much non-hedonistic good was realized in their lives, since that could not *ex hypothesi* be infinite. Yet surely if we had the power either to create a universe in which there existed only one being with a consciousness like that of a lower animal which lived for ever and enjoyed itself in its own way continually, or to create one in which there were a number of beings with finite lives possessed of goodness, happiness, love, knowledge, and aesthetic experience far beyond that of the best and most fortunate men we know, it would be fitting and our duty to create not the former but the latter? This may be used as an argument against utilitarianism, whether hedonistic or ideal; but a difficulty is left even if we discard utilitarianism, because it is almost or quite as paradoxical to say that the first universe would be a better universe than the second as it would be to say that we ought to create the first universe rather than the second. The difficulty seems to arise from taking too quantitative a view of good and to disappear if we realise that to call something good is not to say that it has a quality, goodness, of which you can have more or less, but to say that we ought to have certain attitudes towards it. If so, it ceases to seem evident that an infinite amount of certain good kinds of experience would be better than a finite amount of certain other good kinds. It does not by any means follow that, if we ought to produce something, other things being equal, we ought to produce an infinite amount of it in preference to a finite amount of any other kind of thing which we ought to produce. This seems to follow only if we assume that the sole reason for producing something is because it has a certain quality, goodness, distinct from the fact that we ought to produce it. In that case, since the only legitimate reason for action is constituted by this quality, goodness, the only reason for choosing A rather than B must be because A possesses or is likely to bring into existence a greater amount of this quality than B. But it need not be, on my view. Similarly, if goodness is a quality, A must have more of this quality than B if it is to be better than B; but, if to say that something is good is to say that we ought to take a pro attitude to it, it is again not evident that the strength of our pro attitude towards an infinite series ought to be greater than the strength of our pro attitude towards any finite series. We cannot in any case be expected to approve or welcome infinitely the infinite series.

My analysis thus removes what seems to me a serious difficulty for ethics, and I do not see how it can be removed as long as we hold that goodness is a quality possessed by all good things. Two other solutions have been suggested, but neither of them seems to be acceptable. One is to say that the goodness of pleasure and the higher kinds of goodness are incommensurable, so that no amount of pleasure, however great, can exceed in value any amount of moral goodness, however small. But this seems to me totally incredible. It surely would be less of an evil for me to do something slightly immoral, for example, not make as much effort as I morally ought to concentrate on my work during the next half-hour, than it would be for the whole human race to suffer intense agony or even to lose all pleasure for the space of a year, even if this made no difference for good or evil to their moral character? Another suggested solution is that, though pleasure is always in some degree good, so that the longer the hypothetical lower animal lived the better, the degree of goodness attached to a given amount of pleasure enjoyed by it might diminish progressively after a certain point, so that, when its existence had gone on for a very long time, the goodness of each successive increment of pleasure asymptotically approached zero.[8] But this also seems to me very difficult to hold, for I cannot see why the animal's pleasures should be supposed to diminish in value the longer it lived, provided their intensity as pleasures did not diminish. The animal could not be morally blamed for confining itself to the lower pleasures. We need not suppose it to be dissatisfied or bored with them; and, if it were, this would contradict the hypothesis by showing itself in a diminution of pleasure. No doubt the value of a total life may be

---

[8] V. McTaggart, *The Nature of Existence*, Vol. II, § 852.

viewed as dependent not only on the value of its parts but on the way in which these are related, and the value, if any, dependent on the relation of the successive stages of the animal's life might conceivably diminish to zero as its monotonous life continued. But this would not affect the value of its successive pleasant states of consciousness in themselves, which would surely be as great in the later as in the earlier ones, provided they were equally pleasant. It might still be argued that, however small the value of each specious present was, the total value of the infinite series would surpass any finite quantity of another good, whether or not it was augmented by any value due to the relation of its parts. The success of my theory in solving the difficulty where other objective theories fail is in my opinion an argument in its favour. This is not the only point in regard to which difficulty has been felt about a quantitative treatment of good. Yet the ordinary view is bound to treat good quantitatively, for choice between alternatives must depend on one alternative having more of this quality, goodness, than another in so far as the choice is dependent on the quality goodness at all, as it must in some cases be dependent, even on Ross's view. But, if to say that A is better than B is not to say that it has more of a certain quality, goodness, than B, but only that we ought to adopt a certain attitude towards it, that is, prefer it to B, this explains why a quantitative treatment is not satisfactory.

Another argument in favour of my view is that it explains the fact that goodness is on the face of it a quite different concept from that of any ordinary quality. There is obviously a sense in which one could give a complete description of something without saying whether it was good or bad, which fact shows goodness to be something different from an ordinary quality of the thing which is pronounced good. The naturalist recognises this, but there is another condition which his account does not fulfil. He makes goodness consist in a relation to certain psychological states, but not a relation of a kind which we could see to follow necessarily from the other characteristics of the thing which is good. It does not follow necessarily from the nature of anything, as far as we can see, that it will in fact be admired or approved or desired or pursued by human beings. But the relation in which I hold goodness to consist, that of being a fitting object of a pro attitude, can be seen to follow necessarily from the factual nature of anything that we rightly pronounce to be intrinsically good. If something is a fitting object of a pro attitude at all, it could not fail to be so without its factual nature being different from what it is. Yet fittingness is still not itself a part of its factual nature. The analysis I have accepted thus does provide a considerable amount of real help in solving philosophical puzzles about ethics.

But many people will remain unsatisfied with a theory like mine, because instead of explaining our duties by reference to the good it leaves us with a set of *prima facie* duties for performing which no reason has been given. They will have the feeling that the theory gives no real ground why we ought to do one thing rather than another, while utilitarianism at least does that. It is important not to state this objection wrongly. We must not express it by saying that the fact that something ought to be produced, chosen, approved or pursued, etc., is not the reason why it is good. For my theory is not that this constitutes the reason why something is good, but that this is what is meant by saying that it is good. The reason why something, A, is good, that is, why we ought to adopt these attitudes to A, lies in the natural, factual characteristics of A itself, for instance the characteristic of pleasantness possessed by certain experiences or the characteristic which certain acts have of being the fulfilment of promises. The value judgements which we see to be true are judgements that, because of certain natural characteristics which it has, A ought to be chosen, approved, or pursued. The non-natural, specifically valuational element comes in with the "ought" and only there.

Thus in regard to a particular action that I ought to do there will always be reasons in favour of doing it in the shape of general characteristics which it shares with other actions, for example, the characteristic of fulfilling a contract or that of increasing a neighbour's pleasure. But the objection still has some weight, since I have given no further, more ultimate reason for the general principle that it is fitting to fulfil contracts or to give pleasure to others but just relied on the fact that we see it to be true. It will still be objected that my theory like Ross's does leave the fact that we ought to do one kind of thing rather than another unexplained, while utilitarianism explains it further by reference to the good. True, the utilitarian, if asked to explain why certain things are good-in-themselves, cannot do so, but just has to say that he sees them to be good; but at any rate he does carry the explanation one stage further back. And it does to many seem somehow more rational to take propositions such as "this kind of thing is good" as ultimate and self-vindicating than to hold this view about propositions like "this kind of thing is what I ought to do." It may be objected that I am left with nothing but a chaos of *prima facie* duties for none of which there is any reason beyond themselves, and that I have thus abandoned the essential purpose of Ethics, which is to make coherent our ethical beliefs. It is true that the advantage of utilitarianism relatively to my theory is much less than might appear at first sight, because, unless he is a hedonist, the utilitarian will have to admit an ultimate variety of intrinsic goods, and it might be argued that this is as bad as to admit an ultimate variety of *prima facie* duties. Further, if there are no general rules available for balancing different conflicting *prima facie* duties against each other, neither are there for balancing the different goods and evils of the utilitarian against each other. There is a good deal of force in this reply, but I cannot be satisfied with my position unless it is possible on principle to bring the *prima facie* duties into some kind of system.

Now there are different kinds of system. If we could deduce all ethical duties from a single principle, for example that I ought always to do what I could will everybody else to do, or from one single type of good, for instance pleasure, we should have a system of a certain kind. Such systems in ethics seem to me impracticable. They either give only a pretence of explanation, because they leave outside any concrete idea of the good, which has to be smuggled in unnoticed if the system is to work, or they conflict with moral judgements which we see to be true. They do not do justice to the complexity of ethics or of life.

But you may have a system of another kind. The systematic character of a body of beliefs may lie not in the fact that they are all deducible from one and the same principle but in the fact that, although no one of the beliefs can occupy the exalted position of being premise for all the rest, they are all logically related to each other so that you could not alter any one without contradicting others. It is a system of this sort that is envisaged in the coherence theory of truth. Could the true propositions of ethics form a system of this kind? Clearly not in the full sense. For one could certainly deny some true ethical propositions without logically contradicting any others. But there is still, I think, a sense in which they may be said to form a system. They form a system in the sense that the different ultimate *prima facie* duties are so connected that to fulfil any one harmonizes with and forwards in general and on principle the fulfilment of others. The utilitarians hold that it is generally a duty to tell the truth, keep promises, be just, make reparation for wrong one has done, treat our parents with love, etc.; but, as is well known, they maintain that what makes these kinds of action duties is that they further other goods. The view that this is the only reason for their being duties has been challenged by non-utilitarians, but hardly the view that they do further other goods and on the whole make for the best state of society attainable all round. Now "further other goods" becomes on the view I have suggested "further what ought, other things being equal, to be furthered on its own account," that is, fulfil other *prima facie* duties. But if the different *prima facie* duties play into each others' hands in this way, that may well serve as a confirmation that we are on the right lines in admitting them, so that we are not wholly dependent on intuition, but have also this "coherence" test.

But what about the undoubted clashes that do occur at times between different *prima facie* duties? Surely I may easily be placed in a situation in which I have to break one of two promises because the two are incompatible with each other, or to neglect either my *prima facie* duty to a relative or my *prima facie* duty to the state? Is not this sufficient to show that the line of argument suggested is a *cul-de-sac*, and that the *prima facie* duties cannot possibly be regarded as con- stituting a system?

It may be retorted, however, that, if we investigate such clashes, we find that, so far from refuting, they support the view that the *prima facie* duties constitute a system in some sense like the one I suggested. Let us take one of the acutest possible clashes, that arising in the case of war. Suppose one's country has promised to help another country against aggres- sion and that country is wrongfully attacked by a Power whose mode of government we cannot help regarding as a tyranny which has deliberately and persistently set aside in theory and practice principles of justice and liberty that we consider quite fundamental to civilisation. What are we to do? If we fight, we are certainly violating *prima facie* duties by the killing and other evil practices which war involves. If we do not fight, we are breaking our solemn word and letting a higher form of civilisation be overthrown by a lower and injustice and wrong triumph over right. Whichever answer we give, it is quite clear that we shall be violating some *prima facie* duties. But this does not disprove the view that the *prima facie* duties constitute a system. On the contrary it supports it. For why does this acute clash arise? Only because somebody has done wrong first. In every war at least one party is to blame. But, if the *prima facie* duties do constitute a system, surely the only thing to expect is that, if you violate one, you or someone else will tend to be brought into a position in which others have to be violated. To take an analogy, nobody would put forward as an objection to the systematic or coherent character of arithmetic that, if you start by believing that two plus two equals five or five plus seven equals eleven, or (without believing these propositions) wilfully proceed in your calculations as if they were true you will arrive at a host of other false propositions by arguing consistently from your premises. This will happen just because the different arithmetical propositions do constitute a system in which they all hang together.

Similarly the occurrence of clashes as a result of violating one *prima facie* duty is not a contradiction but a confirmation of the view that the *prima facie* duties constitute a system. If they do constitute a system, clashes are just what one ought to expect under these circumstances; and most of the serious clashes which occur in fact are due to previous violations of duty on the part of some person, or at least to mistakes as to what was his duty. If I make two inconsistent promises I must break one, but then I have already, intentionally or unintentionally, acted wrongly in making them. Again I may have to choose between lying and exposing to punishment as a criminal a person whom I love, but then either he has already done wrong in committing a crime or the government or administration has done wrong in treating as a crime the kind of act he has done. A man lives under a social system such that he cannot give satisfactory opportunities to his family without grasping after material gain somewhat more zealously than is desirable; that is because the social system is morally evil in so far as, through being too competitive, it encourages selfishness and makes money too much the standard of success. One cannot rapidly overthrow an existing bad political or economic system in some country without a violent revolution which will involve great misery and injustice; but that clash arises because the people who think they benefit by it are too much concerned for their own interests and too little for the welfare of others to let it be amended peaceably, and perhaps because the people who lose by it are too bitter and not disciplined enough to avoid revolutionary excesses. We must not indeed go too far on these lines. All clashes cannot be explained in this way. Natural disasters, as well as wars and bad social systems, may cause grave clashes; for example there is the well known case of lying in order to save some invalid from hearing bad news, or again a man might through an earthquake be placed in a position in which he had to choose between saving the life of his child and the lives of two other persons unknown to him. So the most we can say is that in general and on principle the *prima facie* duties fit together, that to fulfil one tends, of its intrinsic nature, to fulfil others, and to violate one tends to the violation of others. But this much we can say, and this helps to confirm the belief that any one of them is a genuine *prima facie* duty.

We need not therefore confine ourselves to saying that the ultimate *prima facie* duties are known intuitively; we can add that our intuitions of them are confirmed by the fact that to further one on the whole furthers others and to violate one tends to involve sooner or later violating others. There is thus a kind of coherence test available after all to supplement intuition. To this it may be objected that to see something to be an ultimate *prima facie* duty is to see that it ought to be done on its own account, and that the fact that to do it will have the effect of facilitating the fulfilment of other *prima facie duties* is therefore quite irrelevant to the question whether it is an ultimate *prima facie* duty or not. It is relevant to the question whether it ought to be done, but not to the question whether it ought to be done on its own account, and the latter is the question we are asking when we ask whether it is an ultimate *prima facie* duty, for instance, to keep promises or not. Obviously we cannot show that we ought to keep promises just because we have made them by showing that there are other good reasons for keeping them.

But the different goods are more closely connected with each other than this objection assumes. To recognise that we have a *prima facie* duty to keep promises is to recognise that keeping promises is intrinsically good; but to say this is not to say that keeping promises would be good altogether apart from its relations to anything else. When we say that something is good-in-itself we certainly mean that it really has the property of goodness itself and not only that its effects have it. We mean that it is to be valued for itself and not merely as a means to something else, but it does not follow that it would have this property in a quite different context. This, it seems to me, would not necessarily follow even if good were a quality; [9] *a fortiori* it does not follow if to call something good just means that it is fitting that we should have a certain attitude towards it. Consequently the fact that something which we seem to see intuitively to be intrinsically good is linked up with other goods may still help to provide a confirmation of our intuitive belief that it is intrinsically good. This would

---

[9] V. above, p. 114.

be the case to some extent even if the connection were only one of cause and effect, for we must expect good on principle and *per se* to produce good rather than evil and *vice versa*. No doubt good can be wrung out of evil but only by conquering it, for instance by bearing it well, and in that case the cause of the good gained does not lie wholly in the evil. Fresh good is produced by the furtherance of good and the conquering of evil.

But the connection between the different goods is closer than these remarks about causation suggest. It is not only that, for example, the keeping of promises is a cause which produces good effects. It can be seen to be linked up with the other kinds of good in respect of its essential nature and not merely by causal laws. In the first place, it follows necessarily that a person who has a fitting regard for the intrinsic value of true cognition will be averse to thus deceiving people. In the second place, it follows from any real sense of regard for the well-being of others that we shall not wish to cheat and disappoint them by breaking our promises, promise-keeping is bound up necessarily with the good of benevolence or love. In the third place, there would be no point in keeping a promise if it did not give any satisfaction at all to anybody, even the promisee. It is therefore bound up with hedonistic good. Fourthly, it is unfair to benefit by the promises of others, as we cannot help doing, and yet not keep our own, an argument which links promise-keeping with the good of justice. If you ask me whether promise-keeping would still be a good if it did not stand in any of these relations I could not say that it would, or rather I should answer that the question is absurd. It would not then be promise-keeping at all. It does not follow that we ought absolutely without exception to keep promises, for what follows from the nature of promise-keeping is that it has a general inherent tendency to be associated with these goods, not that this tendency is in all cases realised more strongly by keeping than by breaking a particular promise. It may happen that an action which is an example of promise-keeping has other characteristics which are not of such a desirable nature, for instance I may have promised to commit a murder. If in a particular case to break a promise is really for the good of the promisee, it may be more in accord with benevolence to break it than to keep it and more in accord with hedonistic good.

Now, if we had an ostensible intuition of the goodness of promise-keeping and not of the goodness of true cognition, benevolence and fairness, our intuitive conviction that promise-keeping is good (a *prima facie* duty) would be in a less strong position than is the case as things are, for now it is also supported by the ostensible intuitions that each of these other things is good. If any of them are intrinsically good; promise-keeping is in so far good and should in so far be pursued on its own account. For I am not merely saying that promise-keeping is good as a means for producing certain effects. The attitude to truth, to other persons, to the general happiness, and to the requirements of reciprocal justice, involved in promise-keeping is such that it must be better *per se* than promise-breaking if a right attitude to any of the above-mentioned itself has intrinsic value. So we now have not just one ostensible intuition, but a number of such intuitions confirming each other. That something like this confirmation, perhaps not always so complete, can be given of all genuine *prima facie* duties seems to me likely. It is significant how often the same action may be rightly recommended on different grounds, and this fact, which incidentally has made a multitude of conflicting ethical theories possible, shows the fundamental coherence of different *prima facie* duties. Benevolence can itself be commended on grounds of justice because it is unfair to expect kindness from others in case of need and yet not be prepared to give it when others are in need. All or most of the other *prima facie* duties may indeed be commended on the ground that they are bound up with the duty of promise-keeping; that is, they must be fulfilled if we are to keep faith with the community by fulfilling reasonable expectations, including the expectation that members of a community will sometimes devote themselves to the benefit of the community in ways the particular character of which cannot from the nature of the case be foreseen by others. But this is not to say that all other duties should be deduced from the duty of promise-keeping as their ultimate *raison d'être*. The different *prima facie* duties may confirm each other without any one being supreme. Similarly the goods of intellectual, aesthetic, and moral development are not just alien and indifferent to each other. They may accidentally clash, but this will be either because a man has not time to develop all sides of his nature as much as he would like or because the development of one side may become more or less warped and perverse. It is generally realised on the contrary that each side of human nature has something to give to the others, and that they cannot be sharply separated from each other. Thus artists who have written on the purpose of their art generally claim to be not merely creating beauty but conveying some kind of truth and thus benefiting also the intellectual side of man as well as cultivating and ennobling the emotions and making men more sensitive to the good. It is the belief of thinkers, defended in this book by the very emphasis I am giving to the coherence test, that thought can help the ethical side of our nature, and the intellectual quality of rationality and consistency is essentially connected with at least such a virtue as justice. In other quarters emphasis has been rightly laid on a certain aesthetic quality possessed by coherent theories and well rounded arguments and on the effect on one's emotional and aesthetic sides of the disinterested contemplation of truth whether in science or philosophy. There is essentially an aesthetic and moral quality about good intellectual development, an intellectual and moral quality about good aesthetic development and an aesthetic and intellectual quality about good moral development. To work out in full these suggestions towards a coherent theory of ethics would be to carry me far beyond the scope of this book, but what I have said at any rate shows that I am not necessarily reduced to a mere chaos of unrelated and unconfirmable *prima facie* duties.

Some thinkers have stressed intuition and some coherence, but both are needed in ethics. The coherence test plays an essential part in confirming, amending, clarifying and extending what first presents itself as a more or less confused intuition. Thus it is by the use of the coherence test that humanity passes —alas how slowly!—from moral principles almost confined to dealings with other members of the agent's small tribal group to a really universal application of these principles, since men gradually come to recognize that the limits imposed by themselves on the classes of those towards whom they have duties of benevolence and justice are arbitrary and inconsistent. On the other hand without ethical intuition there would be no material to which the coherence test could be applied. Similarly, we need both intuition and inference not only for the establishment and justification of general principles but in order to make adequate moral decisions in particular cases.[10] In emphasising coherence I do not indeed mean to imply that intellectual consistency is of chief value in ethics. It is very important as a help to finding what is right, but practical ethics does not lie merely in finding out what is right, it lies in the often much more difficult and much less pleasant task of doing what is right. Further, even for the purpose of find-

---

[10] For the part played by inference here and the different modes of inference used v. my book on *The Morality of Punishment with Some Suggestions for a General Theory of Ethics*. (Kegan Paul, London, 1929), pp. 195–215.

ing out what is right, empirical knowledge of the likely consequences is another factor which cannot be supplied by the philosopher as such and is yet of the extremest importance.

This book has been a discussion of what good is, not of what things are good, and it is therefore neither an attempt to commend certain values (good things) nor to give advice on the solution of concrete ethical problems.   It is a doubtful point how much the philosopher can do in either direction, though he can do something, but anything he does will not be a direct deduction from the analysis of good.   Still less could I be expected by such a deduction to persuade people to do what they know to be their duty, but in any case this is the task not of the philosopher but of the preacher. But this is not to say that I think my book of no practical value. I think that it is an extremely important task, both practically and theoretically, to stem the tide of subjectivism and naturalism in ethics, for the development of such beliefs seems to me bound to weaken seriously the sense of moral obligation by taking away any rational basis for ethics. To stem this tide we need three things—criticism of the subjectivists and naturalists, reply to their criticisms, and a positive opposing theory as to what good is. These I have tried to supply; and if I have at all succeeded it seems to me that I have done something of practical as well as theoretical importance, though a philosopher must be careful to avoid the error of overestimating the effects on practice of his theories.

He could have "stood in bed."

Index

Admiration, 154 ff., 157–58, 173, 180 n.

Aesthetic value, 164, 173, 211.

Analysis in philosophy, 31–2, 37–8, 43 ff., 49. See Definition.

Anti attitude, 168.

Approval, as basis of definition of good, and ought, 4 ff., 58 ff., 100 ff., 154 ff., 177.

Argument, in ethics, 5, 30, 34. See Coherence test.

Aristotle, 34.

Bad, different senses of, 117; definition of, 167–68.

Biological definitions of ethical concepts, 41, 73–4.

Bosanquet, B., 80 n.

Bradley, F. H., 80 n.

Brandt, Prof. R. B., 25.

Broad, Prof. C. D., 11, 23, 40 ff., 73 n., 100 ff., 118 n., 132.

Butler, Bishop, 57–8.

Carritt, E. F., 11 n., 112 n.

Children, ethical development in, 23–4, 56, 182–83.

Class-relation, definition of good in terms of, 104–6, 117.

Coherence theory of ethics, 13, 79–101; coherence test, 203–12.

Commands, theory reducing ethical judgements to, 10, 13–17, 56–7, 75–6, 106 ff.

Commonsense, 31–2, 54–5.

Consequences, in ethics, 19, 21, 118 ff., 125–26, 187 ff.

Cruelty, 64, 163–64, 165.

Definition, general nature of, 41 ff., 46–8, 78–9, 99–100; final definition of good, 146 ff.; the indefinable, 45 ff., 78, 83, 146–47, 178.

Descriptive theory of good, 100 ff.

Desire, as basis of definition of good, 17–18, 62–70, 97–8, 101 ff., 166; as motive for action, 51–2, 137 ff.

Determinism, 135.

Differences of belief in ethics, 18–22, 25 ff., 120–21.

Disapproval. See Approval.

Duty, meaning of term, 123–25, 170–71; sense of duty as motive, 141 ff. See Moral obligation.

Education, ethical, 182–83.

Efficient, 113.

Egoism, 18, 50, 111.

Emotion, connection with ethics, 4 ff., 12–13, 24 ff., 56 ff., 76, 101 ff., 151, 164 ff., 178 ff., 182–83.

Empiricism, in ethics, 38 ff., 44, 51–3.

End, as opposed to means. See Intrinsic goodness.

Evil, 117, 208.

Evolution, 73–4, 105–6.

Exclamations, theory reducing "ethical judgements" to, 10 ff.

Experience, relevance to ethics of, 20, 38 ff., 49–51, 52–3.

Feeling, 2 ff. See Emotion.

Field, Prof. G. C., 51.

Fittingness, 132–33, 135–36, 150 ff., 156–58, 169–73, 176 ff., 184–85, 189 ff., 201.

Function, definition of good in terms of, 105–6.

God, 106–11, 123, 134–35, 170.

Greatest good, 188 ff.

Harmony, 81, 98–9.

Hedonism, 50, 186. See Utilitarianism.

Hume, David, 41, 52, 88, 165.

Hypothetical imperatives, 135, 177 n.

213